Casey Scalf

JOE JACKSON is the author of five works of nonfiction and one novel. His most recent book, *The Thief at the End of the World: Rubber, Power, and the Seeds of Empire*, was named one of *Time* magazine's Top Ten Nonfiction Books of 2008.

ALSO BY JOE JACKSON

The Thief at the End of the World

A World on Fire

A Furnace Afloat

Dead Run (with William F. Burke Jr.)

Leavenworth Train

How I Left the Great State of Tennessee and
Went On to Better Things

ATLANTIC FEVER

LINDBERGH, HIS COMPETITORS,

AND THE RACE TO CROSS THE ATLANTIC

JOE JACKSON

PICADOR

FARRAR, STRAUS AND GIROUX
NEW YORK

www.picadorusa.com
www.twitter.com/picadorusa • www.facebook.com/picadorusa
picadorbookroom.tumblr.com

Picador® is a U.S. registered trademark and is used by Farrar, Straus and Giroux
under license from Pan Books Limited.

For book club information, please visit www.facebook.com/picadorbookclub
or e-mail marketing@picadorusa.com.

Designed by Jonathan D. Lippincott

The Library of Congress has cataloged the Farrar,
Straus and Giroux edition as follows·

Jackson, Joe.
    Atlantic fever · Lindbergh, his competitors, and the race to cross
the Atlantic / Joe Jackson.
        p.   cm.
    ISBN 978-0-374-10675-1 (hardback)
    1. Transatlantic flights—History—20th century.   2. Aeronautics—
Competitions—History—20th century.   3. Air pilots—Biography.
4. Lindbergh, Charles A. (Charles Augustus), 1902–1974.   I. Title.
TL531 .J33 2012
629.13092—dc23

                                                              2011046068

Picador ISBN 978-1-250-03330-7

Picador books may be purchased for educational, business, or promotional use.
For information on bulk purchases, please contact Macmillan Corporate
and Premium Sales Department at 1-800-221-7945, extension 5442,
or write specialmarkets@macmillan.com.

First published in the United States by Farrar, Straus and Giroux

First Picador Edition. May 2013

As always, to Kathy and Nick

Who are these that fly as a cloud, and as the doves
to their windows?   —Isaiah 60:8

CONTENTS

ATLANTIC FEVER

PROLOGUE:
WINGED MESSENGERS

Charles Augustus Lindbergh lined up the church in his gun sights and fired.

It was 1944 in the South Pacific, seventeen years after the transatlantic flight that made him a household name. The world had called him a messenger of peace, the forerunner of a scientific Utopia. Now he was a killing machine. His Lockheed P-38 Lightning carried 1,600 rounds of .50-caliber ammunition; the bullets spewed forth at 83 rounds per second from his plane's four machine guns. He zoomed over tiny Duke of York Island in eastern Papua New Guinea; military intelligence reported that Japanese troops were quartered in the church. The man who was once called the "supreme navigator" of his generation watched as his tracer bullets chewed the quaint wooden building to pieces.

The strafing run was a success. He flew back to base, wondering where he had lost his way.

"If God has the power over man claimed by his Disciples," he wrote, "why does He permit the strafing of churches and the atrocities of war? How can one return from battle and believe that an all-powerful God desires 'peace on earth, good will toward men'? One questions the extent of God's power. One questions the very existence of God."

It was not supposed to be like this. For the first three decades of the twentieth century, mankind believed that science, and especially flight, would bring peace to the world. Lindbergh had grown up a disciple of science and knew its spiritual fascination. "I have felt the godlike power man derives from his machines—the strength of a thousand horses at one's fingertips; the conquest of distance through mercurial speed; the immortal viewpoint of the higher air." As he flew nonstop across the

Atlantic for two days in May 1927, he felt a "harmony of muscle, mind, and mechanism" that bespoke a higher existence—and not just for him, but for all mankind. "[T]he rhythm of an engine is geared to the beat of one's own heart," he wrote. A wing "in turning flight seems an extension of one's own body."

It seemed a modern prayer.

Between 1910 and 1950 two generations of Americans and Europeans believed in what has been called "the winged gospel"; their reverence for flight and fliers resembled deification. To many, Lindbergh was the exemplar of this worship, and journalists tried to interpret the "Lindbergh religion" that sprang from thin air. Yet Lindbergh was a symbol of a belief that was barely understood. Adherents held faith in a wondrous tomorrow, an "Air Age" with no limitations. Flight would allow man to transcend boundaries that had confined him for centuries: no longer checked by time or distance, men and women could accomplish anything they dreamed.

But aviation was more than a mere subset of the greater technological advancement dominating the early twentieth century. To many, it changed the entire game. To be "air-minded" meant one was farsighted. Aviation was "the greatest factor for progress that has ever existed in the history of civilization," proclaimed U.S. Air Services magazine in 1923. "Of all the agencies that influenced men's minds, that made the average man of 1925 intellectually different from him of 1900, by far the greatest was the sight of a human being in an airplane," wrote Mark Sullivan in his 1927 reflection on American society, Our Times. As the earthbound gazed upon the airplane, they saw more than another mass-produced marvel. They saw freedom incarnate. In the flier, they saw freedom personified.

The meanings assigned to the flier could be wide-ranging and intensely personal. Any race could pilot an airplane. Any nationality. For the 1920s "New Woman," the aviator represented a long-sought sexual equality. No other technological advance spoke to young women like the airplane. Gender did not matter in the cockpit—only skill.

Finally, flying spawned a hope that an era of reason and peace had dawned. National boundaries would become obsolete in an age of flight. Warfare would end. Who would be so mad as to threaten conflict when unchecked retribution could rain from the sky? Planes would help populate those parts of the world previously deemed inaccessible; they'd end urban congestion, curtailing poverty and disease. Some suggested that increased contact with a rarified atmosphere would accelerate evolution and, in the process, create a superhuman "Alti-Man" by A.D. 3000. Like the angels, he'd rarely come to earth; instead, he'd make "the upper stratas" his home. Long before that, predicted a 1921 article entitled "The Therapeutic Value of Flying," man would establish "private air sanatoria and state and municipal air hospitals" in the "pure microbless [sic] air."

The rivals in the Great Atlantic Derby of 1927 were the incarnations of this hope. Richard Byrd, René Fonck, Clarence Chamberlin, Bert Acosta, George Noville, Bernt Balchen, even the often disparaged Charles Levine—those who survived the Derby were hailed as the supreme navigators of their generation. Although Lindbergh would be proclaimed the greatest, all were called the archetype of modern man. "Modern man is always solitary," wrote Carl Jung in 1933, and the solitary navigator became the most compelling existential image of its day.

"My cockpit is small, and its walls are thin," Lindbergh wrote, "but inside this cocoon I feel secure." Detached from care and history, the solitary messengers imagined themselves reborn. They brought a new gospel as they winged above the world.

Many followed, hypnotized. For the devout, their faith would be their ruin.

•

Flying in a light, rickety plane *is* hypnotic, but it is demonstrably perilous, too. Of the 2,501 fatal accidents among private and student pilots in single-engine airplanes from 1983 to 2000, 57 percent occurred when the pilot had between 50 to 350 hours of flight experience beneath his or her belt. This inescapable learning period has been termed the "Killing Zone" by pilot and author Paul Craig. In 1974 the National Transportation Safety Board noted a similar spike between 100 and 299 flight hours: "Perhaps the explanation for that peak is that by the time a pilot has accumulated [this many hours], he is confident of his ability even though his actual flying experience is low."

Craig put it another way: "[The pilot's] ego is writing checks that his experience can't cash!" Experienced pilots, he said, have "simply survived themselves."

It's hard to argue with statistics, especially when expressed so bluntly.

Yet it is important to understand the mystical power that flight has held over mankind. Even with our modern understanding of aerodynamics, the experience of going aloft still seems a miracle. God, in Western thought, is a creature of the air. Winged messengers surround Him, bringing the Word to man. The earliest legends of flight involved either men of exceptional gifts or those touched by angels or demons. Either way, they bent the rules. Flight meant power over the elements, a subjugation of the natural order of the world.

In important ways, early powered flight did seem unnatural. The first planes certainly *appeared* that way to landlocked observers. Orville and Wilbur Wright's original 1903 Flyer was a fragile, ungainly contraption: an incredible-looking box kite with rudders fore and aft, limited in scope and shape by the restraints of a very weak engine. Yet in just a few years, nothing much was left of the Wrights' original design. Engineers have a saying—"It's not right until it looks right"—and by 1909 the box kite had been replaced by a birdlike form with a body and tail. The Blériot monoplane that first crossed the English Channel to Dover on July 25, 1909, had the basic design of most planes throughout the first half of the century: long fuselage with a tail; wings sticking at a right angle from that body; propeller up front; and landing wheels.

There was a reason for such symmetry. Aircraft designers of this period had a fairly straighforward attitude: Change was defined as "farther and faster and bigger and better." Yet to reach such a goal meant developing greatly improved engines, bigger gas tanks, and more durable parts that could withstand the stress of higher speeds. Flying at high speed introduced the new problem of overcoming air resistance, or drag. The exposed positions of the pilot, tanks, and engine found in the early Wright Flyer were abandoned for streamlining: Now a tractor propeller was mounted to the front of the engine, which in turn was mounted to the front of the enclosed fuselage. And this surrounded and protected the pilots, gas tanks, and passengers from the cold and wind.

Yet increased performance also increased the dangers of the air. The greatest danger was the flier himself. "Flying releases something almost uncontrollable in the average pilot," wrote Leighton Collins in the 1944 flier's bible, *Stick and Rudder*. At the time, nearly 70 percent of all fatal accidents occurred from an onrush of joy. The pilot pushed his plane too far. He circled low over his friends and spun out; dove at his house and could not pull up; stalled at low altitude when he turned too sharply and lost control. "[O]nce on his own, there surges within a pilot a powerful impulse to break the bonds of every restraint," Collins observed. Flying was more than a mode of conveyance; it was a new type of language whose means of expression included "infinite freedom of motion" and speed. A pilot unleashed "wants to give vent to all the suppressed feelings of his innermost self," Collins warned.

Just where did those early aeronauts think they were headed once they managed to rise? Some had firm ideas. An aviator would hit a lower region warmed by the sun, then a region of cold. This was a chaotic domain, responsible for the birth of clouds, wind, and comets. Finally, he would enter an uppermost region of fire that was dry and dangerous, but also serene—for it was here that the aviator would come closest to God.

Solitude. Serenity. The idea that one's soul might continue even as the body fades. "I am above them and the plane roars in a sobbing world, but it imparts no sadness in me," wrote Beryl Markham in September 1936 as she became the first aviatrix to cross the Atlantic solo from Europe to North America. She is alone in her plane and the lights of Cork, Ireland, shine below. "I feel the security of solitude, the exhilaration of escape . . . as if I have eluded care and left even the small sorrow of rain . . ."

•

On October 20, 2009, I decided to try it for myself, going up with veteran crop duster Harvey "Windy" Belote over Virginia's Eastern Shore. Windy is a soft-spoken man, thirty years in the business but still nimble when vaulting around his plane. You fly by feel, he said: A good pilot reads the air the way a sailor reads the sea. Antoine de Saint-Exupéry, the French Aéropostale pilot and poet, thought the atmosphere as deep and mysterious as the ocean. A plane, like a sailing ship, was a mere speck in an immense gulf, a "sparkling fish" swimming through the air.

We climb into Windy's 1947 Piper Cub, parked on the nearby landing field. It is a lighter plane than his crop duster; I'll feel the air more intimately, he says. We take off in a cross breeze, one wing down into the wind. That wind catches the wings and pushes us up and back like a sheet lifted off a clothesline. At 50 feet, the little Piper bumps and squeaks. It's a bit disconcerting.

But then we're over the Chesapeake Bay, and the initial turbulence fades. This is a calmer place: at 250 feet, the boats and cars beneath us look like Matchbox toys. The higher we go, the more I lose my sense of speed. Our shadow, a cross, flies beneath us on the water like a protective charm.

I feel as if my trivial, earthbound problems have been left behind. This is the narcotic effect described by so many aviators. I feel the pulse of my arteries: all seems a realm of quickening currents—the sea, the sky, my blood. Then a gust from the west pushes us sideways, as if to chide me for succumbing to an overused cliché.

Perhaps the most seductive aspect of flight is how much sharper my senses seem. There's always the smell of gas, always the roar of the engine. Steering appears rather easy: left wing down, left pedal down and left on the stick to turn in that direction. The opposite for starboard. I feel the engine's vibrations through the stick more readily than one feels the road in a long, low sports car. I feel the river of air in my belly, the slight changes of speed in the catch of my breath, a change of direction in my inner ear.

"Want to spray that field of soybeans?"

We can't, of course—the Piper is not built for crop dusting—but we can mimic the run. This soybean field is boxed on three sides by tall oaks and pines. We execute a wingover into the wind, dipping the wing until we almost stand on it and then pirouette in a tight two-to-two-and-a-half G turn. Down we go, into the green, the first line of trees already behind us, the far one coming up faster than seems possible. A wall of trees towers before us and we angle up at what must be forty-five degrees. We climb until the light glitters around us, do another wingover, and dive again.

High above the ground, I feel transformed.

•

As early as 1919, a standing prize of $25,000 had been offered to the first aviator to cross the Atlantic, in either direction, from America to France or France to America. Sponsored by expatriate French hotelier Raymond Orteig, his "Orteig Prize" was one of the most coveted prizes in the flying world. Yet it lay unclaimed for eight long years. Then, during five incredibly tense weeks in the spring of 1927, a window in history opened when seemingly unconnected strands of technology, finance, fanfare, and character met and merged. This convergence of place, time, and people created what *The New York Times* christened "the most spectacular race ever held."

Because he won, the story of what newspapers called "Atlantic Fever" has regularly been framed as Lindbergh's. The losers' accomplishments have been largely forgotten by history. That is the American way. "People who succeed are loved because they exude some magical formula for fending off destruction, fending off death," said Arthur Miller in a 1999 interview about his archetypal loser, Willy Loman, in *Death of a Salesman*. "It's the most brutal way of looking at life that one can imagine, because it discards anyone who does not measure up...You are beyond the blessing of God." The American Dream of rising from obscurity, like Lindbergh, to the pinnacle of fame is built on the suspicion that our dream of triumph and fear of failure are linked—that the fairy tale rarely comes true. Failure is not the embarrassing footnote to the American myth of success. It is its foundation.

Lindbergh's success was made possible by the discoveries and mistakes of his rivals. From September 21, 1926, to May 20, 1927, sixteen fliers—ten American, four French, one Norwegian, and one Russian—competed in the race. This international flavor was part of the appeal: The rivalries played out the nationalism that led to World War I, and continued unabated during the postwar years. Most of these fliers were more experienced than Lindbergh, and all were better equipped. It was their efforts—not Lindbergh's—that dominated world news. The American press had only recently learned the technique of maintaining a long-term news story and turning it into modern myth; each flier was presented to the world in what today looks like a publicity campaign. Lindbergh's victory was not foreordained, and a close examination of the coverage shows that almost every one of the rivals could have been "Lindbergh" instead. Indeed, Charles Lindbergh was barely mentioned at first, a single short story in the reams produced by major papers such as *The New York Times*. One read of the exploits of the Cowboy, the cool and dedicated Professional, the Sheikh, the Ace of Aces, the romantic Knights of the Air. The Cowboy flew with his beautiful wife, who planned to serve as his copilot: They, not Lindbergh and his future wife, Anne Morrow, were the original "first couple of the air."

In fact, the early odds-on favorite was polar explorer Richard Byrd. He was certainly the most widely known. With copilot Floyd Bennett, he received the Congressional Medal of Honor for being the first to fly over the North Pole. For a while he was even the best-funded, backed to the tune of $100,000 by the scion of the Wanamaker department store chain. Byrd said it did not matter to him whether he won or lost; he was making the transatlantic attempt in the name of science. Like most of the rivals, Byrd saw himself as the herald of a greater tomorrow. And like most, he came to believe in his own publicity.

If nothing else, the quest for the $25,000 Orteig Prize turned into one of the most perilous races in history. Five crashes occurred before Lindbergh took off, two world records were set, and several fliers were injured and scarred. Of the sixteen competitors, six would die. Lindbergh found that fame was a nightmare, and that one could plummet just as fast from public opinion as from the clouds. Byrd went on to torment himself in a "sinister Ice Age at the bottom of the world." Others died early, pushed to the brink by their fame. The race Lindbergh won was so big, obsessive, and dangerous—the hero worship surrounding it so far beyond anything ever seen to that point—that every competitor was changed. If an aviator wasn't killed, he somehow lost his soul.

Flight meant freedom, the oldest dream of man. Deep in the bowels of the Labyrinth, Daedalus offered hope to his overeager son. "Escape may be checked by water and land," he counseled, "but the air and sea are free." Above the clouds, Icarus thinks he can rise forever. Everyone knows how that story ends.

PART I

PHANTOM TRAVELERS

In flying, I tasted the wine of the gods.
—Charles Lindbergh

ONE

STRANGE DAYS

Charles Lindbergh hooked his leg over the right side of the cockpit and prepared to throw himself from his plane. Only a day earlier he'd fretted that his life had stalled, and now, as if to prove the point, his army-salvage DH-4 had run out of gas somewhere on the mail run between St. Louis and Chicago. It was the night of September 16, 1926: Overhead, the clear midwestern sky glinted with stars; below him, a fog bank obliterated all trace of the ground. He balanced for a second, then launched himself over the side.

Landing "blind" in a fog was suicide, the leading cause of death among airmail pilots. But parachute jumps were almost as dicey. If a parachutist failed to jump out far enough, he'd be caught by the plane's control wires and stabilizers. The wings hissing past at 100 miles per hour could slice through a man like a knife through cheese. Since 'chutes were often defective, a jumper could hit the earth at tremendous speed. The tall and lanky flier called "Slim" by his pals would have been remembered as a "twisted and horribly distorted thing."

He did not drop immediately. One of the strangest sensations discovered by a jumper was that, for the first few seconds, he slid through the air like a bird. The 100 mph impetus given to him by the hurtling ship shot him forward with it, facedown, hands and feet extended, about 30 feet beneath the wing of the plane. It was not an unpleasant sensation. The cold wind whistled past one's face; instead of a breathless descent, you cut through the air like a projectile.

Then gravity took over and Lindbergh dropped, turning somersaults for two or three seconds before pulling the ripcord.

He'd been through this before. The *idea* of floating to earth beneath a huge canopy of silk was not particularly new. Leonardo da Vinci first sketched out the possibility in one of his many notebooks; the idea of a "Fall Breaker" came to him in a dream. The first successful experiment occurred in 1779, when Joseph and Étienne Montgolfier loaded a sheep into a basket hung beneath a large parasol. They pushed it off a high tower, and though the sheep lived, it voiced its objections the entire way down. More often than not, barnstormers used parachutes for "stunts," and Slim's entry into aviation in May 1922 was as a wing walker and parachutist to draw paying crowds. This was his third jump to save his life: he'd ditched once in 1925, as an army flight cadet, then once earlier this year near St. Louis, when his controls had jammed. Yet he didn't like to jump, and was more likely than most pilots to stick with his plane as it went down.

The 'chute boomed above him. He jerked up in the harness, then swayed back and forth as the shrouds rustled overhead. He pulled out his flashlight and pointed it past his feet. He saw an endless quilt of fog covering the farmland somewhere north of Peoria.

Until this point, the summer had been uneventful. Barely a year out of army flight school, Lindbergh had been named chief pilot when the Robertson Aircraft Corporation inaugurated its St. Louis–Chicago airmail run on April 25, 1926. It was quite an honor for the twenty-four-year-old former barnstormer, and the most responsibility he'd ever had. The "CAM-2" route, with its unpredictable weather, was considered one of the most dangerous runs in the country, but the skies during the summer of 1926 had been clear. He flew five round trips a week, following railroad tracks, rivers, and, at night, the soft glowing lights of farm towns. He lived at the edge of Lambert Field, in a room rented from an airport mechanic; he cooked two meals a day, and for the first time in his short career as a flier, felt he had found a permanent home.

But permanence made him uneasy. When his mother, in Detroit, sent his weekly package of candy, cheese, and nuts, she sometimes included magazines filled with the exploits of other fliers. The mid-1920s had suddenly turned into the glory days of long-distance flying: in 1924 six army aviators flew 27,553 miles around the globe, the first to do so in an airplane; the Italian flier Francesco de Pinedo flew from Rome to Tokyo by way of Australia. In May, Lindbergh had read how navy commander Richard Byrd had been the first to fly over the North Pole; Lindbergh had applied to take part in Byrd's expedition, but was turned down. He dreamed of flying to Alaska or entering the next long-distance race, wherever that might be. It seemed that another age of exploration was taking shape, like that of Columbus and Magellen, only this time in the air. And he was getting left behind.

This night's run had started as inauspiciously as others in this long, boring summer. He left Lambert Field at 5:55 p.m. and noted a light ground haze, though the skies were practically clear. Night arrived twenty-five miles north of Peoria, and with it came the fog. It rolled over the countryside, wiping out all features. By Maywood, which was Chicago's airmail field, the fog reached an altitude of 900 feet; the field crew set searchlights out and burned two barrels of gas, but Slim was still unable to find clear ground. He circled back, and his engine stopped at 8:20 p.m. He thought he had more gas, and did not learn till later that when a mechanic had repaired a leak, he'd switched the normal 110-gallon tank for an 85-gallon replacement without telling anyone. Lindbergh switched to his reserve tank and released a parachute flare, but this, too, was swallowed by the fog. He climbed to 5,000 feet. At 8:40 p.m. the reserve tank died.

Lindbergh went over the side and pulled the ripcord; he swayed in his harness, watching the fog approach below. Though this was his first night jump, everything initially seemed "like pie." But as he sank into the clouds, things turned strange. All of a sudden, he heard the burbling engine of his abandoned plane. He'd neglected to cut the switches when he bailed out, thinking all the gas was depleted. Instead, the DH-4's nose dipped down and the last cupfuls of gas had evidently trickled into the motor. Lindbergh and his plane were spiraling to earth at the same level and at the same rate of speed.

Then he saw her, apparently coming for him out of the fog. The fabric wings, painted silver, caught light from the stars; the maroon fuselage looked black in the night, U.S. AIR MAIL painted in big white letters on the side. She flew as straight as if a phantom pilot sat at the controls. He grabbed the risers of his parachute, ready to swing the 'chute aside.

But the plane passed harmlessly about a hundred yards away.

Then she returned. Slim realized he was on the outside of the spiral, and each time the plane came back, she was a little farther away. The plane returned five times: he listened as the engine grew faint, then loud, until once again her slow, steady bulk reappeared at his level. She was like some poor lost pet that couldn't give him up and kept searching for him.

He sank deeper into the fog. It was cold in the cloudbank, and he felt the chill through his heavy flight suit. He reached again for his flashlight, but realized he had dropped it in the excitement when the plane first appeared. All sound was hushed; the ground rushed up, but he could not judge how far away it was. The DH-4 passed once more, but too far away this time for him to see. He held his feet together so he wouldn't straddle some farmer's wall or barbed-wire fence, and covered his face with his hands. Shrouded in white between heaven and earth, Lindbergh waited in silence to land.

•

Nine hundred fifty-five miles to the east, New York's typical hot and humid summer had proved anything but boring. Summers in the city were always murder, but this year an inexplicable unrest had developed that no one could quite explain. Social commentators dubbed it the "American nervousness," but something more basic was going on. Perhaps, they theorized, six years of Prohibition had taken their toll.

If people weren't dying for a drink, they were dying in unexpected ways. In June three policemen were murdered. The first officer was shot to death in a holdup; the second, during a traffic stop in Brooklyn. The third killing occured, amazingly, while a detective was booking a car thief at police headquarters in the Tombs. In mid-August Rodolfo Alfonso Guglielmi di Valentina d'Antonguolla, known to the world as Rudolph Valentino, checked into Polyclinic Hospital for severe stomach pains. Surgeons removed an inflamed appendix and closed two perforated gastric ulcers, and the thirty-one-year-old screen icon seemed on the mend. But then he developed peritonitis and slipped into a coma. Worried fans gathered on the sidewalk outside the hospital. On August 23, Valentino seemed to rally; his eyes fluttered and he gazed at the head of United Artists, seated by his bed. "Don't worry, chief, I'll be all right," Valentino promised. Then he died.

Maybe Mayor James J. Walker should have predicted what followed. The dapper, flamboyant face of Tammany Hall, the political machine that ran New York and its five boroughs, "Beau James" had an innate sense of the public mood. He could feel its pulse in his sleep, he said. New York loved its characters, and he was happy to meet the demand. Rather than spend his days behind a desk, Walker held court at the Central Park Casino, the supper club whose entrance fee was $22,000.

It was there he wined and dined his mistress, Betty Compton, who'd appeared on Broadway with Fred Astaire. Before politics Walker had been a songwriter: his biggest hit, "Will You Love Me in December (As You Do in May)?" To him, politics and entertainment weren't a far remove.

But who could have known? Valentino's death released a worldwide flood of mourning, and New York determined its style. Some Hawaiian fans may have set the standard for the most melodramatic response when they threw themselves into a live volcano, but in Manhattan, gestures like that of Mrs. Angelina Celestina—a twenty-year-old mother of two who drank iodine, shot herself twice, then collapsed on her pile of Valentino photos and magazines—were more common. New Yorkers believed in overkill. The next day, a riot broke out—the first celebrity-inspired riot in the city's history—when Valentino's body was laid out in an ornate silver-bronze coffin displayed behind the huge plate-glass windows of mortician Frank E. Campbell's funeral home. Thirty thousand mourners lined the street. When they pressed against the window glass, it shattered, and mounted police charged the mob in an attempt to drive them away. Instead, the mourners rubbed soap on the street so the horses would slip and fall.

Two days later, on August 27, the city gave a lavish ticker tape parade. Gertrude Ederle, the twenty-one-year-old daughter of an Amsterdam Avenue butcher, had just swum the English Channel, which made her the first woman ever to do so. A teenage Olympian, Ederle had trained for the feat for most of the decade, and on August 6 swam from Cap Gris-Nez in France to Kingsdown in England in 14.5 hours, beating the times of some of the men who preceded her. She debarked from the Cunard liner Berengaria and was met by Walker's official greeter, the equally dapper Grover Whalen, who then squired her on the one-mile route on Lower Broadway dubbed "the Canyon of Heroes." It was the city's biggest ticker tape parade up to that point—bigger than the one in June for Commander Byrd and copilot Floyd Bennett after they conquered the North Pole. It was even bigger than the one in 1910 for Teddy Roosevelt, when he returned from his African safari; bigger than in 1919, when General Pershing and the troops returned home from the Great War. A blizzard of shredded stock market tape rained down on the young woman's head. In nervy times like these, people wanted a hero.

So when a thirty-two-year-old Frenchman marched into Walker's office and announced his plan to win the Orteig Prize, it was entirely within the spirit of that strange summer. The audacious visitor was, in fact, one of the world's most famous fliers: M. le Capitaine René Fonck, the Allies' "Ace of Aces" in the Great War. With seventy-five official German kills to his credit, Fonck was the youngest-ever officer of the Legion of Honor, the "D'Artagnan of the Air." Known as the "Unpuncturable," since—if he was to be believed—only one bullet had ever pierced his plane, Fonck portrayed himself as an instrument of ruthless precision, expending the least ammo necessary to make a kill. "I put my bullets into a target as if by hand," he bragged.

"One must be in constant training," he once told his admirers, "always fit, always sure of oneself, always in perfect health. Muscles must be in good condition, nerves in perfect equilibrium, all the organs exercising naturally." Preparing for battle was like preparing for a prize fight—he did a series of sit-ups before entering the cockpit, did not carouse the night before battle, and was perceived as a show-off by fellow aviators. But he had a point. Aerial encounters often took place at altitudes of 20,000 to 25,000 feet, and such heights tested the healthiest of men. "Alcohol becomes an enemy—even wine. All abuses must be avoided. It is indispensable that one goes to a combat without fatigue, without any disquietude, either physical or mental."

"Constantly I watch myself," Fonck said.

He watched himself that day. He wore a dark, double-breasted suit—not the army uniform most photographs captured him in, the chest draped with the more than fifty palms, medals, and citations awarded by the grateful governments of Belgium, England, France, Italy, Japan, Poland, Portugal, Romania, Serbia, Spain, Sweden, and the United States. He spoke in quick bursts, "and it is doubtful if he could talk at all were his hands tied," a writer observed. He was a short man, about the same height as Walker, and the showboat mayor knew that short people tried harder. Fonck sported a short, stiff moustache like that of Chaplin's tramp and the confident, jaunty stride of a college quarterback. He smiled easily at Walker and remarked that he, too, had been a mayor—an eight-day honorary term after the war in Saulcy-sur-Meurthe, his birthplace in the Vosges Mountains. Alas, said Fonck, the job had been too hard.

"I am surprised you didn't make a good mayor," Walker said, laughing. "A mayor is up in the air a good deal of the time."

•

Indeed, Fonck had prepared for this meeting as carefully as he'd once prepared for the dawn patrol. To succeed in a desperate endeavor, he wrote, one must condition both the mind *and* the machine. All that summer, he had lived alone in his room at the Hotel Roosevelt on Long Island, where he regularly took his meals. He spent his afternoons working at nearby Roosevelt Field. If he went out at all, it was to attend a movie, alone. He drank nothing but red wine with his meals; his one observable vice was his chain-smoking. *The New Yorker*, the Jazz Age's best source of local gossip, proclaimed him "the quietest celebrity ever to visit these shores."

His purpose was single-minded: the construction of a "beautifully proportioned ship," a "monstrous silver gull" designed to carry 13,840 pounds of fuel, cruise at 120 miles per hour, and climb more than 800 feet a minute. Only such a beast could traverse the Atlantic Ocean, he claimed. His Sikorsky S-35 was one of the biggest planes of its time, and it was designed solely for one purpose: to fly from New York to Paris without stopping, and win Raymond Orteig's $25,000 prize.

But let this be clear, Fonck declared. He was not doing it for the money. Or the glory. He was doing it for progress, to prove that "the science of aeronautics has progressed to the point where such a non-stop flight can be undertaken with virtual certainty of achievement." He was doing it for international relations. "[O]nce more, the American and French flags will be triumphant in a mutual venture for the glory of these two great liberty-loving republics."

It was a theme that would be repeated ad infinitum for the duration of the race, and Fonck created the mold. He was the first to portray the $25,000 quest as a great leap forward for scientific progress and peace, not an enormous boost for the winner's bank account. Those who knew Fonck best—his fellow pilots and partners—had their own opinions. But they held their tongues, at least initially.

In some ways, Fonck had done wonders before ever leaving the ground. No one else had seen that piloting skill, business acumen, and technical genius were the necessary components to succeed in what, to that point, was considered impossible. There had been two previous transatlantic "hops," both in 1919, but neither flew nonstop over the same unforgiving span of ocean as required by the Orteig Prize. The first was made by a U.S. Navy seaplane in May of that year: four navy flying boats, or "Nancys," left Newfoundland, but only one made it to England, after sixteen days, multiple stops, and several repairs. The second hop occurred in June, when a war surplus Vickers Vimy bomber made the 1,800-mile trip from Newfoundland to Ireland in 16 hours and 2 minutes. The British pilots, Captain John "Jack" Alcock and Lieutenant Arthur "Teddy" Brown, were just one team out of many competing for a £10,000 prize by Lord Northcliffe, owner of both the *Daily Mail* and *The Times*. As Lord Northcliffe awarded them the check, he told the assembled newsmen that someday their papers would be published in the morning on Fleet Street and read that evening in Manhattan. The reporters laughed in disbelief and shook their heads.

But these flights were ancient history. The route from New York to Paris stretched approximately 3,600 miles, doubling the miles flown by Alcock and Brown. According to Fonck, the idea to make such a flight came to him in October 1925, when he attended the Pulitzer Trophy Air Races at Mitchel Field, an army air base running parallel to the civilian Roosevelt Field. Everyone seemed to be talking about Orteig's unattainable prize. Fonck had entertained the idea earlier, in France, but no one had taken him seriously; now he literally stumbled into a group considering the attempt right outside Manhattan. Igor Sikorsky, the Russian designer of large bombers, was designing a ship for a group called the Argonauts. When Fonck arrived, bedecked in ribbons and medals and suggesting they all join forces, the Americans swooned.

Fonck returned home on January 23, 1926, and for two months sought additional French backing for his shot at the prize. On March 24 he revealed his plans to the world. He would fly from Central Park in New York to rue du Bois-de-Boulogne in Paris in an American-made plane. The engines would be French—three huge Gnome-Rhône Jupiter radial engines able to achieve 400 horsepower, which, he added, would be loaned to the Argonauts by the French government. French war minister Paul Painlevé, the first Frenchman to fly with Wilbur Wright, had promised the government's support, Fonck proclaimed. Though he hoped to take off as early as May, caution dictated that the date be

pushed back to June or July. He anticipated that the flight would take
about thirty-five hours.

Fonck's announcement stunned the flying world, and spurred a
handful of French and American competitors. He was not, however, the
first aviator to apply officially for the prize. In 1923 fellow French aces
François Coli and Paul Tarascon had investigated a transatlantic flight,
and in August 1925 the two formally applied. But their fund-raising
hit roadblocks, and by 1926 Fonck was miles ahead. Lucien Bossoutrot,
the world record holder for high-altitude flight, also announced his intent, though he never officially entered. In the United States, a lieutenant commander, Noel Davis of the U.S. Naval Reserve, and former
barnstormer Clarence D. Chamberlin said that they had also sought
funding.

Few paid them any mind. It was Fonck, Fonck, Fonck, from the moment he stepped off the liner in New York Harbor in early May. He
visited Washington and asked Navy Secretary Curtis Wilbur for a list of
naval aviators who might serve as his copilot. The applicant had "better
be a good swimmer," he quipped. He planned to fly northeast from
Long Island to Newfoundland, then east across the North Atlantic. The
next land he'd see would be Cape Clear, in Ireland, followed by Cornwall, Cherbourg, and Paris. If he made it, he hoped to fly over Mount
Everest in 1927. He reminded reporters again that he was not in it for the
glory—he was in it for mankind.

"Air transportation, bringing speed in communication between the
nations of the world . . . will be a paramount factor in establishing world
peace," he declaimed.

All that summer, the plane took shape in her hangar at Roosevelt
Field. Foreign workmen clung to her sides, speaking in Russian and
French. Most were former military; many, expatriate Russians bearing
titles that meant little after the Revolution. Each day, Fonck picked up
the paper; each day, people he'd never met said they were going with
him. They seemed to hope that if they spoke loudly enough, Fonck
would be forced to listen, and to take them along.

Designed by Russian genius, built with American dollars, fueled by
French élan—Fonck's silver gull was an international effort, the best
the world could offer. They'd make it across with no problem. It was a
sure thing.

•

At first the general public did not seem to care.

By 1926 Americans seemed oddly divided in their attitudes regarding airplanes. They could wax poetic about aviation's future in one breath, then state as common sense the "fact" that the technology would never touch their lives. The March 1926 *Popular Science* showed a flying car on its cover, its wings folded up to fit in the family garage. Yet for most Americans such dreams were not practical—not like those other modern wonders, the telephone, the radio, or the Ford Model T. Flying was "wildcat stuff," the realm of death-defying stunts and war ace glamor. It was unnecessary and dangerous, even when evoked in the name of progress, as evidenced by the sobering loss of life in flying the cross-country mail. To the average American, flying seemed a daredevil dream played out by adventurers costumed in goggles, leather flying suits, and long, flowing scarves.

Despite their fabled inventiveness, Americans historically distrusted flight. In the United States, inventions had to be practical to catch fire. As early as 1784, a British visitor observed that "the people of America have a saying—that God is Himself a mechanic ... and He is respected and admired more for the variety, ingenuity and utility of His handiwork than for the antiquity of His family." Yet this inventiveness had to be grounded in the everyday. "Those who cultivate the sciences amongst a democratic people are always afraid of losing their way in visionary speculation," wrote Alexis de Tocqueville in 1831. Even Thomas Jefferson, who did more to establish colonial science than anyone, distrusted aerial flights of fancy. In 1822, four years before his death, he discussed his reservations with a certain D. B. Lee, who had apparently proposed a "heavier-than-air machine." To fly "by macanacal [sic] means alone in a medium so rare and unassisting as air must have the aid of some principal not yet generally known," Jefferson predicted. He wished Lee success "with more good will than confidence."

Not everyone subscribed to such views. When Benjamin Franklin saw the Montgolfier brothers rise in a hot air balloon, he predicted that such experiments "may possibly give a new Turn to Human Affairs." War might be eliminated, he said, for where "is the Prince who can afford to so cover his Country with Troops for its Defense, as that Ten Thousand Men descending from the Clouds, might not in many Places do an infinite deal of Mischief, before a Force could be brought together to repel them?"

On the whole, however, the idea of a transatlantic flight remained an object of ridicule. An 1894 "Pass on the Trans-Atlantic Air Line Railway," by the Emigrant Publishing Company, pictured a steam locomotive crossing the ocean on a train track suspended from hot air balloons. New immigrants and smugglers were encouraged to ride, since they would bypass the "inquisitions and nuisances of the emigration commissioner and custom house officials." Passengers were asked not to spit tobacco out the windows "as ocean steamers may be passing below." As late as 1908, the Harvard astronomer William Pickering doubted whether "aeroplanes will ever cross the ocean, and despite the Wright success, they offer little menace to warfare. The public has greatly overestimated the possibilities of the aeroplane, imagining that in another generation they will be able to fly over to London in a day. This is manifestly impossible."

All this talk about making the world a smaller place did not hit home. Americans in the 1920s were not ready to become citizens of the world. The comfort of "withdrawing into one's private America" was rarely debated; the world was a dangerous place, filled with dictators, Bolsheviks, anarchists, and mad bombers. Most Americans believed that after they won the Great War for the Allies, the victorious troops brought home the Spanish influenza—which killed 500,000 to 675,000 people in the United States and 50 to 100 million worldwide. This was a warning of the dangers of international involvement. It was safer to stay within their country's borders, a place they understood.

That spring and early summer, as Fonck's shining gull took shape, a curious lack of excitement hovered over the venture. Few stories appeared on the front pages; "briefs" about its progress were buried deep inside the scientific and transportation sections of The New York Times. A human factor was needed to make the story come alive.

Despite Fonck's assurances, the transatlantic quest still seemed a flight of fancy. The North Atlantic is one of the harshest places on earth, an environment of bleak winds and monstrous winter waves. In 1872 the Scottish town of Wick watched huge breakers carry off rock and concrete barriers weighing more than 1,350 tons. The world's highest tides are found in Canada's Bay of Fundy, where the water rises 50 feet in the spring. More ships lie buried beneath those waves than in any other ocean, their hulls split open by mountains of water, or picked up like toys and capsized.

The North Atlantic is also one of Nature's great battlegrounds, where warm air masses heading north crash into the polar air mass flowing in the opposite direction. The front of this atmospheric war zone stretches three thousand miles, from Canada's Cape Chidley to Norway's North Cape, an inhospitable expanse longer than the trenches of the Great War. The Norsemen, more intimate with the Atlantic than other ancient seafarers, foresaw the end of the world in her waves. According to Norse myth, Ragnarök, the apocalypse, would start with the relentless Fimbulwinter, a time when "snow drives from all quarters, the frosts are so severe, the winds so keen and piercing, that there is no joy in the sun."

Flying over those waves would immediately bring an aviator in conflict with these winds. Sea currents flow clockwise in the North Atlantic, driven by prevailing westerlies. This is the realm of the North American Gyre: The Gulf Stream moves north along the coast, turns toward Europe, flows south toward the equator, and then west toward Florida. The north edge of that circle has some of the world's most consistently turbulent weather. An airman would encounter huge anvils of cumuli blocking his path, loaded with rain, snow, ice, lightning, and hail. The high winds in those clouds were known to push aircraft backward in flight, giving them a negative ground speed.

Flying over the clouds was not an option either. Since the atmosphere grows less dense with height, an aviator could get the bends. He would fall prey to the crushing fatigue of diminished oxygen supply. Temperature dropped by one degree Fahrenheit for every 300 feet in altitude: in an open cockpit, he would freeze.

Then there was fog. The most fogbound region of the Atlantic is off Newfoundland's Grand Banks, where the cold Labrador Current meets the warm, northbound Gulf Stream. The spring and summer fogs are typically thick and unyielding. Ships and planes enter and disappear. As warm surface currents move in one direction, the cold North Atlantic Deep Water mass rushes beneath it at a depth of two thousand to four thousand meters, an automated conveyor belt working on a global scale.

What was the point of flying? The dangers were real by water, but at least on a ship one could face them in luxury. A traveler made the six-day New York–Liverpool run in a floating hotel, replete with dance halls, casinos, eight-course menus, and fully stocked bars, an added plus in Prohibition-era America. Although the *Titanic* disaster was still recent, Cunard liners such as the *Mauretania* made steady profits. There was something reassuring about a ship, its officers and crew decked out in uniform, centuries of sea lore anchoring each action. Aviators, on the other hand, acted like big kids in a secret club. They spoke in strange tongues of *slipstreams, Immelmanns, dead sticks,* and *aspect ratios.* They wore jodphurs, as if ready to jump on a horse and gallop away.

Yet the dream of flying the Atlantic had persisted for nearly a hundred years. In 1836 the British balloonist Charles Green proposed floating across the ocean, but no financial backers took him seriously. Seven years later, America's premier nineteenth-century balloonist, John Wise, proposed riding the west winds to Europe, then around the world. If it rose high enough, he said, a balloon would hitch a ride on a giant river of air—one of the earliest references to stratospheric "jet streams." Congress ignored his $15,000 petition.

From 1840 to 1900 not a decade passed without a proposed crossing, but all to no avail. The first transatlantic flight to be reported as fact was by balloon, but this turned out to be no more than a fraud. On April 13, 1844, *The New York Daily Sun* led with the headline "ASTOUNDING NEWS!!," then described the crossing of aeronaut Monck Mason and seven crewmen. Their trip from Britain to Sullivan's Island, South Carolina, was said to have taken seventy-five hours aboard the "steering Balloon" *Victoria,* and even the *Sun's* editors were fooled. Yet no *Victoria* existed, and no Monck Mason. The story was instead a convincing hoax written by the young and still unknown Edgar Allan Poe.

Tales of the fantastic attached themselves to the Atlantic like lampreys. First mentioned in Herodotus's *Histories* as the "sea of Atlas," the Atlantic was the home of Atlantis, nine rings of land surrounded by another nine of water. The ocean's average depth is two and a half miles: from these depths, bizarre life forms emerge. In 1938 fishermen caught the coelacanth, a plated prehistoric fish thought extinct for sixty million years. Storms off the Grand Banks have disgorged the legendary giant squid. There have been human mysteries, too. In December 1872 the 282-ton brigantine *Mary Celeste* was found sailing off the coast of Gibraltar, her crew of seven, captain, his wife, and daughter gone. They'd simply disappeared.

Tales of the first transatlantic voyage had a similar phantasmal ring. Between A.D. 512 and 530, St. Brendan of Clonfert sailed from Ardfert, in Ireland, with fourteen to sixty other pilgrims in search of the Garden of Eden. For seven years he encountered the world's wonders and horrors: Judas frozen on one side of his body, afire on the other; people with the heads of swine and the teeth of wolves; an enormous fish that encircled their boat by holding its tail in its mouth.

Yet Brendan's most enduring legend was that of the phantom isle. Rumored to lie west of the Canary Islands, San Borondón, the "Isle of the Blessed," appeared on numerous maps and served as one of the mysteries spurring Christopher Columbus to head west into the unknown. Though it hid behind a wall of mist, thousands swore they'd seen it. St. Brendan said he landed there in A.D. 512 and lingered fifteen days. When he returned to his flagship, he discovered that he'd entered some kind of time warp and had been missing for a year. The monk Barino claimed that when he visited this paradise, trees bore rich fruit and rivers ran with sweet water. Columbus searched for the island, without luck. In his ship's diary of August 9, 1492, he wrote of receiving "the assurance of many respectable Castilian inhabitants of the island of El Hierro... that every year they saw land to the west." Witnesses said the island appeared at dawn and sunset, when they watched the sun set behind it. Sailors called it the "Insubstantial" and the "Inaccessible." The moment it was glimpsed, it would disappear in a fogbank or be swallowed by a storm.

Like most Atlantic phantoms, it seemed within reach until the very last moment—when it slipped away.

•

A good meal changes everything. The French, who turned the act of eating into something sacred, said one must "rise above the table." At that moment, one's vision expanded. The walls melted away.

One spring night in 1919, a short, bald, and risible Frenchman rose above the table in ways he could not at first comprehend. Raymond Orteig co-owned two Manhattan fixtures: the hotels Brevoort and Lafayette. His partner, Elie Daution, ran the Brevoort, known even during Prohibition for its excellent wine cellar, while Orteig managed the

the Lafayette, originally the Hotel Martin, featured marble-topped tables, space for its elderly dominoes players, exquisite French cuisine, and a sidewalk café. The list of notables passing through its doors reads like a crash course in the city's history: Mark Twain, Lillian Russell, Jay Gould, Anna Held. During the Great War, the two hotels became headquarters for French officials visiting New York, many of them army officers and aviators. The excitement of his hotels lifted Orteig's spirit at the same time that it filled his rooms. But now he missed the young French and Allied airmen, and pined for their tales of individual combat in the skies above the no-man's-land.

Like many immigrants, Raymond Orteig was stuck between two worlds. Born in the shadow of the Pyrenees to a family of shepherds, he came to the United States at the age of twelve when his grandmother told him, "See what you can do." It was 1882, America's "Gilded Age," and Orteig arrived in Manhattan with thirteen francs sewn in his clothes. He landed a job as a bar porter that paid two dollars per week; by 1897 he was headwaiter at the old Hotel Martin's café, and five years later he had bought both the café and hotel and renamed it the Lafayette, in honor of his native land.

The Lafayette and Orteig would be society fixtures for the next forty years. Yet in 1919 the hotelier still did not feel accepted by his peers. The best hotels in America were found in New York City, and their owners belonged to the Tavern Club, "the most exclusive and powerful hotel men's club in the USA," they liked to say. The members hailed from Germanic and Anglo-Saxon stock, with names such as Quinn, Bowman, Baumann, Biggs, and Muschenheim. No French, Italian, or Latin hoteliers filled the early rolls. Such exclusion seems to have burrowed under Orteig's skin.

On May 21, 1919, the Aero Club of America hosted a banquet at the Lafayette for the top American air ace Eddie Rickenbacker. The night was filled with speeches and fine French cuisine. There was talk of the flying season in Newfoundland, where the four navy seaplanes had departed on their voyage five days earlier, and a host of rivals, including Alcock and Brown, prepared their planes in hopes of winning Lord Northcliffe's £10,000 prize. The long and lean Rickenbacker spoke of his nostalgia for the Franco-American friendship that had existed between the wartime fliers, a chivalric "brotherhood of the air." Longing filled his voice, a feeling Orteig recognized. There would be a day, the ace predicted, when airplanes would link the two nations—not in war, but in peace, by means of regular commercial flights winging over the sea.

Orteig was inspired. He joined the Aero Club that night, then the next morning composed the note that started it all. "Gentlemen," he wrote, "As a stimulus for the courageous aviators, I desire to offer through the auspices and regulations of the Aero Club of America a prize of $25,000 to the first aviator of any allied country crossing the Atlantic, in one flight, from Paris to New York or New York to Paris, all other details in your care."

He could not foresee the consequences. At first the check lay in limbo, and for five years there were no serious takers. No airplane engine then built could endure the stress of a nonstop flight across the sea. When the prize expired in May 1924, Orteig, egged on by a French newspaper, renewed it without a time limit. The sum was placed in the hands of seven trustees, and the law firm of Delafield, Thorne and Burleigh served as counsel. The Bryant Park Bank, at 220 West Forty-second Street, stored the money in its vault; the National Aeronautic Association, on H Street in Washington, D.C., finalized and administered the rules. They handled all queries—from whether landing gear could be dropped in flight to save weight to the means by which a pilot raised funds.

At the time of its renewal, Orteig's $25,000 prize was worth about $305,000 in 2010 dollars. He could not know that several people would die in its quest, or that gods would be made of the young fliers competing for his prize. He was not aware that his rashness could have been his ruin. Only later did he learn that, when he made the original offer, the $25,000 represented about one-eighth his personal fortune and most of his liquid funds. His enthusiasm placed him at financial risk had there been an emergency.

•

Not everyone remembered the "war to end all wars" as fondly as Orteig or Eddie Rickenbacker. The two nations whose hopes would be most tied up in Orteig's prize could not have fared more differently. In France, the Great War was a catastrophe. Nearly 1.7 million of her citizens died, or roughly 4.29 percent of the total population. The war decimated an entire generation and caused untold millions in property damage. Shielded by the Atlantic, the United States suffered a fraction of this—

117,465 deaths, or 0.13 percent of its population. In fact, in many ways the United States actually benefitted from the war. It stimulated the economy, increased employment and wages, and brought huge profits to industry. Before World War I, England had been the world's greatest creditor nation, providing global insurance and shipping nearly everywhere. But the costs of war would be so great that England consumed all her credit and became heavily indebted to the United States to survive. Within four short years, the financial center of the world shifted from London to New York. The United States emerged from the war as both the greatest economic power on earth and the world's main creditor.

There was a European backlash against America's sudden rise on the world stage—and nowhere more so than in France, the center of ruin. The conflict had not been the time-honored clash of man versus man, but an unholy nightmare of man versus the Machine: *the Machine*, which knew no honor, and had transformed the battlefield into a scorched wasteland. New and soulless ways of killing had come into being. The machine gun fired up to 600 bullets a minute, the equivalent of 250 rifle-bearing men; massive 8.4-inch cannons known as "Big Berthas" were able to fire projectiles 76 or more miles. There were flamethrowers and U-boats; tanks capable of carrying a crew of 8 while firing 208 shells and 13,000 bullets. There was green chlorine gas, first used in the Battle of Ypres, which swept through the trenches and soon exhausted each soldier's five-minute supply of oxygen in his gas mask.

Men were not replaceable, but should a metal juggernaut be destroyed in battle, another could soon roll forth from the assembly line. And no other nation had more avidly or efficiently embraced mass production in the new century than the United States of America. In model year 1909/1910, Henry Ford rolled 18,664 Model Ts from his Detroit plants; by 1920/1921, that number swelled to 1.25 million. No other nation erected skyscrapers with such alacrity: the forty-one-story Singer Building, built in 1908; the fifty-story Metropolitan Tower; the sixty-story Woolworth Building in 1913. They were the new cathedrals.

Such veneration of the assembly line and large-scale industrialization led many French observers to see America as the personification of The Machine. "This devouring civilization," philosopher Georges Duhamel christened postwar America. "As yet, no nation has thrown itself into the excesses of industrial civilization more deliberately" than the

United States, he claimed. Across the ocean from France lay the dark continent of technology, driven by the ironclad logic of mass production. Even Alexis de Tocqueville, with his famous observation of America's genius for invention, could not have predicted what the young nation would accomplish in so short a time.

Americans themselves seemed slow to notice, but by the 1920s some native critics began describing the new gods, which seemed to spring from a machine aesthetic. They were, as Lewis Mumford wrote, "Clean, devoid of archaic ornaments, polished, efficient, carefully adapted to every human need." Success, said social critic Waldo Frank, was "an exercise of power visible to the world. If some one else can't see it, it is not success." The Machine was the symbol of that success and a form of self-adulation, the "creature of [one's] need." Like the family car, "its body of surfaces must shine, as if it were the body of the beloved."

One machine sailed above all others: the airplane.

On the surface, this seemed strange. The airplane, like the tank and U-boat, had been used as a killing machine in the war. Yet some human element remained. The combat "dogfights" of the English, French, German, and American pilots became romanticized. The popular press lionized pilots of all nations, feeding a frenzy that mutated quickly from the "cult of the aviator" to the "cult of the ace." In a war seen as an apocalyptic confrontation of men and machines, the immediate recognition of the individual flier lifted him above the mud-soaked trench soldier. Aces such as Manfred von Richthofen, René Fonck, Georges Guynemer, Eddie Rickenbacker, Billy Bishop, Charles Nungesser, and Frank Luke were front-page fodder. French tabloids kept daily records of the aces' "kills." A German newspaper published the letter that ace Kurt Wissemann sent to his mother in which he claimed to have shot down the top French ace Georges Guynemer. National Geographic published a long article on the fliers and their combat styles. While mentioning their skill and ruthlessness, the writers especially dwelt upon their chivalry, comparing them to warriors of a pre-machine age. They became something greater than soldiers; they became "knights of the air."

With the war, we see a change in the public's perception of all fliers, and not just aces. No longer was the aviator an oddball or a dangerously obsessed inventor, a rich man playing with an expensive toy. As early as 1914, in a series of quickly mimicked adventure books christened The Aeroplane Boys, the flier was set apart, a protohuman of extraordinary skill and nerve. Aviators must be athletes, something Fonck had voiced: "[T]heir very lives," observed one character, "may depend upon instantaneous action and speedy thought that springs from intuition." A 1916 ad for the Wright Flying School proclaimed, "Red-blooded, sturdy manhood has become imbued with the spirit of flight. The world has its eye on the flying man—and woman...A Fall or Winter vacation at a flying school will increase the red corpuscles and make you over into a new being—a superman in physique as well as fact."

Suddenly, more than ever, the act of flying was portrayed as something unique in human history. There was a sense of freedom, a mystical bond between man and machine. "The stars at night," observed one character in the 1913 *The Flying Machine Boys*, "seem clearer, larger, brighter, than when seen through the heavy atmosphere which surrounds the lower levels of the air."

•

As the flier's image changed, so did his importance to his nation. In the immediate postwar years, breaking world records and, increasingly, the idea of flying the Atlantic would become the badge of a country's greatness—or at least its potential. The European powers were exhausted—drained of capital, of an entire generation of men. America was content to stay within her shores. The most comforting view was of the future, not of the past or present. Progress in aviation was the yardstick of modernity; the rush to conquer the unconquerable signaled what a nation could someday be.

No nation took this idea more to heart than Orteig's homeland. "Airmindedness" became a profession of faith in the nation's future; it served as a kind of litmus test for the Gallic soul. The French invented human flight in 1783, when the Montgolfier brothers went aloft in a hot air balloon; eleven years later the nation was the first to use flight in warfare, one more manifestation of its strong tradition of allying technology with the military. Aviation resonated with the public in a special way. By the mid-nineteenth century, the balloon as an icon of science and freedom fired the nation's imagination; by the turn of the century, the airplane had taken its place.

The French were ahead of their time in aviation and aeronautics, more so even than the Americans. By 1912 French engineers had already envisioned rocket- and ramjet-powered propulsion systems, producing designs for aircraft and engines that would not appear for another forty years. The language of flying—words such as *fuselage, aileron, nacelle, hangar,* and *chandelle*—was French. Even the basic identity itself: *aviation* and *aviator.* France could boast of the dirigible flights of Brazilian expatriate Alberto Santos-Dumont, the glider trials of Ferdinand Ferber, and Blériot's crossing of the English Channel. French enthusiasts worked continuously on "product improvement," refining their theories of aerodynamics and aircraft design. During the Great War, every Allied nation either flew some French aircraft or a plane that incorporated French parts and design.

More than in any other nation, aviation had become part of the French national identity. Even before the war, citizens read and heard that they were the "winged nation," the people best suited for locomotion through the air. Flying required dash, valor, imagination, subtlety, a sense of adventure, and élan—all French qualities. In 1914 a prominent novelist claimed that, as heirs to classical antiquity, the French must avenge Icarus's fall. If France was the world's "most refined and intellectual nation," and flight was the apex of civilization, this meant that every Frenchman had aviation in his blood.

So *why,* people wondered, were the French not the first to go aloft in a motorized plane? How had the Wright brothers beaten them on December 17, 1903? No one asked this more than the French themselves. Perhaps by making the first nonstop, 3,600-mile flight across the Atlantic—a flight that many still thought impossible—France would prove to the world, and to herself, that she was still the premier "winged nation."

For all this, a visitor to the United States in 1918 could not have known that fifteen years earlier, two American bicycle shop owners had invented the airplane. At the outbreak of the war, the United States possessed a mere 2.5 percent of the world's military aircraft. Before 1914 Europeans had built ten wind tunnels for testing and design, while the United States had built only two—one of those of European design. In 1917 Theodore Roosevelt complained that the United States did not have "a single machine competent to fight the war machines of our enemies," a statement of prophetic poignancy since, in 1918, his youngest son, Quentin, would be shot down in a dogfight over German lines. By Armistice Day, the U.S. Army and Navy had nearly fourteen thousand American-made planes in service, but most were obsolete trainers that would soon be offered for sale.

After the war, aircraft production flagged. The military auctioned its surplus, selling the ubiquitous Curtiss JN-4, or "Jenny," models for $1,500 or less. Unflown Curtiss "Speed Scouts," still packed in their crates with new Gnome engines, went for $2,000. Such easy availability created a new class of aviator, the nomadic and death-defying "barn-stormers."

Some commercial interest did take shape, though usually as con-tracts for the airmail. But companies often operated on a shoestring. Government airmail flights began in May 1918; the following April, the U.S. Post Office Department called for ten specialized planes, each able to carry 1,500 to 3,000 pounds of mail. In 1920 the government announced plans for transcontinental service and called for bids on a number of routes; five years later it planned for night delivery. By 1926 a line of beacons stretched from New York City to Salt Lake City, Utah.

The military also began to realize the importance of aviation in any future warfare. In 1921 Billy Mitchell's all-American-built bombers sank the captured German warship *Ostfriesland*. In 1924 army aviators flew around the world via the coasts and short island hops using Doug-las biplanes. In 1925 army aviator Jimmy Doolittle won the prestigious Schneider Trophy in a Curtiss racer, the first time an American pilot, flying an American plane, had won the important international cup since 1909.

A curious tunnel vision had developed in both French and American aviators. While the French could not forget that the United States had invented powered flight, Americans, especially military fliers, resented what they saw as France's "air ascendancy." After the war French aces held more world records than any other group of fliers on earth. The one-eyed François Coli completed the first circle of the Mediterranean in twenty-four hours. Coli and his one-legged partner, Paul Tarascon, flew successfully from Paris to Casablanca in record time. In the sum-mer of 1925, French aces Maurice Drouhin and Jules Landry set the world record for nonstop flight at 2,734 miles. Some of the world's great-est airplane manufacturers were French: Blériot, Farman, Hanriot, Le-vasseur, and Nieuport-Delage. In 1926 the French government set aside 860,000 francs for bonuses to French aviators who set and retained world records. The funds were awarded only if their aircraft were en-tirely of French manufacture and design; premiums were even greater for seaplane records, since, in this sphere, the nation had fallen behind.

No other Western nation offered such incentives. France was already the world leader in flight: with such public support, she could remain ahead for decades.

And now René Fonck, the French ace of aces, arrived on the scene, confidently claiming he would be the first to cross the ocean and claim Orteig's prize. Almost as soon as Fonck stepped off the liner, the hotelier hosted a dinner for him at the Lafayette Hotel.

Fonck's words that night echoed the lofty sentiments that had led Orteig to sponsor his prize seven years earlier. "I am not out for the money," the famous ace declared. "I want to see the bonds between France and America, forged by Lafayette, strengthened... I will give the money, when I win it, to the men who built the plane."

Not *if* he won, but *when*. Orteig was charmed. As an afterthought, Fonck added that the plane would not have floats or pontoons for landing in water.

"It is either fly or sink," he said.

TWO

THE SURE THING

Fonck charmed the sporting crowd as effortlessly as he had Beau James. Success seemed so certain that bookies gave even odds that he would make it to Paris as claimed. Wall Street banker Jesse Winburn put down $1,000 that the flight would go as planned, an amount approximately equal to $12,000 in today's dollars. Fonck's friends bet $6,000 that he would make the flight on schedule—which was stipulated in his contract with the Argonauts to be completed on or before September 25, 1926. Their optimism got a boost when Richard Byrd and his copilot, Floyd Bennett, inspected and endorsed Fonck's plane. Even a German dirigible expert said Fonck's transatlantic flight was a sure thing.

The plane's first flight over New York only increased this certainty. The Sikorsky S-35 was billed as one of the largest and probably most advanced airplanes of its day. It was a huge silver beast, dwarfing the workers and spectators crowded around its unveiling on August 24 at Roosevelt Field. Their heads could not reach the cowlings of the three air-cooled engines; the wingspan was 101 feet, and the length of the fuselage was 45 feet. It was a "sesquiplane," a biplane whose top wing was longer than the lower, giving it a look from the front of an inverted triangle. The sound of the three engines roaring to life—one in the nose, the others suspended between the two wings like giant eggs—drowned out everything else on the field. A wide yellow-and-white stripe ran from front to back, bracketing the four cabin windows and the NEW YORK–PARIS legend painted on each side. It was a winged dynamo, the perfect image of aviation's power and promise in the Machine Age.

At 9:00 a.m. that clear Tuesday, Fonck and designer Igor Sikorsky climbed into the elevated cockpit and strapped themselves in. The plane carried four thousand pounds, one-quarter of its full-loaded rating. As the S-35 taxied down the runway, Mayor Walker and his entourage clapped their hands to their ears. Some cameramen for the papers and newsreels stood in a line some distance in front of the plane. As it came down the field at them, they dropped their cameras in panic and ran. At the last minute, Fonck pulled back on the stick and the S-35 cleared the cameras by several feet. He'd gotten rather tired of the press that summer. This was his revenge.

They stayed up thirty minutes, circling the field. At 4:00 p.m., they took off again, tracing a big oval around Manhattan. This time they took on a passenger, Lieutenant Allan Snoddy of the navy, and all three took their turns at the controls. The plane headed west, up the Harlem River and over Yankee Stadium, then turned down the Hudson River and back east, around the Statue of Liberty. They headed up the East River and back over Brooklyn, then made their final approach into the breeze. The $100,000 plane glided to a stop in the soft green grass of the runway.

There was silence when the propellers stopped; a pause, then the three pilots emerged. A mob of Sikorsky's countrymen hoisted the grinning Igor Ivanovich on their shoulders and took him for yet another circuit around the field.

•

For Sikorsky, winning the prize meant everything. A plump, balding refugee of the Russian Revolution with a pencil-thin moustache and a perpetual worried look, Sikorsky feared he would be ruined if the S-35 did not win. Approximately $80,000 in the hole over its construction, he prayed that the publicity would lead to lucrative military contracts. His financial survival depended upon that successful landing in Paris.

Yet, from the beginning, conflict and doubt filled his days. When he signed the contract with Fonck and the Argonauts in December 1925, he'd been pressured to build the transatlantic plane for $43,000. It was immediately apparent to him that the cost would far exceed that, but he needed the contract so desperately that he signed anyway. By late August 1926, the Argonauts had paid only $20,000, and when he demanded payment, they played hardball. They would pay in time, they promised, and he had to take their word. If not, they would pay the current balance due of $8,000, fire Fonck, and send the S-35 to Paris with a U.S. crew. Maybe Richard Byrd, they said.

What could he do? He was a prisoner of his dreams. Not just him, but his wife, Elizabeth, his sons, and a dozen White Russian refugees, mechanics, and tinkerers who worked with him in the leaky hangar at the edge of Roosevelt Field. Sikorsky's ride atop their shoulders was not showboating, but expressed the team's relief that their efforts had not been in vain.

It was amazing to Sikorsky how quickly dreams could sour: it was a constant pattern of his life, one he'd watched unfold before. He had come to the United States in 1919, the same year Orteig first offered his prize, when he was just under thirty. Two years earlier he had been Russia's leading aircraft designer, in charge of building his nation's bombing fleet for the Great War. The result had been seventy-three "Ilya Muromets" bombers, so big that they had observation decks where the crew could stroll out and watch the clouds. So tough that only one was shot down. They formed the heart of the EVK, the world's first bomber squadron, which had run a number of sorties over the Kaiser's Germany.

Sikorsky feared the little things. In 1911 during a demonstration of the S-5, his first plane completely of his own design, the engine quit and he nearly pancaked into a wall. He took apart the engine and discovered that a mosquito had been sucked into the carburetor, starving the engine of fuel. One engine was never enough, he decided. Bigger was better. Redundancy became his creed.

As his planes became behemoths, he was honored by the tsar. Those unimpressed by the size of his airplanes could not ignore their speed. In 1914 he set the world speed record when he flew at an average of 70 miles per hour from St. Petersburg to Kiev. He grew rich from the sale of his airplane designs. At age twenty-three, his future seemed assured.

It all crumbled in 1917. After the Revolution, he fled first to Paris, where as a youth he'd attended the world-renowned École Supérieure des Techniques Aéronautiques et de Construction Automobile. Yet too many unemployed aircraft designers lived in the City of Light, and he moved to New York a year later. He arrived with only a few hundred dollars and no English to speak of. Few knew of his accomplishments there; even if they had, American military aviation was experiencing a postwar slump and commercial aviation had barely gotten under way.

There was no capital and little work for a man of his skills. Major Alexander de Seversky, a Russian ace who now acted as general manager for a small New York aircraft firm, hired him as chief engineer at $12,000, but the company dissolved almost immediately, and Sikorsky was on the street again. He taught himself English and gave lectures to men's clubs on aviation, mathematics, and astronomy; he lived in furnished rooms in Brooklyn and the Lower East Side, limiting himself to eighty cents daily for coffee, rolls, and baked beans.

Vertical flight had been Sikorsky's first love, one that had inspired him even as a boy. Under his mother's tutelage in Kiev, he'd studied the works of Leonardo da Vinci and Jules Verne. At age twelve he'd devised a rubber-band-powered model of a helicopter; in 1909, at age twenty, he'd built his first working prototype, which at best hopped across the field. Sikorsky still dreamed of fathering the helicopter, but Americans weren't interested. Helicopters seemed impractical. As talk in the early Jazz Age veered toward commercial transport, Sikorsky saw the writing on the wall and began designing airplanes capable of carrying forty to fifty people at a time.

In 1922 he showed these plans to W. A. Bary, an American oilman raised in Russia, and his luck began to change. Bary knew of Sikorsky's big Russian bombers—he, too, had fled the Revolution—and put up $600 seed money for what would become the Sikorsky Aero Engineering Corporation. Sikorsky's workforce filled quickly with Russian expatriates who'd attended his lectures on the Lower East Side; many were Russian naval officers who had spent their youth with him in the naval college at St. Petersburg. Several hailed from royalty. Their first objective was to build a four-engine passenger plane, the first American-made Sikorsky, dubbed the S-29. One of the Russians owned a chicken farm at the edge of Roosevelt Field, so the coop became their machine shop and the farm their commune. They salvaged hospital beds from junkyards for the angle iron and pipe that formed 90 percent of the aircraft frame; the pieces were bolted together and braced with wire. Rivets were scarce, and the chickens often swallowed them for grist. Each Saturday featured a chicken feast, which also served as a way to retrieve the rivets. As winter approached, expatriate composer Sergei Rachmaninoff donated $5,000 to the effort, and was named company vice president in recognition of his largesse.

The S-29-A (A for "American") took its maiden flight from Roosevelt

Field on May 4, 1924. It stretched 49 feet, 10 inches from nose to tail, and stood 13.5 feet tall. Although the plane was designed to hold fourteen people, Sikorsky feared it was underpowered with its two 300-horsepower Hispano-Suiza engines. He wanted only two passengers to ride with him on the maiden flight, but instead eight excited Russians crowded inside. This was Sikorsky's great weakness: he could not say no. The overloaded plane struggled aloft to 100 feet. Then one engine failed, and the plane crashed on a golf course near the end of the field.

No one was hurt, but Sikorsky once again feared ruin. He rebuilt the plane, but by midsummer he'd run out of money for wheels, propellers, and the two 400-horsepower Liberty engines he wanted to replace the weak Hispano-Suizas. He called a meeting of fifty stockholders, most of them Russian, and locked the door; he would not unlock it, he announced, until they donated $2,500. The honor of Mother Russia was at stake, he declared. The captive stockholders dug into their pockets, and he let them go home. That September, he climbed 1,000 feet and pirouetted for ten minutes before his appreciative audience. This time only three people rode along.

The S-29 would be Sikorsky's American savior. By now he understood the importance of publicity in his new home. He granted demonstration flights for the public, the military, and the press, and by the end of 1924, the 14-passenger plane had made 45 flights and clocked 15 hours and 37 minutes in the air. More than 420 passengers flew with him that year, including members of the Army Air Service and an aeronautics professor at New York University. The professor and five students conducted tests, including a cruise with only one engine. The favorable results were published in *Aviation* magazine.

By 1925 Sikorsky had made more than two hundred flights, most of these charter trips for aviation enthusiasts. He transported two baby grand pianos from New York to Washington, D.C.; he arranged publicity stunts, from air photography to airborne radio broadcasts. One passenger was World War I ace Harold Hartney, vice president of the General Airways System of New York, who had visions of using the S-29 for an airline that would link Boston, New York, Detroit, Chicago, and Minneapolis–St. Paul.

Sikorsky had every reason to think that the lean days were over. He secured the financial backing of Arnold C. Dickinson of Fitchburg, Massachusetts. Over the next five years, Dickinson, his friends, and family invested several hundred thousand dollars, allowing Sikorsky to move his company from the chicken farm to a real hangar on Roosevelt Field. Sikorsky reorganized and started building seaplanes and some smaller biplanes. His old passenger Harold Hartney sent a wire asking him to build a prototype of what would become the S-35.

Although this early S-35 was somewhat different from Fonck's, its original purpose was to make the Atlantic hop and win the Orteig Prize. In a memo to the U.S. Department of Commerce, Hartney said he began planning the project as early as June 1925. He lined up financing, met with Washington officials, and approached Sikorsky with the idea. The early S-35 would be a three-engine transport with a three-man crew and room for sixteen passengers. Hartney considered himself a pragmatist. Winning the prize, he wrote, would create "an all-metal multimotored plane suitable for the future airlines of this country." He believed that victory would buck up public confidence in air travel, and that in the afterglow he could make his planes available to buyers "at a reasonable price." Finally, it would "demonstrate to the world that air travel was rapidly bringing all the countries of the globe closer together to standardize economic practices and to stimulate our commerce with the world." To Hartney, globalism began with the transatlantic plane.

Hartney could talk a good game, but his postwar flying career had not been illustrious. He was one of six aviators in July 1920 to fly the first transcontinental airmail route from the East Coast to San Francisco, but his journey proved a litany of misfortune. In Cleveland he tangled with a telephone pole, ruining one of the planes. In Omaha he tried to take off with Eddie Rickenbacker aboard. Instead, he rolled past the end of the runway and into a nearby home. Fortunately, the residents were outside watching the takeoff. The only injury, Rickenbacker said, was "a severely fractured straw hat."

To curb liability and seduce potential stockholders, Hartney formed the Argonauts, Inc., the New York–based group providing limited backing to Sikorsky. Despite the assistance, Sikorsky still assumed a greater risk, but hoped it would be worth it with time. The Argonauts assured him that the publicity would make him famous; the navy was interested in trimotor planes and would pound on his door for contracts once the S-35 landed in Paris. They told him that he ought to be willing to shoulder a temporary loss for all the future benefits, and he desperately wanted to believe them. After all, the principal shareholders were men whom he trusted or who were successful in their own right: they included Sikorsky's benefactor Arnold Dickinson; Hartney, who held 25 percent; Robert B. Jackson, a newspaper magnate from Concord, New Hampshire, who also held 25 percent; and Hartney's friend and fellow pilot Captain Homer Berry, a 10-percent stockholder.

Of all the Argonauts, Berry saw the project as more than just a business proposition. A military flier for Pancho Villa and during the Great War, he was the original choice as pilot. He would be famous, the first aviator to cross the Atlantic nonstop. In September 1925 he tested one of Sikorsky's prototypes; as late as the summer of 1926, he would be shown in news photos, arms wrapped around Richard Byrd and Floyd Bennett in their dress whites during a dinner honoring them for their flight to the North Pole. Even then, some newspapers called him the heir apparent for the Orteig Prize.

Then Fonck arrived and everything changed.

·

In addition to Fonck's other pioneering work in the transatlantic race, he introduced a theme that would arise repeatedly: bitter dissension within the teams.

For Sikorsky, the little Frenchman was a godsend. Sikorsky's recent and sudden success in the States was based on big planes, but his heart still lay with the idea of creating a craft that could rise and fall like a window shade. No one took him seriously. But if one of his planes won the Orteig Prize, everything would change.

Besides, Fonck represented a flair that filled Sikorsky with longing. He'd breathed it in like air during his student days and his later exile in Paris; though he loved his new country and had already become naturalized, it sometimes seemed to him as if Americans were born without a soul. Everything came down to the bottom line. He missed the romance of the French more than he cared to admit, and in the controversies surrounding the flight, he would support Fonck in everything.

Fonck had moved quickly from the very beginning. He first walked into Sikorsky's hangar in October 1925 while attending the Pulitzer Trophy Air Races; by that December he was meeting with Hartney in Washington. The kind of publicity Fonck would bring to the project was "alluring to me at the time," Hartney later said. On January 15, 1926,

Fonck signed a contract with the Argonauts: it named him lead pilot, paid him a salary of $250 per week, gave him control of the $25,000 prize to distribute among the crew as he saw fit, and promised him 10 percent of the Argonauts' common stock should he land in Paris by the end of the summer. If Fonck succeeded, he would be rich. Homer Berry stepped down as lead pilot, but a clause in the contract assured him a place should more than two people take off in the plane.

In addition to flying the plane and publicizing the flight, Fonck vowed to deliver three powerful Gnome-Rhône Jupiter engines from the French government in the spirit of Franco-American cooperation. He insisted on this: the S-35 already had three Liberty engines, but Fonck felt they were not powerful enough for the ocean flight. Fonck "was to furnish the motors free and I would furnish the plane," Hartney said.

It didn't work that way. By March 1926 Hartney had arranged for the transport of the motors from France, still believing they would be free. But by May 1, Fonck's promise had fallen through. The French underwrote a loan for the engines, but the Argonauts had to pay a $27,000 bond. This was more than the Orteig Prize itself (and worth $330,539 in today's dollars).

Why was Fonck unable to keep his word when it seemed, on the surface at least, that he could do no wrong? In a world of death and romantic gestures, he displayed a rare ability to apply mathematical principles to aerodynamics, a skill he'd picked up as an engineering student in the school of arts and sciences in Paris. His knowledge of the strengths and weaknesses of his aircraft surpassed that of most other pilots, and he used that knowledge with lethal results as he approached his foe. While other pilots jousted for position behind an enemy plane, Fonck dove straight into its face, knowing how much stress his own plane could stand. When the enemy broke off first, he fell prey to Fonck's guns. The tactic led to the day that made him internationally famous: May 7, 1918, when he downed six enemy planes in a massive dogfight, three of them within forty-five seconds.

But the focus and confidence that had made Fonck so deadly in war looked more like rampaging ego in the peace that followed. As with so many who are driven, he could not imagine that people ever doubted him; he seemed incapable of doubting himself.

Yet he did have detractors, even during the war. Other pilots did not like him at the same time that they valued his unerring skill. One author referred to Fonck as "a dreadful show-off, intolerable, always bragging, egotistical, ham-like, a poseur, gaudy, loud, hard to take, expressionless at times, morose, deliberately cruel, over-neat, tightly tailored, etc." Even his best friend, twenty-two-kill ace Claude Haegelen, admitted: "He is not a truthful man. He is a tiresome braggart, and even a bore, but in the air, a slashing rapier, a steel blade tempered with un-blemished courage and priceless skill... But afterwards he can't forget how he rescued you, nor let you forget it. He can almost make you wish he hadn't helped you in the first place."

Such resentment seemed to continue after the war. While several authors and journalists wrote books about France's many aerial heroes, no one wrote about Fonck but Fonck, in his appropriately titled *Ace of Aces*. Several French pilots wrote memoirs about their service without once mentioning Fonck; among the survivors, the "pilot's pilot" was not Fonck but the dashing Charles Nungesser, who had been wounded sev-enteen times.

Similar tensions began to peek from beneath the fabric in the sum-mer of 1926, after Fonck returned to New York. In June and July all seemed calm. Every day, Sikorsky wore his greasy checkered cap to the leaky hangar where his old twin-engine, medium-range passenger plane was turning into a trimotor monster. New designs meant tests for stress; extra length was added to the middle sections of the top and bottom wings. He redesigned the fuselage to handle the third engine; he cre-ated a complicated fuel system to deliver the huge amount of fuel needed to fly 3,600 miles. Gas would be stored in nacelles behind the wing en-gines, in fuel tanks forming the top wing's leading edge, and in tanks inside the cabin separating the pilots from the tail. Not unexpectedly, the plane was becoming huge. It was ungainly and ugly, critics said. "Most people think a plane should be like an eagle, with a broad wing-span and slight body," Sikorsky responded. "But, no, an eagle has a very short range. My plane is constructed like an albatross, with a powerful body and great wings. The albatross flies great distances against heavy winds in all weather, and that is what my plane will do."

Fonck did his part. He gave interviews to newspapers and maga-zines, and appeared in the newsreels. There were lunches at country clubs and chambers of commerce, speeches on Franco-American ac-cord. Letters arrived from strangers asking to be taken aboard, includ-ing a Brooklyn salvage dealer named Charles Levine, who offered

$25,000 to ride along as a passenger. Fonck turned them all down. In addition, hundreds of fliers and mechanics applied for the crew, but by July the roster seemed set. Fonck would be pilot; Homer Berry, copilot; the navigator would be Lieutenant Allan P. Snoddy, and the radio operator would be Captain John R. Irwin, a friend of Hartney's.

Despite the calm, Hartney's patience wore thin. Most of his rancor seemed directed at Fonck; he was probably still steaming over the $27,000 bond for engines that had yet to arrive. The plane was not finished on May 1, despite a contract deadline; in mid-August, the engines finally arrived, accompanied by an engineer to help install them. On August 17, Sikorsky announced that the S-35 was ready for her maiden flight, but rain delayed it. Seven days later the plane flew for the first time, over Manhattan.

It was a triumphant debut, but it came too late to patch the divisions assailing the team. The original crew began to shed like dead skin. The first to go was Berry: on August 10, Fonck told him his services were no longer needed. Though Fonck never gave his reasons, the dismissal occurred around the time that newspapers revealed that Berry had been made a captain not by the U.S. Army, but by Pancho Villa. Berry always assumed he would fly, and his stock ownership seemed to give him the right, at least in his own mind. The rift did not become public until August 29, but when it did, Berry said he planned to sue. "No Frenchman, no matter how many medals he has, can come over here and push me out of this flight," Berry told a pack of reporters. Hartney stood by his side.

So much for Franco-American accord. "The best thing for Capt. Berry to do is to keep quiet," Fonck shot back. "I won't say anymore. I won't talk to newspaper men. There is so much damned nonsense in the newspapers."

Soon others departed. Irwin left next, privately telling Hartney that after watching Fonck "handle the big ship, he did not want to commit suicide." Snoddy fell ill with bronchitis. A possible replacement was George O. Noville, the flight engineer in Richard Byrd's polar venture. But Noville stomped off the scene when he disapproved of Fonck's choice of lubricating oil—a number of endorsements had been signed to help finance the flight, and Noville's employer, Vacuum Oil Company of California, was not one of them.

On Labor Day, Hartney called a meeting of the Argonauts' board.

"Fonck is irresponsible, and not competent to pilot this ship," he declared, citing the broken promises, lack of testing, problems with the crew, and delays. "To permit him to attempt [the flight] would jeopardize human life. Either he withdraws from this project, or I do."

Hartney's statement split the board down the middle, and it seemed there might not be a flight. Hartney and Berry stood on one side; Sikorsky's partner Dickinson and Robert Johnson, the newspaper magnate who held the largest share of stock, backed Fonck. Their 50 percent of the voting shares outweighed Hartney's and Berry's 35 percent. Dickinson said that relations between France and America should not be threatened. Hartney shot back that the threat to human life was greater if Fonck stayed on.

The row became so public that *The New York Times* felt called to weigh in. Fonck had a perfect right to select his crew, an editor wrote. He was the captain, wasn't he? "Without the support of public opinion the development of commercial aviation would be hopeless," the *Times* warned. If this attempt collapsed due to internal squabbles, "a long time may pass before Americans will concern themselves about transatlantic flying."

In the end, neither Hartney nor Berry prevailed. Hartney sold his shares and resigned from the Argonauts. "[T]he success of the flight is more important than my personal feelings," said Berry, and he, too, withdrew.

Through it all the ship performed admirably, even if the people did not. During an August 30 test, the plane flew steadily with only the nose engine running, and climbed a little as well. Sikorsky switched between engines as he idled the others. The plane's performance was flawless each time.

Eight days later, a group of army observers came aboard. This time the plane carried 20,000 pounds—7,000 less than the full-rated load. It climbed to 2,000 feet in just under three minutes. Sikorsky throttled back on the center engine so that only the wing engines ran. In two minutes, the S-35 climbed another 500 feet. The army brass was amazed. Their best bombers could not climb at that rate, even at full power.

The next day, the plane was christened at Roosevelt Field. A Protestant minister and Catholic priest placed icons in the cabin—St. Nicholas, patron saint of Russia, and St. Christopher, the traveler's guardian. Mayor Jimmy Walker held aloft a big bottle of mineral water (since champagne was illegal) and yelled, "I christen you the *New York to Paris.*" He struck the metal exhaust pipe. The bottle stayed intact.

He swung the bottle again. A third time, at a metal propellor. He dented the blade.

A mechanic ran up with a huge Stillson wrench; he swung it hard as Walker held the bottle against an exhaust pipe. The bottle shattered. The crowd cheered.

"Nothing'll ever sink this ship," cracked Walker.

"Some bottle!" cried a wag.

•

Around midnight on September 21, Igor Sikorsky climbed into the cockpit and taxied his "huge, beautiful ship" from the leaking factory hangar to the end of the runway. It was a black September night; the sky was overcast, no moon or stars. Fonck planned to leave near dawn. They had decided that it would be best to load and fuel the plane at the starting point rather than roll her from the hangar full of petrol. Workers swarmed around and over the S-35, grooming her like a thoroughbred. Bathed in floodlights, she glittered like a giant dragonfly, her wings silver and pure. Lights flashed in and out of the cockpit as contacts were tested; the shadowy figure of a mechanic could be seen on the top wing as he crawled back and forth with a flashlight, checking connections. Others went over every inch of the body, wiping off dust, tightening every nut and bolt, polishing the wings.

Time and again that night, Sikorsky climbed to the top of a small hill bordering Roosevelt Field. He watched as hundreds of cars drove from the west, from the city. The feuds and delays, the tests and gradual construction of his great silver albatross had turned this flight from a barely noticed footnote in the *Times* to a page-one daily feature in every paper. He checked for wind. Even a little breeze from the right direction would help her lift off. But there was nothing. Only calm.

One frets about one's children: a million ills may beset them, and for the S-35 the big problem was obesity. The weight had piled on over the last few days. Sikorsky's plane weighed 8,000 pounds empty, and with a full complement of equipment, crew, gas, and oil, was rated for a takeoff weight of 24,200 pounds. The 50 barrels of gas, a full 2,380 gallons, were sufficient to keep the three engines running for the trip; the filled barrels alone weighed 15,200 pounds. Sikorsky had tested the plane empty; then in increasing weights, until he reached 20,000 pounds; and each time the S-35 performed beautifully. By September 14, she had made 23 flights covering 2,500 miles in 23 hours and 50 minutes of flight, but none had been made at full rating.

Now she was overloaded, tipping the scales at 28,160 pounds, 4,000 pounds heavier than expected. When Sikorsky taxied the plane from the hangar to the end of the runway, there were problems. To compensate for the weight, a temporary wheeled platform, or "dolly," had been added: this lifted up the tail as the plane took off down the field. Two small wheels were placed behind the original landing gear to redistribute the load. The dolly had never been tested in takeoff, and as Sikorsky taxied the plane into position, the tail skid slipped off, slightly damaging the lower end of the center rudder. One small landing wheel was bent when the plane was turned around. As he watched the mechanics straighten the wheel and reattach the dolly, he could see the ground beneath the wheels dimple from the excess pounds.

How had this excess weight piled on? In the excitement, an enormous amount of last-minute baggage had been added. An interior designer installed mahogany chairs, a red leather hide-a-bed, a miniature food cabinet and table on which a victory dinner would be served on arrival at Paris's main airport, Le Bourget. A hot dinner, stored in a vacuum container and cooked at the Hotel McAlpin, was loaded for Robert Johnson and Parisian officials; they would eat Manhattan clam chowder, roast Long Island duck, wild Vermont turkey, and Baltimore terrapin.

Sikorsky had wanted more tests, mimicking the takeoff weight by filling the gas tanks with water. They would be completed by spring 1927, but his backers balked at the idea. There had already been too many delays, they said. The flight had been pushed back several times already due to bad weather. On September 15, they were gassed up and ready to go when a leak in one fuel tank was discovered. While they were forced to wait for repairs and tests, other aviators threatened to make the "hop"—from Paris, Paul Tarascon, François Coli, and French air force commandant Pierre Weiss; from New York, Clarence Chamberlin and Noel Davis. None of these pilots was anywhere close to being able to take off, but the Argonauts got scared. The days were growing shorter, and the window for good weather was closing. It was time to go.

Fonck felt the pressure, too. Four days earlier, Commandant Weiss sent a telegram urging him to start at all costs. "ABSOLUTELY START THE FLIGHT," read the cable, "EVEN IF YOU DROP INTO THE OCEAN." French newspapers clamored for him to get in the air; their editorial writers groused that he should either take off or call the flight off entirely.

Sikorsky looked down from his perch and felt a chill. The Argonauts were being pushed by a force that was new to him. They'd made decisions against their better judgment, based upon the demands of publicity. An urgency arose that was neither real nor necessary. More cars arrived. By 5:00 a.m., an estimated two thousand spectators had gathered. Indistinct forms hovered at the edge of the lights, pointing at the painted stork on the fuselage honoring Fonck's wartime squadron, at the crossed American and French flags by the words NEW YORK TO PARIS. Police formed a cordon between the dark mass and the plane.

At least the crew was not an issue: after the departure of Snoddy, Irwin, and Noville, Fonck had assembled a new one. Snoddy was replaced by Lieutenant Lawrence W. Curtin of the navy; he was principal navigator and for the last few days had been working on his charts and monitoring a storm off Newfoundland. Though it would probably pass before their takeoff, storms like this often meant fog. If necessary, they'd go around.

Charles Clavier had replaced Irwin as radioman. Fonck had brought him over from France in May to install the radio, designed by Radio des Industries, and the short, jovial thirty-three-year-old quickly became a favorite. He lounged around the plane with his hands in his brown leather jacket, incessantly chatting with friends. He'd joined the French navy in 1908 and served eighteen years, a period that included four flights across the Mediterranean. He was elated to return to Paris, where his wife and two children awaited him. He'd bought presents for all, and held up his last thirty-five cents as proof. "Dinner in Paris on Wednesday," he laughed. "I will never leave France again."

Jacob Islamoff, twenty-eight, had been made flight engineer. He was tall and reserved, the opposite of the short and outgoing Clavier, with whom he'd become pals. Islamoff was one of Sikorsky's core Russians, a longtime friend and one of the naval graduates from St. Petersburg. He knew the S-35 inside and out, especially the complicated fuel system. Now he stood in the glare of the floodlights in a snow-white jumpsuit, studying the unstable dolly. Like Sikorsky, he worried that it had never been tested; it was his job to pull a lever to release the dolly once they got airborne. Still, he felt lucky to be on the flight; his parents lived in exile in Constantinople, and this was the quickest way back to see them.

Shortly after 4:00 a.m., Sikorsky called the New York weather service, based in a Midtown skyscraper. The weathermen had been in contact with about a dozen oceangoing ships to the east, and it seemed that for the next twenty-four hours reasonably good weather could be expected over most of the Atlantic. After that, bad weather would close in. The flight would then be impossible, and it might very well mean the end of the flying season. Sikorsky called Fonck and gave him the news. They would start just before dawn, Fonck said.

At 5:00 a.m., Sikorsky declared the plane ready. A low-throated rumble arose from the crowd. Homer Berry stood in the mob, unable to keep away; Harold Hartney sat in his car at the edge of the field, thinking his presence might disrupt things. Automobiles lined both sides of the runway. One of Sikorsky's engineers drove a car down the flight path to drive back the crowds, barely clearing enough room for the passage of the plane. The tension seemed too great; one last time, Sikorsky climbed the little knoll overlooking the field. He hoped to stay there until his beautiful plane was but a speck in the sky. A breeze *had* blown up, about 14 miles per hour, but though it helped clear the weather, it was also a crosswind and a little aft, not a headwind, which would have helped lift the plane.

At 6:00 a.m., the three huge motors roared to life, kicked into motion by a little outboard engine. The French engineer who'd supervised their installation sat in the cockpit and listened for any odd sound. In the end he seemed satisfied. The plane quivered behind the wheel chocks. The engineer cut power and climbed from the plane.

The gray of dawn began to show. Islamoff stepped from the hangar, followed by Clavier. A big car drove up and pulled into the light; Fonck stepped out, clad in brown puttees and his blue service uniform coat and medals. Curtin followed. They changed into their heavy flying suits and leather helmets, storing the uniforms in the aircraft's cabin.

Fonck stood by the door and threw away his last cigarette. A woman stepped from the crowd and put out her hand. "Bon voyage," she said, as easily as if she were seeing a friend off for holiday.

Fonck liked the gesture. He smiled. "Merci, madame," he replied. "Au revoir."

A man with a long beard stepped up next and handed Fonck a large box of freshly baked croissants, compliments of Raymond Orteig. Fonck lifted it in his hand to test the weight. With a rueful grimace, he placed it aboard the overloaded plane.

Islamoff and Clavier crawled into the back of the fuselage; Fonck and Curtin, into the front, considered the most perilous place, since they would sit in slightly elevated seats right behind the spinning nose propeller. Friends had urged Curtin to ride in the back with the others, but he declined, saying his place was beside Fonck, in case of trouble.

The pilots closed the door behind them. It was not locked, and could easily open from inside, so long as nothing jammed. Fonck started the engines again and let them warm for a couple of minutes. The mass of automobiles began to move, speeding down the runway so they would be as close as possible to the S-35's liftoff. Sikorsky watched the frenzy from atop his knoll. He had calculated that it would take his heavily laden plane 50 seconds to reach a flying speed of 80 miles per hour. But that had been at its full rating. At its overburdened weight, who could really know?

It was 6:20 a.m. The light was now sharp. Sikorsky could see everything.

•

Roosevelt Field stretched 5,180 feet before them, nearly a mile. It was laid out east to west, to take advantage of the prevailing westerly winds. At the eastern end of the strip, behind the S-35, a line of telegraph wires formed a mental hazard for those piloting heavily loaded planes. Beyond that lay a golf course, then the length of Long Island. The western end seemed friendlier, at least for takeoff, but at its edge lay a forty-foot bank that dropped into a gully. Beyond that lay neighboring Curtiss Field.

Roosevelt's runway was 200 feet wide and made of sand and clay. Paved strips were still a rarity; the landing gear of planes at that time were delicate structures, and dirt and grass tended to cushion landings. Three dirt tracks crossed the field—one 300 yards from the starting point, another two-thirds down the course, and finally a third 50 yards from the high bank. The S-35 had hopped over these in earlier tests—when it was considerably lighter—with no problem.

Fonck opened the throttle, and the plane roared. Sikorsky's Russians put their shoulders to the wings. Clouds of dust streamed behind the S-35 as she rolled down the field.

The plane reached the first road, hitting the ruts and bouncing over them. Suddenly one wheel of the dolly tore loose and leapt into the air. The plane lurched to the left, but Fonck straightened it back out. "Lift the tail, lift the tail!" cried a pilot in the crowd, jumping up and down in excitement. The second set of ruts approached at 3,200 feet, but the S-35 was only making 70 miles per hour, not enough to get airborne.

When it hit the second road, the plane began to come apart. The right wheel of the dolly collapsed, then spun and whirled away. The wheel beneath the tail skid leapt into the air, and the skid itself hit the ground. One of these spinning wheels struck the lower left rudder, which broke loose and dragged behind, further slowing the plane.

In the cockpit, Fonck knew he was in trouble. Brakes in planes did not then exist, and if he turned, the 14-ton S-35 would plow through the mob on either side. If he throttled down and cut his speed, he'd lose control and veer into the cars. The carnage would be incredible. All he could do was keep going. The bluff was coming up: if they were going fast enough, he hoped, the plane might hit the dirt and hop over, then skid to a level stop on the grass beyond.

But the rudder dragging behind them made even that last-ditch maneuver impossible. The plane hit the embankment, her great wings outspread. She slid over the top and disappeared into the gully. Then she cartwheeled on her right wing and began breaking into pieces.

"Oh my God!" cried someone in the crowd. "He's crashed!"

Sikorsky began running from the top of his hill. His face was pale as death, his eyes fixed in horror. There was a moment of silence as the first cars pulled up to the bank, then flames shot up at least forty feet high. He heard the roar of the flames and the screams of a hysterical woman as he ran. He made it to the bank before many others, then stopped at the wall of fire. He turned away and doubled over. He didn't remember anything after that. Friends later told him he was incoherent. They bundled him up and took him home.

Homer Berry was close behind Sikorsky. He plunged past the designer and slid down the embankment. "Oh, what a shame! What a shame!" he cried. "Those poor men!" Orange flames and black smoke engulfed the wreck. Everyone must be dead.

Then, miraculously, Curtin and Fonck were seen clambering up the bank, covered with soot, oil, and grime. Fonck was bleeding from a cut on his forehead; he staggered when he reached the top, unable to speak. Curtin talked for both of them: When the plane had flipped up and over to the right, the opening in the front of the cockpit was nearly blocked, leaving a gap of only a few feet, he said. The center motor, three feet in front of them, was in flames. Curtin spotted gasoline pouring from the wing tanks toward the burning motor; the smell of gas washed over them. They dodged the spinning propeller and had barely crawled clear when the gas reached the fire. There was silence, then a *whumpf!*, and the shock wave knocked them down. They heard nothing from the fuselage. Clavier and Islamoff, they thought, must have escaped through the side door.

But the two crewmen in the back never made it out. It was believed they had been knocked out by loose baggage, and the flames made it impossible to rescue them. An ambulance from Mitchel Field pulled up within five minutes; a fire engine from Hempstead soon afterward. By then there was nothing to do. The plane burned for hours before the flames could be extinguished; a black mushroom cloud of smoke rose high in the air. When firemen finally entered the wreck, they found the charred hand, shoulder, and leg of one of the men. His crewmate's hip lay nearby. Both were burned beyond recognition. A charred Koran and crucifix were found near the bodies.

Later that day, Fonck spoke to reporters in the Sikorsky hangar; Curtin stood beside him. "I tried to slacken the speed because I knew that if I stopped too quickly after the first accident to the landing gear, the wheels would give way altogether," he tried to explain. "But I could not do so. When the right wheel gave way after the drop I knew it was all over. It is the fortune of the air. It could not be helped."

That seemed cold, a form of wartime fatalism quite alien to civilian tragedies. But Curtin understood, and broke in. He had stayed with a friend after the wreck and tried to calm himself for the explanations that would follow. It was hard for him to speak; he fought to control his nerves, and his voice trembled. "Now is the time for you fellows to get us another plane," he told the subdued little group of newsmen. "I will try it again with Capt. Fonck as pilot in a plane built by Mr. Sikorsky. How about that, Captain?"

Curtin's words were translated for Fonck, and he nodded quickly.

"*Absolument,*" Fonck replied.

Sikorsky could not speak so easily. Newsmen found him in his cottage in nearby Mineola, a green sanctuary where he raised cucumbers and plowed his garden with a small tractor. Now he sat in his high-backed leather chair, hands in his lap. He greeted his visitors with a glance, and tried to smile. But he could not speak, and his wife, Elizabeth, laid her hand on his arm and asked the reporters to come back later in the day.

When they did, he was more composed, though just barely. He shook hands with each of them. He was calm, but very pale, and his lip trembled as he spoke. Jacob Islamoff was his good friend, he said, and "no one can ever take his place." Charles Clavier had been with them only a few months, but "his unfailing smile was a great asset." And Fonck?

"We believe that Captain Fonck did all in his power."

•

The recriminations began immediately. French aviation experts blamed Sikorsky for faulty construction of the giant plane, saying the S-35 did not have sufficient lifting capacity. Hartney called Fonck "incompetent." Fonck blamed Islamoff for releasing the dolly too quickly, causing it to break off and damage the rudder, thus making the plane unmanageable.

Still, in the end, everyone was cleared of wrongdoing. Nassau County district attorney Elvin N. Edwards said, after a brief inquest, that no criminal negligence was involved. There would be no charges. If any single factor was responsible, he said, it was the central fact of overloading. There was a brief investigation into Commandant Weiss's wire to Fonck to leave at all costs. But in the end, sorrow took over. The few isolated calls for retribution were ignored.

A few days after the wreck, Clavier's body was sent by ship back home. Islamoff's was buried closer to where he died. He was a Muslim, and twelve pallbearers carried the six hundred-pound red leaden coffin a mile and a half from the funeral home in nearby Westbury to the Sikorsky hangar at Roosevelt Field. His pallbearers laid the coffin on the three scorched Gnome-Rhône Jupiter engines of the S-35. A local mullah read from the Koran. ·

Fonck and Curtin said they would try again, and Sikorsky returned to his drawing board. But in truth, Fonck and Sikorsky would never again be serious contenders for the Orteig Prize. Fonck continued to plan, but Sikorsky thought he himself was bankrupt, and his heart was no longer in the competition. Once again, as so many times in the past, his life had jumped quickly from hope to gloom and uncertainty.

Until the day of his death, Sikorsky believed that his friends, and his plane, had been sacrificed at the altar of publicity.

THREE

"THIS HERO BUSINESS"

Fonck's calamity was an opportunity for others.

The next to give the transatlantic challenge serious thought were French aces François Coli and Paul Tarascon. The two made an exotic pair: Coli had lost his right eye and Tarascon his right leg in crashes. Both were part of the French quest for long-distance records, pushing their postwar planes farther than seemed possible.

Coli was especially successful. Son of a Corsican seafarer, he knew the ways of the weather and the sea. He joined the French Air Service in March 1916 and rose to command Escadrille N.62 by February 1917. After the war, he flew for records, often with his old war friend Lieutenant Henry Roget. On January 26, 1919, the two flew 457 miles in 5 hours to make the first round-trip jump across the Mediterranean; four months later, on May 24, they flew 1,365 miles from Paris to Morocco, setting another long-distance record. Coli was injured in a crash at the end of the flight, but by 1920 he was back in the cockpit, making further long-distance flights around the Mediterranean. By 1923 he and Tarascon began planning a nonstop transatlantic flight, and though Tarascon briefly bowed out, by 1925 they had reunited with plans to win the Orteig Prize.

Coli was a careful man. The loss of his eye meant the loss of his depth perception; thus he transformed himself from a pilot to a first-class navigator. He studied every route from Paris to New York, poring over maps and charts, plundering the Navigation Almanac for data on weather, tides, and prevailing winds—especially near the North American coast, where a forced landing might be necessary. He became expert with a sextant and versed in the calculus of air navigation. He practiced keeping awake in the air for twenty, thirty, or more hours.

Coli and Tarascon rebuilt a French Potez 25 biplane for the flight, a sesquiplane like the S-35, with the upper wing much larger than the lower, for added lift. Their air-cooled, nose-mounted Gnome Jupiter engine provided 450 horsepower, and their fuel tanks could carry 3,500 pounds of gasoline. They planned to drop the wheels once aloft, to save weight and cut drag, and land on a golf course in Rye, near New York City, using skids built into the belly of the plane. They heard rumors that the Germans were preparing for a hop; in addition, two French rivals flying a twin-engine Farman Goliath airliner announced that they would take off soon. The challenge by their fellow countrymen worried them most: The Goliath had been built with extra fuel tanks and had recently set a world endurance record with forty hours in the air. In response, Coli and Tarascon hastened their plans, but soon after Fonck's disaster, their heavily loaded biplane crashed during a test, and Tarascon was badly burned. The Goliath never took off; the rumored German attempt never materialized. The window of opportunity still existed, but Coli had to find another flying partner.

•

Four thousand miles to the west, Charles Lindbergh once again flew the night route between St. Louis and Chicago. The sun had just set; a blue moon lit the world below. The sky was clear, and he was bored. The parachute jump into limbo two weeks earlier, on September 16, had been a break in the monotony. He'd landed without mishap, found his plane torn up in a cornfield, and shipped the mail by train to Chicago. The next day, still feeling a bit agitated, he left his room at the Congress Hotel in Chicago's Loop and went to see the movie *What Price Glory?* In the newsreel before the feature, Fonck's S-35 taxied down the runway for a test over Manhattan. Like everyone else, Lindbergh assumed the Frenchman would win the Orteig Prize.

Now it was the end of September, about a week after the ace's hopes had ended in flames. The moon reflected off a bend in the Illinois River, and shone off Lindbergh's biplane's silver wings. He lightly touched the stick and watched the lighted farmhouse windows below. This was a night for beginners. He resented the fact that he'd have to come to earth: He liked to think of himself as a creature of the air. He was like the moon itself: a satellite passing overhead, free of gravity. "I can fly on forever through space," he thought, "past the mail field in Chicago, beyond the state of Illinois, over mountains, over oceans, independent of the world below."

He'd had the same dreams as a boy on his family's Minnesota farm. He'd spend hours on his back, hidden from others, sunk into the prairie grass—the high timothy and redtop that spread west across the plains. The clouds drifted overhead. "Those clouds, how far away were they?" he wondered. "Nearer than the neighbor's house, untouchable as the moon—unless you had an airplane!" With a plane, he could explore the cloud caves and canyons, or circle like a hawk hunting prey. "I would ride on the wind and be part of the sky, and acorns and bits of twigs would stop pressing into my skin."

Suppose he did keep flying tonight...suppose gas did not weigh so much and he could stay up in this plane for days. He could go anywhere he wanted in the world. How much *could* a plane carry if its fuselage were filled with gas tanks? Fonck had tried just that a few days earlier, and look what happened. The man had been one of Lindbergh's aviation heroes. René Fonck, he had thought, could do no wrong.

And yet he had. Disastrously.

Lindbergh wondered how he might have done things differently. He'd fly alone, for starters, cutting out the crew and all the troublesome personalities. He'd discard any and all inessentials: upholstery in the cabin, bulky equipment and furniture. He'd take a few concentrated rations, a rubber boat for a sea landing, a little extra water. Why *couldn't* he succeed where Fonck had failed? "I'm about twenty-five," he thought. "I have more than four years of aviation behind me, and close to two thousand hours in the air. I've barnstormed over half of the forty-eight states. I've flown my mail through the worst of nights." When it came to flying, Lindbergh didn't lack confidence. He decided that a nonstop flight between New York and Paris would be far less risky than the winter mail run between St. Louis and Chicago.

Still, he would need a special plane for such an attempt—and that meant money, of which he had very little. He had maybe $2,000 in savings, and that was all. The very best plane for such a long flight would be the new Wright-Bellanca he'd read about, with a small body and a single, high wing. It had been built specifically to showcase the newest Wright Whirlwind radial engine, reportedly the best source of power available for long-distance flight. But the Wright-Bellanca was expensive—exactly how much, he didn't know. And who would back an unknown airmail pilot whose reputation barely extended beyond Lambert Field?

He sat quietly in the cockpit, suspended in the air. The magnitude of the undertaking seemed overwhelming. He needed a plan, a plan that would convince others to back him and not think him crazy.

The Chicago beacon flashed before him. Ten more minutes and he must land.

•

While Coli crashed and Lindbergh dreamed, Richard Byrd made plans.

Flying the Atlantic had long been one of his goals. He'd held his peace during Fonck's preparations, never admitting his desires. He'd served on the committee inspecting the S-35, sealing its tanks after fueling in preparation for takeoff on September 21. He fulfilled his sad duty as witness in the inquest held that same day. On September 22, he wrote a letter of condolence to Sikorsky. Ten days later, Sikorsky thanked him. "This terrible accident was certainly a great blow to us but the only way to overcome this is to continue our work with renewed vigor and hope that next time we will have better luck," the designer replied.

It was apparently what Byrd wanted to hear. He might not have a backer yet for entering the race, but he knew what he wanted when it came to a plane. "I'm looking for an aeroplane that will do about 3,500 or 3,600 miles with a good factor of safety," he told Sikorsky on October 6, writing from his Beacon Hill home in Boston. "I am very serious about the matter. How quickly could you build such a plane? How much would it cost? I realize that if it is built in a big hurry it will probably cost more. Would you be willing to undertake the contract?"

Sikorsky did not waste time. "[W]E WILL BE VERY GLAD TO BUILD YOUR PLANE ABLE TO FLY DISTANCE REQUIRED OR MORE HAVING [A] GOOD SAFETY FACTOR," he telegraphed back on October 11. Twelve days later, on October 23, he mailed Byrd estimates of three separate trimotor planes he could build. All could make it to Paris and ranged in cost from $40,000 to $60,000, depending upon the type of engine.

Byrd hedged his bets even as he wrote Sikorsky. Sometime in late September, after Fonck's crash, he wrote Anthony H. G. Fokker with the same proposal. It was a natural choice—Fokker had built the *Josephine Ford*, the trimotor in which Byrd and Floyd Bennett had flown over the North Pole earlier that year. But the "Flying Dutchman," as the press called him, was not as immediately receptive as Sikorsky. On September 28, Fokker replied that he could not guarantee the flight range of the kind of ship Byrd imagined.

Sitting in his brownstone study surrounded by the mementoes and honors of his career, Byrd remembered that he and Tony Fokker did not always get along. The Dutchman tended to speak his mind. His blunt ways irritated Byrd. "I am trying to buy a plane from you for a transatlantic flight," he replied on October 11, a glimpse of Byrd that rarely leaked into his manicured image. "If you are as reluctant to sell this plane as you were to sell the polar plane, let me know for I have no desire to cause you to inconvenience yourself as you did in selling us the plane for the North Pole flight."

●

In the hundreds of guides for self-improvement published between 1900 and 1920, one need becomes clear. We live in a mob from which we cannot escape. The problem is simple: How can we distinguish ourselves in an overcrowded world?

The standard answer these books offered was to create an image, a carefully crafted character or "personality" that one turned like a bright face to the crowd. "To create a personality is power," insisted one writer. "[M]an's mysterious atmosphere" can "sway great masses," claimed Orison Swett Marden, one of the genre's greatest stars. Every American must be a performer, such self-help gurus proclaimed.

Every field of endeavor had its celebrities, and by 1926 Richard Byrd was the poster boy of "this hero business," as he so often called it—the movie star of the air. He stared at the camera in countless magazine spreads and newspapers photos, clad in the sheep-wool parka, sealskin mittens, polar-bear pants, and Eskimo mukluks that he had worn to the Pole. His gaze was direct; his features seemed chiseled from marble: a high brow, deep-set eyes, and dark hair that swept forward in breaking waves. In articles appearing in 1925 and 1926 in *National Geographic* and *The New York Times*, Byrd began "an ongoing dialogue with the public about his own life and aims," observed his biographer Lisle Rose. "He would be no lone eagle, no romantic figure on a distant hilltop, but a public creature of his own making, inviting the people to share his adventures, however vicariously, through print, media, and film."

There was something machinelike in the presentation: well oiled
and tightly controlled. After the 1926 polar flight, he was portrayed as a
hero, philosopher, explorer, and a role model for red-blooded American
boys. "Byrd is essentially a mystic, deeply concerned with the meanings
of life," began the first page of *Struggle*, his first full-blown biography. Yet, a distinction was made. He was not the "carefully nurtured
type...who holds forth in lectures before Ladies' Clubs." He was a scientist, a man among men, able "to translate into muscle the concepts of
his mind."

Friends and family helped form the image. When Byrd finally made
public his intent to enter the race, he received instructions from Fitzhugh Green, an old friend from the navy and, some said, the ghost
writer of his first book, *Skyward*. "We must keep this up, Dick," Green
said. "It crystallizes your personality in the minds of the American public. If we do it right the effect will be lasting"—as if flying the Atlantic
were merely a step to greater things.

Yet beneath the shine lay a welter of contradictions. By 1926 these
could already be seen. Byrd was brave, intelligent, a "straight-shooter";
he drank heavily, was ruthlessly political, and lied. He was loyal to constant friends, and more than willing to destroy those who strayed from
the fold. Ambition drove him onward at the same time he complained
how wearisome the "hero business" had become.

"He was very sensitive, and as gentle as a woman with people he
loved," said his niece Margaret Byrd Stimpson. "But he was completely
motivated with a one-track mind; when he wanted something he would
climb over people. Great men like Uncle Dick have to be more motivated than other people. To accomplish great things you have to walk
over a few people."

•

"Wherever men live in contact with one another, they are inevitably in
competition and are bound to struggle for their interests and ambitions,
for prestige, and the satisfactions of their passions."

Seven years before his death, Byrd sat down and wrote out hundreds
of "miscellaneous thoughts" that would create a window into his mind.
By then he was Rear Admiral Byrd, the "Admiral of the Arctic," the
"Final Explorer." He had explored both ends of the earth, written four
bestsellers, and participated in one of the most famous competitions of

the twentieth century. He had accomplished more than most men ever dreamed, but instead of being content, he appears, from these random scribbles, to have been a lonely, embittered man. Something had always eluded him. It was always beyond his fingertips...just beyond his reach. "The world is sick," he wrote. "What I have tried to do is make a diagnosis of the patient."

Richard Byrd was born in Winchester, Virginia, on October 25, 1888, the second son of Richard Evelyn Byrd and Eleanor Bolling Flood Byrd, scions of two "First Families of Virginia." The Byrds had been part of Virginia's ruling class since the founding of the colony, and a sense of entitlement passed through the generations. Yet the Civil War had ruined Byrds and Floods alike, and they were desperate to regain their place in society. The first son, Harry, would become governor of Virginia and later a U.S. senator; the third son, Tom, was the businessman of the three, running the family's lucrative Winchester apple business and town newspaper while his older brothers left to seek their fame.

"I'll name this one," Richard's father declared at Dick's birth, supposedly miffed that his firstborn had been named after his wife's brother. He named his second son after himself—and never understood him. By all accounts, Richard Sr. was a prickly, argumentative man with a discerning intelligence and an acute sense of duty. He would serve as attorney, judge, and state representative, becoming, according to some, "the greatest speaker the Virginia House of Delegates" had had "in two generations." That view must be tempered by the post-Reconstruction politics of the time. A rabid defender of states' rights, he wrote a brief challenging the state's ratification of the federal income tax that conservatives called brilliant; he was an unapologetic white supremacist, opposed to "race-mixing." Once he threw an inkwell at an opposing lawyer in court, drawing blood. Another time, he rode alone into the mountains to judge a clan who had been terrorizing the countryside. He arrived, sentenced the guilty, packed them off to jail, and then rode home—all in a day, faster than the clan could marshal its forces to seek revenge.

Winchester at the time of Richard's birth was the kind of rural southern town that boosters called progressive. A tree-lined county seat of five or six thousand, it nestled between the Appalachians to the west and the Blue Ridge Mountains to the east. City fathers pursued railroads and industry, and laid telephone and electrical lines in the sloping downtown. The economic engine was apples, and orchard owners were shipping their produce up and down the East Coast and even into Europe by the 1920s.

Tom, Dick, and Harry came of age when the creed of the "Lost Cause" was in full steam. According to this version of history, the South was superior in all things except manpower and industrial might, and thus the Confederacy had lost because she was rolled over by an implacable, inhuman machine. Boys especially were filled with notions of southern honor, a concept of manhood that had its hooks deep in Byrd. Though he never stated it boldly, the hallmarks were obvious: good sportsmanship, physical bravery, the idea of "breeding," education, and of being a gentleman. Yet southern honor could be a volatile thing. Based on an "unshakeable conviction of self-worth," honor ultimately became a slave to the opinions of society. One became a performer, a personality. The southern male vibrated like a tuning fork, endlessly sensitive to insult or discord. Southern honor demanded satisfaction for every real or perceived slight; while bolstering the cult of pure southern womanhood, it allowed and excused violence against blacks as a check against "miscegenation."

Such "honor" sprang from violence, and Richard Byrd was raised in a violent family. Most accounts treat the violence condoned by his father as a colorful joke, but some of the tales are alarming, probably exacerbated by Richard Sr.'s alcoholism. He taught the boys to box, then staged boxing matches for black and white spectators. The two greatest rivals were Tom and Dick, separated in birth by a year. Dick was the elder, but puny, while Tom would grow quickly to six feet two inches and two hundred pounds. Their rivalry was not handled well. After one bout, Tom dashed into the house and came back with a pair of brass knuckles. "Come on, Dick," he said, "and see who gets a licking now." Another time, after Dick rubbed Tom's head in the dirt, Tom charged back with a knife in his hand. Dick fled into the house and locked himself in the bathroom; Tom hacked at the wood, trying to get in. Once, Dick set fire to a barn, and his father rushed in, thinking his sons were inside. Believing Harry had set it, Richard Sr. beat the boy on the front porch in the presence of spectators.

The boys adored their mother, Eleanor, probably because she was an island of peace, but it was their father they emulated. "I never expect to meet a man with the scintillating brilliance my father possessed," Dick later said. But the feeling was not mutual. Dick was a small, frail boy, and Richard Sr. was repulsed by frailty. Dick "is keen as a blade," he once told his wife. "He seems to know what he is doing. But he is too impatient, too erratic." He consigned his son to failure.

Dick apparently found solace in dreams of adventure. It was said that he devoured tales of exploration and, in 1900, at the age of eleven, wrote in his diary that he would be the first to reach the North Pole. Nine years later, the navy's Robert Peary beat him there, but by then he'd thrown in his lot with aviation. Thanks to the airplane, he wrote, man could "move and fly faster than the bird, and as he soars above the earth he catches glimpses" of a time when all things are possible and "he may gain mastery of his fate."

His father believed otherwise. "You know what I think about airplanes," Richard Sr. said in 1925, just before Dick left on his first Arctic exploration. "I know you will go, regardless of what I say. But I want you to understand that I have not changed my mind—that I believe you are undertaking a dangerous and inconsequential career."

Richard Sr. died a few months later, before Dick returned. The one whose approval Dick craved most had died convinced that his namesake was a fool.

•

Early in Dick's life, two patterns emerged. The first was risk taking. "Danger was all that pleased him," his mother later said. He seemed absolutely fearless, and was often found atop a house or tree. He took long solitary walks in the woods of the Shenandoah Valley and, according to one biographer, discovered "a lost river in a forgotten cave in the hills around Staunton, Va." He was supposedly so engrossed that time passed without his knowledge, and a dozen search parties were called out while he slept at the site of his discovery. Exploration had an extra benefit for him: he could be alone.

He also discovered a gift for self-promotion, a fondness for telling tales that were not always true. It is not unusual for a youth to stretch the truth; what is more unusual is for that youth to be aided and abetted by his family. On August 9, 1902, eleven weeks before his fourteenth birthday, he was sent to visit a family friend in the Philippines. His mother accompanied him to Washington, and then a family acquaintance took him as far as Manila. Yet he and his family always told the press that he left when he was twelve, and that he set out alone—a far more romantic version. The newly installed American government was still battling Filipino insurgents, and Dick's letters back home cast him in the center of action. These invariably landed on the front page of *The Winchester Star*, by then owned by the Byrds. "Winchester Boy Captures a Spy," a typical headline blazed.

He was training in restlessness, and in the mechanics of celebrity. When returning home, he shipped in the opposite direction so as to circumnavigate the globe. After high school he briefly attended the University of Virginia, then, in 1908, entered Annapolis, at which time a new pattern emerged. He may have been fearless, but he was also injury-prone. He joined the navy football squad and broke his ankle during a pileup in a game against Princeton. During his midshipman cruise to Europe, he contracted typhus and nearly died. As a senior, he broke the same ankle when performing a gymnastic stunt on the overhead rings. The injury ended his athletic career and hindered him forever after. Assigned to the battleship fleet after graduation, he fell down a gangway and aggravated the old injury. Doctors nailed his shattered bones together—for years he and his family would alternately insist that he was patched together with a silver nail or by some silver thread. The truth was more prosaic.

By March 1916, on the eve of America's entry into the Great War, Byrd's health had deteriorated to the point where he asked to be placed on inactive duty at three-quarters pay. For most, that would have meant the end of a career. But Byrd was too restless to sit idle, and he had learned persistence through his many trials. By May 1916 he had cajoled and harassed his superiors into placing him back on active duty, first as inspector general of the Rhode Island Militia, then to the navy's Personnel Bureau in Washington, D.C. He soon found shuffling papers as burdensome as retirement, and by 1918 he had badgered his superiors again to be transferred, this time to the Naval Aviation School at Pensacola, Florida. Reminded of his bad leg, Byrd snapped back, "But you don't fly with your legs!"

He desperately needed something to turn his life around. He had married his childhood sweetheart, Marie Ames, and the two moved to Pensacola. But their new home was fraught with anxiety. Richard had lost twenty-five pounds from worry over the "uselessness of what I had become—just a high-class clerk." He was on the verge of a breakdown, aware that he might once again be shelved. He begged for a month's training at the air base to see if this would whip him into shape, but on his first day in Pensacola he witnessed a fatal crash. Flying was not some vague romance from his boyhood dreams—it was a truly dangerous business. He took long, gloomy strolls on the beach. He knew that taking control of the stick meant holding his life in his hands.

•

Pensacola's influence cannot be underestimated. Just as its graduates midwived the navy's gestating "air-mindedness," they shaped the course and issues of the Orteig Prize. More than half the Americans who entered the Great Atlantic Derby were navy fliers. They had earned their wings at Pensacola, and left with its values. These included a devotion to the science of flying, and an elevation of navigation to the same pinnacle as piloting. They all knew one another, for naval aviation was still a very small world. They downplayed the daredevil image still attached to early aviation, presenting themselves to the world as technocrats united by an obsession with advanced machinery and a devotion to the sacred mysteries of flight. Without ever actually admitting it, they saw themselves as holy priests who explored, suffered, and died. The race for the North Pole had been a navy grail, as would the future South Pole expeditions. The stop-and-go transatlantic flight of the four navy seaplanes would be an all-navy affair. Navy-funded research into long-distance air-cooled engines would make the *idea* of the nonstop flight possible. If the Atlantic was their personal domain, why shouldn't they own the Orteig Prize?

By Armistice Day 1918, military strategists had begun to see that future wars would be won or lost in the air. The Great War had spawned the development of countless land-based aircraft: seaplanes and dirigibles used in everything from dogfights to bombing, scouting, and strafing foot soldiers. Which of these aircraft would reign supreme, and which service would control the purse strings? The role of air power in U.S. military policy was a debate that was just heating up, and the battle between the army and navy for its control was one into which Byrd and his fellows would be thrown.

Four flags had flown over Pensacola Bay since the seventeenth century—those of France, Great Britain, Spain, and the United States. All four nations considered the bay crucial for control of the Caribbean and the Gulf of Mexico. On February 21, 1825, the Senate authorized the building of a navy yard and depot at Pensacola, but over time its importance dwindled, and in October 1911 it was officially closed. Flight breathed new life into the facility: In January 1914 the navy's small aviation unit moved from Annapolis to Pensacola to establish a flying school.

Unfortunately, the school's early seaplane trainers were man killers. The pilot sat unprotected in the front, his feet propped on a bar, dangling over the waves hundreds of feet below. These were "pusher" planes, whose propellers were located behind the pilot, rather than in front, as in more modern "tractor" designs, where the engine is in the front and pulls the plane along. The navy's first fatality at Pensacola occurred on February 16, 1913, when Ensign W. D. Billingsley was thrown from his trainer at 1,600 feet. Lieutenant John H. Towers, later in charge of the navy's 1919 transatlantic attempt, was riding as passenger and somehow survived the crash in the Pensacola Bay.

By March 1918, when Lieutenant Byrd arrived in Pensacola as administrative aide to the base commander, there were 38 planes in service and 129 students. The air base was a little town in itself, with 438 officers and 5,559 enlisted men. It boasted a YMCA and a Knights of Columbus; dances and boxing matches; and amateur vaudeville. Prostitution was so rampant that a sweep by the local sheriff netted more than one hundred women, and moonshine flooded from the piney woods of Escambia County.

When Byrd arrived, the planes had changed as well, evolving from motorized box kites to more stable machines with long, graceful wings, working rudders and enclosed fuselages. But they were still deadly. During the war months of 1918, base records revealed 148 crashes and 21 student deaths. Byrd sat on the Crash Evaluation Board, studying the mangled planes and crushed bodies of men who had been his friends. His wife, Marie, used to hear over and over that Richard had crashed, only to learn at the end of the day that this was not so. One crash—that of Ensign Morgan Draper—especially hit home. Byrd and Marie ate dinner often with Draper and his wife. One day he and a copilot vanished over the horizon; a few hours later, a clerk in Pensacola called to report that a plane had nosed straight into the water, shooting spray a hundred feet in the air. The copilot's body was tangled in the wreckage, but Draper had been thrown out before he died. Draper had often speculated during dinner whether it was possible to switch seats while a plane was in the air, and Byrd deduced that he had been attempting this when he lost control. From this and other incidents, Byrd concluded that over half the crashes resulted from almost criminally bad judgment by cocky young men.

Clinicians in the budding field of aviation psychology began to notice the same trend. The war was a dangerous drug for young men already high on flying. "The World War changed the status of airplane pilots from crazy fools to national heroes," wrote army doctor Harry G. Armstrong. "The public changed its attitude from one of curiosity and scorn to one of honor and respect. Thus for the first years the military pilot had his ego tremendously stimulated."

This held implications for every flier seeking the Orteig Prize. Lindbergh was not the only one to face the stigma of being called suicidal or a "flying fool." They'd all started flying during the war or in the years immediately afterward, and every one—except the one last-minute passenger—had been trained by either the army or navy—and now, all of a sudden, they'd been elevated to the status of gods.

Byrd was probably the most careful, because of his crash board experiences. He had seen death up close too many times to be cocky or reckless. In later years, critics said he feared to fly, but in his eyes he was merely practicing common sense.

In mid-April 1918, Byrd earned his wings, becoming Naval Aviator 608. He took another three weeks to qualify as a seaplane pilot. Heading to the front, however, was not in the cards. His superiors valued his gifts as an administrator too highly and sent him to Halifax, Nova Scotia, to direct the construction of a new U.S. Naval air base. It was during this time, in the daily presence of the North Atlantic, that he first conceived of flying across the ocean, sometimes with others, sometimes alone. He lobbied to be included in the 1919 "Nancy" flights across the Atlantic, but was turned down.

On July 30, 1921, he tried again, asking the chief of naval operations for approval to fly alone across the Atlantic, from Newfoundland to England, in a Navy hydroplane. "I have made a deep study of Trans-Atlantic flying since I first received my orders to Aviation in 1917," he said. Prevailing westerly winds would be in his favor and give him a push; he would not need a copilot, destroyer escort, or any other help but the standard drift indicator and a bubble sextant that he had designed. He claimed that the flight would further science and the service, a claim he would use repeatedly when "selling" high-priced expeditions to navy brass and private financial backers. In this earliest case, he said an ocean crossing would demonstrate that a "pilot can both navigate and pilot his machine at the same time," thus making possible "long distance reconnaissance flights from battleships." The argument seemed to work, and he was endorsed by W. A. Moffett, the head of Naval Aviation, but once again his idea was turned down.

In 1921 Byrd received orders to fly the British dirigible R-38 from England to America, but on the day of its last test flight, his London-to-Howden train was delayed. He arrived too late to come aboard and watched in despair as the huge silver ship floated into the rosy sunrise without him. Hours later, the R-38 split in two while turning too sharply, and only fourteen of the forty-nine-man crew survived.

Byrd returned to Washington, D.C., to become the navy's point man for the growth of naval aviation. By now, his brother Harry had been elected to Virginia's state senate, a familial fact that also expanded Richard's list of political contacts. Dick needed the help, for his chief opponent was Brigadier General William Mitchell, the army apostle of air war. Air power was the force of the future, Mitchell wrote in *The Saturday Evening Post*: "Where there is no vision, the people perish," he warned, quoting from Proverbs. That in itself was not a threat: where Mitchell made enemies was in his assertion that naval warfare was a thing of the past. An air force could sink battleships and turn cities into infernos, he claimed, and nothing could stop them except other planes. In 1921 he seemed to prove his point when a fleet of his bombers smashed and sank a captured German battleship off the Virginia Capes. But the general's foresight was better than his discretion, and he was not prepared for the kind of infighting waged by the suave and handsome Byrd.

When Mitchell pushed a bill before Congress urging a United Air Service that would absorb the navy's coastal air patrol, Byrd was charged by his superiors with killing its chances. He played golf with the rich and important, and within a year was calling forty-eight U.S. congressmen by their first names. He persuaded them all that Mitchell was infringing upon the navy's sacred reserves. When Mitchell's bill was defeated, the general's enemies in both service branches smelled weakness: They condemned him for his outspokenness and, in 1925, court-martialed him for insubordination. Like many other prophets, Mitchell was cast out—and Byrd contributed directly to his ruin.

By 1924 Byrd felt that some favors were owed him. He lobbied to fly aboard the dirigible *Shenandoah* in an expedition to the North Pole, but Congress killed the venture as too expensive. But a new seed had been planted in Byrd's mind. If he had not been the first to cross the Atlantic, maybe he could be first to fly over the Pole. He'd heard that the Norwegian explorer Roald Amundsen planned a similar quest, and he meant to beat him there. His reach now extended into some of America's wealthiest families, and he persuaded Edsel Ford and John D. Rockefeller Jr. to pledge $15,000 each, and an unnamed benefactor, $10,000. The plan was to follow Peary's route as far as the Pole, then fly to an unexplored region that lay beyond.

It was the first step in a flight that would make him world-famous—and haunt him until the day he died.

FOUR

THE EXPLORER

What magnet in the poles drew obsessed and troubled souls? The men remembered today for seeking out the white wastes were temperamental loners who attracted fanatically loyal subordinates even as they made the most ardent enemies. Sometimes the loyalists switched sides; thrown together in the most extreme conditions on earth, they saw minor differences and quirks mutate into bold rivalry and hatred. Frederick Cook claimed to have reached the North Pole, but his claim was disproved and he was humiliated; Robert Peary made the same claim and was hailed by the National Geographic Society, which had funded him. Robert Falcon Scott listened to no one in his quest for the South Pole, and died for his hubris; Roald Amundsen had gotten there earlier with clockwork efficiency. A polar voyage was a quest for many things—riches, land, a new passage, social position, or lasting fame—and the explorers often fell victim to several deadly sins, especially pride and cupidity. Detractors condemned them as bunglers, swindlers, liars, and cheats; partisans portrayed them as saints and heroes. Anyone seeking an unvarnished account of their exploits encountered silence, condemnation, or threats. Those drawn to the poles soon found that a singular hunger consumed their lives.

The first attempt to conquer the Pole by air occurred in 1897, with the flight of the hot air balloon *Eagle*. But instead of success, Salomon Andrée and his two companions became the first victims of aerial icing, the future bane of fixed-wing planes. Under certain conditions, water vapor collects and freezes on the forward "leading" surfaces of a fuselage or wing, creating a mass that can weigh hundreds of pounds. When ice built up atop the *Eagle's* air bag, the ship went down. The three explorers had hoped to float from Spitzbergen, an ice-locked island on the edge of the Arctic Circle, across the Pole, and on to Alaska. Instead they crashed two days out and tried to walk back. Thirty-three years later, their bodies were found 250 miles due east from where they began.

Take Robert Peary, Byrd's personal hero. On April 6, 1909, when Peary took a latitude reading of 89°57', he was standing on top of the world. He had fought to get to this point through eight expeditions spanning twenty-three years. As the years progressed, he grew rigid and desperate; he called his own actions "criminally foolish," was often assailed by doubt, and repeatedly considered suicide. Loneliness clung to him like a pall, and his quest left physical scars. After 1902 all ten toes were missing joints because of frostbite. He could be recognized from afar as he walked with a strange, shuffling glide.

The similarities between Peary's career and Byrd's are eerie. Both took nearly continuous extended leave from the navy for their quests; both were made rear admirals afterward. Both men's claims of being first across the North Pole were widely credited for most of the twentieth century—though not without controversy—and are widely doubted today. Both created a network of influential donors: like Byrd and his industrialists, Peary depended on the "Peary Arctic Club," formed in 1898 to fund his expeditions. The "PAC" included such New York graybeards as Morris K. Jesup, who made a fortune in banking and railroads, and Henry W. Cannon, president of the Chase National Bank. When others questioned their claims, both Peary and Byrd were defended by the powerful National Geographic Society, which had funded their expeditions.

The reasons for doubting Peary were legion. He claimed to have stood at true north with five men, five sledges, and thirty-eight dogs, yet not one of his companions could vouch for his solar observations, which determined the latitude. Peary replied that he was not about to share his glory with someone who hadn't earned the right to be there. In fact, he'd sent back to base camp five days before his triumph the one man capable of checking his readings: Captain Robert Bartlett, commander of the expedition's supply ship, the *Roosevelt*.

Other claims by Peary were also suspect, but most suspicious of all was his mysterious burst of speed—an issue that would also dog Byrd. From Ellesmere Island to 87°47', the point where Bartlett was sent back, Peary averaged 9.3 miles a day. Arctic travel is some of the hardest on earth: the ice always shifts, throwing up pressure ridges and forming deep cracks that force explorers to make wide detours. Suddenly, without Bartlett around as a witness, Peary said he sledged 26 miles per day for 5 days in a row. When he reached the Pole and turned back, he traveled 133 miles, at the very minimum, in two and a quarter days, or more than double his previous speed. This was impossible in such conditions, and no one since has been able to approach such mileage. The world record—of 36.6 miles a day—was set in 1912 by Danish explorer Knud Rasmussen, and that was on smooth ice.

This was Peary's last chance at greatness, and his actions spoke volumes. Matthew Henson, Peary's black manservant, had been with him through years of disappointment and pain. Now, at what he thought was the Pole, Henson took off his glove to shake his leader's hand. But Peary's face grew "long and serious," and he turned away. From that moment on, Peary scarcely spoke to his old comrade. "It nearly broke my heart on the return journey from the Pole that he would rise in the morning and slip away on the homeward trail without rapping on the ice for me, as was his established custom," wrote Henson. "On board the ship he addressed me a few times. When he left the ship [for good], he did not speak."

Obsession can make liars of us all—and these were the actions of a troubled man. In the same bleak and deadly landscape, Richard Byrd would face similar temptations.

Sixteen years after Peary's triumph, Byrd began work on his own Arctic plans. By 1925 he'd persuaded rich friends to donate $40,000. He convinced Secretary of the Navy Curtis D. Wilbur that it was in the navy's interest to map the Far North, since military and commercial flights would eventually cross the Pole. To that end, the navy supplied Byrd with three open-cockpit biplanes powered by an inverted 400-horsepower Liberty engine; these had a maximum speed of 122 miles per hour and a cruising range of 500 miles. He teamed with Robert Bartlett, Peary's ship's captain; when he learned that Roald Amundsen also planned a polar flight, Byrd used international rivalries as leverage to raise money.

But now a third team had entered the race, and this one was American. Like Bartlett, professor-explorer Donald B. MacMillan had been with Peary on his epic voyage of 1909. Byrd had inside information that MacMillan's goal was a phantom place called Crocker Land.

As late as the 1920s there was thought to be land in the center of the Arctic Ocean that went by several names: Crocker-, Keenan-, or Bradley Land, and sometimes "the Lost Continent." It appeared on charts as an empty spot filled with question marks. Its existence, like Saint Brendan's "Isle of the Blessed," was surmised by glimpses from afar and the supposed trajectory of ice floes. It lay in an Arctic "blind spot," a point equidistant from all land masses and about four hundred miles south of the Pole. Whoever found Crocker Land first could claim it for his nation, and in the process win everlasting fame.

While MacMillan had substantial backing from the National Geographic Society and Chicago millionaire E. F. McDonald Jr., head of Zenith Radio, Byrd had the navy's planes. He approached MacMillan about combining their efforts, and the veteran explorer reluctantly agreed. Yet the chemistry was bad. MacMillan insisted that he be in charge, and dropped Bartlett from the expedition. Byrd and McDonald clashed, and their goals would never mesh: MacMillan wanted to push only five hundred miles into the blind spot, while Byrd hoped to follow Peary's route, even as far as the Pole.

A gloom fell over Byrd before the expedition began. His father opposed his suicidal folly and lobbied the navy brass to deep-six his plans. The president of the American Legion of Massachusetts did not think his young friend would return: "[T]hose millions of square miles of snow and ice are terrible things to contemplate," he wrote. The normally organized Byrd fell behind on the mechanics of daily living: he missed a tax deadline; began a long, overwrought squabble about alterations for a new suit; and could barely deal with an onslaught of mice and roaches in his Boston brownstone.

Sometime during the wait, Byrd's quest for the Pole became spiritual. He had seen himself as a mystic, but his longings had always been free-floating and vague. Now, suddenly, an undated, typed note appeared on pink paper, sent by someone who signed him- or herself "Ederi." The pink note had a tremendous effect on him. Ederi advised him of the "law of Infinite Life," of how "the Supreme Intelligence meets the *human need* in every instance; whether it be in mid-ocean or mid-air; whether in fire or in ice." Byrd should never doubt his purpose, Ederi said, for it was the face of God's. "The laws of the Spirit are continuously harmonious," the note explained: "[T]here need be no engine trouble; atmospheric conditions can be annulled—for it is Intelligence which is operating—not mere man." Nine years later, when Byrd stared into the Antarctic night and contemplated his imminent death, Ederi's exact words rang in his mind.

The note may have given him confidence, but it did not save the expedition. On June 25, 1925, MacMillan and crew left Wiscasset, Maine, packed aboard two small ships. On August 1, they reached the port of Etah, a small village on Greenland's northeast coast, about seven hundred miles south of the Pole. MacMillan and his National Geographic Society scientists would study natural phenomena, while the navy planes would search for Crocker's Land. Yet bad luck plagued the group from the beginning. Gas on the water surrounding a ship caught fire, and one plane suffered substantial damage. Storms moved in, and the fjords began to freeze. The planes were ill prepared for these conditions, and they had less than four days of good flying. Nevertheless, they covered 6,000 miles and glimpsed 36,000 square miles uncharted by man. Byrd told MacMillan that he wanted to fly farther north, unescorted. Appalled by the risk, the professor moved south and ordered that the expedition end.

Yet the quest was not a complete failure for Byrd. It marked the first productive use of aircraft by Americans in the Arctic, and it thrust him into the limelight as its spokesman. In the fall of 1925, several articles ran in *National Geographic* describing the expedition. One of these, written by Byrd, cast him in the role of aviator-explorer.

He also paired for the first time with Warrant Officer Floyd Bennett, the pilot of his seaplane. No man could be more unlike Byrd. Before the expedition, the plainspoken, thirty-one-year-old machinist's mate from Warrensburg, New York, had wandered no farther from home than flight school in Pensacola. Of the many photos taken of the two of them together, Byrd gazes directly into the lens as if trying to charm the viewer, while Bennett seems uncomfortable and glances aside. Like many early pilots, Bennett was an auto mechanic, and owned a prosperous little taxi business in his hometown. He fell in love with his wife, Cora, when she became the first woman in town to own and drive her own car. Bennett volunteered for the Great War and was sent to the Norfolk Naval Base, where his experience with engines made him a natural fit as an aviation mechanic. Enlisted men were not supposed to go to flight school, so he taught himself to fly.

One day he took Cora aloft with him. "[A]fter my first flight, I understood," she later said. "Never, but for one moment, in a plane did I ever feel anything but the ecstasy of it. But on that first trip, as the plane left the ground, I had the ghastly sensation one gets when an elevator drops too quickly—like a clutch at one's very heart-strings.... Then, like a flash—it was gone, and we went soaring high, high, up into the blue." She knew why Floyd loved flying—she loved it, too. She described it as an addiction: "I never had enough of it. Always I was dreaming of my last flight and looking forward to the next one."

After the war, enlisted men were allowed to earn their wings, and Bennett graduated from Pensacola. He returned to Norfolk and bought a green-shingled house in the city, a tiny bungalow surrounded by chinaberry and sycamore trees. He seemed content with the obscure life of a navy "greaseball" as long as he and Cora could fly. It seemed idyllic to her, until one day in early 1924 Floyd came home and said he had been ordered to Greenland aboard the cruiser *Richmond*, assigned to act as a station ship for some army fliers circumnavigating the globe. "Floyd, what shall I do?" Cora asked, and started crying. A chill settled over her that would continue for the next four years.

"Dear," he answered, "I have my own decisions to make. This one is yours. Whatever you do will be right with me."

The job needed doing: that seemed his basic philosophy. He wasn't much for words, but others trusted him. Pilots watched his big-knuckled hands move lightly over the throttles, his fingertips trail back and forth across the instrument panel, attuned to the rhythm of the plane. Bennett was serving one night as the *Richmond*'s lookout when he saw a spot in the sea that seemed blacker than the night; it was one of the army planes, floating on the ocean after its oil pump had failed. Bennett's superiors took note, and in early 1925 asked him to volunteer for the MacMillan expedition.

Soon Byrd learned how much he needed this quiet cipher of a man. They were flying over ice north of Greenland when Bennett signaled to him. Since it was hard to be heard above the engines, he wrote in the logbook, "Will you fly for a few minutes?" Byrd took the stick, simply thinking it was his turn to fly. He turned when he heard a noise, and saw Bennett climb onto the wing in the stream of frigid air. Byrd realized for the first time that the engine was in trouble; he looked around for a landing place but could see nothing but jagged ice for miles. Landing in this was impossible. Bennett began to fiddle with the starboard oil tank. Byrd glanced at the oil gauge and realized suddenly that the pressure was too high. So high, in fact, that the tank could have burst at any moment. Without a word, Bennett was trying to release the pressure to save their lives, but if he wasn't fast enough the explosion would blow him off the wing. Byrd tried to keep the seaplane steady and watched in agony until finally Bennett pried off the oil cap and the pressure needle fell. Bennett returned to the pilot's seat, smiled at Byrd as if he'd just been out for a stroll, and turned the plane back to base.

It was the most remarkable repair job Byrd had ever seen. He never found out what had caused the pressure spike—some pernicious effect of the cold was all anyone could say—but he did know this: if Bennett hadn't crawled on the wing like a spider, they both would have died.

•

In May 1926 Byrd tried again. And he made sure Bennett came with him.

This time, he was better prepared. The brush with death had focused his attention, and for the first time one caught a glimpse of the mature explorer of later years. From henceforth, he freely delegated responsibility. Gone were the days when he had to do everything alone. Now he divided the labor. Bennett would fly, Byrd would do everything else: plan, promote, administrate, and navigate. Byrd might get the lion's share of the credit, but Bennett always piloted, and Byrd always acknowledged Bennett's superior ability. Bennett was not home from Greenland a week when he told Cora that he and Byrd planned to fly over the North Pole.

This time, however, Byrd made sure that he was in charge. The navy granted him and Bennett a six-month leave; Byrd raised nearly $100,000 from William Vincent Astor, John D. Rockefeller Jr., Dwight Morrow, department store heir Rodman Wanamaker, Edsel Ford, and others. The National Geographic Society donated heavily through contracts for future articles. Byrd leased the steel steamer U.S.S. *Chantier* for six months at the price of $5,312.50, plus repairs and port charges. And he changed planes.

As late as January 1926, when Fonck declared to the world that he planned to win the Orteig Prize, Byrd thought he might use a dirigible to fly over the North Pole. But then a three-engine Fokker with an enclosed cabin became available. A trimotor airplane could still fly safely if one engine failed, while a two-motor plane could not; in addition, the Fokker had won the 1,600-mile Ford Reliability Tour of 1925. Byrd purchased air-cooled engines from Wright Aeronautical, which were considered less likely to break down in harsh conditions, and named his new plane *Josephine Ford*, in honor of his first donor's three-year-old daughter.

Byrd also changed bases. Greenland had been a bad choice—good flying conditions were possible only from late in the summer to a few weeks afterward. Spitzbergen, in Norway, the launching point for Salomon Andrée's doomed balloon flight, seemed a better idea. It lay four hundred miles closer to the Pole than Alaska or Greenland, and its harbor, warmed by the Gulf Stream, was open to shipping by April or May. The Fokker, after being loaded into the ship and reassembled on land, could start for the Pole well before flying was even possible in Greenland.

Yet Spitzbergen presented another challenge, in the form of Norwegian explorer Roald Amundsen. He, too, was based there. Amundsen was one of the most famous polar explorers in the world. In 1903–06 he had completed the first continuous traverse of the Northwest Passage; then, five years later, he beat Scott to the South Pole. Yet the Arctic could play deadly tricks, even on a veteran like Amundsen. In 1925, as Bennett and Byrd fought their own battles in Greenland, Amundsen tried flying over the Pole but never made it, falling 156 miles short of the goal. In mid-April 1926, he and a crew of Norwegians—along with the young, rich American adventurer Lincoln Ellsworth—set up a base camp at Spitzbergen, determined to try again. This time they would man an Italian-made dirigible named the *Norge*. They were still awaiting its arrival over the horizon when, instead, on April 29, Byrd's long black ship appeared.

For the Norwegians, this was an unwelcome surprise. Nevertheless, Amundsen told his men to help the newcomers. Most important, he offered the services of a young Norwegian navy pilot with hundreds of hours' experience flying in Arctic conditions. Lieutenant Bernt Balchen was quiet, athletic, blond, and wavy-haired; the son of a doctor, he had survived the Great War only to be bayoneted when the Russian Red Army invaded Finland in early 1919. He'd cast around after that first brush with death, searching for meaning—ski competitions, Olympic boxing, forestry—but by his mid-twenties had settled on flight, which made use of his talents for math and tinkering. Everywhere he went, he carried a pocket slide rule; he was as prone to drag it out for a quick calculation as other men a pipe or a pack of cigarettes.

Balchen watched the men from the *Chantier* gather around the long mess table as they talked to Amundsen. There was Byrd, dashing and suave. The bespectacled George Noville, a former naval officer and flight engineer with knowledge of airplane oils, had been Byrd's executive officer in Greenland. Thomas "Doc" Kinkade of the Curtiss-Wright Company was assigned to keep the Fokker's engines in trim. And there was Byrd's pilot, Floyd Bennett, who spoke softly and seemed painfully shy. Bennett admitted that he'd piloted plenty of seaplanes, but never one fitted with skis. How did that change an aircraft's lift and drag?

These four—Byrd, Noville, Bennett, and Balchen—would be the original crew of Byrd's Orteig bid, though they could not know it now. On first impression, Balchen liked Bennett best. Byrd's pilot was quiet, intent, mechanically minded, and cared little for publicity. He seemed far more interested in the challenge than in fame.

Problems beset Byrd immediately. When the *Chantier* arrived, the Norwegian gunboat *Heimdahl* refused to leave the pier to make room for her for fear of nearby pack ice, so Byrd's crew nailed planks across the *Chantier*'s lifeboats and hauled the disassembled plane to shore. The hard crystalline snow acted like sandpaper on the skis, threatening to end Byrd's hopes before he even took off. On the first test flight, the friction was so great that *Josephine Ford* could not build sufficient speed to rise. Balchen watched as Byrd's crew waxed the skis with black shoe polish, an endeavor he knew to be a waste of time.

On the second test, the inevitable occurred: one ski cracked, and the Fokker crumpled. Amundsen asked Balchen to help them. Although the *Chantier* carried a spare set of skis, they were just as soft and flimsy. Balchen suggested an alternative: cannibalizing the ship's hardwood oars, then waxing them with a mix of pine tar and resin burned into the wood with a blowtorch. On May 8, the same day that Amundsen's *Norge* finally arrived from Italy, Bennett started the *Jo Ford* for one last test. She still handled sluggishly. Balchen suggested that they take off at midnight, when the cold would freeze the runway. There would be less friction then.

Balchen saved Byrd's plane and his career. Shortly after midnight Greenwich time on May 9, 1926, Bennett started the Fokker's engines for its all-out effort to reach the Pole. The sun was low on the northern horizon; the temperature was below freezing. Shortly before entering the cockpit, Byrd told a Norwegian reporter that he expected the round-trip flight to take at least seventeen hours, and maybe even twenty. He had fuel enough in his tanks for twenty to twenty-four hours of flight, he said.

Balchen watched Bennett roll down the ice. This time, the plane lifted easily into the air. Balchen reached into his shirt pocket for the small notebook he never went without, and wrote, "9 May. Jo. Ford, B & B, depart Kings Bay, 0037." He watched with mixed emotions as the plane headed north and faded over the horizon.

Shortly after 4:00 p.m., an Italian workman accompanying the dirigible rushed into the mess hall where Amundsen and his crew had gathered. "She come! They here!" he shouted. Balchen and the others rushed outside. The *Josephine Ford* rolled to a stop on the snow; some noticed an oil leak from the tank under the right wing. When Byrd and Bennett opened the cabin door, Amundsen rushed up and smothered them both in bear hugs. Byrd's crew hoisted the fliers on their shoulders and rushed them to the *Chantier*, where Byrd announced to the world via ship's radio that he was the first to have reached the North Pole by air. Balchen plucked the notebook from his shirt pocket and wrote, "9 May. Jo. Ford returns King's Bay, 1607."

She had been gone exactly 15 hours and 30 minutes, an hour and a half less than the minimum predicted time. The distance to the Pole and back was 1,330 nautical miles, or 1,529.5 statute miles. This meant that in order for the plane to have covered that distance, its average speed had to have been 98.67 miles per hour. Balchen thought about the figures briefly, then dismissed them. He'd never flown a trimotor Fokker. An average ground speed of nearly 100 miles per hour with heavy skis and a full load of gas was indeed an excellent time. He'd heard about the famous Fokkers during the war. He hoped to fly one someday.

Those simple scribbles in his notebook would embrace Balchen in controversy, damage his future, become front-page news, and follow him after his death. Years later, these air speed calculations would be villified. While Balchen would be called an ingrate and worse, Byrd would be called a fraud.

•

The crux of the matter was simple: flying time and the plane's top speed. Later that same year, Balchen himself would calculate the Fokker's top speed as he flew it with Bennett in a cross-country tour. He could never exceed an average speed of 75 miles per hour, he realized, and this was in a lighter plane, without skis. In fact, tests later revealed that these slowed the plane by another 5 miles per hour. The times for takeoff and return were never in dispute, since there were so many witnesses. The question was blunt: Had they actually made it to the Pole? Or had they turned back when they discovered the potentially fatal oil leak under the right wing?

Bennett thought they *had* reached the Pole, at least at first—but he was not the navigator. In an account he gave to his wife, he said they had been out about seven and a half hours when they noticed the oil leak on the starboard side. He handed the controls to Byrd, went back, and traced the leak to a connection at the bottom of the tank. "It is a bad leak and we may lose the motor at any time," Bennett scrawled on his pad for Byrd to read. They cut back on power, flying on the two remaining engines. One hour and thirty-five minutes after first noticing the leak—eight hours and thirty-five minutes into the flight—Byrd came forward and shook hands with Bennett. "I knew that we had reached the Pole," Bennett told Cora.

Yet Byrd's claims could not be true—*unless* they hit 100 miles per hour on only two engines. Byrd would later write that the unprecedented speed was made possible by a tailwind, which pushed them to the Pole. Then, once they reached there, the wind "began to freshen and changed direction." It did so, he claimed, by 180 degrees, thus boosting their speed to more than 100 miles per hour all the way home. The miraculous tailwind sounded very much like Peary's claims to lightning-fast sledding over ice—based on his word alone, and unsupported by independent verification. Though meticulous in everything else, Bennett never mentioned Byrd's fortuitous tailwind in his account to Cora.

Two days later, on May 11, Amundsen's dirigible cast off from its moorings with sixteen men and a dog aboard. Balchen did not accompany them. He watched the giant gray whale rise slowly then glide from view over the northern horizon. The good weather held, and at 1:25 a.m. on May 12, the *Norge* passed directly over the North Pole. Two days later, it landed safely at Telli, Alaska, north of Nome.

With Amundsen's departure, Balchen suddenly found himself with plenty of spare time on his hands. Bennett made several short flights in the Fokker, and he asked Balchen along. Balchen was impressed by the aircraft's handling. He told Bennett when they landed that she was one of the nicest planes he'd ever flown.

The next day, Balchen watched as the Fokker was dismantled for the long trip home. Byrd, Bennett, and Noville walked up and asked Balchen what he thought of the plane. Once again, he bragged about its handling. Byrd said he was planning another expedition in Greenland for 1927. Would Balchen like to go?

"*Ja*, you bet," Balchen replied immediately.

Byrd asked if he'd like to return to the United States with them until the expedition was ready. If the Norwegian navy gave him leave, Balchen said, he'd be happy to go. But how would he live in America?

"Don't worry about that," Byrd replied. Bennett would need a copilot for a series of cross-country exhibitions planned for their famous plane. If that did not work out, he promised to find him a job.

They boarded the *Chantier* and steamed first to England, landing in London on May 27. The press and public lionized Byrd, while Bennett was named as an ancillary. The young Virginian dined with the king and queen. Yet amid the celebrations, Byrd glimpsed for the first time the controversy that would follow him the rest of his days. The first skeptics now surfaced: Italian and Scandinavian journalists asked how the crippled Fokker had made it to the Pole in such a short time. Questions were taking shape: Had Byrd and Bennett turned back when they discovered the oil leak, then lied about the conquest? Had Byrd lied to Bennett about reaching the Pole, when in fact he'd turned back early and concealed the fact from the world? Or had Byrd simply miscalculated his position, thinking he had *indeed* reached the Pole?

Given Byrd's fierce pride and the importance he placed upon his honor—given the fact that the straightforward Bennett did not seem the least bit uncertain or guilty in his account to his wife—the last scenario is probably the most likely. Friends and colleagues would later note that Byrd was barely better as a navigator than he was as a pilot, and it's not unreasonable to think that doubt arose in his mind as early as London. If so, he began to wonder whether they'd fallen 150 miles short of the goal.

As Byrd's official biographer wrote, "the carping of foreigners made no difference to Americans." But it apparently mattered to Byrd. He immediately held a press conference and said that as soon as he returned to the United States, he would hand his report and diary to the National Geographic Society for review. Just as it had seventeen years earlier with Peary's report, the Society appointed a committee headed by President Gilbert Grosvenor. After five days of "nonstop scrutiny," as Grosvenor called it, the Society verified Byrd's claims. The committee's June 28, 1926, report concluded that the *Josephine Ford*'s flight records "substantiate in every particular the claim of Commander Byrd that on May 9, 1926, he reached the North Pole by airplane, thus being the first person to reach the North Pole by aerial navigation." Then, just as it had done with Peary, the Society made the records unavailable for independent scrutiny. Calls by researchers to look at the records and diary would be rebuffed by the Society for decades.

That summer and fall, Byrd set the groundwork for protecting his image. Doubts had apparently begun to assail him. He certainly did not appear completely confident when, on November 24, 1926, he wrote to Dr. Isaiah Bowman, director of the American Geographical Society in New York. The AGS was a rival of the National Geographic Society— while the NGS was better known, thanks to its fantastically popular magazine, the AGS was more scientific and less political. When Bowman asked Byrd about the controversy, Byrd replied, "But do you think perhaps it would be better for me to preserve to myself the privilege of giving out the data?"

It was a strange thing to say. "Should I not pass on applications from engineers from certain European countries . . . and certain would-be explorers . . . who have declared themselves very much on the other side of the fence?" Byrd continued. "Should I not protect myself from academic discussions with such people—discussions which would have no scientific bearing?" Rather than release his diaries and flight logs to the public when the National Geographic Society finished with them, he asked Bowman, "will you not keep them in your own personal files?"

Though Bowman was diplomatic, subsequent actions showed that Byrd had piqued his curiosity. Five days later, on November 29, 1926, Bowman wrote back, "There is not the slightest doubt that you are wise in taking a conservative position in respect to the giving out of data." He added, "If there was one thing more important than flying in the case of your expedition it was that you had previously established a reputation as a navigator and no sane person can question your flight."

Whether or not Byrd had actually found true north, one thing was certain: he was learning to navigate the rocky shoals of fame.

•

And, in truth, the American public did not care. They wanted a hero. Readers of *The New York Times* opened the May 11 edition to see screaming across the front page, in twelve-point type, the headline "Byrd Saw No Sign of Life Near the North Pole, Neither Bird Nor Seals." The last time an event rated that size type was when England declared war in 1914. It marked "the first time in the history of journalism that seals have rated an eight-column head," although in this case it was the absence of seals that made the news, noted *The New Yorker*.

As Byrd's ship hurried home from London, his brother Harry, now Virginia's governor, informed the state's national delegation that Byrd and Bennett should receive promotions and the Congressional Medal of Honor, a medal usually reserved for battlefield heroism. Yet the full force of the hero worship would not hit them until the *Chantier* steamed into New York Harbor on June 22, 1926. Municipal fireboats shot aloft seven or eight high-powered streams of water; the air was filled with cheers and sirens; Battery Park was black with people as the *Chantier* settled in its berth. The square-jawed, black-mustached Grover Whalen strode aboard; he swept Byrd and his men ashore into the confusion, and Byrd would later say he felt "tossed about like a leaf in a storm."

It was the first of Byrd's three ticker tape parades, and perhaps the most surreal. He and Bennett walked from the Battery to City Hall, with three hundred of New York's most distinguished citizens following at a respectful distance. They started at 12:00 noon sharp, one of the details Whalen had insisted upon. He'd discovered a few years earlier that a man could not walk up Broadway at noon without finding the sidewalks packed for lunch. It was, he realized, a ready-made audience for any grand parade.

Planes roared overhead in formation. "I believe aviation has pulled the teeth of the Arctic," Byrd declared at the podium on the steps of City Hall. "There is no place on the face of the earth a plane cannot fly." Mayor Walker handed out medals to Byrd, Bennett, and three others, including Joe de Ganahl, a collier who had shoveled coal sixteen hours a day throughout the expedition. Byrd whispered in Walker's ear, and the mayor led de Ganahl to a prominent spot. "And if anything else is necessary to prove the courage of this young man," Beau James added, "let me tell you he's just getting ready to be married."

Others were honored in their own special way. As the parade made its way up Broadway, twenty young women stepped forward strumming furiously on ukuleles. They were the students of Dick Konter, better known as "Ukulele Dick," author of the popular *Dick's Ukulele Guide*. Konter had shipped aboard the *Chantier* as an able-bodied seaman and flourished a signed ukulele that he claimed had been taken to the Pole aboard Byrd's plane. Konter certainly needed a boost. He'd gone to the Pole to teach the ukulele to the Eskimos, but when he got to Spitzbergen he discovered that not a single Eskimo lived within several hundred miles.

That night, Byrd and Bennett left by train for Washington, where they were hailed by President Coolidge, the National Geographic Society, and apparently every government official in D.C. It seemed that everyone was honored—except Bernt Balchen, without whose expertise Byrd would never have gotten off the ground. Only Bennett seemed to notice that Balchen looked glum. Before stepping on the train, he mentioned that it might be nice if someone took Balchen on a guided tour of the city.

The next day, Whalen showed up again aboard the *Chantier* and took Balchen in hand. He whisked him aboard his chauffeured limousine and showed him the sights. They passed Wanamaker's, at Astor Place between Broadway and Fourth Avenue, the grandest department store in town. In it was a music hall that could seat 1,500 people, an eleventh-floor cold storage vault that could store 50,000 furs, and a subbasement with one of the largest private electrical and ice-making plants in the city. Balchen learned that in addition to all he did with the city, Whalen handled the store's publicity.

Balchen learned something else. Wanamaker had promised Byrd $30,000 if his stores in New York and Philadelphia could display the *Josephine Ford*. Someone was needed to answer customers' questions. Whalen smiled suavely. Guess who that was?

Balchen blanched. Here was the job Byrd had promised—the last thing in the world Balchen wanted. Within a day or two he found himself standing behind a red velvet rope signing autographs, trying not to blush when teenage girls said how handsome he was. He was billed as the "Flying Viking," and the girls squealed with delight when he stammered something in Norwegian. He felt like a "prize bull at a country fair."

•

Summer turned into autumn, and the "hero business" intensified for Byrd. The Medal of Honor, Navy Cross, Distinguished Flying Cross—he was recommended for them all, and then some. September was interrupted briefly by his ceremonial part in the Fonck preparations, then his testimony in the inquest.

By October he was somewhat free—free enough to go back on the lecture circuit, free enough to start planning for his next expedition, maybe this time to the South Pole.

In late October all that changed. At a dinner he hosted for Byrd, Rodman Wanamaker rose and dared the explorer to fly across the Atlantic in a single bound. Wanamaker chafed at the idea that some little Frenchman was sponsoring the greatest aviation challenge in history. He read from a letter proposing the very same venture, which Wanamaker had sent to the Aero Club of America in 1914—five years, he reminded the audience, before Orteig's original proposal. Wanamaker had also sponsored Glenn Curtiss's original *America* flying boat, and now he proposed a reborn *America*, one that would achieve the impossible.

Would Byrd do it? Would he cross the ocean in a Fokker trimotor, just like the one that he and Bennett had used to conquer the Pole? Just like the one tucked behind red velvet ropes in Wanamaker's stores? If Byrd dared take up the challenge, Wanamaker added, he would donate $100,000.

There was a hush. Byrd had little choice: by now, he was the symbol of man's growing mastery of the air. He didn't ponder long. The idea was as dangerous and impossible as anything out there at the moment. If he succeeded, the whisper campaign would stop.

Yes, he told Wanamaker, he would accept the challenge. One way or another, no one would ever question his courage again.

FIVE

"THE MOST SPECTACULAR RACE EVER HELD"

Byrd's acceptance of Wanamaker's dinner challenge was one of the worst-kept secrets in aviation. The rumors that circulated in the press were fueled in part by Byrd's inability to pass up any chance to burnish his fame. On October 28, he told reporters that the Atlantic would be conquered during the summer of 1927; he played coy, stating he was more interested in heading an expedition to Antarctica than anything else, yet could not help but hint that he would be the one to fly first across the sea. "He could make no announcement of the exact plans for an expedition which he admitted was being formulated at present," declared *The New York Times*. Simultaneously, he criticized Fonck for overloading his plane and said that more testing would have been wiser. The day after he said this, on October 29, the paper announced in a small inside story, almost like a whisper, "Byrd Hints at Flying Across the Atlantic."

Byrd's interest sparked the American public's in the Orteig Prize, and a sense of patriotic ownership began to form. It was slow in the building, but one can see this humble October 29 "brief" as the beginning of all that would follow. The American public was strangely ambivalent when Fonck seemed so certain to win. A French ace, riding a Russian-built plane, paid for by American money—Fonck's team was portrayed as a spicy international goulash. Somehow it did not seem an *American* prize. The public grew interested only when the squabbles began within the team.

But Richard Byrd was a bona fide American hero, honored by the president, fêted by high society. If the rumors were true—and why wouldn't they be?—this would be two historic and impossible "firsts" by the same American flyer in little more than a year. If that didn't prove that this would be the "American century," what would?

Being "first" was important in the hero business—the most important thing. No one remembered the also-ran. If one was first, he was a pioneer. He was a part of history. Byrd was already hailed as the all-American man, barely a year before the same theme would begin for Lindbergh. George Palmer Putnam wrote a tribute to Byrd's "qualities" that appeared in the December 16, 1926, *New York Times*. Citing a recent flare-up between Amundsen and the *Norge's* Italian pilot, Putnam said Byrd "seems almost the only major explorer of today who continues to keep out of the rows, criticism and backbiting." He was fearless, imaginative, generous, and forgiving: "Essentially he is a gentleman," Putnam wrote, "and an extraordinarily modest one, with a rare ability to keep his head on his shoulders and his feet on the ground." These were the best qualities of practical, hardworking America, and they were what had "endeared him to the American public, which revels in his good sportsmanship as much as it admires his heroic attainments."

It was hard to avoid Richard Byrd during this time. In 1925 he'd gone on the national circuit with a photo lecture of the MacMillan Expedition. In October 1926 he started again, with "motion and still pictures" for a new lecture called "The First North Pole Flight." He "performed" in movie theaters, such as the Times Square Theatre in New York, and in churches and school auditoriums. His schedule, handled by the Pond Bureau of New York, was booked solid through March 1927, partly to pay off a debt of $30,000 remaining on his polar venture. The series was a hit; the debt would be paid by February 18, 1927, thanks to the sold-out crowds.

He told of the ice and killing cold, the fact that there was nowhere for his plane to land. If they had, they would never have taken off again. It would have been their death warrant, he said. He showed movies of the *Josephine Ford's* unloading and assembly; of the early tests, his take-off, and return from the Pole. He tried to soften his image with humor. "My Grandmother Byrd, 87 years old, was the principal objector," he told the crowds. "I argued as eloquently as I could but I could not budge her. When I got through, all she said was, 'What are you going to do with the North Pole, when you get it?'"

Though he believed that science offered new freedoms for everyone, there were places he would not go. On October 9, 1926, early in the lecture schedule, his handler, James Pond, begged him to speak before "the colored Methodist Episcopal Church in Ithaca, NY. They are a very good crowd...They are very anxious to have you." But Byrd would not bend: on October 10, he wrote a one-line reply: "No, I believe that I would rather not lecture at Ithaca as you suggested—I am sorry."

To do so would have meant editing his lecture. His notes included a segment entitled "Mess Attendants," which suggested to his audience that blacks did not like to fly. It was a gratuitous "bit," since the story involved Byrd's black mess attendants during the Great War and had nothing to do with the Pole. "My mess boy was a very good one and I wanted to reward him by taking him up for a flight," Byrd said. "But I could not get him on the plane. I told him how great it was to be flying around in the air like a bird. He answered: 'Boss, I would a lot rather run around on the ground like a rabbit.'"

Byrd wanted to see if other mess boys would fly, but his luck was no better. "This fellow said he did not care even to go near the planes," Byrd said. "He was going to stay right on terra firma. So I asked him why. 'Captain,' he answered, ' 'cause de less de firma, the more the terror.'"

The joke probably would not have gone over as well in Ithaca as it would before the Grand Rapids Junior League.

Prejudice was woven into the times—these were still the Jim Crow years, and in 1924 the Ku Klux Klan reached its political peak with 4.5 million members. Yet there was a purpose to Byrd's seemingly gratuitous segment about "mess boys." Blacks in the Roaring Twenties were portrayed as the ultimate comic Luddites, ruled by superstition, resistant to technological change. Byrd was making a subtle point to his audience: Are you white, scientific, and progressive, or black, superstitious, and backward?

He had started making the same point—without the racial overtones—as early as August 1926, when it still appeared that Fonck would win the Orteig Prize. In "Have Spectacular Flights Value?," an article he wrote for the magazine *World's Work*, Byrd acknowledged the protests against "stunt" flights, which he defined not as barnstorming tricks but as "pioneer spectacular flights" like his. Stunt flights appeared useless, expensive, and dangerous: they seemed a potential waste of money, men, and machines. However, Byrd countered, "apparently useless events may have their meaning for progress." They fit into a larger, more "cosmological" design. He saw his destiny as an agent of progress, and he attacked it with a missionary's zeal. "Spectacular flights accelerate progress," he preached. "Man needs this spur of necessity—a powerful impetus due to the risk of life involved."

Were there any benefits besides that of personal glory? Most definitely, Byrd said. Stunt flights brought prestige to America, a nation "specially adapted to aviation by its great distances" and the "temperament of its people." In time, he promised, "aviation will be shown not to be an instrument of war, but of peace." Successful trips across the oceans would "bring us closer to the nations of the world both in distance and in sympathy."

Byrd's plane was also a star. Much would be made of Lindbergh and his *Spirit of St. Louis*, a molding of man and machine that Lindbergh reinforced by referring to the plane and himself as "we." But Byrd set that template a year earlier with his identification with the *Josephine Ford*. In 1926 he personified the American faith in scientism, the belief that a culture wedded to science and technology would rule the world. "A civilization," wrote scientism's architect, sociologist Thorstein Veblen, "which is dominated by this matter-of-fact insight must prevail." Byrd's conquest of the Pole brought world attention to man's ability to master, and not be enslaved, by the Machine.

It was in this proselytizing spirit that, on October 7, 1926, the *Josephine Ford* began a 7,000-mile cross-country tour funded by the Guggenheim Foundation and sponsored by the U.S. Department of Commerce. The *Josephine Ford*'s cabin was refitted with carpets and chairs; it was repainted, and the engines were reconditioned to be "practically as good as new." The plane would start in Washington, D.C., and for the next six weeks would fly coast to coast on its grand tour. After leaving Washington, it would fly to New York, then Albany, Syracuse, Rochester, Buffalo, cities along the Great Lakes to Chicago, then down through the Midwest to St. Louis and on to Texas. It would turn north to Salt Lake City, land in cities in the Rockies, cross to the Pacific and cruise south along the coast, then return via Denver and the southern states to D.C. It was seen as an investment: "The tour," said the Guggenheim Foundation's official release, "is to show the people of the United States how safe commercial operation of airways may be."

Floyd Bennett piloted the three-engine Fokker, Bernt Balchen by his side. Balchen jumped at the chance to escape his position as "prize bull." True, they'd stop and speak at fifty cities, and it seemed to Balchen that he would never be free of big crowds. But at least between banquets he would be in the cockpit and watch the huge nation he'd heard about since childhood scroll past beneath their wings.

Balchen soon found that he and Bennett were from two different flying "schools." Bennett was "old school," as were many American pilots at the time. He flew at low altitudes so he could follow roads, railroad tracks, and rivers to their destinations. Balchen had taught himself the newer technique of instrument flying, an essential in Norway, where the weather was rarely clear. He was experienced in "dead reckoning," flying a compass course for a certain length of time while observing wind drift to make course corrections. Though airmail pilots were learning this new technique, few others were. On October 8, they left New York and skirted a suburb when Bennett asked whether, on the way to Albany, they would follow the river or railroad.

"Why not fly across country direct?" Balchen said. "I'll give you a compass course, and after a while I'll check the ground speed and tell you when we'll be there." He took out his pocket slide rule and made his calculations.

They droned over Westchester, passing woods and mountains that Bennett had never seen. Balchen could tell that his friend was uneasy. "Sure you're on the right course?" he finally said.

"Ja, ja, don't worry one thing: we'll be in Albany in just forty minutes."

They landed within a minute of the estimated time. Bennett gave him a sidelong glance as they climbed into the waiting auto. They drove straight to a lunch hosted by the Albany Chamber of Commerce, where Bennett was introduced and read a speech written for him by Harry A. Bruno, a New York public relations man hired by Byrd for the tour. "I'm an aviator, not an orator," he opened before launching into the reason for the tour: Byrd's polar flight had proven that aviation had come of age. Someday, hourly flights would take off between major cities; no place in the world would be inaccessible by plane. Balchen listened intently, glad he was not at the lectern, still shy about his command of the English language. The applause had barely died before they were back in the limo, back at the airport, back in the cockpit, and on their way to Syracuse.

The itinerary at each city was the same: crowds at the airport, a hurried ride through the city, a lunch or dinner, a meeting with local reporters. They passed out a press kit, then went to the hotel for the night or climbed in the cockpit again.

Their friendship grew, partly based upon friendly rivalry. On the way to Cleveland, Balchen wondered aloud whether there would be any variation this time. Always the same food; always the same speech from Harry Bruno. One day, Balchen bet he could recite Bennett's speech by heart.

"Okay," said Bennett. "If you know it so well, you can give it yourself tonight."

Balchen couldn't back down. That night in Cleveland, he faced a roomful of suited dignitaries. He cleared his throat, remembering how Bennett always started. "I am an aviator, okay, not an oriay-tor, you bet."

Bennett doubled up with laughter, and the audience quickly followed. That night in their hotel room, Bennett insisted that Balchen was the biggest hit yet. "From now on you're the oriaytor, Bernt, I'm only the aviator, you bet."

Balchen stood in the open window, listening to the rumble of traffic below. He stared at the smoking stacks of the steel mills lining the Ohio River. Somehow he felt lonely and strange. "We're both only aviators," he replied. He turned and asked Bennett about that flight to Greenland that Byrd had mentioned back in Spitzbergen.

There was a brief space of silence, then Bennett spoke quietly. "I've got a better idea," he said. "How would you like to fly the Atlantic?" Byrd had spoken to him before they left about entering the Orteig Prize. Since then, nothing had been said. Maybe the two of them could do it, Bennett suggested. Maybe they could convince the Fords and Guggenheims to let them take the *Josephine Ford*. They'd need better data on its range, and for the rest of the trip they should keep accurate tabs in their logbooks on maximum speed and fuel use to see if she could actually fly nonstop across the ocean.

The rest of the trip passed quickly. They tested the plane wherever they could. They flew by compass, making allowance for drift. Balchen had been cautioned not to fly over the Rockies and to follow the railroads, but he ignored the warnings. He set a course and flew at 15,000 feet through fog and over mountains without difficulty. By late November they had covered the West Coast and were returning to Washington, D.C. When they arrived, they'd phone Harry Bruno with their plans.

But a telegram was waiting when they landed. Bennett read it and handed it to Bernt without a word. Byrd had ordered them to deliver the plane to Detroit. He was presenting it to the permanent collection of the Ford Museum.

The next day, they sat silently in the cockpit while flying to the Motor City, where Byrd awaited for the ceremony. They'd gone farther than they'd expected on the tour, logging 9,601 miles in 117 hours of flight. The *Josephine Ford* had handled smoothly the whole time. Balchen's eyes ran over the instrument panel and he wrote down the speed and fuel consumption in his logbook one last time. "Tell me," he asked, "what do you get for the average cruising speed in these trips?"

Bennett drew a logbook from the leg pocket of his overalls. "Let's see. About seventy miles an hour."

"So do I," Balchen said. At that rate, it would take 53 hours' flying time to cover the 3,600 miles from New York to Paris. That would mean breaking the world record for sustained flight, something the aviation world doubted was even possible. Still, if they put in bigger engines— say, the new Wright Whirlwind J-5 that had just come on the market, with its extra 30 horsepowers per engine—they might be able to do it.

But they knew this was a pipe dream. They circled the Detroit landing strip, and the *Josephine Ford* rolled to a stop one last time. Only later did it occur to them that the 70 mph average speed of the two-month flight fell far short of the nearly 100 mph Byrd had claimed on his flight to the Pole.

At the time, neither said a word.

•

Byrd had not been idle while Bennett and Balchen winged across the country. After Rodman Wanamaker's dinner challenge, he shopped for three-engine planes that could fly nonstop for four thousand miles. He wrote Edsel Ford, who said that his father's company had never built anything that could fly that distance. He queried Sikorsky again, but despite the Russian's assurances that he could build such a craft for $40,000 to $60,000, Byrd was unconvinced. The crash of the S-35 was still fresh in his mind.

One company could do the job. The Atlantic Aircraft Corporation of

Hasbrouck Heights, New Jersey, had built the *Josephine Ford*. In a letter dated October 25, the company made extensive recommendations regarding an ocean-hopping plane. Such a craft would be like the *Jo Ford*, with changes. It would have three air-cooled Wright Whirlwind engines, the best around; that way, a coolant leak was not a factor at a time when overheating was still the death of many aircraft engines. The company would stretch the *Ford*'s wingspan from 63 to 71 feet, thus adding more lift at takeoff to carry the huge and necessary load of fuel.

But once again, Byrd had reservations. Relations between Byrd and Anthony H. G. Fokker, the company's founder, were not particularly cordial. The Flying Dutchman had little regard for Byrd as a pilot, and did not like him personally. He did, however, recognize Floyd Bennett as a first-class flyer. Fokker had wanted more involvement in the North Pole flight, and detested the fact that his plane would be displayed like a stuffed turkey in some dusty Ford museum. Even though he'd sold her for $40,000, Fokker still regarded the *Josephine Ford* as his. "Little Miss Ford rode to and from the North Pole on the wings of Mr. Fokker," he later said.

Byrd's dislike of Fokker went further than simple business disagreements. He thought "Uncle Tony" was uncouth, absentminded, and profane. Seated, Fokker resembled a Dutch Buddha, short and stout; when he rose to make a point, he threw his hands about and paced wildly. His statements were fragmentary and abrupt, filled with long silences. At times the man seemed out of his mind. He didn't smoke, didn't drink, avoided the theater, and abhorred nightclubs. In meetings with the navy brass, he nibbled peppermints, took naps when sessions grew long-winded, and told racy anecdotes at exactly the wrong time. Sometimes, in the midst of a deal, he would vanish for two or three days, then be found tinkering on some new plane. He loved to swim and, when the weather grew sultry, would sometimes jump into the Hudson River fully clothed. Byrd did not know what to think of him, but this much was obvious: he was not a gentleman.

How could one be a gentleman in the brutal twentieth century?, Fokker would have replied. Born on April 6, 1890, to a wealthy Dutch coffee planter in Java, he showed early on the impatience and mechanical genius that would make his fortune. By age ten, his experiments with gas engines and Bunsen burners led him to tap into his house's gas line; when his father called a halt to the experiment, Anthony tapped the neighbor's. He electrified the doorknob to his workshop after young relatives broke in to play with his inventions. He built his first plane at eighteen, and two years later, in 1910, entered his homemade craft in the Russian Military Competition in St. Petersburg. It won easily. In 1911 one of his ships made a well-publicized flight from Berlin to the Hague. These early planes showed later hallmarks of Fokker's brand: speed, flexibility, and ease of handling. Efficiency was his god. Fokker offered his designs to the Belgian, Dutch, English, and French governments, but only the Germans paid attention. In 1913 they offered him a three-year contract; the war began the next year. The pink-cheeked youngster of twenty-four became a vital part of the German war machine: his planes were faster, easier to maneuver, and more effective in action than anything else in the sky. He devised the first synchronized machine gun, using a simple interrupter gear; he designed the famous triplane, used by Baron von Richthofen and the Flying Circus. By the end of the war, Fokker had made eight thousand planes for the German government and another six thousand were built under plans he approved.

But the Germans lost. The Armistice placed an embargo on the export of German property, and everything Fokker owned was there. Postwar inflation left him penniless; his fate was in his own hands. He bought quantities of rugs, furniture, and bedding, acquired a sixty-car train, and packed his purchases around plane parts, blueprints, and proprietary machinery. During the confusion of the Ten-Day Revolution, his train secretly crossed the Dutch border, not many days behind the Kaiser. On the journey, he staged a mock antismuggling raid on his train, throwing the real custom officials off his scent. By the time they realized they'd been fooled and tried to extradite Fokker, he was safely in Holland, setting up his Netherlands aircraft company. After selling the U.S. Army a number of D-7 planes, he came to New Jersey in 1922 to set up his American factory.

Byrd might not have liked Tony Fokker, but when it came to costs, material, and labor, the man was honest. On October 31, Byrd wrote Wanamaker that the "total cost of the expedition, including the airplane engines, mechanical and other personnel employed, meteorological organization—for weather prognostications, radios, etc., will amount to approximately $100,000." Two months later, he broke it down further, in what remains the best surviving record of estimated costs for seeking the Orteig Prize:

Total cost of plane with all equipment	60,000.00
Hangar for erecting and housing plane and flying-field	5,000.00
Fuel & oil for any test-flights and trans-atlantic flight	2,000.00
Navigation equipment	2,000.00
Assembly plane	1,500.00
Radio equipment	500.00
Pay of mechanics, workmen, meteorologist, etc., etc.	2,500.00

Innumerable miscellaneous matters such as preparation of flying-field near New York; trucks for taking parts to the plane from factory to our hangar; hiring of trucks for transportation to hangar of gasoline, sandbags; purchase of flying-gear and special rubberized boots; flares for use on the water at night; telephones, telegraphs, stationary, etc., etc.; the preparation of the field and the placing of fuel at St. John's, Newfoundland, in case of necessity of landing there en route to Europe, etc.; the hiring of a plane to refill the trans-atlantic flight with gasoline in the air if necessary. We had better allow for all of these things. Shipping of plane back to the United States (in case we don't continue on around the world).   10,000.00
TOTAL   83,500.00

No other flyer in the race outlined the costs so systematically. Byrd approached the prize like a navy quartermaster outfitting his ship for a world cruise. Perhaps because of such care, other flyers (except Lindbergh) would use his approximate range of total costs as their own. Even Lindbergh would piggyback off Byrd's infrastructure, using his field, meteorologists, and innumerable tweaks. Byrd tried to cover every eventuality.

But such mammoth logistics scared Wanamaker. He got cold feet and started to rescind his offer. On November 15, his liaison Grover Whalen sent Byrd a telegram: "MR. W. FEARS COMMERCIALISM MAY CREEP INTO EXPEDITION UNDER PRESENT PLAN HIS INTEREST IS SOLELY FOR THE GLORIFICATION OF AMERICA AND THE SCIENTIFIC VALUE OF SUCH AN ENTERPRISE . . ."

Byrd was thunderstruck by the news. He was on the road, on his lecture circuit, and unable to return to New York until December 8 at the earliest. On November 16, he fired off two letters, one to Wanamaker and one to Whalen. To Wanamaker, he was the soul of diplomacy, taking the blame for whatever misunderstandings might have arisen. "Possibly the statements I made in my letters to you were too conservative," he demurred. "I am well aware that you desired to make the trans-Atlantic flight from patriotic motives and for science, and I have felt the same way about it."

But to Whalen he didn't try to hide his outrage. "If we should buy the plane outright from the Atlantic Aircraft Corporation I cannot see how there could be any charge of commercialism," he wrote. "Did Mr. Wanamaker think that *I* would commercialize the project?"

Instinctively, with the facility he'd developed in Washington, Byrd knew who played adviser to the king. Wanamaker had the money, but Whalen had his boss's ear. November and December faded into secret negotiations, so that by January 14, 1927, Bennett wired Byrd: "WANAMAKER APPROVES PLAN. MEETING TOMORROW TO AUTHORIZE PURCHASE OF PLANE." The word had leaked the previous day—*The Detroit News* wired Byrd on January 13, "WE HAVE REPORT YOU CONTEMPLATE NONSTOP FLIGHT TO PARIS AND PROJECT IS FINANCED CAN YOU GIVE DETAILS BY WIRE?" Byrd didn't answer, for Wanamaker prized secrecy. Bennett sat at the table with Fokker and Wanamaker while Byrd remained on the road selling himself. On January 15, there were some last-minute flare-ups: Bennett wired, "WOULD YOU FAVOR SIKORSKY IF WE CANNOT DO BUSINESS WITH FOKKER?" But even Tony Fokker could see the advantages of this marriage. By January 21, Bennett wired Byrd: "CONTRACT CLOSED. WORK STARTED. MUST NOT HAVE PUBLICITY."

Byrd was in the race, if still secretly. Funding was always his worry, and now he seemed to breathe a sigh of relief. In his soul he thought he would be the first man to fly the Atlantic nonstop; his name would go down through the ages.

But his fate, he would learn, was not his own. If he had not exactly sold his soul to the devil, he had shackled his ambition to the man holding the purse strings.

●

Consciously or not, Byrd's sign-up with Wanamaker would send a powerful message: Winning the Orteig Prize was a rich man's game. Except for Lindbergh, every other flyer sought backers in an attempt to match

Byrd's $100,000 price tag. Lindbergh sought rich backers, too, but his ultimate pool of $15,000 from St. Louis investors seemed more down-to-earth, the kind of benchmark a determined Average Joe could achieve.

Byrd also had to know what kind of world he had entered by cultivating Wanamaker. He had radar for the rich; he'd already befriended Edsel Ford, John D. Rockefeller Jr., and William Vincent Astor. But with Wanamaker, heir to the exclusive department store chain with stores in New York, Philadelphia, and Paris, he had entered the upper echelons of New York society. Wanamaker's personal wealth was closely guarded. Still, there were hints. In 1907 he was the first man in North America to take out a $1 million life insurance policy. In 1927 he topped the list with personal coverage totaling $7.5 million. Only movie producer William Fox came anywhere close, with $6 million in coverage. Such policies were an attempt to "regulate the future," explained *The New York Times*: business empires in America had a way of dissipating after a generation or two, and multimillion-dollar coverage, taken out to satisfy both heirs and creditors after the "great man's death," was a way of ensuring that the name and legacy remained.

But Wanamaker wanted to be more than rich. It wasn't enough to own the grandest department store in New York. His actions and associations suggest he craved the role of the power behind the power. His instrument was the suave and ubiquitous Grover Whalen, a vice president in his company, who served double duty as Mayor Walker's greeter and as police commissioner. Under Whalen, Wanamaker was named special deputy police commissioner from 1918 to 1925, a largely honorary title, but one that he used to align himself with the forces of progress and order. In 1923, for example, he spearheaded a referendum to raise by $200 the annual pay of New York's firefighters and policemen, whom he called "The Iron Lions of Bravery." The increase would give them an annual salary of $2,100 a year. They deserved it, Wanamaker wrote in a four-page broadsheet passed out at his store. "They protect you from harm. They save you from destruction." They were essential guardians for the property of "All Businessmen, Bankers, Brokers, Manufacturers, and Real Estate Owners." He appealed to melodrama: "Always staunch of heart, they are soldiers to the death for you."

A strange, querulous air seems to envelop the man. He stares from his photos, impeccably dressed in bow tie and stiff collar, never smiling, hair combed over his bald spot, moustache crimped at the waxed ends.

He would turn sixty-four in February 1927 and he had heart problems. In an earlier day and place he would have been a merchant prince, a patron of the arts and science, a sponsor for a Michelangelo or a Da Vinci. In his brief five years as head of the Wanamaker stores, he turned entire floors into concert halls and museums. He held after-hour organ solos and orchestra recitals featuring luminaries such as Leopold Stokowski. He erected a chapel in Philadelphia to his first wife and buried her there. He donated paintings, altars, jeweled Bibles, gem-studded crosses, murals, and Wanamaker Organs to churches and hotels throughout the United States and Europe. From 1908 to 1914 he sent photographers out to the West to snap the vanishing Indian. In 1916 he founded the Professional Golf Association and donated its trophy.

Despite all that he accomplished, he always lived in the shadow of his father, John Wanamaker, the "Founder" of the department store chain. It was only at his death in 1922, at age eighty-four, that the son took control. Even today, John Wanamaker is considered a retail pioneer. In 1876 he ran a large general store that included a restaurant and mail-order business; in 1878 he held the first "white sale." In 1882 he installed the first soda fountains and elevators. Fourteen years later, in 1896, he expanded to New York, turning the old A. T. Stewart Store at Broadway and Tenth into a thirty-two-acre palace complete with furniture store, piano salon, and mattress and pillow factory. His advertising was designed "not to sell, but to help people buy," and he always spoke in superlatives: the bridge between the old Stewart store and the new addition was "The Bridge of Progress"; the furniture store was "The House Palatial," the "house of ideas." His sons, Thomas and Rodman, entered the business in 1885 and 1888, respectively; both felt crushed by his legacy and died much younger than their father had.

More than anything, Rodman resented the way that time had forgotten him. He had been a proponent of commercial aviation long before the Great War. In 1909 he bought a $2,200 replica of Blériot's Channel-hopping monoplane, then sold it to aircraft enthusiast Louis Bergdoll for $5,000. In 1911 he planned a balloon flight from the roof of his New York store—the balloon landed safely in New Jersey—supposedly the first time a balloon ever rose from a high building. In 1918 one of his first acts as special deputy police commissioner was to create the city's first aviation section. Five years later, he offered Henry and Edsel Ford's first all-metal plane, the Stout, for sale in his store.

What galled him especially was the way Raymond Orteig's "stunt" eclipsed his own earlier attempt to cross the Atlantic. In February 1914 Wanamaker had proposed to the Aero Club of America a nonstop Atlantic crossing from St. John's, Newfoundland, to London, a distance of about 1,900 miles. To do this, he hired early airplane designer Glenn H. Curtiss to build an enormous flying boat, 35 feet long with a 72-foot wingspan. Though Wanamaker claimed that this had nothing to do with any contest, he neglected to mention that if he did cross the ocean, he would win Lord Northcliffe's £10,000 prize. The flight, he said, was planned solely "in the cause of science and in the interest of world peace." A successful crossing would be as important as Columbus's voyage to the New World. The plane would be ready by the summer of 1914; he'd already paid Curtiss $50,000 and had christened the plane *America*.

But the Great War intervened, and the plane was donated to the Allied war effort. In 1919 Alcock and Brown accomplished what Wanamaker had only dreamed. Soon afterward, the little French innkeeper stole his thunder, too.

But now he was back, with an authentic American hero at the helm. When they finally went public, Wanamaker would remind reporters of his earlier attempt in almost every interview. "I have been planning a transatlantic flight since some time before 1914," he would say.

The purpose was the same as before: not for glory, but for science. Not even the name would change. Byrd's plane, Wanamaker stipulated, would be the *America*.

•

On November 2, as Balchen and Bennett winged across the country on their show tour and Byrd hinted that he would fly across the Atlantic, Lindbergh once again bailed out of his plane.

It was six weeks after his last parachute jump, and it occurred to him as he floated to earth that he could not keep this up forever and survive. This jump was made under much the same circumstances as the last one. He was on the night run, 25 miles beyond Springfield, when again he hit fog. This time he flew under the 400-foot cloud ceiling for several minutes before the fog dropped so low that he could no longer fly under it safely. Peoria and Springfield were blotted out; his only hope was to fly on to Chicago and pray for a gap in the clouds. He found such a gap, but when he dropped a magnesium flare to light his path, its tiny 'chute caught on his rudder. The flare tore off and fell like a stone.

With only ten minutes of gas left in his tank, he turned away from Chicago in search of open country. He had climbed to 14,000 feet when the reserve tank went dry. He didn't want the plane to circle him again, so this time he took precautions before jumping over the side: he cut the switches, stalled the plane, and put it into a level heading. He jumped at 13,000 feet; as his 'chute opened, his plane disappeared into the clouds. Snow whirled around him and the wind was freezing.

This was getting discouraging, he thought as he swayed in the harness. As he'd predicted, his enthusiasm for airmail was diminishing, and these jumps didn't help matters any. Just four days earlier, he'd written to his mother: "I'm working on a new proposition in St. Louis and have been very busy lately." The "proposition" was his idea about entering the Orteig race, but at this point it consisted of little else than a "To Do" list and some appointments with possible financial backers. If anything, this newest jump seemed to him a reflection of how his future floated in limbo.

He played his light below him, and landed on a barbed-wire fence; the barbs did not penetrate his heavy leather suit, and the fence broke his fall. It was his fourth jump in twenty months, making him the only man in America to save his life by parachute that many times. The exploit made news, and one midwestern paper described him as "a supple, young, blond giant just past twenty-four." His former sergeant from flight school wrote, "I don't know whether you possess any angelistic instincts, but it appears to me as though you are favored by the angels."

•

As the New Year dawned, the country seemed gripped by a bad case of nerves.

The Roaring Twenties, historians tend to point out, was a decade in which nothing big occurred. There were no cataclysms or "big events"— no wars or plagues, rebellions or economic tsunamis, at least until the 1929 stock market crash. Yet it may have been the decade of greatest change in U.S. history. In a sense it was a reactionary time: rising from the disillusionment of the Great War, Americans entered a riotous age of spending, profit, cheap goods, and consumerism. Everything and everyone seemed to be on a roll; they revolted against all the chains of Victorian culture, seemingly abandoning old ideas overnight to adopt new ones wholesale. The press was filled with tales of deep division: anti-Prohibition "wets" versus "drys," town versus city, progressives versus conservatives, men versus women.

Nothing served as a greater symbol of this general restlessness than the "New Woman." Continuing the revolt from old social patterns they had begun before the war, women in the 1920s raised their hemlines, smoked in public, and sipped Prohibition whiskey with the men. As late as 1919 they had still worn ample ankle-length dresses over corsets, chemises, and petticoats; now they preferred flesh-colored stockings whose cheesecake color gave rise to the term for the familiar leggy pinup photography. There was a lot more talk of sex, though later studies suggested there was more talk than action. In any case, "it" was on everyone's mind.

The "Jazz Age" itself suggested an unfamiliar hedonism. "The word jazz in its progress toward respectability has first meant sex, then dancing, then music," wrote F. Scott Fitzgerald, the decade's unofficial scribe. "It is associated with a state of nervous stimulation, not unlike that of big cities behind the lines of a war." By 1926 Fitzgerald had grown fed up with this "universal preoccupation with sex." He recalled a "perfectly mated, content young mother" asking his wife, Zelda, about "having an affair right now," even if she had no one particular in mind. The mother considered it a problem only since, over thirty, adultery seemed "sort of undignified."

While Americans were throwing what Fitzgerald called "the most expensive orgy in history," Europe was still wrestling with the ruins of war. Dictators replaced democracies, and their rise seemed to bring an uneasy order. In 1922 Benito Mussolini formed a Fascist government; two years later, Joseph Stalin began his thirty-one-year rule of the Soviet Union. In the democracies, things got worse. A 1926 general strike in Britain brought the nation to a halt. The German economy collapsed. In Vienna, socialists rioted.

The New Year would prove to be one of technical wonders. The first "talkie" would be released in October: *The Jazz Singer* astounded audiences across America. Philo T. Farnsworth demonstrated the first long-range television transmission. The NBC radio network went on the air in November 1926, followed by CBS in September 1927, making radio a national conduit for news, sports, and entertainment. The Holland Tunnel opened under the Hudson River. Even Kool-Aid hit the shelves, though it was spelled "Kool-Ade" then. It was a year when anything seemed possible, the year Babe Ruth batted .356 with 60 home runs and 164 RBIs. When told he made more money than President Coolidge, the Babe answered, "I had a better year."

It would be a "year of wonders" especially for aviation, though it started in a slump with the aircraft industry faced with an unshakeable conundrum. Though hailed by futurists as the symbol of "the new," U.S. aircraft manufacturers by December 1926 had produced among them a total of only about a thousand planes. They needed something to give the public, and investors, a nudge.

In fact, American planes were more technically ready than ever to attempt a sea crossing. All manner of improvements had occurred since the war. A carved slot on the wing's leading edge forced air over its upper surface and smoothed out drag. The increased use of steel and aluminum alloys strengthened the frame. Metal propellers and electric ignitions became realities; the 1926 synthesis of the isooctane hydrocarbon reduced engine knock, the bane of greater propulsion. By the mid-1920s, more single-engine monoplanes that carried six to eight passengers were being built than ever before. With their 100 mph cruising speed and 500-mile flight range, commercial aviation finally seemed more than a dream. The airplane's use grew monthly: it was now used for medical evacuations, crop-dusting, moving freight, aerial photography, and advertising.

Yet the most heralded improvement was the perfection of the air-cooled radial engine. The 1920s saw the birth of small fast planes—forerunners of the World War II fighter—due to the new sport of air racing. If aviation was becoming the symbol of a nation's technological future, the Pulitzer Trophy races in the United States and the Schneider Trophy races in Europe were the arenas where those nations tested one another. The flying arm of every Western military service entered these contests; in the United States, the navy especially poured money into research, and many of the race entrants were navy fliers. The new air-cooled engines transferred the heat of combustion directly from the cylinder to the atmosphere, whereas traditional water-cooled engines transferred heat to the cooling water, then out through the radiator. Air-cooled engines eliminated the water, radiator, pipes, and shutters—for an average 200-horsepower engine, this lowered the weight by about 120 pounds. They were reliable, durable, and required less maintenance than water-cooled engines, and by December 20, 1926, air-cooled American planes had flown 1,774,268 miles with only three forced landings due to motor-part failure.

As the Jazz Age started, only one American company produced air-cooled engines: the tiny Lawrance Aero-Engine Corporation of New York City. In the high-profile world of aircraft design and racing, Yale graduate Charles L. Lawrance was something of a recluse, but he didn't mind obscurity. "Everybody remembers Paul Revere, but no one knows the name of his horse," he once said. The navy saw the future in him: it wanted planes that could be packed aboard aircraft carriers; light, small, and fast without the weight and maintenance problems of water-cooled systems. But the Lawrance Corp. was small itself and did not have the resources for large-scale production. In 1923 the navy strong-armed the larger Wright Corp. into buying Lawrance; by the next year, the Wright J-3 and J-4 engines, better known as "Whirlwinds," were being sold. These were the engines that had powered Byrd's *Josephine Ford*—and that was the best advertisement in the world. By New Year's Day of 1927, the improved Wright J-5 was heralded as "the world's first truly reliable aero-engine," and all long-distance fliers wanted it in their planes.

●

If more was better, Jazz Age Americans should have been the happiest in the nation's history. And, in fact, this cornucopia of new inventions and their cheap production did unleash a cult of prosperity unlike anything ever seen. Everyone seemed to own everything. Radios, autos, ready-to-wear clothing, appliances, gadgets—they made their way into more and more homes. By 1925 a Ford Model-T sold for $295; a Victrola cabinet phonograph went for $250; an RCA Radiola radio, $175. This might seem a lot on an average annual salary (in 1930) of $1,368, but to this had been added a new way of buying: the installment plan.

After 1920 the old values of saving and thrift gave way to the idea that spending was a virtue, maybe the highest economic duty of all. Between 1920 and 1929, installment purchases quadrupled; in 1929 they accounted for 60 percent of auto sales, 70 percent of furniture sales, and a whopping 90 percent of all radio, refrigerator, and vacuum cleaner sales. The old stigma of buying on credit disappeared. Advertising became more intimate, feeding fears of how we looked and smelled. Ads for "Odor-o-no" deodorant reminded us that underarm odor could be an impediment to love. Where Americans once defined themselves by their religion, occupation, and politics, we now were what we bought. As John Wanamaker had foreseen, possessions made the man.

A new mantra entered the national discourse: mass production and consumption could lead to permanent prosperity. The Machine could make Man happy, and if this were so, 1927 would prove a red-letter year. Every economic indicator seemed strong. The national debt was being paid off; there was near-full employment, almost no inflation, and President Coolidge imposed three big tax cuts during his administration. For the first time in history, Americans bought stocks in great volume. Euphoria reigned in the 1927 market, and on December 19, 1927, the Dow Jones Industrial Average would pass 200 for the first time. Unlike other economic upswings, this era of prosperity seemed driven by the "average man."

But who exactly was he? It was an important question, if such prosperity were to continue. What were his hopes, worries, convictions, and prejudices? In May 1927 *The Literary Digest* released a report based upon the standardized test results of 93,000 soldiers taken during the Great War, combined with actuarial tables. The average man stood 5 foot 7 inches, weighed 150 pounds, and had a brain of 1,300 grams, or twice that of a chimpanzee. He had a pulse rate of 70 beats a minute and an active vocabulary of 7,500 words. He left school after the 8th grade, and scored the same as the average boy of 14 on intelligence tests. In all likelihood, he would drift into a skilled trade. He married young, had three to five children, held set ideas about morality, and respected "common sense," which he believed he had in spades. "He is a Democrat and a Methodist," wrote the author, a psychologist at Columbia University, "or a Republican and a Baptist, because his father was." He fell prey to salesmen with get-rich-quick investments, and though he had no great interest in religion, he was superstitious. He died at age 53, his wife at 54.

By 1927 the average man felt blue. He did not know why, but the prediction that "more was better" had not come true. Perhaps Fitzgerald saw it first—at least he was the first to pinpoint the year. Before, it had been merely a general malaise, a vague restlessness "like a nervous beating of the feet," but in 1927, Fitzgerald suddenly realized that "contem-

poraries of mine had begun to disappear into the dark maw of violence."
A classmate killed his wife and himself on Long Island; two more tumbled from skyscrapers. Two died in speakeasies; another was committed to an insane asylum, where he got an axe to the head. "These are not catastrophes that I went out of my way to find," Fitzgerald mourned, "these were my friends." Strangest of all to him was the fact that they happened "not during the depression, but during the boom."

What could cause such darkness in the nation that called itself the "mansion on the hill"? Princeton historian John Ward would blame it on "a philosophy of relativism," but it was probably more vague than that, a roiling in the gut that might have been indigestion or something far more serious, those sleepless spells at 5:00 a.m. when a man wondered what he had become. Had we traded something vital for prosperity? And what about those installment loans hanging over our heads?

Maybe it struck more intimately than that, in the marriage bed. "That something is wrong with marriage today is universally admitted and deplored," wrote Paul Popenoe, the father of marriage counseling, in his 1925 *Modern Marriage: A Handbook.* "The number of celibates, of mismatched couples, of divorces, of childless homes, of wife deserters, of mental and nervous wrecks; the frequency of marital discord, of prostitution and adultery, of perversions, of juvenile delinquency, tells the story." Once, the nation had been young and idealistic. Now we had deserted some basic vision of ourselves.

Perhaps our values were skewed. Theologian Reinhold Niebuhr watched from the Bethel Evangelical Church in Detroit and cried, "What a civilization this is!" Rich gentlemen who made a killing in the stock market were sought out for their wisdom in all matters: "Isn't it strange how gambler's luck gives men the assurance of wisdom for which philosophers search in vain?" he wrote that year. Money didn't buy just happiness—it bought wisdom, worth, and the adulation of millions in this new, dynamic America.

Maybe the weakness lay within. This would be the year that the U.S. Supreme Court legalized compulsory sterilization by upholding *Buck v. Bell,* a case challenging the constitutionality of a Virginia sterilization law. The ruling reflected a widespread fear. According to the 1927 *World Almanac,* the number of "feeble-minded" people committed to American institutions was 39.3 percent per 100,000 of the total population, a number that had increased from 22.5 percent in 1910. "The stock of the entire country is being constantly poisoned and vitiated," wrote *The Twin City Sentinel* of Winston-Salem, North Carolina. Given a national sterilization program, "this nation could be pretty well rid of the usual types of mental weaklings within the next two generations."

So much prosperity, so much fear. What was one to do? Something was needed. A guidepost. An anodyne.

"In the spring of '27," wrote Fitzgerald, "something bright and alien flashed across the sky."

•

The bright flash was Lindbergh, but on January 1, 1927, few knew he existed. Yet the way was being prepared. The gears of the hero business had already started to grind.

All nations and cultures have their heroes: the "average man" holds them up as a mirror to "adjust and adorn" his own life, Plutarch wrote around A.D. 75. The Roman biographer's primary interest lay in the means by which character shaped destiny. Eighteen centuries later the basic pattern remained unchanged, only now they were the "human interest stories" that dominated twentieth-century journalism.

By the 1920s a new spin had attached to the ancient form. Daniel Boorstin, in his classic study *The Image*, chronicled biographical articles in *The Saturday Evening Post* and *Collier's* in five sample years from 1901 to 1914. During that time, 74 percent of the subjects—people the editors deemed worthy of notice—came from politics, business, and professions such as medicine and law. After 1922 well over half came from the entertainment world. The machinery of information changed the rules. Where the old-style hero was known for achievement, the 1920s version—now called the "celebrity"—was known for being known. Where the hero "created himself," said Boorstin, "the celebrity is created by the media." Somewhere in the mid-1920s the two merged.

The change reflected the growing supply and demand of news. An information hunger existed in America, a daily "news hole" that had to be filled. It began with late nineteenth-century technical innovations such as the rotary press, which could print both sides of a continuous sheet of paper; this vastly increased a paper's daily circulation while cutting its price, but also created the daily race to fill that space. Writing in *Collier's* in 1911, American journalist Will Irwin described this endless demand for news as "a crying primal want of the mind, like hunger of the body."

Words were mass-produced, which meant more pages to fill than ever before. In 1902 *The Saturday Evening Post* sold 314,671 copies of each issue. By 1922 that figure had exploded to 2,187,024 copies per issue, for an advertising revenue of $28,278,255.

The rise of other media added to the need. Photojournalism was still new; *The New York Times* had just organized World Wide Photos in 1919, while the first wire photo to attract wide comment was Coolidge's nomination as president in Cleveland in 1924. The newsreel, invented in France by Pathé, came to the United States in 1910. In 1926 and '27, competing radio news networks, NBC and CBS, filled the airwaves.

At this point no one quite understood the role of the hero or the celebrity. What need did he or she fill? But intuition told storytellers—the novelists and journalists—that somehow it was an essential one. Walter Winchell, the great gossip columnist and broadcaster, understood intuitively that fame lay at the heart of a daily moral conversation. Somehow it was therapeutic, even if those turned into gods were later crucified. This explosion of mass hero worship in the 1920s shaped every form of journalism for the rest of the century, and the great flowering that began in 1925 and reached its apotheosis in 1927 would serve as its template. The media-made hero lived a narrative of sublime importance to those who witnessed—and they witnessed by the millions.

But *why?* Two decades later, scholars took a stab at defining the American hero. "An age of mass hero worship is an age of instability," wrote sociologist Orrin Klapp in 1948. He and others noticed several characteristics of the American hero. He was an underdog, often poor, and recently off the farm. However, his was not a debasing poverty, but rather the era's common struggle to make ends meet. By hailing from a farm, he learned at an early age a kind of business management, one that could make him a success as an adult. He had a "good mother," a paragon of virtue like the Virgin Mary. Such narratives formed a web of "truths disguised for us," wrote Joseph Campbell in his 1949 *The Hero with a Thousand Faces*, but Oriental or Occidental, modern, ancient, or primitive, they all ultimately exposed a need. We saw ourselves in the hero—not in the "bright moments of his...great victories, but in the silences of his personal despair."

The journalist of 1927 might not have known the theory of hero-making, but he certainly knew its practice. It was the "Year of the Big Shriek," declared journalist Herbert Asbury. "The remarkable prosperity of the newspapers during the year was accomplished by the most terrific bombination of personal publicity in the history of American journalism," he observed. "For in truth, the news and editorial columns throughout the twelve months were just one scream after another. 'He has exalted the race of men!' cried the Baltimore *Sun*...'He has performed the greatest feat of a solitary man in the records of the human race!' shouted the New York *Evening World.*" That year, American newspapers grew rich off hero tales. The top three selling issues, on May 21, June 6, and July 1, all contained stories about the Orteig Prize, while the runners-up on July 21 and September 22 followed the exploits of sports heroes—the Jack Dempsey–Jack Sharkey fight in New York, and the Jack Dempsey–Gene Tunney battle in Chicago. In New York alone, newspaper readership increased by four hundred thousand; nationwide, by two million. People "whose principal reading matter had hitherto been the titles of moving pictures, began to buy newspapers and eagerly spell out the headlines."

Two years earlier, American journalists had learned the art of grabbing a reader's interest and holding it over the course of a long, sustained hero tale. On Friday, January 30, 1925, the spelunker Floyd Collins was exploring a passage in Sand Cave, a largely unmapped cavern in south central Kentucky, when a rock fell on his foot and he could not climb clear. On February 1, two of nearby Louisville's four dailies published a short account of his predicament. The Louisville *Courier-Journal* sent reporter William "Skeets" Miller to cover the story. Miller was not the only reporter on the scene, but he was the smallest, and on February 2, he scooted down the narrow passage. He reached Collins, getting an interview at the same time he developed empathy for the trapped man. Over the next few days, Miller repeated the trip, becoming one of the heroes of the tale.

For the next two weeks, *The Courier-Journal* and papers across the nation began running front-page accounts of the effort to save Collins. This was not only an entrapment story, it was also a race against time, and Miller's accounts were carried by the Associated Press and printed in more than 1,200 papers. Movie theaters, restaurants, and hotels posted reports on the efforts to save Collins; plays were interrupted with bulletins. On February 6, four hundred cars jammed the road to Sand Cave. The next day, a Saturday, authorities counted two thousand people. Estimates for Sunday, February 8, a week into the ordeal, placed the number anywhere from ten thousand to fifty thousand people. The suspense grew as great as the crowd, which had to be held back by state troopers and barbed wire.

Collins was neither the first nor the last person to be trapped in a cave. Yet the nation's connection to him grew with each story. On February 4, a cave-in had made direct rescue impossible. Only Skeets Miller could still wiggle back and forth between Collins and the surface, and he, too, was in danger of ending up trapped or buried. Several plans to get Collins out proved fruitless—including one that involved the amputation of his pinned foot. Rescuers sent in food via Miller, as well as a makeshift light. As it became evident that he was doomed, Collins resorted to prayer.

A few days later, there was silence. On Monday, February 16, when an alternate shaft finally reached him, it was obvious that Collins had been dead for several days. Two days after that, he was buried in a simple ceremony inside the cave that had killed him.

Why did so many people care? The size of the story took even veteran journalists by surprise. Nothing quite like this had ever happened before. Yet when they looked back, they could see quite clearly the elements that had sucked people in. The most important was the narrative arc: the attempt to save Collins was a race against time. There are no ambiguities in a race; there is a clearly delineated beginning and end, and you either win or you lose. As Miller crawled down to Collins and they talked about life and death, those up top argued about the proper way to rescue the trapped man. The tone in media reports seesawed between hope and despair: Collins's chances looked good on February 3, 4, 6, 8, 10, 11, 14, and 15. On February 2, 5, 7, 9, 12, and 13, hopes sank, keeping the public on edge. On any given day, both possibilities were held out: escape was near, while death was certain, or vice versa. Collins's extended plight grew bigger than he: in time, writers translated the ordeal into universals: man versus nature, loss of hope versus a faith in something greater.

Moreover, the story was filled with people the readers thought they "knew." First and foremost there was the everyman, Collins: able, hardworking, religious. "I'm not afraid to die," he said. "I believe I would go to Heaven." Then there was Skeets Miller, the cynical reporter human-ized by Collins's courage. Finally, there were the supporting players: Lee Collins, Floyd's father, portrayed as a cantankerous, stereotypical moun-taineer; Collins's hardworking stepmother, Miss Jane, her shoulders sagging from "years behind the plow"; Floyd's dog, "Old Shep"; and his "girlfriend," Alma Clark, who waited for his release at the mouth of the cave. The dog and the girlfriend were fictions: "Old Shep" was really named Obie, while Alma was merely a friend and was never romanti-cally involved with the doomed man.

•

At the dawn of 1927, journalists sensed another race with life and death in the balance. They pursued the characters, though at the time only two, Fonck and Byrd, were known to the general public. Byrd's entry was expected at any moment; Fonck appeared weekly in the papers with some new, vague plan to try again. Across the ocean, several French fliers said they would soon enter. A German flier planned to take off from Bremen; an Italian aviator, from Rome.

"The hallmark of the American journalist is a direct and coarse at-tack, without any subtleties," said Alexis de Tocqueville in 1827. One hundred years later the basic technique had not changed. "I was shad-owed," Byrd wrote of this time. "Questions were put to my family and friends about me to find out what I had 'up my sleeve.' Exaggerations and rumors flew about thick and fast. Caustic criticism of other en-trants was attributed to me."

Despite the media attention, Byrd would not be the first to apply for the race in the New Year. On January 28, the first entry arrived: Lieu-tenant Commander Noel Davis of the navy sent in his application, along with his copilot's, Stanton Wooster, also a navy man. The American Le-gion backed them for $100,000, a pledge equal to Wanamaker's.

On February 28, the National Aeronautic Association announced its second entry: the unknown C. A. Lindbergh, a mail pilot from St. Louis. The story ran on March 1 and was buried on page 16 of *The New York Times*. Little was known about the man other than that he flew the mail between St. Louis and Chicago and had been "forced to make para-chute descents, abandoning his plane in a fog at night when the motor failed him." He would fly a Ryan monoplane "equipped with Wright J-5 Whirlwind engines" that was being built somewhere on the Pacific

Coast. One read the brief story and shrugged. The mail pilot's chances didn't seem good, even if the plane was finished on time.

On March 3, Byrd did as expected and announced that he would make the attempt, revealing, finally, that he was being backed by Rodman Wanamaker for $100,000. Floyd Bennett would be his copilot; the plane, the *America*, designed by Anthony Fokker, would be a bigger version of the *Josephine Ford*. Byrd had not sent in his application yet; perhaps he would not at all! "We want to set right one thing," he said at a press conference held later in March. "If we attempt a transatlantic flight, it will not be for the Orteig or any other prize...Our desire is to help the progress of aviation." He reminded the world that Wanamaker was "the first man to propose a transatlantic flight from the United States to Europe." The general impression at the end of the speech was that Byrd and Wanamaker were above such mundanities as winning a race and taking home a prize.

Then, in late March, a dispatch from Paris announced that Captain Charles Nungesser would attempt the transatlantic hop in the opposite direction—from Paris to New York—sometime in the late spring or early summer. Nungesser was France's great hero, a living legend on par with Byrd. He was brave, skilled as a combat pilot, and, by official count, had shot down forty-seven German planes and two observation balloons during the war. True, that count was less than Fonck's, but unlike Fonck, Nungesser had suffered in the war, bearing the scars of seventeen wounds. His copilot would be François Coli, the one-eyed ace, who'd started much earlier with Paul Tarascon but had been plagued by misfortune and delay. Nungesser and Coli would fly a single-engine Levasseur, a French-built biplane with a 450-horsepower engine that should be ready to fly by early April.

Of all the international rivals, Nungesser was easily the most glamorous. And like Lindbergh, he wanted to fly alone. But Pierre Levasseur, his backer and designer, demanded that he take a navigator. It was a stipulation, he said, if Nungesser planned to fly a Levasseur. Nungesser relented when he heard the designer's suggestion—François Coli, who had been looking for another partner after the 1926 crash that had left Paul Tarascon so badly burned. Coli probably had bragging rights to more distance records than anyone on the Continent, and he was known as one of France's best navigators. Besides, the fellow aces knew each other from the war.

Suddenly, what started out as René Fonck's one-man exhibition had transformed into an international rivalry. A substantial feature published in the Sunday, March 20, *New York Times* dwelt upon the entries of Byrd, Davis, and Fonck, while barely mentioning the others. Davis and Byrd were "crack Navy fliers" who at one point had been rumored to be flying together; Fonck still seemed in the running, especially after announcing that Sikorsky would build another plane for him. Lindbergh was mentioned deep in the story: it was mistakenly reported that he intended "to fly with only one other pilot, and such a venture would perhaps be the most spectacular of all." The glamorous Italian flier Francesco de Pinedo, then in the middle of his transoceanic trip from Africa to the United States, was rumored as a possibility: "Whether he will compete for the Orteig Prize is not yet known, although he could not do it in the flying boat he has been using." The exact identity of the French entrants was still uncertain, though it was assumed that at least one team of aces would attempt the jump from Paris to Manhattan, considered more difficult because of nearly constant headwinds.

One thing was certain, said the *Times*, "Those in close touch with aviation have no doubt that somebody will fly from New York to Paris this Spring. The question is, Who?" The story had finally found its arc, and the narrative had begun:

Big planes and little planes are being built; planes with three and two motors, and with only one. Some of the airmen who are planning to hop to Europe have the backing of large manufacturers and business men who are eager to show that long-distance flying is comparatively safe. Others intend to go it alone, in ships that are so small that their adventure will be a pure gamble against fate.

It would be, the *Times* promised, "the most spectacular race ever held."

SIX

THE FARM BOY

On the morning of February 24, 1927, Douglas G. Corrigan walked onto the landing field of Ryan Aircraft Corporation in San Diego. Normally, the twenty-year-old Corrigan—who would one day be known as "Wrong Way"—would be flying at this hour. Though he was one of Ryan's test pilots, he had a penchant for getting into trouble. One day in January he'd been reprimanded for flying too low and scraping his wing on a telephone line. A week later he made a vertical turn on his wingtip two feet from the ground, and for that was grounded. He spotted a tall, slim fellow standing beside a Ryan prototype while talking to company owner Benjamin Franklin Mahoney and sales manager A. J. Edwards. Corrigan asked his boss, chief pilot John J. "Red" Harrigan, about the tall stranger.

"That's a fellow from St. Louis that wants to fly from New York to Paris," Red replied. His name was Lindbergh, a mail route flier out of Lambert Field. His friends called him "Slim," which, except for the bad haircut, just about described him.

"Gosh," said Corrigan, "he looks like a farmer. Do you suppose he can fly?"

"We'll find out pretty soon. He's going to take the ship up."

Corrigan watched as the Farm Boy took up Ryan's single-engine Hisso monoplane. He buzzed around a few minutes, came back over the field, headed upwind at 200 feet, and looped seven consecutive times. He ended with a wingover, then brought the plane down for a good landing. It was the most perfect low-altitude stunt flying Corrigan had ever seen.

"Well, I guess he can fly all right," Red Harrigan said.

•

The Farm Boy could fly, all right, one of the few things he could do quite well. When it came to flying, Lindbergh knew his mind. He liked the Ryan plane so much that he wanted one like it, though with a few changes. It needed to fly nonstop for 3,700 miles, he said. Could Ryan build such a machine?

Who was this Farm Boy who appeared out of nowhere with his odd ideas for planes? Decades after the flight that brought him "Fame— Opportunity—Wealth—and also tragedy & loneliness & frustration," Charles Augustus Lindbergh Jr. remains a mystery. Millions of words have been written about him, yet no one has quite been able to pin him down. It is impossible to examine the history of the Orteig Prize and not fall within his shadow: he was the "the hero" to every author who wrote about him on or after May 21, 1927, and that colored every fact, even when he fell from grace in his worshipers' eyes. He was "Lindbergh Alone," the "Lone Eagle," the ultimate Boy Scout to scores of contemporaries. Though the same adulation would have attached to many of his rivals if they had won, his triumph came at exactly the right moment in a growing worldwide expansion of competing technologies. That year, telephones, the Bartlane Cable Process, radio, and radiographs could transmit voices and pictures around the world in moments; motion pictures mastered the technique of synchronizing sound and image; the printed word was read by more people than ever before. Progress made Lindbergh mass communication's first international superstar.

Every decade sees a reevaluating of the man. In the 1940s, Dixon Wecter's *The Hero in America* claimed that the twenty-five-year-old flier's sudden appearance turned the race "into an issue between Death and the boy." In 1959 Kenneth Davis published his celebrated *The Hero: Charles A. Lindbergh and the American Dream*. Lindbergh was no longer just a hero, he was Joseph Campbell's ur-hero in rough midwestern clothes. A. Scott Berg, whose 1998 biography won the Pulitzer Prize, could still not shake off the worship: when "Lindy" sped across the ocean, he wrote, "no man before him had ever been so much alone in the cosmos...placing him in the unique position of overshadowing every other living hero." It was a moment unique in history, for "not even Columbus sailed alone."

Alone. That is the key word. Richard Byrd, conversant in the "hero business," recognized the appeal. Facing death in the world's worst places was not enough; one had to do it like a modern knight, single-handedly. "By the mechanics of hero worship," noted Wecter, "a single-handed victory is far better than the combined effects of two." People revere the heroes, saints, and sages that face the world alone.

Some tried to see past the glow. "Except for the fact of his flight," wrote Daniel Boorstin in his study of celebrity, "Lindbergh was a commonplace person. He was not a great inventor or a leader of men. He was not extraordinarily intelligent, eloquent, or ingenious. Like many another young man in those years, he had a fanatical love of flying. The air was his element."

Yet in trying to drown out the hero worship, Boorstin neglects the positives. "Slim" *was* intelligent, in a very focused way. His was a specialist's grasp of knowledge: he had to be interested in something first, then he would learn about it thoroughly. He *was* eloquent, but only on the page, as his Pulitzer Prize–winning memoir, *The Spirit of St. Louis*, would prove. He was shy and solitary, afraid of girls. Like many of that ilk, he often came off as dismissive and taciturn. He made endless lists—everything from the contents of his steamer trunk and self-improvement pointers to a plan for luring St. Louis backers into his transatlantic scheme. He would prove himself quite self-disciplined.

Perhaps his father saw him best. Charles A. Lindbergh Sr., or "C.A." to his friends, was the radical pacifist congressman from Minnesota who for ten years represented the state's rural Sixth District; like many country lawyers, he could size up others quickly and accurately. In a 1922 letter, when Slim was twenty, C.A. wrote that his son was "uncommonly sensible" but also "neglectful" of personal relations, since he "dislikes to write a letter." If anything, Slim lived in a world of his own.

Not surprisingly, for one so introspective, he was, like Byrd, a bit of a mystic. Unlike Byrd, he did not believe in a Supreme Intelligence that planned and oversaw all. He was a determinist, convinced that all the elements of earth and humanity were linked through space and time. How atoms lined up one moment determined the next; what happened today proceeded from yesterday and led to tomorrow. Success did not spring from thin air, but evolved from one's observations of previous successes—and failures.

He'd known failure and discord while growing up, which bred in him self-sufficiency and a distrust of others. The only child of badly

mismatched parents, he withdrew into himself to filter out the unpleas-
antness. His mother, Evangeline Lodge Land, was the child of two
medical families—one dental, one homeopathic, both inventive and
ambitious—and she would become a high school chemistry teacher at a
time when many women stayed home. C.A. was a country lawyer who
liked farmers and found that they liked him. Slim was born on February 4, 1902, heir to an assortment of family skeletons that included
"financial malfeasance, flight from justice, bigamy, illegitimacy, melan-
cholia, manic-depression, alcoholism, grievous generational conflicts,
and wanton abandonment of families." His mother doted on him all her
life; he got his looks from C.A.: a lean handsome face with deep eyes
and a firm mouth; a long, lanky frame. Although an affectionate father,
C.A. never understood his dreamy son.

Neither could he comprehend the boy's mechanical obsessions,
which passed from bicycles and motorcycles to Model T jalopies and
planes. Though he staked Charles $800 for his first plane, he never
really liked the idea. "I don't like this flying business," C.A. said to his
law partner, Walter E. Quigley. "See if you can't get the boy to come into
our office, study law, and join the firm."

When Quigley brought it up, Charles smiled and said the law was
not for him.

In 1906, when Charles was four, his father ran for Congress and
won. He would stay until 1916, when he ran for the Senate and lost
badly. Charles spent the bulk of those years in Washington, shuffled
between the separate residences of his mother and father. He was quiet
and lonely, and did badly in school. In 1913 he entered the Sidwell
Friends School, where it was later said he became pals with Theodore
Roosevelt's sons, but this was just another moment of de facto mythmaking. He was not part of the "Roosevelt Gang" or any other. The only
friend he made was the boy with whom he shared a desk.

His life in Washington was so upsetting that he virtually rubbed it
from his memory. In his six autobiographies, he barely mentions those
years at all. Instead, he saw himself as a farm boy, though from 1906 to
1917 he rarely visited the family farm back in Little Falls, Minnesota, for
more than two or three months each year. He was happiest when alone.
He collected arrowheads, cigar bands, or just about anything, and became an obsessive list maker, always updating his running tab of possessions. He spent hours on his back in high weeds or corn, staring at the

clouds. Years later he would write to his mother, "That farm was one of the most important things in my life. It taught me the value of water, trees, and sky—and solitude."

It was also the first place where he ever saw an airplane. One day, while playing alone upstairs, he heard an engine that kept getting louder. It sounded different from an automobile. He climbed out the window and up on the roof, and there, above the treetops, passed an early pusher biplane, with the pilot perched precariously at the front end of an oblong box without side walls. The whole thing seemed held together with struts and wires. His mother explained that the aviator had come to Little Falls to give rides and exhibitions. Flying, she pointed out, was both dangerous and expensive.

Little Falls was also where he developed his daredevil ways. One of the farmhands, Bill Thompson, recalled the day Lindbergh climbed a sixty-foot tree and, after scanning the horizon for Indians, declared he would jump down. "You'll be killed!" Thompson cried, but Charles seemed determined, so the farmhand screamed for Evangeline, who ordered her son to climb down. He did as commanded, until ten feet overhead, when he leapt out, landing heavily, though unhurt. "He came the nearest to getting a spanking that afternoon than he ever did," Thompson's brother later told a newspaper. But Lindbergh was never punished physically, unusual in itself for the time. "Neither his mother nor his father ever laid a hand on him," he said.

He had fears, though. One was a horror of heights that took form only in his dreams. He'd have nightmares of falling, plunging into darkness, nauseated with fear. This helplessness frightened him most of all. "It was what I couldn't see that frightened me," he later wrote, "the python slithering overhead, the face beyond the curtain."

He learned to lock away the fear, and did so by watching his father. In 1915 C.A. helped found the Minnesota Farmer–Labor Party, a progressive, socialistic, "anti-money" political party that traced its roots to the Farmer's Nonpartisan League; by the next year, the Minnesota party had acquired an antiwar and anti-British flavor. Members suspected that Wall Street and Britain would lead America into war. In 1918 Charles drove his father across the state in the family jalopy as C.A. stumped for governor on the Farmers League ticket. It was a wild and bitter campaign. Mobs booed him and threw eggs. Newspapers branded him pro-German. Justice Department agents broke the plates of his books denouncing "the money trust," and he was arrested three times. In the lumber town of Cloquet, he was nearly lynched at a theater where the owner declared, "There ain't going to be no pro-German meeting here." Hundreds milled around C.A., and it was later said that half a dozen carried ropes. C.A. stared them down and, after minutes that seemed like hours, declared, "Step aside." The crowd "parted like water before a swimmer," one witness recalled. C.A. and his group entered their car and drove off to hoots and shouts, but without injury.

His father believed that a certain sternness was required in life, a Spartan quality Charles absorbed and adopted. In 1917 C.A. asked a friend to take him to the hospital for a "little operation." This turned out to be major abdominal surgery, which he underwent without anesthesia. The ordeal lasted an hour and a half, and during that time C. A. discussed international banking and the Federal Reserve with his friend.

It was his obsession. On the campaign trail, C.A. denounced the sale of Liberty Bonds as a hoax, and believed that a cabal of bankers and politicians was dragging the United States into war. "I believe I have proved that a certain 'inner circle'...maneuvered things to bring about conditions that would make it practically certain that some of the belligerents would violate our international rights and bring us into war," he said in 1918. Twenty-two years later, his son would repeat the "maneuvered" theme, but there were no "supermen" or "yellow breeds" in C.A.'s rhetoric—and no finger-pointing at Jews.

C.A. ran for office one last time, in 1923, in a campaign for a special Senate primary, and by then Charles had been flying for seven months. He flew campaign literature and speakers around for his dad, and sometimes took C.A. up with him. Once, when taking off from a field near Glencoe, Missouri, a wheel hit a ditch and Slim's old surplus Jenny bomber upended. No one was hurt, but C.A. did not go aloft again.

C.A. died of a brain tumor the following year. Charles was able to visit him only once as he lingered in the hospital; he was in army flight school, and his leave was up before C.A. died. Walter Quigley, C.A.'s old law partner, encountered Slim as he left. "I could see he was deeply moved," Quigley later recalled, "but outwardly he was stoical." His father left him a legacy of "stifled anger and sadness," one biographer said, baggage he would never really put away. Already distant and lonely, he became a chameleon, able to blend in anywhere and absorb the ways of those around him. But he was always apart, and he could call few his friend.

One day in 1925, Lindbergh carried out one final promise to his father. He circled the family farm in Little Falls in his Jenny and scattered his father's ashes over their old homestead.

•

The only place Slim really came to life was in a plane. He graduated from high school in Little Falls, took three semesters of engineering at the University of Wisconsin, then dropped out before he could be expelled. He enrolled in a flight school in Lincoln, Nebraska, taking his first flight on April 9, 1922. He knew he'd found his calling. That summer he bought a salvaged Jenny with the $800 his father staked him, and for the next two years lived as a "barnstormer."

The word itself was a misnomer, originally applied to itinerant actors who used local barns as their stages. The aviators called themselves "gypsy fliers" and, like modern surf and ski bums, lived a nomadic existence. They dropped into town to give informal exhibitions and sightseeing flights for between five and fifteen dollars, performed some death-defying stunts and then took off for the next venue, often with the wind at their tail to save on the cost of fuel. "This sure is a great life," Lindbergh wrote his mother as he barnstormed the Lower 48. "The states seem small with a plane." Slim was a daredevil, performing wing walks and parachute jumps, wowing the audience below. He and Randy Enshaw, one of his partners, would fly over a town with one on a wing to attract attention, then drop hundreds of little handbills printed on yellow paper:

COME OUT AND GET ACQUAINTED

THE SHIP IS MADE OF WOOD
AND WIRED TOGETHER

THE WINGS ARE NOT
COVERED WITH TIN

IT DON'T BACK UP

Much would be made of Lindbergh's army training and his experience as a mail pilot, but barnstorming served as his college and turned him into a jack-of-all-trades. The Jenny was a patchwork plane, kept aloft by a crude Curtiss OX-5 engine. The plane had its benefits: it could be landed at 45 miles per hour, and a pilot about to crash could usually aim at a haystack or between two trees and walk away. Yet its problems were legion, and the barnstormer had to be able to jury-rig a fix wherever and whenever it was necessary. The OX-5 was undependable and tended to shatter in flight, and most of a pilot's money went into upgrades and repairs.

A good barnstormer learned to read the signs of the earth and sky, just like a nineteenth-century mariner. He used cows as weather vanes, since they turned their tails to the wind. He searched for rural garages, which were his source of fuel. He fine-tuned his sense of balance, listening to the wires and engine for information about his plane. If caught in a cloud and flying blind, he listened to the engine to determine if it labored with the strain of climbing; to the ringing of the wires, which meant his speed was building and he was pointed at the ground. The idea was to maintain balance; to stay on an even keel.

A barnstormer also learned to be a salesman, in order to coax people into the cockpit and make a living. It was a trait that seemed to go against Slim's solitary nature, but that would serve him well when he entered the race for the Orteig Prize. "It's a sociable place, under a wing," Lindbergh would recall, "and good business, too: People like to come and sit beside you. They start asking questions about flying, and talking about their farms. Pretty soon they begin kidding each other into taking a flight over town. If you help them along a little, they're the best salesmen you could have."

Partners such as Randy Enshaw quickly learned that traveling with Slim was a good idea. He was honest, reliable, and cool under pressure. People seemed drawn to him. Yet Lindbergh had his eccentricities. One was his infamous practical joking, which had a cruel edge. Enshaw had been out with Slim only a week before learning to check his bed every night; if not, he might lie on a cocklebur or feel a June bug crawl up his leg. He started watching him during the day: "If I saw him stoop and pick up anything as we walked across a field, I knew it was another cocklebur or bug, and governed myself accordingly." The worst was the "booster," a little electric generator attached to a wire. If Enshaw was late in rising some mornings, Slim "would slip the wire between my toes and crank. He always managed to get outside the door before I could reach him."

Another oddity had to do with girls: Slim kept away from them. Sexual promiscuity came easily for aviators; they were young and exciting, and as Lindbergh later said, "Girls were everywhere." He tended to intellectualize his reticence, at one point describing the act of choosing a wife like that of a farmer choosing good breeding stock, but in fact he was shy and inexperienced and didn't want to deal with the social graces of socializing with women: "[Y]ou had to learn to dance, to talk their language, to escort them properly to restaurants and theaters." It was easier to seem distant, or simply to disappear. One time Enshaw set up a double date, but Lindbergh vanished. "I had to take both girls myself," Enshaw recalled. "When I got home, he was sound asleep and the next morning he got me up with his 'booster' just as though nothing had happened."

Despite his eccentricities, Lindbergh developed a reputation after two years of barnstorming as a very able aviator. His name must have been known in that very small world, for near the end of this period, he was approached by talent scouts at Pathé motion pictures. They offered him a part in a feature about adventures in the air. Lindbergh agreed to the offer, but only under certain conditions. They would pay him a salary, give him an advance of $5,000, and "not require him to do any kissing or love-making." Pathé agreed to everything but the $5,000. Lindbergh would not yield, so they parted ways.

It seemed a missed opportunity, but Lindbergh was apparently thinking of his future. He could not stay a barnstormer forever. He needed to learn more. The army was the great practical school for flying, so he enlisted in March 1924 in what was known as the "War Department's Air Service," and was commissioned the next spring as a second lieutenant, graduating first in a class of nineteen. He barnstormed a bit more, then joined the 110th Squadron of the 35th Division, Missouri National Guard, rising to captain in December 1925. His flying had given him contacts in St. Louis, so he went to work there early in 1926 for Major William B. Robertson, whose company had just been licensed to fly the mail between St. Louis and Chicago.

Lindbergh was paid a salary of $350 a month, received another $100 a month for expenses, and completed his flying education. A mail pilot had to fly by night, something he'd never done as a barnstormer. Flying at night left him more likely to fly in the great dangers—ice, storms, and fog. For the year ending June 30, 1927, the Transcontinental Air Mail

Service had an "efficiency" rating of 94.2 percent nationwide; of those 5.8 percent of flights that did not make it, all were stopped en route by bad weather. Of the five pilots killed from 1924 through 1927, all were killed while flying "blind."

•

And so, in October and November, after Fonck's crash, Lindbergh planned his strategy for entering the Orteig Prize. How did one approach such a problem? Sure, *he* believed in his ability to cross the Atlantic, but how would he convince others?

One thing was certain: money was needed, much more than his $2,000 savings. Still, it wasn't particularly hard for Slim to find backers in St. Louis, where he was known. So he made some lists, jotting down the names of prospective investors, necessary equipment, advantages to his victory, and maps he would need. He wrote out a long page entitled "Propaganda," which clarified for him why local boosters should sink money into his scheme. "The future of aeronautics in St. Louis is in the ballance [*sic*] to-day," he warned. "St. Louis has been asleep." But his flight would "advertise" the city and "show people what airplanes can do." Under "Results" he listed two options: "Successful completion, winning $25,000 prize to cover expense," and "Complete failure." What all the latter implied was left unsaid.

In some ways, his plan was vague; in others, it made sense. He'd fly a single-engine plane stripped of everything but the pilot, instrument panel, and a small amount of equipment to save room and weight for extra fuel. This was an engineering problem to him. An air-cooled engine such as the Wright J-5 Whirlwind would make the journey easily, and by flying alone, he'd dodge the squabbles that had plagued Fonck. Lindbergh did not trust collaborations: he remembered his father's old saying, "One boy is a boy, two boys are half a boy, and three boys are no boy at all." He anticipated a major objection: How could a single pilot stay awake for the thirty to forty hours necessary to get across? He'd done this as an airmail pilot, he would say. He'd make his case before those St. Louis businessmen who knew his abilities. After all, he'd taught many of them to fly.

He started with Earl Thompson, a local insurance broker who had been one of his students. When Lindbergh succeeded with the broker, he proceeded to others he knew. Major Albert Lambert pledged $1,000, and said his brother Winston might, too. Slim's boss, Bill Robertson, could barely make ends meet, but said he'd support him if the other pilots could cover for him; in addition, he allowed Lindbergh to use the company name in appeals. Two private pilots—Harry Knight, a wealthy stockbroker, and Harold Bixby, vice president of the State National Bank of St. Louis and president of the local Chamber of Commerce—came aboard. When Lindbergh approached the city's influential *Post-Dispatch*, however, he was rebuffed. "To fly across the Atlantic Ocean with one pilot and a single-engine plane!" stormed an editor. "We have our reputation to consider. We couldn't possibly be associated with such a venture." Soon afterward, though, the rival *Globe-Democrat* signed on.

It was even harder to find a plane. One day that fall a Fokker representative appeared at Lambert Field, and Lindbergh cornered him at a local diner. The salesman talked about the safety of multi-engine planes; Lindbergh asked whether the company would make a one-engine plane for the New York–Paris flight and was told Fokker had already "made a study" of the challenge and it would take a trimotor to win. "You should plan on over $100,000 for such a project," added the salesman. "In fact, you should have almost unlimited financial backing."

Lindbergh was floored. He'd raised $10,000 from his local consortium, and that had been a challenge. He could *never* raise such an astronomical sum. He tried to dicker, saying that the group he represented was more interested in single-engine planes. The Fokker salesman cut him off immediately. "Mr. Fokker wouldn't consider selling a single-engine for a flight over the Atlantic Ocean."

What Lindbergh really wanted was a single-engine Wright-Bellanca with a Wright J-5 Whirlwind in the nose. He spent $100 on a tailored suit, silk necktie and scarf, blue overcoat, and felt hat, and on November 29, 1926, showed up at the Wright Aeronautical Corporation factory in Paterson, New Jersey, hoping to make a good impression. An executive told him that the Wright-Bellanca was just a demonstration plane: they'd never intended to make aircraft, and built it just to show off their engine. He should talk to the designer, Giuseppe Mario Bellanca, who was staying in Manhattan at the Waldorf-Astoria.

Lindbergh visited Bellanca the next day, and he liked him from the start. He was "a serious, slender man—straight black hair, sharp-cut features, medium height. One feels, in his presence, genius, capability, confidence." There'd be no "feinting for position," and that was a relief. "What he says, you can believe."

Like Sikorsky and Fokker, Bellanca was an immigrant. He was born in 1886 in Sicily, in the town of Sciacca, which rose literally from the sea and was awhirl with wind. The sea breezes rushed up the cliffs, poured down the streets, flooded his father's small house, and gyred in little eddies. Even as a boy he saw air as a "fluid," which is exactly how it behaves. The whole town was addicted to flying kites, but Bellanca was an experimenter, slicing holes in the fabric, devising crude airfoils. A potter's shop near his house was littered with discarded porcelain chips; he skipped them at angles into the wind, watching them scale up and over his head. He said to his parents, "I can *see* the air."

He attended the Technical Institute of Milan, where he studied mathematics and aviation engineering. His first two planes were polar opposites: a "pusher-" and a "tractor-type," with propellers in the back and front, respectively. He never suffered for ideas, but always for lack of money. All Italy did—southern Italy was deeply impoverished then, so badly so that in 1913, 872,598 people immigrated. He left home with his parents, six brothers, and a sister two years before that, in 1911, at the urging of his brother Carlo, who'd already settled in Brooklyn.

By the end of that year, Bellanca had built his third plane. It was a parasol monoplane, built in his basement with the help of his mother and father. He took it to nearby Mineola Field, where it hopped around the grass in long strides. He taught himself to fly, and from 1912 to 1916 operated the Bellanca Flying School. One of his students was the young Fiorello La Guardia, the future mayor of New York. La Guardia was too poor to pay, so he taught Bellanca how to drive a car in exchange for his lessons.

During the war, Bellanca designed trainer planes for a Maryland steel company. His designs were too far ahead of their time, and in 1917 the War and Navy departments thought he was just another crazy inventor. But by 1921 he'd gained a reputation for original designs, and a group of investors lured him to Omaha, Nebraska, in hopes of turning the old cow-and-railroad hub into the commercial airline center of the world.

All Bellanca planes had certain design characteristics that departed from ordinary practice. The plane he built in Omaha, the Bellanca CF, was called by *Jane's All the World's Aircraft* "the first up-to-date transport airplane that was designed, built, and flown with success in the United States." It was so stable that the test pilot released the stick at 400 feet and flew four complete circles using only the footbar controlling the rudder. Bellanca used air-cooled engines long before any other designer. The fuselage of the Wright-Bellanca desired so ardently by Lindbergh had the same cross-section as a normal airplane wing: convex on top and flat underneath. This imparted tremendous lift, and at a high enough speed the ship could theoretically fly without wings because of the lifting power of the body alone.

Yet for all his genius, Bellanca was a mess personally. He needed a babysitter. He didn't cut his hair; he owned one tie and a single pair of socks and shoes, all black. His brothers said he looked like Charlie Chaplin. Others called him "the Professor," or by his initials, G.M. He often forgot to eat, and was an atrocious businessman. His Bellanca CF, for example, sold for $5,000 at a time when the rock-bottom price of a secondhand Jenny was $250. It didn't take long for the Omaha venture to die.

While there, he fell in love with Dorothy Brown, the daughter of his landlord. But Bellanca distrusted love. He distrusted all emotion as inefficient, far less elegant than a well-designed wing. Dorothy was tall, attractive, and confident, the very epitome of the restless "New Woman" in attitude, if not necessarily in outward fashion. She wanted out of Omaha, and envisioned an exciting future with this eccentric if lovable little genius. Still, it must have rankled when she had to beg him to get married. "I just can't wait any longer," she pleaded in early 1921. "I do everything for you that a wife would do and as you have no objection to that, you can't object to the other. I cannot go on this way indefinitely...I am not asking anything unreasonable, am I?"

It was a logical argument, but the Professor was a hard sell. Love, he said, was too distracting. "I have noticed that when I am close to you, I am unable to do what is really the best thing for us both," he replied.

But Dorothy was no quitter, and chipped away more furiously. "There are one of two things I would seriously advise you to do if you want to make a success of the Plane and of the future," she wrote on February 8, 1921. "Either give me [up] entirely or marry me...If you give me up you will have more time for work, and if you marry me you will have more time for work; but the way we are doing now is neither one thing or another and is doing us both harm."

Who could argue against such logic? On November 18, 1922, they wed.

After Omaha, Bellanca designed wings for the Post Office Department's DH-4s, then in 1925 was lured to the Wright Corporation to build a craft highlighting its Whirlwinds. The first version of his plane, the WB-1, had already won one special race and an efficiency competition when it crashed during preparations to break the world's nonstop endurance record. Luckily, Bellanca was already working on the improved WB-2, and in 1926 this won two efficiency trophies at the National Air Races in Philadelphia. Wright considered putting the WB-2 into production, but at the last moment decided against it: to do so might alienate other aircraft companies that would otherwise buy Wright engines. The disappointed Bellanca left Wright and joined with a young Brooklyn millionaire named Charles Levine to form the Columbia Aircraft Company.

The fates of the plane and of Bellanca were both in limbo when Lindbergh met him in the hotel. "My plane is fully capable of flying nonstop from New York to Paris," Bellanca claimed. "I should like very much to have it make the flight." But he didn't own it; the Wright Corporation still did. His partner was trying to buy it from Wright, but they'd had no luck so far. They also did not have a factory yet in which to build another, though they were looking at property in Brooklyn. Nonetheless, winning the prize "would be of great value," Bellanca said. They shook hands as Lindbergh rose to go.

"I hope you have success with your organization, Captain Lindbergh," Bellanca added. "I hope you are able to buy my plane."

Lindbergh was hopeful, but soon he, too, was once again in limbo. In December, Bellanca wired him that the WB-2 was still tied up in negotiations. The best he could offer at the moment was a new trimotor he had designed for $29,000. Around the same time, Lindbergh heard that Byrd was considering the race, bad news for him since the Explorer knew "how to get financing." He fired off telegrams to every manufacturer in the country; like Fokker, they turned him down. All except one, the tiny Ryan Aircraft Corporation in San Diego, which didn't have much of a track record. In wires dated February 3, 4, and 5, Ryan informed Lindbergh that they could make a plane similar to the Wright-

Bellanca, but with bigger wings. It could carry 350 gallons of gas and cruise at 100 miles per hour, enough to get him to Paris. They could build it in less than three months, but their $6,000 bid was so low that even the frugal Lindbergh suspected something must be wrong.

By the turn of the New Year, Slim had grown disheartened. He went to talk to stockbroker Harry Knight, and told him that it couldn't be done. The plane, even if started, would not be finished in time. He suggested that their syndicate abandon the transatlantic plan and go after another project. They could fly the Pacific, and maybe convince somebody to stake a huge prize.

Knight looked at Lindbergh and felt sorry for him. Slim was as proud as they came; Knight knew that such an admission was one of personal failure. But he also knew the business of business, and how quickly the wheel can turn. It was too early to give in.

"Let's stick to the Paris flight, Slim," he said. "That's the idea we started out with." Knight told him to go wait in the outer office, and he called Harold Bixby. Slim needed a boost. Maybe they could take him out to lunch and raise his spirits.

As they talked, Lindbergh ate hungrily. Depression didn't seem to bother his appetite. Knight suggested that Lindbergh give up his airmail job for the time being and see whether Ryan could build that plane as it said it could. The food and the offer cheered Lindbergh considerably.

All during that time, Lindbergh hinted to his mother in Detroit that something big was going on. After the meeting with Bellanca on November 30, he revealed to her that the trip's purpose concerned "a contemplated St. Louis NY to Paris flight next Spring," revealing more about his plan than in the earlier letter. By the day after Christmas, he as much as told her he'd do the flying, but not to worry because "plans will be entirely different from those of Sikorsky."

Yet by January his early optimism had plummeted, and his mother tried to cheer him up. "The experiences you are having seem very hard ones," she wrote on January 20, 1927. "Sometimes I can scarcely believe what you write." She imagined his nighttime airmail flights as "a magic carpet where you just wish yourself there and you are." Still, the plan worried her. "It will take a very trust-worthy plane to be so long in the air," she wrote on January 31.

By February 4, his birthday, Lindbergh had grown desperate and began to cast around for extra funds. He wired his mother to withdraw

$1,000 from his savings account. "I can raise on my own securities the additional amount in the telegram," she wrote back, then added, "As you know, I am with you to the limit."

Then the wheel turned. At 11:10 a.m. on February 6, the day after Ryan wired that it could build a plane in less than three months, Giuseppe Bellanca wired with good news. "WILLING TO MAKE MORE ATTRACTIVE PROPOSITION ON THE BELLANCA AIRPLANE FOR PARIS FLIGHT," he wrote. Wright had just sold the plane to him and his partner for $15,500. "SUGGEST YOU COME NEW YORK SOON POSSIBLE SO WE CAN GET TOGETHER QUICKEST MANNER."

Lindbergh wired back that he was coming, grabbed his suit and hat, and jumped on the train. Next stop, Manhattan, where in a sumptuous office in the prestigious Woolworth Building, he would meet the man he forever cast as his nemesis: Charles A. Levine.

•

No one would be more reviled in the Great Atlantic Derby, or more disparaged, than Charles Albert Levine. Despite the many moments of pettiness and indecision among almost every actor in the race, only Levine would be branded a "Brooklyn wheeler and dealer," a "perverse middleman," a "crank," and a "madman." No one else would be pilloried for misunderstanding "the rules of the world of sportsmanship," or for introducing "crude materialism" into the race for the prize. No one else would be pressured to deny his religion in order to prove his patriotism; no other flier would be ignored by President Coolidge when he returned. Though Grover Whalen shook his hand when Levine stepped off the liner, no other flier would be so ignored during his bare-bones ticker tape parade. Levine "was not surprised that New York did not toot its horns at him and get wildly excited," Time magazine observed. "It was raining."

It seems no small coincidence that Levine was also a Jew.

He did have supporters, but they were ignored. The Brooklyn Jewish community loved him, though there was a divide between the young and old. The highly respected Thomas "Doc" Kinkade, the lead engineer at Wright who serviced the Whirlwind engines on every rival plane, called his flight "one of the nerviest things in the history of aviation," and added, "I never saw a man with so much courage in my life." The problem, Kinkade implied, was that Levine did not have a press agent— like Lindbergh's Harry Bruno and Byrd's Fitzhugh Green—to tweak his image and curb him from saying the first thing that entered his mind. *Time* under Henry Luce leapt to Levine's defense, as did *The Literary Digest*, which said that he "revealed a soul of flaming courage when put to the test."

He was impulsive and combative, traits that led both to his success and to his downfall. At times he seemed congenitally unable to make up his mind, a flaw that cost him the race and cast him forever as "the man who wasn't Lindbergh." Yet of all the rivals, no two were more similar than Lindbergh and Levine. While all the other fliers mouthed platitudes about peace and science, Lindbergh and Levine unashamedly focused on the prize. Both were awkward in society, and preferred to keep to themselves. Both doted on their planes like lovers. Both were gamblers, and did not fear death. They even shared the same initials: C.A.L.

It was an anti-Semitic time. Anti-Jewish prejudice surged throughout the late 1910s and 1920s on many levels of society. Klan membership climbed higher in the twenties than it had in the previous fifty years, or ever would again. Henry Ford railed against the Jews in his *Dearborn Independent*, and quoted from *The Protocols of the Learned Elders of Zion*, a forged tsarist document purporting to outline a Zionist plot to conquer the world. The 1919 Black Sox scandal—a World Series "fix" allegedly engineered by New York gangster Arnold Rothstein—lingered in people's minds. "If fans wish to know the trouble with American baseball," said Henry Ford, "they have it in three words—too much Jew." Many businesses and law firms were closed to those of the faith, as were government posts and neighborhoods. When FDR invited Harvard law professor Felix Frankfurter home for lunch, Eleanor Roosevelt later wrote, "An interesting little man, but very jew."

Levine did not advertise his Judaism, but neither did he hide it. If he fit into any stereotypes, he was a portrait of the young Jazz Age entrepreneur, the "New Money" that Wanamaker's class disparaged and Fitzgerald's Tom Buchanan raged about in *The Great Gatsby*. Born on St. Patrick's Day 1897 in northwest Massachusetts, Levine moved with his parents to the Williamsburg section of Brooklyn when he was two. At the time, Jews by the thousands were migrating across the East River from the Lower East Side. From 1880 to 1920, 3.5 million immigrants had filled the Manhattan ghetto, and the old group moved out as the new group moved in. The Germans came first, followed by the Irish, then Jews from Eastern Europe and Russia, many of whom were fleeing the tsar. Now as waves of Italians and Poles settled into the Lower East Side, the Jewish community trekked across the newly finished Williamsburg Bridge to Brooklyn.

There was tension between father and son. Levine's father was a junk man, and when Levine graduated from P.S. 122 at age fourteen, his father pulled him out of further schooling to work in the family business salvaging worn-out machines. Levine lasted two years, then one day disappeared. Six months later, the family learned that he'd taken a job as an apprentice mechanic at the Morrisant Aviation Company in Long Island. The boy had developed a love for flying and would be taken up for rides. His father yanked him out of Morrisant and demanded that he return to the junk metal trade.

Levine stayed until he turned eighteen, then broke away again, to sell secondhand autos. But he always had bigger goals. He used his profits to develop high-speed racing engines, and although never successful in this venture, he made good money in the auto trade. He became a speed demon and owned a custom-built Stutz racer. He raced it up and down the Motor Parkway at 80 to 90 miles per hour. He cut quite a figure and in 1917 married Grace B. Nova, known as "the belle of Williamsburg" after winning two beauty contests. They'd met a few years earlier, when she was thirteen, and Charlie, as his friends called him, pursued her relentlessly. In 1916 she went to work for him as a secretary at the Peerless Iron Pipe Company in Manhattan. They eloped the next year.

In 1921 Levine started the Columbia Salvage Company, which bought up old copper shell casings and ammunition from war surplus stockpiles. He'd heard that the government was loading barges full of old ammunition and dumping them into the sea; he hurried to Washington with an offer to salvage the metal and powder, then sell it back to the government at a 60/40 return. It could be a dangerous business: in Charleston, South Carolina, he'd just inspected some ammo when the shells exploded, killing three in the arsenal. The contract brought him $3.5 million in the first two years. Yet even capitalism had its perils: The government disagreed with Levine's accounting methods, and the amount was under litigation.

In 1926 Levine heard from old aircraft contacts that Giuseppe Bellanca and Wright were parting ways. The two men may have known each other: they had both resided in Brooklyn, were only ten years apart in age, and few aviators lived in the neighborhood. Levine moved fast: he bought the WB-2, formed the Columbia Aircraft Corporation, and brought in Bellanca and his longtime friend and test pilot, Clarence Chamberlin. They opened offices on the forty-sixth floor of the Woolworth Building. Levine realized the plane was a gold mine, but he didn't know exactly how to proceed. He bid for a New York–Chicago mail route, but the Post Office turned him down. He thought about starting a private airline, or building planes for the army. But to do anything, he needed to publicize Bellanca's plane.

Then Lindbergh appeared, and the perfect way to publicize his company began to form in Levine's mind.

Lindbergh met twice with Levine. The first time was on February 10, as soon as he could get to New York after receiving Bellanca's February 6 wire. The only account we have of this meeting is the one presented in Lindbergh's *Spirit of St. Louis*, published three decades later. In attendance are Bellanca, Lindbergh, Clarence Chamberlin, and Levine. From the beginning Bellanca is gracious and Chamberlin watchful—but Levine is adversarial. While the others discuss the plane and its qualities, Levine is interested only in business. "Mr. Levine's eyes size me up as he speaks," is Lindbergh's first introduction of the man in his autobiography. Levine says the plane is worth $25,000, but they will sell it for $15,000. "That will be a contribution of $10,000," he says.

Lindbergh says he must discuss this with his backers, since the price is higher than any considered previously. But on the train ride home he writes to his mother that "My trip to N.Y. ended very satisfactorily." He already plans his strategy: he could make the flight around April 1, but tell the press that takeoff would not occur until sometime "before late fall." That way he could "mislead any rival attempts."

The second meeting occurs six days later, on February 16. Lindbergh holds the $15,000 check in his hand. His backers were happy with the price, their only stipulation that the plane be named the *Spirit of St. Louis*. Lindbergh agreed.

This time, Lindbergh and Levine are alone. That should raise flags in itself, for up to this point Bellanca has always been involved. But Bellanca does not like messy emotional exchanges, and no doubt he and Levine have discussed the fate of their plane. "We will sell our plane," Levine tells him, "but of course we reserve the right to select the crew that flies it." Lindbergh stands dumbfounded, and immediately realizes that Levine means Chamberlin. The check stares back at him from atop Levine's polished desk. "You understand we cannot let just anybody pilot our airplane across the ocean," Levine says.

"Here's a point there can be no trading over," Lindbergh writes three decades later. The moment is still fresh in his mind. As far as he can see, his backers are paying $15,000 for the mere privilege of naming the plane. That's no deal at all.

Once again his hopes are dashed, just when he thought he'd secured the perfect plane. His anger starts to rise. "Is the Bellanca for sale or not?" he snaps. If it is, they can trade; if not, "there's no use wasting any more time."

Levine tries to calm him down. It is for sale, but why won't Lindbergh let them select the crew? "We know better than anybody else how to fly the Bellanca." He's only trying to be sensible. Lindbergh picks up the check. "Levine's eyes follow it," Lindbergh writes. The aviator starts for the door.

Levine tries one last time, and suggests they speak again at eleven o'clock the next morning. Maybe, by then, tempers will have cooled. That night, Lindbergh wanders the streets in a daze. As arranged, he calls the next morning and Levine answers. "Well, have you changed your mind?" Levine says. Lindbergh slams down the phone, too enraged to reply. And without actually writing the words, Lindbergh paints the picture that will follow Levine forever: *duplicitous Jew.*

How much can we trust Lindbergh's version? How faithful to the truth is he? No one has ever asked this question; it is like doubting the word of God. Yet there is a very good chance that he misrepresented that last meeting, painting Levine in the worst light possible. One decade after this meeting, Lindbergh would condemn "Jewish groups in this country" for pushing the United States to the brink of war with Germany. In his radio address for the isolationist "America First," he would say that a "few far-sighted Jews" realized the danger of war, but most did not, and "their greatest danger to this country lies in their large ownership and influence in our motion pictures, our press, our radio, and our Government." By then he was great friends with Henry Ford, absorbing—as he so often did with those around him—the opinions and prejudices of the man he called his boyhood hero. In July 1940 Ford said it more blatantly to former Detroit FBI chief John S. Bugas: "When Charles comes out here, we only talk about the Jews."

Nothing in the reams stored in archives across the country reveals that Lindbergh held any strong anti-Jewish animus before his face-off with Levine. True, his "America First" address echoes those of his charismatic father, but when C.A. railed against the "money trust," his sights were set on J. P. Morgan and Wall Street bankers, with no mention of the Jews. The only hint in Slim's family correspondence of this period actually comes from his mother, and this fails to rise above the general anti-Semitism of the time. On January 20, 1927, she quotes a joke she heard from a fellow teacher concerning "Ikey," who tries to join the Catholic Knights of Columbus. He is kicked out when he says, "[M]y father was a Catholic priest." Eleven days later, on January 31, she tells about a fight between a black man who works for a mutual acquaintance and "the Jews." The seeds of bigotry are there, but no extraordinary virulence is evident, and none of the many acquaintances who later write about their days with the young Lindbergh ever mention a thing. Chronologically, the first moment arises forty-six stories up in the Manhattan skyline, when two men see their futures tethered to the same plane.

•

So it was that on February 24, Lindbergh found himself on the landing field of San Diego's Ryan Aircraft investigating the second-best plane.

Ryan was Lindbergh's last chance—and he was theirs. The office was in an old fish cannery on the San Diego waterfront, a small, cluttered room in a faded Mission-style building smelling of mold and dead fish. The company was days away from bankruptcy; they had orders for planes but not enough money for materials and payroll. If they did not find new capital quickly, they would fold.

After his test flight, Lindbergh got down to business with the owner, B. F. Mahoney, a Pennsylvania bond salesman with a build like a boxer's and what appears in photos to be a broken nose. Though Lindbergh felt more relaxed than he had with Levine, he did not like everything he heard. Mahoney stood by his stated price of $6,000, and would provide the engine and extra equipment at cost, charging nothing extra for installation. But when Lindbergh asked if he could guarantee the plane's cruising range, Mahoney said he did not see how they could. The risks were too high—and, candidly, they were not a big company with a lot of capital to spare.

Lindbergh's decision to go with Ryan would rest on what he thought of the designer, Donald Hall.

But Lindbergh liked Hall almost immediately. They spoke the same language, thought in the same way. The twenty-eight-year-old designer had signed on with Ryan in late January; he'd graduated from the Pratt Institute, then worked for the Santa Monica–based Douglas Company before coming to Ryan. Hall and Lindbergh were both independent and loved the outdoors; while at Douglas, Hall took a leave of absence in 1926 to become an Air Corps cadet at Brooks Field in Texas, where Lindbergh earned his army wings. Hall's flight handbook bore the signature of its previous owner, "C. A. Lindbergh." They laughed when Hall mentioned the coincidence.

They sat on the long, curving beach at Coronado Strand and discussed design. The Pacific breeze blew in their faces; it was a perfect flying day. Hall paused when Slim said he wanted only one cockpit— he meant to fly the Atlantic alone, something he had not mentioned in his telegrams. But once he explained that he would rather "have extra gasoline than an extra man," Hall was on board. He sketched and re-sketched as they talked—cutting down to one pilot meant reallocating 350 pounds, and that meant another 50 gallons of fuel. Lindbergh wanted the cockpit behind the gas tank so that he would not be sand-wiched between the engine and the tank in case of a crack-up. If he wanted to see, he could always look out the window.

Hall kept asking questions. Did Lindbergh want a passenger arrangement for after the flight? Night-flying equipment? A parachute? All no. Hall's job kept getting easier, yet any one change would always affect the others. He said they'd probably have to increase the wingspan of Ryan's standard M-2 plane, move the tail surfaces, and replace the engine. What was the range?

Lindbergh wasn't exactly sure. They drove in Hall's Buick to the public library, where they stood before a globe. Lindbergh pulled from his pocket a piece of white string. He stretched it from New York to Newfoundland, then over the ocean to Europe. Though it wasn't the most scientific means of measurement, they figured the total distance at about 3,600 miles. Just to be safe, they increased that by another 400.

Hall made further calculations on an envelope, figuring in a 10 percent reserve. When he looked up, he suggested that the plane carry 400 gallons of gasoline.

When they returned to the Ryan plant, they learned that Mahoney had drawn up the figures. His company could deliver one special monoplane with a Wright J-5 engine in sixty days. The cost, $10,580. Lindbergh wired the details to Henry Knight from the office. The next day, Knight wired back: "YOUR WIRE STOP SUGGEST YOU CLOSE WITH RYAN FOLLOWING TERMS."

A wave of relief seemed to wash over Lindbergh. "The chafing, frustrating weeks of hunting, first for finance and then for a plane, are over," he later said. He could turn his attention to the flight—the design and construction, the details and study that lay ahead. The order was written up, with specifics—a plane with a fuel capacity of 400 gallons and a minimum cruising range of 3,500 miles at 1,500 rpm. Instruments: an oil gauge, temperature gauge, and altimeter. He put $1,000 down, with a second payment of $6,580 a week later and $3,000 upon delivery. He signed the order that afternoon.

Soon afterward, he wrote to his mother and told her what had transpired. She slept on the fact that her son had entered the "most spectacular race ever held," then woke and wrote to him. "The 'publicity' is in the St. Louis papers," she said. "They emphasize the dangers connected with your trip." She admitted she was like any mother; she worried about her child. She wondered if she could see him once before he started, or if that would make his life more difficult.

"But for the first time in my life," she added, "I realize that Columbus also had a mother."

SEVEN

THE COWBOY

The first aviator actually to be declared the front-runner rode out of the West like a tin-starred avenger. So much attention had been paid to Fonck, then to Byrd, that it came as a shock when the first flier to have a plane in working order was an unknown: Lieutenant Commander Noel Davis, U.S.N. As a youth, the Cowboy had jogged along the Utah grazing lands on horseback, textbooks on math crammed in his saddlebags. Now, as March flowed into April, he rode into the American consciousness on page one of *The New York Times*. While others mouthed cliches of progress and peace, Davis spoke softly, with moral clarity. Once upon a time, he said, America led the world in aviation records, but the Old World crept in and stole them away.

"A few years ago, we had 70 percent of all aviation records, and now we hold less than 20 percent of them. Last year, they took two more of them away," he said in his first extended interview, on March 14. The Italians took the seaplane record; the French, the record for altitude. Americans did not hold a single important record, he claimed. "This seemed a shame to me, for I am convinced that American airplane engines are the best in the world, and that we have the best planes." Winning the Orteig Prize was not just a quest, Davis asserted. It was necessary for national pride.

There is an interesting difference in Davis's portrayal in the press as compared to that of his rivals. Byrd frustrated reporters with his coy sidesteps and manipulation of the truth. By March, Fonck still received mention in longer stories or the occasional "brief," but his second attempt had stalled from lack of funding and he was treated as a has-been. French fliers were the unreal but ever-present threat. "Lindberg" was misspelled.

But no such criticism or contempt, implied or direct, rubbed off on the Cowboy. The press seemed a little intimidated by Davis. Reporters held him in awe. They might ask questions, but they never challenged him outright; late in the game, one journalist made that mistake, and he was slapped down. At thirty-six, Davis was the oldest flier in the race, and reporters portrayed his decisions in the light of hard-won maturity: he was unpretentious but smart, and had "an instinct for the key to a difficult situation," the *Times* profile proclaimed. He spoke "deliberately and with humor, and is able to laugh at himself and his own mistakes," of which, Davis would admit, there were many. He looks out from the photos taken for this story with a long, plain, honest face, smile lines feathering the eyes and mouth, a direct gaze. He is short like Fonck, "concealing a quick and powerful muscular development under an almost chubby exterior." One could not help but like this man; reporters certainly did. "He talks best with his feet on a desk," the *Times* said.

He was the most educated flier in the race, and possibly the smartest. In 1914 he had graduated third in his class at the Naval Academy; three years later, he was made chief of staff to the admiral in charge of laying fifty-six thousand mines between Scotland and Norway during the Great War. With the Armistice, he had to take them out. To do this, he developed an ingenious remote-control method for disarming them by radio before dragging them from the water; afterward, he wrote several books on laying and disarming mines that became standards in the field. He applied to Pensacola for aviation training and on August 11, 1921, was designated Naval Aviator No. 2944; while still a student, he was appointed officer-in-charge of the ground school and wrote the facility's first training manual. One year later he resigned his commission to attend Harvard Law School and specialize in the new field of aviation law; he entered the Naval Reserve, ran its airfield at nearby Squantum, and wrote more training manuals. In his spare moments, he invented the first aerial sextant able to draw together the horizon, sun, and stars during flight and keep them in position—not an easy thing to do in an airplane. After graduating from Harvard, he moved to Washington to run the Naval Reserve.

He was the first to admit that he had done nothing spectacular in the air—he had not shot down seventy-five enemy fliers or flown over the North Pole. After leaving the West, he'd devoted himself to military routine: flying in formation, learning his plane and engine inside and out, putting them through the stress of unusual situations. He rarely strayed long distances except by plane, usually big navy bombers or seaplanes.

Just like its pilot, Davis quipped, his chosen plane for the oceanic hop was nothing special to look at—but it would get the job done. It was a "stock plane," built by the Keystone Aircraft Corporation of Bristol, Pennsylvania, a big biplane with a 67-foot wingspan, originally designed as a bomber. If his plane made it, there should be no reason why others of the same make could not do so, too. The main modifications were the substitution of three 240-horsepower Wright Whirlwinds and an increased gas capacity. She'd take off weighing 16,000 pounds and burn 9,000 pounds of gas in flight, landing in Paris at a svelte 7,000·pounds. At that weight, Davis calculated, the plane would take off in 2,400 feet in about 40 seconds, then climb at a rate of 270 feet per second. He'd done the figures, he said. Fonck's plane had carried a fatal load of 27 pounds per square foot in the wing area when she took off. His plane would have half that, 14 pounds per square foot, he said.

The numbers told the tale; equations didn't lie. Davis exuded easygoing confidence as he went through the calculations. "On paper, at least," said the *Times*, the Cowboy's chances for success were "much greater than those of his competitors."

•

Unlike the others, Davis had apparently never dreamed of the possibility of flying as a boy. He had chanced into the pilot's seat as he chanced into many things. It was his luck, he'd say. At the end of the day, when he'd sprawl beside the campfire and stare into the night, the idea of one day sitting in a cockpit was as far away from his mind as the stars. Like the West, the night sky was endless and huge, and one tended to get lost in it if not careful. Like the West, its immensity could humble a man.

And like many in the West, Noel Davis's family knew hard times. He was born on Christmas Day 1891, hence his given name. His birthplace, the little town of Nephi, lay seventy miles south of Salt Lake City, nestled at the foot of Mount Nebo, the southern end of the Wasatch Mountains. To the north, around Ogden and Salt Lake City, what the Mormons called the intermountain empire spread green and lush, but around Mount Nebo the land rose in arid steppes circumscribed by jagged ranges. Very few towns sank roots out here. Those that did hold on, such as Nephi, seemed simultaneously forlorn and proud, tiny and self-sufficient—islands in the plains.

The West might be a dangerous place, but in the Utah Valley, order prevailed. The marks of Mormon settlement were planted everywhere: in the fields of alfalfa and beets; the grids of irrigation ditches; the solid houses and wide streets. Most of all, one saw order in the long lines of Lombardy poplars that marched along the streets and ditches. Their presence imposed order on the landscape, just as the Church did to men's souls.

To the north, in the irrigated valley close to Salt Lake City, the Church of Jesus Christ of Latter-Day Saints held more sway. "The Mormons were never, in their church organization or in their social patterns, what we think of as democratic," said Western writer Wallace Stegner, himself a Presbyterian who grew up in Salt Lake City. Down south, however, in sheep and cattle country, that changed. Stock raising was always more individualistic than farming; people were alone with their thoughts for greater periods of time. On the ranches, Saints and Gentiles, as non-Mormons are known, worked side by side, drinking from the same tin cup, rolling cigarettes from the same pouch of tobacco. There, the Church's control did not extend as far. Young men broke away, not because they were persuaded by others, but simply because they drifted. Social control is difficult in a place where hardly any society can be found.

From what few sparse accounts still exist, Davis seemed to hail from a family given to wanderlust, hard times, and speed. One grandfather was a gold miner who lost his claim to an oil company. Noel's father, Garwood Davis, was identified either as a drifter or a boat pilot on the Great Salt Lake; in the 1900 census, he listed his birthplace as "At Sea," and ten years later, Noel's mother said that he was dead. Noel had a younger sister, Bessie, while his older brother, Harry, died in Salt Lake City's "saucer track" during a motorcycle race. His mother seemed the one most saddled with Noel's upbringing: she raised her children within walking distance of the Salt Lake Temple, in a tiny cottage belonging to her father, Harry Sampson, who had followed Brigham Young across the frontier to this Promised Land.

When Davis turned thirteen, he signed on with a cattle outfit in the south, and spent much of his youth riding the range. Despite what people thought, little romance existed in a life among cows. Davis pounded postholes in the red earth, then strung rusty barbed wire between those posts; far more dangerous than rustlers was the invisible threat of sepsis or infection should he cut himself on the rusted metal barbs. His days were filled with the endless maintenance of domestic animals: branding, dehorning, castrating, dipping, finding strays, and replacing worn horseshoes. He was a hired hand on horseback, as underpaid as any modern crop worker, and his fabled independence was chiefly the right to quit and find another job that paid just as abysmally.

Davis was a Mormon, "though not a very good one," his wife would later say. Still, a Mormon upbringing had imposed order on his mind. When Davis stated his purpose for entering the Orteig race, he phrased his thoughts in terms of order and control. Just as Mormon towns and homesteads imposed order upon the wilderness, he would impose order upon the air. By making the transatlantic hop for his nation, he would shorten the distance between continents, making the world smaller and more livable. Like any good engineer, he was simply fixing things.

His youthful hopes for the future seemed focused on engineering. He attended school when he could, and on the range, math texts were his companion. By nineteen, he'd absorbed an odd assortment of practical mechanics—gleaned from conversations with prospectors in the hills and from facing the everyday mechanical problems of harvesting and irrigation. Westerners understood to what extent industrialization made their survival possible in this harsh land. It would be impossible without the Colt revolver, barbed wire to control cattle, windmills for filling stock tanks, gang machinery to plant and harvest fields, and the railroads. Westerners had few problems with the idea of The Machine.

By 1910 Davis had cobbled together a high school education, possibly because his mother dragged him off the range and into Salt Lake City to attend Latter Day Saints High School. His education was spotty, but by then she recognized that he was sharp as a tack when it came to figures. In February of that year, when Noel learned that Utah would be allowed three slots for the Naval Academy at Annapolis, he abruptly decided to apply. He could not say why; if anything, the novelty appealed to him. Six applicants competed for appointments in examinations that took nearly a week. The first page asked, "When did you decide to enter Annapolis?"

"Yesterday," he answered.

"What are your educational qualifications?"

"None."

There were seven sections, and in four—history, grammar, literature, and geography—Davis knew next to nothing. But, as he told his mother, the math problems "were pie." In Annapolis, the examiners were clearly intrigued. Any youngster who knew math so thoroughly and could be so frank about his limitations would probably catch up in the easier subjects. Besides, math comprised a large part of naval education. Davis was admitted in May, but his mother kept it a secret until the night of his high school graduation. His classmates cheered and predicted that "someday he would add further honors to the state of Utah by being made an admiral."

Davis joked that he'd meant to go to Indianapolis to be a race car driver, but ended up in Annapolis instead. He worked hard, and to his surprise ranked 7th in a class of 250 by the end of his first year. Although they were contemporaries at the Academy, Byrd and Davis were apparently not acquainted at this early point. Byrd was a year ahead of Davis, and involved in the sports that would make his name among cadets and cause many of his injuries. Davis was a quieter sort, and did not seek renown.

Instead, a measure of respect found him. During his second summer cruise, Davis berthed aboard the U.S.S. *Illinois*, the old battleship that had been part of the Great White Fleet's round-the-world cruise. One day, a turret gun was raised too high and stuck in place; there seemed no choice but to go into dry dock, remove the armor from the turret top, and lift the gun from its trunions, a laborious process that gave the crew nightmares. Davis approached the gunnery officers and asked if he might try something instead.

He improvised a pipe wrench from a link of chain and a pivot bar, and with this took a turn around the pin connecting to the gun's elevating screw. When he gave a yank, the screw popped loose. Down came the gun. With that, he was elevated from obscurity to respect; when he returned for his junior year, he was made student regiment commander, a "five-striper." Though his classmates still called him "Percy" and "The Mormon," they would also write in the school yearbook that "this sturdy little giant can do anything and do it exceptionally well."

He called it luck—the "Davis luck"—as if his hard-won mechanical instincts had nothing to do with the matter. In 1914 he graduated third in his class, and three years later, when the nation declared war, he was assigned as aide to Admiral Joseph Strauss, who commanded the U.S. mine-laying forces overseas.

Strauss took Davis to Great Britain, where they were based in Inverness, Scotland, on the firth opening into the wild North Sea. From May to September 1918, Davis helped supervise the laying of 56,000 mines in a 6,000-square-mile stretch from Scotland to Norway, a "wall" of more than 10,500 tons of TNT designed to keep the German U-boats bottled up in the North Sea. But with the Armistice, that wall had to be removed if commercial shipping were to start up again. Each nation was required to remove its part, and the United States had laid 80 percent. For Davis, this meant locating and raising the mines, a seemingly impossible job.

One particularly perilous type of mine vexed him. Although its explosive charge floated underwater, a copper antenna stretched to the surface, kept afloat by two copper buoys. When any steel or iron vessel brushed past the antenna, the water served as an electrolyte to create a current; this in turn started a tiny motor inside the mine. The motor rotated a cup, which dropped a golden ball; the ball fell between two forks of a switch, which closed the circuit and detonated the mine.

The same process that made this mine a danger to German submarines during the war now made it deadly for any metal-hulled ship attempting to clear the minefield. Wooden boats were the only alternative. Davis chose a pair of two-masted, fifty-foot wooden ketches that would not awaken the mines. Each boat had a crew of ten. Davis skippered the *Red Rose*, while the *Red Fern* was under the command of Lieutenant Olaf Maatson.

Davis also assigned two tugs to follow behind as the *Red Rose* and *Red Fern* sailed into the minefield. The ketches dragged between them a long copper sweep, which they hoped would snare the mines and pull them to the surface, or at least detonate them harmlessly far astern. Yet, as they sailed out of Inverness, the barometer began to fall. The sea grew choppy. They detonated one mine as planned, but the shock set off a second, then a third, the last under Davis's *Red Rose*. His ketch lifted up and slammed down hard enough to loosen her seams and rigging. Luckily the mine was deep enough that it did not scatter his boat and crew all over the sea.

The explosion did, however, scare the tugs. Within minutes, they'd disappeared over the horizon, back to Scotland. Bad luck came in threes: the tugs had hardly vanished when the wind freshened into a gale. Davis ordered Maatson to head back home and report, while his wounded *Red Rose* limped behind.

It seemed less likely as the night wore on that they would reach shore. By midnight, the staysail had washed over, and the jigger mast worked loose. The topmast broke free, but instead of washing over, it got caught in the halyards. Davis watched it swing back and forth like a battering ram against the remaining masts and shrouds. The only way to save the ship was to chop it free, but when Davis began to climb up the mast, Philip Strahan, the quartermaster and only other man on deck, stopped him. "You are needed to navigate this boat," Strahan cried. "If anybody is to get that topmast, it'd better be me."

As Strahan climbed up to free the topmast, Davis tried to tame the *Red Rose*. Suddenly the wind shifted and another shroud tore loose. He struggled forward to fasten the sail, but as he moved back, the seas bucked up and a high wave swept him overboard.

He immediately started to sink. Well, that's the end, he thought. What's the use of fighting? He was wearing heavy boots, sweaters, and a hooded cape, which weighed him down. There was no chance to swim; he wondered how long he could hold his breath as he descended. *Not very long*, he figured. Suddenly something grabbed his sweater and pulled. Strahan had seen him go over and reached in after him. By luck, the boat did not lift at that moment, and Strahan was able to get a firm grip on Davis's clothes.

Five days after leaving Inverness, the crippled *Red Rose* limped into harbor at Peterhead, on a cape sticking out into the North Sea. Everyone had given up on them. It was Christmas Day, Davis's birthday, and he figured his luck had saved him again.

He had survived, but the puzzle of the mines remained. He struggled with the problem until radioman Dudley Nichols strolled into his office one day. "If these mines can be exploded by one kind of current, that turns over the cup, that drops the ball and closes the current," suggested Nichols, "why not drop an opposite current overboard, reverse the motor in the mine and jam it so that it won't work?"

Nichols's idea made perfect sense; Davis wondered why he hadn't thought of it himself. Davis rigged a ship's generator so that one pole was grounded to the side of the ship and the other dropped overboard on a long wire trailing astern. The reverse polarity jammed most of the mines, rendering them harmless. In six months, the mines were all swept up with the loss of only one ship. Davis was awarded the Distinguished Service Medal; Nichols, who would be a reporter in Manhattan during the transatlantic race, was decorated and received a letter of commendation from President Wilson.

Like many veterans, Davis seemed unsure of his future. He needed a change. In 1921 he applied for flight school in Pensacola, and while there met and married Mary Elizabeth Merritt, oldest daughter of a prominent Pensacola shipbuilder. She was small and dark, and something of a southern belle, chosen at least once as queen of Pensacola's Mardi Gras. Two years younger than Davis, she took to his dry sense of humor. "You always had to take whatever he said with a grain of salt," she later told her son, Noel Jr. "He was the second-most plausible liar I ever met." The first, she said, was her son.

After earning his wings, Davis moved with his wife to Boston; he attended Harvard Law School, passed the bar, authored books, and co-invented the "Davis-Radford Mark II Octant," U.S. patent number 1,743,979. He took command of the Squantum Naval Air Reserve Base from Richard Byrd, a meeting that apparently led to their close friendship. He flew Dr. Paul Bartsch of the Smithsonian Institute around the Florida Keys in search of the *Cerion casablanca* snail. His mind first turned to the possibilities of the transatlantic flight in 1925, and the challenge seemed to focus him.

He started haltingly, as had Lindbergh. He tried to find a plane and backers, but always received a polite "no." He finally decided to abandon the project, at least for the year, but kept making inquiries, always very quietly. He did not want news of his venture to leak out until the arrangements were nearly 100 percent certain.

In the summer of 1925 he met a like-minded ally, Lieutenant Stanton Hall Wooster, who'd graduated from Pensacola a couple of years behind Davis. Wooster was the navy's expert on propellers, in charge of its propeller research center at Langley Field in Hampton, Virginia. Both the Navy and Army air services called on him to argue propeller patent claims in court, and he even had one of his own—patent number 1,674,674, a design for a metal propeller filed on August 16, 1925, which he signed over to the navy.

Wooster was also the navy's expert on piloting big planes. He had flown the first reconnaissance flight off the navy's first aircraft carrier, the U.S.S. *Langley*; in 1926 his name was bandied about as a copilot for René Fonck after Fonck dumped Homer Berry. Though this proved little more than a rumor, Wooster had caught the Orteig bug. When Davis broached the subject of an ocean flight, Wooster pounced, saying he'd thought of little else since his name had first made the gossip page.

They formed the first of several odd couples seeking the Orteig Prize. Where Davis was reserved, Wooster epitomized the kind of free spirit common in American aviation during its "Golden Age." His father, Rollin, was an attorney and a preacher; the family settled in Connecticut in 1650 and included several churchmen and a brigadier general in the Revolutionary War. Born near Hartford on April Fool's Day 1895, Wooster seemed destined for a serious route through life. But after a year in Yale he transferred to Annapolis, graduating in 1917. He spent the war in convoy duty aboard the battleship *Nebraska*, and then, like Davis, entered flight school. In a December 1920 navy fitness report required for promotion he was described as "calm, eventempered [*sic*], forceful, active, [and] careless," the latter added because he had too much fun in the air. During flight training on February 19, 1920, he kept his seaplane up for more than the prescribed hour; for that, he was confined to base for five days. Two months later, he was confined for ten days after taxiing his plane too fast across the water, resulting in a burned-out radiator. The navy seemed unconcerned about such stunts: it promoted him from ensign to lieutenant, with the gentle admonition "that you will show by your future conduct that you have entirely overcome the defects noted."

The warning was soon forgotten. Wooster appears to have quickly gained a reputation as a swashbuckler, and always seems on the verge of laughter in his photos. He was a big, dark-complected fellow with apple cheeks and hair parted down the middle and peaked on each side like the pop crooner Rudy Vallee. After earning his wings, he was posted to Panama, where he crashed in the jungle. He'd been ordered to fly across the mountains in a plane that could not reach high altitudes; rather than point this out, he carried out his orders with a quizzical acquiescence. He found his way across the range by following valleys, but on the way back, he turned down the wrong ravine. He found himself in a cul-de-sac, unable to turn back, unable to go forward without eventually crashing. He flew on until the sides closed in, and he landed as gently as possible. His emergence from the jungle four days later, after living off the land and navigating by the sun and stars, was the stuff of pulp fiction. He had a wife, Marjorie, but no children; like many aviation marriages, theirs didn't last. The two were separated and in the process of divorce when Davis entered his life.

Despite Davis's circumspection, word of his intention to seek the Orteig Prize leaked out. As early as May 5, 1926, his plans were mentioned in an article printed deep inside *The New York Times*. Byrd would later write to him that he knew "in a general way something about what has been going on." He'd learned this either through navy scuttlebutt or from their mutual friend Fitzhugh Green. "I kept out of things . . . on account of the fact that you were in the race," Byrd added. When it seemed that Davis's plans had faltered, Byrd said that only then did he decide to enter the race himself.

It was not unusual for navy fliers to write back and forth like this, even if they were potential rivals. Navy flying was a very small world. Before the disastrous takeoff of the S-35, Davis wrote his friend Lieutenant Bill Curtin, who had recently been chosen as Fonck's copilot. When Wooster returned to Washington from New York, he apparently brought tales of the chaos surrounding the upcoming flight. "Since [Wooster] came back from New York with some of the details of the S-35," Davis wrote on September 18, 1926, three days before the fatal take-off, "I have begun to worry whether you have a sufficiently even break to justify attempting the flight. The plane is loaded to the gills . . . These wing tanks have always bothered me—too much weight inadequately supported and too close to the engine. Lord knows I don't want to see the flight fizzle with you in it." Davis was worried enough to recommend replacing the Jupiter engines with Wright Whirlwinds, and even called Wright to have the company provide Sikorsky with three J-5s. His concerns proved well founded, but by then it was too late and the S-35 sped to its doom.

There would be problems with Davis's plans. He first attempted to buy a Fokker trimotor similar to Byrd's *Josephine Ford*. To raise money, he signed a publicity agreement with Putnam: the publisher would handle all print and movie rights, and lectures. The deal was put together by the ubiquitous Fitzhugh Green. But when Davis went to collect the airplane, there was a large lien against it, and the deal fell through.

He tried again, with more secrecy. After Fonck's crash, Davis took a trip to Washington to speak to Major General Mason M. Patrick, chief of the Army Air Services and the organizer of its 1924 round-the-world flight. It was both interesting and telling that a navy man like Davis would approach an army officer for aid. By the fall of 1926, so many navy fliers had either entered or been rumored to have entered the Orteig race that it had begun to resemble an all-navy affair. Considering the interservice warfare over the fate of military aviation, the army wanted its own men involved. Within a week, Patrick told Davis that he could buy a stripped-down version of the Huff-Daland Company's Keystone Pathfinder, a versatile plane being produced as both a bomber and an airliner.

Patrick promised secrecy, and Davis sped to Bristol, Pennsylvania, the company's new headquarters, where he made his case before Richard F. Hoyt, chairman of the board. Huff-Daland was a new company, but extremely influential. Founded in 1921 by engineering partners Thomas Huff and Elliot Daland, the company originally built open-cockpit crop dusters for the war against the boll weevil in the Mississippi Delta. But the two aimed for bigger prey, including contracts for large military and civilian passenger planes. In March 1925 they closed their plants in New York and Louisiana and moved all operations to a former shipbuilding site in Bristol. It was billed as the largest airplane factory in the world, and at 200,000 square feet, it may well have been. Planes with wingspans of 70 to 100 feet could easily fit inside. This was a company committed to the gargantuan, and Huff-Daland churned out planes weighing 6 to 10 tons with regularity. They specialized in heavy bombers, and their Cyclops was said to be the world's largest single-engine bomber of its time. Another large plane, the LB-3A twin-engine bomber, soon became the backbone of the Army Air Corps' bomber fleet. In 1926 the company changed its name to the Keystone Aviation Corporation.

Davis got his plane, but he still needed backers. He turned to the American Legion, the fledgling organization of Great War veterans that so strongly supported military aviation that it stood up to Congress over the firing of General Billy Mitchell. The Legion urged all posts to paint their roofs with the name of the town and an arrow pointing to the nearest landing field; it believed that the best way to establish military aviation was by encouraging flight in the civilian world. Davis approached the national executive committee and spoke to the editors of the Legion's monthly magazine, which drummed up support among the rank-and-file. He hired the Wall Street firm of Hayden, Stone and Co. to oversee all publicity, and set up the "New York–Paris Non-Stop Flight Corp." to handle details. Hayden, Stone lost no time. They advertised the flight as something distinctly and completely American: this was an "all-American" plane, built entirely in America, flown by an all-American crew. Finally, as a way to finance the flight, Davis planned to carry twenty thousand postcards aboard the plane to Paris. He'd sell them by mail order at two dollars apiece, and reserved 100 pounds in the final load for that purpose.

When Davis filed his Orteig Prize application with the NAA on January 27, 1927, all the pieces seemed in place. His Keystone K-47 Pathfinder was in production in the cavernous factory, and he'd registered it as NX179. He was the first new applicant in the race after Fonck's crash; Lindbergh would not apply until February, followed in March by Byrd. The application of the French ace Paul Tarascon was still in good standing, but his actual effort was in limbo. Fonck had not yet reapplied with a new plane, though this was anticipated. Davis had the edge. The veterans' organization pledged $100,000 to his effort, and planned to showcase the plane at its annual summer convention in Paris. In exchange, Davis named it the *American Legion*.

•

Davis's plane was big, even in a field of big planes. The idea of "bigness" in international flight was a given among these navy fliers, a perceived necessity that approached the status of doctrine. The idea of redundant systems, of extra engines should one give out, was drilled into their heads. Davis believed he would need three engines at takeoff and for the first ten hours of flight, then two for the remainder. In an emergency, one engine could keep the ship in the air. By mid-March, the *American Legion*'s skeleton began to fill the huge, half-lit factory. Workers swarmed around its frame like elves.

The plane stretched nearly 45 feet from nose to rudder, 67 feet from wing to wing. Three 225-horsepower Wright Whirlwind J-5s replaced the war surplus Liberty engines, which had more power but tended to rust from within. One engine sprouted from the nose; one was mounted to each lower wing. Together, they should be able to drive the plane at

120 mph at full power, while the cruising speed was slightly less than 90. The *American Legion* weighed 16,558 pounds when fully loaded, and had an effective flying range of 4,500 miles. The fuselage was made of welded steel tubing; the wings were extra-thick wood, to provide the necessary lift. She was painted a light, bright yellow with red trim; on the fuselage, American flags crossed beside the name. The press called her the "Yellow Bird."

The cockpit was roomy and open, partially encased by a glass canopy; the pilots sat side by side, close behind the whirling steel propeller at the nose. The standard control stick was replaced by a big wooden wheel that could be flipped from one seat to the other, depending upon who was in control. The 900-gallon brass gas tank—the world's largest, built by Alcoa—filled up the cabin directly behind the cockpit; three more 200-gallon "gravity tanks" were set in the top wing, giving the plane a 1,500-gallon capacity. To get from the front to the back, Davis had to crawl atop the fuselage in the open air, his progress aided by two handrails and a wire rope with a safety clip. The idea of such a walk did not seem to bother him; he would crawl back every hour to take a reading with his newly invented sextant. It would be pie, he said. He'd then drop through a hole in the roof into the navigator's cabin, equipped with a chart table and an RCA radio that could send and receive for 1,000 miles. Two compasses were set between the tail and that roof access; a glass dome could slide across the hole in bad weather.

When the *American Legion* rolled from her hangar on April 9, 1927, her appearance surprised everyone. The construction had been a closely guarded secret; no one else in the race had a completed plane. Not Byrd, not far-flung Lindbergh, not even the French flier Charles Nungesser. Charles Levine's Wright-Bellanca, believed the closest to completion, was still a couple of weeks shy of its first test. Even *The New York Times* was caught off-guard. "[A]ccording to present indications," it wrote in a front-page article, "the *American Legion* may be the first of the transatlantic fliers to get off."

It was a gray, cloudy day. The doors rolled open and she appeared, "a massive, heavy, powerful machine," standing in relief against the yellow turf of the field. The previous week, Davis had been confined to bed with tonsillitis; nonetheless, he arrived for the unveiling, pale and unsteady but still determined to see what his Yellow Bird could do. The Keystone employees gathered outside: they had worked nonstop for four months and were as anxious as Davis and Wooster. The two climbed into the cockpit and taxied up the runway. Davis opened the throttles and the big plane tore forward down the field.

Before the spectators realized it, the *American Legion* sprang into the air. "It fairly spurned the ground," the *Times* enthused. A small plane with a cameraman filming for the newsreels took off after her, but was unable to catch up. "Round and round it chased the big sturdy shape of the transatlantic flier, which was apparently not hurrying but just couldn't settle down to a slower pace," the *Times* said. After two complete circuits the slower plane finally cut across the circle and caught up. Soon afterward, the *American Legion* eased back to earth and lightly touched the ground.

"The plane handles beautifully," Davis said. Even he was surprised. She responded quickly to the lightest touch and was easy to control. At full power, she had flown over 120 miles per hour; how much over, he did not know. They flew her on three motors, then two, and finally one, and even climbed a little on one engine, something unusual for such a big ship. Keystone's owner, Richard Hoyt, was even more effusive. "The plane is as safe as can be," he beamed. "Crossing in it from New York to Paris would not be any more venturesome than taking a Pennsylvania train from here to New York. I would just as sooner [sic] do it as not. I wish I could."

On April 10, the day after his plane's unveiling, Davis pressed his advantage and took off from Bristol to Washington. A crowd of 1,500 cheered, many of them Keystone employees. The company declared a holiday, and many brought their families. Five people rode aboard, including Mary; there was already talk that she would make the transatlantic flight with Wooster and her husband. She would serve as radio operator, sending shortwave reports back to *The New York Times*. If they made it, Noel and Mary would be called the First Couple of the Air.

The *American Legion* flew the 160 miles from Bristol to Washington in 2 hours. Admiral William A. Moffett inspected the plane when she landed. "She is a perfect ship," he said. The next day, Davis and Wooster pointed the plane south for several days of tests at Langley Field. They rotated the propellers to various angles to find the most efficient setting: a low angle would boost a plane at takeoff, but cut into fuel economy; a high angle had the opposite effect. Each time they incrementally added weight to the ship, she flew like a charm. Early tests suggested they could take off in 9 seconds from Langley, crossing 310 feet of runway with a wind speed of 16 miles per hour.

The "Davis luck" seemed to be holding steady, he thought, maybe even better than usual. In a few short weeks he'd gone from dark horse to front-runner.

•

Yet beginning with the *American Legion*'s sudden unveiling, everything began to change—as if Davis sent a jolt of adrenaline through the competitors, who'd been absent from the news. Previously, the Great Atlantic Derby had followed at its own leisurely pace; now, every week, then every few days, saw a sudden sea change. On April 13, the press anointed Davis as the front-runner. Yet even as they did so, two previously ignored hopefuls—pilots who had not even officially submitted their applications—were in the midst of breaking a world record. The normally cautious Davis decided to move up his timetable. At 10:55 a.m. on April 16, the *American Legion* took off from Langley for a 300-mile trip to Long Island's Mitchel Field.

The trip lasted three and a quarter hours, on a gray, cloudy day. The plane headed north, over the Chesapeake Bay, and was laden with passengers: Kenneth "Spoons" Boedecker, engine mechanic for the Wright Corporation; an RCA engineer, there to test the shortwave; a moving-picture photographer; and a reporter for *The New York Times*. The air was bumpy at first: as the wings swept back and forth in great arcs, the plane yawed like a boat at sea. As Davis steered over water and climbed to 2,000 feet, the ride grew more comfortable. They flew up the spine of the Maryland Peninsula, the broad fields and stretches of forest like a gray-and-green checkerboard. On the edges of the water the mudflats were hatched "with queer silver crosses and crescents of water, like some strange batik work," the *Times* reporter wrote. It was as if he'd fallen under a spell.

The passengers were far from idle. The moving-picture photographer crawled from one window to another and up the hatch to get pictures. Boedecker crawled out of the hatch and crept up the catwalk, blown by the windstream of the forward engine. The wind jerked at his mouth and nostrils and battered his eardrums. He poked his head inside the open cockpit and asked the pilots how they thought the engines were faring.

The three Whirlwinds made such a "monotonous clashing" that it was nearly impossible to talk. "At first one's system fought against the noise," explained the *Times* reporter, "and then came a sleepy hypnosis and finally a nonchalance that made flying over the ocean seem the most commonplace thing in the world." He looked out the window and watched the white line of sand pass beneath. The delicate white lines of waves seemed like etchings; the plane was so high that the breakers hardly seemed to move.

The reporter no longer felt connected to the earth; the trip seemed otherworldly. He rode on "a heavy, cumbersome piece of machinery churning its way through the atmosphere by brute force," he mused. "And yet, when one looked at the big, broad wings, shining yellow in the sunlight that occasionally broke through the clouds, they were like the wings of a great bird."

Boedecker, the engine expert, spent most of his time on the catwalk. He liked it out there, despite the fact that it was only a three-inch rail that kept him from rolling over the side. One unexpected dip or air pocket and he'd be the "former" engine man. The wind split his overalls and blew his helmet overboard. He smiled and hung on.

They cruised over Atlantic City, the hotels like toy houses at this altitude. The wooden boardwalk seemed an inconsequential reed. They turned out to sea and left all sight of land. Steamships passed underneath, now boats in a bathtub, white wake trailing behind. They angled back to land and passed the lightship *Ambrose*, first sign of New York's sheltered harbor. Around Long Island beach, Davis throttled back and coasted down. He left the cockpit and crawled back, facing the rudder. He stayed like this awhile, watching the surfaces, hoping they would give him some hint of the weight of the tail. After a few minutes, he crawled back to the cockpit and picked up speed. He roared over Mitchel Field, described a half circle, then set her down "so easily that it wouldn't have overturned a glass of water on the [cabin's] calculating table."

Cheering army officers and Legion officials surrounded the plane; they led it between two hangars for its official christening. Mary Davis had arrived earlier by train and now waited by a stepladder. She climbed the steps, a bottle of ginger ale in her hand. When she cracked the bottle over the center propeller, the contents exploded over her coat and her face. As Noel helped her descend, he laughed at her unexpected shower.

EIGHT

THE PROFESSIONALS

Even as the Cowboy and his sidekick planned their test flight to New York, a silver-and-yellow Wright-Bellanca with a single J-5 engine traced long, lazy circles over Broadway. Although it was the plane so coveted by Lindbergh, the Farm Boy was not aboard. Two "professionals," Clarence Chamberlin and Bert Acosta, had the helm.

From Tuesday, April 12, through Thursday, April 14, the plane, now named *Columbia*, droned back and forth over Long Island, circled the Woolworth Building, buzzed Hadley Field in New Jersey, and dropped notes to those below. Sometimes they flew over the ocean to practice compass flying. The goal: to stay aloft for more than fifty hours. If successful, they'd set a new world record for nonstop flight by a gas-powered plane.

A lively debate raged among experts around this flight, and many thought it was not possible. There is a delicate balance between a plane's "lift" capabilities and its "load," and in order to stay aloft for fifty hours, *Columbia* needed to carry 375 gallons of gasoline. Every Orteig rival balanced on this tightrope, but *Columbia* was the first to make the attempt. More dramatically, she was the first single-engine plane to try to do so. Many experts thought a single engine was not powerful enough to get that weight off the ground or keep it up that long.

In addition to pushing the known limits of technology, Chamberlin and Acosta were challenging a psychological barrier. Critics recalled what had happened when Fonck's overloaded plane tried to take off. Many expected a similar fate for *Columbia* at the end of Roosevelt Field. The experts were not alone in the debate: a number of gamblers bet anywhere from 30 cents to $100 that the plane could not stay up that long.

The steel *Columbia* rose with ease. She rolled down the runway at 9:30:40 on Tuesday morning; after 1,200 feet, or less than a quarter of Roosevelt's length, she slid into the air. The pilots passed over "Fonck's bluff" with 100 feet to spare. Chamberlin had the helm. They were 400 feet up when they passed the end of Curtiss Field. The pilots nursed the throttle and the fuel mixture controls, trying to find the point where the motor would use the least possible fuel. After all, they planned to stay up for a long time.

The world record the two hoped to beat had been set in August 1925 by French fliers Maurice Drouhin and Jules Landry. They'd flown for 45 hours, 11 minutes, and 59 seconds, dramatically surpassing the previous benchmark of 36 hours, 4 minutes, and 34 seconds set by American army lieutenants John A. Macready and Oakley G. Kelly in April 1923. This was one of the records taken by European fliers that Noel Davis said should come home to America. Though aviation experts did not dispute the point, they did not think it could be accomplished by a small, single-engine plane. This opinion was probably influenced by the navy's line of thinking: big, multi-engine planes such as Byrd's *America* or Davis's *American Legion* would be the ones to break the record and, by inference, first to cross the ocean. Those who conceded that *Columbia* would even take off at all thought she'd stay up for thirty, maybe thirty-five hours. No more.

Breaking the French record by a mere five hours might not seem like much to a layman, but former record holder Macready sympathized with the pilots over what lay ahead. After a certain point, every hour became a trial. "I can feel for Acosta and Chamberlin up there," he said, "counting off the trips—watching for the dawn or darkness or anything to relieve the monotony." His thirty-six-hour flight had been a strain on the nerves, but not enough to keep him from the cockpit forever. "I know the fascination of flying. It gets into your blood."

Aviators often said that when the unexpected occurred, "a flier discovers whether he is running a ship or it is running him." Chamberlin and Acosta had to prove quickly who was in charge. Soon after takeoff, they nursed *Columbia* up to 1,000 feet, then cut back on power to save gasoline. They'd circled Long Island and had flown back over Mitchel Field when the engine died. They looked at each other in shock; the sudden quiet was frightening. Chamberlin prepared for a "dead stick" landing as Acosta searched desperately for the cause.

Dead stick landings called up every ounce of a pilot's skill. If the motor died at 500 feet, he had less than three seconds to decide where to land. That usually meant straight ahead. At 2,000 feet, he had the luxury to spiral as he scouted for the straightest, softest field. No matter at what altitude he was flying, the great question never changed: *How far can I glide?* With a dead engine, the average ship could glide 6 to 8 feet ahead for every foot it descended; thus, if it was a mile up, it could glide 6 or 8 miles before reaching ground. The best bet was usually to sight along the nose. Any field below the nose was easily reached, while one beyond that was impractical. A great mistake of novice pilots was the illusion that if they could see something ahead, no doubt they could get there, too.

As Chamberlin steered toward Mitchel Field, he ran through the mental checklist necessary for a forced landing. He stripped off his goggles, to save his eyes from splinters. He checked his safety belt. Just before impact, he must remember to cut the ignition switch, lessening the danger of fire. He must keep his eyes open until the last second, so he'd know how the plane would hit and could brace himself accordingly.

While going through this, either he or Acosta discovered the cause of the engine failure. Just after takeoff, one of them had accidentally tripped the gasoline cutoff valve with his elbow or knee, probably while adjusting controls for the long haul. Chamberlin flipped the switch back on and prayed for the best. The engine roared back to life.

Cockpits were often tight, but the *Columbia* was a sardine tin. She had originally been designed to hold six passengers, but the seats and flooring had been replaced by a long, low, piano-shaped gas tank located directly behind the pilots' chairs. They had thrown a mattress atop the tank in case either wanted some sleep during the long ordeal, which had made things even tighter. At 210 pounds, Acosta would be the burliest flier in the Orteig race, and in these tight planes, where every inch of space was filled with equipment, tanks, and fuel, such heft made him miserable. Worse, the highest part of the tank sat directly behind him, wedging him in place, at least for the first day.

To save space, their seats were placed directly above the 17-gallon oil tank. A few hours into flight, Acosta noticed that the oil temperature gauge had failed. In most cases, this would have been a concern, since the dial was their main check for engine overheating. For this flight, however, the failed gauge was only a minor difficulty. They could gauge by the seat of their pants the temperature of the oil.

"Anyone who thought flying was glamorous," growled Chamberlin, "oughta be here."

They leveled out at 2,000 feet and tried to get comfortable. The first day proved to be a dreary, bumpy ride. Clouds piled up, and the wind seesawed from the south, to the west, then back again. They kept in sight of the flying fields in case more trouble developed and they needed to land. Occasionally, to break the tedium, they set a course over the Atlantic or Long Island Sound. Acosta, especially, needed practice with instrument flying. From time to time, planes filled with reporters or dignitaries flew up beside them. They shouted questions through a megaphone, but could not be heard over the motors and the wind.

After seven hours, they swooped low over Curtiss Field and dropped a message: "Aboard the Bellanca monoplane, 4:31 p.m., April 12, Mr. C.A. Levine, Woolworth Building, New York," it read. "Seven hours and all is well. The old Wright J-5 doesn't seem any worse for the wear of the 200–300 hours it has had. Hasn't missed a shot yet." They threw down other notes during the first twenty-four hours, but only a couple were retrieved.

They calculated their time constantly on the several clocks and watches they'd brought aboard. In order to beat the record, they'd have to stay up until 6:45 a.m. on Thursday, April 14. As each hour passed, they scratched a mark on a piece of paper between their seats.

Daylight waned, replaced by a night of low clouds. They held *Columbia* down to her lowest possible speed to husband fuel, a choice that made them easy prey to small air pockets or fine shifts in the wind. Then the food and drink began to go. Chamberlin reached for his container of milk: that and roast chicken were his great comfort foods. But he'd set the container between their two seats on the oil tank, and the heat had turned the milk sour. The water went next: someone had forgotten to rinse out their canteens, and neither cared to drink the brown solution that poured from the lip. They'd underestimated their appetites: by 9:30 p.m. Tuesday, they'd eaten all the sandwiches they had brought. For the next day and a half, all they had to eat or drink was cold coffee, some vegetable soup, four apples, and four oranges.

The floodlights switched on at the three landing fields. A light breeze sprang up from the southwest, and they circled, ever wider, over Long

Island, eastern New Jersey, and Manhattan. Far to the west they could make out the lights of Hadley Field. A big revolving beacon at Mitchel Field traced circles in the low clouds. They could see the lights of Broadway, and that was comforting. This was the greatest city in the world, and tonight it seemed all theirs as they circled the Woolworth Building and Times Square. Some pedestrians later said they thought they heard the *Columbia* through the din of the city at night. This was the night the Sherry-Netherland hotel, on Fifth Avenue, caught fire and went up in a spectacular blaze. Acosta and Chamberlin wheeled overhead and watched the fire below.

•

The fact that *Columbia* had made it up at all was in itself a minor miracle. Uncertainty plagued Charles Levine and his airplane from the very beginning. After Lindbergh stormed from his office on February 16, Levine realized how far ahead he was of everyone else who'd shown an interest in the Orteig Prize. He alone owned a finished plane. His partner, Bellanca, and test pilot, Chamberlin, both wanted to enter the plane in the race, and both felt that *Columbia* could cross the ocean with ease. Yet there were dangers in entering. Bellanca's monoplane was a valuable commodity. Potential investors lined up at airfields to settle into the handsome cabin with its red velour chairs. Levine spun marvelous tales of the future, where businessmen sipped Manhattans and traveled coast to coast in a fraction of the time the trip took by train. But if *Columbia* crashed, all that was gone. If she disappeared over the ocean, Levine would lose everything.

Maybe he could show her worth in other ways. The company hoped to build more machines like *Columbia*, then expand to a trimotor version and introduce a transoceanic flying boat, so Levine had Bellanca and Chamberlin fly the plane to meet with potential investors in Richmond, Atlanta, and Charleston. Yet these were distractions, and by March all three knew they were losing their lead. The teams of Davis and Wooster, and Nungesser and Coli, were feverishly catching up, as was the dark horse loner Lindbergh. Rumor had it that Byrd's trimotor Fokker would be ready in April.

Finally, Levine made up his mind—sort of. He released *Columbia* from her duties as a show horse and sent her to a shop in Amityville, Long Island, for modifications. The seats and flooring were ripped out and the big gas tank installed. New fuel and oil lines were added; the engine overhauled. He gave in to Bellanca's insistence to let his plane beat the endurance record. If she succeeded, the Columbia Aircraft Corporation would be on the map. After that, there would be plenty of time to think about the Orteig Prize.

It took nearly a month to ready the plane, and in that month Levine's search for an edge spawned a series of dramas. He seemed to view pilots as finely tuned parts of an intricate machine. Where Fonck juggled copilots like hot potatoes, Levine pitted them against one another like glamorous fighting cocks. The episode with Lindbergh in the Woolworth Building was a perfect example of Levine's management style. Although Bellanca's contract stipulated that he had final say over all flying matters, in truth, the retiring Sicilian avoided disputes with his hard-charging partner. Bellanca believed *Columbia* needed a pilot such as Chamberlin, who had been with him since 1921 and instinctively understood his planes. Levine, on the other hand, preferred "headliners."

To this end, he signed the thirty-year-old Leigh Wade, one of the aviators who'd flown in the army's celebrated round-the-world tour. Wade was a "name." Bellanca didn't mind having him pilot his plane as long as Chamberlin flew, too, but soon after signing, Wade tried to replace Chamberlin with an army friend. Then he tried to bring in a second friend as "general manager," plus his own publicity man.

Levine may have had a weakness for "headliners," but he held strong feelings about who was in charge. On April 8, Wade "withdrew." By now the proposed endurance flight had progressed in the papers from a simple record breaker to a walk to the Orteig Prize. Weekend drivers from New York wended the narrow road to Mineola to watch the final touches on the sturdy monoplane. Bellanca's ground crew, under head mechanic John Carisi, painted "140" on her fuselage, and "NX-237" on her wing. She was a pretty craft, yellow with silver trim. Before he left, Wade said he had been named pilot for both the record flight and the transatlantic hop, but without his knowledge. "I withdrew from these flights because I realized there was not time for adequate and proper arrangements to successfully carry out so serious an undertaking," he claimed. "To successfully cross the ocean, it is necessary to regard the flight as a scientific problem and not one of a 'stunt' character."

Thus began a theme: Blame Levine. Levine was not "serious." He was not as "high-minded" as aviators. One could read a lot of preening between the lines. Levine began a pattern, too. While aviators squawked, he grew taciturn, keeping all his plans to himself. In Wade's place he hired Bert Acosta, who'd taught him to fly in a surplus Jenny and had been the army's chief test pilot during the Great War. Four days after Wade quit, Acosta and Chamberlin took off from Roosevelt Field.

The fliers were as different as two men could be: the fact that they'd be trapped together in a small cockpit for more than two days seemed incomprehensible. Perhaps because their boss was so contentious, Chamberlin and Acosta got along famously.

Clarence Duncan Chamberlin was a flier's flier, a slow-talking, meticulous mechanical wizard from Iowa with a healthy sense of the absurd. Years later, when the giant Portly Pig balloon floated off from the Macy's Christmas Parade, he snared it with a towrope and brought it home. But he was not glamorous, like Davis, Byrd, or Lindbergh. The sandy-haired Chamberlin was not blessed with a movie star face, an otherwise inconsequential trait for a flier that would become more important as the race shifted from being a test of skill to a spectacle of celebrity.

The *Columbia* was not that different in design from Bellanca's 1922 prototype built in Omaha, and Chamberlin had flown each evolving version. In her newest form, she was a high-winged monoplane, stretching 20 feet 9 inches from end to end, with a wingspan of 46 feet 6 inches. Thus, she was not as massive as Fonck's S-35, Byrd's Fokker trimotor, or Davis's *American Legion*. She stood only 8 feet off the ground at her highest point; the pilots stared forward over the Whirlwind engine behind a glass windshield, and the control panel was set directly beneath the glass. Bellanca equipped the plane with a dump valve, which could empty a ton of gas in seconds, minimizing the risk of fire during a crash. A magnetic compass hung down from the transparent cockpit roof; brackets were attached to both side windows for a drift indicator.

In her present incarnation, *Columbia* boasted a top speed of 132.5 miles per hour and cruised at 110 miles per hour. When cruising, she used a gallon of gas for every 10 miles, a low consumption rate that drew raves. She weighed 1,850 pounds empty, 3,454 pounds full.

Chamberlin's career as a pilot was welded to Bellanca's machines. He bought his first Bellanca in 1919, when the Sicilian "Professor" began working for the Maryland steel company. When he took that plane up, "a tremendous respect for [Bellanca's] ability began to grow in my mind," Chamberlin said. For the next couple years, Chamberlin barnstormed for the Franco-American Aero Exposition Company of New York, then in 1922 he flew Bellanca's Omaha-built monoplane for high marks in the Pulitzer Trophy Air Races. Two years later he formed the Chamberlin-Rowe Aircraft Corporation, but this quickly folded: like Bellanca's, his talents did not lie in the business world. In 1925 he tested planes for both Anthony Fokker and the Wright Aircraft Corporation, and was instrumental in bringing Bellanca under Wright's wing. After that, Chamberlin and Bellanca became inseparable.

When others bailed out, often with good reason, Chamberlin bulled ahead without fanfare. His closest brush with death came in 1925, when he rebuilt one of Bellanca's biplanes and entered her in an air race at Mitchel Field. At high speeds, the plane tended to drop her wing. Before the race, a friend asked to ride along, and Chamberlin unwisely agreed. During the race the wing dropped—he lost control and hit a telephone line. Chamberlin strained his back, and broke his leg and ankle. The friend died.

At first, authorities did not know which man had died. By then, Chamberlin was married to the former Willda Bogert of Denison. When she rushed to the field, a pilot blurted, "Chamberlin was bumped off in a crash an hour ago." A local newspaper ran a story with his photo under the headline "Killed in Crash at Mitchel Field."

Soon after Chamberlin woke up in the hospital, doctors told him he would never fly again. "A man never got over a bad crack-up," they said. "His bones would mend, and his bruises heal, but his nerve would never be the same." This made Chamberlin mad. How did they know what he would do? On the first day that he felt well enough, he slipped out of the hospital, caught a ride to the airport, and hobbled into the nearest cockpit, even though his leg was still in a cast. He felt right at home. He later estimated that he had crashed ten times in his flying life. Where others might have seen a warning in so many crack-ups, Chamberlin always blamed them on "faulty motors" or "poor landing fields," and climbed in the cockpit again.

In *Record Flights*, his autobiography, Chamberlin attributed such behavior to midwestern stubbornness, but in fact he'd picked it up from his father. Elzie Chamberlin was the town watchmaker in Denison, a west central Iowa county seat with a population of 2,771 residents in

1900—an island of peace in a sea of corn. Father and son both found the Norman Rockwell life too dull. Born on November 11, 1893, Clarence earned extra money tinkering with old watches in his father's shop, then graduated to automobiles when his father bought the first-ever car in Denison. This "asthmatic, one-cylinder Oldsmobile" panicked the farmers' horses whenever it wheezed by. The farmers held a town meeting to condemn "Elzie Chamberlin and that infernal contraption his boy, Clarence, drives through the streets of Denison." They voted to boycott the store unless Elzie abandoned his folly, but backed off when a local attorney said the watchmaker could possibly sue them for damages.

Clarence's love of mechanics grew on him like a second skin. He attended Iowa State College to study electrical engineering, but left after his sophomore year to open an auto and motorcycle shop back in Denison. He preferred Harley-Davidsons, and once crashed in a race only to hop back on the bike and win. Soon the town fathers declared Clarence the newest snake in their vale of contentment: in 1915 the town council met to put a stop to the din from his motorcycles. He was charged with disturbing the peace, but still refused to stop riding through town. Instead, he made himself useful: he added a sidecar to his bike and delivered packages for a dime. He drove passengers to nearby towns for $1.00 to $2.50 and was apparently so helpful that the complaints soon died.

Like others in the race—Bennett, Lindbergh, Nungesser, and Levine—Chamberlin was obsessed with the century's new sensations: fast cars and fast planes. Chamberlin often served as chauffeur for Charles W. Taber, one of the richest men in town. It was while driving Taber on a cross-country trip to see the 1915 San Francisco World's Fair that Chamberlin decided to become an aviator. He'd seen an old-style "pusher" plane five years earlier and was not impressed, but now he saw a flying boat in San Diego and asked his boss to spring for the twenty-five-dollar ride. "You can risk your fool neck in one of them some other time, but right now I've got a lot more places on the Coast that I want to visit," Taber fired back. "What's more, I don't intend looking around for another driver to get me back home. None of this flying business for you, young fellow!"

This kept Chamberlin out of the air only for a little while. In 1917 he enlisted in the aviation section of the Army Signal Corps, but got trans-

ferred to balloon school instead. By June 12, 1918, he wrangled a billet
back to flight school at Chanute Field in Illinois, where an instructor
promptly told him he was "about the worst student they had ever seen."
He got seasick his first time up: "There are waves in the air just like in
the ocean, only you go up and down much faster," he wrote to his parents. At one point he felt as if he'd hit a springboard and shot straight in
the air, followed by a 900-foot dive by his instructor. "After we landed,
the instructor asked me how I liked it," Chamberlin wrote. "I had a hard
time telling him it was fine."

Flying changed him. He'd always been quiet; now, however, he
would lapse into long silences in which he seemed far away. But the
moment he entered a cockpit, he transformed. He wiggled the stick,
warmed up the motor, and his face lit up with joy. His body language
became vivid and eager. In the air, he rolled his plane about, sideslipped
1,000 feet, pitched up, and zoomed ahead. He'd laugh from sheer happiness while others prayed that they would live through the ordeal.

On November 1, 1918, he received orders to take the first available
troop transport to France, but before he could leave, the Armistice was
signed. "Oh hell, war over," he wrote home.

His father made him an offer: give up this flying nonsense and he'd
take him on as a partner in the watch and jewelry business. In 1919
Chamberlin returned to Denison and gave it a try. But cleaning watches
proved too tame for him. One day, when he heard the sound of an
airplane passing overhead, he rushed into the street and looked up. He
felt "utterly miserable," he admitted. "The flying fever was still in my
blood."

Soon afterward, he bought his first Bellanca, moved to the East
Coast, and became a barnstormer.

He was not well known, but in the very small world of New York and
New Jersey flying, he developed a reputation for a unique set of skills.
He would do or try just about anything; the more unusual, the better. At
a time when black aviators were almost nonexistent, Chamberlin was
the only white flyer to have anything to do with "Colonel Hubert
Fauntleroy Julian, M.D., World's Greatest Parachute Jumper," better
known as the Black Eagle. Saturday after Saturday in 1923 and 1924,
Chamberlin would take Julian up. Dressed in a red devil suit and paid
by some merchant, Julian would jump from Chamberlin's plane trailing
a giant advertising banner as he parachuted over Harlem.

Chamberlin also became the first-known pilot to take aerial photos for the news. He'd fly overhead and snap photos of fires or accidents from the cowling of his cockpit while the unattended plane made a steep dive or began to bank sharply. In one case, he photographed a fire while sitting on the edge of the cockpit and holding the stick with his legs. His most notorious photo was an overhead shot of the World Series opener at the Polo Grounds. He parachuted the photographic plate to a man waiting at Riverside Park and got the picture in the next edition of *The New York Times*.

More than anything, Chamberlin became known for his ability to land on a dime. He would prove this, often, while flying Levine to meetings and then back home to Belle Harbor, Rockaway. He'd check his speed, land on the concrete foundation of a small, abandoned hanger, then bring the plane to a quick stop. The most famous instance occurred in 1926, when Clarence and Willda flew to an air meet in Camden, New Jersey. As had Cora Bennett with her future husband, Willda fell for Clarence back in Denision, through their mutual love of fast cars; ever since, they'd been flying companions. But this day would test her resolve. They'd entered a stiff headwind on the way to the meet and the gas cap worked loose; unknown to them, a fine spray of fuel was sucked from the tank. The motor sputtered. Chamberlin banked sharply, crested a stone wall, and landed. It turned out they had set down in a potato patch inside the walls of Philadelphia's Eastern State Penitentiary. A group of convicts walked up, followed by three or four guards with guns.

But they were just curious. Some convicts brought up five gallons of gas and helped turn the plane around. Everyone congratulated him for this feat—everyone but Willda. "I have flown often with Clarence, but I have never banked or side-slipped as we did that day," she told the *Brooklyn Daily Eagle*. "I was almost thrown out. We came down fast, but we leveled off, slowed down and landed in a potato patch. It made me ill and I had to lie down and rest in the jail."

•

In some ways, Chamberlin and his copilot, Bert Acosta, were very much alike. Both were in their thirties and had been flying most of their working lives. Where the press portrayed Lindbergh as the spirit of youth, military pilots such as Byrd and Davis as crusading technocrats, and the

French as romantic "knights of the air," Acosta and Chamberlin were "professionals"—skilled civilian aviators who made their living in the air. True, barnstormers had been around since war's end, but they were basically seen as circus performers and not taken seriously by society. A professional pilot was a new idea: he could test any new plane, fly the mail or other cargo in any weather, and read the sky like a book. In keeping with the thirteenth-century origins of the word "profession," his very presence overhead was a public declaration of his faith, and the terms he used, clothes he wore, and arcane skills he practiced attested to his admittance into an order that set him apart from other men.

In other important ways, Bertrand Blanchard Acosta, known as the "Bad Boy of the Air," was Chamberlin's polar opposite. By 1927 he was probably the most famous professional pilot in America. Born in 1895 in San Diego to Spanish American parents, he built a working glider at age thirteen; three years later he entered Pasadena's Throop Polytechnic Institute, where he earned a degree in mechanical engineering. He was nineteen when he graduated and hired on as a pilot for the still-unknown Glenn Curtiss, testing "hydro-aeroplanes" off San Diego's North Island. His association with Curtiss lasted several years and would bring them both fame.

By 1927 the dark and handsome Acosta had done about everything available for an aviator to do except fly in the war. He'd flown *all* the light American-made planes of the 1910s and '20s, then flew the first working transport planes. In 1914, the same year he graduated, he was named chief flight instructor for the Canadian Air Service, where he trained four hundred aviators who fought in the Great War. He tried to go to the front himself, but was told he was too valuable for the war effort and was appointed chief flight instructor for the Army Air Service in Mineola, at what would become Curtiss, Roosevelt, and Mitchel fields. After the war he surveyed the nation's first airmail routes, then, in July 1920, laid the first route from New York to San Francisco with war ace Eddie Rickenbacker. He was simultaneously an inventor, barnstormer, mechanic, designer, and America's first acknowledged "test pilot." His records were legendary. During the war, he set the U.S. altitude record by climbing to 22,500 feet—over 4 miles—without oxygen. On June 27, 1920, he set the American nonstop distance record by flying 1,200 miles from Omaha to Lancaster, Pennsylvania; the next year, he won first place in the Pulitzer Trophy Race, and set the American speed record at 197.8 miles per hour, 3.3 miles per hour short of the world record held by French flier Joseph Sadi-Lecointe. At the ripe age of twenty-six he had flown a dozen years, accumulated some seven thousand hours of flying time, and had probably flown more types of aircraft than any other flier on earth.

But 1921 saw the beginning of a long plunge. Many temptations offered themselves for those who spent their lives on the edge. It was easy to grow addicted and easy to fall. Acosta's favorite cocktail was an equal mix of women, thrills and booze, a combination that apparently did not stop after he married his second wife, Helen Belmont Pearsoll, in August 1921.

The first hint that he'd sipped too freely surfaced two months before his wedding. That June a group of navy brass gathered at Curtiss Field to watch Acosta test their record-breaking CR-1. Spectators choked the road leading to the field, and as usual, Acosta did not disappoint. As soon as he took off, he pulled the nose up in a loop, executed a series of rolls while climbing to 7,000 feet, then pointed the nose back to earth and began a shrieking dive. He pulled out just in time, right over the heads of the navy brass, then rolled the tiny plane on its back and thundered over the field.

But when he landed, the reaction was not quite what he'd expected. Though he'd proven the worth of the little navy racer in a number of unexpected ways, he was roundly criticized in the papers for his reckless endangerment of the suburbs.

That was not the day's biggest surprise. When he stepped from the cockpit, one of his students, an attractive and rich married woman, told surrounding reporters that she and Bert were marrying soon. Her announcement was news to Acosta. His two-year marriage to his childhood sweetheart, Mary Louise Brumley, had ended in 1920, and his marriage to Helen Pearsoll was being planned. He didn't need more complications, and denied the woman's claims. Nevertheless, the next day's headlines trumpeted the fact that Acosta had stolen the wife of a millionaire.

One can see this simply as a messy entanglement, or as an early sign of a social obsession that would crest when Lindbergh appeared. The aviator represented in a vague but powerful way a liberating freedom that the 1920s New Woman tried to put into words. Lindbergh felt it as a barnstormer when he said, "Girls were everywhere." When he arrived in New York, he would be besieged. There were several tales of women throwing themselves at Acosta, apparently drawn to his movie star looks and his dark magnetism. In France, Charles Nungesser played the same role. Byrd would be deluged with letters. In every nation, people looked up and recognized the plane and pilot as the symbol of a freedom that only seemed a dream. Now the Orteig Prize focused such longing, and the response surprised everyone.

At this point, however, Acosta's problem came too early to be recognized as part of a gathering wave. Instead, he found himself in the kind of situation that fired jealous passions and got people killed. He'd played the cuckold before, but it had never been announced in the news. The next day, he arranged to meet the husband in a Long Island speakeasy. He'd expected the man, at the very least, to see red; instead, the millionaire laughed and said his wife craved publicity. They got drunk together and parted as friends. "What's one more publicity gag to a guy like you?" the husband said.

No one could tell at first that his luck was finally turning bad. In April 1922 a national flying meet held at Curtiss Field attracted twenty thousand spectators, and Acosta was the star performer. During the meet, he opened the throttle on a supercharged Curtiss triplane, the *Cactus Kitten*, and hit 208 miles per hour, unofficially topping the world speed record. But such luck would not hold. Three months later, on June 22, 1922, he took up the *Messenger*, an untested Sperry biplane. Showboating as usual, he rolled her on her back and glided 50 feet above Mitchel Field. Everyone clapped. Then the engine died.

At that altitude, there is nowhere to land but straight ahead. Acosta managed to roll the *Messenger* back upright before it plowed into the field. It took ten minutes for rescuers to free him; no bones were broken, but he lay unconscious with a severe concussion. The fuselage had split down its length, and the engine lay on his feet. The cowl was dented from where he'd rammed it with his head.

Acosta spent six weeks in the hospital, floating in and out of consciousness. In his more lucid moments, he saw a woman, vaguely familiar, sitting by his bed. She held his hand and called him darling. He seemed to recognize her, but... who was she? It made him uneasy. Perhaps she was a hallucination, an angel born of confusion and drugs.

His visitor was anything but an angel. The press styled her a glamor-smitten "mad divorcee." In fact, she was a woman whom Acosta had romanced in 1920 during his cross-country flight to lay the airmail. She'd traveled cross-country to Reno, Nevada, from Beechhurst, Long Island, for one of the quick and easy divorces that were Reno's claim to fame. Acosta landed there also, for a scheduled stop; somehow they met and had a fling. But the divorcee apparently did not see it as ended. As Acosta and his copilot taxied their lumbering German Junkers JL-6 across the Reno airfield to begin the final leg of their journey, the love-smitten Long Islander burst from the crowd and rushed toward the plane. Acosta jerked the wing over and up, missing the woman but damaging the landing gear. He flew low over the desert to make out the shadow of the damage on the sand below; he landed successfully on a dry lakebed to make repairs. Then he flew back to Reno, but did not dare land. Instead, he dropped a note to his ground crew. With that, he thought he'd shaken the divorcee forever.

He'd badly misjudged her. She returned home to Beechhurst and later read about his crash in the Long Island newspapers. By 1922 Acosta and Helen Pearsoll had apparently separated, but only briefly. The Beechhurst divorcee, who was not yet identified in the papers, apparently saw her chance: she bundled Acosta into her house for a long convalescence upon his release from the hospital. Jokes circulated in the press that Acosta received the kind of service "normally unobtainable in a hospital." True or not, when his strength returned he slipped away in the early hours, hoping to be rid of her forever.

The crash that summer changed his life in fundamental ways. Friends noticed it and worried about him. His courage never wavered, but a desperation arose, as if he felt hunted by something. His drinking bouts grew more frequent, and were no longer just for fun. His behavior, still hailed in the press as the mark of a swashbuckler, turned bizarre.

He began taking too many unnecessary chances. Fellow pilots laughed it off, but often uneasily. Too often, the stunts were associated with drinking. He flew his plane beneath the Brooklyn, Williamsburg, and Manhattan bridges along New York's East River, then just missed a collision with the Queensboro Bridge. He crashed his plane in a mock dogfight. He frightened a cabinful of passengers, potential financial backers, whom he felt did not properly worship aviators.

The most famous was the "What time is it?" episode. Several versions of this anecdote circulated. In one, Acosta and fellow mail pilot Lloyd Bertaud were stepping into the night from a speakeasy; in another, they were drinking late around the stove at Roosevelt Field. "What time is it?" someone asked, and Acosta, who wanted to go into New York, maintained that it was early. Bertaud said it was late, since he wanted to go home.

"I'll settle this argument," Acosta said. "Come along, Lloyd."

They took off west, toward the lights of the city. Manhattan opened beneath them; the two planes roared south along the Great White Way, Acosta in front, Bertaud behind. Madison Square came in sight and there in the center thrust the spire of the Metropolitan Tower with its huge clock faces. The northern face read 10:20 p.m. The planes circled the tower and headed back east toward the aerodrome. But it was night, and the two had trouble relocating Roosevelt; it was touch-and-go getting through the ground haze to safety.

Photos of Acosta from that time seemed to show the strain. There are dark pools under his eyes; he seems a tall, gaunt shell. In 1925 he was grounded temporarily for drunk driving; his fourteen-year association with Glenn Curtiss ended abruptly for unstated reasons. Though he tried to clean up his act, he had entered his thirties and he must have seen that something fundamental was changing in aviation. The new generation of flier was more commercially minded. Daredevils such as Acosta were becoming dinosaurs.

Then 1927 dawned, and with it the Orteig frenzy. Acosta was back in the cockpit, struggling to break another record. However briefly, the glory days had returned.

•

The first night passed, uncomfortably. The low clouds and shifting winds made for a bumpy ride, but in the early morning hours, a northeast breeze cleared away the clouds. The moon and stars peeked out, and the plane climbed. Chamberlin and Acosta plugged along at a gas-saving 80 miles per hour. At first, when the plane was heavy and hard to control, they switched shifts every thirty minutes, but as they used up gas and *Columbia* lightened, they switched every two hours. Neither man left his seat, but catnapped briefly when his partner had the wheel.

Down on the airfields, the big floodlights blazed. The rotating beacon slowly turned. Bellanca's mechanic John Carisi stayed up through the night, watching his "boys" in their endless gyres. Levine joined him, as did Carl Schory of the National Aeronautic Association, who acted as official timekeeper. Only Bellanca went home. He felt sure of success, a calm based upon his calculations.

The French were less sanguine. When the *Columbia* took off, the nation's airmen seemed to think that Chamberlin and Acosta hoped to break the world speed record, set in 1924 by their own Florentin Bonnet at 278.5 miles per hour. It was a logical guess—Acosta was always nudging against that record, at times even breaking it unofficially. But as the first night passed, they realized the Americans were after bigger game. Between this and the several entrants in the Orteig Prize, they saw it as a warning that America had begun a campaign to regain air dominance.

Wednesday, April 13, dawned pink. Hunger was their main complaint. They tortured each other with meals they would order when they came down. Around 8:30 a.m., after twenty-three hours aloft, they penned a note to Bellanca and dropped it on the field:

> Everything running fine, holding our own. Last night from midnight on was not so very good. However, we experienced no difficulty. We are continuously on minimum R.P.M. and expect to stick it out all right. Our present R.P.M. is 1235-1250. Just finished light breakfast of soup and water. Pretty good.—Bert Acosta

The note proved too tempting for the assembled reporters. Several boarded a plane and flew alongside. As before, they shouted questions through megaphones. They flew up several times that day, always with the same result. During one trip, only Acosta could be seen in the pilot's seat; Chamberlin was in the back, on the mattress, trying to catch some shut-eye. In a moment, he crawled into view beside his partner. Both looked oil smeared and disheveled; neither paid the least attention to the flying reporters.

By now both were battling sleep deprivation, though the occasional catnaps mitigated the effects. They had been up for twenty-four hours without any appreciable periods of sleep, and both experienced the frequent cramps in their limbs known to come with long periods of waking. In a 2000 study published in the *British Medical Journal*, researchers in New Zealand and Australia found that sleep deprivation had the same hazardous effects as heavy drinking. People who drove after 17–19 hours of sleeplessness performed worse than those with a blood alcohol level of .05 percent, the legal limit for drunk driving in most Western European nations. Test subjects had intermittent trouble focusing their eyes. Sometimes they would fall asleep without warning and pop back to wakefulness with a jerk. They were a danger to themselves and others on the road.

The second day passed, and shortly before sundown, John Carisi went up to see how his boys were doing. His plane flew beside theirs, and he saw both pilots sitting at the controls. They lowered the cockpit windows and waved. He came back down convinced they would reach their goal.

"Those boys are just chugging along, taking things easy and saving their gas," Carisi said. "They look fine, too."

At fifteen seconds past 9:35 p.m. that second night, Schory checked his stopwatch and congratulated Bellanca. His plane had just established the new American record.

Giuseppe Bellanca smiled. "That's all right, now for the big record," he said.

That record lay in their sights as Thursday, April 14, dawned. It was a sunlit spring morning. The two nursed their plane, keeping close to Roosevelt Field, where, according to the rules, they must land. Up, down, and around they flew, the motor thrumming slowly as the crowds listened below. By daybreak, hundreds had collected; they watched the monoplane bump along in the uneven air like a rowboat on choppy seas. At times, *Columbia* looked clumsy. But to the experts, including those who had said she could never take off, the sight was reassuring. The aviators were merely "doing their stuff, saving the precious gas, making the record that will stand," one said.

Shortly after daybreak, the spectators had a scare. As the plane flew west, it swung about in the sun. The cockpit gleamed like flame. "She's afire!" someone cried, and the crowd leapt into their cars, speeding across country after the *Columbia*. But there was never any fire, just the sun's reflection on the glass. The plane kept on. Observers attributed the scare to nerves frayed by the long vigil, but it was also something more. Underneath their excitement, the crowd expected the worst. They'd seen Fonck's sure bet end in disaster, and they waited for it to happen again.

At 6:42:40 a.m., Carl Schory announced that the world record had been broken. He turned to the crowd on the field behind him and waved his hand. The spectators cheered and threw their hats in the air. Some danced on the runway.

And still *Columbia* kept on. The engine maintained a smooth purr. The two were tired when they passed the French record, tired enough to quit, but decided to keep going as long as their gas remained. They'd felt sure the plane could go for fifty hours, but how much longer after that was a mystery. At 10:15 a.m., a little plane went up with the message "HOW MUCH GAS?" chalked on its fuselage. Chamberlin held up ten fingers: 10 gallons. The little plane descended to report there would be at least two more hours of waiting.

By then, the crowd had increased to thousands. Nassau County police roped off the runway and drove off trespassers and officials. Bellanca himself had trouble parking his car. The ground wasn't the only site of traffic jams. Shortly after noon, the air buzzed with press and army planes, all swooping and racing about, edging close to the *Columbia* to talk to the pilots or take pictures. Suddenly she picked up speed. Acosta chased one army plane, raced beyond another, and started to climb. "We knew we had made the fifty hours and we decided to show those army fliers that we had some speed," he later said.

It was the fifty-first hour and they started a slow climb to 4,000 feet, to add every second to their final glide home. At 12:37 p.m., the engine gave a last gasp and a strange silence filled the cabin. The wind whistled past the cockpit with a plaint of longing. Chamberlin turned to Acosta. "Well, Bert, I guess that's it," he said. They pointed the nose towards earth and glided back to Roosevelt Field.

A prolonged roar rose from the crowd. A small biplane landed ahead of *Columbia* and swerved to one side. Motorcycle cops sped about, chasing photographers out of the way. At 41 minutes and 5 seconds past noon, *Columbia* touched down. It had been in the air 51 hours, 11 minutes, and 25 seconds, or nearly 6 hours longer than the French record-holders. Acosta and Chamberlin had averaged 80 miles per hour and had covered approximately 4,100 miles—500 miles more than the flight from New York to Paris.

The propeller whirled to a stop, and a mob of three thousand swarmed about the plane. They fought with one another and the police to be the first to shake the pilots' hands. Somehow, John Carisi beat them all and climbed to Chamberlin's window. When Clarence slid back the panel, Carisi kissed him on both cheeks. The chief mechanic then swung like a monkey beneath the engine to greet Acosta in the same way. The screaming crowd hoisted the pilots atop their shoulders and marched them around the field. The two finally escaped when a score of policemen stowed them beside their wives and friends and raced off in two cars to the nearby Garden City Hotel. The first thing they did was eat. Acosta ordered orange juice, two helpings of oatmeal and cream, four lamb chops, rolls, coffee, and a double order of French fries. Chamberlin was more moderate. He ate only rolls, coffee, fries, and a whole roast chicken.

Then both went to bed.

•

The news was wired immediately overseas. Most European fliers responded with admiration, but the French tempered their praise. They knew the race for the Orteig Prize between the two countries was now in earnest. French aviators hastened to point out that flying circles for fifty-one hours above Manhattan was not the same as crossing the North Atlantic, the graveyard of the sea. Henri Farman, France's premier aircraft designer, said his nation's aircraft were fully capable of staying "in constant motion" for fifty-five hours, though as far as he knew no one had tried it or planned to do so anytime soon.

But back in New York, *Columbia*'s backers had no questions about who would win. "In three days, we should be ready to start for Paris," Bellanca announced happily. He ordered a new J-5 engine that should be installed within twenty-four hours, he said.

Levine was even more blunt. "We intend to be the first across," he declared. "[T]hat means that if another flier should start, and our plane is ready, we would be able to go after him with as much as a three-hour handicap and beat him across. Our plane is the fastest of those now heading toward Paris."

Then he played up the rivalry for the assembled media. "Boys, it's a race. Let the great Byrd have a three-hour head start. We'll catch up to him and still win."

NINE

THE LORD OF DISTANCES

Perhaps the condors were a sign.

Commander Francesco de Pinedo was not particularly religious, but the vision of the huge birds wheeling above the Brazilian jungle, then rising in a black cloud toward his plane, was enough to make him pray. There would be many chilling sights during his famous Four Continents Flight, but the giant, silent vultures swirling about his seaplane were perhaps the weirdest and most deadly.

It was mid-March 1927, the second month of his 43,071-mile goodwill tour. He was already famous, having completed a record-breaking, 35,000-mile circuit of the Orient in 1925. De Pinedo was "Messaggero d'Italianità," Italy's winged ambassador. Benito Mussolini called him the exemplar of the *Civus Romanus*, the new breed of Italian who merged the glories of imperial Rome with those of the modern world.

De Pinedo did not like politics, yet to be an airman in 1920s Italy meant belonging to the Fascisti and navigating Mussolini's whims. In January 1927 Britain's Chancellor of the Exchequer Winston S. Churchill applauded Il Duce's "triumphant struggle against the bestial appetites of Leninism"; the Great Powers held no grudge against fascism at this point, and so long as it opposed communism, even approved it. To many Italians overseas, Il Duce was a hero.

By the mid-1920s, Mussolini had absorbed Italy's fledging air corps to transform it into a force envied by the world. To Il Duce, flying had a profound spiritual meaning. His goal was the creation of an aviation consciousness among Italians, and to this end he staged spectacular displays of air power, such as the October 1923 flight of 263 planes over Rome to commemorate the nation's victory in the Great War. He authorized a huge expansion of the air budget, raising it from 200 million lire in 1923/24 to 630 million in 1926/27; funded de Pinedo's epic flights in 1925 and 1927; and proclaimed de Pinedo "The Lord of Distances," the prototype of the new Fascist man.

Il Duce grasped the idea of the flier as a natural leader early in his career. In 1909 he wrote in the newspaper *Il Popolo* that flying expressed the deepest traits of the new century. The age was a heroic one, he wrote, characterized by *movement*: "Movement toward the icy solitude of the poles and toward the virgin peaks of the mountains, movement toward the stars...Movement everywhere and acceleration in the rhythm of our lives." When Blériot flew across the English Channel, Mussolini called him the first in a new race of Nietzschean supermen destined to rule the world. In March 1920 Mussolini, then thirty-seven, signed up for flying lessons so that he, too, could be a superman.

But Mussolini was not alone in such beliefs: they gained wide credence in the years preceding World War II. In 1928, German playwright Bertolt Brecht wrote a radio play, set to the music of Kurt Weill, in which the flyer was mankind's hope for the future. Who better than an aviator to solve society's ills? He saw farther than most, and sat like Prometheus above the clouds. That same year, the American publisher of *Aviation* magazine dubbed the flyer "the evangelist of a new creed of conduct." In Italy, the journalist Guido Mattioli called the aviator man's natural leader, for "no other machine requires such a concentration of the human spirit, of man's will." Since the flyer raised his body and spirit above the dull masses, he knew what it meant to govern.

"Every aviator is a born fascist," the journalist declared.

•

Such pieties sounded noble in the marble halls of Rome, but had little meaning over the Brazilian Amazon. De Pinedo's twin-hulled seaplane, the *Santa Maria*, had steered north from Asunción, the capital of Paraguay, over Brazil's vast Mato Grosso, the densest jungle in the hemisphere. De Pinedo stared at the uninterrupted green carpet below, the branches of the huge trees so closely woven that he could not see the forest floor. The scenery never changed; no sign of human life was visible for hundreds of miles. In Africa's jungles, one could see paths or natural means of travel from above; light broke through the trees. In the Amazon, there was the green canopy above and the darkness underneath. De Pinedo knew that those outsiders foolhardy enough to invade its depths were often never heard from again. His only hope of survival was to stay above it all.

But the gods apparently had other plans. In the skies between Corumbá and Cáceres, he spotted sunlight glinting on what seemed white, metallic wings. "What?" he exclaimed in surprise to his two companions, navigator Carlo del Prete and Vitale Zacchetti, his chief engineer. "Airplanes away up here?"

As he watched, the mysterious fliers floated in perfect spirals above the trees. From a distance, they resembled planes, but as he drew closer, he saw they were prodigious birds: huge South American condors far from their Andean range. They were grand and gruesome at once: the nine-to-eleven-foot wings effortlessly keeping them aloft; the white ruff around the neck; the bald, warty heads. The large feathered patches of white on their wings reflected the sunlight, creating from afar the illusion of white metal.

The giant birds did not seem alarmed when the Santa Maria appeared. On the contrary, they were drawn to the plane as if she were just another condor, albeit one they'd never encountered before. De Pinedo grew alarmed by their wheeling curiosity. They sped toward him, growing bigger, and in a few seconds were so close that his seaplane's wings almost struck them. If one flew into a propeller, it would not only kill the bird but also wreck or disable the plane. That would force a forest landing, which could only be upon the treetops. And that would be their last good-bye.

De Pinedo soared high, then dove, again and again, in an effort to dodge the birds. Sometimes, frightened by the roar of the engine, they scattered, only to wheel about and dip within yards of the blades. One flew so close that he could see a bald patch among the feathers, from some disease. He increased power and shot forward, but still they followed. He'd lose one flock only to meet another that emerged from behind the clouds.

How long this continued he could not tell. Time compressed in the chase: The condors came and went, reappeared and vanished again. They stopped only when he was five miles from Cáceres. He saw below him the silver ribbon of the Paraguay River, barely visible through the trees. He landed the seaplane on the waterway, thanking God for his escape until he looked around. They'd dropped into a tree-lined pocket of the river, and there was no way out. He'd landed in a green tunnel of trees and liana vines from which it was impossible to rise.

•

Of all the rumored "rivals" in the Transatlantic Derby, Francesco de Pinedo (along with his journeys) was the most surreal. On March 20, as he picked his way through the jungle, his fate and location unknown, *The New York Times* dubbed him a possible threat to the front-runners, "although he could not do it in the flying boat he has been using," the newspaper said. His protestations that he neither was in the race nor intended to enter often went unheard. Amid the explosions, riots, and cries of sabotage attending what started as a goodwill tour, he must have wondered if America had gone mad.

America was not alone in such madness. In Italy, a cult formed around his name. He'd been inscribed in the registers of nobility, made a marquis by His Majesty Vittorio Emanuele III, king of Italy, for his service to his country. Newspapers displayed his daily wanderings on the front page. In every bank, café, and hotel lobby, maps were hung and studded with pins to track his voyage. Fans talked of his steady nerves and level head; Mussolini held him up as an inspiration for Italian youths, turning him into a symbol of Italy's aerial empire. Recruiting posters displayed the flier's face, framed by the words "DON'T YOU WANT TO BECOME A DE PINEDO?"

Like every aviator, de Pinedo knew the Icarus myth, and what happened when you presumed to climb too high. One was safer lost in the Amazon than fixed in the public eye. By early March, as the world press paid more and more attention to the Orteig race, a sore realization began to dawn on him. He was in a race, all right, but not against the other fliers. He was racing the Orteig Prize itself. If he did not return to Rome before an American or Frenchman winged across the Atlantic, his round-the-world journey would be forgotten in the delirium that ensued.

That simple fact meant that his survival as an aviator was at stake. Although he was the Air Corps chief of staff, he was envied by General Italo Balbo, the newly appointed undersecretary of the Air Ministry. Any fall from grace, real or imagined, and Balbo would use it as an excuse to bring him down. Mussolini expected results, something record-breaking and earth-shattering that he could broadcast to the world.

Anything less would be an anticlimax that would spell the end to de Pinedo's days as a trendsetting aviator.

In some respects, Il Duce and Balbo already harbored suspicions about de Pinedo's devotion to fascism. The aviator was too modest for his own good, a constraint that exasperated the dictator. His initial shyness made him seem reserved, even stiff, at public functions. Like Chamberlin and Lindbergh, he shunned publicity, convinced that talking too much about himself to reporters invited misfortune.

If the Four Continents Flight was a goodwill tour to South and North America, then the *Santa Maria* was an impressive ambassador. An Italian-made Savoia-Marchetti S-55, she was a twin-hulled flying boat with a 78-foot, 9-inch wingspan and a 52-foot, 6-inch stretch from nose to tail. Originally designed as a torpedo bomber for the Italian Royal Navy, she was a world-class machine, as good as any other seaplane of her time, but graced with the Italian sense of style. Her two sleek hulls resembled oversize boots, joined by a broad, sweeping V-wing; the cockpit nestled in the wing's center, while above that sat two tandem-mounted Isotta-Fraschini V-6 engines able to deliver 1,000 horsepower or more.

De Pinedo's choice of transport expressed its own logic. There was a faith in the 1920s that the future of intercontinental flight belonged to seaplanes. Since water covered two-thirds of the earth, planes that could land on the vast expanse of ocean seemed the best bet for commercial aviation. "Civilization is built on water," de Pinedo often preached. "The world's principal cities are mirrored by seas, rivers, or lakes. Why not utilize these immense, ready-to-use, natural airstrips in place of costly airports?"

He had started, appropriately enough, as a sailor. Born in Naples in 1890 to a wealthy patrician lawyer, he joined the Royal Navy in his teens, saw action aboard a destroyer in the 1911 Italo-Turkish War, then six years later volunteered for the navy's new air division. He spent most of the Great War flying scouting missions.

By the beginning of the Four Continents Flight, de Pinedo had developed a trademark style. Whether conscious of it or not, famous aviators reflected a romanticized national image. Despite the best efforts of Byrd and other "scientists," American fliers were seen as cowboys— they traveled light, calling no place home but the patch of ground beneath a wing. English fliers were more cultured, if less optimistic, than their American cousins: theirs was a daring insouciance, for they'd learned in the Great War that nothing, not even youth and life, lasted forever. Most of France's famous aviators were war aces, and would have fit easily into a Dumas novel about winged musketeers.

But de Pinedo was different: he projected the air of a cultured Italian gentleman. Schooled in music, literature, and the arts, he had little in common with the daredevil image so loved by other nations. Life in the air was not necessarily short, sweet, and brutal; rather, it was an art that could be learned and refined. He was short, slender, and always neatly combed; his belief in spit and polish went far beyond the code of the navy. It was said that to find a scuff on de Pinedo's shoes or a wrinkle in his tailored suits indicated the approaching end of the world.

The original idea for the Four Continents Flight had been Mussolini's, and it was not a bad one. The propaganda value could be immense, especially in North America. In 1927 Italian immigrants were seen by the average American as gangsters, anarchists, and fruit peddlers. Names such as Charles "Lucky" Luciano, Frank Costello, and Al Capone sprang to mind—or, even worse, Nicola Sacco and Bartolomeo Vanzetti. For the world to see a cultured Italian gentleman who had just braved oceans and jungles step off a plane would do wonders to reverse such negative images.

By now the papers had a name for the quest to conquer the ocean: "Atlantic Fever." De Pinedo was part of a second path in pushing that envelope, one that wasn't well covered in the United States but that had a ferocious pedigree in Europe and Latin America. The battle for the South Atlantic was just as hotly contested as its northern counterpart—the route from Portugal or Africa to Brazil was a shorter hop than the one from New York to Paris, and usually taken in stages from the continent to the coast of Brazil. Although the southern crossing didn't seem as glamorous, in some ways it was harder. This was an endurance test, often expressed as a "world tour"—a tour across the continents, from Europe to Africa to South or North America. Or one flew from Europe to Asia and back, stopping at Australia along the way.

Like its northern counterpart, the conquest of the South Atlantic started soon after the Great War. In 1922 two Portuguese fliers, Captain Sacadura Cabral and Captain Gago Coutinho, flew from Portugal to Brazil. This was a qualified success, since it took three machines and two months filled with crashes and breakdowns. Four years later, a Spanish hydroplane, the *Plus Ultra*, made the trip from Spain to Buenos Aires after seventeen days of mishaps and delays. Though de Pinedo would follow their route, he hoped to do so more quickly, then add thousands of miles to the return. He proposed flying over the Amazon, then north to the United States and Canada, where he hoped to visit most of the continent's major cities. He'd return to Italy via the North Atlantic, a round-trip crossing that had never been accomplished and would place him in the record books forever.

On January 20, 1927—eight days before Davis officially entered the Orteig Race and one day before Tony Fokker signed the contract with Byrd—de Pinedo met for the last time with Mussolini. "Go ahead," urged the premier. He clapped de Pinedo on the shoulder and assumed his famous "magnetic look," with the wildly staring eyes. "Carry Italy's greetings to the New World."

Ten days later, on January 30, the Savoia-Marchetti was christened the *Santa Maria* and moved to the southern tip of Sardinia. Two weeks after that, in the frigid early hours of February 13, de Pinedo and his companions took off under the stars. They flew across the Mediterranean and west over the Algerian and Moroccan coasts, then turned south along the desolate beaches of the Spanish Sahara. They reached Bolama in Portuguese Guinea at 8:00 a.m. and prepared to tackle the Atlantic on February 16, de Pinedo's birthday. But the weather was so hot that their engines consistently overheated, and they were forced to head north to the cooler climes of the Cape Verde Islands. On February 23, they finally took off for Brazil.

At first the crossing went well. De Pinedo entrusted the *Santa Maria* to the same gentle trade winds that had carried her namesake over the sea. They cruised southwest toward the Brazilian island of Fernando de Noronha, 1,450 miles away. From there, the mainland lay another 270 miles off. They uncorked a bottle of red wine and relaxed. The moon peeked through the clouds, silvering the sea 2,000 feet below.

But once they crossed the equator, they hit a downpour so violent it resembled a waterfall. De Pinedo had dropped to within 150 feet of the surface when suddenly the engines again overheated; hissing clouds of steam enveloped the cockpit as the deluge struck the radiator. The mechanic, Zachetti, pumped water back into the radiator from the reserves, then from the crew's drinking water, and finally from the rainwater leaking through the open cockpit, which he and the navigator squeezed into buckets with a sponge.

This saved the engine, but when they shot from a cloudbank, they found themselves face-to-face with a huge waterspout that churned straight toward them. De Pinedo seemed frozen in awe: he later called the sight "Brobdingnagian," a 1,500-foot funnel rising from the surface like a giant mushroom. The spout changed color as he watched, stark white against gray clouds, so white it seemed to glow with an internal fire. Its winds shrieked as the funnel writhed across the water toward them. If they got caught in its vortex, he realized, theirs would be "just one more Atlantic flight that failed."

They veered off, yet the storm went on and on. By midafternoon, they spotted tiny Fernando de Noronha, but the storm had apparently weakened, and they flew on to the mainland. They reached the Port of Natal an hour later, but the vengeful storm had caught up, kicking up such high seas that it was impossible to land. Their only hope was to turn back to the island, where at least there had been calm seas.

But when they returned, the storm had enveloped even this last pocket of calm. Worse, their fuel was gone. Their one chance lay with the *Barroso*, a Brazilian crusier that had been sent out to save them. If she headed into the wind, they might be able to land in the sheltering calm of her wake without too much damage to the plane. De Pinedo pulled behind the ship, but when the sailors threw out a towline, the cruiser swung about in the heading seas. De Pinedo watched helplessly as the stern loomed over them; he heard a crunch, and the *Santa Maria*'s right wing flap floated beside them in splinters.

The Brazilians were aghast; they towed the plane to port, and in less than twenty-four hours she was restored. At 4:00 p.m. the next day, de Pinedo reached Natal, officially beginning his tour of the Americas. The *Santa Maria* landed at all major Brazilian ports, attended by banquets and parades. Rio de Janiero's carnival welcome was so festive that the aviators did not want to leave. They flew to Buenos Aires, Montevideo, and Asunción, where city officials closed every business and school.

Word of their arrival set Rome afire. Even Pope Pius XI was impressed: perhaps the Vatican should incorporate airplanes into official Church business, the pontiff said. No American or Australian cardinal

had ever been able to attend the fifteen-day conclave to choose a new
pope, but now the great distance should no longer bar them. More sig-
nificantly, His Holiness could see the world—and it could see him.
Since 1870 each succeeding pontiff had been a voluntary prisoner of the
Vatican because of his unwillingness to enter Italy. Now, claimed the
Vatican paper *L'Impero*, the Pope could fly over the Eternal City and
"past the limits of the Italian frontier."

It was mid-March. Five teams had entered the Orteig competition,
officially or otherwise, and *The New York Times* hinted that de Pinedo
might be the sixth. The Lord of Distances was not saying. Instead, he
flew into the Amazon and disappeared.

•

What were people getting out of such high-flying adventures? What did
these stories mean to them? By now every flier even remotely connected
to the Orteig Prize was being given a public persona, a process that
started slowly and built to a crescendo with more news ink and time. A
flier's machine was described as lovingly as any Triple Crown thoroughbred: it was a winged Pegasus powered by modern technology and en-
hanced by antiknock fuel additives. Each culminating flight built on a
particular narrative of danger and death that drew writers like flies.
True, the journalists watched their subjects and reported their acts, but
the stories also served them as a public dialogue. A continuous murmur
of print, radio, and newsreel told and retold each event, always inter-
preting, reinterpreting, as if the drama itself could be distilled to some
formula defining the essence of winners and losers.

By 1927 the guideposts of narrative theory were not really that old.
Literary criticism as a discipline, with its academic rules and standards,
had developed in the Victorian and Edwardian eras simultaneously with
the study of myth and folklore. The theory was simple: we told ourselves
stories that held import for our lives. There was the story, and the meaning behind the story, and digging out the latter was the critic's job. It
wasn't as impossible as it sounded; some maps existed. In 1863, German
writer Gustav Freytag spotted common patterns in stories and sketched
out what is still taught today as Freytag's Pyramid. It is a simple and
elegant model, probably drawn on millions of chalkboards across the
literary world:

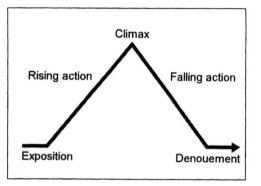

It looks very much like poor Icarus's fate: what goes up, must come down.

A few decades later, the Cambridge don and writer Sir Arthur Quiller-Couch divided Freytag's "rising action" into seven conflicts, each of which represented a basic human condition and thus a vital narrative: Man versus Man, God, Nature, Himself, Society, Woman, and one he called "Man Caught in the Middle." The labels changed with time and fashion, the latter two especially, but this idea of conflict assumed increased importance in almost every template of drafting a story. As 1927 progressed, conflict shaped the way people thought of the Orteig rivalry.

Who were the characters in this tale? By March the media had begun its mythmaking. Each flier seemed larger than life, and unreal. Each had a foe who had to be bested. Lindbergh's conflict was man against himself, his struggle against the seduction of sleep, which could kill him. Byrd and Nungesser would pit themselves against a natural world ruthlessly intent on their personal destruction. Everything about Levine suggested man pitched against his fellow man. Davis and Wooster labored to control The Machine, the same contest Fonck had entered, and lost.

De Pinedo's conflict was different, and initially deceptive. On the surface, his struggle also seemed to be against the elements: the waterspout, the jungle, the deluge, and circling birds of prey. As he conquered each, Nature threw another challenge at him. But the greatest danger lay at the end of the journey, where Il Duce waited. The premier expected great results from this flight; he must be satisfied. It was de

Pinedo's fate to be born and to fly in the nation that had introduced fascism to the troubled world. Could he conquer his fate? Could any of them?

At 6:57 a.m. on March 16, de Pinedo pointed the *Santa Maria* north "across the stretches of Brazilian jungles over which no man ever before had flown." It was a region inhabited by alligators, snakes, and "fierce semi-savage Indians," said the *Times*, a land of swamp where any forced landing meant never rising again. To those following his progress, the Lord of Distances had been swallowed by the Amazon.

It wasn't *that* bad, but he certainly had his troubles. After landing on the Paraguay at Saõ Luiz de Cáceres, de Pinedo and his crew were able to refuel. Yet it would be impossible to take off from this twisting, overhung stretch of river. A small river gunboat lay idling in port, and de Pinedo told the captain of his plight. "I can tow you somewhere, till we find enough open water," the amiable officer agreed.

The gunboat crew tied a line to the *Santa Maria*, and for three days the strange little procession searched for a straight stretch of river. Brazilians called the Mato Grosso the biggest forest in the world, and de Pinedo could believe it. "Through this eternal green jungle, damp and emitting strange odors hinting at rotting wood, mud, odd fruits, and plants new to us, we wound our way," he later said.

Bugs tormented them. They spent hours fighting off mosquitoes and flies. De Pinedo's navigator found it helpful to snap a pair of plastic gloves over his hands as armor; the three fliers took their meals in shifts, one eating while the others blasted away at the bugs with kerosene. At one point de Pinedo suggested fighting the bugs and heat by taking a swim; he had just pulled off his trousers when an alligator surfaced at the very spot where he proposed to dive. Someone shot it, and de Pinedo pulled his trousers back on.

Alligators weren't the worst things lurking, the Brazilians warned. "[I]t's not alligators that kill swimmers here," one said. "It's that voracious little fish you see swimming there, in that school. His teeth are like a wolf's. If you put your hand in the water he may grab it, and it's hard to shake him off." De Pinedo tied a piece of meat to a string and dropped it over the side. He felt a tug and brought up several piranhas.

Just before midnight on March 18, after cruising more than two hundred slow and winding miles, they finally hit a straight stretch of river.

The aviators bedded down for the night and took off at the first light of dawn.

They swung west on the Guaporé River, which formed the northern border between Bolivia and Brazil. The river was their road: they followed the Guaporé to its meeting with the Madeira, one of the Amazon's major tributaries. Covering 540,000 square miles, the Madeira Valley encompassed nearly 20 percent of the Amazon Basin and was larger than any Amazonian country but Brazil.

On March 20, the *Santa Maria* emerged from the jungle and landed in the provincial capital of Manaus, the largest city on the Amazon and at one time the world capital of the rubber trade. In 1910, at the peak of the rubber boom, every ball of smoked rubber from the forest's estimated 21.4 million rubber trees came to the floating docks of Manaus before shipment to the industrialized world. Two years later the bubble burst, and the world trade shifted to Singapore. Manaus was now a shell of its former self: the docks and rubber warehouses had deteriorated. The cages in the Zoological Garden stood empty. The suburbs at the edge of town were overgrown. The jungle had crept in.

For de Pinedo's arrival, Manaus reopened its Teatro Amazonas, the famous opera house inspired by Paris's Opéra Garnier. It rose above the river like a Gothic cathedral dwarfing a medieval town. This night, a special performance of *Madama Butterfly* was held in de Pinedo's honor. He sat in a thickly upholstered chair reserved for him in the center of the house, right before the stage, settled in the cushions, and sank into slumber; his hosts realized he had not slept for more than four straight hours since leaving Asunción. Though his snores competed with Puccini, the audience let him dream.

•

They started at dawn the next morning, hoping to make the 1,000-mile trip to Pará at the Atlantic mouth of the river before nightfall. By 11:30 a.m., they'd passed the ancient Indian site of Monte Alegre, a little over halfway there. The morning had been clear, but now the weather turned ugly. The mist and rain grew so thick that de Pinedo had to fly close to the southern bank, under the treeline, just to stay oriented. The river seemed a clear-cut road, but tributaries kept branching off, and no other landmarks existed to guide him. Pitch darkness descended, and de Pinedo could not see 150 feet ahead. Chain lightning darted around them, one stroke landing so close they were temporarily blinded. They feared they'd been hit; a strange vibration shook the *Santa Maria's* frame. Raindrops pelted the plane like rocks, and the open cockpit began to flood. Their battered radiator sprang twenty leaks; their maps, notebooks, and food floated inside the cabin. Ahead he thought he spotted a strip of silver; he headed for what turned out to be the ocean—and clear weather. They finally reached Pará after eleven punishing hours aloft. As soon as they pulled into the dock, de Pinedo inspected his plane and found that the propellers were bent out of shape. He told his companions quietly that they would not have survived another thirty minutes in the air.

They spent three days in Pará to make repairs. The city was the gateway for those steaming upriver, a crumbling provincial capital plagued by bouts of yellow fever. De Pinedo witnessed an alligator drive, where hundreds of the reptiles were rounded up and slaughtered; he visited the Zoological Gardens, where he observed a condor up close and judged it as "husky and heavy as a fat young boy." Outside the zoo he saw perched on the rooftops the condor's smaller cousin, the Urubu turkey vulture. After the daily showers, they stood erect with their wings outstretched, their feathers clacking in the breeze.

The rest of the trip should have been easy. On March 25, they flew north along the coast to Georgetown, Guyana, then crossed the Caribbean the next day. They followed the chain of islands to Pointe-à-Pitre, Guadeloupe; Port-au-Prince, Haiti; and Havana, Cuba. On March 29, they flew the 700 miles from Havana to New Orleans, reaching the mouth of the Mississippi in six and a quarter hours.

They touched down on the city's banks shortly after noon, making the *Santa Maria* the first foreign airplane ever to fly to the United States. De Pinedo had to look the part for such an occasion: he'd shaved with a straight razor while flying over the city, listening as the plane's phonograph played their only record, a foxtrot titled "Who." He'd donned golf knickers and polished his shoes. Their hosts expected haggard aviators to emerge from the seaplane. Instead, three trim, tanned, and stylish officers stepped ashore.

Reporters and photographers swarmed around the flier; the Italian consul and half the city's Italian population lined the shore. "Viva de Pinedo!" they cried out. "Viva Italia! Viva Mussolini!"

The questions began. What was the significance of his flight? It was a preview of the future, de Pinedo replied. In ten years, one would need only an airplane ticket to repeat his itinerary. What was their diet in the air? Bread, cheese, and wine. When some eyebrows rose at the last item, de Pinedo remembered America's Prohibition laws and added that they'd polished off the wine before touchdown.

They stayed in New Orleans three days before beginning the American leg of their tour. They attended the usual banquets and receptions, and de Pinedo spent hours answering a sack of telegrams from home. American papers trumpeted the fact that, with the Orteig Prize and de Pinedo's feat, the new day of the airplane had dawned. Aviation promised a new world, they predicted. Life would never be the same.

Some papers noted that even if de Pinedo did not *enter* the Orteig race, he still might win—at least symbolically. "The greatest performance is yet to come...the passage of the Atlantic," observed *The New York Times*. "It would be the irony of fate if Pinedo, to whom in his wanderings through the air nothing has yet been impossible, were to take the Northern Atlantic in his stride, as it were, while his rivals were still elaborately planning to make the crossing."

That was the heart of the matter: A symbolic victory held as much meaning as an actual one. A symbolic win would show the world that Europe, and Italy, mattered—that, indeed, the future lay in their hands. Long before the sky became a battleground in the Second World War, it became one for international prestige. France and the United States might be the only contestants so far in the Orteig race, but that did not mean the other Great Powers were sitting idle. In England, Captain W. H. Johnson-Wreford, an army veteran and cousin of the home secretary, had ordered from Tony Fokker's Amsterdam plant a single-engine monoplane capable of crossing the ocean in one hop. He predicted a flight by early summer. In Ireland, thirty-three-year-old Frank T. Courtney journeyed to the Dornier factory in Germany to order the Whale, an all-metal flying boat with a 72-foot wingspan. Also in Germany, Professor Hugo Junkers dusted off plans for an all-metal, low-winged monoplane able to cross the ocean; he ordered his factory to make two, and began searching for aviators capable of making such a flight.

The English and Germans were so far behind the leaders that there seemed little chance they could win. But the French were just as likely to be the first across as the Americans. At first the French fliers seemed hobbled, not by expertise or skill, but by lack of money. Yet as March became April, several former war aces appeared close to takeoff dates. Fonck was still searching for a second chance, while Nungesser was working steadily on his *L'Oiseau Blanc*, or *White Bird*. Even now it was undergoing tests at the Chartres Aerodrome. He and partner François Coli expected to take off sometime between May 10 and 15. There were others, too. Paul Tarascon, the first flier to register for the Orteig Prize, had recovered from his earlier crash and joined with Captain Dieudonné Costes for an attempt in a Potez biplane, *L'Oiseau Tango*. Maurice Drouhin and Jules Landry announced they would make the Paris–New York hop in a huge Farman Goliath, *L'Oiseau Bleu*. All assumed that within the next couple months, someone would win the prize. The question was, who?

Maybe de Pinedo, in his meandering way. On April 2, five weeks after Lindbergh placed his order for the *Spirit of St. Louis* and a week before the huge *American Legion* rolled from its hangar, de Pinedo turned west on his American tour. He flew to Galveston and San Antonio, and trailed the Rio Grande into New Mexico. He followed the Southern Pacific Railroad through the Rockies. On April 6, he cut through Arizona, landing at Roosevelt Reservoir, a manmade lake about sixty miles east of Phoenix, where he stopped to refuel. He planned to be in San Diego by the end of the day.

The *Santa Maria* pulled up to the dock at 10:14 a.m. The fliers were greeted by some local officials and the state manager of Standard Oil, the plane's official fuel. Standard Oil had built the temporary depot for this moment, and some local residents volunteered to lend a hand with the refueling. A carnival atmosphere prevailed; de Pinedo watched as motorboats filled with the curious buzzed nearby. Refueling would take two hours: Zacchetti and Del Prete supervised while the local contingent squired de Pinedo into the Apache Lodge, a shore-side hotel, where a quick lunch was scheduled. It was beautiful here in the desert: the sky was peregrine blue, and one could see for miles. It was 12:05 and de Pinedo was following his hosts into the rustic lodge when they all heard a commotion behind them. De Pinedo turned and looked back. The blood, he later said, curdled in his veins.

A wall of flame had risen up around his plane. He ran to the water's edge, unbelieving. The *Santa Maria* was burning from stem to stern. He watched in horror as Del Prete and Zacchetti jumped overboard to save themselves; an open manhole on the port side created such a draft that oxygen was audibly sucked into the inferno. The fire was too intense even to think of diving for the plane's extinguishers; anyone entering the cabin would have been turned to cinders. Others rushed extinguishers from the lodge, but by the time they got there it was too late. De Pinedo turned to the frozen crowd behind him and implored, "Somebody take some photographs! I want a final memory of my child!"

Nothing could be saved. Weakened by the flames, the engine supports collapsed, sending the two V-6 engines crashing to the lake bottom, sixty feet down. De Pinedo stood in silence and watched the plane burn. Soon all that remained was a blackened skeleton on charred pontoons, bumping pathetically against the banks of the reservoir.

Within minutes, the wireless sent the news across the world. "Sabotage!" the Italian papers cried: the fact that the flight was under Mussolini's wing lent credence to the rumor that this was the work of antifascist saboteurs. In the Italian Senate there were speeches, while the Pope compared de Pinedo to Napoleon in exile. The rumor was further fueled by onlookers who reported seeing someone flee the scene. "A curious kind of match thrown by an individual in a motor boat" led to the disaster, read the original communique. The same suspicion occurred to U.S. ambassador Henry Fletcher, who wired his condolences to Mussolini. "If a cowardly crime has been committed, the guilty will be discovered and punished," Fletcher vowed.

It took hours to get the whole story: the truth was more mundane. The cause was nothing more sinister than a tossed cigarette and a teenage boy. During refueling, the surface of Roosevelt Reservoir had glistened with a sheen of oil. A reporter for *The Arizona Republic* tracked down the boat from which the inferno was seen to spread. James Gibson, one of the volunteers, said several boys had been quarreling inside. One of them, a stranger, had lit a cigarette; they told him to extinguish it, and he did just that—by tossing it into the oil-slicked water. They watched in horror as the flames spread from their boat to the *Santa Maria*, the concentric center of the sheen.

It didn't take long to track down the fugitive, an eighteen-year-old volunteer named John Thomason. He admitted tossing the cigarette; he didn't mean anything by it, he pleaded; it was just instinct, tossing the fag end in the lake as he had a hundred times. He panicked when the plane went up; he lost his head and lit out in fear.

The fact that a discarded butt destroyed the *Santa Maria* after

18,000 miles of some of nature's cruelest assaults was more than a little absurd, but de Pinedo realized he had an international crisis on his hands if he did not say the right thing. On April 7, the day after the accident, he held a news conference at the Apache Lodge. The smell of the inferno still lingered in the air.

"The misfortune which overtook the *Santa Maria*," he told the assembled crowd, "was the result of carelessness by a small boy. In no way could the tragedy be connected with a plot against Fascism. It was purely an accident, and I am sure my Government will regard it in no other light."

Mussolini agreed: "I wish to express full assurances that Italy, linked by such strong chains of friendship to America, sees absolutely no connection between this painful incident and the fact that it occurred on American soil."

Il Duce knew a good opportunity when he saw one. Until the explosion, de Pinedo had been a free agent, an ambassador without a portfolio representing Italy. But now Mussolini stepped in as benefactor, and the gesture changed the nature of de Pinedo's tour. While the orphaned fliers caught a commercial airliner to San Diego, then a cross-country train to New York, he, Il Duce, would personally send a replacement plane to America. It would come to New York by steamer and be rebuilt in the hangars lining the East River. It would be an exact duplicate of de Pinedo's plane, and be christened the *Santa Maria II*. And if by that point the transatlantic race were still undecided, he hinted, who was to say whether the Lord of Distances might not consider taking part?

Stranger things had happened. The skies, like the future, belonged to everyone.

PART II

FIVE WEEKS

I always feel I am a traveler, going somewhere and to some destination. If I tell myself that the somewhere and the destination do not exist, that seems to me very reasonable and likely enough...I shall find then that not only the Arts, but everything else as well, were only dreams, that one's self was nothing at all.   —Vincent van Gogh to his brother, August 6, 1888

TEN

CRUEL DAYS

By mid-April, Atlantic Fever was infectious. Every entrant was described as a hero; each plane, a chariot of the gods. The rush to win the Great Atlantic Derby began to affect peoples' judgment, and veteran aviators made choices they may not have made otherwise.

By April 16, it seemed the entire aviation world was in or coming to New York, landing at the adjacent Roosevelt, Mitchel, and Curtiss fields. De Pinedo was on the West Coast, scheduled to board a train for Manhattan. Davis and Wooster were flying from Virginia to Long Island. Chamberlin and Acosta's *Columbia* nestled in a hangar by the landing field, going through an overhaul after its record flight. Richard Byrd's *America*, just released from Fokker's shop, waited for its introduction to the world.

A strange giddiness began to set in, almost like oxygen deprivation. Charles Levine set the tone: he felt that he was on a roll. His plane had set a record. A new engine should be installed in *Columbia* within a week, after which preparations for the Paris hop would be full speed ahead.

Levine and his pilots also seemed strangely unconcerned about the $25,000 cash prize. According to the rules, the NAA had to receive an entrant's application sixty days before his team made the hop, and the Bellanca team had not even filed. Levine tried to get the provision waived, but the rules committee would not bend. "It is hardly likely that the rules would be changed on a few days' notice," sniffed Captain R. R. Blythe, vice president of the NAA's New York chapter. "The matter would have to be taken up by Peter Adams of Boston, President of the Association, and a meeting called by him in Washington would have to sit on the matter."

That was too slow for Levine. For Bert Acosta, too, who told the press he soon hoped to be off. He and Chamberlin were both deluged with invitations to receptions and honors after their record flight; one, hosted by Mayor Walker, was scheduled for the following Monday. All rode the crest of the wave. Bellanca alone seemed unconcerned by the excitement: he refused to utter another word about the Paris flight until Walker's reception. Until then, he said, he hoped to catch up on the sleep he'd missed while Chamberlin and Acosta spent fifty-one hours in the air.

Forgoing the prize might seem impulsive, but Levine knew what he was doing. What was a mere $25,000 compared to the value of owning the first plane to fly nonstop across the ocean? To win the race, he'd spurn the prize.

Levine's presence in the race would create more turmoil than that of any other single participant, except perhaps Lindbergh. People expected financial backers to stay in the background—they might exert influence, but they did not seek publicity. In that way, Levine and Rodman Wanamaker were as different as night and day. Wanamaker was "old money"—conservative and stodgy, rarely appearing before the cameras and preferring to direct Byrd's progress through his lieutenant, Grover Whalen. Levine was wild and gambling, a new kind of venture capitalist who got involved firsthand. Unlike Wanamaker, he participated in the day-to-day operations, and unlike Wanamaker, he grasped the power of publicity. Before anyone else, Levine saw that the winner would be *more* than just a winner. He'd be an international phenomenon, bigger than any movie star—bigger than Valentino; bigger, even, than Chaplin. Those hitched to his coattails—the designer, the owner, the plane itself— would be just as big.

But what Levine had over his rivals in vision, he lacked in interpersonal skills. He seemed unable to hide his intentions. Chamberlin had heard the rumor that Levine did not consider him the "movie-type," probably from Bellanca. Someone had convinced Levine that Hollywood did not "like" blue-eyed actors, since they did not "film well." Chamberlin's eyes shone as blue as cornflowers. But Acosta was dark and swarthy, and loved by the ladies. Acosta was like Douglas Fairbanks Sr. and Rudolph Valentino mashed together and equipped with wings. Chamberlin was, at best, Harry Langdon.

Chamberlin and Acosta may have won a world record, but they had not won the right to fly the Bellanca to Paris. *Columbia's* cockpit and cabin had room for only two, and Levine said one of the fliers would have to be an experienced navigator. While Chamberlin held his peace, Acosta lobbied for them *both* to go. They'd already broken one world record—why not two? "Contrary to what has been said," he remarked, "I know quite a little about navigation, and we won't need any navigator. I studied it at the Throop Polytechnic School in Los Angeles before I ever became a pilot."

But on April 15, the day after the record flight, Levine revealed his cards. There was some talk of rigging *Columbia's* undercarriage to drop free after takeoff to cut wind resistance: "A man like Acosta would not need the undercarriage to land," he said. To save weight, Levine speculated, a compass might be the plane's only instrument for navigation. "A man like Acosta could take the plane across easily in thirty-two hours," he said. Chamberlin's name was conspicuously absent from these remarks. It was not hard for the blue-eyed Iowan to read the writing on the wall.

Others were out there, waiting to compete, though the world had largely forgotten them. There was the handsome Leigh Wade, fresh from his split with Levine. He said he would take off for Paris in six weeks if he could find a company to back him in time. And there was still the mail pilot, Lindbergh, with his crazy idea of flying alone. Fonck was in Paris, searching for engines, while Sikorsky planned the S-37, a variation of the doomed S-35, but with two engines instead of three.

And there was twenty-three-year-old lieutenant Winston W. Ehrgott, a West Pointer who flew with the New York National Guard. Ehrgott submitted his application on April 18; he was backed by the Aircraft Corporation of America, which claimed to be building a two-engine amphibious plane at the Sikorsky plant in College Point, New York. Ehrgott proposed that all the competitors postpone their flights until summer, when his plane would be ready; they could all race to Paris under a handicap system, he said. But the Sikorsky officials said they knew nothing of plans to build a plane at College Point, and the other aviators showed little interest in Ehrgott's suggestions.

So began a rolling series of mishaps and tragedies that changed the entire tenor of the race and convinced every pilot that he flew under a cloud of doom.

•

Richard Byrd, the expert planner, erred first, felled by an unchecked burst of joy.

Like Lindbergh and Davis, Byrd kept the *America*'s progress close to his vest—*extremely* close, considering his love of publicity. Even insiders were kept in the dark. On April 15, the day after the *Columbia*'s record flight, Byrd's biographer Charles J. V. Murphy asked Floyd Bennett whether the *America* wasn't in danger of being left behind. Bennett smiled. "The *America* is in a much more advanced stage of construction than most people know," he said without elaborating. "We're not worried. Besides, we're not in any race."

Was Bennett attempting irony? His wife portrayed him as a sphinx, keeping his opinions to himself. "We're not in any race" was indeed the team's standard fallback line, repeated like a mantra by Byrd. Yet Byrd's letters and actions from mid-January, when he signed the construction contract with Tony Fokker, until mid-April belie his words and show how desperately he wanted to win. In a letter dated January 15, Byrd told Bennett to "[K]eep the project absolutely confidential" and "First and most important, get the plane ahead of any other people who contemplate a similar project."

They were not above a little industrial spying: when Bennett heard in January that another trimotor Fokker was being built on the West Coast, Byrd hurried to California while mining his sources for details. It turned out that the mystery Fokker was being prepared for a flight from San Francisco to Honolulu, a distance of 2,400 miles. This team expected to fly in March. "If they make it successfully," wrote Byrd, "there is some danger of their attempting the Transatlantic flight and beating us to it. If Mr. Wanamaker had ordered the plane when we suggested it [back in November 1926], this would not have happened. I warned him what probably would happen."

There also was the question of the *America*'s crew. By January 1927 it seemed it would consist of Byrd, Bennett, and George "Rex" Noville, their flight engineer at the North Pole. But who would be the fourth? They needed two pilots for relief, an engineer, and a radioman. Bernt Balchen seemed the perfect pick, but Wanamaker was adamant that this be an all-American crew. At loose ends for a job and seemingly frozen out of the *America*, Balchen leapt at an offer to serve in Canada's first large-scale airlift operation, flying a ton of freight to miners and prospectors in Churchill, then the nation's northernmost outpost of civilization. From March 22 to April 17 he and three other pilots flew passengers, dynamite, motors, and wooden crates a total of 12,724 miles in frequent snowblind conditions. It reminded Bernt of Norway, and he felt right at home.

Although Wanamaker essentially killed Balchen's hopes of participating in the Derby, Byrd saw his one-month Canadian adventure as a desertion. Byrd could be loyal, but in exchange he demanded a fealty that seemed medieval. "I can't say much for Balchen if he wants to desert us at the first attractive proposition offered him," he wrote to Bennett. "Those are the folks that don't go very far in life. Of course, he might go up there and find an island, but certainly it is he [who] hasn't played the game with us."

If Balchen's doubts of Byrd's veracity began while flying the *Josephine Ford* cross-country, Byrd's doubts about Balchen began now. His was not a reasoned suspicion, however; it ran much deeper and opened a window into his character. Byrd could be generous, but only when the recipient played by his rules.

His distrust extended to Tony Fokker's motives and reliability. In January, Fokker started building the *America*'s fuselage in his Atlantic Aircraft factory. He ordered the giant 74-foot wing to be shipped from his factory in Holland. On March 18, construction was far enough along that Byrd told Wanamaker that the plane should be finished by April 15 and all tests completed by the first week of May. In the same letter, he told Wanamaker that he had made friends with Atlantic Aircraft's chief stockholder, a Mr. Llorillard Spencer, whom Byrd called "a reasonable man." Spencer assured the Explorer that "the company will not permit Mr. Fokker to embarrass us with any unreasonable calls for commercialization of our project," Byrd wrote.

The dislike swung both ways. As the *America* took shape, Byrd met with Fokker to inspect his monoplane. Fitzhugh Green, who would soon depart for Paris to arrange a grand reception when Byrd arrived, tagged along. Fokker was gruff; Green asked the questions; Byrd didn't say a word. "Suppose he falls into the water?" Green asked.

"He'll sink in thirty minutes," Fokker replied.

"Suppose he is forced to come down on land in the darkness—can't see the ground?"

"Probably kill the whole crew."

Byrd didn't bat an eyelash. Finally, after a beat, he raised a long forefinger to his cheek. "When will she be finished?" he asked.

Now he was appealing to Fokker's professional vanity, which was considerable, and the answer was straightforward. It would be finished on time.

The plane looked like the *Josephine Ford*, only bigger, in order to accommodate the three J-5 engines and huge load of fuel. They expected it to be at least 3,000 pounds heavier than on the flight over the Pole. The *America* carried its 1,200-gallon tank behind the cockpit, able to carry over 7,000 pounds of gasoline; the tank had a dump valve in case of an impending crash, and the empty tank could serve for flotation if they came down in the ocean. They planned to pack a special waterproof radio set, two rubber lifeboats, emergency food and equipment, some Very pistols for night flares, and a kite for the wireless antenna. A short platform connected the cockpit to each outboard engine so that, in an emergency, a man could lie flat and make repairs. The cockpit sat farther forward than the *Josephine Ford*'s, and was fitted with dual controls; like the *American Legion*, the pilots sat side by side.

Construction was out of Byrd's hands, but not so the myriad other details. In February and March, Byrd was all over the place. Through Grover Whalen, he arranged for Wanamaker to lease Roosevelt Field and smooth out the runway, filling in the three dirt tracks and shoring up the soft spots that had doomed Fonck's S-35. He walked every inch of the ground, obsessively, repeatedly, striving for the same ice-slick smoothness they'd achieved at Spitzbergen for the *Josephine Ford*. He asked the U.S. Weather Bureau to make weather predictions for the transatlantic flights and to draw up daily weather maps of the North Atlantic. The bureau assigned Dr. James H. Kimball of its New York office to the task, which he did by procuring radio reports from seagoing ships in the region. Byrd did this all while finishing up his cross-country lecture tour to pay off the remaining bills from the North Pole: from January 3 to February 5 he visited Charlotte, New Orleans, San Antonio, and Austin; he returned to San Antonio, then hit El Paso, Maricopa, Phoenix, San Diego, Los Angeles, Glendale, Long Beach, Pasadena, Santa Barbara, Bakersfield, San Francisco, Eugene, Portland, and Tacoma. He sped back east through Illnois and Ohio, and by March 1, he was in Virginia. In mid-March, Byrd formed a "publicity control organization" for the race—two former newspapermen named "Klemfus and Gillespie" who were loved, or at least tolerated, by fellow journalists and who "would have your interests at heart," he assured the ever-skittish Wanamaker. Gillespie especially "fully understands how you are desirous of disassociating the expedition from any commercial aspects, and thinks he can so control publicity that your objects and aims can be realized."

That was the crux of the matter: control. Byrd seemed to feel that with enough planning, every obstacle, emergency, and criticism—even every bowel movement—could be anticipated and controlled. He sent Fitzhugh Green to France to try to organize things on the other side of the Atlantic. On April 12, Green arrived in Paris and began meeting with French and American authorities. Within two days, French naval, army, and civil air services all gave him charts and documents that could aid the *America* in a safe landing. Byrd also smoothed over hurt feelings when they arose. "We are simply in this thing together," he wrote to Grover Whalen, "and the big thing is to play the game with each other and to not misunderstand." He designed a "Low Protein Diet" for his crew—heavy on the cereals and fruit, no hot coffee or soup, meat only once a day. "In this age . . . we get too much protein, not enough of the natural mineral salts, and nowhere near enough 'roughage,'" he said. He woke every morning at five and was often early to bed. "For the intestines, a teaspoon of lactose or sugar of milk, in a glass of milk, with meals will do wonders for constipation."

Yet not everything could be controlled: his time and the demands made on it, for one. Fans wanted Byrd's time; they wanted to ride in his plane, to accompany him on his historic flight across the sea. Hundreds of letters, mostly from women, streamed in from all over the nation. From Ruth Haviland of Kansas City: "Would you consider taking me with you as a first female passenger to Europe. I had flying experience. Am 21 years of age. Please give me your serious consideration. Wire me collect." From Beatrice Evelyn Byrd, who claimed to be a distant cousin and thus deserved a seat; from a waitress in Pittsburgh, who promised to bring a lot of food. From Virginia Castle, who said "if you won't take me, will you at least take me for a 5-mile ride in the plane?" From another Evelyn Byrd, this one a twenty-seven-year-old schoolteacher in Seattle: "[T]o be different, why don't you take the first lady passenger? And why not an Evelyn Byrd?"

Byrd's press corps answered them with a standard reply: "I have your telegram [or letter] but am very sorry that I cannot take you along with me on the flight as we have to take along all the gasoline we possibly can and one extra person would add materially to the weight of the plane. However, your courage is to be admired."

What was happening? Byrd was not the only rival to receive such cards and telegrams. Lindbergh would be famously flooded with fan mail, for this flight and future ones. Bernt Balchen, once he entered the race, got pleas from girls—especially those of Norwegian ancestry. Fonck had received his share in 1926, but not as many since "Atlantic Fever" at that time had not yet captured the public's imagination.

But something bigger than fan worship was taking form. Byrd, usually so sensitive to the public pulse, missed the signs. None of the American fliers really understood the public dreams tapped into by the Orteig Prize. Most of the pleas came from women in their twenties and thirties (when they provided details). These women felt trapped by their roles in society—the schoolteacher; the waitress; the Pennsylvania woman who had given birth to twelve children, seven of whom had died. There was so much talk then about the "New Woman"—a dynamo of sex and self-assertion—but where was *their* runway to this new lifestyle? There wasn't one, that was the brutal truth, and they were trapped, unless, as Daedelus said, "the air and sea are free." They looked to the sky and pleaded—

Please take me along.

•

On April 16, two days after the Bellanca's record flight, Fokker's mechanics trundled the *America* out the doors of his factory at Hasbrouck Heights, New Jersey, and pushed her to a nearby landing field. They were four weeks ahead of their publicly announced unveiling; a mere one day behind the target date set in Byrd's March 18 letter to Wanamaker. The New York journalists assigned to the race were usually a shrewd lot, but they had been completely fooled this time. So casually was this first test undertaken that none was present to cover the event. Charles Murphy, Byrd's publicist, called the deception "malicious," probably because he was as much in the dark as anyone. The news of what had happened did not break until two hours later.

Tony Fokker took the helm, as he usually did when testing a new plane for the first time. His mechanics had only partially filled one of the wing tanks with gas and did not put any in the enormous 1,200-

gallon tank in the fuselage. He could not stay up long with so little gas, only an hour or so. That was okay, since he planned only to circle the field, testing the handling in the air and during takeoff and landing. A haze had settled over the field, so the ceiling was low. But that was fine, too, for Fokker's main concern at this point was a possible problem with design. He suspected that the *America* was nose-heavy, and he hoped to determine why.

Bennett had worried about that, too. Two days earlier, Noville and he had spent the day eliminating weight from the cabin and testing the radio. Bennett lightened the load by about 200 pounds when he installed smaller or lighter parts or cut equipment down to bare bones. For example, he cut out dust caps on the motor, since he did not think they would be bothered much by dust when they flew over the ocean.

But at the last minute, Byrd wanted to ride. Having heard that Fokker was taking her up, he contacted Bennett and Noville, and they clambered aboard. Several people tried to dissuade him, but Byrd was too excited. He would later say, "I did not want to accept the plane without personally observing its performance." Yet there was still plenty of time for that. This was nothing more than a case of boyish enthusiasm.

Fokker and Bennett sat side by side in the cockpit, Fokker closest to the door. Byrd stood behind Fokker's seat and Noville behind Bennett's, holding on. They took off at 5:17 p.m., clearing the runway in less than four seconds and soaring aloft without difficulty. Fokker kept her up for forty minutes, then banked for a return to the runway. He beamed: these planes were his children, and this one had performed well. Byrd, Bennett, and Noville exchanged smiles.

But as Fokker cut power in preparation for landing, the ship pitched nose down with breathtaking abruptness and hurtled toward the ground at dangerous speed. More by instinct than conscious thought, Fokker gave the engine full power, yanking the nose back up and regaining control. The plane arced up to a safe altitude.

They circled the field while Fokker tried to think of a way out of their dilemma. He realized that he should have said no to the extra weight, but he'd given in. The huge gas tank blocked the passage back from the cockpit, making it impossible for Byrd and Noville to crawl back and equalize the load. Fokker wet his lips and throttled back again. The instant that power diminished, the ship slipped into a vertical dive.

Fokker glanced back at Byrd. "We've got to come down anyway," Byrd said.

In a minute, Byrd realized, his $100,000 assemblage of machinery might be reduced to splinters and twisted metal, and there was nothing he could do. Fokker brought *America* down with all his skill. A hundred feet above the ground, he cut the engine and the grace of the controlled descent ebbed away. He turned to Bennett and asked him to turn the handle controlling the stabilizer to its lowest position; Bennett complied, but unknown to any of them the line had jammed. The great wing wobbled. Time slowed for Noville, and he knew a crash was inevitable. But that fraction of a second seemed to drag on forever, like the "condensation of a century," he later said. Byrd held on to the heavy steel upright behind Fokker's seat with all his strength; Noville grasped the back of Bennett's chair.

America touched down with her tail up and slid along the field for 50 yards. Fokker pulled the wheel into his lap and tried to wrestle down the tail. The relatively low landing speed of 60 miles per hour made the elevators only partially effective: instead of dropping, as it should have, the tail continued to rise. The plane's nose swung low as she stumbled across the field; soon the propeller would chew into the ground. Fokker could imagine the result: the framework would telescope back; the engine would crush them; the giant tank would rip from its straps and tumble forward, squashing them like bugs.

Instead, the unexpected occurred. The plane hit a soft spot and the center propeller struck the ground at an angle, pushing the motor to the right. The ship became a pinwheel with the nose as its axis. The plane bumped up and over in a somersault and crashed onto its back. Hot oil from a broken tank streamed over the pilots' compartment. The forward motor sprang from its steel housing and smashed into Bennett's lap.

There was an eerie silence, then Bennett's voice, racked by pain: "Look out—she might catch fire!"

The *America's* interior resembled a slow-motion merry-go-round, where each man saw and remembered particulars in a different way. In there, the world flipped over, rather than the plane. There came a horrific *crack* as if every inch of the ship were being reduced to kindling, and something struck Byrd a stunning blow to the small of his back and his head. Noville pitched forward against Bennett's seat; a pipe buckled and hit him in the side. The impact snapped Byrd's right arm. He later told others that, as soon as the wheels touched the ground, Fokker bolted from his chair and made a frantic effort to open the trapdoor above them in the cockpit's canopy and jump out. However, this would have been impossible, since the outline of the broken steering column was imprinted in Fokker's abdomen, showing that he'd wrestled with the wheel all the way to the end. He may, however, have risen and tried to open the door when they began to flip, because of all of them, Fokker alone was thrown clear and fell headfirst to the ground.

The others worried about fire, the death of Fonck's two crewmen uppermost in their minds. Oily smoke hissed around them, and this increased their terror. Noville thought the oil dripping on his face was blood; he was sure he'd been cut in two. Though in agony, he tore a hole in the fuselage with his hands and crawled from the plane. Byrd followed, and looked around. Fokker lay facedown on the grass, unconscious, stunned, or dead. Noville writhed in agony from his injuries, then fainted from the pain. Grover Whalen, Doc Kinkade, and half a dozen others sprinted toward them from a nearby hangar. Byrd did not see flames—someone at the last moment had the presence of mind to cut the gas switch, though neither Fokker nor Bennett ever remembered . doing so. Then it hit him: Where was Floyd?

For all Byrd's faults, he could be truly heroic when a friend or colleague was in danger. He was at his best at moments like these—such as the time when, as a young officer visiting the Mexican coast, he dove into a riptide to save a drowning sailor. Now he dove back into the *America* to save Floyd Bennett. Despite his broken arm, he picked his way through a jumble of rods, seats, frame, and gear to find his old friend. What he saw would haunt him forever. Bennett hung upside down in the wreck, held in place in his seat by the strap and the weight of the motor pinned against him. Both his legs were broken; his face streamed with blood. Oil covered his eyes; at first, Byrd thought that, too, was blood and that Floyd was blind.

Byrd leaned over Bennett and said he was there. Bennett tried to open his eyes, but failed. "Guess I'm done for," he whispered. "I'm all broken up. I can't see, and I have no feeling in my left arm."

"Nonsense, old man," Byrd replied, but to himself admitted his friend might be right. It helped a bit when he wiped away the oil and Floyd could see again. By now, others had arrived, and helped cut Bennett free. They carried him from the plane, then righted the *America*.

There were reports by now that Fokker had come to, and that he and Byrd stood outside the plane shouting at one another. Ambulances screamed up and rushed the injured men to the Hackensack hospital.

The injuries to Fokker, Byrd, and Noville proved less serious than expected. Fokker sustained bumps, bruises, and a slight concussion, and was released from the hospital the next day. X rays showed that Byrd's right wrist was broken, but that would heal. Even Noville, first thought close to death from unexplained internal injuries, recuperated fast: he suffered a concussion, a badly strained muscle in his groin, and a blood clot in his leg, which was quickly removed in an operation. All were expected to fly again within a few weeks.

But Bennett's injuries were truly serious, even life-threatening. He was out of the race for good. In addition to a broken leg and a tremendous gash across his forehead, his skull was fractured and his left lung punctured by a broken rib. When he learned he was out of the race, his heart broke too.

What about the *America?* Would she fly again? After an inspection, Fokker thought she would. Though the center engine, propeller, and cockpit were all smashed up, the giant wing and wing engines remained unscathed. The principal damage had occurred to the tubular steel molding that cradled the center engine: this had telescoped back inside the fuselage and to one side, and it was this that had injured Bennett and Noville. There was some disagreement over whether the *America* had crashed after hitting a soft spot in the runway or because of the lift of the tail, but engineers at the scene figured the problem could be fixed by adding ballast aft in the fuselage. Fokker told the press he expected to return the *America* to racing shape within four days. Clarence Noorduyn, the president of Atlantic Aircraft, was a little more cautious. It would take three weeks before she was ready to fly again, he predicted.

The *America* might be patched up, but any working relationship between Byrd and Fokker was ruined. Byrd immediately began to spread the tale that Fokker had panicked and tried to abandon the plane before they came to a stop: he told this to Cora Bennett, who believed him, and printed the story in his autobiography, *Skyward.* "Maybe Byrd was excited and imagined this," countered Fokker, "a description more worthy of a layman than a supposed technician." What had before been a controlled irritation between the two now developed into full-blown hatred.

Byrd fell into despondency. He would never admit it, but he had to know that his insistence on riding in the test flight had led to the crash and to Floyd's injuries. He had difficulty admitting fault and tended to blame others—in this case, Fokker. He doubted he could continue without his friend and said as much to Wanamaker, who adopted a wait-and-see attitude. But Byrd was an emotional man, perhaps more so than any other flier in the race, and he could not keep his doubts hidden. Within a day of the crash, every rival either visited Byrd in the hospital or sent his condolences. "We feel it deeply," Acosta said. "It is too bad that the fates which apparently control the destinies of men in our business should have so treated Commander Byrd and his associates."

A week after the crash, Balchen flew from Canada to New Jersey. Byrd and Noville had already checked out of the hospital; only Bennett remained, alone in his room. His right leg was in a plaster cast, stretched to the ceiling by weights; the top half of his mechanical bed was elevated to support his bandaged shoulders. His eyes drooped from sedatives. Still, he managed a grin when he saw Balchen walk in, and he pointed to the cables and pulleys around him. "Ever fly in a cockpit like this?" he said.

Bennett was glad for the company. Cora had not visited yet, laid up herself with a bout of pneumonia in a Manhattan hospital. Byrd visited when he could, but the *America*'s crew and sponsors were running around like maddened ants trying to rebuild their colony. Bennett grabbed the trapeze bar above his head and hoisted himself up. It hurt him to talk, but he took a sip from the glass beside him and explained what had happened.

Bennett winced as he talked, not simply from the physical pain. It would be a long time before he could fly again, and he might never again be strong enough for another major expedition. He had talked often of Byrd's plans for a flight over the South Pole once the Derby was history, but things would be far different now for Byrd with Floyd out of the picture. Balchen tried to avoid mentioning the transatlantic race, but Bennett was not one for evasion.

"Byrd's getting another pilot," he said.

"Who will it be?"

Bennett shrugged. It was uncertain. There was trouble in the Bellanca camp; it could be one of the two nonstop fliers. Personally, he thought it would be Acosta, but who could tell? There was a pause: Bennett looked in Balchen's face and saw the question.

"Probably you wonder why your name isn't on the list," he said. "Rodman Wanamaker is putting up the money for the flight. He named the ship *America*, and he wants an all-American crew. You're not a citizen." Bennett's eyes began to droop. "So that's the way the wind sock blows."

Balchen crept toward the door, but Bennett opened his eyes and called after him. "You've seen the ship at the factory. How long will it take to get up in the air again?"

"A month maybe."

Bennett nodded, and his head dropped on the pillow. Balchen closed the door.

•

There *was* trouble in the Bellanca camp, and it grew worse by the day. The team that should have been the closest to takeoff was instead the most rocked by internal dissension. On April 17, one day after the *America's* crash, the new Whirlwind engine was installed in *Columbia*. Two days later Levine dropped a bomb. He announced that either Chamberlin or Acosta would be replaced by an experienced navigator. Such an addition, he explained, was indispensable and could not be avoided. "The choice [of pilot] will not be made until the last minute before the flight, and it will then be determined by lot," Levine told the press in his office on Broadway. "Both pilots will appear upon the field in flying togs. Their names will be written separately on slips of paper. One slip will be drawn. The name on it will decide the flyer."

For navigator, Levine tapped Lloyd Bertaud, whom he believed one of the best around. Bertaud was well known in flying circles: an aviator since 1912, he was tall and powerfully built like Acosta, with a large shock of sandy hair. He had the same devil-may-care attitude as Bert, and in some versions was the second pilot in Acosta's infamous night flight around the Metropolitan clock tower. He was a veteran of the airmail service and had been flying a route between Cleveland and New Jersey when Levine took him on. The two had a history: after Bertaud organized the Eastern Division's airmail pilots into a bargaining group, Levine became a member, then bid, unsuccessfully, on the new route between New York and Chicago.

People liked the thirty-one-year-old Bertaud: his happy-go-lucky

reputation was second only to Acosta's. That he was considered so af-
fable is surprising, since today he is primarily remembered for the ac-
rimony he introduced into the Bellanca team. He'd flown since age
twelve, barnstormed with the famous "lady-flyer" Katie Stinson, trained
Great War air cadets, won an air race in Kansas City, and set an endurance record in 1922 with Stinson's younger brother Eddie by staying
aloft for twenty-two hours. The famous "Flying Parson" Belvin Maynard
wed Bertaud to Helen Lent in a well-publicized flight over New York
City. He was pals with both Chamberlin and Acosta, and dined with
them frequently, cracking jokes about the exploits of their employer,
Charles Levine.

Despite the public pronouncements of fairness, Clarence Chamberlin held no illusions about whom Levine wanted in the cockpit for the
flight to Paris. Clarence was *not* Levine's idea of a flier, he'd been heard
to say. Instead of shiny boots and riding breeches, Chamberlin wore a
bow tie, loud socks, and "plus-fours," those trousers extending four
inches below the knee favored by golf pros. Levine declared privately
that Acosta and Bertaud would make much better screen impressions
than Chamberlin—he thought they should make the flight together because of the movie offers that would pour in as soon as they landed.

In this case, however, Levine underestimated Giuseppe Bellanca.

When it came to his old friend the little Sicilian stood his ground.
He was willing to see Bertaud replace Acosta for the sake of harmony,
but regarding Chamberlin, he delivered his own ultimatum. Bellanca
sent Levine a registered letter in which he declared that unless Chamberlin made the flight, he was through with the whole undertaking and
would leave the Columbia Aircraft Corporation as well.

While this was playing out behind the scenes, the other rivals were
moving forward with their plans. Charles Nungesser declared he would
take off from Paris on Sunday, April 24, though bad weather eventually
scotched his plans. Maurice Drouhin announced that he had paired
with a French navy navigator and would take off in a 1,000-horsepower
Farman Goliath before mid-May. Noel Davis looked ready to leave in
the *American Legion* at any time. To counter these threats, it was believed the Bellanca would try to take off as quickly and quietly as possible: in the early morning—perhaps even by the light of an automobile's
headlights—when the plane could taxi to the end of Roosevelt Field
and gas up before anyone knew it.

The French threat caused Bellanca the greatest worry, he admitted. He wanted his plane always ready to take off should a wire come across the Atlantic saying that Nungesser or Drouhin had flown. "If it were an American plane," he said, "then we would have nothing but best wishes, but as she is of another nationality, the spirit of competition is heightened. We want the honor of the first non-stop flight to come here."

They planned their route and groomed their plane. Chamberlin studied the North American weather maps, lent to all rivals by Byrd. Acosta arranged the delivery and installation of a high-powered radio. Bertaud mapped a new flight route, one somewhat south of the Great Circle and closer to the steamship lanes. The new route, he hoped, would lessen the chance of their flying through low-temperature fog or mist, the ideal conditions for icing. Ice was a killer: it changed a wing's contour and decreased its lifting power, which could mean a sudden plummet to the sea. Ice had formed on the wings of five mail planes during the previous winter, and all had gone down.

The Brooklyn Chamber of Commerce even did its part to prepare for a departure. Levine surmised correctly that whoever made it to Paris first would win the $25,000, whether or not they adhered to the sixty-day rule. But Raymond Orteig would not say as much until the following month, so Levine was working on instinct, not guarantees. On Saturday, April 23, the Chamber made his life easier. It announced that it would give $15,000 to the crew of the *Columbia* if they succeeded in the Paris hop. The offer would last thirty days. Ralph Jonas, the chairman, said the Chamber made its offer because of civic pride and the "magnificent feat" of the endurance record. The announcement came after a nighttime meeting with Levine, who also belonged to the Chamber.

Sunday, April 24, was set as the plane's official christening, scheduled·for 4:00 p.m. Crowds from New York and Long Island gathered early on this bright, clear day, many toting picnic baskets. The New York *World* estimated that five thousand people showed up; Curtiss Field had all the semblance of a county fair. Between 3:00 and 4:00 p.m., the dignitaries arrived: Levine, his wife, Grace, and their nine-year-old daughter, Eloyse; the Chamberlins, Acostas, Bellancas, Bertauds; chief mechanic John Carisi and his crew; and the Brooklyn Chamber president Ralph Jonas and his fifteen-year-old daughter, Grace.

At 4:00 p.m., Eloyse Levine climbed a stool positioned at the nose of the plane. She carried a beribboned bottle of ginger ale. A left-hander, she struck the propeller with such force that she got a good drenching, not to mention a few scratches from shattered glass. "I christen you *Columbia!*" she yelled. A burst of applause rose from the spectators. Undaunted by the soaking, Eloyse turned to her father and asked if she could go for a ride in the plane she'd just named. And how about her friend Grace, too? It seemed a reasonable request, and a good climax to the ceremony.

Chamberlin smiled. What was a little spin around the field? He climbed into the cockpit, then John Carisi started up the engine and climbed into the cabin behind him, settling onto the "shelf" of the big gas tank for the ride. The two girls were lifted up to sit in the chair beside Chamberlin. They smoothed down their dresses and set their hats on straight. They were quite pleased with themselves. This would be fun.

And so began the flight that would define Chamberlin—not so much as a competitor, but as something more. The girls waved to their parents as *Columbia* taxied down Curtiss Field. As the plane turned and headed back, it lurched while lifting from the ground. Those inside felt nothing but the slightest bump. But one landing strut hung loose beneath them and the left wheel tipped in, now a useless appendage.

"Oh, my God," whispered a pilot in the crowd. He knew what this meant, and passed the word back to *Columbia*'s hangar. As it later turned out, a pin in the left shock absorber had sheered off as the plane took its last bounce, causing the front strut to drop from the fuselage. The left wheel wobbled uselessly. In Bellanca's planes, the landing gear spread down from the bottom of the fuselage; two struts held the wheel, extending away from the body at a forty-five-degree angle. The dangling wheel would not hold any weight when the plane landed.

In the air, Chamberlin and his passengers had no idea of the danger. Neither did the girls' parents or the crowd. They watched the plane with interested but unconcerned eyes. But behind them in the hangar, John Carisi's mechanics were tearing at the wheel of a dolly, trying to get it off so that Chamberlin could be made to understand what had gone awry. As the mechanics ran out with the wheel, veteran airmail pilot Dean Smith climbed into the cockpit of a nearby Curtiss Oriole and started the engine. Paul Herman, his mechanic, grabbed the wheel and climbed inside.

In a minute they were in the air; in another minute, they'd pulled beside *Columbia*. Trouble was the last thing on Chamberlin's mind. It had been a pleasant few minutes aloft and the girls were chatting away. Chamberlin enjoyed being around the Levines. True, his boss could be difficult, but the little bald-headed bulldog did have vision and, like Chamberlin, loved the two great toys of the new century, wings and wheels. While others grew red in the face or turned white with rage, Chamberlin would sit quietly, a slight smile on his lips. And he liked Grace Levine and her girls. She'd insist he come in for a snack whenever he flew Charlie home. Now he saw the little biplane pull beside him; the passenger held a tire out the window and pointed down. "I wonder why those damn fools are waving a tire at me?" he thought. "Probably they want a race." He leapt ahead of the Oriole, but both Smith and Herman kept waving so frantically that he knew something was wrong. He glanced down at his landing gear and spotted the problem immediately. He nodded to the Oriole to let them know he understood.

"I guess we have lost our landing gear, John," he said over his shoulder to Carisi. A second plane hummed up; the new pilot also pointed to make sure Chamberlin knew the danger. The Bellanca circled smoothly, escorted by the two planes; word began to spread among the thousands on the field. Spectators jumped from their cars and turned their faces up. "What will he do?" they asked one another.

Inside the plane, the girls were still having the time of their lives. They got a great kick out of the behavior of their escorts, especially the guy waving the tire around. As they talked, Chamberlin figured the odds. He had to tell the girls what was happening, yet at the same time he couldn't scare them. He turned to the seat beside him and smiled. "One of the wheels is loose," he said. "When we come down we may turn around or turn over and get jammed up a little, but I won't let you be hurt. You will be safe enough." He laughed reassuringly, as if this happened every day, and the girls smiled.

Down on the ground, matters were considerably tenser. People had begun to realize what might happen if the big plane turned over with the two girls inside. The escorts landed, and the field was cleared by motorcycle cops. Men dashed off for fire extinguishers; they piled into two cars to chase the plane should it heel over and catch fire. A field ambulance arrived from Mitchel Field, its big red cross aglow in the setting sun. Grace Levine twisted a handkerchief and softly began to cry. When Charles Levine and Ralph Jonas saw the ambulance pull up, they shuddered and turned away.

Carisi leaned out the side of the cabin and wondered whether he might not be able to pull out the landing gear enough that it might bear *some* weight, no matter how briefly. He crawled over Chamberlin's lap and hung, head down, in the blast of the propeller; Clarence held on to his legs with both hands while clutching the control stick between his knees. If he slipped or let go, Carisi would be a goner. But the head mechanic found there was not much he could do. He crawled back in, and they tried to find another solution.

The first thing to do was lighten the plane. They carried about 350–400 pounds of sand by the tail to serve as ballast to keep *Columbia* nose up when she landed "light"; Chamberlin told Carisi to start passing him those bags one at a time. He wanted as little weight as possible in the plane when he brought her down. He circled far from the crowd over Roosevelt and dumped the ballast over the side, but each time he dropped a bag from the cockpit, an energetic motorcycle cop would speed from sandbag to sandbag, evidently thinking Chamberlin was dropping messages. He dashed from one to another like a dog chasing sticks, and Chamberlin was scared to death one would drop on his head and kill him. Finally, the policeman found a manufacturer's "O.K." tag fastened to one of the bags; he rushed back to the crowd to tell them everything was okay in the plane.

Soon all the ballast was overboard. Carisi and Grace Jonas had grown airsick from the circling. They'd been in the air nearly fifty minutes, and now they had to land. Chamberlin figured Roosevelt would be best, since it was longer and smoother, but just about then a third plane flew up with "MITCHEL" chalked on the side. The pilots and mechanics down below had come to the conclusion that this would be best, since the crowds and their cars could not get there as easily. Chamberlin waved his hand and headed to the army field, as did the army ambulance beneath him.

Chamberlin told Carisi and Eloyse to crawl back in the cabin, behind the big gas tank. Place yourself on the side of the ship where the wheel is good, he said. Carisi piled some remaining sandbags in front of the tank, and Eloyse crawled over. "Is this far enough?" Carisi asked, and Chamberlin motioned them a little farther back, two-thirds of the way to the tail. Carisi sat with his back to the rear partition and lifted

Eloyse into his arms. He tucked her head into his chest, put her arms under his arms, and waited. He had done all he could.

Now Chamberlin turned to Grace Jonas, who sat up front beside him. She still thought this was all a lark. He told her to take his seat pad and hold it against her face so that if she were thrown forward she'd still be somewhat protected. With her other hand, she braced herself against the instrument panel before her. Chamberlin loosened all the windows in front so that if there was a crash, they had a slim chance of being thrown clear.

Grace did as she was told. It was scary, sure, but Mr. Chamberlin didn't seem frightened, so it was exciting, too. Besides, Eloyse was being so brave in the back, and she was six years younger. Grace had no choice but be brave.

Everything now depended upon Chamberlin. He noticed strange things about himself: his eyesight grew sharper; his breathing seemed to slow. He maneuvered over Mitchel Field and waited until the ambulance arrived. He banked and headed into the wind. Those below knew the critical moment had come. A mass of cars roared from Curtiss Field toward Mitchel, jamming the road. Grace Levine sat with a strained face as her husband's chauffeur drove at full speed to where *Columbia* would land. Bellanca had watched through binoculars as the plane circled for nearly an hour; he started his car, and a reporter rushed up. What effect will this have on the Paris flight if the plane is damaged? the man asked.

Bellanca stared at the reporter in disbelief. "To hell with the Paris flight if those girls and those boys are not [sic] hurt," he said.

Chamberlin swooped lower in a big circle, closer to the field. He heard nothing except the wind and the engines. It was strangely peaceful inside. He cut speed gradually. When he was finally around 30 feet above the field, he banked to the right so that when the plane came down on the slick, wet grass, she'd land on the tail, right wheel, and right tip of the wing—a "three-point landing." The plane touched down and rolled about 200 feet, then the wing scraped the grass and *Columbia* wheeled gently to the right. As she lost speed, she settled on her broken left wheel, causing the left wing to drop and touch the ground. In an unexpected way, this straightened the plane, causing her to angle back to the left again. *Columbia* slid to a stop without pitching on her nose or even tearing the fabric of her wings as they scraped the ground.

The crowd converged upon them. Grace and Eloyse were lifted out and ushered to a car. They turned back to Chamberlin, who was just exiting the plane.

"Thank you for the ride, Mr. Chamberlin," said one of the girls. They held out their hands. Chamberlin took them and laughed.

"Glad you liked it," he said.

"Oh, we did, and we would like to go with you again some time."

The mob descended on Chamberlin. Mitchel Field's commandant called the landing "the most adept work I have ever seen." Bellanca ran up and pounded his old friend on the back: "I knew you could do it," he cried. Acosta and Bertaud got him to one side and pumped him for details.

It would indeed be one of the most deft and amazing maneuvers of the race—though one quickly forgotten in all the uproar over winners and losers. The crowd flowed to the officers' club, where the girls had been taken to be checked out by doctors. The two had heard by then what Chamberlin had really done, how close they had come to death or serious injury. They came up to him again, a little more solemnly than earlier, and thanked him for saving their lives. At that, Grace Levine could no longer hold herself back. Tears in her eyes, she kissed Chamberlin, who grew red as a beet. It seemed the only time he had been flustered that day.

Did this assure Chamberlin a place in the race? The next day, *The New York Times* had this to say: "Clarence Chamberlin may never fly to Paris, but he did a far better thing yesterday afternoon with the Wright-Bellanca monoplane." Another reporter asked if this settled the question of Bertaud's companion.

"Why should it?" snapped Levine. But he was getting pressure from all sides. Several friends on the Chamber of Commerce had taken the same attitude, including President Ralph Jonas, whose daughter the pilot had saved.

Chamberlin knew he had dodged a bullet, but he did not talk about it to others. One day around this time, he was poking about in the old Sikorsky hangar when he came across the two charred motors that had been on Fonck's S-35 when it crashed and burned the previous year. They were probably the ones upon which Islamoff's casket had lain. Chamberlin stood still and seemed to ponder them.

A reporter passed by, spotted Chamberlin, and hesitated in the hangar door. He remained silent as he contemplated the aviator. What passes through the mind of a man, he wondered, when he stumbles upon a hint of his own mortality? Chamberlin woke from his reverie. He turned and spotted the writer's silhouette in the door.

He said nothing as he passed him and walked outside.

ELEVEN

A LITTLE PATCH OF GREEN

"A singular fatality seems to hang over the transatlantic attempts," mused *The New York Times* in its April 25 write-up of Chamberlin's heroics. "Every one [*sic*] was hoping yesterday that this would end the jinx which seems to cling to these flights." The paper did not realize how wrong it would be.

The damage to *Columbia* left the field open, if only for a brief window, to Noel Davis and Stanton Wooster. The *American Legion's* tests in New York had been a success, and the two had flown back to Langley; more and more weight was added to the plane in 500-pound increments, and each time, the big yellow bird soared into the air. They scheduled the final test, with the plane fully loaded, for Tuesday, April 26. If that passed without a hitch, they'd take off for New York, and then for Paris.

By April 21, it was already assumed in many quarters that Davis would win. Though Chamberlin's crack-up three days later was not that serious, it put the *Columbia* behind—a fact that merely seemed to confirm the *American Legion's* lead. The Legion post in Paris asked the French government to light up the aerodrome, because Davis, like Byrd, expected to arrive around midnight. They requested the same promises made to Fitzhugh Green: keep several French destroyers at full steam off the coast should Davis need help at the end of his trip; ask all merchant ships to stay on the alert for a big yellow plane.

Parisians began laying bets on the winner. By April 22, they had put even money on Davis and Wooster, the damaged *Columbia*, and hometown heroes Nungesser and Coli. That changed the next day: the odds increased 2 to 1 against Davis, since his chances of winning were "frankly believed to be more brilliant than those of his rival."

Not that the French had suddenly given up on their fellow countrymen. On the same day that the new odds against Davis came out, Paris's *Le Matin* predicted that Nungesser and Coli would win. "Coli understands the sea even better than the air, for he spent many years in the merchant marine, while Nungesser is more at home in the air than on the ground and knows all the ins and outs of flying," *Le Matin* observed. "With two such admirably equipped airmen, France should be the first to gain the honor."

On Monday, April 25, Davis gave an impromptu news conference at Virginia's Langley Field. They'd planned to make the final test that day with a full load, but the winds were unfavorable, and they postponed it a day. The field made a pleasant setting. The air station covered six square miles, and the landing field itself, flanked by several large hangars, including some for dirigibles, was said to be the finest on the Atlantic Coast. The field overlooked the southern branch of the Back River, known for its oysters, and across the stream lay the little fishing village of Messick. Airplanes circled over oystermen planting seed oysters in the blue water.

"We are almost ready to get away," Davis told the journalists, "but there is no hurry about the trip. We want to have everything in our favor and I think the May full moon will give us favorable weather." He gazed at the Keystone and smiled. "I have never piloted a better plane. Some of us feared that when the machine was loaded to capacity, as she will be when we start on our long trip, a big field would be necessary to get her up, but the machine rises in less space than is required for some smaller planes. It is the best mechanical brand I have ever seen, and I believe we will make the flight to Paris with few difficulties."

One reporter was not completely sold and directed a question at Davis. "Do you really believe these big flying machines, manufactured in this country, are capable—?"

Davis cut him off and stared at the man. "A few years ago, we held all the aviation records. We have lost nearly all of them. We make as good planes and motors as any country in the world, and we have as good pilots. I want to see some prestige in the air return to our country."

This was unusual for Davis—not the words so much, which he'd repeated in other forms, but the tone. By all appearances Davis enjoyed the company of reporters, and they, in turn, gave him favorable cover-age. He didn't mind an occasional verbal joust, but this time he'd simply cut the man off. It was known that he'd moved the tests forward in response to the French threat, and maybe the strain on his nerves was beginning to show.

"Are you ready?" another reporter asked, more gently.

"No pilots," said Davis, "are better prepared."

•

That night, Noel and Mary Davis played cards. They and Wooster were staying at the home of Marine lieutenant Walter Farrell; they had left sixteen-month-old Noel Jr. with a nurse at their home in Lee Heights, Virginia. According to the papers, Davis asked his wife not to leave the house during this last, fully loaded test, which was known to be the most dangerous of all. The papers made it seem that she agreed.

This would not be Mary's version of the tale. She wanted to be on the plane. She'd bowed out gracefully from the Paris flight to make room for Wooster after she and Noel agreed it would be unwise for both to go with an infant son. Even so, she would not stay away. She prepared emergency rations—peanut butter sandwiches, sliced bacon, dried beef, beans, and other foods donated by the Beech-Nut Packing Co.—enough to last her husband and Wooster eight days at sea. She was not the sort to think that women should sit meekly while the menfolk changed the world. Years later she told her son that they had a nice night of cards and talk, but she drank too much as the night wore on. When she went to bed, it apparently wasn't settled whether she'd fly with Noel the next day. But come the morning, the alcohol had had its effect. She felt queasy and hung over. It was better not to fly, she said.

Tuesday, April 26, looked like it would be a go. At 5:00 a.m. there was little wind; Davis woke his men and said they would give this last test a try. Wright engineer "Spoons" Boedecker was present, along with a mechanic from the Keystone Company and members of the ground crew. They started the engines and warmed them up: the huge yellow plane trembled against its chocks as the motor roared. The tires bulged under the great load. To this point, the plane had lifted easily from the ground with a load of 13,000 pounds. This morning's test would put her at the full load of 17,000 pounds, 9,000 of that fuel. The huge center tank was completely filled, as were the big tanks in the wings.

Davis and Wooster walked around the plane, looking at the motors and listening for any hint of trouble. They climbed into the cockpit and tested the controls. The wings shook from the thrust of the propellers as if the plane were alive. Davis climbed back out and gave his mechanics their last-minute instructions: he wanted them to go down the field and stand far apart so they could measure his takeoff. He'd pointed before to the spot where he wanted to lift off; if he did not leave the ground by that point, he said, he would cut the engines and try again. Their course stretched a mile before them: it started in front of their hangar, then swept in a wide, smooth swathe toward open space between a dirigible hangar and some trees.

Wooster sat at the controls: Today he'd have to live up to his reputation as one of the nation's best pilots of heavy planes. Davis joined him in the cockpit and waved his hand for the chocks to be dragged from the wheels. Wooster rolled the *American Legion* from the hangar and idled her engine as they made one last preflight check. There still was no wind. The nose of the plane stuck out like a snout, with the center motor at the end. The cockpit was directly behind this, where Davis and Wooster sat side by side. The huge fuel tank hung in a web of straps and supports directly behind them.

Wooster gave the plane full power. The engines roared with their combined 700 horsepower, creating a horrific din. The mechanics spread out in a long line before them; at the dirigible hangar, a small crowd of officers and officials waited. The big yellow ship started down the field, gathering speed. She grew lighter on her wheels as the wings began to lift and the tail stuck out straight behind her.

But she would not rise.

Sometimes it was hard for pilots in these huge machines to know when they'd left the ground. Forty seconds passed and they sped 200 feet beyond the spot from which Davis said he wanted to lift off. Only then, very slowly, could one see daylight beneath the wheels. Wooster kept her close, gathering speed before he attempted to climb. But she did not respond as quickly as in the past. She'd lifted up about 50 feet by the time she passed the dirigible hangar, and slowly, excruciatingly, seemed to be climbing.

Everything would have worked out if not for the line of trees. They stood in front of the bomb pits, and day after day Davis had risen easily over them in his tests. But now with the slow climb and tremendous weight, the trees stared them in the face. They could not clear them this time.

The *American Legion* had become the plaything of the "ground effect," a phenomenon little understood at the time. It feels like smooth sailing: the pilot does not experience the bumps and updrafts he suddenly feels when cresting this limit, and even overloaded planes seem to lift effortlessly. Sometimes called the "wing in ground effect," this generally occurs when an airplane flies no more than the length of its wingspan off the ground: thus, the typical light airplane with a wingspan of 35 feet will feel the ground effect when it flies 35 feet or lower above the ground or water. Since the *American Legion* had a wingspan of 67 feet, she was safe within that zone.

But the line of trees ahead was apparently taller than the wingspan.

It is known today that ground effect results from the physics of wingtip vortices at low altitudes. Higher pressure from beneath a wingtip swirls up and around the tip to the zone of lower pressure over the wing. Usually these vortices spiral behind the plane, creating drag. But when the plane's altitude measures less than her wingspan, the ground breaks up these vortices, reducing the drag.

Simultaneously, the very presence of the airplane changes the shape of the surrounding air. The normal pressure pattern of the air surrounding a ship resembles a big cylinder; it is as if the craft travels in an elongated bubble. But once that bubble gets close to the ground, it flattens and spreads out on the bottom. This has two effects. First, it effectively lengthens the wingspan, increasing lift within a very narrow zone. Second, it creates a cushion of air beneath the craft, allowing the plane to skim calmly along the ground.

But there is a flip side to this: the plane encounters trouble once she starts to rise. A heavily loaded plane can suddenly find it difficult or even impossible to rise above her wingspan. She will edge slowly to the upper limits of the ground effect, then refuse to climb any higher. Below this upper boundary, the effects of drag had been negligible; now, all of a sudden, drag increases exponentially. The pilot feels this transition as a sudden loss of thrust, and unless the plane has dramatic reserves of power, as much as 50 percent or greater, what had seemed an easy takeoff now becomes one that abruptly ends.

This was exactly the situation in which Davis and Wooster found themselves. They could not rise, but if they continued forward, they'd

crash into the line of trees. Wooster turned right, very slightly, but turning a big plane with a full load at such a low altitude is a dangerous
choice, for when a ship turns, she loses speed. The 8.5-ton *American Legion* began to slip sideways and lose height, and Wooster straightened
her out again. Those watching on the ground were still close enough to
see the pilots; the two sat side by side in the cockpit working frantically
at the controls. The spectators were rooted in place, watching a familiar
slow-motion nightmare. The plane lumbered over the Back River, and
the oystermen looked up, aware that something was very wrong. Directly
to the east, Wooster could see the village of Messick; near that, he saw
a peninsula and a little patch of green. A pond, maybe 75 feet across, lay
beyond the green patch, and a salt marsh stretched from the pond to a
line of trees that borders present-day Poquoson. There was no way in the
world that he could clear this second line of trees. Once more, he turned
right, ever so slightly, and again the plane lost altitude. Wooster headed
straight for the green patch, hoping that it was firm ground.

He came down well: the right wheel touched, the left still in the air.
The tail dropped, and the plane began to slide across the wet ground.
Then the left wheel touched, and as it did, one of the pilots cut the
switches. Two fishermen standing on the point were so close that they
nearly had to jump aside. There was a huge splash and a plume of water
as the *American Legion* plowed through the pond. She reached the
other side and piled up against the edge, then in a blink turned on her
nose. The tail stuck up at forty-five degrees and the nose sank in the
mud. No sound came from the cockpit. No fire broke out, because
of the flipped switch. The takeoff and crash had taken less than fifteen minutes. All was still.

Suddenly there was movement again. Some oystermen waded
through the marsh and tried to right the plane, but she was too heavy.
Across the Back River at Langley, Spoons Boedecker and others piled
into a boat and rowed as fast as they could. They could see the long,
plowed furrow where the plane had landed. The left wing was shattered; the front engine, buried in the marsh. No movement could be
seen in the cockpit; water was inside, but not so much that it looked like
it might drown the fliers.

The rescuers climbed up and tried to smash the canopy. Davis and
Wooster were still in their seats, slung forward against their straps, sitting side by side in a pool of gloomy water. The main tank had cracked

and some gas was leaking forward, but the huge copper tank had only shifted forward in its straps and had not moved more than an inch. Yet the entire forward part of the fuselage, from the engine to the cockpit, had been smashed, the front motor buried in the mud. Wooster's neck was broken, and Davis's face was crushed. Death for both appeared to have been instantaneous.

When word came back to Langley of what had happened, the *American Legion*'s ground crew was overcome by grief. The mechanics had worked with both officers for so long that few of the barriers of rank still existed. Someone remembered that Davis's wife had to be told. For all her vibrancy, Mary was not a public person; she took the news that every flier's wife dreaded stoically. She called Noel Jr.'s nurse in Lee Heights and told her what had happened; she made arrangements for the Cowboy to be buried in the family plot in Pensacola. Wooster would be buried in Arlington National Cemetery.

She never wrote or spoke publicly about how she felt, Noel Jr. later said. She watched as her son grew up, joined the service, went through flight training, earned his wings. But the feelings were always there. Two years later, Cora Bennett would write about the fears that every pilot's wife prayed would never come true: "[F]or every young man whose eyes are fixed on some far limit of space which is the goal of his ambition, there is a girl who must stand on the ground and wait while he soars into unfathomable space where she can never follow him. Sometimes he does not come back—and she must wait on and on forever."

The afternoon of the accident, a reporter with the Associated Press called a little town in Utah to speak to Davis's mother. She now lived on a small ranch 150 miles east of Salt Lake City, at the edge of the Mormon Valley; his call was the first time she had heard the news. She'd already lost her eldest son in a motorcycle accident. Now another machine had taken her Noel.

She spoke to the AP reporter long-distance over the phone. "It is terrible, the death of my boy," she said. "I have the knowledge, though, that at least he died as he had lived—in the service of his country."

A click came over the wire. She had hung up. There were some crackles on the line, and then dead air.

TWELVE

THE MAIDEN FLIGHT

The deaths of Davis and Wooster threw a pall over everything and everyone. On the afternoon following the crash, many associated with the Derby felt compelled to comment upon the tragedy. Fokker, Sikorsky, Wanamaker, and officials in Washington all conveyed their sadness. But what could be said? The mystery of death was beyond easy expression, and their words all sounded the same. "The accident was not the fault of either pilots, plane or engine," said the president of Keystone Aircraft. Davis and Wooster "made the supreme sacrifice as a contribution to the advance of aviation," assured Rodman Wanamaker. *They died in the cause of science and progress*, many echoed. *They were great men.*

Byrd's tribute was the most poignant, because it was the most personal. "The death of Davis and Wooster came as a distinct shock," he said. "We were rooting for each other. We hoped that both would make Paris for the advancement of science...Only several days ago I wrote him offering what assistance he cared to ask of me, and his last message to me before taking off was to offer some good advice."

He paused a moment, and when he resumed, his voice was a little thicker. "They were my old friends."

What would be the ultimate cost of this race? Was it really worth it? Byrd spoke of science, and early on in the buildup to the Derby had addressed the lure of the unknown. Those trying to cross the ocean "do it because they know that someday it will be done. Man cannot stand the lure of the almost unpossible [*sic*]," he tried to explain. Man's supreme purpose was "to push back the limitations of his activity, of his life."

"Pioneers are always foolhardy," declared *The New York Times*, "if

one cares to look at it that way. But sometimes they accomplish significant things." One heard the same tributes in September 1926 after the
deaths of Charles Clavier and Jacob Islamoff, but now a more troubling
note crept in.

The flying fraternity knew that the whole truth was not being told.
For all the talk of science, the men who laid down the money—the
Harold Hartneys, Rodman Wanamakers, and Charles Levines—were
driven by commercial motivations. Speed and ease of movement meant
money, and whoever invested early in transatlantic airlines stood to
make millions. As for the pilots—sure, they flew for progress, but more
than that, they flew for the sheer adventure. But in their darkest hours,
they could not escape another truth: they had become the glorified advance men for capital interests. They risked their lives in the service
of PR.

For the first time, in addition to the barely uttered doubts, superstition raised its head. *The New York Times* discussed it seriously, an unusual departure for a publication that rarely mentioned such things
except in irony:

[P]ilots are hoping that the jinx—rising from mechanical miscal-
culations—which has been hanging over this transatlantic flight
to Paris is forever banished. They are believers in the sequence
of three, and there have been three bad crashes so far. Chamberlin's is not included because he saved himself and his passengers by consummate skill and his plane was light at the time.
Pilots will not light three cigarettes with the same match, and
although many of them joke at superstition, like Nungesser, who
puts a skull and crossbones on the side of his plane, they nevertheless have a healthy respect for it, and joke even while they
watch.

Religion and magical thinking are as old as mankind, attempts to
control or placate a hostile universe when rationality fails. The rivals in
the Orteig race had run up against one such epistemological wall. Their
calculations assured them that, given sufficient space and force, they
should be able to lift these massive, heavy birds. Davis had been the
truest believer—his calculations *told* him that he could rise, and in
test after test, one additional 500-pound increment after another, his calcu-

lations had proven true. Even at full load, he had lifted off—but then *something* held him fast, and he was unable to climb higher. That wasn't magic, of course, but some unknown physical principle. Still, would future calculations be sabotaged by other forces they could not yet comprehend?

"Transocean Flight Dogged by Bad Luck," the headline read. Four people had died, and Floyd Bennett would never fully recover. Islamoff and Clavier were bad enough, but they had not been part of the East Coast flying fraternity; though mourned, they were barely known. But Davis, Wooster, and Bennett were friends, and the grief hit close to home. Plus, there was the collateral damage: Davis's widow, his sixteen-month-old son, their immediate family. Was such "progress" worth the price? people began asking.

The fatal events affected spirits on both sides of the Atlantic. "Profound gloom" settled over the French fliers, newspapers declared. The French still believed they held an ace card with their runway—the field at Le Bourget was two miles long and "almost perfect," allowing more space for takeoff than American fields—but the fatalities tempered much of their excitement. Fonck said he would not be rushed. Nungesser and Coli scheduled more tests, saying in all probability they would not take off until May 15 or 16, and maybe not even then. Drouhin changed his plans completely, declaring that after a careful study of the winds, he'd concluded that a nonstop flight from Paris to New York was suicide. Instead, he would fly his Farman Goliath in a series of short hops from Le Bourget to Mitchel Field, then, after a ten-day rest, turn around and fly back to Paris nonstop. In essence, he was out of the competition.

That left the *Columbia*, which more by default than anything else was now the acknowledged front-runner. The landing gear was fixed by Thursday, April 28, and only bad weather prevented the pilots from making a test that day. Levine told the press that he would probably announce his choice between Chamberlin and Acosta on the following night. All the hangar mechanics were betting on Chamberlin. The decision had to be soon: it was already rumored that *Columbia* would be ready for Paris by Friday, May 6—only eight days away.

That night, the twenty-eighth, Chamberlin and Acosta sat alone at the Lambs Club on West Forty-fourth Street in Manhattan. This was a sad affair, kind of a wake, since the two fliers knew their fate would be decided the next day. One of them would be out of the race. They had become good friends during and after their fifty-one hours in the air; this was not a competition they relished. It seemed unbelievable that they could break a world record and still be treated this way.

Pilots had a saying for the wiles of fate: "That's the way the wind sock blows." One day the wind was in your face, joyously lifting you up; the next day, the wind was against you and you were nose over in the ground.

Chamberlin left his friend at the club at about 11:00 p.m. and went home. When Chamberlin left, Acosta asked the waiter for a pen and paper. He thought for a moment, then wrote a letter to Charles Levine. It was short and sweet, seven paragraphs long, the gist coming early in the first three. He'd obviously thought this out, and he mailed it right away. It reached Levine's office in the Woolworth Building the next afternoon:

Dear Mr. Levine:

As the hour for the "hop-off" for Paris in the Bellanca monoplane draws near, I feel that as a matter of fairness and sportsmanship I can no longer withhold a decision which I feel the circumstances make necessary.

I have watched the useful load of the plane increase day by day as navigation and other instruments necessary to the flight's success have been installed. It seems that every pound counts.

I cannot help but realize that the sixty pounds difference in weight between Clarence and myself gives him an advantage that can materially advance the possibilities of success, and for that reason I wish to withdraw in his favor.

This was a noble thing to do—though, in truth, it may not have been as self-sacrificing as it first appeared. Acosta was already talking to Byrd, or Fokker, about filling in for Bennett. Floyd had hinted as much to Bernt Balchen, though, amazingly enough, this was one of the few rumors associated with the flight that did not leak to the press. Acosta may also have known what was in the wind. On April 23, the day before Chamberlin's lifesaving landing, Bellanca had written a letter to Levine that raised the same point about weight. He put his foot down about Chamberlin, and although he preferred Acosta, he would leave the choice between the big man and Bertaud to his partner. He added:

to play safe we should take advantage of every possible reduction in weight. Now, you know well that C. Chamberlin is sixty pounds lighter than anyone [sic] of the other two pilots and sixty pounds of weight are equivalent to about 100 miles distance. Further, you know that the pilot seats are very close together even for average size men and would be therefore very much cramped for two big fellows.

Nevertheless, it was still a painful decision for Acosta. He needed this flight to restore his reputation as a great pilot. He could be known through history as the "First Flier Across the Atlantic," rather than as the "Bad Boy of the Air." Though he had a fallback option when he penned the note, it seemed at that point that the *Columbia* would be first across. Chamberlin seemed the obvious favorite after saving those two girls, but he still wasn't Levine's favorite, who wanted a pilot *and* a movie star. By bowing out, Acosta assured that both he and Clarence would have a shot at the transatlantic flight, but by doing so, he risked being remembered by history as an also-ran.

The next day, Chamberlin came down from a long test flight of the *Columbia*; before he could even leave the cockpit, someone handed him a typewritten copy of Acosta's letter. He read it without saying a word. He reread the paragraph in which Bert compared their weights, then looked across the field and dropped the letter on his lap.

"It must have been hard to write that," he said in a sad tribute to his friend.

There are different kinds of tribute, some touching in their oddity. On Tuesday, April 26, the morning of the Langley disaster, George Hughes of Elizabeth, New Jersey, crawled behind the wheel of his car. George had been inspired by Chamberlin and Acosta's endurance feat, and felt something stir within him, perhaps for the first time. He admitted he was just an ordinary fellow, the "average man" talked about so much by social commentators but who seemed destined for obscurity. George wanted to show that ordinary men were also capable of extraordinary things. So he bet his friends that he could drive his car longer than the famous aviators had stayed in the air.

And so George drove. He got odds of 3 to 1 and won $2,000 when he completed sixty hours on the road. By then the press had gotten wind of George's quest, and were present for what they thought would be the end. But George kept going, wondering how long a man could drive. His wrists were manacled, then the manacles connected to the steering wheel by a foot of steel chain. He ate chocolate and drank hot cocoa from a thermos; the car was gassed up "on the go." Journalists began to ride with him as he cruised the roads of South Jersey. At 9:00 p.m. on Saturday, April 30, after 107 hours on the road, he pulled before his house and killed the engine. He opened the door and the shackles were unlocked, then he crumpled to the ground. Friends rushed him to the hospital. They expected the worst: What would 107 hours in the driver's seat do to a man? But George Hughes was simply exhausted. Doctors kept him overnight, assuring New Jersey that its long-distance driver was in no physical danger.

The next day, the Automobile Association of America released a statement. Since no AAA timekeeper had been officially present, the marathon drive of George Hughes must pass into obscurity.

•

Almost every history written about the Orteig Prize asserts that Lindbergh's arrival in Long Island became the turning point of the race. If anything, this is history written from the perspective of his victory. But it is not actually true. The disaster at Langley was really the turning point, the point at which the entire tempo of the race sped up, strange things began to happen, and emotions became rarified. Even in the measured tones of the *Times*, one can sense the change. The furrow plowed by the *American Legion* becomes Colonel William B. Travis's "line in the sand": step over, and there is no return. Before the crash, this was just a race—a spectacular race, to be sure, one that pitted nation against nation, more epic and important than anyone could recall—but a race just the same. But after the crash, the race was transformed. The pilots were now players on a very public stage. All of a sudden, these technocrats, adventurers, and barnstormers found themselves thrust into some primal modern fable that was bigger than anyone had predicted or could have imagined. Later, some would call the race a metaphor for the American myth of success, but that interpretation discounted the involvement of the French and ignored the fact that winning and losing had become a drama of life and death—a narrative that transcended national boundaries.

Still, the race was very American. Henry David Thoreau wrote in

Walden that among all American merchants, "a very large majority, even ninety-seven in a hundred, are sure to fail." There was the winner, and in his shadow, the deadbeats, the bankrupts, the flunkies, the flops, the nobodies and has-beens. This was just as true for the Orteig Prize as it was when Thoreau first said it in 1854.

Francesco de Pinedo was the next person to be swept away by the Orteig fable. When he arrived in New York on Monday, April 25, the public mania for the race had become palpable. He'd come to Manhattan to meet his new seaplane, the *Santa Maria II*, yet his early morning arrival at Pennsylvania Station would not be announced in the news until hours later for fear of antifascist protestors. He was met by the Italian consul general, his staff, and a handful of reporters and photographers who'd been alerted just a few hours earlier. De Pinedo gave a brief statement, but when a photographer attempted a candid shot, the consul general bundled the aviator into a waiting auto.

All de Pinedo wanted was his plane. Instead, he was forced to play a role. At no other stop in his four-continent wanderings had he worn the black shirt of the Fascisti or felt obligated to mention politics. He spoke of what he had seen and of the future of flying. Now he had to defend his politics, just as Levine would feel forced to defend his religion. He was no longer just a man or an aviator; he was a symbol of Il Duce's Italy.

His political tour started that afternoon at City Hall. De Pinedo arrived at Jimmy Walker's office wearing the black-collared shirt of the party. His gray-streaked hair was slicked back; he looked tan and fit, and stood even shorter than Beau James. De Pinedo was thirty-eight; the mayor, forty-four. "Looking at you," said the mayor, "I am glad that another little fellow has made a great name. You come from a people famous for courage. While you were braving the dangers of the air, hundreds of thousands of Italian-American citizens of New York face the dangers of New York's subways every day."

De Pinedo grinned and said he'd first come to New York in 1909, when he was barely twenty. The city had changed since then. He said that Mussolini was anxious to build goodwill between the United States and Italy, and that the accident in Arizona had been far from a disaster, since his countrymen had witnessed the kindness of the Americans.

"I think New York is the best Fascist city in the whole world," he continued. "It's people love activity, work, energy—and these are things

I love, and things we Fascisti stand for. People think the Fascisti are a political party, but they are not. We are not a party, but we stand for a way of life.

"I know Mussolini would like New York. He would love it for its activity and its intensity."

The speech was a mistake, and more than a little naïve. Outside, on the City Hall steps, he got a glimpse of the hatred directed at what people thought he symbolized. Thousands of Italians cheered and raised their arms in the Fascist salute when he appeared with Jimmy Walker; about 200 wore black shirts and stood at attention. More than 170 police, mounted and on foot, guarded the park outside City Hall. But there were also hisses from the crowd. Detectives and members of the bomb squad mingled among this mass, and one man carrying a bouquet of red roses was thrown to the ground. The roses dropped and spectators gasped, but the bouquet failed to explode. The man was an admirer, he said. The roses were a present.

Three days later, at 10:00 p.m. on Thursday, April 28, de Pinedo spoke before the Italian Legion at 215 Second Avenue. As he spoke, about two thousand antifascists tried to break in. There had been warnings, and the police saw them marching in tight order through the intersection of Sixteenth Street and Second Avenue. "Come out and face us," someone shouted to de Pinedo; others took up the chant, and their voices could be heard blocks away. Four officers formed a hopelessly outnumbered line across the street, but they were soon joined by twenty others, armed with billy clubs. The shouts could be heard inside the Italian Legion; a large part of de Pinedo's audience piled outside and threw themselves upon the protestors. The riot rolled up and down the street as officers clubbed everyone.

"Come out and face us!" the antifascists cried, but de Pinedo kept speaking, paying no attention as others left the audience to join the fray. A stone crashed through the front window. He did not stop. When he finished, the few left in the audience clapped. Then they, too, ran outside.

By then police reserves had arrived. City officials later guessed this was as big as the riot by Valentino's mourners. Nearly ten thousand Fascists, antifascists, police and spectators fought, shoved, shouted, or fled within a one-block radius. One group of bluecoats chased a man into a drugstore. When they searched him, they found a loaded pistol.

They had it all wrong, the man pleaded; he'd brought the gun to protect de Pinedo, his hero. He would not let these *bastardi* harm a hair on the head of the Lord of Distances.

The police were not impressed. They beat the man with their nightsticks, then dragged him to the station.

This was madness in the extreme, de Pinedo realized. He had survived lightning, tornadoes, deluges, and deserts; he and his men had escaped an explosion, and he'd evaded the close scrutiny of giant prehistoric birds. But never had he seen anything like what he encountered in New York City. He breathed a great sigh of relief when, on May 2, his replacement plane finally arrived. On May 8, it was fully assembled, and he took off for Boston on his way to the Midwest and then Canada.

At least in the mind of the press, the question still remained whether de Pinedo would register for the Orteig Prize. Would he or wouldn't he? Time was running out for the Lord of Distances to make a decision. Writers observed that, even if he did choose to compete, the 1,300-mile range of his new ship meant he'd need another to qualify.

But de Pinedo had decided privately that it was far better to flee. A madness was building in New York, and he wanted out of there. Moreover, everything he'd accomplished in the past four months would be eclipsed unless he beat these aviators across the Atlantic.

Unless he hurried, every mile he'd flown would be swallowed by the Orteig Prize.

•

In San Diego, Lindbergh saw an opportunity. Unlike his rivals, he took advantage of every mishap the moment it occurred. He'd seen an opportunity with Fonck's crash; he doubled the efforts of Ryan's mechanics when the newest dispatches arrived concerning the *American Legion*, *America*, and *Columbia*. All of a sudden, he had a chance—one he'd barely had before. While others grieved, Lindbergh pushed ahead.

That may seem a harsh judgment, but Lindbergh was always a distant, driven man. Death was part of aviation. He'd stared into its face several times: he'd crashed more airplanes than most Americans would ever board. Victory in this business was not for the common good: it was deeply personal.

Lindbergh's strategy had also developed along a different line from that of his rivals'. When he had his first vision of the race, the night after

Fonck's disaster, a rare sense of power washed over him. He thought he saw the problem in a nutshell, and every subsequent crash, except Chamberlin's, seemed to confirm his suspicions. The key to winning lay in lightening the load. Since the limiting factor on any long-distance flight was the load of gas a plane could carry and lift, the obvious conclusion was that every excess ounce of weight must be stripped. While Fonck's Sikorsky had been loaded down with luxury, Byrd had succumbed to the "luxury" of too many safety devices. Davis's Keystone had been so massive that it barely got off the ground. The perfect design would be a gas tank, a man, and a wing.

It helped that Lindbergh was alone and, in general, isolated from his rivals and peers. Every other flier in the Orteig race lived and worked in a seething world of fellow pilots, financial backers, mechanics, journalists, PR men, race officials, and spectators. They visited the same clubs, frequented the same restaurants, and read the same magazines and newspapers. However, of the many so-called differences between Lindbergh and the others that have been cited over the years, only two really matter: he was physically isolated from all the other fliers during the critical period of his planning and preparation, and he was willing to fly the ocean alone. His intelligence, upbringing, age, experience as a flier, and mechanical ability were really no different from those of the other fliers; the main qualitative difference lay in his insistence that the best way to cut weight was to fly alone across the ocean. Every other flier shuddered at the thought, but Lindbergh had stayed awake close to forty hours in some of his solo mail runs, he insisted. It had been dangerous, but he had survived.

If Lindbergh had purchased the two-seated Bellanca, as he originally intended, he might easily have flown with a copilot. If he had made his plans on the East Coast, like the others, he might have been convinced, for one of the few things that mattered to him was the esteem of his peers. He was always portrayed as the "Lone Eagle," the man who flew alone, but in truth he was easily swayed throughout his life by those he considered wiser or richer. His isolationist friends in the group America First, the anti-Semitic Henry Ford—he absorbed their prejudices like a sponge, then repeated them to the world as if they were his own.

Yet in 1927 the simple fact of geography placed him a continent away from his peers and their prevailing attitudes on flying. He was too far away, and too far along in his own plans, for his mind to be changed. With his geographic and emotional distance, he could look at prevailing wisdom with fresh eyes and see how it had killed or injured the others. He pounced on his opponents' weaknesses and learned from their tragedies. That was a truth of the winner that no one wanted to admit. Everyone gloried in the winner's skill, strategy, stamina, and courage, but few ever mentioned the grisly truth: the winner climbed over the bodies of those who had gone first. This was rarely mentioned in the American myth of success. If Lindbergh didn't pay heed to the mistakes made before him, the next guy would learn from the failures of Charles Lindbergh.

•

On April 28, 1927, the completed *Spirit of St. Louis* idled at the edge of San Diego's Dutch Flat runway, ready for her first trial run. It was a warm and sunny Thursday, with blue skies and a slight breeze off the sea. It was sixty days exactly since Lindbergh had ordered the plane from Ryan, and two days after Davis and Wooster had died in a salt marsh in Virginia. Across the Pacific, Russia and China threatened war along the border; on the Mississippi River, dozens of towns were underwater and tens of thousands left homeless as a 100-year flood surged down its length, requiring $2.6 million in aid. There was trouble all over the world, but in California, Charles Lindbergh breathed deeply and climbed for the first time into the cockpit of his new plane.

He liked what he saw. The windows were set on either side of the cockpit; a small periscope—suggested by a Ryan worker with submarine experience—was built into the instrument panel and could be projected sideways from the fuselage, giving Slim a view of the area directly in front of the nose. In landing, he would operate as most contemporary pilots did, craning his neck out the window to keep an eye on the ground. The stick and rudder pedals were set in their normal positions; the trim lever, which fine-tuned the motion of the nose up and down, was to his left, just below the window. The throttle lever was just behind that. The instrument panel included dials for air speed, bank and turn, speed, and drift; two types of compass; tachometer; altimeter; fuel and oil pressure; and oil temperature. A wooden map case was mounted on the fuselage, behind his seat to the right. His chair was woven wicker and the padded armrests brown velveteen. There was plenty of room for his long legs.

The other distinctive feature of the cockpit was that the pilot essentially flew blind. Five gas tanks were spread about *Spirit*, but the biggest, at 425 gallons, was placed directly in front of the pilot's seat. Lindbergh could not see straight ahead. He would have to fly on instruments, by sticking his head out the window, and with the help of the little periscope. He'd flown blind many times on mail runs, because of night and fog, and was confident he could do so again. Most planes in the race had the big gas tank built right behind the pilot's seat, but Lindbergh felt his self-imposed blindness was a small trade-off for the assurance that he would not be caught between the engine and an exploding gas tank during a forced landing, the cause of death for many pilots. Discarded due to weight concerns were a radio, a parachute, navigation lights, a sextant, and a gas gauge. He'd navigate by dead reckoning, using his maps and eyes for visual checks; he'd track fuel consumption with his watch.

If the interior was Spartan practicality, the exterior was distinctive style. *Spirit* was a tiny silver thing, futuristic in the fashion of the popular "boys' adventures" of the day. Superficially, the plane resembled the Bellanca that Lindbergh coveted: Deeply streamlined struts dropped from the wing beneath the fuselage, just as on the *Columbia*. Beyond that, the resemblance ended. The plane stood at only 9 feet 8 inches high; she was 28 feet long, with a high, one-piece wing measuring 46 feet from tip to tip. The 9-cylinder, air-cooled Wright J-5C Whirlwind engine could develop 220 horsepower. The Whirlwind had been "super-inspected" by Wright Aeronautical and fitted with a special magazine that kept it greased in flight. The plane weighed 2,000 pounds empty and 5,200 pounds with a full load of fuel. The most distinctive feature was the nose, which was covered with an intricate swirling pattern of overlapping aluminum circles known as damascene. Upon the nose was painted "SPIRIT OF ST. LOUIS," a name borrowed from a 1922 movie highlighting the city's achievements. The surface of the plane, from the point where the wing joined the body then back to the tail, was covered with a "doped" silver fabric. The effect was one of aerodynamic sleekness: every strut was streamlined with light aluminum; even the wheels were covered with fabric, then doped and laced tight. It was believed that such streamlining would add an extra 10 miles per hour to the plane's speed.

She was certainly striking, and Lindbergh was taken with her immediately. He would later say that *Spirit* was totally unique: designing the aircraft wholly from scratch meant that every single part was built specifically for the Paris flight. "I can inspect each detail before it's covered with fabric and fairings," he claimed. "By working closely with the engineer, I can build my own experience into the plane's structure and make the utmost use of the theories he expounds."

But later research disproves that claim. In the summer 2005 *Journal of the American Aviation Historical Society*, historian Nick Sparks uncovered a photo of Ryan Airline's B-1 Brougham, a successor to the company's popular M-1 and M-2 monoplanes that was still on the drawing board when work began on *Spirit*. The two planes look almost exactly alike: same fuselage and rudder; same high wing, cowling, and Fokker-style landing gear. Spark asks:

> Could it be that the staff at Ryan effectively pulled the wool over Lindbergh's eyes, convincing him his plane was "special" when it was really a modified, pre-existing design? Or could it be that Lindbergh exaggerated his level of control over the design and construction of the aircraft? Is it possible that by the time Lindbergh finished his book—a quarter century after the fact—that he had begun to buy into some of the legends surrounding the construction of the aircraft?

Modified or unique, the sight of *Spirit* ready for flight seemed to take Slim's breath away. Ryan's mechanics, designers, and other employees had worked like maniacs to get to this point on time. Lindbergh was usually right beside them. About thirty-five people worked for Ryan: twenty of them mechanics and helpers in the factory; the others, in the office and on the field. At first none of them was quite sure what the rush was about; it was, to them, the "mystery airplane." By early April, though, they knew it was an entrant in the Orteig Prize, and they knew they were in a race against time. Douglas Corrigan and others often worked past midnight, then came in at eight the next morning. "If any of those planes with their experienced crews made the flight and won the prize," Corrigan remembered, "that would have meant the plane we were building wouldn't have been in the race. And that would have meant the factory wouldn't have any more work and we mechanics would be out of a job."

By early April, construction was in high gear, but reports kept coming in about the progress of the other fliers. When Chamberlin and Acosta completed their record flight on April 14, Lindbergh grew concerned that he could not win unless all the other competitors failed. It might not even be worthwhile to fly to New York, so in desperation he went out and bought charts to lay out a flight across the Pacific by way of Hawaii.

He appeared at the factory almost every day. While Donald Hall computed performance curves, Lindbergh taught himself the fine points of navigation. He chose 100-mile intervals as the distance between course changes, figuring that he could cover that distance each hour. His route was basically the same as that of all the others except Bertaud—he'd follow the Great Circle from Newfoundland to the southern tip of Ireland, then cut across a narrow strip of England to France. If he left Newfoundland at dusk, he could hit Ireland before nightfall of the second day. He aimed for a mid-May takeoff, when there would be a full moon. Hall's figures showed Spirit's theoretical range to be 4,100 miles: under dead wind conditions, he could come in over the coastline as far north as Scandinavia or as far south as southern Spain and still have enough fuel to reach Paris.

Lindbergh's mother wrote faithfully during this time. "People are all asking about you," she wrote on March 18. "One man, Mr. Keal, one of the superintendents, yesterday said, 'All my life I have longed to do something—that I could do alone and that I wanted to—but I have never been free.' He is very interested...He felt that you are right—so I feel grateful to him."

His flight had entered his mother's imagination as well. "If I were capable, I would go in another plane right beside you all the way," she wrote on March 21. On April 8, she wondered, "Do you think I am too dumb ever to learn to fly? Please be honest. They are going to build foolproof machines."

On April 27, at two in the morning, all factory work on Spirit was pronounced done. By now it had an official license number: N-X-211 (N for United States, X for experimental). As the sun went up, the fuselage was slowly towed a couple of miles behind owner Claude Ryan's Studebaker to the Dutch Flats field on the edge of town. The wing was bolted on, and soon after that, the propeller from Standard Steel Propeller with its damascened spinner was attached. On Thursday, April 28, Spirit was ready.

•

Lindbergh crawled into the cockpit knowing that all his theories about the perfect plane for the trip, all his visions of flying eternally since that moonlit night the previous fall, all would now be put to the test. The entire factory staff looked on: this was their test, too. "For me," he later said, Spirit "seems to contain the whole future of aviation."

In an important sense, more was at stake in this first test than on that day in the future when he took off alone across the ocean. Then, the most he could lose was his life, but at this moment, if all his theories were wrong, he would lose everything that mattered to him: his respect and reputation. He would look like a fool. None of the other pilots' fates so depended upon their own designs, and if their first tests failed, they had options. Byrd was already talking about exploring the South Pole; Chamberlin seemed content to test planes for Bellanca forever. But if he failed at this moment, Lindbergh would go back to where he had been. The papers already portrayed him as reckless, in over his head. A young man with more bravura than brains. A "Flying Fool," in the words of an old barnstorming moniker.

Spirit had already been gassed up when he crawled in. Lindbergh watched as the mechanics and helpers walked around the plane, checking their handiwork for any unseen imperfection. The check was a ceremony, a transfer of the aircraft from Ryan to Lindbergh. It was as much their plane as his.

The factory workers cheered as chief mechanic John van der Linde stepped to the propeller and primed it a few times. Douglas Corrigan hand-propped it next, followed by Frank Saye, a small fellow, who got it started when Lindbergh yelled, "Contact!" Slim ran the engine up to 1,400 rpm. Spirit vibrated like a horse at the gate; Lindbergh gave the signal to remove the wheel chocks, and Corrigan ducked under the wing to pull them free. Lindbergh taxied out and pointed the nose to the west. He glanced at the wind sock and at the blue sky above him, then opened the throttle. It was about 3:00 p.m.

He had never felt an airplane accelerate so fast. The tires were off the ground before he had rolled 100 yards. Spirit climbed quickly, though he tried to keep her nose down. The plane, it seemed, was impatient to be in the air. He spiraled up carefully, leveling off at 2,000 feet, then circled over the field. Little stick figures ran beneath him. He rocked his wings in acknowledgment and headed west toward San Diego Bay.

Lindbergh had fallen in love. More than that, he felt like a boy again—on his back in the tall grass, watching the hawk pass overhead. But now he was the hawk, and nothing could catch him. He flew over North Island with its big navy hangars, its planes in a line and seaplanes at anchor. The Naval Air Station was on one side of the island and the army's Rockwell Field on the other. He noted that his ailerons rode a bit high and the fin needed a bit of adjustment; the single big problem he could identify was instability, due to the small tail surfaces. But this might actually be to his advantage, since it meant that he would have to actively fly *Spirit* every minute. Correcting the instability would keep him awake while over the Atlantic. He tested his top speed and accelerated to 128 miles per hour, which exceeded Don Hall's calculations by 3.5 miles per hour. He cut power and circled back east toward the white houses of San Diego. That was enough for a first flight. There was no need to push his luck just yet.

Suddenly a navy Curtiss Hawk dove on him from above. The pilot pulled alongside to check out this strange silver bird. He banked for position, and then the two staged a mock dogfight over San Diego Bay. The Hawk had greater speed, but *Spirit* had a tighter turning radius and kept cutting inside, lining up on the Hawk's tail. "We spiral, zoom, and dive for several minutes, while we try to get imaginary guns on one another," Lindbergh wrote. Finally Slim broke off and headed back to Dutch Flats. He made a three-point landing and taxied in; he'd been up for only 20 minutes. The ground crew ran up and said he'd taken off in 165 feet, 61⅛ seconds, an unbelievable time. Maybe he did have a chance of winning.

Lindbergh stepped from the cockpit and smiled.

"This is a very good airplane," he said.

THIRTEEN

THE WHITE BIRD

A Frenchman would win the Orteig Prize. It was written in the stars, according to a famous soothsayer quoted in *L'Auto*, a leading Paris sports tabloid. The appearance of a psychic in the sports pages seemed to surprise no one. Paris's magazines and newspapers were devoting more space to the race than to the World Economic Conference or to the events on the border between Russia and China.

"There will be many attempts on both sides of the Atlantic," the psychic declared. "Several will fall into the water, others will crash." But she was happy to assure the people of France and the United States that no would else would die, though several contestants would have narrow escapes.

But the winner? pressed *L'Auto*. Who would be the winner?

She would not be rushed in these matters. Though the details were vague, victory would be delayed, she said. Neither did she know the name of the winner. But she knew this: "A handsome young Frenchman will finally be the one to triumph."

All Paris knew whom she meant: Charles Eugène Jules Marie Nungesser.

•

Everything—his life, fortune, and love—depended upon victory.

But when would he actually start? That question was a mania, an idée fixe that dogged Parisians from the first light of morning until they closed their eyes at night in bed. Nungesser's *White Bird*, the *L'Oiseau Blanc*, sat in a hangar at the edge of Le Bourget, two miles of runway stretching before it, as the pilots and the entire population of the City of Light waited for a break in the weather. For the entire week of May 1–7, that weather had been abysmal: thunderstorms, dripping fog and mist, an anticyclone spinning out to sea. The wait and the weather put a strain on everyone.

No object of adoration was ever uglier. The *White Bird* was an ungainly ship; "ponderous," as the French press said. She was a reconfigured Levasseur PL.8, with three enormous fuel tanks, able to carry 1,063 gallons, which replaced the front two cockpits. Fully loaded, she would weigh 11,000 pounds, 6,000 pounds less than the *American Legion*. As in Noel Davis's ship, the pilot and navigator sat side by side. The 12-cylinder, 450-horsepower Lorraine-Dietrich engine had a reduction gear that made it capable of developing up to 550 horsepower; it had already been run for 40 hours in the Paris Levasseur factory and was judged sound. The wings stretched 48 feet; the landing gear would jettison after takeoff to save 271 pounds in weight; the fuselage was reinforced to allow a water landing in New York Harbor. Nungesser had painted it white, so it could be seen from a distance, and put the French tricolor on its tail. His old flying logo from the war was emblazoned on the fuselage: a skull and crossbones, candles, and a coffin, enclosed in a black heart. The press called it "gruesome." Nungesser called it his good luck charm.

Everything about the *White Bird* had become a national obsession. While the United States had several fliers in the race, the French invested all their hopes in Nungesser and Coli. Just as the American press tracked every move of the U.S. entrants, so the French press breathlessly followed the *White Bird*.

On April 20, *Le Petit Parisien* reported that the aviators would leave in four days. They'd carefully planned their route: across the Channel to southern Ireland and out to sea, following the Fifty-fourth Parallel to Newfoundland, then south to New York. They expected to maintain an average cruising speed of 100 miles per hour, which meant they should cover the route in about 36 hours. If they left Paris at 4:00 a.m., said Nungesser, they should reach New York the next morning.

But bad weather and bad luck set in. The diverse crosswinds on their route could be deadly. That week a heavy fog blanketed the northeast skies. The aviators delayed. On Tuesday, May 3, they made a five-hour flight between Paris and Chartres to test the speed of their plane. At 3:00 a.m. the next morning, an electric light bulb fell from their hangar's ceiling at Villacoublay Aerodrome and ignited 200 liters of gasoline. Though some mechanics were able to roll the *White Bird* free of danger, a lower wing was badly burned. Pierre Levasseur, her builder, declared the damage slight: a new cover of varnished silk would do the trick. The wing was repaired in just a few hours.

That did not stop the false rumors. Tales circulated in Paris that the plane had been burned to a cinder and was out of the race. A report arrived from New York that Chamberlin and Bertaud had taken off in the *Columbia.* These were soon squelched by more accurate news: an anticyclone had formed over the North Atlantic, covering the American coast in fog and rain. All American flights were cancelled. Nungesser and Coli breathed easier.

But not for long. At 6:00 p.m. on Friday, May 6, the *White Bird* was seen circling Paris, then appeared over the field at Le Bourget. Nungesser had mentioned in passing that he would not leave Villacoublay until he was ready to start for New York. He circled the field for twenty minutes, testing his plane's lifting power in the air's upper currents; as he did so, thousands streamed from Paris to catch a glimpse of the airmen. When the *White Bird* started to land, the mob rushed the plane. It took French soldiers to clear the field; fifty sentries charged the crowd with leveled bayonets, driving the fans off the runway.

One minute, Parisians swooned with concern; the next, they launched into hysteria. Such madness could get on a flier's nerves. Fonck had grown snappish while preparing for his flight, though the French media treated it simply as a case of the little man's big ego showing through. But the constant nattering now got on Nungesser's nerves. "Every place I go all I hear is, 'Are you ready?,' 'Are you going?,' 'Will you make it?'" he complained. "I really don't know when I shall leave but what I do know is that all this talk has created an atmosphere of nervousness which is not at all helpful."

"I am aware," he continued, "that each night in well-known Paris bars numerous aviators successfully cross the Atlantic between cocktails. But so far as I am concerned, I have been carefully preparing for three years and do not intend to take off until I am certain of my plane and as certain of the weather as it is physically possible to be."

So much depended upon the weather. Ninety-five percent of the days in April, May, and June were windy, government officials told *Le Matin.* During these blustery days, 33 percent of the winds came from the west,

23 percent from the south, 22 percent from the north, and 17 percent from the east. The remaining 5 percent were days of calm. A wind from the west favored an American flier, since it served as a tailwind and pushed him along. A wind from the east favored a Frenchman. Thus, the odds favoring an American victory were 33 to 17, said the sporting crowd.

The local winds were not the only factor affecting Nungesser and Coli. Cyclonic and anticyclonic zones lie over the ocean, and these behave differently. Cyclonic zones are regions of high barometric pressure, and they favor an easterly flight. Anticyclonic zones are regions of low pressure, and they favor a westerly flight—so long as the pilot rides the edge of the zone. With so much riding on an ability to interpret weather over the ocean, it was no wonder that many pilots and navigators started in the navy.

But that Saturday, May 7, the French meteorological service told them that east winds were forming off the coast, possibly clearing the skies. The fliers looked at each other and grinned. At dawn on Sunday, they determined, they would go.

At noon that Saturday, Nungesser had lunch with his mother, Leontine, at her flat on the boulevard Voltaire. His portrait, news clippings, war decorations, and other mementoes dominated the little salon. She kissed him and gave him *pommes frites* and *crème au chocolat*, his favorite treats. She noted that he seemed more cheerful than usual, as if a great weight had lifted from his shoulders. He had coffee, then rose to go.

"You're always dashing off somewhere or other," she said, sighing. "And how's this famous airplane of yours getting on? I've got a feeling you'll be going off with Coli before long."

Charles laughed, and lied. "For the mother of an airman, you're a bit naive," he needled her. "Look at the weather! You couldn't fly far in this. I'll be here for your birthday," on the thirtieth of May.

She followed him to the landing and waved goodbye. "You'll be coming back?" Something scared her that she could not put her finger on, and that scared her even more.

"Of course," he said. "I'm one of those who always turn up—like a bad penny."

•

The cavalier remark, the joke to diminish death—such had been his trademark for more than a decade. But Nungesser had his fears, not so much of death as of failure. He'd barely escaped death so many times that its imminence brought neither terror nor mystery. The black heart painted on the side of *L'Oiseau Blanc* was his way of thumbing his nose at the Reaper: "A black heart doesn't fear death," he'd say. But a mundane life where all his visions for the future failed—his line of seaplanes, starring roles in movies, plans to win back his wife and support her in the style to which she'd grown accustomed—all that would come crashing down if he were an also-ran. "I will open up a way that will change the world," he liked to say of his flight, and a part of him was as idealistic as the grand statement implied. Yet unlike those of so many of his American counterparts, his motives were also quite worldly. Victory or death were his only options.

It is surprising how one famous, glamorous, and adored man could steer himself into such a cul-de-sac, yet that is exactly what Nungesser had done. Sometimes the trajectory of his life seemed to overwhelm him. Born in Paris on March 15, 1892, and raised in the small village of Valenciennes, to the northeast, Nungesser came from a troubled background. His father, a butcher from the town of Saint-Mandé, seemed to have little time for the boy. Charles's mother was the opposite, and early on doted on the child, entering him in the local "Most Beautiful Baby" contests of 1892, 1893, and 1894, one of which he won. Charles was still a boy when his parents parted: he moved with his mother to Paris, while his father remained the butcher of Saint-Mandé.

Charles seemed determined to distinguish himself at an early age. He gravitated toward and excelled at competitive sports, especially boxing. Unfortunately, he was a middling student in every subject except, perhaps, girls. He dropped out—or was forced to do so—at age sixteen, right around the time his father discovered that he had been having an affair with a married woman. "But *mon papa*," the boy reportedly said, "if one excludes the married women for morals, the unmarried ones for virtue, then there's no one left but widows and divorcees." Fine logic for one so young, but his father sent him to Brazil to visit an uncle.

It seems an extreme form of punishment, made worse by the fact that the uncle had disappeared, moving on without leaving a forwarding address. To support himself, Charles went to work in a factory as an auto mechanic. To fill his time, he lifted weights, swam, and entered the world of auto racing, competing in the grueling twenty-four-hour Cordillera de los Andes across its namesake mountain range. Between races, he fought in exhibition matches in Uruguay and Argentina. He was seventeen.

It was during this time in Argentina that one of the earliest apocryphal stories about him appeared. One night, he attended a boxing match between the Argentinian champ and a French contender, and the Frenchman went down in the first round. The champ was not gracious in victory: he called all Frenchmen cowards, at which point the teenage Nungesser stripped off his coat and hopped in the ring. He went down in a minute, then came up again. The champ knocked him down fifteen times, but each time Nungesser rose, bloodier than before. There were two endings to this tale: the first, that Nungesser fought until he could no longer get up; the second, that he made a feint and felled the champ with a surprise right hook to the jaw.

Soon after this, Nungesser finally found his uncle, now a rancher in Argentina. For five years Charles lived the life of a gaucho, riding the range and herding cattle like Davis in Utah. Then, in 1914, the Great War began. Nungesser returned to France and joined the cavalry, convinced it was the natural place for a young man in search of action.

A month after signing up, he was on patrol with his squad when they ambushed a German staff car. Inside they found some important military plans. Nungesser got a medal and the car for that feat, and was assigned the job of a rear-line driver—a safe, boring assignment that he hated. "I don't like chauffeuring every officer around when other Frenchmen are fighting," he wrote in his transfer request to the newly formed air service. He earned his wings in April 1915; three months later, he shot down his first plane, a German Albatross, after leaving the aerodrome without permission. For this, he was awarded the Croix de Guerre and confined to the barracks for eight days.

Thus began a pattern. By the end of the war, Nungesser would be awarded almost every decoration for bravery from every Allied nation, but he would be disciplined innumerable times. He became an ace in April 1916 and finished the war with forty-five official victories, ranking behind Georges Guynemer, who did not survive the war, and Fonck. Nungesser's own personal kill list included between 103 and 106 downed planes; he always ran neck and neck with Guynemer on the front-page tallies religiously kept by *Le Petit Journal* and other newspapers. They named him "The Indestructible Nungesser," and his rugged good looks, flamboyant personality, and appetite for danger, wine, beautiful women, and fast cars made him a regular feature in the gossip columns.

But fame came with a price. The list of his injuries amazed the medical profession. Doctors more than once predicted he would not survive the latest bullet wound or crash, only to see him rise from his bed in bandages and hobble to a plane. By the end of the war, he'd been wounded seventeen times and had a platinum knee, foot, and lower jaw: he could boast of a fractured skull, a concussion, five fractures to the upper jaw, two to the lower, and shell splinters in the right arm; dislocations of both knees, a collar bone, his right ankle, and left wrist; a bullet wound to the mouth, an atrophied calf, and injured lower tendons of the left leg; and finally, contusions to the chest, a punctured palate, and two broken legs. In one 1916 crash, his last sensation before blacking out was that of the control stick impaling his face. He was not expected to live, and a priest gave him last rites in the cockpit. Doctors trepanned his skull and inserted a gold plate in his palate. A week later, still swathed in bandages, he was up and hobbling around.

There was an emotional cost to the physical injuries. In the air, his flying style was free and fluent, punctuated by the same bursts of exuberance that made Bert Acosta famous in America. But on the ground, he was moody and drank heavily. The Germans were as scared of him as the Allies were of Manfred von Richthofen; like the Red Baron's plane, Nungesser's Nieuport 17 sported distinct markings as if daring the enemy to fight. "We began to recognize this pilot and sensed something different about him, almost grotesque," said a German pilot after the war. "There was no mistaking his style. He was a magnificent pilot, but only a madman would attack our ships in a Voisin," an unsturdy little plane used for scouting and light bombing. "[W]e wanted no part of him," the German added. "You had to be careful, never knowing what to expect when he came to you."

Tales of Nungesser's exploits were legion, but two in particular explain the person he was as well as why so many pilots admired him. The horror that shaped him came early, when he first transferred from bombers to a fighter squadron in Nancy. He'd taken his Nieuport up to 8,000 feet when he spotted two German Albatrosses flying over German lines. He dove out of the sun. The Albatross was a slow two-seater, and he traded shots with a gunner standing in the gun-ring behind the pilot; at 30 feet, Nungesser pressed the trigger and watched the pilot

The hotel owner Raymond
Orteig, originator of the
$25,000 Orteig Prize
(Courtesy of the Library of
Congress)

The French World War I ace
René Fonck, the first pilot to
attempt to win the Orteig Prize
(Courtesy of the Library of Congress)

Richard Byrd and Floyd Bennett, February 1927, receiving the Congressional Medal of Honor from President Coolidge for their flight over the North Pole (Courtesy of the Library of Congress)

The department store scion Rodman Wanamaker, who donated $100,000 toward Byrd's attempt to cross the Atlantic (Courtesy of the Library of Congress)

Anthony H. G. Fokker, the designer of Byrd's *America* (Courtesy of the Library of Congress)

The navy pilots Noel Davis and Stanton Wooster, standing on the *American Leg*
(Courtesy of the Library of Congress)

Left to right. Bert Acosta (in flying clothes with scarf around his neck), Cla Chamberlin, Willda Chamberlin, and the designer Giuseppe Mario Bellanca. The photo was taken at Roosevelt Field on April 14, 1927, after Acosta and Chamberlin beat the world endurance record aloft in the *Columbia*. (CORBIS Images)

Charles Augustus Lindbergh Jr., 1923, in the open cockpit of a plane at Lambert Field, St. Louis, Missouri (Courtesy of the Library of Congress)

Lindbergh's *Spirit of St. Louis* in its hangar at Curtiss Field (Courtesy of the Library of Congress)

Lindbergh, Byrd, and Chamberlin, posing for photographers in the long week before Lindbergh's flight on May 20, 1927. The *Spirit of St. Louis* is behind them. (Courtesy of the Library of Congress)

The French World War I ace Charles Nungesser and his wife, the American heiress Consuelo Hatmaker. They are attending an unspecified ceremony in France honoring the nation's war dead. (William Louis Nungesser Photo Collection)

Clarence Chamberlin and Charles Levine, standing before the *Columbia* shortly after landing in Germany on June 6, 1927 (National Air and Space Museum, Smithsonian Institution [SI 88-8613])

Left to right: Bert Acosta, Richard Byrd, George Noville, and Bernt Balchen, standing before the *America* as they wait for the skies to clear (Getty Images)

Ruth Elder at Roosevelt Field. Of all the pilots who attempted a 1927 transatlantic crossing after the end of the Orteig Prize, none generated as much excitement as the Southern aviatrix Ruth Elder. Although her plane, *American Girl*, crashed at sea, Elder became famous and was catapulted to Hollywood stardom.

slump forward and the nose go down. The gunner clung to the ring for dear life, but the metal suddenly ripped loose and he tumbled into space, his arms flailing. He turned his face, and Nungesser was close enough to look into his eyes. The doomed man's expression often came back to haunt him. Sleeping was a trial after this, for he saw that face whenever he closed his eyes.

Nearly a year later, Nungesser demonstrated the skill that would endear him to other pilots. On April 27, 1916, he spotted three single-seat Fokker scouts escorting an equal number of two-seat observation planes above the forests of Spincourt. He dove into the midst of them and a two-seater immediately went down. Five ships still remained. The enemy circled him, and he realized that his only chance of survival lay in staying in their midst, always keeping between two planes. If they fired, they might hit their own. Nungesser fluttered from spot to spot like a drunken bat, one eye always in a rearview mirror he had installed to check his position. Finally the Germans tired of the game and flew off. Nungesser limped home with his engines coughing and most of his controls shot away. His mechanics counted twenty-eight bullet holes in his plane.

As the war continued, his injuries began to catch up with him. He fell behind Fonck and Guynemer in the race for top ace. He acquired a roving commission training volunteer American aviators in the famous Lafayette Escadrille: he liked these uninhibited *Americains* and they liked him. He spent more and more time in Paris with his American friends, in clubs such as Maxim's, Harry's, the Chathams, and the Musée Guimet, and less time in the air. He became a favorite of the Paris social set, including the Dutch exotic dancer Margaretha Zelle, better known by her stage name Mata Hari.

Then the war ended. At first Nungesser lived in the social whirl that befitted a hero; he was revered, and when he wore his full-dress uniform, his Croix de Guerre stretched down to his navel thanks to the twenty-one attached silver palms. One beautiful spring day in 1919 he drank two bottles of champagne and swam the Seine through Paris in an open competition, finishing fifth. He dedicated his swim to the war's wounded veterans: "I want to show them that once a man wants to do something, they can," he said.

Despite his fame, peace was not kind to him. Nungesser struggled to find a place in the postwar world. In 1919 he opened a flying school at

Orly airport, but few people wanted to fly, and his school closed the same year. He designed an egg-shaped monoplane with 700-horsepower engines and V-shaped wings that swept forward in a 120-degree angle. Experts predicted she could reach the unheard-of speed of 250 miles per hour, but the plane never got off the drawing board. He designed amphibian "flivver" planes for the consumer market; a hundred were built with a selling price of $4,000, but very few were sold.

He even tried to make a living as a barnstormer. He bought a dozen surplus biplanes to stage epic mock dogfights, but they reminded people too much of the war, and this venture also failed. Such memories were too painful: the government held a mass burning of its warplanes, just to get rid of them. But in the United States such dogfights were a romantic rarity. Maybe, like so many Europeans in the past, he could reinvent himself in the New World. He kept three planes from his original fleet—a Hanriot HD.1, Potez, and Pioneer—and shipped them by liner to the United States.

And, as so often happens, love unexpectedly found him. Twelve years his junior, Consuelo Hatmaker was a Manhattan socialite with a Park Avenue address. Fluent in French, she was attending school in Paris when she met the dashing flier. She was dark, petite, adventurous, and rich; her mother, Nellie Sands, had married well. Nellie's first husband was the wealthy captain Joseph DeLamar, who'd made millions in 1898 in the gold mines around Leadville, Colorado. Her second husband (and Consuelo's father) was James R. Hatmaker, onetime confidential secretary to Cornelius Vanderbilt, which gave both women instant entry into New York society. It was a storybook match—the glamorous aviator, the beautiful socialite—but her father considered fliers frivolous and dissolute, and objected to Nungesser's attentions. Consuelo ignored her father. They were engaged in May 1923 after a whirlwind romance and filed for the marriage certificate with a Paris magistrate. James Hatmaker insisted that Consuelo postpone the ceremony, but on July 28, 1923, Consuelo and Charles wed in the English church at Dinard, in Brittany.

Consuelo accompanied Charles when he took the United States by storm. He built a modified "rumble seat" into the Hanriot's cockpit. Consuelo donned her leather flying suit as he barnstormed from Maine to Cuba, and as far west as St. Louis, where Lindbergh apparently saw him perform. Because of his marriage to Consuelo, Nungesser now had dual citizenship, which meant he could negotiate business deals. Sometime in 1925–26, he built a prototype for the "Nungesser Amphibian N.U.A.," a two-winged seaplane he planned to sell to the U.S. Air Mail. Built in North Point, Long Island, it could cruise at 73 miles per hour with a top speed of 100 miles per hour. Around this same time, the Cuban government asked for his help in building an air force. Nungesser inquired about purchasing some SPAD biplanes, and planned to serve as consultant once the Cuban venture began.

He went to Hollywood and, in April 1925, starred in the silent feature *The Sky Raider*, a tale about thieves hijacking the airmail, opposite Jacqueline Logan. Reviews were mixed. "The captain struggles through the leading role but it is easy to see that he would be more at ease in the face of a flock of enemies in the air than he is before the camera," commented *The Motion Picture News*. "However, it is not fair to expect an ace to be an actor also, so we'll have to overlook the acting part of his career."

Despite the lukewarm notices, the film did well. It was shot at Roosevelt Field, and Igor Sikorsky served as cameraman. The premiere was held in Grauman's Chinese Theatre with Nungesser's Nieuport parked out front. The movie moguls must have liked his style, for in 1926, he flew his Hanriot HD.1 with his "KNIGHT OF DEATH" emblem in the dogfight scenes of Howard Hawks's Oscar-winning *The Dawn Patrol*.

By 1926 the future seemed bright for Nungesser, but appearances were deceptive. Sales of his flivver plane and the N.U.A. amphibian had not taken off; the Cuban Air Force had yet to buy a single fighter; the barnstorming shows were losing steam. Much worse was the situation with Consuelo. Her father hated Nungesser: he threatened to cut off her allowance and write her out of his will if she did not get the marriage annulled. She was a child of privilege, and had no intention of living in what she considered poverty. Their divorce was granted by a Paris court on September 9, 1926, on the grounds of desertion.

Winning the Orteig Prize seemed the best way for Nungesser to pull out of this spiral. In 1919 he had joked that "I want to take a trip to America, but since the ship takes too long, I'll go by plane." In 1927 he was no longer joking: when he spoke of the trip, he did so in all seriousness. He and Consuelo continued seeing each other secretly after the divorce—though how well kept a secret it was is up for dispute, as a 1927 photo shows her on an airfield in France standing beside the *White*

Bird. He sent her back to the United States before he took off. If he won the $25,000, he would be rich, not only from the prize money but also from the endorsements and other business that would roll in. The airmail contract, the Cuban Air Force—all that would become real. He would be independently wealthy and able to give Consuelo the kind of life she'd always known. They'd thumb their noses at her father and be free.

Consuelo took an ocean liner back to the United States sometime in April. She knew her ace would take off sometime in May. She'd been living in Philadelphia since the divorce; it would be world news when Charles took off from Le Bourget. She could hop a train to New York and be there in just a few short hours.

This is what he would do, he told her. He would put his medals in a leather case and stick that case beneath his seat for the flight. When he landed at the foot of Lady Liberty, he would don his medals, then stand straight in the cockpit for all to see. Thousands would be watching as his plane was towed through the harbor to the end of the Battery. She would be there, waiting. Planes would roar overhead; fireboats would arc jets of water in a graceful curve. Thousands would cheer. But he would stand and search until he saw her face, then he would smile and wave.

Then nothing, and no one, would come between them again.

•

On the night of May 7, General Delcambre of the French meteorological service had good news and bad news. For the first third of their crossing, he told the fliers, the sky should be clear. The Americans had postponed their flights because of the rain and mist shrouding the East Coast. But those same conditions were good for French fliers: as an anticyclone formed over the North Atlantic, it had cut a clear lane between Iceland and the Azores, a favorable tailwind from the west coast of Ireland that would push them to Newfoundland. After that, however, Delcambre could not tell them what they might find. Weather reports from Greenland were inaudible, and he did not know the exact conditions in the northwest quadrant, around Newfoundland. Yet it was the best weather news they'd had for weeks, and might be the best news they would have for the immediate future. Lightning flashed outside.

Thunder boomed, but those were just local conditions. "You'll have 500 miles of favorable wind," said the general, "and you'll have to wait a long time for that to happen again."

"How about it?" Nungesser asked Coli. As navigator, his was the final say.

Coli is reported to have experienced a moment's hesitation. There were still many uncertainties. Yet the wait had been so long. He glared at Delcambre and said, "Very well, I will take the responsibility. We will go." He asked Nungesser if everything was ready, and it was. "All right, then we're off." They grasped one another's hand. Nungesser went home to try to sleep; Coli as well.

Paris subsisted on caffeine that night as the word spread. The early-edition French and English newspapers said that fueling would begin at 1:00 a.m. and takeoff at 4:00. It may even have been broadcast on the radio. The crowds streamed from the city to Le Bourget. It was a warm night; the rain let up and the stars appeared. Cars clogged the road leading to the airfield; many had come straight from the clubs in Montmartre and Montparnasse and were still dressed in dinner jackets or suits, satins, and furs. Others brought picnic baskets and bottles of wine or champagne. It was a national holiday, the Feast Day of St. Jeanne d'Arc. By 2:00 a.m. "many thousands" had crowded the edge of the airfield, separated from the hangar by a cordon of *poilus* with steel helmets and fixed bayonets.

Mechanics prepared the plane. They poured gas into the tanks from nearby drums, 880 gallons precisely. Provisions were loaded: dried fruit and vegetables, caviar, bananas, sardines, cold coffee, and a bottle of cognac for when they arrived. There would be no life raft or radio, to save weight; the only safety equipment, their watertight flying suits and a light under the fuselage that flashed the letter *N* in Morse code. Coli took a fishing line, with which he said he would catch cod, at Cape Cod.

At 3:00 a.m. the *White Bird* was wheeled from the hangar and onto the field. She looked silvery in the rays of the searchlights. The crowd cheered. Minutes later, Nungesser and Coli drove up dressed in street clothes. Nungesser, Levasseur, and several mechanics gave the plane one last check; Nungesser climbed in the cockpit and checked the instruments. The two were then escorted to a small room off the hangar, where Nungesser's personal physician gave him a massage and an injection of caffeine. They donned their warm yellow flying suits, and Coli tucked his old flying license in his pocket for luck, as well as a comb "to make myself handsome when we arrive and not disappoint the girls."

It was 5:00 a.m. Levasseur's chief mechanic started the machine. The propeller was so massive that it could not be hand-cranked, but had to be started with an injection of steam or compressed air. There was a deep and steady roar as the mechanic opened the throttle; when it did not miss a beat, he powered down.

They left the hangar. Nungesser limped from his old war wounds; Coli fell in behind him. A cheer rose from the crowd. Nungesser kissed two women, then joked with Maurice Chevalier and the boxer Georges Carpentier. A young woman threw him a rose; he caught it and blew her a kiss. The dancer Mistinguett embraced him. Madame Coli embraced her husband less theatrically, but tears rolled down her cheeks. He tenderly brushed them away. Pierre Levasseur kissed both pilots, and there were handshakes. "Allons!" said Nungesser, and the fliers climbed behind the controls.

It was 5:10 a.m. A fire blazed to the west; on the horizon, lightning flashed from the looming storm. An orderly ran up with a final forecast: a minor trough of depression had formed. Coli said they'd have to alter course a little to the north. "Contact!" cried Nungesser, and the propeller began to turn. The engine gave off little mauve flames. The mechanics pulled away the chocks, and the *White Bird* began to move.

At first the spectators feared that the plane would suffer the fate of the *American Legion*: five tons of plane had to lift up, and she'd never flown with a full load. Four small planes, propellers spinning, prepared to accompany the *White Bird* to the coast. It did not seem at first as if she could rise. The plane gathered speed, and after 1,000 yards Nungesser lifted her up. Then she sank back down. "My God, he'll never make it," one of Nungesser's wartime commanders said. But the plane roared on. Nungesser had said he would cut the switch if they were not airborne at 2,000 yards—and at 1,750 he tried again. She rose heavily, dipped, and straightened out at 50 feet. She fought the ground effect for altitude. It was 5:17 a.m. when she left the ground. The other planes tore after her as she passed over a ravine at the end of the field. One escort flier saw the detachable landing gear drop off as Nungesser fought to lighten his ship. She climbed to 700 feet and headed toward the Seine, twisting and turning to avoid the nearby hills.

Silence embraced the thousands assembled on the field. They had awaited this moment for months, and now they were stunned. When the *White Bird* vanished in the dark, they seemed to wake. A ragged cheer rose up. Then the storm that had threatened to break all night rumbled close and everyone ran for cover.

With four planes flanking her, the *White Bird* headed west. She passed Mantes-la-Jolie at 6:05 a.m., then veered slightly north to strike the coast at Etretat at 6:45. By then Nungesser, aided by a slight western breeze, had coaxed her up to 1,200 feet. The fliers who accompanied them estimated her speed at 115 miles per hour. The escorts dipped their wings in salute and turned back to Paris. Their last sight of the *White Bird* was a poignant one: she seemed fragile and small as she headed west northwest toward the southern coasts of England and Ireland.

The British saw her, too. Her Majesty's submarine H50 spotted a plane matching the description of the *White Bird* near Plymouth at around 8:30 a.m. Between 10:00 and 11:00 a.m. she was spotted by a vicar and his son, and by a coastal ship, near Fastnet Rock, near the southern coast of Ireland. Then she sped west, beyond the eyes of men.

•

Nungesser's American rivals were taken completely by surprise. They had all been grounded by the bad weather off the Northeast coast, and lulled into a complacent routine of tests and preparations. Wires describing the *White Bird*'s takeoff flooded New York immediately. Byrd's camp was strangely quiet, but the *Columbia* team was free with their feelings. Lloyd Bertaud called the Weather Bureau. Good weather did, in fact, exist off France, but closer to Newfoundland there were storms and headwinds. He knew the danger of such conditions, yet his ancestors were from France, and he could not help but feel proud. "They are brave men and have all my best wishes," he said. Chamberlin was more skeptical. "I don't see how they can make it," he said flat out, "but I wish them luck, and the best of it!" Bellanca added that "if the French fliers were successful, *Columbia* likely will not try the flight."

Levine was most admiring. He hoped they landed safely, he told the *Herald.* "They deserve to win. They are intrepid flyers and success should award their daring."

The suspense loosened many tongues. In his concern, Raymond Orteig finally put to words what Levine had already guessed: the rules no longer mattered. Although Nungesser had not officially registered for the Orteig Prize, Orteig admitted that whoever made it across the Atlantic first would get the $25,000, regardless of technicalities.

When the news made it to San Diego, Ryan's employees drifted in to console Lindbergh. No distress showed on his face, but Mahoney and Donald Hall had grown close to Slim, and the forced blankness of his expression said everything. The factory was as quiet as a funeral home. "I almost hope they don't make it," Hall said softly.

"Don't say that!" Lindbergh cried, his voice rising sharply. His face flushed, and the two men knew in an instant that he had been thinking the same thing.

"Aw, Charlie, I know how you feel," Mahoney said.

Lindbergh looked down at the maps and data pads that he still had clutched in his hands. "I've been going over the transpacific idea again," he said, attempting to change the subject. He spread the maps over the hood of Mahoney's black Studebaker and started jabbing at islands with his finger. "It's the route beyond Honolulu I'm worried about," he said. "I can arrange for gasoline drops on the islands, but how can I find them? I don't suppose anyone has a radio out there for me to pinpoint on."

There was only silence. It was one of the saddest things Hall and Mahoney had ever seen. "Charlie, let's wait to see whether they make it," Hall finally said.

Before he left, Nungesser wired Captain René Bouygée, president of the Federation of French War Veterans of New York, with his plans. The flier said he would land between the Statue of Liberty and the French line's Pier 57, berthage for the liner *De Grasse*. He estimated his arrival at 2:00 p.m. EST, or 8:00 p.m. Paris time, on Monday, May 9, though experts estimated that he had enough gas to last until 6:00 p.m. EST. The official New York greeting boat *Mecam* would stand ready at the Battery, all decked out in brightly colored flags. Grover Whalen, as usual, had arranged everything. Accompanying Whalen on the boat were Mayor Jimmy Walker, Richard Byrd, state and city notables, and Robert Nungesser, the flier's half brother, who lived in the suburbs of Washington, D.C. Five army pursuit planes from Mitchel Field would fly up the coast to meet *L'Oiseau Blanc* when she was sighted and guide her in. Bertaud, Chamberlin, and others made their own arrangements to take off when she neared the coast of Maine. A massive air armada would fly over New York from Teterboro Field. The Grand Ballroom of the hotel Astor was hired out for a huge reception on Friday the thirteenth, four days after their scheduled arrival.

One person was left out of the official lineup, but evidence exists that she was present. A photo in the *New York Daily News* showed Consuelo Hatmaker staring up at the sky. Although the caption does not expressly say that she waited at the Battery with the thousands of others who began assembling at 7:00 a.m., her snapshot was included in a photo montage of all those waiting to catch a glimpse of the *White Bird.* A later story in the *Daily Mirror* seemed to confirm it, too. Dressed in her furs, a hand held to her chest, she gazed overhead. They were divorced, she said, because Charles lived to fly, but "there would be a reconciliation if he succeeded in flying across the Atlantic."

The crowds waited in miserable conditions. The day was misty and gray, and from the Battery the Statue of Liberty was just a fuzzy, insubstantial shadow. Sometimes the mist turned into a gentle, soaking rain. Noon came, then one o'clock, and two. By then, Lady Liberty was concealed in mist, and the crowd strained to hear the faintest purr of a motor. Three o'clock arrived and there was still only the thick and quiet fog, turning the harbor into a gray field of ghosts, hiding the tops of skyscrapers. At 3:01 p.m. a report arrived of a sighting off Portland, Maine; a flash from Portsmouth, Massachusetts, of a white plane without wheels seen flying off the Isle of Shoals at 3:30. But these were false reports: the plane seen in Portland probably had pontoons, while the one south of Portsmouth was a Coast Guard amphibian eventually forced down by the weather.

James Kimball of the Weather Bureau said it was very likely that they had been delayed by the foul conditions. Their speed had probably been 100 to 115 miles per hour during the first part of the journey, but when they reached the mid-Atlantic they met headwinds of at least 25 miles per hour. These strengthened as they approached Newfoundland, cutting their speed to as low as 85 miles per hour. Though their original plan called for them to come off the ocean south of Newfoundland, the fog could have forced Coli to make a course correction, curving north above the steamer lanes, then dropping south in a wide arc to avoid a disorienting region of mist that in 1919 had nearly ended the flight of Alcock and Brown.

But conditions were worse than Kimball let on. Reports of a huge storm in the mid-Atlantic arrived via wireless from dozens of liners. A low-pressure cell that cut Newfoundland in half stretched far into the Atlantic. The storm was probably 500 to 1,000 miles across, with westerly winds of 30 miles per hour that would slow any plane in it to a speed of less than 70 mph. At 10:00 p.m. on the night of May 8, Nungesser and Coli would have been in the middle of that storm, fighting strong headwinds. If they'd detoured to the north of the cell and kept at low altitudes, the winds would have helped, but as they neared the North American coast, they almost certainly ran headlong into sleet and heavy clouds.

Four o'clock came and went in New York with a lifting of the fog but no further news. At 4:58 p.m. three navy seaplanes left Staten Island to search the Long Island coast for the missing plane. That day, 3,345 people called *The New York Times* asking about Nungesser and Coli. A few diehards remained at the Battery past 6:00 p.m., but most went home. At 6:20 p.m., *The New York Herald* posted a cable to its office in Paris: "Defying dangers and low visibility three fliers are skirting Long Island coast in search of Nungesser. It is doubted whether the French fliers have sufficient gasoline to remain longer in the air."

In Paris, *Le Presse* came out with an "extra" edition in the early evening, shortly after the 2:00 p.m. mark in Manhattan, when the *White Bird* was supposed to have landed. "THE ATLANTIC IS CONQUERED!" read its banner headline. "THE GOLDEN HOUR OF FRENCH AVIATION!" The story told of the plane's smooth landing in front of the Statue of Liberty; of the wild crowds cheering at the Battery; of the ticker tape parade down Broadway. Every ship in New York Harbor blew its siren; French and American flags hung from windows in every skyscraper. The fliers' families were contacted: "Luck has always been with my son," said Leontine Nungesser. Cried Coli's mother: "I knew my son would make it, because he told me he would." Cheering crowds poured onto the streets; cannons boomed at the Invalides. When photos of the fliers were flashed across the screens in theaters and cinemas, members of the audience stood and wept.

Unfortunately, *Le Presse* was wrong, its stories written in advance to beat the competition. Under pressure, other French dailies followed its lead. One paper did not—the Paris edition of the *Herald*, which had been receiving depressing cables from New York all day. A crowd swirled before its office at the Avenue de l'Opéra, demanding an explanation as to why the paper had not printed the joyous news. Voices from the crowd accused the Americans of silence in an attempt to belittle France's achievement; at last Albert Jannette, the paper's white-haired advertising manager, faced the crowd from an upper-story window. He was as proud of the fliers as any Frenchman, he said, but they could not run the story. The *White Bird*'s arrival had not been confirmed.

As the night dragged on, other French papers admitted that confirmation was lacking. Celebration turned to grief; someone must be held to blame. At first it was the Americans: *they'd* sent the false reports of the *White Bird*'s arrival. Either that, or the U.S. Weather Bureau had sent Nungesser and Coli to their deaths by reporting clear weather in the western Atlantic when in fact it was deadly. Both rumors were quickly disproved. The Paris office of the Météorologique National, under General Delcambre, leapt to the defense of their American brothers, saying its reports had been as detailed as possible.

Le Presse suffered most, and the resulting scandal eventually led to the paper's bankruptcy. Parisians seized all offending copies of the paper and burned them. They demonstrated wildly, at one point breaking into its offices. It was a frightening sight, and in a rearguard action, the French evening papers that had followed *Le Presse*'s lead tried to save themselves by signing a collective note shifting the blame to the government.

●

Though the loss was French, the grief was international. Something about their quest, and the loss, touched everyone. Some have said that the rejoicing over Lindbergh's flight would not have been so frenzied if not for the mourning over Nungesser and Coli. When the "Lindbergh religion" burst forth, and Slim was portrayed as Christ, Americans tended to forget that the *White Bird* had gone before him. But the Americans were not completely hardened. "Man is still thrilled and a little exalted by great daring in the face of death," wrote Russell Owen in *The New Yorker*. "Nungesser and Coli did not fail—for a moment they lifted the world out of its shabby materialism into the realm of romance."

Yet that does not answer the question of what happened to the *White Bird*. On the night of May 9 and into May 10 there still was no word. Searchlights swept the sky above New Jersey's Sandy Hook; fishermen scoured the Newfoundland coast; ocean liners watched for floating debris. In time, Floyd Bennett would come out of the hospital and, sponsored by *Aviation Magazine*, for nine days backtrack the area between Maine and Newfoundland where the *White Bird* might have gone down. Hundreds of private and military pilots did the same. The Canadian Ministry of Lands and Forests sent up two float planes, which crashed and required their own rescue. Hunters and fishermen searched the forests and coasts for signs of life or hints of wreckage.

But there never was a sign. Nungesser and Coli had simply vanished. Their disappearance remains one of the great mysteries of aviation, as equal in import and as subject to speculation as Amelia Earhart's disappearance in the Pacific ten years later.

Ironically, the two aviators apparently did conquer the Atlantic, considered the deadliest part of the journey. On the early morning of May 9, seventy-year-old Anna Kelly walked outside her home near Harbor Grace either to hang her laundry or to do some gardening, depending on the account. She heard a loud noise and looked up; she saw what she said were two "white birds" flying south. She'd never heard of Nungesser and Coli, and authorities later guessed that she had seen the double wings of a biplane. It came off the ocean in the fog and flew between two cliffs that other rivals would later use to align their flights across the ocean. Smoke streamed from the strange apparition, she said. This, too, would make sense: the engine did not have valve covers, and the oil that bathed it was continuously pumped up from the bottom of the housing. After thirty hours of flight, the engine would have been hot. When this hit the cool Newfoundland mist, the rising condensation would have resembled smoke streaming from the engine.

Another eight to twelve people would tell authorities they heard or saw a plane pass overhead that morning in Newfoundland. The reports followed a straight line south and west, from Harbor Grace toward the Gulf of St. Lawrence, New Brunswick, and Maine. Ebeneezer Peddle and his eighteen-year-old son, James, were working in the fields a mile past Harbor Grace when they saw "a large white machine in the air" at about 9:00 a.m. Elizabeth Munn heard it pass as she fed her chickens. Sergeant Roberts heard a drone and what sounded like a blast over Conception Bay. Some lobstermen saw a white airplane heading west over the Bay of Fundy, which separates New Brunswick and Nova Scotia.

After that she disappeared.

The search for the "Ghost Plane" continues today. A current theory has the *White Bird* leaving Newfoundland and heading southwest toward the French islands of Saint-Pierre and Miquelon, not far west off the Burin Peninsula. The rum boat *Amistad* lay in anchor nearby, loaded with bootleg rum. The crew of eight heard a motor overhead, in the fog. Thinking it was U.S. Treasury agents, they fired into the sky, and heard a loud bang. A fisherman on shore also heard the shots and explosion, but kept quiet for fear of retaliation. He told his story two years later, when Dieudonné Costes and Maurice Bellonte became the first French fliers to survive the Paris–New York passage. They stopped in Newfoundland and asked about rumors of the *White Bird*; at that point, the fisherman came forward.

This seems supported by a recently discovered clue, found in a Washington archive by French aviation enthusiast Bernard Decré. An internal Coast Guard telegram dated August 18, 1927, mentioned the remains of a white aircraft that "may be the wreck of the Coli-Nungesser airplane." Spotted 200 miles off New York, it had apparently drifted south with the currents. If this story is true, the fifth and sixth casualties in the Orteig race were not victims of overloading or bad weather but of American Prohibition.

It is only a mystery now, covered by woods or waves, but during that summer of 1927, and in the years immediately following, it was much more. Numerous ocean pilots dropped flowers, wreaths, and other mementoes in mid-ocean to honor Nungesser and Coli. The rumors continued. Not all gave up hope, including Nungesser's mother.

She sat in her apartment at 33 boulevard du Temple surrounded by memories of her son. The parlor was covered with his photos and decorations, and was dominated by a huge portrait that stood on an easel in the center of the room. One had to walk around it to get anywhere else. Until October 24, 1940, when she stepped onto a Paris street and was run down and killed by a sixteen-year-old boy on a bicycle delivering bread, she never truly believed he was dead. On February 23, 1928, nine months after he had taken Paris by storm, she wrote to Lindbergh. "I am still waiting for my poor son," she said:

I feel that he is *so unhappy* that the wait has made me ill, especially not knowing at all the place he could be. We have searched a lot, it's true, but my son was maybe wounded and will not maybe have the strength to get in touch. We were searching *too high*. It's *lower* that we have to search.

You are an ace and a bird. Could you, yourself, look for my poor Charles? (He doesn't have any identification on him.) You are so admirable, you could maybe find his location or some kind of clue, to where he is.

Canada is big—is he maybe there in a weakened state with hardly anything to protect him from the cold and very little food and it seems that you could know something about that. I'm putting all my hope in you—my life at present is so sad.

FOURTEEN

CURTISS FIELD

By Tuesday, May 10, the *White Bird* was officially listed as missing. Paris spent the following day mourning its loss. Some had hoped that Nungesser and Coli would be rescued by a fishing vessel off Newfoundland's Grand Banks, but these hopes were destroyed when dispatches from Halifax explained that, because of the threat of ice, few boats ventured out at this time of year. "Charles will come back," his mother said. "He has never failed." She waved her right hand dismissively when a reporter asked whether she was upset by the news. She walked to the window and looked up at the sky. "If he doesn't come back, I'll go look for him myself," she said.

But on the street, the French shook their heads. "Another loss," they said—another loss in a nation that had suffered so many losses during the Great War. Among those who'd flown with the two aces, one could hear the traditional refrain uttered when a squadron member died: "This is another man who won't go out on Sunday patrol."

That Monday, May 9, while everyone waited for the *White Bird*, Byrd finally came out of seclusion. His wrist had healed, his plane was fixed, and he would head for Paris as early as Saturday, May 14, he said. It was announced for the first time that Bert Acosta would take Floyd Bennett's place in the cockpit. The Bellanca team countered that *they* would take off as soon as the weather cleared.

Some did not think this a good idea. French newspapers still blamed America for sending misleading weather reports and for news cables that erroneously announced the *White Bird*'s arrival. It took a few more days for them to admit that the mistake was closer to home. As the full nature of their loss finally settled on France, Myron T. Herrick, the U.S.

ambassador in Paris, warned the State Department that the immediate start of any plane for Le Bourget might be "misunderstood and misinterpreted." He advised all fliers to wait until the *White Bird*'s fate was known.

As the wait stretched on, desperation grew. The French government offered a $2,000 reward for credible news of their fate. Raymond Orteig, in his grief and guilt, offered $5,000 to the aviator who discovered the fliers or traces of their plane. Not to be outdone, Rodman Wanamaker posted $25,000 for anyone who found them dead or alive.

In California, Lindbergh saw another reprieve. On May 8, when word first arrived about the *White Bird*'s takeoff, he was ready to ditch the competition and cross the Pacific. On May 10, when it was obvious the Frenchmen were lost, he changed his mind.

•

From the day of its maiden flight until May 8, Lindbergh put *Spirit* through twenty-three test flights that lasted anywhere from five minutes to a little over an hour. He took off from Dutch Flat, Rockwell Field on North Island, and Camp Kearney, testing speed and load. He increased the amount of gas he carried in increments, starting at 38 and ending at 300 gallons. During the last test, *Spirit* rose in 20 seconds, but the field at Camp Kearney was rough and stony, and the plane sustained some minor damage: the wheel bearings overheated, the tail skid broke, and the shock absorbers bottomed out. He'd intended to make tests up to the full load of 400 gallons, but if he did that and blew out a tire, he could wreck the plane. When he took off for Paris, he decided, he would either make it up or not. The final test for full capacity would be a make-or-break affair.

Stories began to circulate that he had trained himself to stay awake by taking long nightly walks around San Diego, though biographers maintain that such stories were false. But he did intend to fly at night from San Diego to St. Louis, the first 1,500 miles of his journey to New York. He'd never flown through an entire night, and he wanted to check several things before the final flight to Paris. He wanted to test how well he could hold a course in the dark by compass and dead reckoning, knowing that success would put paid to the critics who brought up his lack of experience in long-distance flying.

Those final days in San Diego passed in a happy haze. *Spirit* was a triumph, more nimble and responsive than he had dreamed possible. Yet those days also played on his nerves. Persistent rumors of the *Columbia*'s imminent departure reached him from the east. News of Nungesser's takeoff hit him hard, while news of the Frenchman's failure was a guilt-laden relief. Lindbergh began to change. He started to harden.

The change in him became noticeable after the first report of his maiden flight came back. He responded to the perceived criticism with a mistrust and distance that would define his relationship with the media for the rest of his days. The article that started it all read "Lindbergh Escapes Crash, Plane Near Collision," and was a small "brief" reported in the San Diego paper on April 29, one day after *Spirit*'s maiden flight. Picked up the next day by *The New York Times* as "Lindbergh Plane Near Disaster," the story ran deep inside, on page 21. It claimed that he had "narrowly escaped disaster" when he "almost collided" with the Curtiss Hawk over North Island. Slim felt the piece disparaged his flying skill. His early feeling of triumph turned to one of bitterness. As he read the San Diego story over breakfast, his attitude toward the press began to change. In St. Louis he'd liked the reporters covering Lambert Field and was always eager to describe the St. Louis–Chicago mail run. But nothing was worse in Lindbergh's book than questioning his skill as a pilot, no matter how innocently or inadvertently. On this he could be remarkably thin-skinned. It is around this time that he starts to complain that reporters distract him from the important matters of life: the details of his flight and his plane. Reporters, photographers—and later the public—become alien creatures for him; his standard response around them, to hide.

This illustrates a part of Slim's personality that would become more evident with fame. There was little give-and-take with Lindbergh—it was all black and white, with only the occasional shade of gray. His relations with the press were the first glimmer of this Manichean worldview. His dealings with the San Diego press, when viewed in this light, are doubly ironic since that city's reporters had been unusually accommodating to him. He'd essentially asked San Diego reporters to work for him, keeping quiet about his progress while keeping him informed on that of Byrd and Levine. When he sold his story exclusively to *The New York Times* a few weeks later, they felt cheated.

By Saturday, May 7, the day before Nungesser's surprise flight, Lindbergh was clearly ready to go. It was only the "storms, rain and fog along nearly the entire route from here to St. Louis" that held him up. By May 10, the bad weather had cleared and a low pressure area was spreading east from the Pacific, bringing with it clear skies and tailwinds. That morning, he packed a small suitcase and dropped into the Ryan factory to say goodbye. He then flew to North Island, where he gassed up and, at 3:55 p.m., started the engine. *Spirit* climbed to the left as two army observation planes and a Ryan M-2 monoplane took off after him. Lindbergh circled North Island, the Ryan factory, and San Diego, and then headed east. At 4:30 p.m. the escort planes dipped their wings in a final salute and turned back. Lindbergh was finally off.

The first part of the trip passed easily. Lindbergh stared at the coastal mountains below as he flew inland: they were strewn with boulders and laced with crevices. "What a hopeless place for a forced landing," he mused. He flew over Arizona at 5,000 feet as the sun went down; the terrain glowed in the moonlight, and he held his compass course at about 55 degrees. He eased the ship up to 8,000 feet and settled back in the cockpit, watching the luminous dials.

Without warning, the engine vibrated and sputtered. *Spirit*, though very slowly, began to descend. His imagination took over: landing in the night, in the mountains, would be the end. Fortunately the rate of descent was slow enough that he had time to analyze the problem. He set the throttle and fuel mixture controls in various combinations and finally concluded that altitude and the cold night air had caused ice to form in the carburetor. Finally the sputtering ceased and the Whirlwind ran smoothly again. He climbed slowly to 13,000 feet and, at 10:00 p.m., cleared the peak of the Continental Divide by 500 feet. He sat back and relaxed, vowing to install a carburetor heater once he landed in Long Island. Soon he watched the sun peek over Kansas. He saw windmills, oil derricks, the smoke of a train, and at 8:20 a.m. Central Time, 14 hours and 21 minutes after leaving North Island, he powered down and landed at Lambert Field.

He taxied up to the black hangars of his old National Guard squadron at the edge of the field. Frank and Bill Robertson, plus a small clutch of friends, aviators, and reporters, watched as he climbed from the cockpit. He'd just set a new record for a nonstop flight over this course, averaging over 100 miles per hour. Lindbergh's backers arrived and admired their new plane for the first time. Though he was pleased with the flight as a whole, he neglected to tell his backers about the engine trouble over the Rockies. He'd been only 50 miles off course through the night, and that without the aid of his earth inductor compass, which had stopped working over the mountains. A new compass and the carburetor heater could be installed once he landed in New York.

The small crowd escorted Lindbergh to Louie Dehatre's lunch shack next to the hangar, where Slim ordered ham and eggs. Harold Bixby arrived while he was still chowing down, and Lindbergh quizzed him and others about the progress of his rivals, especially his greatest threat, the Bellanca. How about Nungesser and Coli? There was a rumor that they'd been picked up by a British ship, but no confirmation. They handed him his new transport pilot's license and asked if he'd heard the State Department's warning not to fly to France until something definite was known about the *White Bird*.

"Has the government put any restrictions on taking off?" Lindbergh asked.

"No," came the answer. "That's apparently up to the pilots. There weren't any restrictions issued, just the warning." What would he do? someone asked. Lindbergh said he'd figure it out when he got to New York, though to reporters he said, "I am very sorry that Nungesser and Coli seem to have failed in their brave attempt to cross the Atlantic in the wrong direction. I hope they will be picked up. But their experience, whatever it proves to be, will not affect my plans."

He spent the night at his old boardinghouse, preparing for the final cross-country flight. He catalogued his few possessions and packed them in a steamer trunk with instructions should he never return. They included a gift from his father, a collapsible rod and reel he had used as a boy in Little Falls, made by the Rainbow Company. He folded his khaki and olive shirts with the "CAL" laundry mark inside the collar. He stowed a booby-trap practical joke that sprung at the unwary, a collection of news clippings about the crashes and deaths of other pilots, a toothbrush, shaving kit, straight razor, keys to the room in his boardinghouse, and some pocket change. He wrapped the possessions in brown paper, stuck on a label and bound them in twine. He rolled his last will and testament in a mailing tube and addressed it to his mother.

He rose at five the next morning, Thursday, May 12, and ate sirloin steak and four eggs at Louie's. *Spirit* was fueled up with Red Crown gas and serviced with Mobiloil "B." He took off at 8:13 a.m. and headed east into a clear blue sky. Over the Alleghenies he hit clouds low enough to hide the peaks, so he flew through the passes. At the end of the seventh hour, he saw Manhattan below him, where millions of people lived and worked, "each one surrounded by a little aura of his problems and his thoughts, hardly conscious of earth's expanse beyond." He thought of the huge country he'd just crossed, characterized by long, lonely spaces. "I feel cooped up just looking at it," he said.

From the air, the three airfields involved in the Derby looked peaceful. On one side lay Long Island's suburbs; on the other, farmers' fields. Curtiss, Roosevelt, and Mitchel fields were so close they seemed—from Slim's vantage point—side by side. Mitchel was the best kept, since it was an army field, but the sod was too rough for takeoff and landing. Curtiss, where Lindbergh would now land, was too small for the takeoff of a heavy plane. Only Roosevelt's runway met the requirements: a mile-long strip running east to west that put the plane straight into a head-wind coming off the sea.

Lindbergh touched down at Curtiss at 5:33 p.m. He'd flown 7 hours and 20 minutes from St. Louis to New York, for a total elapsed time in the air of 21 hours and 20 minutes, beating the old transcontinental record set in 1923 by 5.5 hours. As he checked the wind sock for landing, he noticed a crowd of two or three hundred staring up at him. Photographers fanned out, some right where he wanted to land. He banked to the side and came down at an angle to the wind. *Spirit* was immediately surrounded by news- and cameramen. He shouted at them to stay clear of the propeller, but no one paid attention. Spectators began pushing and shoving one another. Dick Blythe, co-owner of the PR firm Blythe and Bruno, which handled press relations for Wright Aeronautical, introduced himself and told Lindbergh that a team of Wright mechanics headed by Spoons Boedecker and Ed Mulligan had been assigned to his plane. Since all three planes in the race used Wright J-5 engines, the company had decided to assign mechanics to every flier and not play favorites. Lindbergh climbed from his cockpit and the cameramen crowded around. They stood, knelt, or lay on the dirt for the best angle, and shouted instructions:

"Smile!"

"Look this way, will you?"

"Say something."

Chamberlin and Bertaud strolled over from their hangar, unable to contain their curiosity. The newsmen cajoled Slim and Clarence to pose for a picture together. "May the best man win!" someone shouted from the crowd.

Lindbergh grinned down at the shorter Chamberlin. "I guess that goes both ways."

"You bet it does," Chamberlin replied.

•

Chamberlin gazed at the blond newcomer towering over him and knew that everything had changed.

Even before Lindbergh's arrival, the *Columbia* and her crew found themselves in a race against time. They'd announced on May 10, the day the young flier took off from San Diego, that they planned to leave for Paris the coming Saturday, May 14. The weather guided that decision: the first letup in the rain and fog that had plagued them for so long would come over the weekend, James Kimball predicted. Superstition also figured into the decision: nobody wanted to fly on Friday the thirteenth, Levine told the press. There'd already been too much bad luck in this race. No point tempting fate again.

Still, agreeing to go, and when, had been painful. They'd reached their decision late on Monday, May 9, after a long debate in the hangar among Levine, Bellanca, and the pilots. They'd just received word of Ambassador Herrick's warning about anti-American feelings, and stopped all work in astonishment. Bellanca didn't believe it at first; he called *The New York Times* and had a friendly reporter read Herrick's dispatch to him. "We seem to be going up and down," he groaned, "making altitude but no distance."

By 11:00 p.m. they had decided to go. "Any anti-American feeling which may exist in France is so ill-founded that it can exist only with a few and will quickly pass," Levine said carefully. "Our flight will not start before Saturday, at which time we have a promise of better weather and a full moon." They hoped that Nungesser and Coli would be found by then, he added.

Bertaud and Chamberlin were more outspoken in their desire to leave. More delays would merely give the French more time to prepare another plane. "We won't go to Paris if they don't want us," said Bertaud. "We'll fly over and around the Eiffel Tower, land our wheels at Le Bourget and then go to London and land at Cobham Field." Nungesser and Coli were brave men and great fliers, they said, but they had known the risks. "They tried to get the jump on us and we hoped for their success as much as anyone in France did. Now is our chance. Let's go."

On Wednesday, May 11, as Lindbergh was landing in St. Louis, the *Columbia* team was preparing to leave. Willda Chamberlin and Helen Bertaud spent the afternoon making sandwiches and thermoses of hot chocolate at the Garden City Hotel, which had become their headquarters. A technician for the Pioneer Instrument Company made adjustments on the compasses. Doc Kinkade of Wright Aeronautical tested the engine. John Carisi and his mechanics went over every inch of the exterior for flaws in the fabric covering or loose bolts, rivets, and cords. The wheels of the landing gear were painted red, white, and blue.

All the gears seemed to be meshing smoothly. Yet Chamberlin could see three points of discord within his team.

The first point of contention was the radio—whether they should have one. The debate had no clear-cut winner. A sophisticated transmitting and receiving set with its own generator added at least 30 pounds to the total load. Even a simple transmitter, which relayed an SOS, required a heavy generator. But if the plane went down, that same radio could be a lifesaver.

The wireless debate caused huge discord. Both Levine and Bertaud wanted a radio: each, without the other's knowledge, hoped to sell the story of the flight to the newspapers, and real-time bulletins from the airplane hiked up the asking price by adding drama. Levine had a second reason: he justifiably felt he could be blamed if his fliers came down in the ocean and were unable to call for aid. Chamberlin was against a radio because of the weight factor, and Bellanca sided with him.

Bellanca was the most upset. The best radios could still be received only 125–150 miles away; the set weighed 10 pounds, while the generator weighed another 20. The latter gave him nightmares. This generator was powered by a blade whirling in the air, and the best place to attach it was on one of the wing struts. But doing so cut 3 miles per hour from total speed and caused the strut—and the entire wing—to vibrate. Over the course of 3,600 miles, that could lead to an unseen host of potentially catastrophic problems.

As the debate raged, Bellanca's mechanics mounted, dismounted, and remounted the generator to the wing—which delayed the takeoff. Each time the generator was mounted, the compass needed to be reset, a process that cost seventy-five dollars. In the end, Bellanca and Chamberlin prevailed, and the only radio included in the cabin was a small battery-powered set able to transmit an SOS for up to 25 miles.

Two other debates raged simultaneously with the radio issue. Chamberlin and Bertaud wanted Levine to provide them with $50,000 life insurance coverage to protect their wives should they be lost at sea. Levine resisted. Also, Chamberlin and Bertaud argued among themselves about the route. Should they follow the shorter Great Circle Route along the top of the North Atlantic, as Chamberlin wished, or should they take Bertaud's more southerly choice, which lessened the threat of icing?

With Lindbergh's arrival, the media madness seemed to increase exponentially. Chamberlin was used to seeing the public act wildly, but in this case it was normally brash journalists, whose cynicism seemed a point of pride, who acted crazy. He felt a little sorry for Lindbergh; they wouldn't let him get away. When the young arrival turned to walk to the hangar, the cameramen snapped photos three feet away from his face. They closed in around him, firing questions.

"When're you going to start for Paris?"

"Tell us something about your flight from California."

"Did you have any close calls?"

It was actually a little frightening. Chamberlin was pushed to the side. The only thing missing, he thought, was Richard Byrd. As if on cue, a deep drone passed overhead. They all glanced up. "Look! There's the *America!*" a journalist cried.

The big trimotor Fokker circled Roosevelt Field and landed. It was the first time anyone had seen it since the crash; its arrival, at nearly the same moment as the *Spirit of St. Louis*, felt like a challenge.

"That's the first time it's been over here," said one reporter.

"Byrd must be ready to go again," another replied.

•

It wasn't Richard Byrd who ferried *America* from Fokker's shop to Roosevelt Field, but Bernt Balchen. He sat in the cockpit with Leroy Thompson of Colonial Air Transport and looked down at the sleek silver gull resting on the grass at Curtiss. With all the gawkers swirling around it, he knew the mail pilot from San Diego must have arrived. He landed at Roosevelt and taxied to the main hangar.

Balchen had not left Uncle Tony's factory for eleven days. After leaving Bennett's hospital room, he had hurried to Fokker's shop, where the Dutchman hired him on the spot as his test pilot. Balchen lived, ate, and slept there, working around the clock with the others to make the *America* airworthy again. He had a cot in the factory and grabbed meals at a quick-lunch counter across the field. To overcome the nose-heavy condition that had caused the crash, they relocated the navigator's compartment behind the main fuel tank, thus redistributing weight more evenly fore and aft. They built a catwalk connecting the cockpit to the back cabin; it led under one side of the oval tank, so that a man could slide back and forth on his belly. Day and night the work continued. On May 12, the *America* rolled out the factory doors for the first time since the crash and Balchen made a couple of short takeoffs and landings. They made some minor adjustments and then he flew her to Roosevelt Field.

Balchen had rarely seen Byrd during the refitting. Acosta sometimes dropped by to inspect the plane, and Bernt liked the man. He seemed a decent guy, if a little reckless. With that olive skin and close-cropped black moustache, Acosta reminded Balchen of a Hollywood sheikh, and he could see why women fell for him. Acosta's addition to the team was no longer a secret, though it hadn't yet been made official. Now, as Balchen rolled to the hangar, he saw Byrd dressed in full flying regalia. The commander had come over from Hasbrouck Heights in an earlier plane. He looked "slim and handsome in his flying clothes," Balchen later wrote, "high-topped boots and regulation breeches, and his dark curly hair is unruffled by the wind." George Noville stood behind him, dressed the same way. George, as always, was a sphinx—his eyes behind his horn-rimmed glasses rarely gave away his feelings; the straight line of his mouth was expressionless.

This was a photo shoot to introduce Acosta officially as the newest member of the team. Whereas Byrd and Noville wore their aviators' pants and boots for the photographers, Acosta was more casually dressed, in a gray tweed suit and tweed cap. He looked like an English lord going for a Sunday drive. The cameramen posed Byrd and Noville in front of the *America*, and Byrd called Acosta over to join them. But Lindbergh had stolen their thunder, and few could stop talking about the newcomer parked in the next field.

Though Byrd looked as picture perfect as ever, Balchen knew that something in him had changed. Davis's death and Bennett's injury had damaged him more than any physical blow could have. He no longer seemed interested in the race. He could put on a good show, but he didn't seem to care if he ever took off for Paris. The old fire was gone.

He seemed like a man reaching out for help, and it would be at times like this that his famous self-pitying drinking bouts occurred. "Where can I get another man like Bennett, who is a combination mechanic and pilot?" he pled on April 28 to Captain Jerry Land of the navy's Bureau of Aeronautics. "I expect after this terrible disaster and our mishap, the Navy will not allow anyone else to go into any spectacular flights, and I do not blame them a bit for that." He expected to rebuild the *America*, he said, but after that he was "not sure just what we will do. It is a long story." If anything, he sounded tired. The race had sucked him dry.

He rallied a bit on Wednesday, May 11, the day Lindbergh landed in St. Louis, two days after Nungesser and Coli disappeared. Maybe he'd felt the approach of the new rival; maybe he had simply grown tired of sitting around. He knew that the *America* was almost ready, and that Acosta had joined as their pilot; after all his waiting, he wanted to do something. He wired Wanamaker: "After the test flight tomorrow, would you be willing to consider the practicability of sending the *America* on a searching expedition [for Nungesser and Coli]? My personal services are at your disposal."

By all accounts, Wanamaker was intrigued, though he eventually replied, "I cannot give you that permission." The French were earnestly pursuing a search with the Canadians. They would see Byrd as an intrusion, he said.

So Byrd tried again. If he couldn't go on the search, why leave *America* idle? She was ready to go. Once the plane went through her tests, Wanamaker should give him permission to take off for Paris. But Wanamaker disagreed. No flight until the fate of the two Frenchmen was determined. No flight until more "scientific" tests were performed.

One must take chances, Byrd argued.

No flight, the reclusive millionaire said.

It must have been a heated exchange between the two. Wanamaker rarely explained his reasons to the press, and on the rare occasions he did, he did so very tersely, giving only a brief sentence or two. But on May 12, the day after his refusal of Byrd, he explicitly told the papers that *America* would not fly until Nungesser and Coli had been found or until "the world accepted their loss as the supreme sacrifice to·the science of aviation." Even then, his ship would not fly until every safeguard had been installed and tested. His plane was not in a race, he reminded everyone. His flight was "solely in the cause of scientific progress."

He ended his statement like a man grown tired of addressing the same questions again and again. "The *America* has not yet been accepted by me and will not be until its test flights prove its scientific soundness," he said. "And when it does come into my hands, I shall not release it for the transatlantic flight until the uncertainty over the French aviators is dispelled. Pioneering requires boldness, but it should be guided as far as possible by the slower but surer hand of science."

The press was too preoccupied with Lindbergh's arrival to notice the feuding within the team. Lindbergh's situation with the press was veering toward the absurd. He was momentarily rescued from the reporters by Dick Blythe, only to be steered right back in front of the pack. "Good Lord," Slim wailed, "haven't they got enough photographs?"

"I know," Blythe said, trying to soothe him, "but they say it will only take five minutes, and that they won't take any more."

The questions came fast and furious. First they asked about the plane. But then the questions got even stranger:

"Do you carry a rabbit's foot?"

"What's your favorite pie?"

"Have you got a sweetheart?"

"How do you feel about girls?"

Chamberlin left the madness and walked back to his hangar before he, too, got drawn in. He shook his head.

No doubt about it. Things were going to get crazy.

FIFTEEN

THE WAITING GAME

Soon after his arrival in New York, Lindbergh was taken to the nearby Garden City Hotel, temporary home for many of the rivals. Although he wanted to stay at the field near *Spirit*, there was no place in the hangar to sleep. He rode to the hotel with Joe Hartson, his liaison with Wright, and asked about Dick Blythe and Harry Bruno, whom he knew nothing about but who would play an important role in his flight preparations. "They're your buffers," Hartson said. "Both fliers. They're O.K." He suggested that Slim and Blythe take a double room on the third floor. Lindbergh nodded his acceptance but apparently didn't warm to the idea. That night and for the next three days, Blythe later remembered, "We bedded down like two strange wildcats, each in his own hole."

Although Lindbergh didn't know it, the Garden City provided a glimpse into his life to come. Located twenty miles from Manhattan, the fifty-three-year-old hotel still clung fast to its connections with New York's Gilded Age. It was the de rigueur home away from home for the Vanderbilts, Astors, Pierpont Morgans, and other stars of the Social Register when they flocked to Long Island for the sporting season. The pilots could drive to their hangars in five minutes; for most, the hotel would be the most palatial quarters they had ever known. But there was a downside to such luxury, since the Garden City's lobby filled daily with businessmen, reporters, and the curious.

Lindbergh got a taste of this on his first night there. He'd eaten dinner and joined Bertaud and Chamberlin on the porch outside overlooking the great lawn. There was no moon or stars that night; all were hidden by low-hanging clouds. Crickets whirred in the background; in the distance, they could see the glow of the city. They leaned upon the rail and talked about Coli and Nungesser. What had happened to them? Had they made it to Newfoundland or perished out at sea? In a couple of days, they knew, they could just as easily be the topic of the same conversation.

On the fringes stood some bankers listening to them talk. They'd come to the Garden City to attend a convention, but when they saw the three move outside, all their thoughts of finance were abandoned. They clustered near and "listened with evident wonder at their quiet and unassuming courage," wrote *The New York Times* in the next day's edition, as if such eavesdropping were the most natural occurrence in the world.

A curious shift takes place at this moment, as if the old rules of privacy no longer applied. For the first time in the race—and possibly in celebrity culture—a private conversation was reported in a "serious" paper as news. Yet all parties had to agree on the intrusion, the fliers especially, for instead of moving their discussion to a more private place, they continued as "normally" as actors on a stage.

With Lindbergh's arrival and the continuing string of tragedies, we begin to see the fliers portrayed in a new way. They are painted as a different breed of men, an idea that hearkens back to the "Alti-Men" who would lead mankind to a new and better age. Their difference from the average man made them subject to constant curiosity that broke down the old walls of privacy. "When airmen talk, as they rarely do, you discern something that sets them off as a race apart," mused Russell Owen in *The New Yorker*, one of the few journalists allowed into their inner circle. "They actually live in another world," he wrote, probably referring to what he'd heard about this conversation:

Gradually you understand that it is *necessary* for these men to attempt the impossible. It is a necessity as impelling as that of breathing. They must see if they and their planes can do it. And each one of them thinks that failure, death even, of the other man was due to some mistake on his part: he didn't have quite so good a plane, or he went west because his time had come. Something inside them drives them on.

As the fliers' privacy diminished, the level of public interest soared. On Curtiss and Roosevelt fields, the black sedans gathered in the night.

Most cars of that time were the black square boxes of the Model T. Some parked at the fields, while scores more parked along the roads. Their owners stood quietly, watching mechanics work on the Bellanca-, Ryan-, and Fokker-designed planes. Who would win?, they asked. Who would die? No light shone from the moon or stars. All were cast in shadow and gloom.

"It was an unusual spectacle on a flying field," observed the Times, "for perhaps never before has there been such interest in a long distance contest."

•

The Times's front-page story announcing Spirit's arrival read like a love letter to Charles Lindbergh. Without any buildup or gradual transition, he was presented as a pure and sturdy youth straight out of The Aeroplane Boys and other adventure series; a corn-fed, red-blooded, all-American boy. It was an amazing moment for the otherwise sober "paper of record." New York's first introduction to Lindbergh reads like something from a romance novel. Spirit lands and taxies to a stop: "A window opened and the smiling face of a man who seemed little more than a boy appeared. His pink cheeks, dancing eyes and merry grin seemed to say: 'Hello, folks. Here I am and all ready to go.'

"No moving picture director could have planned a better entrance for the youngster," the paper continued. His landing was the finale to a cross-country hop "that made spectators chuckle and slap each other on the back." Lindbergh's "bashful and infectious smile won the heart of every one who saw him." One could not help but love him. "Pink-cheeked, fresh and smiling, he looked the embodiment of youthful health and confidence. Even his collar was spotless, and his flying suit was immaculate."

This description goes from the sychophantic to the bizarre, and eventually borders on hagiography. Not only was Lindbergh pure and spotless, but his shirt was, too, an impressive feat considering the number of miles he'd worn it in a cramped cockpit. It was the opening note of a chorus that swelled quickly as Slim prepared his plane. Lindbergh could do no wrong. When it later became evident that he was less than perfect and could do wrong, evidence of his imperfections was obscured; it would not appear in print for years and even then only in cautiously worded code. Time magazine called him a "sudden, romantic national hero" who grinned "like a schoolboy emerging from a showerbath" when he arrived. "Romantic speculators soon placed bets that Lone Pilot Lindbergh, 25 and tousled-haired, would be the first to reach Paris." Will Rogers said, "This lad is our biggest national asset. He is our prince and president combined." According to *Current History,* Lindbergh "so typifies the spirit of clean knighthood that men have honored him greatly." More than one publication would dust off the old appellation for Great War aces and deem him a "knight of the air."

Given such adoration, it seemed but an instant before Lindbergh was turned into an object of desire. Take, for example, the incident of the "mirror girl." May 13 was a busy day for Lindbergh in Hangar 16. He talked with his Wright engine experts about his problems over the Rockies, and they decided to install a carburetor air intake heater. A technician from Pioneer Instruments fixed the compass; the press asked for photographs; Lindbergh took *Spirit* up to test his propeller's new spinner assembly. A sizable crowd collected outside the hangar. When a specialist mentioned the need for a mirror, a young woman dug into her purse, held up a standard compact, and cried, "Will this do?" The guards lifted the rope so she could enter the work area. The mechanic stuck the mirror to the top center of the instrument panel with a wad of gum. It was perfect, he said.

Her name was Mrs. Loma Oliver Jr., and she was twenty-two or twenty-three. A press photographer snapped a shot as Lindbergh accepted the compact from her. Loma is a little overweight and no great beauty, but she is well dressed and well groomed, clad in a necktie and sports jacket, fake pearls, a black cloche hat pulled over her ears. Her dark hair is bobbed; like many young women in this period, she has adopted a flapper style. She hands the mirror to Lindbergh, who stares at her intently. Her eyes are wide, glistening, and doelike; it's easy to interpret her expression as one of adoration—or love. She disappeared into the crowd after the shot was taken, and was never heard from again.

One cannot discount the importance of Lindbergh's availability in such adoration—even if the chances of bagging the young flier existed only in fantasy. All the other aviators were married; only Bernt Balchen was young and single like Lindbergh—but at this point he was not yet part of Byrd's crew and not officially in the race.

Such attraction was recorded one month later in the Brooklyn Yiddish paper *Der Tog.* "On Second Avenue near a theater, several Jewish girls and boys stood looking at a poster of Lindbergh displayed in a window of an ice cream parlor. The girls can't take their eyes off Lindbergh," the writer observed. The boys argued over who was braver, Lindbergh or Levine (who by then had flown). The fact that Lindbergh flew alone made him the bravest, the girls claimed. "[I]t's not such a big thing when two fly together," they said, since one can sleep while the other flies. "That's right!" another girl shouted, with "half-closed lids." She added: "I would love to sit by Lindbergh's right side and help him stay awake." The young men bellowed in jealousy: Levine was "a thousand times more of a hero," and girls "who are 'crazy' about Lindbergh are fools."

"But Levine is already married," a previously silent girl piped up, an observation that ended the debate once and for all.

Yet the spark that existed between Lindbergh and his fans was completely one-sided. There'd been some talk in the press that no romantic idol had filled Valentino's shoes after his death; now, suddenly, that same kind of longing emerged full-blown. But Lindbergh, unlike Valentino, did not smolder. He was the exact opposite: on his second day in Long Island, he was called "girl-shy." "Lindbergh's only love is his monoplane," the *St. Louis Post-Dispatch* declared. "Feminine admirers surround him whenever he appears at Curtiss Field to tinker with his plane, and have observed that the airman is apparently 'girl-shy.'" Finally, a "girl reporter" asked if he had a sweetheart, a "question that seemed to be worrying her sisterhood." Lindbergh answered, "My airplane is my only girl. Don't know any others. I'm not married, engaged, or divorced."

Such aloofness with women only deepened his mystery and seemed to make him more attractive. One woman stole his half-eaten corncob; he had problems with laundry, since everything he sent out was stolen. Even mothers and matrons found his silence endearing. He was an "intrepid, virile youth," the "best we have to offer in clean-cut masculinity... the boy who lives near to Nature's heart—the out-of-doors boy, of sound body and mind." Mothers could feel safe with such a boy around their daughters; they held him up "as an example for their sons," declared "The Social Peek-a-Boo," a society column in the St. Louis *Censor.* "He has set many of the gin-toting, jazz mad dissipated youths of the country thinking, and if nothing more comes of his startling prowess, he will have done a valuable service to his country in this respect alone."

Lindbergh might have tired of reporters, but whether they took him seriously as an aviator or not, the press had not tired of him. He was new, so he was "news." Many writers couldn't resist the inherent possibilities of an "unvarnished Midwesterner" who planned to cross the ocean alone. The longer the weather stayed lousy, the more his star built up in the papers. The public interest in him began to resemble that of a freak show. Some opportunists, looking to make a quick buck, ran a shuttle service between Manhattan and Long Island, filling the airfields with clients, offering them the chance to pose with a famous aviator. At one point, a middle-aged woman broke through the security cordon, grazed Lindbergh's leather flying jacket with her fingers, and ran off screaming, "I touched him! I touched him!" Another matron bet $1,000 to $100, or 10-to-1 odds, that Lindbergh would win. One PR man tried to get a photo of his starlet client doing the splits on Lindbergh's propeller. Slim wondered, What were these "splits"? He laughed when someone explained, but still refused.

One media theme with staying power was his identification as an underdog. It lasted as long, or longer, than his sex appeal. Like Floyd Collins stuck in his Kentucky cave, having the odds stacked against him is what gave his story "legs." Commentators liked to say that Americans loved their underdogs, but by branding Lindbergh as the "dark horse"—by harping on it in almost every story—the press turned Slim into a mythical version of the "average American." Sometime during that week, all over the city and country, people picked up their papers and said to themselves, "He could be Me."

He could be me. He could be anyone, and that public anonymity was a big part of the appeal. Dick Blythe, his handler, expressed it in a nutshell when Lindbergh came back home and tried to don his air service uniform prior to appearing before adoring crowds. Harry Bruno, Blythe's partner, recalled the conversation:

"You can't wear it," Dick said.
"What do you mean, I can't wear it?"
"It'll label you," Dick explained.
"I don't get you."
Dick sighed. "Look, dumb-bell," he said patiently. "Up to now

you've not been labeled as Protestant, Catholic, or Jew. You've had no stated politics. You've not been listed as Republican, Democrat, or Socialist. You were identified with no movements or causes. You were young, healthy, good looking, and single—a possible future husband for every American girl. And you weren't an army man or a navy man but a plain civilian with a job, and your way to make in the world. Nobody could claim you and nobody could be against you. This army uniform would spoil that picture."

In the language of behavioral economics, Lindbergh's sudden and surprising popularity was a case of "informational cascade." Producers—in this case, journalists—talk, either among themselves or on the page. This talk is of prime importance, because there is so much uncertainty and ambiguity in what they do. Many cultural industries work like this: Who knows what has value unless it's on the tip of everyone's tongue? But the problem with such value is that it needs frequent transfusions. With each new story, readers want more. The old information isn't enough; a new "angle" is required.

On the night of May 13, Lindbergh returned to his hotel after a day in the hangar and found that no matter how much he tried to hide from the public, he was their property now. If that was not enough, he received a telegram that night from his mother as he relaxed in his room. She planned to arrive the next morning, via train from Detroit, to see him one last time before he flew.

•

None of this would have mattered if Lindbergh had not won. The fuse would have sputtered; the cult of Lindbergh would have died. On the night of May 13, this was a real possibility, since Chamberlin and Bertaud planned to fly to Paris the next day.

They'd already put off their flight because of the weather. They'd wanted to take off on the twelfth, but on that day, Bertaud got a weather report that made him change his mind. A low-pressure cell lingered off the Grand Banks; another lurked to the north. If they met, they'd create a nasty storm. Southeast winds wailed off the European coast, which would blow right in their faces as they started the last leg of their journey. For 1,800 miles in the middle of the Atlantic, ships reported rain and fog with low temperatures. Flying into all that was a foolhardy choice. Bertaud decided to wait until Saturday, the fourteenth, when the Weather Bureau believed the clouds might clear.

So much noise was made about Lindbergh's arrival that it's easy to forget the excitement generated by *Columbia*'s imminent departure. Lindbergh may have been the new kid on the block, but his plane needed repairs and *Columbia* was ready to go. Bertaud's mother was contacted in Alameda City, California: "He was born to be an aviator," she said proudly. Chamberlin's father wired his son: "FLY THE IOWA FLAG ACROSS THE ATLANTIC." Bellanca's younger sister Concetina wrote in late April from their native Sicily: "I have never been so thrilled as when I saw your happy face smiling at me from our daily paper," she said. "In the last two weeks it has been an inspiration to me...The moving picture houses showed your monoplane in detail, and both the aviators and you. Everybody is talking about it, and I am so proud."

The biggest noise came from Brooklyn, in praise of Levine. The local and Yiddish papers were filled with stories and pictures; his name came up where people were talking, in stores and around newsstands. It went like this: someone would shell out a few pennies for a paper; a crowd would gather; some snuff would be passed about; and then the discussion would turn to "airplanepilotology" and the owner Levine. Some skeptics thought it was all a bluff—that *no* plane would ever make it to Paris—but many admired the man. A well-known cantor at a synagogue wondered whether Levine's role in the Orteig race would ease America's closed-door policy with regard to Jewish immigrants. "Charlie Levine is himself the child of immigrants and, who knows, maybe one of my sons could grow up to be as big a hero as Levine."

There were even songs praising Levine. They were published as sheet music in both Yiddish and English translation, and sung in Yiddish vaudeville and the Yiddish theater. They were sold as records and on the music rolls that snapped into player pianos. The most popular, it seems, was "Levine! With His Flying Machine," written by Sam Coslow, Saul Bernie, and Joseph Tanzman:

> Brave are those who fly the great Atlantic
> Of their deeds our sons and stories tell.
> But there's one whose name is not romantic.
> . Let us sing a song for him as well.

Levine! Levine!
You're the hero of your race!
Levine! Levine!
You're the greatest Hebrew ace! . . .
We're proud of you, Levine! . . .
Levine, with your flying machine!

Columbia's pilots did not find him nearly as endearing as Brooklyn's Jewish community. On the night they were supposed to take off, Chamberlin, Bertaud, and the mechanics worked like maniacs in their hangar, "up to our necks in the inevitable last-minute preparations." Levine walked in carrying a contract; it had been drawn up by his lawyer, and he wanted the men there to sign it. They glanced at it hurriedly, then read it again. The provisions were exacting. If they signed, they'd receive $150 a week for the year following the flight, while Levine acted as their manager. He would decide and negotiate all speaking engagements; publishing, movie, and vaudeville contracts; and newspaper serial rights and product endorsements. If these earnings exceeded their weekly salary, he would distribute unspecified "bonuses" to them. He would get half of all "prize money," which included Orteig's $25,000, the Brooklyn Chamber's $15,000, and the awards offered by the gas and equipment companies for using their products. The contract did not address insurance protection for their wives.

They were stunned. They felt they were being cheated. The hesitation must have shown on their faces, since Levine immediately added, "You can sign it or not, just as you please, but if you don't sign, you don't fly."

Chamberlin knew they had little choice or leverage. There was no doubt that Levine could stop the flight: Bellanca had input, but only if *Columbia* took off. Bertaud and Chamberlin talked, then signed reluctantly.

Levine was a "shrewd psychologist," Chamberlin realized. "We were a pair of pilots on the brink of our greatest adventure, our minds occupied with a thousand and one details which might mean the difference between success and failure. What was to happen to us during the next year seemed of little consequence; our chief concern was for the next forty-eight hours."

Like Lindbergh and Byrd, Levine wanted complete control—but

his was a world of contracts and deals, not planes and their parameters. He'd won, but it would be a Pyrrhic victory. He might control his pilots, but he could not control the weather.

•

There were many turning points in this race, determined by good and bad luck, disaster, generous acts, and brief windows of reprieve. But Saturday, May 14, was the day that truly determined the course of the race. The weather was supposed to clear that day. If it had, the *Columbia* would have taken off, leaving the others behind. The plane was in perfect shape, and would never be more ready. Instead, the weather turned for the worse.

Every day, it was Dr. James Kimball who told the pilots whether the alignment of forces over the ocean was favorable. He took his duties seriously, and it showed. He was middle-aged and nearsighted, with stooped shoulders and a graying mop of once-black hair. He'd never married, and had lived alone for years, with a quiet family in Washington Square. The pilots called him "Doc Kimball," and only one friend called him "Jim."

Kimball's office was perched on the twenty-fourth floor of the Whitehall Building, overlooking the Battery, and from this eyrie he drew his twice-daily "Upper Air Charts" with predictions concerning wind, temperature, visibility, and humidity. As the rivals waited for good weather, Kimball adopted the role of the man at a racetrack holding the starting gun. He did not choose the role, and did not like it, but he took it seriously. Before he pulled the trigger, he had to be sure of two things. First, that the flyer had a wind coming from the west, which would help get his heavy ship off the ground and push it toward Europe once it was in the air. Second, there must be reasonably settled weather over the ocean, and an absence of destructive storms.

The Weather Bureau maintained 210 "first-class" fixed-land weather stations across the nation and its possessions, which were staffed with 1 to 15 men apiece and packed with the latest scientific devices to measure temperature, wind direction and velocity, precipitation, cloud ceiling, and other indicators. On top of that, there were thousands of other "second-class" stations manned with part-time employees.

But corralling these same indicators from the ocean was a sketchy affair. Kimball might hear from only four or five widely scattered vessels on any given day. He received their readings at eight in the morning and at night; he transcribed the data onto a blank map of the Atlantic, then sent his maps to the fliers at noon and midnight. Lines called isobars flowed from his pencil until the map was covered with a topology of ripples. These connected and swirled to form zones, or "cells," of high and low pressure. The lows were bad news, indicating the centers of storms.

One could never feel entirely secure with Kimball's predictions: in twelve hours the ocean could transform. One of the most serious problems was the high percentage of foggy days. Newfoundland was notorious for this: fog crept in for 50 to 60 percent of the days during summer; 60 to 65 percent in June. Though fog rolled in during only 30 to 35 percent of the winter, by then the persistence of ice spelled death to an aviator. These Newfoundland fogs owed their existence to the rush of warm, moist winds from the Gulf Stream over the colder water of the Labrador Current. These fogs were broad, spreading hundreds of miles, but not deep, averaging only 500 feet above sea level.

The best news that Kimball could give an Atlantic flier was that a high barometer reading lay to the south of his course, and a low to his north. The average wind in the summer blew from the west-southwest at a speed of about 15–20 miles per hour; he could ride this wind between the two pressure cells and hopefully encounter blue skies. On the Thursday that Lindbergh arrived from St. Louis, such skies prevailed during the morning across most of the northern sea. But by that afternoon, storms started blowing down from Greenland. Nine ocean liners reported gloomy skies and high seas far off the coast, and one reported fog so thick it had to reduce speed. Two lows were slanting from the north—one over the Grand Banks and one farther out in mid-ocean—and if those two met, it promised a huge storm filled with strong winds, falling temperatures, and rain that would easily turn to ice on a ship's wings.

On Friday night, as *Columbia* made ready, Kimball guessed that these conditions would improve in the next twenty-four hours. But when Saturday dawned, the weather grew worse, and it remained bad for the entire week. From Saturday, May 14, until Friday, May 20, the fliers were grounded. The wait turned into a great equalizer. Within two days, the advantage held by *Columbia* over *Spirit* was eaten up; within three or four days, Byrd's wrist had healed and he could fly again. By the week's end, no single plane held a natural advantage. Weather permitting, all three planes could take off simultaneously.

•

From Saturday, May 14, until the night of Thursday, May 19, local conditions over New York and Newfoundland and widespread conditions across the entire North Atlantic were as bad or worse than they had been all season. That weekend was a preview of the waiting game they would all endure. The pilots hunkered down in their hangars, testing and calibrating their machines. There were at least nine test flights that weekend: five by Lindbergh, three by Byrd, and a long one over Long Island by Chamberlin. Spectators watched from the other side of the ropes strung before the hangar doors. Hundreds and thousands had come to Curtiss and Roosevelt fields for past tests and takeoffs, but this was different. On Saturday, 7,500 to 10,000 people converged on the airfields in 4,000 cars; the number on Sunday blossomed to 30,000 spectators. It was as if a spell had been cast over the curious, and they could not break away. They were usually kept back by Captain Frank McCahill and Sergeant Wilson of the Nassau County Police Department, but occasionally a fan would slip beneath the ropes to touch or speak to his or her hero. The total cash package awaiting the winner was now estimated at between $46,000 and $100,000, including the Orteig and Brooklyn prizes, product endorsements, and newspaper serials. Forty-five Western Union linesmen spent the weekend stringing telegraph wire to the fields in anticipation of the expected crush of reporters when the first plane rolled down the runway.

The rivals rarely mixed; instead, they orbited tightly within the gravity of their planes. Yet despite not communicating directly, it was easy for them to know what the others were up to. The fliers passed the others' hangars every morning and night; they knew when the others went up for tests; they read the detailed accounts of each team in papers such as *The New York Times*, New York *Daily World*, *New York Post*, *New York Herald Tribune*, *Brooklyn Daily Eagle*, and *Nassau Daily Review*. They received the same twice-daily weather maps from Doc Kimball.

Byrd seemed to handle the week-long wait better than the others: Wanamaker's demands for further tests and some kind of knowledge of Nungesser's fate before takeoff seemed to free him from the demands of decision making. On Friday, May 13, he strolled over to Lindbergh's hangar and offered him the use of Doc Kimball's daily weather reports and Roosevelt Field. He did the same with Chamberlin. The *America* was run from the hangar for what Byrd called his "laboratory work," a full series of "scientific tests of plane and equipment, fuel and engine, in order that we should know exactly what our machine would do." Lindbergh and Chamberlin planned to fly single-engine planes for which ample data already existed; they already knew their planes' lifting capacities, while "No one knew just what a three-engined plane the size of ours could lift, or what its cruising radius would be," Byrd said.

Every evening, he retreated into his hangar to interpret new data. This hangar was a "beautiful place," admired *The New York Times*: its interior was painted white, with shiny red fire extinguishers hanging from the walls. There was a kitchen, mess hall, special room for reporters, and sleeping quarters for the thirty to forty mechanics, telegraph operators, and other skilled workmen staffing the camp. Byrd's own office was neatly arranged with charts, compasses, sextants, and weather tables.

Early in the week, Byrd determined that *America* should have an average speed of 120 miles per hour and use 30 gallons of gas per hour; he spent the rest of the week confirming this. He did not want the fate of the *American Legion* to repeat itself with his plane.

Yet even with such care, there was one near-tragedy during this period of tests that did not make the news. Early in the week, Acosta and Noville took *America* up about a mile. Noville rose to look around the cockpit; the seats were so placed that when a pilot got up, he had to step backward. When Noville stepped back, he stepped into air.

He began to plunge as if pulled down to earth, but at the last second was able to recover. Noville realized that he had stepped through a trapdoor in the bottom of the ship that must have opened because of vibrations. One leg was hanging in space, jammed against the bottom of the plane by the force of the wind. If he'd been thinner, he might have dropped through; for once, he was thankful for the extra pounds. Acosta laughed when he understood his copilot's predicament, but Noville was not amused.

Fokker called Byrd's hangar his "boudoir." The Explorer had been seduced by his science; no sense of urgency remained. Almost every day, Fokker drove to the airfield from his New Jersey plant in his low-slung

Lancia sports car. A big bulb horn was set by his window; he honked it loudly as he drove in. Every day, he confronted Byrd about taking off. The explanation—that the weather prevented it—was always the same.

The issue came to a head on Tuesday, May 17. By then every test flight had confirmed the team's estimations of speed and lift; the day's weather forecast was the most promising yet, and the sky, though not clear, was less overcast than it had been in days. "Look at the sky," Fokker fumed to Balchen, whom he liked with the same intensity with which he detested Byrd. "Just a little mist only. Any fool could fly it blindfolded with both eyes shut." If Byrd didn't start soon, he sputtered, "I myself will buy the plane back and fly it over the ocean, by Gott!"

That afternoon, Acosta and Balchen took *America* up for another test flight, and Fokker went along to see how she performed. The weather grew soupy as they gained altitude. At first, Balchen sat at the controls. Fokker told Bernt to take the plane into a cloud and fly level, then told Acosta to take over. Suddenly Balchen felt himself forced down into his seat; when he glanced at the instrument panel, the turn indicator's needle was pointed all the way over to one side. Acosta had fallen into the classic foul-weather trap: he'd trusted his senses instead of the instruments and had plunged into a spin. Balchen grabbed for the wheel, and Acosta let his hand drop from the controls in relief.

"You don't know anything about instrument flying, do you?" Fokker asked.

"This is one thing I don't know anything about," the big man admitted. "I'm strictly a fair-weather boy. If there's any thick stuff, I stay on the ground."

Balchen righted the plane and they landed without further incident. Once on the ground, Fokker dragged Balchen into a secluded hangar and exploded in rapid-fire German. Now he knew why the flight had been held up, he yelled, stabbing Balchen's chest with his forefinger. There was only one thing to do. "You, Bernt, must go along in the crew to handle instrument flying and bad weather, or all summer the *America* will still be waiting here, and I am the laughing stock of the whole United States!"

Balchen pointed out what Floyd Bennett had mentioned: he was Norwegian, and Wanamaker would sponsor only an American crew. Fokker would have none of it. "Poof! That is nothing," he spat in disgust, and told him to get his citizenship papers.

Then Fokker went after Byrd, and told him what had happened. "If you're going to make the flight and come through alive," Fokker said, "I offer you Balchen. If you don't take him, I'll buy the plane and fly it with him myself."

If Byrd remembered his earlier dislike for Balchen, he said nothing now. He looked at the Norwegian, apparently without comment, and said he'd take him along. Balchen was still reluctant, so Fokker offered him $500 from his own pocket to go.

That night, Balchen lay on his cot in Byrd's hangar. The idea of becoming a U.S. citizen had never crossed his mind. Was he turning his back on his native land? But as he thought about it, he realized it was possible to love two countries at once. It was strange how casually big changes like this occurred in one's lifetime.

The next morning, May 18, he took a car into the city to the office of the Bureau of Naturalization. He hesitated before the desk, and the girl siting behind it smiled when she heard his Norwegian accent. "My mother comes from Oslo," she said. "You want to be a citizen of this country, too?"

Balchen smiled as he picked up the form printed "Declaration of Intention."

"You bet," he said.

That night, he returned to the field. It was late, but Byrd's hangar was more active than it had been in days. The *America* was to be christened on Saturday afternoon, May 21, and Wanamaker had invited two thousand people. A speakers' platform was being built at one end of the cavernous hangar; red-white-and-blue bunting draped the walls. There would be speeches and tributes, and some words about the upcoming flight from Byrd.

Balchen looked for Byrd, but the commander was not around. He was speaking that night in the city at Carnegie Hall, at a Red Cross fund-raiser for Mississippi flood victims. He did not seem worried that the weather would turn.

Balchen stretched out on his cot and sighed. It had been a confusing, if amazing day. He listened to the drip of the rain on the hangar's tin roof. The sound was hypnotic. Maybe, he thought, as he drifted off to sleep, maybe they would take off soon.

Maybe they'd be first. Like his citizenship, stranger things had occurred.

•

As that week progressed, Lindbergh tried to face his problems. Some he handled with ease. Others grated at him, especially the constant publicity.

"It wouldn't be so bad if I could go off quietly for an hour by my-self—if I could walk over the field alone and feel earth beneath the soles of my shoes while I let the wind blow confusion from my mind," he later wrote. "But the moment I step outside the hangar I'm surrounded by people and protected by police. Somebody shouts my name, and im-mediately I'm surrounded by a crowd." He'd been lonely as a boy and then as a youth transformed the loneliness into a love of solitude; it was his sanctuary, his wall from the world, and now that wall was crum-bling. In all his 501-page *The Spirit of St. Louis*, this is probably the most poignant and telling passage. In time he would begin to push back, in ways that were bitter, unlikable, and, at least once, even dangerous, but at this particular moment he was lost in the crowd, and his only desire was to hide.

But there was nowhere to hide. On the night of May 13, he ordered room service for himself, Dick Blythe, Ed Mulligan, and another when the door burst open and two cameramen walked into the room. The men all jumped up, then asked what the hell was going on.

"We're here to get a picture of 'Lucky Lindy' shaving and sitting on the bed in his pajamas," one of them said. They grinned, looked at Lind-bergh, and began adjusting their lenses. Lindbergh's group pushed them out the door.

Slim had already been on edge when they barged in. He'd gotten a telegram from his mother that she would arrive the next day by train. The press has done this, he thought: they'd phoned and filled her with fear. How would she handle this chaos, he worried.

She handled it better than Slim. He collected her in the morning from the train station and took her to his hangar at Curtiss Field. She watched as he made his test flights; in the afternoon, he took her back to the Garden City railroad station to catch her Detroit-bound train. She patted him lightly on the shoulder before she boarded the car. "Well, son," she said, and smiled, "good-bye and good luck."

A cameraman asked her to kiss him, so they would have a goodbye picture.

"No," she said, firmly. One gets the idea she looked on them as un-
ruly but malleable schoolboys, and treated them accordingly. "I wouldn't
mind if we were used to that, but we come from an undemonstrative
Nordic race."

Her stoicism seems to have affected Slim. She had come "to make
sure I really wanted to go and felt it was the right thing to do," and then
she simply said she would go home. As she said goodbye, an excited boy
ran up with an autograph book. While her son signed it, Evangeline
stepped onto the train. She smiled once from a window, knowing full
well she might never see him again, and then she was gone.

On the day of this visit, an incident occurred that Lindbergh would
always use to justify his hatred of the press. He was landing after the
morning's first test when some photographers ran in front of the plane
to get a better angle. He turned *Spirit* quickly, but the swerve broke her
tail skid and damaged the rear end of the fuselage. At first the damage
seemed serious—"It looked like a hopeless mess," said the man who
repaired it—but with the help of a welder and two Curtiss mechanics,
it was fixed in plenty of time.

Despite this avowed disdain for the press, he began to make his own
newspaper deals. After Lindbergh gave the St. Louis rights of his story
to the *Globe-Democrat*, Harry Knight phoned Arthur Sulzberger and
sold syndication rights to *The New York Times*. The *Times* paid $1,000 up
front for signing, $4,000 for world rights if the flight was a success, and
only $1,000 if Lindbergh did not make it within 50 miles of Paris. If Slim
never made the flight, he'd have to return the signing fee.

Lindbergh didn't hate all reporters—he liked those who appreciated
the technical aspects of his plane. He preferred those reporters who
adhered solely to questions about his plane and his flight. His name appeared so frequently in the papers during this week that it was hard to
get away from him. He was more than a newsmaker; he was a constant
presence, and everything associated with him took on a special significance. He chose Felix the Cat as his mascot, with his can-do spirit,
inventiveness, and, ironically, his plastic identity always subject to
change. The "Spirit of Me Too," coined by E. B. White, appeared among
manufacturers and suppliers: his oil was Gargoyle Mobiloil "B"; the plywood in his wing and fuselage, laminated Haskelite, one-eighth of an
inch thick; his gasoline, Red Crown, courtesy of Standard Oil; his tires,
Goodrich Silvertown.

Even the French press took an interest in Lindbergh. His solo attempt appealed to their imagination; they interpreted his shyness as nonchalance, and compared him to their own flier Vedrines, who did "crazy things like landing on the roof of the Lafayette store." Although the odds stood at fifty-fifty between Lindbergh and the *Columbia*, French airmen preferred Slim. "It is that kind that often have the most luck," one French flier said.

An interest in and respect for detail often ensured a pilot's survival, but for Lindbergh and Byrd, they were also a refuge away from the uproar. Lindbergh meticulously attended to the installation of the new carburetor heater and repairs to the earth induction compass; he watched with amazement as the Curtiss Company fixed a crack in his propeller for free. The passengers he took up in test flights were all aviation technicians—Spoons Boedecker and Ed Mulligan for Wright; Pioneer Instrument's Brice Goldsborough. Some others might sit in the cockpit, but none flew.

This obsession with detail extended to every aspect of the flight, including an examination of Roosevelt Field. By Monday, May 16, most of the repairs to *Spirit* had been completed, as were most of the test flights. With nothing to keep him in the hangar, Lindbergh climbed the hill where Sikorsky had watched his beloved S-35 burst into flames. He began to examine the field with the intensity of a treasure hunter scanning a beach with a metal detector. He bent down to examine soft spots in the grass, testing the spring of the turf with the palm of his hand. He gazed around at the runway. The ground was flat; there were few telephone wires that might be hazards; treacherous crosswinds seemed rare.

By that Monday, Lindbergh had begun to relax. He even took up practical joking again. At 5:00 a.m. on Sunday, Blythe was wakened by a shower of ice water. His eyes snapped open and he saw Lindbergh above him holding a pitcher. "That'll teach you to wear pajamas," Slim reportedly said. A couple of mornings later, Blythe woke to another morning assault, this time as Lindbergh tried to shave off half his pencil-thin moustache. He managed to save it, but in the struggle, he got shaving cream up his nose.

Lindbergh even loosened up enough to deal with selected celebrities. A smattering of the rich and famous linked to aviation dropped by Hangar 16. By Monday, Slim had met Fonck, Tony Fokker, and Wil-

liam P. MacCracken Jr., assistant secretary of commerce for aeronautics. He'd eaten lunch with Colonel Theodore Roosevelt Jr., the former
president's son, and met Charles Lawrance, the developer of the Wright
Whirlwind engine.

Even Harry F. Guggenheim had dropped by. Guggenheim was an
important presence in the growing world of commerical aviation; he
was president of the Guggenheim Foundation for the Promotion of
Aeronautics, and on April 29, three days after the *American Legion* disaster, he had offered a $100,000 prize for the safest plane built in the
nation. Though the two would eventually become good friends, Guggenheim thought at first that Slim was doomed. He sat in the *Spirit's* cockpit and wished Lindbergh luck, but all the while he thought, "He'll never
make it."

•

The wait weighed heaviest on *Columbia's* team. As the weather grew
worse, so did Bertaud's temper. On Saturday, May 14, when it was finally evident that conditions over the Atlantic were too dangerous to
make the hop, Chamberlin took the plane on an extended flight over
Long Island. The weather was choppy, but he could handle it, and it
gave him plenty of time to think.

He thought about Bertaud. The navigator resented Levine's contract.
The more he thought about it, the angrier he grew. His old job as an
airmail pilot paid more in a year than what he'd agreed to accept from
Levine. Lloyd looked on that contract as nothing but a moneymaking
scheme, with the pilots "as the cat's-paws that were to fork over the
chestnuts," Chamberlin later wrote. Sometime on Saturday morning,
Charlie had told the papers that "every nickel of the prize money goes to
the *Columbia's* pilots," and with that statement, Chamberlin watched
the navigator's fury climb. Chamberlin held his peace when the reporters
asked for a comment, but Bertaud could not keep his anger bottled up.
"Why, that lying son of a bitch," he hissed, and told the whole story.

What was Charlie's game? Chamberlin actually liked the little
guy...or at least tolerated him better than anyone else in the competition. Even Bellanca was getting fed up, and it took a lot to make the
little Sicilian mad. But Chamberlin also had no illusions about his boss.
He could turn on you quickly, given the right provocation. The tendency

that all men had to resent being told what to do was highly developed in Levine. Maybe it was his circumstances, Chamberlin thought—rising from nothing by fighting for everything. Yet he never knew when to stop fighting; he'd never learned to recognize when he was hurting himself. At times he just seemed naturally contrary: if anyone made him go somewhere he wanted to go anyway, he would find a way to reverse the direction.

Chamberlin felt caught in the middle. Levine was a problem, true, but Chamberlin had never really trusted Bertaud. He felt the airmail pilot had tried to edge him out, and they could not agree on such fundamental points as the radio and the route across the Atlantic. Bertaud said he planned to hire a lawyer and wanted Chamberlin to go in with him, but the soft-spoken Iowan quietly said that he'd probably get his own.

While the *Columbia* team fought, Lindbergh perched on the sidelines watching. If the squabble went to court, they'd never take off, and the dark horse would win. "Fly first and fight later," Chamberlin pleaded with them both: if we get across first and make history, these differences will seem small. Everything will work out in the aftermath.

But no one was listening.

By the time Chamberlin landed that Saturday afternoon, the rift had developed exactly as he'd feared it would. The fight had landed in the papers. Bertaud had hired as his attorney the Honorable Clarence W. Nutt. A meeting of all parties was set for Sunday at the Garden City Hotel. In desperation, and probably with the help and advice of Bellanca, Chamberlin hired his own attorney, former state senator Charles C. Lockwood, a director of the Brooklyn Chamber of Commerce who had once represented Levine.

And so began a fight that resembled the breakup of a long, unhappy marriage. Levine and Bertaud were the principals, and neither agreed with anything the other said. There was no room for compromise. The long, stormy conference stretched throughout Sunday at the grand hotel. In attendance sat Bertaud and his attorney, Nutt; Chamberlin and his attorney, Lockwood; Brooklyn Chamber of Commerce president Ralph Jonas; and Levine, representing himself. Bellanca stayed out of it, at least at first: "I have only one enemy now, and that is the Atlantic Ocean," he said. "Mr. Levine is just as enthusiastic as I am, and merely wants to prove that our plane can cross the Atlantic."

The meeting wore on everyone. Levine took a beating from his fellow Chamber members Jonas and Lockwood for the hard bargain he'd forced upon his pilots the night before they were supposed to fly. At one point, Bertaud barged out of the meeting and shouted, "I'll be damned if I'll work for Levine for a year! I may want to do something else." But he was soon coaxed back inside.

Of them all, Chamberlin seemed even-tempered and best able to weather the storm. A *Times* reporter who was either in the room with them or conveniently placed so he could watch the proceedings wrote that through it all Chamberlin wore a grin. "[M]ost of the day when the others were scrapping...Chamberlin's nerves seldom show any evidence of strain, no matter what is going on, and little mundane matters don't seem to appeal to him nearly as much as the business of flying."

At 10:30 that night the meeting broke up, and things finally looked settled. Levine agreed reluctantly to draw up a new contract to be signed the next day. The pilots would receive all the prize money, and the proviso that they would work exclusively for Levine in the year that followed would be discarded. In addition, Willda Chamberlin and Helen Bertaud would receive $50,000 apiece in life insurance if their husbands died.

Everyone seemed happy, said Chamberlin, "but the illusion was short-lived." It was now Levine's turn to get rankled. The next morning, Monday, May 16, he returned to the Garden City Hotel with his own attorney, Samuel Hartman, and a new "agreement" that was even worse than the first.

In this new version, Levine would provide $12,500 in life insurance to Willda Chamberlin and only $5,000 to Helen Bertaud. And he had added a proviso: the right to withdraw the pilots or plane from the race anytime he wanted, in exchange for a payment of four weeks' expenses. By midday Monday, the meeting had dissolved into a shouting match between Bertaud and his lawyer and Levine and his. The others in the meeting—Chamberlin, Jonas, and Charles Lockwood—all remained silent, like neutral observers.

Finally, Levine's lawyer pulled out the new contracts and demanded that the pilots sign. Bertaud refused, as did Chamberlin, on his attorney's advice. When Bertaud accused Levine of welching on his Sunday-night agreement, Levine's face turned grim.

He told Bertaud to withdraw from the flight.

Bertaud refused, and threatened legal action. He offered to buy the *Columbia* from Levine for a cost set by an independent appraiser. Once they flew the plane to Paris, they'd sell it back to him. Levine said the plane was worth $25,000 and nothing less. They adjourned in the small hours of Monday night with things more unsettled than ever.

Everyone was steamed, but Levine particularly so. He burst from the room and declared to the waiting reporters that he could get "plenty of pilots" to fly his plane. The Paris flight would still commence, "even if not with the present crew." He denied that he'd ever made any sort of verbal agreement with the pilots on Sunday night. As he climbed into his car to drive back home, he said he'd give $25,000 to fly with Lindbergh.

The events of Monday night left everyone in the team demoralized and confused. At an informal dinner held Tuesday, May 17, for Chamberlin and Lindbergh by Frank Tichenor, the publisher of the influential *Aero Digest*, Chamberlin recounted Levine's statement about flying with Slim.

"I will try to think of a place to put Mr. Levine," Lindbergh replied drily.

Everyone laughed, but the statement set off all sorts of speculation. Levine had not been invited to the dinner; when someone caught up with him afterward, he smiled and said he'd made the proposal more or less as a joke, but he was willing to go through with it if Lindbergh would take him. He added that he regretted not selling the Bellanca to the young flier back in February, when he'd first come looking to buy.

As many chuckles from the press as this got, it still provoked discussion about Slim's plans. Should he take a copilot? Was he foolhardy to go it alone? There were plenty in the business who felt that a victory for Lindbergh would be a loss for aviation. The public would see his solo flight as a stunt, and his plane was useless as a commercial vehicle. Even the influential Harry Guggenheim, who'd been publicly encouraging when he met the young flier in his hangar, thought privately that Lindbergh's flight was a terrible idea. He was "indignant with the authorities for letting him go off on this highly *doubtful* adventure," he later confessed, especially without the equipment and navigation aids then available. But when he met Lindbergh, he merely said, "When you get back, look me up at the Fund's office."

During this period, Chamberlin tried to fix the rift on his own. On either Monday or Tuesday morning, he approached Bernt Balchen and made him a private offer. He asked if Bernt would go with him on the *Columbia* as copilot and navigator, and split the Orteig Prize straight down the middle. Balchen was surprised, and apparently tempted: at this point, he was still merely Uncle Tony's test pilot, with no apparent possibility of flying to Paris with Byrd.

He thanked Chamberlin but turned him down. He could not fly the plane of a rival manufacturer while he was still Fokker's test pilot, he said. Besides, he felt obligated to the *America*—not through any loyalty for Byrd, but because of his good friend Floyd Bennett.

That Tuesday the skies opened slightly, then closed again and the rain poured. The storm system that had parked itself over the East Coast and North Atlantic showed no intention of moving. Everyone's mood was as dark as the sky.

In the absence of any more official meetings, the fight among the *Columbia* team turned into a media war waged in the lobby of the Garden City Hotel. Early in the day, Levine announced that he was looking for another navigator; Bertaud responded that he had told his attorney to draw up injunction papers that would legally restrain the *Columbia* from taking off if he was not aboard. Soon after that, he read a letter to a gathering of reporters that was addressed to Levine. "I did not enter this flight because of money," he said:

I did it because I desire to do my part in making aviation history, and because aviation is my life's work. Appreciating as I do the spirit of the donor's prize money, I will accept none for myself, but will donate it to the families of Commander Davis and Lieutenant Wooster, comrades of mine, who died in attempting the flight that I am trying so hard to go on. However, if you insist, I will relinquish to you or your company my share of the prize money. I will not accept one dollar from you or your company for this flight, except for my expenses which I would be glad to pay myself if I were financially able to do so. Although I have asked for protection for my wife in the form of insurance or its equivalent, she does not ask for it and will not accept one dollar.

The message was clear: Levine was not serious. He was in it only for the money, unlike the aviators, who were "high-minded." Bertaud called

on the memory of dead fliers and their grieving families; he brought out
as ammunition his own wife, the potentially widowed Helen Bertaud,
who, like her husband, would not accept one red cent from the merce-
nary Levine.

Not everyone bought Bertaud's performance. Bellanca, who rarely
resorted to sarcasm, wryly congratulated the navigator for "his ability to
land with such glowing success in the newspapers." More interesting is
the fact that the speech may have turned Chamberlin against him.
Around this time, Levine and Chamberlin began talking again on the
sly. After Bertaud's speech, Levine protested to the press that he had
asked Balchen to be navigator, though in truth it had been Chamberlin
who made the offer. This suggests some kind of rapprochment between
Chamberlin and Levine. Chamberlin was also shuttling his boss
between the Levine homestead in Belle Harbor and the Garden City
Hotel. One night—exactly when is uncertain—they were riding in
Chamberlin's flivver when Levine looked over and sighed. He was tired
of being the villain, he said. The newspapers were beating him up, but
when it came down to it, he was like Bellanca and Chamberlin: he just
wanted *Columbia* to get in the air.

"If you'll take me along with you on this flight to Europe instead of
another pilot or navigator, I'll give a $25,000 'prize' myself and you needn't
count on Orteig's money at all," he said. "I'll also put up $50,000 insur-
ance for Mrs. Chamberlin before we start."

"It suits me," Chamberlin said. Levine tore up the old contracts that
night and signed new ones outlining his offer.

Of all the rumored, promised, and abandoned agreements that week,
this was the only one that remained secret and did not make it into the
newspapers. It was also the only one in which the two principal signers
came to an agreement—and stayed in agreement for more than a day.
Not even Bellanca knew what had been agreed. For once in his life,
Charles Levine held his tongue.

As threatened, Bertaud obtained his temporary injunction against
Levine and Columbia Aircraft on Wednesday, May 18. It was signed
by N.Y. State Supreme Court justice Mitchell May in Brooklyn and
returnable before him on Friday, May 20. Until the judge ruled otherwise, the *Columbia* could not fly without Bertaud. Immediately after
the announcement, Bellanca arranged a peace conference. It was held
at Levine's white frame house at Belle Harbor and started on Wednes-

day at 11:15 p.m. Bellanca, Bertaud, Levine, and *Aero Digest* publisher Frank Tichenor attended.

It ended three hours later, at 2:15 a.m. The conference had been a success; the participants beamed. Levine promised that Bertaud would not be replaced; Bertaud promised to withdraw his injunction papers. "I'm awfully glad that the thing has been practically settled," said a relieved, if weary, Bellanca. "I have worked very hard to put this across and did not want to see my efforts go for nothing."

Bertaud, especially, bubbled over with joy. He and Chamberlin were in perfect accord on the route, he told reporters when he returned to the Garden City Hotel. "I am satisfied that as a result of this conference, I will be with Clarence Chamberlin as navigator and copilot in the Bellanca on the transatlantic flight."

And that could take place as early as Friday, May 20, if the weather changed.

SIXTEEN

A BAD CASE OF NERVES

Bertaud's elation lasted at least eight hours, and probably not even that long.

The morning papers for Thursday, May 19, all ran the story that the *Columbia* feud had been settled. Later that day, a reporter for one of the evening papers called Levine at his home. "Well, Mr. Levine," he said. "I hear you bottled things up at that conference you had last night."

"What conference?" Levine replied.

There had been a conference, he finally admitted, but there was no deal. He'd fired Bertaud three days earlier, and the navigator was just trying to get back in his good graces, he said. He still expected *Columbia* to take off once the weather broke, and he had a new copilot. When the reporter asked the man's identity, Levine turned secretive.

"He is known only to three persons. The three are the man himself, Chamberlin, and me."

Bertaud hit the roof when he heard Levine's words. His lawyer served the injunction papers without hesitation. Sheriff's deputies padlocked *Columbia* inside her hangar and hung the court's red tape across the door. There would be no flying the Bellanca until 10:00 a.m. Friday, when the injunction would be heard by Justice May.

What was Levine's game? On the surface his actions made no sense. It was this unpredictability, mixed with a dose of anti-Semitism, that led contemporaries to call him "mad." Wanamaker, for example, was sabotaging *America's* chances to win as much as Levine was *Columbia's*, but if Wanamaker was called anything, it was "prudent." But, for outside observers, Levine seemed to be adopting a scorched-earth policy—his refusal to compromise with Bertaud threatened to destroy every chance of victory. Chamberlin, who knew him best, called his insistence to manage every detail of the *Columbia's* flight a "passion," and compared it to the all-consuming "ambition of a man who 'discovers' a fighter to have the credit of developing him into a world champion."

But there is another way to look at the situation, and that is that Levine had decided to gamble it all. On Thursday, May 19, the weather was not expected to break until the weekend. The injunction would be decided at 10:00 a.m. on Friday, and considering that Bertaud had signed the original contract—legally binding, if objectionable—there was a very good chance that the judge would rule in Levine's favor. If we believe Chamberlin's chronology, it had already been decided who would be the second man: new contracts between the Iowan and Levine had been signed. Levine was playing poker with the *Columbia*, and from his point of view, he held a good hand.

•

On the morning of Thursday, May 19, the sky was gray and low. A light rain covered Roosevelt Field and Long Island. The Weather Bureau reported a dense, impassable fog shrouding the coasts of Nova Scotia and Newfoundland; a storm area had developed in the ocean west of France that could make flying deadly. It had been exactly one week since Lindbergh landed. Seven days of idleness had done strange things to them all. It was as if the rivals' greatest strengths and passions suddenly threatened to become their undoing. Byrd fell prey to the "scientific" solace of order; he became inert, and felt no urgency to leave. Levine's stubbornness—the very thing that had helped him overcome the anti-Jewish obstacles he met time and again in the high-profile world of commercial aviation—now turned against him. Chamberlin's quiet determination had always seen him through, but now he was *too* quiet when the *Columbia's* team needed a strong voice of wisdom to talk sense into the others.

Even Lindbergh was affected. Though the other pilots liked him, he was still an enigma. "I have run into him here and there," said Balchen. "But he keeps to himself, always preoccupied and quiet." Despite the uproar about his arrival, many newsmen still considered him out of his league, and they tried to talk him out of his long-shot flight. "He won't listen to reason," one reporter complained.

Yet backing down and losing face was Lindbergh's greatest fear. In a number of studies done during the 1970s, aviation psychologists discovered that *face*, "the individual's assessment of the way in which others view him," was one of the most powerful and common behavioral characteristics found among pilots as a whole. "[M]ale pilots take up flying for reasons closely allied to their own feelings of identity and masculinity," wrote Stephen R. Murray, "and the anxiety of guilt arising from their own shortcomings is deep-rooted and strong." Several researchers suggested that for aviators, saving face was more important than safety. In extreme, though not uncommon, cases, saving one's reputation was more important than saving one's life.

Dick Blythe and Harry Bruno may not have been psychologists, but they knew Lindbergh better than anyone and quickly realized that losing face was his great terror. They glimpsed through the reticence the fact that the fear of failure and the desire to prove himself were probably *the* driving forces in Lindbergh's life. When he flew the mail for Robertson, he'd been forced three times to bail out of his plane. Though Robertson did not chew him out, the other pilots ribbed him unmercifully. "To be ribbed by other mail flyers, to be treated with patent condescension by famous flyers who looked down upon him," was an insult he could not forget, Harry Bruno saw.

Lindbergh wanted to show everyone who was the cock of the walk, and he'd die before he called off his solo bid. He was extraordinarily sensitive to insult, as his reaction to the small story claiming that he had "narrowly escaped disaster" during his mock dogfight with the Curtiss Hawk in San Diego had proven. He hated the names the New York press linked to him, such as "Lucky Lindy" and the "Flyin' Fool," a show name left over from his barnstorming days. He complained that reporters were intrusive and sacrificed facts for a good story; yet in a passage he later excised from his autobiography, he revealed that the real reason for such antipathy lay in how he began to link pressmen in his mind to failure. He'd see cameramen waiting at the end of the runway and feel certain that they hoped he would crash. It was not an uncommon feeling among aviators. But with Lindbergh, it might have been a main contributor to his hatred of them.

Lindbergh was moody. Blythe and Bruno saw it as part of their job to prevent that moodiness from turning into a bad case of nerves. Blythe planned a tight schedule for that gloomy Thursday so the flier's emotions wouldn't get the best of him. Ryan Aircraft's Frank Mahoney had come to town: Blythe drove Lindbergh, Mahoney, Kenneth Lane of Wright, and Lieutenant George Stumpf of Slim's National Guard unit to visit the Wright plant at Patterson, New Jersey. After that, they planned dinner at the Newspaper Club, on West Forty-second Street, followed by the Ziegfeld Theatre, at Sixth Avenue and Fifty-fourth Street, to catch *Rio Rita*, that season's hit musical comedy by Florenz Ziegfeld. The show involved Texas Rangers, Aztec goddesses, and Montezuma's daughter, and included songs such as "Eight Little Gringitas" and "The Jumping Bean." Lindbergh might get to meet Ethelind Terry, the star. Said Lindbergh, "It ought to be great fun."

The day *had* been fun, despite the weather. A haze hid the tops of the skyscrapers. The streets glistened with rain. On the way to the Newspaper Club, Ken Lane suggested they call Doc Kimball for a weather update. Lindbergh was driving and pulled to the curb by a building with a phone booth in the lobby. Blythe ran inside and made the call.

There'd been a change in the weather, Kimball said. The low pressure area that had hovered for the past week over Newfoundland was retreating, pushed out by a high pressure ridge extending from Bermuda to the British Isles. Conditions over the ocean were clearing; the storm to the west of France had shrunk to small local zones. Yet the weather was far from perfect, Kimball warned. A low-pressure zone over Newfoundland was likely to result in fog and sleet. Still, it was the best news they had had in days.

So much for *Rio Rita*. Blythe called the Newspaper Club and paged his partner. Lindbergh had been scheduled for a dinner interview with some newsmen: Tell 'em a story, Harry, said Blythe—one that won't reveal why the kid's not there. But it's hard to keep secrets on the year's biggest story, especially in a press club. Ed Randall, a cartoonist for the *Daily Mirror*, was in the next telephone booth and overheard everything. He phoned his office with the scoop, and the *Daily Mirror* was on the street at 9:00 p.m. that night with news of Lindbergh's plans.

Blythe ran back in the rain. "You got your weather, Slim," he shouted, diving in his car. "No show tonight."

They turned around and headed back to Long Island. There was a lot to do. Carl Schory of the NAA had to be found to install the reading barograph in the plane. This instrument recorded time and altitude on a revolving paper cylinder, and was designed to show whether *Spirit* landed anywhere between New York and Paris. In Paris, a member of the Aero Club of France would unseal the cylinder and certify the flight. Without the barograph, the record of the flight would not be official.

There were other matters to attend to—too many, it seemed. Blythe ducked into a drugstore in Queensboro Plaza, where he bought two beef, two ham, and one egg sandwich wrapped in wax paper for the flight. The weather was still too rough to move the plane from the hangar to Roosevelt Field for takeoff, but they could make enough preparations now to give him a leg up for an early morning departure. They could pump the first 100 gallons of gas into *Spirit* while she was still in the hangar.

When they got to the field, Lindbergh was amazed to see no activity in his rivals' hangars. Though the *Columbia* was under a court-ordered lockdown and couldn't be moved, Byrd was still a worry. Most of *Spirit's* fueling would have to be done at daybreak, when it was towed to its takeoff position at the end of Roosevelt Field. That would be a tip-off for Byrd, and the *America* could be taxied into position and fueled quickly. Lindbergh knew that the plane's christening was scheduled for Saturday, but if *America* was ready and Lindbergh was preparing to go, he didn't think the Explorer would let the ceremony slow Byrd down.

All Slim could do now was go home and get some sleep. Everything would be ready come morning, and he could decide at daybreak whether to take off or stay. He returned to the Garden City Hotel, but rumors of his plans had already spread, and he had to dodge through reporters and autograph hounds. One man wanted him to sign a $250,000 movie contract; another, a $50,000 deal for a series of stage appearances. He told them he couldn't make commitments until he landed in Paris, then disappeared upstairs.

It was nearly midnight when he finally lay down. He wanted to sleep; he'd learned as a mail pilot that even an hour of sleep could make a world of difference. His friend Lieutenant Stumpf of the National Guard was posted at the door to keep away the curious and had promised to wake him at 2:15 a.m. Lindbergh was usually out the moment his head hit the pillow, but tonight his mind raged with questions: How much crosswind could he master at takeoff? At what angle and velocity? Should he have taken a radio? He'd just begun to drift off when the door slammed open and Stumpf cried out, "Slim, what am I going to do when you're gone?"

Incredibly, Lindbergh held his temper. "I don't know," he said.

"There's plenty of other problems to solve before we have to think about that one."

Stumpf shut the door; Lindbergh lay back down. There was no chance for sleep now. For the next two hours, he lay and worried about everything that could go wrong.

•

Slim arrived at his hangar shortly before 3:00 a.m. Word had leaked of his plans; the roads leading to Curtiss Field were filled with cars. Police later estimated that a crowd of about five hundred people arrived in the very early hours to watch Lindbergh make his attempt. A truck stood by to haul *Spirit* to the starting point at Roosevelt.

"Did my message get through, Slim?" Ken Lane asked.

Lindbergh shook his head. "What was it?"

"I said to let you sleep until just before daybreak, and we'd have everything set for you to take off." Lindbergh winced: though everything seemed to be falling into place for a takeoff, circumstances were conspiring against sleep, the thing he needed most to survive.

At 4:00 a.m. the hangar doors opened and the mechanics wheeled out *Spirit*; at 4:15 the rain had practically stopped, as if confirming Kimball's predictions. The mechanics hoisted the tail onto the truck and towed *Spirit* to Roosevelt Field. A phalanx of motorcycle cops escorted the caravan, which crept from the lights of the hangars up a potholed gravel road. A second truck, loaded with gasoline, followed.

While preparations were being made for Lindbergh's departure, Balchen lay in his cot in Byrd's silent hangar. For some reason he was gripped by the same restlessness he had felt on that night when the *Josephine Ford* waited to take off for the North Pole. He was alone in the *America*'s hangar: the plane was draped with flags, and it seemed obvious to Balchen that the Explorer had no intention of leaving until after the christening on Saturday. He'd asked a mechanic that night about the *Columbia*. It was still tied up in legal battles. What about Lindbergh? Nothing doing, the man said.

Near dawn, Balchen woke from half-sleep and heard the sound of tires on wet concrete. He recognized the source: a plane was being towed by truck across the strip, but the light rain masked further sound. Hours later, it seemed, an automobile drove past rapidly. He struck a match and looked at his watch. It was a little after five.

He rolled over and tried to sleep. The hangar door banged open. Fokker rushed in.

"Get me quick some fire extinguishers," he yelled. "That young fool he is going to take off. Maybe there comes trouble." Uncle Tony ran outside, and Balchen recognized the sound of his Lancia rocketing toward the end of the strip. He followed at a run.

It was nearly dawn. A light rain fell, but there was no wind. *Spirit* sat at the far western end of the runway, its engine covered by a tarpaulin to keep out the rain. Lindbergh stood a little apart, dressed in his flying suit, watching as Ken Lane and Ed Mulligan stood on the engine cowl and poured gas from red five-gallon cans through a chamois strip, filtering the fuel as they topped off the tank. When they finished, *Spirit* carried 451 gallons of gas and weighed close to 5,135 pounds.

To Balchen and the others, Lindbergh seemed oblivious to the stares of the curious. In reality, he felt a little sick. As his ship was being towed to Roosevelt, he thought that she looked awkward and heavy, "completely incapable of flight." The slow trip in the rain reminded him of a funeral. When they had finally arrived, he saw that the runway was soggy and soft, the clay underneath like glue. Extrapolating from the test data at San Diego, he had concluded that, with 450 gallons of gas aboard, *Spirit* should become airborne after a run of 2,500 feet. But this had assumed a run over hard ground.

He stared at the runway before him. Pools of water had collected in the slight depressions. Roosevelt Field stretched 5,000 feet, and at the end sat a steamroller that had been used recently to pack down the runway. Beyond that stretched a line of telephone poles; past that, Merrick Avenue. By now people he recognized were starting to arrive: Balchen, Fokker, René Fonck, Bert Acosta, the pretty "lady flyer" Ruth Nichols, and Chamberlin. He looked at his tires and noticed that, as *Spirit* grew heavier with gas, they seemed to sink into the field.

Then something occurred that can only be called petty and cruel. Though left out of the histories, it is mentioned in the rough draft of Balchen's autobiography and confirmed by *The New York Times*. "As if to prove that he could have made the journey that day," Balchen wrote, "Byrd asked Lindbergh if he might borrow his own runway to make a trial flight in *America*." What could Slim say? He was on the leased field due to Byrd's good graces. For nearly two hours, from 5:30 to 7:30 a.m.,

Byrd flew two short flights, one to test instruments and the other with a load of 12,000 pounds, "probably to test the new rudder," generously commented the *Times*. He flew in and out of the fog, putting *America* through her paces. "Further flights were prevented by the fog."

There is no mention of this incident in Lindbergh's autobiography, nor any indication of the response of the crowd. But as soon as Byrd landed, Lindbergh prepared to go. The tanks were topped off; he settled in the cockpit and then suddenly jumped out. He thought he'd forgotten his passport. One of the crew pointed to a rack behind him that held a flashlight and his important papers. He paused, looked up at the leaden sky, then down at his bulging tires. A schoolteacher named Katie Butler removed the St. Christopher medal from around her neck and called a policeman over. She whispered some words to him. The officer nodded and put the gift in Lindbergh's hand. He nodded but didn't look up; he slipped the medal in his pocket without looking to see what it was.

At 7:40 a.m. Lindbergh reentered his plane. Byrd appeared in the window and shook his hand. Ed Mulligan spun the propeller; Ken Boedecker cranked the booster magneto. Though the engine roared to life, the tachometer registered only 1,470 rpm, thirty revolutions too low. "It's the weather," said a mechanic. "They never rev up on a day like this." Lindbergh buckled his seat belt, pulled down his goggles, and stuffed a wad of cotton in each ear. He turned to Mulligan and Boedecker and said, "What do you say—let's try it." He nodded to the men by the chocks to pull them away. He opened wide the throttle.

The time was 7:51 a.m.

Some of the mechanics pushed on the struts; *Spirit* seemed sluggish at first, but gradually the rudder took effect and he was able to keep the plane in a straight line. He looked over and saw Harry Bruno and Dick Blythe in their familiar yellow roadster. He waved to Bruno, then shouted to Blythe, "So long, Dick. See you later."

The yellow roadster sped after the plane. Nassau police chief Abram Skidmore jumped in a passenger seat, cradling a fire extinguisher. Bruno drew the car abreast of *Spirit*, then fell in behind as she gained speed. Flames leapt from the Whirlwind's exhausts. When the roadster's speedometer touched just under 60 and they'd rolled down the runway for 2,000 feet, the lumbering plane left the ground.

Then she came down. Lindbergh had pulled back on the stick the first time; now he pulled back again. She jumped up once more, then back down. "Kangaroo hops" spectators called them. Then he tried again.

The third time was the charm. *Spirit* lifted up, and at 7:54 a.m. the *Spirit of St. Louis* was airborne. She cleared the steamroller by 10 feet, the telephone wires by 20. Bruno slammed on his brakes to avoid hitting the steamroller. He and the police chief watched as the plane headed into the open air. She dipped, then slowly climbed. They were too wound up to speak. Then, almost in unison, they shouted, "By God, he made it!"

The plane's wing glittered in the sun. Soon *Spirit* was a speck in the murk, then only an after-image. "God be with him," Byrd told reporters gathered around his plane.

"I think he has a three-to-one chance," said Chamberlin. "My heart was in my throat. It was a splendid start, one of the most thrilling I've ever seen."

Balchen was apparently not interviewed. But he let out his breath and whispered to himself his nation's traditional parting for travelers: *"Lykke på reisen!"*

Luck on the voyage.

SEVENTEEN

THE CHOSEN

It is the twenty-second hour of his flight, six hours beyond the midpoint between New York and Paris, what he called his "point of no return." He can only go forward, and he is tired, more tired than he's ever been in his life. Over and over he's fallen asleep with his eyes wide open, "knowing I'm falling asleep, unable to prevent it," then suddenly popping back into reality. It doesn't help that he's flying in a fog. It closes in and his mind closes off; the fog opens up and he spots the sea. He needs that palpable image: the whitecaps on the dark water, proof of a reality outside the plane. He figures he's been awake more than forty-eight hours and doubts he can keep it up. Then the fog closes in again.

It is then that they come to him—"ghostly presences," passing in and out of the fuselage—"vaguely outlined forms, transparent, moving, riding weightless with me on the plane." They come and go at will, first only a few, then many, an entire convention of spirits meeting and greeting in the aft part of his cabin. They do not frighten him, and almost seem expected. "I feel no surprise in their coming," he says later, as if their arrival is the most natural thing in the world.

Scientists who study the psychology and physiology of sleep would say today that Lindbergh experienced a particularly strong "hypnagogic hallucination," a dream occuring at the onset of sleep that seems extraordinarily lifelike and is later recalled in detail. Most such hallucinations are nightmarish, but Lindbergh called his benign. Both, however, seem to exist within the merger of two conscious states. Sometimes, say researchers, dreamers show a simultaneous awareness of the "real" world and that of their dreams.

Lindbergh never said that he was terrified, nor denied what he saw. Quite the opposite. By the time he saw his ghosts, the worst of his battle with sleep had passed. Five hours later he would spot a fishing fleet off the coast of Ireland and try, unsuccessfully, to shout for directions. But the experience with the "visitors" changed something in him. He knew that hallucinations could result from "extreme fatigue and subconscious ravings from a sleepless brain," but these had to be something greater. "The longer I live, the more limited I believe rationality to be," he wrote near the end of his life in his final book, *Autobiography of Values*. Irrationality gave him an insight he had never experienced: "It was the only occasion in my life when I saw and conversed with ghosts... I recognized that vision and reality interchange, like energy and matter."

•

Friday, May 20, and Saturday, May 21, were the kind of days when, years later, people remembered exactly what they had been doing. *Can he do it?* they asked themselves and others. *Can he make it alone?* All day and into the night, the world's thoughts seemed to center on the *Spirit of St. Louis* and Lindbergh. Lloyd's of London, which issued odds on almost every risky venture, refused to quote prices on Slim. "The underwriters believe the risk is too great," a news report said. In Paris, aces and aviators convening at the International Legion of Aviators in the rue du Bois de Boulogne said he took a "crazy" chance, though many admired his bravery. "I do not think that a man can stay awake thirty-six hours by himself with nothing but the sea, sky, and air as an environment and a motor roaring away monotonously," said League president Clifford B. Harmon. "If he could only get five minutes' sleep, two minutes', or any short cat nap now and then, it wouldn't be so bad. But Lindbergh can't afford to risk forty winks. The flight is a desperate thing. But brave!"

In Detroit, Slim's mother started the day with a telegram from Dick Blythe. "CHARLES TOOK OFF AT 7:51 AM TODAY," it read. "HE WILL BE IN PARIS NEXT." A few minutes later her uncle—John C. Lodge, the acting mayor of Detroit—called. He was sure Charles would make it to Paris, he said. She went to school and held her chemistry classes as usual, her only public reaction to the excitement a request to school authorities that she not be disturbed by reporters.

Because his plane was so heavily loaded, Slim flew it low, and his progress over Connecticut, Rhode Island, and eastern Massachusetts was very closely tracked. All along the New England coast, people climbed up trees and on to rooftops to catch a glimpse of the plane. He flew what would be dubbed by air traffic controllers the "Lindbergh Line," a heading of 66 degrees for the first 100 miles. Airliners flying to Europe would file their flight plans under "L/L" until at least December 1957, when the official designation was changed to "North Atlantic Track 101." At 9:05 a.m. Slim was seen over East Greenwich, on Narragansett Bay, in Rhode Island; at 9:15, over Middleboro, Massachusetts; at 9:40, over Halifax, Massachusetts. His air speed was about 100 miles per hour, and he flew barely 100 feet above the ground. Observers said his plane seemed to wobble and his engine to miss, but a spokesman for Wright explained that a radial engine such as the Whirlwind sometimes sounded to those on the ground as if its nine cylinders were "missing fire." The fact that Lindbergh was seen on schedule above Halifax showed that the motor was hitting on all cylinders, he said.

•

At 10:00 a.m. that Friday, Judge Mitchell May of Brooklyn dismissed Bertaud's injunction on all counts, and the *Columbia* was free to fly. Chamberlin rushed from court to the hangar at Curtiss Field, determined to take off as soon as possible. By now, *Spirit* was over Maine. If Chamberlin could leave by 11:00 a.m. or a little after, he'd be within the window in which the more powerful *Columbia* could catch up to the smaller plane. He'd wanted to be first to Paris, but even if too much time had passed for that to be possible, it would be the race of the century. He could wiggle his wings at Lindbergh as he passed above Paris, then break his record by flying farther, possibly to Berlin or Rome.

But the *Columbia* was immediately beset by more trouble. Disgusted by the legal wrangling, the constant bickering, and most important by the fact that another plane was preceding his to Paris, Giuseppe Bellanca had washed his hands of Levine and had resigned from the Columbia Aircraft Company. He told the press, "Two characters like Levine and myself could not continue in the same enterprise." With that, Levine's spirits fell. Chamberlin repeatedly tried to reach him, since he needed Charlie's approval to take off, but Levine hid out for the rest of the day. When he finally showed up at the hangar that night, all the fight seemed kicked out of him. He scanned the next day's weather reports and approved Chamberlin's plan to take off early Saturday if the winds looked favorable. But he left all other decisions with the pilot, something he had never done before.

Chamberlin told John Carisi to have the *Columbia* ready on Saturday morning.

By early afternoon, Lindbergh was winging over Nova Scotia. He had been awake for more than a day, and he was growing tired. "I'd be ashamed to have anyone know I feel tired when I'm just starting," he mused. Still, the sight of the beautiful if rugged coastline boosted his spirits. When he spotted St. Mary's Bay from 1,000 feet, he knew he'd held his course to within two degrees of his original plan. He had averaged 102 miles per hour and had covered 440 statute miles thus far. The wind was good—it pushed him along from the WNW at about 30 miles per hour. He passed Cape Breton Island and headed northeast. Before him lay 200 miles of water, then Newfoundland. With eight hours of flight already behind him, his eyes felt "dry and hard as stones."

The phone calls began after Evangeline arrived home from school. Some were welcome—the *Detroit Free Press* had agreed to phone in the latest bulletins of Charles's flight as soon as they arrived—but many were not. Finally, she felt obliged to make a statement of her own. "Tomorrow, Saturday, a holiday for me, will be either the happiest day of my whole life, or the saddest," she said into the phone. From what she understood, Charles should land in Paris sometime on Saturday afternoon. The wait would be long, but she would be patient, for in the end she knew she would receive "a happy message."

At the same time that she was making this statement, her son was flying over the open stretch of Atlantic between Nova Scotia and Newfoundland where many believe Nungesser and Coli disappeared. It was a taste of the flight to come. He was already fighting sleep, forcing himself to keep his eyes open; he squeezed them together as tightly as possible to force some circulation back into the lids. His mind began to drift. He remembered lying in a Minnesota snowbank when he was seventeen—the clouds outside the cockpit reminded him of the seductive soft snow. Fall asleep in that and you'd die gently. The waves below him were a blur—he saw white spots, and then realized that he had flown over his first ice field. Huge slabs of ice glittered in the sun; their white purity seemed stark and startling against the black sea. He approached Newfoundland just south of the French islands of Saint-Pierre and

Miquelon, where the *White Bird* had possibly met her fate. He headed almost due east, over Placentia Bay and the Avalon Peninsula, then jogged north—his only deliberate deviation during the entire journey— to pass over the provincial capital of St. John's.

By then clear skies and good weather were just a memory. Clouds had started thickening over Cape Breton, Nova Scotia, then grew worse over the 200 miles of open water to Newfoundland. As he neared St. John's, he found himself buffeted by turbulence and hard, driving rains; he questioned his wisdom at leaving his parachute behind. *Spirit*'s long wing seemed fragile in these blasts—would it break from the strain? Should he return to Long Island? But Doc Kimball had predicted such local conditions, and he'd been right about everything else so far. Kimball had said the air would clear to the east when he got over the ocean, so he decided to press on.

Another aviator battled the same bad weather. That morning, Francesco de Pinedo and the *Santa Maria II* had flown from Montreal to Trepassey Bay, at the southeastern tip of the Avalon Peninsula. After leaving New York, de Pinedo had circled quickly from New Orleans, to Chicago, to Canada, still hoping to cross the Atlantic before any of the Orteig rivals. Had conditions been right, de Pinedo would have crossed the Atlantic that afternoon. But the foul weather would push his takeoff back by another two days.

At this point, de Pinedo was still a big name. On May 20, the Newfoundland Post Office had issued the world's first commemorative stamp honoring an individual aviator. Yet his good fortune ended the moment Lindbergh flew overhead. By the time de Pinedo finally lifted off, the storm would grow even worse: he'd drift off course, run out of gas, and have to be towed 200 miles to the Azores by a passing fisherman. It was an ignominious ending to the Four Continents Tour, and when he finally flew into Rome on June 16, the luster had rubbed thin. Italians went crazy with joy, but just as he'd feared, Lindbergh had stolen his thunder and Il Duce was not pleased. Soon afterward he was made air attaché to Buenos Aires, a form of banishment far from Italy and the European air arena.

At 8:15 p.m. local time, 7:15 by his clock, Lindbergh flew low over St. John's, ensuring that he was seen. It would be his last contact with land until Ireland, and he wanted people to know that he had made it this far. If something should happen to him, the search could focus in a straight line between St. John's and the Emerald Isle. It was dusk, and

Lindbergh pointed his plane toward the night. He saw men waving at him; he turned the nose slightly right, shot through the gap between the two hills guarding the harbor, and flew east into the void.

Though now out of sight, he was still on everyone's minds. In New York's Yankee Stadium that night, forty thousand fight fans had gathered to watch a world heavyweight bout between the favorite, Jim Maloney, and his rival, Jack Sharkey. The announcer, Joe Humphreys, told them that Lindbergh was over the ocean; when he asked for a moment of silence, the throng stood as one. That day, the famous "cowboy humorist" Will Rogers wrote in his newspaper column, "No attempt at jokes today." Lindbergh was "somewhere over the middle of the Atlantic Ocean, where no lone human being has ever ventured before. He is being prayed for to every kind of Supreme Being that has a following. If he is lost it will be the most universally regretted loss we ever had."

One wonders at such hyperbole. Would Lindbergh's loss be greater than Lincoln's? Would the nation be as stunned as after the massacre at Little Big Horn? Yet the image of a young man dying alone in the dark rolling water gave everyone pause. The others—Davis and Wooster, Nungesser and Coli, Islamoff and Clavier—had died horribly, but not alone. The image of the lone flier became iconic, and the newspaper artist Daniel R. Fitzpatrick brought it to life in that Friday's edition of *The St. Louis Post-Dispatch*. The drawing was simple. The lower fourth of the panel was a wide, empty sea, and above that, an immense, gloomy sky. And set in the center, vulnerable and defiant, a tiny plane.

•

Night crashed on Lindbergh with sudden impact, as it often does in the northern latitudes. He was flying blind, without lights or flares, with no radio beacon on which to home. He had flown blind as a mail pilot, so he was not particularly worried. The altimeter measured his altitude above the frigid Atlantic, and he had his magnetic compass, though the engine's magneto and the vibration of the plane could severely upset a reading. Out here, without landmarks, he'd need something more to gauge his position.

One of Lindbergh's defenses against veering off course was his Pioneer earth inductor compass. In an ordinary compass, the earth's magnetic field reacts directly on the needle to point north, but a vibrating aircraft could upset that process and result in errors as great as 180 degrees. The Pioneer compass separated the magnet from the needle and steadied the dial. Since he wanted to go east, he twisted the compass face to EAST and turned *Spirit* until the needle steadied on zero. This meant he was on course: if the needle drifted off zero, he turned the plane until the needle returned to its setting, which meant he followed the right heading again.

If this didn't work, there was always dead reckoning. Slim had practiced this art during his San Diego–New York flight and felt comfortable with the procedure. For this to succeed, he must plot a series of compass courses that would keep him on the Great Circle Route, the shortest path between North America and Europe, following the curve of the globe; he'd calculate the moment each leg of the route was completed by using his watch and *Spirit's* speed. Since the plane made about 100 miles per hour, he plotted course changes every hour. In order for this to work, he had to estimate wind drift, which meant he had to keep the ocean in view. One thing that made Lindbergh different from the other ocean fliers was the fact that, whenever possible, he flew close to the surface rather than at a high altitude. Since he often flew as little as 10 feet above the surface, he could watch the sea foam as it blew off the crests of the waves. This way, he could better estimate the wind's direction and speed.

During the thirteenth and fourteenth hours of his flight, he began to climb in order to escape the omnipresent fog. He ascended to 5,000 feet and tried to rise above the billowing clouds. He climbed to 10,000 feet, and still there were clouds; he realized that he might not be able to rise above them. There were mountains and valleys of clouds stretching in all directions. It grew cold, and he zipped up his flying suit and pulled on his mittens and wool-lined helmet. One cloud ahead seemed to be a huge thunderhead, and *Spirit* bounced in the turbulence. He kept climbing—to 10,500 feet—and he thrust his bare hand out the window. It stung, as if it were being hit with tiny pinpricks. He took out his flashlight and pointed the beam outside. He saw ice forming on the strut of one wing.

He had flown right into an ice cloud, and right into danger. Ice has been a deadly threat almost since men began to fly; it clings to a plane like a parasite, and could affect a ship like *Spirit* in myriad ways. It could freeze the wings, struts, wires, and outside fixtures into inflexible chunks, catastrophically increasing air resistance. The entire ship could gain weight as the fabric absorbed water and froze. Ice clung to a wing's leading edge, changing the shape of the airfoil and thus the wing's lifting power. The longer *Spirit* stayed in this cloud, the greater her danger of plunging into the ocean.

Lindbergh fought back panic for the first time in his flight—for the first time, in fact, since he'd considered making the trip alone. Even the battle with sleep was *his* battle, one he fought with himself. But the assault of the ice came from an external obstacle, one that was outside his control. He shone his flashlight out the window and saw, sure enough, that the strut's leading edge was "irregular and shiny." As far as the beam penetrated into the dark, the night was "filled with countless, horizontal, threadlike streaks." If he didn't escape the ice immediately, he would die.

The only defense from icing was to run. Which is exactly what Lindbergh did. But he had to do so slowly. He had no way of knowing how much ice had built up, and he had to make a long slow turn to avoid putting undue stress on his fragile plane. He began to reverse course, turning 180 degrees in a long, slow loop, which brought him out of the cloud and back under the stars. But he was pointed back at Newfoundland. He turned again, slowly, and got back on course, bypassing for the rest of the night the giant thunderheads that boiled up, and droned instead through the canyons of cumuli.

•

Sometime during the sixteenth hour of his flight, he had covered 1,500 miles and passed the halfway point between New York and Ireland. The actual halfway point between New York and *Paris* would not come for another three hours. The continents of cloud still stretched around him, but the ice had melted, and as long as he stayed in the open, that danger had passed. He was grateful for the clouds. They broke the monotony that could lull him to sleep; they forced him to pay attention. Whenever he deviated from his course to get around them, he had to make precise calculations to get back on course again. If he flew 30 degrees to the south to skirt a cloudbank, he would have to fly 30 degrees to the north for an equal number of minutes at the same speed. Neither compass had acted normally since his battle with the ice, but he could see the moon and the North Star. His neck was stiff and cramped, and every muscle in his body ached. He cupped his hands out the window and directed the cold air into his face to stay awake. It had been thirty-nine hours since he last slept. He breathed in frigid air.

From the seventeenth to the twenty-second hours of his flight—from midnight until 5:00 a.m. on his clock—Lindbergh entered a fugue state of sleeplessness, a gray area between waking and dreams. "The deepest sleep resembles death," observed the biblical author of Samuel, and for Lindbergh, sleep at this point would have been fatal. He had no choice but to fight against the temptation. In the hero myth that formed around him, sleep was the monster he conquered, but, in truth, he did not fare quite so well. By the eighteenth hour, strange things began to happen to him. He seemed divorced from his body, as if he were a cloud himself, a liquid awareness spreading through space. His eyes shut of their own accord, even though he fought back by lifting his lids with his fingers. Sleep's onslaught brought comfort, and he almost succumbed. But death and failure would have resulted, and that realization kept him going. He'd maneuvered himself to this position from the start; the choice between life and death had become the essence of this competition. He shook his head until it hurt, rubbed the muscles of his face to regain feeling. He pushed the stick forward and dove, then pulled up sharply at a ridge of clouds.

Lindbergh would not write in detail about his war with sleep until three decades later. Before that, the best account of long-term sleep deficit was made by psychologist S. L. A. Marshall, when observing paratroopers in the 1944 Normandy operation:

They were dull-eyed, bodily worn and too tired to think connectedly. Even a 30 minute flop on the turf with the stars for a blanket would have doubled the power of this body and quickened the minds of its leaders to ideas which they had blanked out. But no one thought to take that precaution. The United States Army is indifferent toward common-sense rules by which the energy of men may be conserved in combat... Said Captain Patch of his people on the far right, "They were so beat that they could not understand words even if an order was clearly expressed. I was too tired to talk straight. Nothing I heard made a firm impression on me. I spoke jerkily in phrases because I could not remember the thoughts which had preceded what I said.

This is probably a good description of Lindbergh's physical and mental state. It is also a good indicator of things to come.

In the twentieth hour of his flight, sleep finally gained the upper hand. He had been asleep, but with his eyes wide open, and woke to find the plane in a spin. The realization came like an electric shock, and within seconds he was in control of himself and back in control of his plane. But he would fall asleep again, his eyes still open, knowing what was happening but unable to stop the inevitable. He hit himself sharply in the face, but barely felt it; he hit himself again, harder, and only felt numb. Not even pain could keep him awake. He broke open an ammonia ampule and took a deep breath, but could not smell a thing. His senses were dead. He'd always abhorred the sobriquet "Lucky Lindy" because he felt that his accomplishments had nothing to do with luck. But during this stretch of the flight, it was only luck that kept him alive.

By the twenty-second hour, the lightness of his body started to affect his mind. The cabin behind him seemed to fill with ghosts. He shook his head, but they did not go away. "I saw them clearly although my eyes were staring straight ahead," he wrote. "Transparent, mistlike, with semihuman form, they moved in and out through the fabric walls at will. One or two of them would come forward to converse with me and then rejoin the group behind. I can still see those phantoms clearly in memory, but after I landed at Paris I could not remember a single word they said."

Lindbergh was not the first to spot such strange visitors: throughout history they have appeared to those alone at sea. Joshua Slocum, the first man to sail solo around the world, wrote of a ghostly stranger that sat in the helm of his boat. Lyn Robertson, a castaway in the doldrums, those becalmed parts of the ocean affected by the Intertropical Convergence Zone, saw a person sitting behind her husband who helped guide them through a long and dangerous storm. In the literature of folklore and the paranormal, Lindbergh, Slocum, and Robertson were describing "phantom travelers," ghosts that haunt roads, vehicles, or way stations. First recorded in Russia and Europe around 1600, such phantoms have hitched rides on every mode of transportation.

These were not the only phantoms Lindbergh saw that night. In the following hour, he thought he spotted a coastline, complete with hills, trees, and islands, under his left wing. He shook his head, and it was gone. This happened several times—he'd approach a landmass and it would melt into mist like the old sightings of St. Brendan's Isle. He knew immediately that these were mirages, products of his sleep-deprived mind.

But until the end of his life, he would believe that his visitors were real. Joshua Slocum, Lyn Robertson, and others believed in the travelers, too. Like Lindbergh, they believed that they'd stood on the "border line of life and a greater realm beyond." They wondered, like Lindbergh, "Is this death? Am I crossing the bridge which one sees only in last, departing moments?" They all described a sense of great and lasting peace.

They all felt that they had been chosen.

•

But chosen for *what?*

If he wanted to find out, he would first have to survive. His extreme fatigue passed with the ghosts, as if they'd taken his exhaustion away. By the twenty-seventh hour, he had spotted signs of life again. He saw black specks in the water and discovered that he was flying over a fleet of fishing boats. He came about and circled a boat. "Which way is Ireland?" he shouted.

The fisherman could not hear.

One hour later, Lindbergh saw land. He was droning over the Dingle Peninsula exactly as he'd planned—an impressive feat of dead reckoning. In another hour he was over St. George's Channel; two hours after that, Cornwall. Twelve-year-old George Reed was working alone in a rock-strewn pasture near his village of St. Bernard when he heard the sound of an engine and looked up. An airplane flew out of the west and passed over the hedgerows. "People raise their heads as I fly over them," Lindbergh noticed. He wondered what they thought. George Reed watched the plane vanish to the east and wondered where it was going.

Forty-five minutes after Cornwall, Lindbergh was over the Cherbourg, or Cotentin, Peninsula of France. He looked down to see French villagers run out of their homes—"blue-jeaned peasants, white-aproned wives, children scrambling between them." He ate his first sandwich since he began, but it tasted flat. He wadded the wax paper and started to throw it out the window when he thought of how "these fields are so clean and fresh it's a shame to scatter the paper." He realized, wisely, that his first contact with France soil should not be the litter from his sandwich wrapper.

Night fell once more, but in the darkness, a circle of light appeared. Lindbergh was drawn to it like a moth, and in its center stood the Eiffel Tower. He looped above it once, then headed northwest to the aerodrome at Le Bourget. A black square was framed by regularly spaced floodlights, and he eased the stick forward to descend. He thought he would be met by some fellow aviators, government officials, and a small group of reporters; he would hand over his letter of introduction, let the Aero Club of France unseal *Spirit's* reading barograph, then ask about a nice, if cheap, hotel. Instead he saw a long string of lights stretching from the city to the aerodrome and realized they were the headlamps of thousands of automobiles stuck in traffic on the road to Le Bourget.

As his wheels touched the ground, Lindbergh became the most famous man in the world. The time was 10:22 p.m. on Saturday, May 21, 1927, and he'd been in the air for 33 hours, 29 minutes, and 30 seconds. He cut his engine, but after nearly a day and a half behind the Whirlwind, his ears still rang. He looked out his side window and saw the strangest thing. Across the lighted space, a dark wave surged toward him, a human tide that engulfed his plane. "Lindbergh! Lindbergh! Lindbergh!" 150,000 throats cried in an unfamiliar tongue. He'd been chosen by the multitude, for reasons he could never quite comprehend. He had entered that twentieth-century state of divinity in which the celebrity's ascendence became his entrapment, and his life would never again be his own.

"Lindbergh! Lindbergh! Lindbergh!" the crowd exulted.

They ripped at the fabric of *Spirit* as if ripping at his skin.

PART III
AM I A LITTLE NOBODY?

Man springs from nowhere, crosses time and disappears forever in the bosom of God; he is seen but for a moment, wandering on the verge of the two abysses, and there he is lost.
—Alexis de Tocqueville, *Democracy in America*

EIGHTEEN

PASSENGERS

Word of Lindbergh's landing arrived back across the Atlantic at the very moment Byrd christened his plane.

It was a bright Saturday afternoon; the clouds had finally broken, and the ceremony at Byrd's hangar was as elaborate as the Explorer and Grover Whalen could arrange. Thousands of excited people had come from the city; the hangar was bedecked with flags and red-white-and-blue bunting; hot dog vendors hawked their wares. A brass band blared "The Star-Spangled Banner" as the American flag was raised. This was immediately followed by "La Marseillaise." Whalen called for a few moments of silence as an honor guard fired a salute in memory of Nungesser and Coli.

Then it was time to christen the plane. Wanamaker's daughters, Mrs. Gurnee Munn and Mrs. Hector Munn, were given the honors: the former had been born in France; the latter, in the United States. Each sister carried a bottle filled with water from the Delaware River at the point where Washington crossed during the Revolutionary War. They broke their bottles over the Fokker's middle propeller and cried, "I christen thee *America!*" Three National Guard biplanes roared overhead and dropped hundreds of tiny American flags.

What happened next is slightly uncertain. Many accounts state that Byrd had come to the lectern and was spreading out his notes when Harry Bruno ran up with a slip of paper stating that Lindbergh had arrived in France at 10:22 p.m., Paris time. Byrd stuffed his notes in his pocket and told the crowd that Lindbergh had arrived. One account had an excited reporter rush into the hangar and broadcast the news.

The most detailed account comes from Byrd's publicist, Fitzhugh

Green. Word reached Byrd before he reached the stage, probably while Wanamaker's daughters were christening the plane. He stood in his office at the back of the hangar, staring out a window. Green walked in. Byrd was surrounded by Whalen, and his brothers, Tom and Harry. The gathering seemed funereal, and Green asked what the problem was.

"Lindbergh has reached Paris," Harry Byrd said.

"What?" Green cried, amazed.

"Yes," Tom Byrd added, "and now Dick says we ought to stop this party."

"It's Lindbergh's day," the Explorer interrupted, turning away from the window. "Why detract from it?"

"But Lindbergh's four thousand miles away," Whalen replied. "And we have a huge audience waiting." The Explorer was overruled. He strode to the podium and began his speech: "It is certainly great news we have just heard about Lindbergh. And my only thought now is about him and his wonderful victory."

Across Roosevelt Field at almost exactly the same moment, members of the *Columbia* team expressed their disappointment less graciously. Levine ordered the plane towed to the field and filled with gas; *Columbia* would take off for Europe that day and surpass Lindbergh's record, he said. But almost immediately, things fell apart. Again.

First, Chamberlin could not find Carl Schory, who needed to install the sealed barograph. That done, the Bellanca's mechanics hitched the plane tail-first to the back of a small truck and towed her to the field. At the gate, the watchman would not let them through. Though he relented enough to allow them on the runway, he refused to let them take off. The Nassau County Police arrived and supported the watchman— no one had told them of the *Columbia*'s plan to fly, they said. The team must get the permission of Grover Whalen, who was at the christening and unavailable. Chamberlin tried to find him, but failed. Carisi's mechanics ignored the police and filled the Bellanca with gas. When the police tried to stop them, Carisi and Captain William Beckett punched each other in the nose. A brawl ensued between the cops and mechanics; cars roared up from the *America*'s christening; crowds swarmed the Bellanca and joined in the melee.

"Take her back to the hangar, John," Chamberlin said to his scrappy mechanic. By now it was 6:00 p.m. and the light was fading. They would have to try another day.

Though Whalen did not apologize for holding up the flight, he did attempt some damage control. True, Byrd had granted use of the field to the *Spirit* and *Columbia*, but it was with the understanding that plenty of notice would be given to clear away spectators, he said. Yet this had not happened when Lindbergh took off, and he never addressed the fact that Levine's group was forced to jump through hoops that Lindbergh had avoided.

So the *Columbia* was hitched again to the truck and towed back to her hangar. Before sending her back, Chamberlin had lightened the strain on the landing gear by opening the dump valve and jettisoning about 150 gallons of fuel. As the plane was towed off, he tossed a match lest a spectator drop a cigarette and became a human torch. A column of fire and smoke ascended; as a fire engine and ambulance wailed up, people at Byrd's hangar thought the *Columbia* had met her end. Rumors flowed all night: Levine had torched his plane out of disappointment, or he'd lost his mind and burned her in a rage.

Willda Chamberlin wondered for an instant whether her husband had set the plane on fire. Clarence had not been himself since Lindbergh took off from Roosevelt Field. He might be able to hide his feelings from the public and the press, but he could not hide them from her. All that long week, she had tried to resolve the insurance dispute between Levine and her husband. She told him not to delay the flight for that reason, but Clarence worried about her. She called Kenneth Collings, a pilot and "fixer" like Dick Blythe and Harry Bruno, and asked if he could use his connections to set up a private insurance fund instead. But underwriting companies weren't covering fliers, especially in this race, and Collings had to tell Willda that he'd failed.

He tried to contact her on Friday, but the Garden Hotel was a madhouse, and he couldn't get through the switchboard. On Saturday he drove there himself and found Chamberlin sitting on the side of his bed turning a coffee thermos over in his hands. He stared out the window, seemingly unaware of Collings's presence.

Willda watched from the side. Collings took her downstairs to explain what had happened with the insurance, then they returned to the room. Chamberlin had stepped out in their absence, but he soon returned. His face was blank and pale. "He made it," he said.

Collings knew he meant Lindbergh. "All the way?"

"All the way—he's in Paris."

That was all he said. Chamberlin gathered up some flying gear, stuffed it in a suitcase, and left without a word. Willda whispered hoarsely that neither money nor anything short of death would stop him now. Collings thought to himself that Lindbergh had won the race because he was a bachelor.

Which meant that Chamberlin had lost it because of love.

•

The week after Lindbergh landed, he seemed like the only flier in the world. Nothing seemed to matter to newspapers except his story; on the morning of his flight, *The New York Times* devoted its first five pages to him, except for a few ads on page 5. On the day that he landed, *The Washington Star* sold 16,000 extra copies; *The St. Louis Post-Dispatch*, 40,000; the *New York Evening World*, 114,000. Papers from Maine to California extolled Lindbergh's virtues: *The Evening World* proclaimed his flight "the greatest feat of a solitary man in the records of the human race," and for a very long time after that no one seemed to disagree. Papers coast to coast used 25,000 more tons of newsprint that day than ever before; newspaper sales skyrocketed five times higher than average. The numbers might have kept climbing, but the presses were already running at top speed.

The joy was not relegated to print. Radio commentators talked about Lindbergh for hours; matinees up and down Broadway interrupted their shows to announce his landing. That night, orchestras everywhere played "The Star-Spangled Banner." In the Roxy Theatre that night, six thousand patrons in the second show heard and saw a Fox film clip that had been taken of Slim's takeoff. In it, Fox tested for the first time a new sound-on-film process called Movietone. The film did not show much: the silver monoplane lumbered across the field from left to right; spectators ran after it, more ghostly than corporeal, followed by Harry Bruno's roadster. The sound of *Spirit's* engines diminished, then returned. There were cheers on the soundtrack as the plane lifted off, and cheers in the theater. Audience members turned and hugged their neighbors.

The joy would spread worldwide. Theater audiences in Berlin burst into applause. A Hindi publication in India called Slim's journey "a matter of glory . . . [for] the entire human race." In Rome, Italians gloried in how Lindbergh could "hurl defiance" at Nature and Destiny. Lindbergh was no ordinary man, declared the London *Sunday Express*, but "the stuff heroes are made of!" Cried the Prince of Wales, "Well done!"

Amid these celebrations, a general theme emerged. Lindbergh reflected the best of humanity—and of America. Mankind was not merely exalted, but made better by what he had done. Possibly the most widely circulated homage in that vein came from the pen of *New York World* columnist Heywood Broun:

> One had only to venture into any city street after the news of Lindbergh's landing to notice that for a little while the aspect of the world and all its people had magnificently altered. We came out of slumps and slouches. There was more brotherhood in being than I have ever seen here since the first morning of the Armistice.

Lindbergh's flight was a "triumph over fear," Broun said; an event that "let us see the potentialities of the human spirit." Man might be "small and fragile and, some would have it, miserable sinners," but when he put his mind to it, he was as big as the cosmos. With science wedded to the human spirit, man would always prevail.

In Paris, Lindbergh was flooded with congratulatory telegrams. President Coolidge sent one of the first, followed by Mussolini; the kings of England, Italy, and Belgium; and the government of Germany and Peru. Western Union provided form telegrams, and 55,000 of these were sent: one from Minnesota contained 17,500 signatures and comprised a scroll 520 feet long. People sent poems, letters, drawings, and sheet music; offers of pets; offers of personal service as his personal secretary, theatrical manager, bodyguard, even masseuse (offering a "good Swedish massage...after a refreshing pine-needle bath"). They offered gifts: a carton of Chesterfield cigarettes; a raccoon coat "made to your measure and selected from twenty thousand pelts"; a new type of garter invented by "Dr. Walter Konigsberger in Berlin," guaranteed to improve the blood flow; a car; a new set of clothes from Famous Barr.

He was offered jobs, most from the entertainment world. Carl Laemmle of Universal Pictures offered $25,000 to $50,000 for two films. Adolph Zukor offered $300,000. William Randolph Hearst offered $500,000 plus 10 percent of the gross for a film in which Lindbergh would play opposite Hearst's mistress, Marion Davies. Goldwyn, Warner

Bros., and United Artists also bid. The manager of Minneapolis's Marigold Ballroom offered $25,000 for six weeks of appearances; the Rialto Theatre in London, $10,000 for a single appearance; the Lyceum of Columbus, Ohio, $15,000; $5,000 a week for 30 weeks in Cincinatti. He was offered the presidency of the Jordan Machine Tool Company of Minneapolis and of the Rush Jones Insurance Company, which specialized in "aviator accident insurance." One of the Gimbel brothers offered him a $100,000 annual salary to serve as the executive of "any airline company."

He turned them all down.

Charles Nungesser had been right: whoever made it across the Atlantic first would be richer than he ever dreamed. Although Lindbergh did not accept the offers and endorsements that flowed in those first weeks—it has been estimated that in the first month alone they totaled $5 million—he did profit from his flight. First and foremost was the $25,000 Orteig Prize, which he would not officially collect until his return to New York. Nevertheless, Rayond Orteig rushed to Paris from Switzerland, where he'd been vacationing, when he heard that Slim had landed. He embraced the flier and laughed in delight. A friend asked him how he felt.

"I feel a lot lighter," Orteig said.

"Lighter by $25,000?"

"Lighter in my heart."

That was the most obvious payout, but there were others. Before leaving New York, he'd signed the $5,000 story contract with *The New York Times*; one week after arrival, he signed a $50,000 contract with G. P. Putnam's Sons for the manuscript that would become the hurriedly written *We*. Soon after landing, he cabled the Vacuum Oil Company, produced by Mobiloil: "In my flight from New York to Paris my engine was lubricated with Gargoyle Mobiloil 'B' and I was happy to say that it gave me every satisfaction," he wrote. "My engine functioned perfectly." The message became the centerpiece of Mobiloil's advertising and promotional campaign for years.

The money only increased once he returned to America. The Guggenheim Fund paid him $50,000 for a 22,350-mile, 82-city tour of the United States in *Spirit*. Within the next few years, he accepted consulting contracts from Pan American World Airways and Transcontinental Air Transport. The latter merged with Western Air Express to become TWA and was known at first as the "Lindbergh Line." By early 1929 he had earned more than $1 million.

Certainly the honors laid at his feet over the next few months would surpass anything up to that time. Governments seemed to compete to see which could bestow the greatest honor. All told, Lindbergh would receive eighteen decorations from presidents and kings; three million letters and three hundred thousand telegrams of congratulations; celebratory postage stamps in thirteen countries; the Legion of Honor, the R.A.F. Cross, and the Congressional Medal of Honor; and paintings, sculptures, and musical compositions dedicated to him. A museum in St. Louis that celebrated his flight would be visited by three million "pilgrims" in its first year. In literature and commentary alike, Lindbergh became a metaphor for the lone individual pitted against tremendous odds. Over and over, in multiple forms and media, one heard of Lindbergh that "He could be Me."

It is during this time that what eventually became known as the "Lindbergh religion" began to emerge. Within a week of his flight, President Coolidge called him America's "ambassador without portfolio." Within a month of that, he was called the "Messenger of Universal Brotherhood." Writers dubbed him an "inspiration" that typified "the spirit of good clean knighthood." In the early days, otherwise objective or even cynical reporters simply lost their heads over Lindbergh.

One feature that surprised everyone was how quickly the worship spread. Despite his fame, Lindbergh remained aloof, so the press had difficulty uncovering his "true" personality. Instead, the coverage built upon his flight, his looks and gestures, all of which were given heroic interpretations. His slim build and youth were signs of manliness and superior talent; his reticence, modesty and honesty. A legend arose that he'd rescued a little girl from a whirling propeller, a rescue that never occurred. He was a tabula rasa for the cult of celebrity, a blank page for the public to fill in as it pleased.

As the worship continued, Lindbergh would show signs of exhaustion. One day, in the midst of yet another reception in New York, he turned a tired face to some of the nation's richest and most powerful businessmen and said, "When this is all over, I think I'd like to run away to some quiet corner where I'm not known and just rest for awhile." A good-natured laugh passed around the room. "Colonel," explained a friend by his side, "just where in the world do you think you could go and not be known? That place, I'm afraid, doesn't exist."

It didn't exist, because "Lindbergh the Hero" was a creation of the media. His photos were on the front page of every paper, and his voice graced the airwaves around the world. But more than that, he was *the* most filmed personality of his day. The amount of movie stock used on Lindbergh was astounding: 7.43 million feet of celluloid, 2 million more than was ever used on the world's previously most filmed person, the Prince of Wales. The scenes of Lindbergh's takeoff, landing in Paris, reception in other European capitals, return to America, and triumphant parades down Broadway and Pennsylvania Avenue—all were building blocks for the inscrutable legend, grist for the movie mill. One of the first, the one-reel *Race to Paris*, was released on May 29, while Slim was still in Paris, and shown to packed movie houses all over the world.

The French, at least at first, were the least taken with Lindbergh and the mythology surrounding his flight. Perhaps in their grief for Nungesser and Coli, an awareness unfolded that France had lost more than two heroic men. "How can a lone American in a ramshackle plane make it," snapped a Frenchman to the American dancer Isadora Duncan, "when two great French pilots of much more experience and in a better plane—the best France could make—failed?" The bitter thought lay not far from the surface in many Frenchmen's minds. This was not pettiness, but a sad realization that a torch of some kind had been passed.

Lindbergh himself did a lot to defuse the bitterness, under the expert tutelage of the U.S. ambassador to France. Myron Herrick was a handsome ex-banker from Cleveland known for his devotion to the French, and they to him. He later denied coaching Lindbergh during that first week in Paris: "I never told him what to say," he wrote. "He did not need to be told." As Herrick wrote in his foreword to *We*, Lindbergh was "the very embodiment of fearless, kindly, cultivated, American youth—unspoiled, unspoilable." Words came naturally to him, Herrick claimed.

According to several reporters, this was untrue. In essence, Herrick housed and groomed Lindbergh in Paris, then presented him to the world. The ambassador rarely left his side. Slim might not yet have known that the eyes of the world were upon him, but Herrick certainly did. Although Herrick would later insist that he had "no plan of any kind regarding Lindbergh"—that, in fact, his first reaction to Slim's takeoff was "who in the devil is Charles Lindbergh?"—he literally took him in hand after he landed. But he had to find him first, and in the madness after *Spirit*'s touchdown, that was a challenge.

Lindbergh's landing in Le Bourget was almost as dangerous for him as the thirty-three-hour flight preceding it. As he taxied toward the terminal, the crowd trampled over a wire fence and broke through the line of gendarmes linking their arms. Men tossed their straw boaters in the air; in the floodlights, they looked like shooting stars. Lindbergh managed to shut off the engine before the propeller sliced the vanguard to pieces; he opened the cockpit door, extended his hand, and was pulled from the plane and hoisted aloft by the crowd. For nearly thirty minutes he bobbed on their backs like a cork at sea. Two *New York Times* reporters cowered under *Spirit* in fear for their lives. At last two French pilots fought their way through the mob. One grabbed Lindbergh's helmet and clapped it on the head of an American standing nearby. "There is Lindbergh!" they cried, then herded the real flier through the darkness and into a waiting Renault.

All this time, Herrick waited to receive Lindbergh in the airport's upper terminal. But strange things began to happen. First, "a little man in white kid gloves" arrived bearing a bouquet of flowers for Lindbergh. He tried to give a speech, but emotion overcame him, so he thrust the flowers at Herrick and disappeared. Then the "fake" Lindbergh was led up. His name was Harry Wheeler, a Brown University student on summer sabbatical, but he was tall, blond, blue-eyed, and American, and even Herrick was fooled. He was badly beaten up from his reception, and still clutched a bunch of red roses that someone had thrust in his hand. Herrick had started his speech when Wheeler interrupted: "But I'm not Lindbergh, Mr. Ambassador," he said.

"Of course you are," Herrick replied, thinking the poor boy must be addled from his long journey and rough reception.

"I tell you, sir, I'm not Lindbergh," insisted Wheeler. "My name is Harry Wheeler. Everyone got confused because of this," and he held up Lindbergh's smashed leather helmet.

"If you're not Lindbergh, then where is he?"

"Some French officers took him away to a hangar on the other side of the field while that crazy mob was almost killing me."

Two hours later Herrick finally met the *real* Lindbergh. After the French fliers had spirited Slim off in the Renault, they took him to the office of Major Pierre Weiss, who commanded a fighter unit located across the field from the civilian air terminal. In essence, Lindbergh was gently if effectively detained until Herrick assumed custody and took him to the U.S. embassy. Slim did not seem to mind: he sat on a camp bed and was drinking water when Herrick arrived. He gave the ambassador his letters of introduction and seemed most worried about the safety of his plane. It was late at night before Major Weiss drove Lindbergh to Herrick's residence, but on the way, Lindbergh insisted on stopping at the Arc de Triomphe, where he bared his head and stood in silence before the Tomb of the Unknown Soldier. Weiss, a writer and celebrity in his own right, was deeply touched, and *Le Matin* featured the gesture in its May 22 story of Lindbergh's arrival.

Even if he was guided by Herrick, Lindbergh seemed to have a natural instinct for winning the hearts of the French. That would make sense; his mother had raised him to be polite, and his father was a Washington politician. Yet public speaking was a trial. Lindbergh rose at around 1:00 p.m. on Sunday, May 22, then stepped out on a balcony to appease the throng yelling, "We want Lindbergh!" He unfurled the French and American flags to loud cheers. Herrick led him back inside to his first meeting with reporters. Waverly Root, a correspondent for the *Chicago Tribune*, remembered that "Lindbergh looked as if he were being led to the electric chair between two husky guards."

He read an opening statement that had obviously been modeled after President Coolidge's cables to Herrick and French president Gaston Doumergue. "I brought with me, gentlemen, the great sorrow of the American people for Nungesser and Coli," he said. The first reporter to speak asked Lindbergh what he thought of French women. "I haven't seen any yet," Slim answered curtly.

According to Root, this was Lindbergh's last contribution to the interview "except for the syllable 'Uh'. . ." If a question offered a chance to score political or diplomatic points, Herrick answered. If it was a technical question, the Ryan representative replied. "Between these answers, Lindbergh was helpless," Root said. Slim may have glimpsed his future at this moment: he was no longer the pilot of his fate, but a passenger.

His only other engagement for that day was a late afternoon visit to

Leontine Nungesser, who from now on would sign herself "la Maman du Capitaine Nungesser." It was a sad, if orchestrated affair. Thousands of people stood on the street outside her door as Lindbergh's entourage pulled up. The visitors climbed the six flights of creaking steps to the small, dark parlor arranged like a mausoleum. Mme. Nungesser opened the door. She took one look at the young aviator who had survived the Atlantic, then hugged him and wept. She begged Lindbergh to find her son.

It was the same request she would make by letter the following year. Lindbergh was clearly moved. He admitted that the searches for her son had not been successful. "But I want you to keep on hoping," he said. She broke into sobs and said she was sorry she had not gone to Le Bourget the night before. "I am a mother, that is all," she said as Herrick translated her words. Lindbergh told her of his own mother and how much he loved her. She embraced him once more as she showed him to the door.

It was the closest thing to genuine emotion he was to show in public. And it was probably at this point that any remaining roadblocks to Lindbergh's acceptance by the French were swept away.

He would remain in Europe until June 4, when he came home on the U.S. Navy cruiser *Memphis*, sent to collect him by order of President Coolidge. Slim had imagined flying all over Europe, but it was not to be—America wanted its hero back home. He stayed in Paris until May 28, then flew to Belgium and Britain, to more cheering crowds and audiences with both nations' royalty. He returned to Paris on June 3 to say farewell and to have the *Spirit of St. Louis* crated up for the voyage home. The next day a French plane flew him to Cherbourg, where the *Memphis* awaited him.

When he left Paris for the first time, on May 28, he flew over the city. The streets were lined with hundreds of thousands of people gazing skyward. He circled the Eiffel Tower twice, then flew over the Arc de Triomphe, the Champs Élysées, and the Place de la Concorde. He dropped a message weighed with a little sandbag tied to the French tricolor. It landed at the foot of the obelisk at Raymond Orteig's hotel, the Crillon. A friend of Orteig's handed it to the hotelier. "Goodbye! Dear Paris," he'd written. "Ten thousand thanks for your kindness to me. Charles A. Lindbergh."

In the Paris *Quotidien*, the French commentator Pierre Bertrand wrote:

It would have been a wonderful thing in human history if tens of thousands of Americans who waited all that tragic afternoon to greet Nungesser's *White Bird* had seen their hopes fulfilled. It was a wonderful thing to see all Paris cheer and rejoice when Lindbergh's plane arrived. Let us do honor to this great sportsman. But what is even better, let us pay homage to the fraternity of men.

•

Lindbergh had won. In the hero myth that would build around him, his success was ordained. In the study of human affairs from the late Renaissance to the present, one's path in life was believed determined by his personal qualities. The winner proved the point: he triumphed, not because of luck, but because he was superior. Americans loved their winners, and had already turned the pursuit of success into the nation's secular religion. Now, at long last, that religion had found its god.

Yet there was a glaring irony here, one that would be ignored for a long time. Lindbergh was not inherently superior to his rivals: he was no smarter than Noel Davis, no better organized than Richard Byrd, no more determined than Charles Levine. He was no better "natural flier" than Bert Acosta, and he never, ever showed the same deftness of handling that allowed Clarence Chamberlin to save the lives of two little girls. Lindbergh never saved a life, except his own.

If anything, Slim's success depended upon the others' failures—their deaths, accidents, and injuries. His victory would seem to bolster the worldview of economists: that randomness prevails. No matter how many times an individual stumbles, there is a good chance of succeeding as long as he hangs in there. Physicists phrase it more poetically: as molecules fly through space, they collide with others, a chaos of Brownian motion that erases all sense of a straight line. An atom's progress through time and space resembles a "drunkard's walk," an apt metaphor for the Orteig Prize.

If René Fonck had not crashed, *if* the line of trees had not risen at the end of Langley's runway, *if* Byrd had not succumbed to boyish enthusiasm, or Levine and Bertaud had not grown to hate one another—*if* these things had not happened, Lindbergh would have been a footnote in another flier's victory. But Lindbergh pressed on, unencumbered by others, and leapt at the chance when others lingered. He did not prevail so much as endure.

•

Yet Lindbergh's rivals refused to be beaten or to fade away. One day after *Spirit* landed in Paris, the other C.A.L. summoned the press corps. His *Columbia* would outdo Lindbergh by flying to Berlin, he said. Maybe even to Moscow. It would do so while carrying a "mystery passenger." Who was this passenger? the reporters demanded, but Levine knew his audience. They'd learn on the day of the flight, he answered. In the midst of all the Lindbergh madness, Charles Levine was back in the papers.

A countercurrent had started against Lindbergh soon after he landed at Le Bourget. It was small, and courteous, if largely ignored. Fonck was the first to go public with the criticism, which came largely from professional pilots, those Lindbergh had most wanted to impress. Lindbergh's feat was courageous, said Fonck, but an anomaly. The lone flier crossing the Atlantic was not the wave of the future. That belonged to multi-engine planes packed with freight and passengers. Fonck said he would take such a plane aloft. Named *Ville de Paris*, it was being built now in the Sikorsky factory on Roosevelt Field. It would carry four in the cabin, two of whom would be passengers.

There was also the question of morality, though this, too, was largely ignored. Around the time that Balchen joined the crew of *America*, General Marie Charles Duval, aviation expert for *Le Figaro*, sounded the first note in a slowly swelling chorus concerning the wisdom of ocean flights. Such flights were no good for sports; nor did they promote aviation, Duval said. The airplane had yet to be built that could justify further attempts. What they were best at, he warned, was getting people killed.

Of course, those getting killed were pilots, and they were used to taking risks. That was their life and their job. But there was something insidious in the spectacle, something that burrowed beneath society's skin. Could there come a time when those less skilled thought they were just as capable? Was society coarsened by it all? "That the crowds of two countries should be passionately roused to a fever of excitement by the possibility of the airman's succeeding and living or failing and dying is both immoral and shameful," wrote Duval.

The Orteig Prize had unleashed something unprecedented, and Lindbergh's victory somehow opened it up for mass consumption. Now others wanted a piece. It was not greed so much as something else: a frenzy people could not understand, though plenty tried. Many rushed to partake of what would become a mad dash for glory, and the first would be Chamberlin and Levine.

But who would fly with Chamberlin? The mystery kept the news alive. After Bertaud left the team, Willda said, "I'd rather come with you than stay at home and worry," to which her husband answered, "Okay, if I can't have a really good pilot, why, I'd as soon take you." So it was somehow leaked that Willda Chamberlin might fly.

But both knew it was not to be. "The truth is, the name of my companion must remain a secret until we actually start," Chamberlin told reporters. It was noted that in the two weeks after Lindbergh's flight, Chamberlin spent a lot of time aloft with Levine. He taught him the fine points of flying the Bellanca, building on the basics he'd learned from Acosta a year earlier. He showed him what the various instruments did. In the process, Chamberlin learned something new about his boss. The flip side of Levine's stubbornness was that he was completely without fear.

No one managed to figure out what Levine was up to. If anyone came close, it was Grace Levine, yet the idea that Charlie might fly himself was a possibility that she kept locked away. One day Levine asked what she would think if he were copilot. She brushed it off as a joke, but later Chamberlin heard her remark, "If I thought my Charlie was going on the airplane, I'd burn it up." Levine never broached the subject again.

In fact, her comment spooked him. One night, as he approached the hangar, he spotted smoke. "Save the plane! Save the plane!" he screamed, but pulled up short when he rounded the corner. The smoke rose from a small trash fire, tended by Chamberlin.

"What's the matter, Charlie?" the pilot asked, poking at the ashes.

"I thought Grace was burning it up," he said, and grinned.

On the afternoon of Friday, June 3, Chamberlin announced he would take off at 4:00 a.m. the next day. He would fly to Europe on the very day the *Memphis* brought Lindbergh home; he would fly as long as his gas held out, in an effort to beat Slim's distance. Doc Kimball advised him that the weather over the Atlantic would be as favorable as that experienced by Lindbergh, so he stayed in the hangar until late, fueling the tanks and supervising the loading. The 65-gallon wing tanks and 390-gallon fuselage tanks were filled up; thirteen 5-gallon cans were stored in the cabin for in-flight fueling. He stowed two sets of flying gear, Very pistols, flares, chicken soup, and a dozen toasted chicken sandwiches on rye bread, half a dozen oranges, navigation charts, and a rubber lifeboat, though he forgot to take the paddles. At 1:30 a.m. he rejoined Willda at the Garden City Hotel to get some rest, but like Lindbergh found sleep impossible. He left word to be wakened at 3:30 a.m.

That same night, Levine called his lawyer Samuel Hartman from his home at Belle Harbor. They chatted awhile. He said he wanted to sail the next day aboard the liner *Franconia*; he'd meet Chamberlin in Europe, and while he was there he hoped to meet Mussolini, whom he idolized. He wanted to have his affairs in order should anything happen on the way; his estate was worth $5 million, and he donated about $20,000 annually to charities and to various needy individuals. He wanted the payments to continue should anything happen to him.

At five in the morning, Chamberlin arrived at Roosevelt Field. He'd said good-bye to Willda at the hotel; like Noel Davis, he did not want her to watch. He'd been awake for about twenty hours without sleep; he was dressed for the flight in his usual leather jacket, knickers, and golf socks. Levine and Grace arrived soon after, and they all stood together in the predawn blackness as the tow truck hauled *Columbia* once again from Curtiss Field. A light wind blew from the east, which meant Chamberlin would have to start from the west, as Lindbergh had. He, too, would have to skirt the telephone poles, though the steamroller had been moved. A crowd began to collect, and a legion of photographers milled around the plane. Levine smiled as the flashbulbs popped; he wore a blue business suit with a leather vest, and Grace stood beside him, happy and proud. A reporter asked him about the navigator. "Not here yet," Levine replied.

The finishing touches were put on the plane. Doc Kinkade stood on a ladder and gave the Wright engine a final once-over. John Carisi crawled all over the *Columbia*, checking controls, wheel bearings, tires. He told Chamberlin that she weighed 5,418 pounds, 350 more than *Spirit*. At 5:45 a.m. Chamberlin climbed into his flying suit, and Carisi started the engine. It screamed, shrill and metallic, breaking the predawn stillness. Kinkade cocked his head to listen, then nodded in satisfaction. The plane was set, but there was still no sign of a navigator. As if on cue, Byrd's chief engineer, George Noville, drove up. The reporters surrounded him, believing the mystery solved. Noville protested that he was merely a spectator. An unidentified man rushed up to Chamberlin with a woman by his side. "Shake hands with my wife!" he pleaded. She'd been the last to shake Lindbergh's hand before he entered the cockpit, and Slim had arrived safely. She was good luck, the man said. As always, Chamberlin obliged.

Just after six, the first signs of light appeared in the sky. Chamberlin climbed into the cockpit, and Levine followed, presumably to discuss some last-minute details. A reporter approached: "Why won't you tell us the name of the second pilot?" he implored. "We have to have his obituary all written, you know, and he may not even get off the ground. Remember the two fellows in Fonck's plane?" Levine, for once, did not respond.

The cockpit door was open, and Levine reached up to close it—but then, with a smile and a wave to his wife, jumped in the seat beside Chamberlin. The crowd gasped and stirred. "Stop him!" cried Grace Levine. "He isn't going! No, he isn't! Stop him!"

John Carisi looked at the plane and cursed, but ran up to Grace and assured her that this was only a test run.

At first that seemed true. Chamberlin fed power to the *Columbia*, and she moved ahead slowly. The plane had always had a tendency to swing from side to side as she taxied down the runway, and she did so now. Chamberlin fought the sway with the rudder's control bar at his feet, but by now the crowd had grown so sizable and tight that it left him only a very narrow lane ahead in which to build up speed. He cut power and stopped the plane, then turned her and rolled slowly back to the west end of the field.

Chamberlin was sore, and for once he showed it, letting the police know that their job was to keep the mob away. Then Carisi ran up, stood on the tire, and yelled at Levine. Grace might be ignorant of what Charlie was up to, but the Italian mechanic was not fooled. "Do you know what you're doing?" he shouted. "Are you in your right mind?" Maybe he thought he could stop Levine's plot by hanging on the door and screaming profanities, but Chamberlin was not going to oblige. He shoved the throttle forward, and Carisi was blown off the tire by the propeller's backwash. The plane started to move.

Once again the *Columbia* started her run, but this time she did not slow. The police managed to drive the crowd to the right side of the runway, and the way seemed clear. The plane gained speed. Chamberlin edged to the left, away from the crowd, and for a second it appeared as if the wheels had left the runway. Straight ahead of the whirling propeller Chamberlin could suddenly see one of the three-foot stakes planted by Wanamaker's crew to mark the runway boundaries. Each stake was topped by a metal star, and if the propeller struck that it would splinter into a thousand pieces of deadly shrapnel. Chamberlin pulled up on the stick. The plane bucked up and down in revolt, but somehow the propeller was just high enough to pass over the stake, or else it passed through the blades between revolutions. At 2,500 feet, the *Columbia* lifted up.

She was officially airborne at 6:05:27. Chamberlin held her at grasstop level for another 1,000 feet, but by the time they reached the telephone wires they zoomed over them with plenty of room to spare.

This time Grace Levine realized what Charlie had done. "He's not going?" she pleaded, apparently stunned. Maybe someone would tell her otherwise. She took one stumbling step toward the plane, then stopped and looked back at her friends. She seemed to melt on the spot. A Nassau County policeman caught her as she fainted.

John Carisi ran up and tried to comfort her. "He's all right!" he shouted. "He'll get there. You should be proud of him. He's a brave boy! A real ball of fire!!"

Grace and Carisi were not the only ones amazed by Levine's ploy. "I'm surprised to see him go," Bertaud spat when told of the takeoff. "I hope he has a nice ride." Bellanca was found in the office of his former flying student Fiorello H. LaGuardia. The Sicilian opened his mouth in amazement, then snapped it shut again. "That plane is part of me," he finally said. "It would make me wince to have it hurt."

Aviators called Levine's move a crazy stunt. He was only a passenger, nothing more than dead weight, unable to help with either the navigation or flying.

They were wrong. He could fly the plane, at least for a short stretch of time. And true, he was a passenger, but one with a vision. He was the *first* transatlantic passenger: passengers might be dead weight, but they were a dead weight that could pay. Pound for pound, they were a more lucrative cargo than regular freight or airmail. Where many criticized Levine's last-minute surprise as nothing more than a stunt, in fact he had demonstrated again just how clearly he foresaw the future. Just as he'd known that the first to fly the Atlantic would be a bigger star than Chaplin or Douglas Fairbanks, he realized that the future of long-distance flight lay in getting people between continents faster than they'd imagined possible. The first air passenger across the Atlantic might be as big as Lindbergh—if he survived.

But few saw that at the time, and his motives were an immediate source of debate. Some said he wanted to prove his courage after the shellacking he'd received at the hands of the press. Others believed he hoped to improve his image after the continuous squabbles with Wade, Bertaud, Acosta, and Bellanca. While many called him mad, others called him mad for publicity. *The New Yorker* dubbed him a hero to husbands: "To a million family men, who after trying, unsuccessfully, to slip away merely to the corner for a can of pipe tobacco without revealing their motive to their women, [Levine's] feat is unparalleled, not merely in the annals of aviation, but in the history of the world."

In Manhattan's and Brooklyn's Jewish neighborhoods, Levine was a hero, though even there one could spot some fracture lines. The main objection came from older, more conservative Jews, who regretted that he'd flown on the Sabbath. By doing so, said one prominent rabbi, Levine had "spurned the holiness of the Sabbath before the whole world." On the whole, however, those interviewed by local papers seemed proud. Here was one of their own, showing he was just as brave and daring as the young Lindbergh or Richard Byrd. "I fear that no matter what we Jews do," said one businessman, "we will never have the complete respect of the non-Jews. But among our children and our grandchildren, Levine's feat has lent prestige to the Jewish name."

Up in the *Columbia*, Levine could not quite believe that he had pulled off his Saturday surprise. The plane leveled off at 200 feet into the eye of a rising sun; Chamberlin zoomed along with an aerial escort that had risen from Mitchel Field. As they cruised toward Connecticut, Levine shrugged into his white flying suit, which had been stowed beneath his chair. In the process, he discovered $300 that he had stuffed into his pocket to give to Carisi. "Perhaps that's why he was swearing," Levine joked. Then he got serious: "Think of taking all that money down with me."

But soon bad luck overtook them. Before they got to Cape Cod, the earth induction compass began to act up. Though Chamberlin had set the dial at zero as instructed, they missed New London by ten miles.

They missed Newport, Rhode Island, passing instead over St. George's prep school, a 5-mile deviation. They continued over Plymouth Bay to Cape Cod, and missed it by 15 miles. Finally, the compass failed altogether, as the needle flopped aimlessly over the dial. Engine vibrations had apparently broken a hairline spring that controlled the indicator needle. They still had the magnetic compass, but couldn't trust it entirely. They circled the Cape while debating their options. Levine cursed Pioneer Instruments for the faulty induction compass: the "damned thing" had cost $1,125. "Should we go back and get it fixed?" Chamberlin asked.

"And meet my wife?" Levine replied.

He also didn't want to face the reporters, some of whom believed he would turn back before striking out across the sea. So they pressed on.

Levine must have rummaged through the cargo, for at this point he discovered that Chamberlin had packed the lifeboat but forgotten the oars. Levine, still fuming about the compass, started to fuss, while Chamberlin kept his usual calm. The oars would only have added weight, he rationalized. "Besides, what was the use? It's too far to row anyway."

For the rest of the trip, Chamberlin would check their position by his compass and watch, the sun, and the stars. In three and a half hours they passed the city of Yarmouth, Nova Scotia, dead on course and right on time. The air was smooth; the weather, clear. At 6:00 p.m. they skirted Newfoundland at Trepassey Bay. It was their last glimpse of land before they headed out to sea.

They followed a path nearly parallel to Lindbergh's, if about 40 miles south, leaving the coast at Cape Race instead of St. John's. Levine took the wheel while Chamberlin pulled heavy woolen drawers over his golf knickers and a fur-lined parka over his leather jacket. He'd been thirty-one hours without sleep, so he stretched out on the piano-shaped gas tank to ease his cramped muscles. They flew at 2,000 feet, and the sun sank behind them. After a brief rest, Chamberlin climbed back in his seat and guided them over the ocean.

Late in the night, they spotted their first field of icebergs. The 'bergs were heading south, and Chamberlin checked his drift against them. For the most part, Charlie sat pensive and quiet, but would launch into excited conversation if he spotted something unusual, such as the lights of a ship or a bright star. The journey's otherworldliness held him enthralled.

After midnight, the weather thickened and solid cloudbanks formed. Chamberlin climbed to stay in the clear, but there seemed no end to these mountains of clouds. The Bellanca rose to 12,000 feet, to 15,000, and still the cloud barrier loomed huge and menacing through the front windshield. Suddenly they were in the thick of it, bumping in the turbulence and unable to see beyond the spinning propeller. At 3:00 a.m. Chamberlin read the outside temperature as 31 degrees Fahrenheit. His vision through the glass grew hazy. He glanced out the port window and saw that the wing's leading edge had collected ice. "We'll have to get out of this, quick!" he said to Levine. He eased the stick forward and nosed down.

They descended slowly, the *Columbia* handling well. At 6,000 feet the air grew warmer, but their visibility remained nil. At 3,000 feet they still could not find a break in the clouds. At 1,000 feet, the same. The altimeter had been set at zero at Roosevelt, but who knew for certain their altitude in such conditions? At 750 feet he finally had brief glimpses of whitecaps beneath them. Chamberlin breathed a sigh of relief and leveled off at 500 feet above the waves.

With the coming of the second day, the weather finally cleared, and they could see 50 miles in every direction. They spotted two steamers in quick succession and knew they were on course and in the shipping lanes. Then a transatlantic liner with four smokestacks and all the trimmings hove into view; she'd come over the horizon under *Columbia*'s nose and seemed to have magically sprung from the depths. They dove until they were even with her top deck, leveled out by her stern, and came about for another pass by her opposite rail.

Levine could read her name—the RMS *Mauretania*, for her time the largest and fastest ship in the world. The rails were jammed tight with cheering passengers as the *Columbia* sped past effortlessly. Chamberlin knew their position would be reported by wireless, but just to be sure, Levine held his hands out the window and mimicked a wireless operator tapping out his keys as they passed a group of officers on the bridge. They stopped waving long enough to nod that they understood.

Chamberlin glanced at the shipping news in the June 4 *Times* that he'd brought with him: the *Mauretania* had left Cherbourg twenty-four hours earlier. If the ship averaged 500 miles a day, that meant the *Columbia* wasn't that far from the coast. They paced the liner for another mile or so, then Chamberlin lined his plane straight down her smokestacks and flew from bow to stern. The trailing white wake was like an arrow pointing their heading. Chamberlin took a compass bearing and made allowances for the wind; this course would take them straight past the Scully Islands at Land's End, into the English Channel, and on to Germany.

Within the hour, another ship appeared to starboard. It was the *Memphis*, carrying Lindbergh back to America. They should change course and "jazz" her, urged Levine, but to do so would waste 20 to 25 miles' worth of fuel, and Chamberlin shook his head. Soon the *Memphis* dropped below the curve of the west, another memory.

Soon it was sunset, the end of the second day. They passed Land's End as predicted, crossed the Channel, and ran into a wall of thick clouds. Chamberlin figured the flight from Plymouth to Berlin would take about five hours, but the clouds piled high and impenetrable over the Continent, and there seemed no way above or around them. Even at 15,000 feet they couldn't get around; he tried climbing higher, but they both grew woozy from lack of oxygen. Since they still had plenty of gas, he decided to wait until daylight and plotted a holding pattern. They would fly north for twenty minutes, then reverse course for the same period, basically flying in place and killing time. Nearing exhaustion after flying at these high altitudes for so long without sleep, Chamberlin decided to take a short nap around dawn. "See what you can do with her for a while," he said. "I've got to get some rest." He handed the controls to Levine.

Chamberlin unbuckled his straps and climbed atop the fuselage tank. Levine had to fly only until daylight, when they could finally get their bearings and head toward Berlin. Chamberlin had barely stretched out on the tank when something felt wrong. The inexperienced Levine had flown into the mist and lost all sense of direction. He pulled *Columbia* up into a stall, then pivoted on her left wing and began spiraling to earth in a deep and dizzy spin. Levine knew something was amiss, but he could not tell what. The blinding mists around him, sweeping past the windows, gave no clue.

Chamberlin's exhaustion dissolved in an instant. In the time it took him to slide from the shelf to his seat, the wings began to shimmy and shudder. It seemed they would tear away from the plane. The rudder bar at his feet whipped back and forth like a scythe. One misstep on his part and it could easily break his legs. The rear of the plane shook with such force that he expected the tail to rip free.

"Never in my life," Chamberlin would write, "have I felt that death was so close or been so badly scared." But Levine was having the time of his life. Maybe he didn't know enough to be frightened; maybe he didn't care. He whooped in delight, like a kid on a roller coaster. When the ship had become unmanageable, Levine had shut off the engine and lifted his hands and feet from the jerking controls. He sat there and laughed. It feels like a bucking bronco, he said.

But Chamberlin understood the dangers. Trying to step down hard on the rudder bar would be suicide. Instead, he pushed his feet down gently at the end of the scythelike arc in order to dampen the terrible vibrations shaking apart the tail. He was as much at a loss for direction as Levine, but the rush of air past the window told him they were going down at a terrible speed. The altimeter needle swept past the 100-foot marks like a plummeting elevator clacking off floors; the airspeed indicator had jammed up against the dial post when they passed 160 miles per hour.'The bank and trim indicator was the only instrument that seemed to make any sense, and it told him they were making a sharp banking spin to the left and continuously going down.

He kept smothering the rudder with both feet to choke off the wild oscillations. The maneuver seemed to take forever, but finally he was able to pull them out of the spin. When the bank and turn indicator told him they were flying straight, he pulled the nose up and the Bellanca lost some of her terrible speed. She leveled off at 4,000 feet—Chamberlin knew they'd started their plunge at around 21,000. In a matter of seconds, they'd dropped more than three miles.

"Charlie," he gasped, "what did you think you were doing?"

He'd thought they were near the Harz Mountains and he'd been trying to clear them, Levine said.

After that, Chamberlin never relinquished the controls.

Though no longer in danger, they had no idea where they were. It was June 6, 1927—two days since they had left New York—and in the near distance they spotted an orange light reflected against the low-hanging clouds. They flew over water, and in the gray mist made out the eerie hot glow of blast furnaces. They must be in the industrial Ruhr Valley, and maybe the river they'd passed over was the Rhine. Considering the past night, it was a miracle they'd made it this far. To the left they saw white flames shoot up, and they buzzed past an airport with the name DORTMUND painted on a hangar roof. Chamberlin spotted a group of workers beneath him and cut power. "Nach Berlin?" he shouted as he glided past in silence. "Nach Berlin?" He banked and turned in the direction they pointed.

It was 4:30 a.m. and, as he watched, the gas needle was dropping lower. After another 65 miles of flight, Levine's dreaded Harz Mountains loomed from the mist, and Chamberlin skirted rather than scaled them. The needle hovered at E. The country was level and flat; the people lived in little villages, and it was too early for even the farmers to be up about their business. He wanted to sit her down near one of the large villages while they still had a few pints of gasoline left and he could use the motor for landing.

"No, we started out to set a long-distance record," Levine demanded. "Run her till she quits."

"You're the doctor," Chamberlin replied. "It's your plane, but I'd hate to bend it up trying to get a few more miles."

He told Levine to get back by the tail, since he figured that with the now-empty fuel tanks the *Columbia* might be nose-heavy on landing. No sooner had Levine clambered over the tank than the engine sputtered, wheezed, and died. Chamberlin glanced down and saw a field that looked level and clear. He maneuvered into the wind for a dead-stick landing in a wheatfield. He touched down, rolled to a road, then bumped over it savagely. It was a severe test for the landing gear, but it held. The plane rolled to a standstill and all was quiet. A bird chirped. Chamberlin heard the whirring of grasshoppers. The time was 6:05 a.m. on June 6, and in 42 hours and 32 minutes, they'd flown 3,905 miles, 295 more than Lindbergh.

Levine jumped out first, followed by Chamberlin. The Iowan was unsteady after so many hours in the air and leaned against the plane. They'd landed near a small village four miles from the town of Eisleben in Saxony. Levine, elated, jumped and hopped in the wheat.

All was quiet for about thirty minutes, until a middle-aged woman and two boys strode through the grain. Chamberlin and Levine asked for gas in halting German, but the woman was not in an obliging mood. She pointed at the wheat. It was her wheat. They'd mashed it flat. Who was going to pay? As they tried to make sense of her claims, her wrath suddenly turned to fear. A band of kidnappers had been terrorizing the region, and it suddenly dawned on her that she stood before foreigners who'd arrived in a new and previously unseen mode for carrying off victims.

Finally one of the boys understood and calmed his mother down. He darted through the field, jumped on his bike, and yelled back that he'd return with 90 liters of gas from Eisleben. As they waited, more people strolled up, then a truck came to a stop with 20 gallons of fuel. The only way to transfer the gas was with a quart-size coffee pot with a curved spout. By now, twenty villagers stood around and gawked: Levine grabbed a paper bag, scribbled the details of the flight, and persuaded them to sign the impromptu affidavit of their flight and time of landing.

By now it was 9:00 a.m. and they still wanted to reach Berlin, 108 miles away, where a huge celebration was planned. They took off again, using the road as a runway; they followed some railroad tracks, hoping they led to the capital. But the tracks skirted Berlin and instead headed to Poland. After ninety minutes of flying, the engine coughed and missed, possibly because of the unfamiliar type of fuel. They passed over a city with the name "KOTTBUS" painted on the flying field. They shot past the runway in hopes of reaching Berlin, but they were still 70 miles away and heading in the wrong direction. The ground grew swampy beneath them, and Chamberlin thought they'd better turn back. Five miles short of the field, the engine cut out for the second time. Chamberlin once again ordered Levine to the back and brought her down in what looked like a green field.

But a few feet over the ground he realized that it was a marsh. It was too late; he could not stop their descent; the wheels struck the muck and clogged up with mud. A black shower of mud rained around them. They plowed a double furrow in the marsh until *Columbia* lurched to a halt and tipped on her nose, snapping off the tip of the metal-sleeved propeller. Every loose item in the cabin rained down upon Chamberlin's shoulders. Powdered milk and chocolate covered his back. He cursed himself for bringing his beloved Bellanca to such an inglorious end.

Levine crawled over the gas tank, shouting Chamberlin's name. But the pilot was so disgusted with himself that he did not answer. Levine called out again, this time in real alarm. He scrambled over the tank and grabbed Chamberlin's hand. "Are you all right, Clarence?" he cried. "Did you hurt yourself?"

"This is a hell of a landing," groaned the veteran pilot. "I'm sorry, but I guess I broke the prop. It looks like we're all through flying."

"Damn the prop," Levine said. "I was afraid something had happened to you. We've flown enough for a while anyway."

A car pulled up with the Bürgermeister of Kottbus inside. Don't worry about the field, he said. It's only beets. Come into town and clean up. Relax and have a beer.

NINETEEN

FOUR MEN IN A FOG

That left only the deeply disappointed Byrd.

Seven months earlier, when Rodman Wanamaker made his dinner-time challenge, such an ending would have been unthinkable. Byrd was the fair-haired boy of the Arctic, America's explorer, the hero of the North Pole. Until the *American Legion*'s surprise unveiling in early April, he'd been the front-runner—and even then, the odds were fifty-fifty over which navy flier would win. But then *America* crashed, followed by Davis's plane—and certainty disappeared. Now Byrd watched from the sidelines as the Farm Boy beat him, followed by a guy wearing golf socks and knickers, and his boss, a Brooklyn Jew.

As Americans watched, Levine and Chamberlin were fêted as grandly in Germany as Lindbergh had been in France. By June 7, the *Columbia* was repaired and gassed up; fifteen to twenty planes escorted her from Kottbus to Berlin's Tempelhofer Feld, where thousands welcomed them. Then they were sped off for their official audience with President Paul von Hindenburg.

In Germany, Levine's Judaism did not seem to be an issue. In the United States, it was. Nothing illustrated this more than his reception, or lack of one, by the two nations' heads of state. Germany's president was far more attentive to Levine than America's. "The Jewish Press was irate because President Coolidge ignored Passenger Levine in cabling congratulations to Pilot Chamberlin," reported *Time* magazine. "Congratulations upon your wonderful feat in setting a new nonstop record in conquest of the air," read Coolidge's wire to Chamberlin. The Jewish daily paper *Der Tog* was slightly more saturnine: "At last we, too, are convinced of the great economy of our President," the paper editorialized. "He is so parsimonious, he watches so closely the cash register of Uncle Sam that even the great sum of 66¢ (the cost of cabling three words to Germany) is of importance to him."

A later piece more directly addressed the president's slap in the face to America's Jews: "Two men left New York; two men risked their lives; two men have shown heroism and created a record even greater than Lindbergh's. Two men left; two men arrived, Americans both. But the President of the United States congratulates only one, and by strange coincidence the one whom the President has not found worthy of being mentioned by name is named Levine." And yet, added *Der Tog*, "why should we wonder? Was ever a man with a Jewish name honored and recognized" by Coolidge?

Being beaten—not once, but twice—was hard for Byrd to bear. A full decade before Lindbergh's great fall from the heights, Byrd glimpsed how quickly a hero could plummet in public opinion. He had gone, in two weeks, from being the presumptive winner to the ultimate loser. Among the continuing wires and letters from young women and scientists begging to ride along on the trip, he began to spot others that were unabashedly hostile. The public seemed to have grown tired of him. "I just want you to know what you may not realize that you are the world's prize boob to get left at the switch as you did," wired a man from North Carolina. "You coward," shot another, "what are you doing out there?" A third called him a "disgrace to America," and fumed "I am sick of seeing your name." The letters came from all parts of the country, from men and women, young and old.

This glimpse of the flip side of fame seems to have caught him off guard. He had faced hardship before, but never disdain—except from his father. The Atlantic crossing hadn't even been his original goal upon returning from Spitzbergen; he'd dreamt of conquering the South Pole. Now people called him a laughingstock. That had to change.

On May 23, two days after Lindbergh's triumph, he proposed something new to Wanamaker. "Has not Lindbergh proved much that we set out to prove?" he wrote:

> It therefore appears to me that science can be better served by utilizing the America for a flight from the United States to Hawaii, which is very strategically important to link up with this country by airplane and has not been accomplished, or another

feasible expedition to promote aviation development. In writing you frankly my views I am solely prompted by my desire to aid international good feeling under the conditions now existing, and the cause of aviation to which I am devoting my life.

Wanamaker cabled back on May 27 from his Philadelphia store. His response was cool: "If it is the desire of yourself and your crew to be relieved I will abide by your decision... There will always be a continuation of the science of aviation but nothing at the present moment can take the place of the great victory of Captain Lindbergh."
After the *Columbia*'s flight, Byrd tried again:

The flights of Lindbergh and Chamberlin-Levine will undoubtedly be made again and again until the day will perhaps come when this will be a regular commercial undertaking. The point is that the pioneer job in this particular line has been done and that the new pioneering now lies in other directions... The North Pole has been conquered from an aviation standpoint. The South Pole remains a problem. The Pacific Ocean remains as yet to be bridged by aircraft.

But Wanamaker would not hear of it. He owned the *America* and thus controlled her fate. Byrd must fly to Paris—or not fly at all.
So Byrd bided his time and tested the *America*. The tests dragged on for days, as did the announcements of their departure. On June 12, Byrd told the press that the final tests would take place the following day and they might leave for Paris on the fifteenth. That day, storms raged over the Atlantic, and he delayed for two days—then two more. On June 19, the storms were still raging, but he said he might start the next morning anyway. By June 22, the *America* was still in the hangar and Byrd went to New Haven to collect an honorary master's degree from Yale. By June 26, the weather finally seemed to be clearing. Byrd said he would leave in two days, at dawn.
Meanwhile, he and his crewmates watched the honors pile up on their rivals. The *Memphis* arrived at the Washington Navy Yard on Saturday, June 11; Lindbergh led a procession to the Washington Monument, where 150,000 awaited their hero. President Coolidge presented him with the Distinguished Flying Cross, promoted him to colonel, and

called the young flier "our messenger of peace and good-will." Thirty-five million listened to Lindbergh's brief words of thanks on their radios.

When Lindbergh returned to New York on June 13, the *Times* devoted its first 16 pages the next morning to the event; the city sank $71,000 into the celebration. Millions of flakes of ticker tape drifted upon Lindbergh and the 10,000 troops marching in his parade. The city's street cleaning department swept up 1,800 tons of paper thrown from office windows. For the ceremonial dinner that night, the Hotel Commodore required 400 tables, 10,000 glasses, 36,000 cups and plates, 50,000 pieces of silver, 15,000 rolls, 300 pounds of butter, 200 bunches of celery, 125 gallons of peas, 2,000 pounds of fish, 6,000 pounds of chicken, 2,000 heads of lettuce, and 800 quarts of ice cream.

Three days later, on June 16, Raymond Orteig officially awarded Lindbergh the $25,000 prize money.

Byrd read the accounts as Willda Chamberlin and Grace Levine took a liner to Europe, then a plane to Bremen to meet their husbands. "Why, your knickers are awful," Willda cried when she saw Clarence. "Didn't you ever have them cleaned?" Levine said he planned a regular airplane service across the ocean: he was ready to invest $2 million, name Chamberlin as a partner, and envisioned starting up "within a year."

The wait to take off drove everyone in the *America's* team a little mad. Their fates were tied to what became known in the press as the "fickle west wind." Twice a day Doc Kimball sent in his weather maps; twice a day they learned that a giant trough of low pressure lay across their path, and the wind was never right. The heavy *America* needed a west wind of at least 8 miles per hour blowing straight down the runway to take off safely. They watched and prayed for a clear horizon and a steady wind at dawn. It was one or the other, but never the perfect pair.

The wait may have been hardest on Acosta. A pair of old demons, drink and women, caught up with him as he idled. In one of the tales from this time, he was drinking scotch at a speakeasy when his anger and frustration boiled over. "I'm going to fly the thing sometime and we might as well get started now," he declared. Some unidentified friends seconded the motion, and they piled into their cars for Roosevelt Field; they opened the hangar doors, pulled loose the chocks, and began to push the *America* outside. They were going to Paris right now, Byrd or no Byrd, Acosta roared. But the team's mechanics reasoned Acosta out of his grand gesture, and he backed down.

As his frustrations boiled up, he succumbed once again to the comforts of female admirers. *The* female admirer, to be exact—Dorothy Walker of Beechhurst, the pursuing divorcee from Reno who had spirited him home from the hospital in 1925. By now she had remarried—to A. C. Walker, a wealthy official with the Fish Tire and Rubber Export Company—but she could not keep away from Acosta and unwisely sent him a batch of love letters that would eventually become evidence in court. Two were written during this time: the first, during the long and maddening wait; the second, when the *America* had just taken off for Paris. "Dearest," she wrote in the first, "when the *America* hops off it will be carrying my heart with it; all my thoughts will be with you." The second was more scandalous, and received wide play in the gossip pages:

> Dear: When you read this you will have reached your destination. How proud I will be of you, Bert, although I have no real right to at all...I will not forget the spanking that I am to receive on your return, nor will I forget your ears...Don't drink too much! And above all, remember that I love you more than anything else in the world.

Byrd used his idle time before the flight to negotiate with newspapers for the rights to his story. On June 17, the North American Newspaper Alliance offered him $15,000 for the story of his trip to Europe; $40,000 if he flew to Paris then turned around and came back; $60,000 if he continued east and flew around the world. The *Times* suggested that he write some dispatches in advance that would appear to have been transmitted from his plane. One dispatch could read, "Wonderful voyage so far but we are in fine shape and going on. Will communicate later."

The delays drove Tony Fokker crazy, too. He had built a 15-foot incline at the end of the field that included wooden wheel tracks and a greased tail-skid slide. Fokker calculated it would increase the *America's* acceleration, adding the equivalent of another 500 to 700 feet to the runway. Two times Doc Kimball predicted good weather; two times the *America* was hauled to the top of his incline. Each time, the takeoff fell through.

At dawn on June 28, the *America* was hauled up the incline again.

For the third time, Byrd called a delay. Acosta wept with frustration. Fokker had been up all night in anticipation of the flight; when Byrd strolled into the hangar later that morning, Uncle Tony flew into "a Dutch rage." Balchen was present, and Fokker's anger was memorable:

His round pink cheeks blow in and out, like the rubber bulb-horn of his Lancia, as he honks with fury. He is sick and tired of all this damn stalling. Byrd can fly the *America* nonstop to hell, for all of him—he is through right now, by Gott. He roars off in his sport car in a cloud of mud and flying grass, and goes for a long cruise in his yacht to cool off.

Later that day, Floyd Bennett showed up at the hangar. His face was thin and gray and he swayed on his crutches, still weak from his ordeal. It was clear that Bennett was upset: whether Fokker had called him, no one ever learned. Nevertheless, he corralled Byrd and Grover Whalen in a corner of the hangar. When all three finally emerged, Bennett limped to Balchen and patted his shoulder. It's all set, he said.

At 1:00 a.m. on June 29, Doc Kimball phoned Byrd one last time. The weather conditions were not ideal, he said, but they were the best they could expect for a long time. A cold front was building along the eastern Atlantic, but until they hit it they should have good visibility. After that, they should be able to fly under the clouds.

Byrd hung up and decided that the wait was over. He walked outside his office to the ever-present gang of reporters. "The transatlantic plane of the future must be able to cope with other than ideal conditions," he said with obvious fatalism. "[P]erhaps we could gain more scientific and practical knowledge if we meet adverse weather."

Balchen lay down on his cot in the hangar to get some rest. At about 3:00 in the morning, Byrd and Noville appeared. A drizzle soaked the field, but this time, Byrd seemed determined. The *America* was cranked to the top of the incline, the tail skid tied to a stake by a rope. Mechanics filled the gas tanks with 1,295 gallons of fuel.

By the gray morning, about a thousand spectators had arrived.

•

What exactly happened during the nightmarish flight of the *America* to Paris has never fully been explained. There were at least eight published accounts of the trip by participants or by those who interviewed them, and they all disagree on important details. Over time the differences grew bizarre. Four accounts were by Byrd, one by Noville, one by Balchen, one by Charles Murphy, and one by Norman Vaughan, who had steamed with Balchen and Byrd to the South Pole in 1928 and would give an account years later based on his conversations with Balchen. Something wild and chaotic happened during the forty-two-hour flight, and although rumors began to leak out almost immediately upon their landing, the fliers seemed to agree, at least at first, that it was better to keep the truth to themselves.

One thing they could agree on was the details of the nearly disastrous takeoff and the fact that Doc Kimball's weather forecast proved horribly wrong. The reports from seagoing ships on June 28–29 were confusing: while most indicated that the wind at Byrd's back would be about 25 miles per hour for most of the trip, the barometric readings were not consistent. A steamship off Newfoundland reported a low and falling barometer—a danger sign of storms—while two land stations on either side of the ship reported more favorable weather conditions. The confusion continued until midnight, when Kimball mistakenly interpreted the discrepancy in favor of better winds. He called Byrd's camp and got his brother Tom. Byrd roused his crew, and they assembled at the field.

Byrd had always insisted that of all the rival planes, the *America* was the forerunner of transatlantic airlines; as spectators huddled against the rain, his pronouncements seemed valid. The three-engine Fokker dwarfed the two single-engine planes that had already made the trip: her wings stretched 25 feet longer than either *Spirit* or *Columbia*; she weighed 15,000 pounds, three times that of her rivals, and carried a crew of four. She also carried a bag of airmail, the first to do so, for which duty Byrd had been named a mailman by the U.S. postmaster. At the last minute Byrd lightened *America*'s load by removing her mudguards and disposing of two 5-gallon cans of gas, four pairs of moccasins, and a 5-pint vacuum thermos of hot tea. Doc Kinkade, the Wright engineer, had contemplated stowing away with Acosta's help, but this final adjustment convinced him that Byrd might not welcome his extra 160 pounds. One thing Byrd could *not* pitch were Wanamaker's treasures: a strongbox containing a letter from the merchant prince to the French president; a copy of the first American flag, sewn by the great-grandniece of Betsy Ross; and the flag Byrd had taken to the North Pole and given to

Wanamaker. These were to be carried over the ocean and then returned to the owner.

By 5:20 a.m. everyone was in the plane. Acosta sat in the left-hand pilot's seat, Noville beside him with his hand on the dump valve, in case they had to abort. Byrd and Balchen climbed through the hatch into the navigator's cabin behind the main fuel tank. As Balchen looked out the port window, he realized the *America* was in the same spot and facing in the same direction as when Fonck sped down the runway. It was not a comfortable feeling. Theirs was the first trimotor to take off since then, and they carried a heavier load than either *Spirit* or *Columbia*. Acosta started all three engines; once they reached full power, he'd give the signal and a mechanic would cut the rope, sending the *America* hurtling off her incline and down the runway at maximum speed.

But as the engines gained power, the aircraft strained forward and broke the rope prematurely. She started down the runway like a slug, rolling forward with insufficient power toward that point where Sikorsky's S-35 had crashed and burned.

Acosta had to make a split-second decision: he could shut down the engines and roll to a safe stop. Instead, he laid on power. The big plane gathered speed, gobbling up the runway. As with *Spirit*, it appeared the Fokker would not rise in time. The end of the strip rushed toward them. Acosta raised his hand to warn Noville to hit the dump valve, but he never gave the command. "This is it, boys," he said, and at 3,270 feet he pulled back with all his might on the stick. The *America* lunged upward, barely clearing the trees.

From Long Island to Nova Scotia, the weather improved. But as they neared Newfoundland, it grew alternately clear and murky. Balchen changed places with Noville up front and, according to several accounts, stayed beside Acosta for the rest of the flight. Around Newfoundland, they received their second scare. The clouds were thickening as Noville handed a slip of paper up front, since the roar of the engines made this the only way he could communicate with the others. Their gas consumption was greater than he'd anticipated, he wrote: the Whirlwinds were sucking gas more ravenously than in the tests at Roosevelt Field. The three others asked Noville to check his figures. They seemed solid, he said. At this rate, if the numbers were correct and they encountered headwinds during the trip, they'd drop into the ocean long before they reached the coast of France.

Byrd eased under the big gas tank and asked the pilots their opinion. Did anyone want to turn back? By now a mist had swallowed them up; the land below the plane was invisible. While flying blind they couldn't come down at St. John's or Harbor Grace, and between Newfoundland and Ireland there was only the sea. Yet Noville's figures so contradicted the earlier tests that he could very well be mistaken.

They chose to keep going, and from Newfoundland to France the trip became an unending mix of rain, wind, darkness, and fog. "It was utterly impossible to navigate," Byrd later wrote. Except for the occasional crackle from Noville's radio, they were cut off from humanity. "We could not tell which way the winds were blowing, which way we were drifting, or what stretch of land or water was below us." If not for the instruments, they could have flown in circles and never known. Byrd's flight diary said it all:

5:30 Thick fog for nearly an hour. Can barely see wingtips. Can't
      navigate.
6:30 Impossible to navigate. Wonder how long this will last.
7:30 Impossible to navigate. Situation terrific.
8:30 Impossible to navigate.

At dawn there was a brief break in the clouds and they witnessed a beautiful sunrise. But soon the sky closed up again:

2:00 Clouds are right up to us. Nothing seen below for 10 hours.
3:30 Ice begins to form.
5:00 Dense fog that can't climb out of. Terribly dangerous. No
      water yet.

He lost track of time and repeated the hours: "5 (?) Haven't seen water or land for 13 hours."

It is at this confusing point in the flight that later accounts diverged. In this unending gray limbo—where the roar of the engines and view from the windows was the same for endless hours—details bled together. The first point of contention was who actually flew the plane, and for how long. Balchen would write that he flew most of the distance that long night, while in *Struggle*, Byrd would assert that he came forward somewhere between two and three in the morning to spell Balchen awhile. It was not an easy journey under the gas tank, he wrote: he got stuck for about ten minutes in the narrow passage before backing out, shedding some of his bulky clothes, and inching forward again. He could tell the incredible strain that Balchen and Acosta experienced from hours of instrument flying: Balchen almost immediately cat-napped, while Acosta tore into a roast chicken like a man who had not eaten for days.

Yet despite Byrd's claims, Balchen was the only aviator on the ship who knew how to fly by instruments alone. It was for this very reason that he had been taken aboard—and it was lucky for all of them that he was there. Soon after they left Newfoundland, at about eight o'clock on the first night, Acosta was dozing in his seat when Balchen began to grow hungry. He remembered some chicken sandwiches he'd stuck beneath the seat and nudged Acosta. "Take the plane a minute, will ya, Bert?" he said.

According to Balchen's account, Acosta rubbed his eyes and took the wheel. The windows still swirled with fog, but it was nice, if even for a minute, to look away from the luminous dials. Balchen bent down and groped for a sandwich when, suddenly, he felt himself pushed down in the seat. He tried to rise but the G forces held him down.

He knew what was happening: they were in a tight spiral, diving toward the sea. Balchen struggled up and looked at the instrument panel. The readings confirmed that they had spun out of control. The air speed indicator said they were going 140 miles per hour. If they reached 160, the wings would rip free.

He grabbed the wheel on his side and waved Acosta off the other. The plane had already lost 1,000 feet and their speed was increasing. Balchen eased back on the wheel and ruddered *America* gently. The plane leveled off, and Balchen climbed up to 8,000 feet, but now they were heading back toward Newfoundland. He made a slow 180-degree turn and got them back on course again.

Once the plane was in control, Byrd crawled forward, tearing his jacket in the tight passageway. "What happened?" he cried. "Oh, nothing much," Balchen said. Maybe a little excitement, but everything was all right now. Byrd left, and Acosta slumped in his seat. "This instrument flying is something I've never bothered with," he groaned. "You'd better handle it for now on, as long as we're fogged in."

Balchen felt sorry for Acosta: he liked the big bear of a man, plus he was so "disarmingly honest about his lack of experience in blind flying" that Balchen couldn't rat on him. Months later, when Byrd wrote about the nearly fatal spiral, he said he thought Acosta took them out of the spin. But he could not see to the front, and Balchen had kept mum about Acosta's loss of control.

At about 1:00 a.m., Noville slipped another piece of paper to Byrd. "Made mistake in first estimate. Have enough gas to fly all the way." They all breathed easier with the message. Noville grinned sheepishly.

It was the only good news they would have. As the night progressed, strange things happened in the plane. The weird sameness did things to Acosta, and maybe to Noville, too. The men tried to keep it secret, but rumors crept out over time. The first public mention came with the 1928 publication of *Struggle*, Charles Murphy's hagiography of Byrd. In this telling, the four had survived the ocean but were lost in the fog over France when Acosta went mad. What set him off is unclear. Murphy does not elaborate, but James Mooney, another Byrd biographer, wrote in 1930 that Acosta cracked after flying for hours without goggles, with his head out the window—a claim that is hard to believe. His colleagues did not realize his condition until he turned to them in the glare of a flashlight and his eyes were "red and blazing." Acosta looked like a savage; he began to act like one, too. He announced that he was doubling back; they tried to stop him and, after a struggle, Byrd laid him out with a flashlight. "[T]he hulking pilot topples from the seat and falls noiselessly into the eight inches or so of leg-room between his chair and Balchen's," Mooney wrote. "Acosta's lips struggle inarticulately; the gale flicks out a few mumbled words. 'Keep her going, Dick,'—then his lips fall shut, and he slips away into the first sleep he has had in more than forty-eight hours."

Though the tale smacks of melodrama, it didn't stop *Time* magazine, in its September 28, 1936, issue, from citing Byrd's novel use of a flashlight as part of a "transatlantic tradition" in which "men who have flown the North Atlantic together shall not long be friends."

Three years later, the story began to change. In a 1939 sketch of Byrd in *Life* magazine, Charles Murphy contended that Acosta did *all* of the flying for the first thirty-eight hours, then went mad. This account left Balchen out of the picture completely. By 1939 Byrd and Balchen had endured the harsh Antarctic winter together and a gulf had opened between them that would never close. If anything, Murphy's account tried to diminish Balchen's importance, in essence writing him out of history.

Not surprisingly, Acosta never mentioned the incident, nor did Noville. That left Balchen, who said nothing in his published accounts. But something happened, and Balchen did eventually tell his version to a friend.

In 1990 polar explorer Norman D. Vaughan published *With Byrd at the Bottom of the World*, his account of Byrd's first Antarctic expedition of 1928–1930. The memoir includes two conversations Vaughan had with Balchen during the long polar winter. By 1990 the war of words over whether Byrd had lied about his conquest of the North Pole was in full swing. Balchen had been dead for seventeen years, yet his reputation was being attacked almost as much as Byrd's. His sin: his questioning of Byrd's veracity, based upon his cross-country flight with Floyd Bennett in the *Josephine Ford*.

In Vaughan's version, Acosta flew the first hours, then Balchen, and finally Noville, when the first two needed a spell of rest. Noville flew low to escape the fog—low enough to clip the tops of the waves. "We can't see anything but ocean," groaned one of the pilots. "We need to turn back."

"Let's have a drink," said the other, probably Acosta. "I think it will steady our nerves." The first pilot thought this sounded like a good idea. They offered a drink to Balchen and Byrd, but neither accepted, so Noville and Acosta had more for themselves. Soon both were drunk and wanted to go home. They begged Byrd and Balchen to turn around and save them from this nightmarish fog. The two refused, and Balchen took the controls. Noville and Acosta crawled to the back and kept drinking until Byrd could stand it no longer. He picked up a wrench and knocked both men out. "They lay in the floor of that place for the rest of the trip," Balchen reportedly said.

This seems far-fetched, but no more far-fetched than a savage, red-eyed Acosta threatening to hijack the plane. Noville's supposed part in this account was barely corroborated when he admitted to Byrd, years later, that he had finally stopped drinking. By 1927 Acosta's alcoholism was out of control; it would be a factor that killed him. And there were details that made no sense unless placed within the jigsaw of Vaughan's tale. Of all publications, *Time* seemed most willing to dredge up odd moments that did not adhere to the official story. Near the end of the flight, it reported in its July 11, 1927, account, only Byrd and Balchen were left standing. Noville was "lying on the floor, exhausted," while Acosta was "so miserable that he did not seem to care what happened."

Something happened on that flight, and it will always remain a mystery. The truth was so damaging to their reputations that all four men agreed it should never be told. And at the center of every account lay Acosta. Most biographers agree today that his daring takeoff at Roosevelt was the apex of his career. Once he got the *America* up, it was all downhill.

•

Despite what may or may not have been happening on the plane, the team wasn't that far off their original flight plan.

At 5:00 p.m. on June 30, nearly twenty-four hours after leaving Newfoundland, they saw a faint smudge ahead of them, a thin line darker than the sea. Soon they recognized it as Brest, the arm of land that points from coastal France straight at the New World.

They were about 200 miles off course, but at least they knew their location. They should have exited the fog near the south end of Ireland; a straight line drawn from there would have taken them to Le Havre for an easy ride up the Seine to Paris. Instead, they crossed a boundary of white breakers and red farmhouses on the French coast, and the weather was clear. Paris was only 300 miles away. They should be in Le Bourget in less than three hours.

But just when they thought the worst was over, Noville received a message from a French meteorological station sent especially to the *America*. It predicted squalls and low clouds for the evening. A second message came from Le Bourget: heavy drizzle and lowering clouds would encase the airport by nightfall.

Yet they could still reach the aerodrome before the clouds closed in. Balchen knew this part of the country; he had flown here two years earlier. If they followed the railroad tracks from Brest to Paris, they could land in Le Bourget before dark, he said. But Byrd chose to ignore him. He told Acosta—who had not yet had his meltdown—to head up the coast to Le Havre, then follow the Seine as they originally planned.

"Commander," Balchen said, "if we do that it'll take us two or two and a half hours longer than if we set a course direct from here to Paris."

"Fly us as I've told you," Byrd commanded.

It was a big mistake, one Byrd never mentioned in his several accounts of the flight. To make things worse, Noville accidentally thrust his foot against some radio wires, tearing them out without his knowledge. From this point on, they could transmit but not receive. They would be flying deaf *and* blind.

They took Byrd's course and by 10:00 p.m. were over Paris, circling in a wide loop, flying blind. At least, they *thought* they were over Paris, since they never really knew. There were no holes in the cloud cover; if Balchen came down to 1,000 feet, he could run into the Eiffel Tower. They couldn't see the fireworks shot off as locators, nor the spotlights placed around the 2-mile-long landing field. Observers at Le Bourget heard *America*'s engines pass; they received Noville's desperate radio transmissions. But the plane circled and headed back west, and the signal grew fainter. Those on the ground asked themselves, Where are they going?

They were heading back to the coast—the one place on this hellish trip where they'd actually been able to see the ground.

•

"[T]here is nothing more glorious than the days which follow a narrow escape from death," George Noville would remember six months after the events of that long, black night. "But the minutes or seconds during which one faces death are not so pleasant. Peculiarly, however, time becomes terribly confused in such an instance, and what may seem years may actually be two or three seconds, and what is actually two or three hours may seem as a flash through the mind."

For five hours that night, the four flew over France like sailors lost at sea, swaddled in a fog so thick that they could not see the tips of *America*'s wings. They flew in a huge circle, from Le Havre to Paris and back, looking for the tiniest glimpse of land or light beneath them, or a lifesaving break in the clouds. All the time, their fuel gauge dropped lower: this was their clock, not the second hand on a stopwatch, but that needle inexorably dropping toward E. Once, they seemed to see a haze of light that might be night-lit Paris or the searchlights of Le Bourget. But no one could tell. "When we got above the clouds," Byrd later wrote, "there were at times some terrible views. We would look hundreds of feet into fog valleys—dark ominous depths. At times the cloud peaks on the horizon looked exactly like a band of mountains. At other times they took on the appearance of a beautiful lake or river."

They were in a parallel world, with no connection to the earth below. Their radio was useless; their earth induction compass spun in meaningless gyres. The only reality was the steady consumption of gasoline. After 2:00 in the morning they saw the line of the shore through a break and in a bright gap of lights spotted an electric sign on the roof of a big building. "DEAUVILLE," it read. They flew south along the coast and saw a long, sandy beach; at 3:00 a.m. they spotted the flicker of a lighthouse beacon beneath them. Byrd scribbled a note and handed it to Noville. The gas was almost gone. "We are going to land." It felt so plain and simple, as if Byrd had just handed him "an invitation to tea."

Byrd crawled up front and showed the note to Balchen, still sitting at the controls. He nodded, and searched for clear ground. Balchen swung about and roared back over the lighthouse; he banked sharply, following the beacon with his eyes. To his right, meadows off the beach were cut up by low stone fences. In front of the nose, he saw a narrow, sloped beach littered with small boats. Only the open water to his left looked clear. He angled over the breakers and the right engine coughed; the gas was about finished.

Balchen and Acosta sat in the cockpit; Byrd and Noville braced themselves in the cabin. Byrd grabbed three carbide drift flares from the stores, opened the hatch, and tossed them into the water at 100-yard intervals. Balchen came around and spotted them burning on the surface. They would be his guides. He planned to pull the nose up at the first flare; to cut speed and come down on the second; then use the third flare to judge distance and time.

In the back, Byrd and Noville ripped out windows so they'd have a means of escape, and tore out the navigator's table so they would not be thrown against its sharp edges. Noville glanced out a window and found that his mind seemed more alert than usual. He was focused on the precious minutes ahead of them: how the plane would hit the water and what flying objects and lethal traps awaited them in the cabin.

They were three or four feet above the water when Balchen cut the engines. The landing gear touched the water—*America* shuddered as the wheels sheared off beneath them. They planed across the water, then a huge wave engulfed the nose. The weight of the front engine drew the airplane down. Balchen watched in slow motion as water closed over the cockpit windows and the *America* settled beneath the waves.

Back in the cabin, Byrd was hurled from a window headfirst. All Noville saw were his boots as he vanished through the opening like a character in a comic strip, then water gushed in. Its force twisted him in somersaults and he became disoriented. One of Noville's horrors had always been of dying in a trap, and now he saw himself drowning underwater like a rat. He thrust out his hand for a window and found an opening; he pulled himself through and shot to the surface. He was temporarily deaf after enduring forty-two hours beside three roaring engines; he called for Byrd but could not hear his voice. The utter absence of noise amazed him, as if he'd been reborn into a world without sound.

Byrd had popped to the surface after being thrown through the window; he was dazed, but knew he was unharmed. He saw Noville shoot up and yelled that he was fine, but Noville just kept yelling for him. Balchen and Acosta were nowhere in sight, and he swam toward the cockpit to find them.

Balchen was having a bad time. He had unhitched his safety belt and squirmed around in the seat to kick off, but somehow had gotten caught. Byrd found him underwater and helped free him. When Byrd asked him how he felt, he began talking "a blue streak" to no one in particular. Byrd grabbed Balchen's hand and pulled him up on the wing, and this somehow seemed to reconnect the young Norwegian with reality.

"Where is Acosta?" Byrd cried. His voice sounded shrill; like Noville, Balchen was experiencing trouble with his hearing after forty-two hours on the plane. They splashed forward, looking for Acosta, and were about to dive back into the cockpit when the big man popped up behind them. He thrashed about in the water and started yelling in the same weird, squeaky tones as Noville had. Two days later, a surgeon in Paris discovered that Bert had fractured his collarbone. It was the closest thing that any of them had to a serious injury.

They had all survived. Noville seemed the most clearheaded now. He ripped open the emergency panel in the wing and hauled out a rubber life raft; they inflated it with a foot pump, then fished from the floundering plane Wanamaker's little strongbox of treasures and a sack containing some of the airmail. They threw these in the raft, crawled in after them, and paddled to shore.

The bottom of the raft grated against the sand. They dragged the raft beyond the breakers and got their bearings, climbing the same dunes that British soldiers would cross seventeen years later on the D-day assault of "Gold Beach." The rain pelted down. They looked across the dune line and spotted the small village of Ver-sur-Mer, about a mile away.

They struggled up a hill. The houses were dark and quiet, surrounded by high fences with locked gates. Somewhere a dog barked. A boy appeared on a bicycle, took one look, and peddled away in terror. They climbed the endless hill to the lighthouse and hammered on its massive wooden door. The keeper's head, topped by a white nightcap, poked from an upper-story window. He saw four men, dripping wet, covered in mud and oil, gabbling in an unknown tongue.

"Go sleep off your hangover somewhere else!" he raged.

Then he slammed the window and returned to bed.

TWENTY

"THE CLOUDS BETWEEN MUST DISAPPEAR"

In the spring of 1927, twenty-five-year-old Myrtle Brown of Omaha decided to fly.

That Myrtle would eventually go aloft was almost a foregone conclusion. She had come from Omaha to New York City to study music; every morning, she sat at breakfast in Staten Island with her older sister, Dorothy, and Dorothy's famous husband Giuseppe Bellanca, whom the family called G.M. Like Dorothy, she was tall, stately, and attractive; like Dorothy, she knew her own mind. Each morning she listened as G.M. prattled about the latest developments in the Orteig race; his joy seemed unbounded when Clarence Chamberlin and Bert Acosta stayed aloft for fifty-one hours; she and Dorothy nursed him through the frustrations wrought by his partner Levine. She was there on the day that Chamberlin saved those two girls, and the drama triggered something inside her. Soon afterward, she asked if Mr. Chamberlin would take her up in the air.

Bellanca could never deny the women of his family anything, and asked Chamberlin for the favor. Soon afterward, Myrtle Brown went on a long, easy ride in the *Columbia* above the fields and suburbs of Long Island. It seemed she could see forever; she had never felt so free. It was like eating ice cream for the first time, she later said—she felt the same sense of childlike excitement, the same surprise of delicious novelty. She thought long and hard about the experience and discovered that her life had changed. She no longer wanted to be a musician. Myrtle Brown wanted to be an aviatrix instead.

Few "lady flyers" existed at the time, and the opportunities for them were even fewer. In 1927 the best known was probably Katie Stinson, with whom Lloyd Bertaud had flown, but Stinson was a daredevil, a performer. There was the blond, blue-eyed Elinor Smith, who earned her wings under Bert Acosta, but at the time she was barely known even in Long Island. There was Ruth Nichols, and the newcomer Amelia Earhart—a midwesterner like Lindbergh—who wanted to be the first woman across the sea. Earhart's closest competition for that title was a European, the flamboyant former actress Mabel Boll, also known as the Queen of Diamonds, for the sparklers she wore. There weren't many others. Jobs for female fliers weren't just hanging on the vine and waiting to be picked, Chamberlin told Myrtle, and Clarence was probably one of the more open-minded and sympathetic aviators around. To him, it didn't matter if you were male or female, black or white, as long as you could fly. But he was a rarity. Most male pilots thought that the aviatrix was a novelty that would eventually disappear. Women just weren't strong enough to handle the physical stress, they said.

Myrtle believed this had to change. People said the female flier was a fluke, but the Orteig Prize had unleashed a new sense of possibility in everyone. Myrtle felt sorry for G.M. when Lindbergh beat him to the punch. Now the flier's photo hung in hundreds of schoolrooms and thousands of homes. He was compared to Columbus. No living American commanded so much loyalty. The global response to Lindbergh only confirmed her suspicion that the old rules no longer applied.

When the *Columbia* took off, Myrtle could see the worry in the face of her brother-in-law. He fretted over his plane as if it were his child. She followed the newspaper accounts as the *Columbia* made a Grand Tour of Europe. Clarence and Charlie stayed awhile in Berlin, then flew to Munich, Vienna, Budapest, Warsaw, Zurich, Berne, and Paris. But too much time together began to wear on them. By June 23 they were in Paris, and their wives predicted a break, despite Levine's announcement of a partnership. By mid-July, when Chamberlin, Willda, and Grace boarded the *Leviathan* for the return to America, Charlie stayed behind.

Once the excitement subsided, Chamberlin reverted to his old ways. He tinkered with new things. On August 8, he took off from the deck of the *Leviathan* and flew to New York, the first time a plane had catapulted from an ocean liner. His purpose: to shave off days from the transatlantic mail. An airplane could take off as far as 1,000 miles from the coast, thus cutting mail transit time from five to four days. He looked for financial backers for a "Chamberlin Flying Service," which offered routes up and down the East Coast. Bellanca told Myrtle and Dorothy that his old friend had always been a better pilot than a businessman. He hoped the fame did not go to Chamberlin's head.

The aftermath of the *Columbia*'s flight certainly did not hurt Bellanca. He started the Bellanca Aircraft Corporation of America and rented factory space on Staten Island near his home. He hoped to produce a commercial version of the *Columbia* while branching out to other designs. John Carisi and his mechanics went with him. By fall the DuPont family of Delaware offered a deal: if Bellanca moved operations to a huge factory and airfield beside the Delaware River, and included seaplanes among his designs, the multimillionaire industrialists would finance everything. There seemed little hesitation: in late 1927, Bellanca, Dorothy, their infant son, August, and Myrtle moved to Wilmington.

Of all of those connected with the *Columbia*, fame most affected Charles Levine. Myrtle watched and listened as wilder and wilder stories of Charlie appeared in the daily papers and on the newsreels. When Chamberlin and the wives sailed home on the *Leviathan*, Charlie stayed behind with his plane. Part of the reason was apparently legal: on July 2, federal authorities announced that they planned to sue Levine for $500,000 in the old dispute over war salvage. They'd actually offered to settle the matter for $300,000 before Levine flew over, and he had accepted the deal. But now, with Levine's newfound notoriety, someone in Coolidge's Justice Department had changed his mind. Why were they bringing this up now? railed an "obviously provoked" Levine. True to form, he added, "I'm entering a counter-suit against them for a still larger sum."

Yet Levine's European dalliance was motivated by more than legalities. His exploits on the Continent kept interest in aviation high throughout the summer and fall. Things began to go south for him in Paris, when the others sailed for home. Like Byrd, he was intrigued with the idea of an Atlantic "round trip," and he hired the French aviator Maurice Drouhin to fly *Columbia* home. But as with almost every flier he had ever hired, the two could not get along. He promised to pay the Frenchman $4,000 for the trip, but when Levine began to sound as if he might back out, Drouhin went to court like Bertaud and filed an injunction to lock *Columbia* away in the airport until Levine made good on the contract. The argument made it to the front pages; Levine got in a fistfight on the streets of Paris with a man he had never met. When he went to Le Bourget, he found his beloved plane under guard by two gendarmes. He paid each off with a 100-franc note, and they helped him roll the plane from the hangar and start the engine.

Levine had never made a takeoff or landing, but he'd watched Chamberlin and thought it was no big deal. When the airport police heard his engines, they rushed up on motorcycles. Figuring he had no choice now but to hijack his own plane, Levine took off. By some miracle, he managed his first takeoff like a pro. He recalled that London was somewhere north of Paris, so he headed in that direction. He crossed a big body of water that he hoped was the English Channel; thirty minutes later, a huge metropolis appeared beneath him that had to be London. He found a runway on the outskirts, but came in with the wind at his back, going 75 miles per hour. Worried that he'd kill himself, the English sent up a plane to show him that he should land with his nose to the wind. Levine tried to land three times and got better with each pass, but always veered off just before touchdown. On the fourth try he went for it, and pulled to a stop inches from the airport fence. He opened the cockpit and asked to phone his lawyer. Maybe he could appease the French now that he was safe in England, he said.

Except, perhaps, for the Parisians, Europeans treated Levine as they had treated Lindbergh: like winged royalty. He was celebrated more widely in Europe than he ever was at home. In early October he showed up unexpectedly at the Schneider Trophy Race in Vienna, where he was greeted with cheers and followed by throngs. He flew to Rome where, on October 3, Pope Pius XI received him in a small throne room of the Vatican. The pontiff said he was greatly pleased to meet the Atlantic flier, then blessed Levine, his family, and all future flights; Levine told His Holiness that this audience was the greatest honor he had ever received. On his way to meet the Pope, he'd passed through five rooms and long halls lined with Vatican guards; every one saluted him as he passed. He broke protocol by going bareheaded—it was the first time an American had been received by the Pope without conforming to the Vatican's rigid dress code—but the Pope did not seem to care. The next day, Levine visited his hero Mussolini.

By late October, Charles Levine was back in Brooklyn. Grover Whalen met him at the dock; there was a parade, but the celebrations were modest compared to those for the other fliers. President Coolidge never congratulated him. But Levine took it all in stride. The transatlantic flight of the *Columbia* and his Grand Tour of Europe had cost him $125,000, he admitted. He grinned from ear to ear.

"It was worth it and I have no regrets," he said.

•

By then, Byrd had come home, too. His receptions in France and the United States had been lavish and grand. Once again, he was the conquering hero; the nightmarish trip, and his survival of it, seemed to make up for the fact that he'd come in third. A rising tide lifts all boats, and like the others, Byrd was canonized.

The night they landed off the coast of France, such adulation did not seem a possibility. The lighthouse keeper left them standing in the rain, but Noville knew a little French and was able to convince the keeper's wife that they were, indeed, downed American aviators, not besotted libertines. She convinced her husband, who apologized profusely, plied them with blankets, and set them by a fire. By morning, villagers had helped salvage what they could from the plane. The tide had gone out and the *America* sat half-submerged on a sandbar; they saved the rest of the mail, unbolted the engines, and removed the big wing. They carried the disassembled plane a section at a time above the tide line. Almost all was saved except one 8-by-40 strip of fuselage. Balchen suspected that it vanished in the hands of souvenir hunters. On it was printed, in big letters, AMERICA.

They received a welcome in Paris that was as grand as Lindbergh's had been. Crowds blocked the streets; the windshield of their car was shattered by Parisians as they reached to touch Byrd or shake his hand. Where the French had loved Lindbergh for his "fresh, youthful modesty" and "engaging smile," Byrd was "more mature, handsome, and the perfect type of officer and gentleman." His crew was also portrayed in heroic terms: the "rough-and-ready Noville, big dashing Acosta, and that little block of Northern granite, Balchen." Telegrams and letters streamed in from all over the world: the secretary of state, Wanamaker, Franklin Roosevelt, Floyd Bennett, Fokker. Byrd and Noville dug out their standard white navy uniforms for the week of tributes, speeches, and banquets, while Balchen and Acosta were rushed to Wanamaker's Paris store, where they were measured by the clothier Herbert Adams Gibbons.

The host of tributes was much the same as what Lindbergh had been through: meetings with famous fliers and President Doumergue; a visit to Madame Nungesser's parlor and the Tomb of the Unknown Soldier; the awarding of the Legion of Honor. Yet distinctions were made between Byrd's flight and Lindbergh's. Where Slim's lone flight was more mythic and brave, Byrd's workhorse ordeal may have been more necessary. Where there had been "something of luck in Lindbergh's great flight," said the *South Bend Tribune*, the world seemed to look upon Byrd's flight as a "successful failure" whose ultimate value might be even greater. It was "upon such work as Byrd has done that the development of aviation depends," claimed the *San Francisco Chronicle*.

There were also subtle differences in the way they were deified. Where Lindbergh's was spontaneous, the crowning of a conquering young god, Byrd was presented to the world as a savior. Several French citizens begged him for charity. On the whole, Byrd's deification seemed less spontaneous and organic, and perhaps more orchestrated. On July 23, soon after his return to the United States, he was called a "Mercury of Modern Flying Science" and described in Olympian terms:

> Physically he suggests a delicate instrument fabricated to the point of frailty. If one chooses to regard him as a product of evolution it is easy to conceive that in the remote past he might have been a frigate bird winging his way on the gales across the seven seas. Even in repose he seems prepared for flight; leaning forward forever into the wind. In action he is Annapolis personified, erect, alert, eager. His eyes are binocular, apparently penetrating to horizons beyond human vision. From his high, Anglo-Saxon, slightly sloping forehead, the hair ripples in wave-lengths that might well have been the offspring of a steady west wind blowing fair upon him from infancy; a buoyant creature born in the breeze.

More flagrant was a scene in Charles Murphy's *Struggle*. No flier but Byrd—not even Lindbergh—was portrayed as a Christ whose touch could heal the lame. Byrd was visiting crippled aviators in Paris's Hôtel des Invalides, "a place of desolate hopes; of wrecks that once were strong, young bodies." He passed down a line of wheelchairs arranged in the court when he came to the injured captain Charles LeGendre. "Take my hand and lift me," LeGendre said:

As Byrd reached for the hand, an attendant rushed up, protesting. The man had not walked in seven years. He had been shot down in an air duel: his limbs were useless. But Captain LeGendre held firmly to Byrd's hand, and pulled himself erect. Byrd felt as if the bones must break, so intensely was his hand held.

Then, with Byrd supporting him by the elbow, the Frenchman tried his limbs, and *walked*...walked thirty paces up the steps to Napoleon's Tomb. The sound of voices was suddenly hushed. And Captain LeGendre, turning from the edge of the pit at the bottom of which lay the Emperor's casket, spoke softly to the naval officer:

"Seven long years I have lived so near it; yet I never saw the Tomb until to-day. Your courage, sir, gave me the courage to walk again."

The message was clear, and not just to Myrtle Brown. New glory awaited, but to achieve it, one must have wings. At the same time that Byrd fought his way across the Atlantic, the army aviator Lester J. Maitland and Albert Hegenberger made the first nonstop flight from the mainland to Hawaii; their 2,400-mile flight from Oakland, California, to Wheeler Field near Honolulu lasted 25 hours and 50 minutes. Yet crossing the Atlantic was still longer and harder, and by June 1927 more than a dozen new flights were planned. "To be in the fashion in the aeronautical world today you must be preparing to fly the Atlantic," said *Flight* magazine. "Everybody is doing it." But this time, the pilots weren't barnstormers, professionals, or military aviators. They were "average men" who learned to fly solely to conquer the sea.

Their explanations, when they tried to make them, were as heartfelt and inarticulate as Myrtle Brown's. She knew she wanted to be the first woman across the Atlantic, and the first aviator to fly nonstop to Rome. But it was hard to say why. She did have a companion—the Reverend James R. Cox of the Old St. Patrick's Church in Pittsburgh, who planned to accompany her to the Vatican—but she had not found a financial backer and she did not have a plane. In fact, she admitted, "I've never piloted an airplane yet, but I've heard so much about them."

It seemed a crazy scheme: a young woman from Omaha who could not fly, crossing the ocean in a plane she did not have, and with a Pittsburgh priest she did not know. When asked what *he* thought about it, her famous brother-in-law said he supported her. He knew from experience that when the female Browns of Omaha set their minds upon a task, nothing could stop them. Myrtle believed in fate, she said. If she met with an accident en route, "it is to be," but death could just as easily happen on her street or in her home. True, hers was a quixotic obsession, and the deck seemed stacked against her. "But if I start, I'm going to get there, and I'm not thinking about anything else," she said.

She proceeded with her plan, taking lessons, slowly earning her wings. By December 19 she had flown under the Brooklyn Bridge with a licensed pilot, a stunt that landed her in the paper. She had yet to find a backer, but she still planned to fly to Rome. By then, others like her had caught a similar obsession, and all had failed. "The Atlantic has beaten so many women now that I feel as if I want to break up a superstition about it so that other women will not be afraid to go over," she said.

And so she persisted. The New Year came and went, and she moved to Wilmington with her famous family. On February 16, 1928, she became the first female solo flier in Delaware history. Five months after that, on July 17, 1928, she soloed over Delaware, Pennsylvania, New Jersey, and New York. She made the skies above the metropolitan corridor her domain. Although she would never cross the Atlantic, she earned her commercial pilot's license in May 1930, at a time when there were only twenty female transport fliers in the entire country.

And as happened to so many, Fate caught up to Myrtle Brown. On March 15, 1930, as she flew over New York farmland, her fuel line broke and she ditched in a spinach field. The impact knocked her out; when she came to, the first thing she saw was a farmer watching from atop his plow. His name was Joseph Fitzgerald, and he owned this field. Myrtle stepped from the cockpit and the freeholder ran over. "Young lady," he declared in a stern voice, "just look at that spinach. That will cost you $100."

Then he seized her plane until she paid.

•

Myrtle Brown was lucky. She realized her dream, at least in part, but she never had the resources to attempt the Atlantic crossing. After Byrd's flight, one would have thought that the Orteig frenzy would be over. After all, the last competitor had run his race. The fatal and dramatic competition was over.

Instead, it did not end. Rather, it evolved into something larger, more personal, and deadlier for many professional and amateur aviators. A strange mania seemed to have taken hold. At the time that Lindbergh made his flight, five planes had already crashed and six aviators had died. From July to December 1927, in the six months after the Orteig race had ended, the death toll of those trying to cross the Atlantic tripled to eighteen. Similar deaths across other large bodies of water during the same period booted the numbers even higher. A significant number of these crashes and fatalities involved female pilots like Myrtle Brown.

The first sign that the Orteig race might unleash a new and troubling era in American aviation came in June, when James D. Dole, president of the Hawaiian Pineapple Company and a board member of the NAA, issued a statement: "Believing that Charles A. Lindbergh's extraordinary feat in crossing the Atlantic is a forerunner of eventual transpacific air transportation, I offer $25,000 for the first flyer and $10,000 to the second flyer to cross from the North American Continent to Honolulu in a non-stop flight." Hollywood showman Sid Grauman posted another $30,000 for a Los Angeles–Tokyo flight, while the San Francisco Citizens' Flight Committee proposed $50,000 to extend the Dole race to Australia. They hoped such sums would tempt Lindbergh, Byrd, or Chamberlin to sign up, but all three declined, saying there was no time to prepare.

Fifteen planes entered, including the biplane *Miss Doran* from Flint, Michigan, which carried as a passenger twenty-two-year-old schoolteacher Mildred Doran. Takeoff was set for August 12, but three pilots died during tests, and the starting date was set back to August 16. On that day, only eight planes started: two crashed on takeoff and two dropped out because of engine trouble. Of the four that headed to Hawaii, two made it and two disappeared at sea, including *Miss Doran*. Three pilots died during the search for survivors, including the stunt flier and air ace "Lonestar Bill" Ervin, who was heard shouting over his radio, "SOS! We are going into a tailspin!"

Ten people died in the race, and reaction was swift. On August 22, Secretary of the Navy Wilbur declared that some federal move was needed to prevent a repeat of the tragedy. Chief of Naval Operations Edward Eberle called for laws preventing hazardous ocean flying. "Was it worth the price—ten lives?" asked the *Winston-Salem Journal*. This was not sport, but "a gamble at long odds against suicide," cried the Syracuse *Post-Standard*. Even the Orteig survivors agreed that such flights, while necessary for progress, should be limited to qualified fliers. "Don't let 'em die!" Byrd famously wrote.

Yet the majority of those who died in the Dole race came from the same backgrounds as Lindbergh and Chamberlin, and some were military fliers like Byrd. Mildred Doran had no experience, but she was a passenger. Despite the official hue and cry, nothing was done. In fact, more than a dozen planes were being readied for long-distance flights on both sides of the ocean, the majority of them trying to repeat the flights of *Spirit*, *Columbia*, and *America*.

If anything, the public wanted more. They wanted more races and they wanted more Lindbergh. Songs such as "Hello Lindy" and "Over the Foaming Billows (To the Land of Parlez-Vous)" were composed in his honor; poems such as "Ave Lindbergh" flooded his mail. Death entered the cockpit, wrote the poetess, but Lindbergh faced Him down:

> And as you flew, just Death and you,
> Your courage made Him shrink,
> 'Twould be a craven deed thought He
> To sweep you o'er the brink.

From June 13 to October 23, Lindbergh toured the United States and parts of Canada in *Spirit*; funded by the Guggenheim Foundation, he covered 82 cities and 22,350 miles. It was estimated that no American was more than 400 miles from the Lindbergh route, and most lived within 50 miles. Cities not originally listed in the tour applied "every imaginable pressure to induce him to include them," said the Norfolk *Virginian-Pilot*. Lindbergh was only a month into his tour, and the strain was starting to show:

> Is there no mercy left for this boy who captured the nation's heart, but who seems to have addled its sense of proportion? Lindbergh is tired. The young face is developing deep lines of fatigue. His shoulders are beginning to show a characteristic sag. The daily receptions weary him. The daily speeches bore him, the formal dinners appall him. He has been "on exhibition" ever

since the hour he landed at Le Bourget. He is entitled to a rest. His countrymen won't give it to him.

Of all the observations made in the rest of that year, this may have been the most perceptive. The nation was killing its hero by degrees. There were plenty of others willing to die for such adulation. Paul Redfern, a young man of barely 108 pounds, took his Stinson De-troiter—a plane much like *Spirit* in many details—up from Brunswick, Georgia, on August 25, three days after the statements of Wilbur and Eberle. He planned to fly nonstop to Rio de Janeiro, a 4,600-mile jour-ney that would outdistance Chamberlin by 700 miles and Lindbergh by 1,000. Somewhere in the Caribbean, his Whirlwind engine died and he was never seen again.

Six days after that, on August 31, the first woman to brave the Atlan-tic by air was ready to go. All summer long, reams of British copy had been devoted to the proposed flight of Imperial Airways captain Leslie Hamilton and Frederick Minchin; they planned to take their sky-blue Fokker monoplane with bright yellow wings from Upavon Airport in southern England to Ottawa in Canada, a distance of 3,300 miles. Ham-ilton and Minchin were experienced aviators with long flying records, but a certain mystery surrounded the flight because the backer had not been revealed. They called the plane the *St. Raphael*, after the patron saint of travelers.

On August 24, a week before the flight, the owner revealed her iden-tity. She was Princess Löwenstein-Wertheim, the sixty-three-year-old widow of a German prince killed in the Philippines while fighting for Spain in the Spanish-American War. Dubbed the "Flying Princess" by the press, she had a colorful past, was one of the first women to fly the English Channel, and once piloted an aircraft from Egypt to France. She now announced she would be the first woman to cross the Atlantic, sitting in a wicker armchair in the enclosed aft cabin while Hamilton and Minchin did the actual flying.

Her family became enraged, especially her titled brother, the Earl of Mexborough, who questioned her sanity. The public and press won-dered aloud if she was senile. When her family tried to stop her, she could not be found; they searched her house in London, and her favorite haunts. They watched the inns and hotels near Upavon, but she eluded

them. On the day of the flight, she just *appeared*, like a spirit, dressed
in flying togs more fashionable and expensive perhaps than any worn
before. Her outfit consisted of a bright-blue suede jacket; blue riding
breeches; high-heeled, yellow, fur-lined boots; and black silk stockings.
She wore a black toque that fit snugly to her head. She posed in the
hatch to the cabin, one arm thrust back for balance, a smirk upon her
lips. The Catholic archbishop of Cardiff blessed the plane and sprinkled holy water on its wings. Despite the report of strong headwinds,
the *St. Raphael* struggled down the runway and lifted off at 7:32 a.m.

Soon afterward, she was seen over southern Ireland, making about
70 miles per hour. This was 30 mph less than the normal cruising speed,
which meant the headwinds were blowing more strongly than expected.
She moved out over the Atlantic in silence, since she did not carry a
radio. At 9:44 p.m. the Standard Oil tanker *Josiah Macy* reported the
lights of a plane in mid-ocean. The *St. Raphael* was never seen again.

The princess had entered the history books, but not in the way she'd
intended. She was the first woman to take off on a transatlantic flight,
and the first to die doing so.

Six days later, another Stinson Detroiter, piloted by veteran British
fliers Terrence Bernard Tully and James Victor Medcalf, left Harbor
Grace for a nonstop flight to London. Their ship, the *Sir John Carling*,
was sponsored by the Carling Brewery of London, Ontario, and named
after the company founder. They were in a friendly race with a plane
from the rival city of Windsor for a $25,000 Canadian prize. The *Sir
John Carling* got off first, and disappeared. The backers of the surviving
Royal Windsor cancelled their effort, but not before the pilots searched
fruitlessly for their friends in the rough waters off Newfoundland.

On the same day that the *Sir John Carling* took off, Lloyd Bertaud
again tried to cross the ocean. His companion was fellow airmail pilot
James Hill, sometimes called the "Father of Fog Flying." Newspaper
magnate William Randolph Hearst backed the attempt; their plane was
a single-engine Fokker monoplane with a 450-horsepower Bristol Jupiter
motor much like the one installed in the vanished *St. Raphael*. The
plane's name was *Old Glory*, and their target was Rome.

Bertaud had fretted ever since the *Columbia*, and Levine, left him
behind. The legal wrangling he had instigated had kept Levine from
winning the race, and he worried that this would be his legacy. Maybe
Old Glory could redeem him. This was basically a promotional flight,

staged to increase readership for Hearst's New York *Daily Mirror*, which was losing a readership war against its morning rival, the New York *Daily News*.

It was planned as a three-man flight, with two pilots and a passenger—the *Mirror's* managing editor, Philip A. Payne. The fliers didn't want him. He would only be dead weight, and *Old Glory* was already overweight by more than 500 pounds when delivered empty from Fokker's factory. This time, however, Bertaud did not fight with his backers. He operated quietly, without prepared statements or verbal duels. He reduced the fuel load by 100 gallons, or about 600 pounds, and changed the runway site from Roosevelt Field to Old Orchard Beach in Maine, reducing the distance by 275 miles. But even with these adjustments, the plane was still too heavy.

Old Orchard Beach had been a bustling holiday spot for northeasterners since the turn of the century. Located 13 miles south of Portland, it arched 2.5 miles from the Scarboro River to a fishing pier in the little town of Old Orchard. The pier boasted a Coney Island–style amusement park and a dance hall, and presented a 50-foot obstacle above which *Old Glory* would have to rise. Yet pilots agreed that at low tide, the hard-packed sand created one of the best, and longest, natural runways in the United States. For a heavy plane such as *Old Glory*, this had advantages.

During the flight, *Old Glory* planned to dip close to the ocean and drop a wreath from the hatch. This was wrapped in a banner that read, "NUNGESSER AND COLI: YOU SHOWED THE WAY. WE FOLLOWED. BERTAUD AND PAYNE AND HILL." The plane would then continue to Rome.

Old Glory lingered at Old Orchard for three days, waiting for good weather and a stiff up-the-beach breeze. During this period, Hearst began to have second thoughts. His *San Francisco Examiner* had sponsored one of the planes that disappeared in the Dole race, and he still smarted from the public criticism after that fiasco. He heard the pilots' warnings that *Old Glory* was dangerously overloaded and cabled Payne, hoping to talk them all out of the flight. "I DO NOT THINK *OLD GLORY* SHOULD START EXCEPT UNDER THE AUSPICES AND WITH THE APPROVAL OF THE GOVERNMENT," he wired from California, knowing full well that the government wouldn't sanction anything after Dole.

But Payne was committed. The future of his newspaper was at stake. He wired Hearst that the two pilots "[w]OULD RATHER GIVE UP ALL

MONEY IN THE WORLD THAN FORGO THEIR FLIGHT," and assured his
boss that they would succeed.

Payne's optimism gave Hearst chills. "DEAR PHIL," he wired back,
"PLEASE THINK OF MY SITUATION:

> HAVE HAD ONE AIRPLANE LOST AND TWO FINE MEN
> DROWNED. IF ANOTHER SUCH DISASTER OCCURRED, EFFECT
> WOULD BE TERRIBLE, NOT ONLY ON MY PEACE OF MIND BUT
> ON PUBLIC OPINION. I TELEGRAPHED YOU ALL THIS AND
> TRIED TO HAVE YOU GET PILOTS TO ACCEPT PRIZE AND GIVE
> UP DANGEROUS ADVENTURE.

But Payne and the pilots were dead set on going. On September 6,
Payne handed one final cable to a friend at Old Orchard: it was to be
wired to Hearst after they had gone. "DEAR CHIEF," he said: "THE PI-
LOTS APPRECIATE YOUR MAGNANIMOUS OFFER, BUT INSIST THEY
BE ALLOWED TO FULFILL THEIR CONTRACTS TO FLY. WEATHER
IDEAL TODAY AND FURTHER DELAY RUINOUS IN MORALE OF PILOTS.
EVERY POSSIBLE PRECAUTION TAKEN . . . I HONOR AND LOVE YOU
AND I KNOW YOU WILL FORGIVE ME ANY MISTAKES I HAVE MADE."

At 12:31 p.m. the *Old Glory* rolled down the strand. It slanted up in
a slight wind, cleared the amusement park, and headed east over the
ocean. Three and a half hours later, at 3:55 p.m., a Canadian freighter
spotted her 10 miles off Digby, Nova Scotia. Twenty-five minutes later,
at 4:20 p.m., Bertaud transmitted his first message: "SHIP IS TAIL HEAVY.
WILL SEND LATER. LOVE TO ALL. WE ARE MAKING OVER 100 MPH."
At 6:30 p.m. the crew of the ocean liner *George Washington* said she
flew past their ship 860 miles east of New York. The liner's radio operator heard the plane's signal, but could not raise Bertaud.

There were other sightings that night. At 9:25 p.m. the S.S. *Berlin*,
about 1,200 miles east of New York, reported hearing the plane in the
dark. At 10:30 p.m. the wireless station at Cape Race, Newfoundland,
received a message: "ALL O.K. MAKING GOOD TIME. BEST REGARDS."
The message was unsigned and no location was relayed.

All was quiet during the early morning hours. But then, at 4:03 a.m.,
nearly sixteen hours after takeoff, the radio operators aboard the S.S.
Carmania and S.S. *Lapland* received the ship's automatic call letters

and a frantic plea: "WRHP [William Randolph Hearst Plane] SOS. WHRP SOS." For six minutes, there was only silence. Then: "FIVE HOURS OUT OF NEWFOUNDLAND EAST." And that was all.

It was later theorized that Payne sent the SOS, since the more experienced Bertaud would have relayed exact coordinates. Ships in the area steamed to the possible crash zone, about 65 miles away. The Pope, who'd arranged a greeting, prayed for their survival; newspapers across the globe printed the SOS. Hearst offered $25,000 to anyone who saved the men. He chartered a Canadian ship, the *Kyle*, to search for wreckage.

Five days later, on the afternoon of September 12, the *Kyle* wired that she had found debris floating some 100 miles outside the original search area. They winched aboard a 34-foot section of *Old Glory's* wing, still painted with the American flag. Three gas tanks, with feed pipes and dangling glass fuel gauges, were still attached, as was a section of the landing gear. And that was all. When experts checked the remains, they guessed that *Old Glory* had hit the water with such force that the wing had been ripped off. The fuselage, weighted by the engine, went down.

The three had carried a rubber life raft, but it apparently never inflated. No trace of the men was ever found.

By mid-September the year's toll for attempting to cross the Atlantic had jumped to fourteen dead and five injured, and the press now called such endeavors "Death Flights." With the death of Bertaud, one of most respected airmen in the business, many male fliers backed off. Into the gap stepped the aviatrixes.

•

The first to try her luck was Ruth Elder, in her bright orange Detroiter, *American Girl*. She and her pilot, George Haldeman, landed unannounced at Roosevelt Field on September 14, little more than a week after *Old Glory's* demise. Out of the cockpit stepped a slim, dark-haired young woman with gray eyes and a husky voice—and reporters were nearly as smitten with her as they were with Lindbergh when he first arrived. She knew how to make an impression: she'd dressed for the flight in a white shirt, checkered sweater and stockings, tan golf knickers, and a multicolor ribbon in her dark bobbed hair. Haldeman had taught her to fly while she worked as a dental assistant in Lakeland, Florida; the moment Lindbergh crossed the Atlantic, she knew her destiny, she said. "I knew some girl would do it, before long," she told the charmed reporters. "I said, 'Why not I?'"

Unlike her male predecessors, Ruth Elder was not reluctant to speak her mind. She planned to fly the Atlantic for the money and the fame. She'd grown up "poor as a church mouse," the second child of a devout couple content with their hardscrabble existence in Anniston, Alabama. That was not for her. All her life she'd been filled with dreams that ended in fortune and glory, but in the rural South, this was considered ridiculous if the dreamer was female. She learned to keep such thoughts to herself.

She wasn't staying silent now. Why, she asked the reporters, was it fine for an American boy like Lindbergh to have big dreams, but not for an American girl? As if to prove it, another obstacle was immediately thrown in her way. Ruth Elder was not the first aviatrix to rent a Roosevelt hangar in preparation for the Atlantic hop. Frances W. Grayson, a wealthy real estate agent and niece of the late president Wilson, was there ahead of her. Grayson was in her thirties, serious, and an ardent feminist; her aircraft of choice was a Sikorsky amphibian that she'd named *Dawn*. Newspapers sprinkled terms such as *curvaceous* in Elder's write-ups, something they did not do with Grayson. To J. J. Lanning, the owner of Roosevelt Field, a public relations disaster loomed if anything happened to the more photogenic *American Girl*.

And so, for the first time since the beginning of the Orteig frenzy, Lanning issued a new set of rules. Anyone wishing to challenge the Atlantic from Roosevelt must have a multi-engine plane able to land on both earth and water. It must carry a navigator and a radio, and pass a government inspection. Though the *Dawn* met these requirements, the *American Girl* did not. *Spirit*, *Columbia*, and *America* would not have either.

So Elder turned on the charm, a tactic she'd learned long ago against recalcitrant men. She requested a private meeting with Lanning, and within a day of imposing the new restrictions, Lanning dropped them for Ruth Elder and her plane.

Aviation's first sex symbol had officially arrived on the scene. Soon girls throughout New York were wearing "Ruth ribbons" in their hair. Every day, Elder showed up at the field to be besieged by reporters. Haldeman was forgotten as he tinkered with his aircraft. So, too, was Frances Grayson.

As it had with Lindbergh, the press spotlighted Ruth's availability.

Was she single? News dispatches from Lakeland claimed she was married to a young salesman named Lyle Womack. Elder denied it. Lyle was just a "very dear friend."

How about Haldeman? Was she engaged to him?

No, George was just her pilot. Although she wanted to be the first woman across the Atlantic, she did not think women were strong enough to make the flight alone.

But the pursuit was relentless, and it soon came out that she *was* married to Womack after all. "I've been married two years," she admitted—she'd wanted to keep it secret for fear of arousing the wrath of housewives. Judging by the disapproval she'd already received in conservative women's publications, there was something to what she said. She'd married Womack when she moved to Lakeland. In fact, he was her second husband. The first was an Alabama schoolteacher.

Suddenly a hint of scandal enveloped the *American Girl*. Not only was she a divorcee, but rumors started that Elder was carrying on an affair with her pilot. Haldeman, at least, ignored the insinuations. It wasn't so easy for Ruth, and every day, the reporters asked her about her love life. Like Lindbergh, she began to feel trapped; she was heard to snap, "Why can't they just let me fly my plane?"

For the rest of September and into October, Haldeman tested the plane over Long Island, often with Ruth at his side. They discovered a gas leak; a new tank was installed. Since the plane sported a Wright J-5 engine, the company's mechanics serviced her as they had every other plane. Since it was so late in the flying season, they decided to forgo the more northerly Great Circle Route taken by Lindbergh and head due east on a warmer course that would pass over more ships and avoid icing. Just to be safe, the two designed a pair of "unsinkable" rubber suits that they would wear should they have to ditch at sea.

All this time, Grayson and Elder eyed each other like boxers in a ring. Another ocean race was in the making, one with a feminine theme. The *Dawn* rested in the Sikorsky Company hangar, right beside Fonck's unfinished plane, the *Ville de Paris*. Crowds mobbed Roosevelt Field in hopes of glimpsing Elder. She was often on hand, smiling and vivacious, chatting with the press and her fans. The *American Girl* was ready to fly, she said, but as so often in the past, bad weather kept them down.

Then, on October 10, Frances Grayson took off for Old Orchard, getting the jump on the *American Girl*. It left the ground in twenty-five seconds, and all systems worked perfectly. Grayson anticipated carrying "the progressive American woman's greeting" to Europe in days, an obvious dig at her rival.

Alarmed by the takeoff, Elder and Haldeman filled their plane with 520 gallons of gas and started down the runway at 5:40 p.m. the next day. It was possibly the most anticipated takeoff since Lindbergh's. Spectators crowded the field; the Nassau County Police had trouble keeping them back. *American Girl* carried 70 more gallons of gas than *Spirit*, but she ran only 3,000 feet before tipping up into the air. She cleared the telephone wires and headed east while the sun sank behind her.

The sudden takeoff elicited a storm of controversy, especially, it seems, among older women. Eleanor Roosevelt was quoted most often: "My personal feeling is that it is very foolish to risk one's life," she said. "All the experts told Miss Elder that she should not try it, but she was determined to go ahead." True, she admitted, there was no denying her courage, but "it seems to me unquestionably foolish for a young woman to fly alone, with only a pilot, over such a long distance."

A storm brewed behind Ruth Elder, and another awaited ahead. At first the air was smooth and the skies clear, but within a few hours they ran into clouds. For eight hours, the *American Girl* battled the elements: the winds made the little plane buck and leap, and it seemed to Elder that Nature was personally bent on her destruction. But then the storm blew itself out, and Elder spelled the exhausted Haldeman at the controls. They flew all day and night of the twelfth; no ships appeared in the sea-lanes beneath them; there was no word of them for twenty-eight hours. At 2:00 a.m. on October 13, Haldeman noticed that the engine had begun to overheat and the oil pressure was dropping. The plane limped along at reduced speed. Nearly six hours later, at 7:46 a.m., he spotted a ship on the horizon. Soon they reached the 3,700-ton Dutch tanker *Barendrecht* and circled overhead.

Elder leaned from the window and dropped a message to the ship. When it fell into the sea, she tried again. The sailors plucked it from the deck: "How far are we from land and which way?" it read. The sailors painted the answer on the deck: "TRUE 40 360 MILES TERCEIRA, AZORES."

Haldeman and Elder circled as they considered their options. Though far off course, they could still reach the islands, yet the engine knocked badly and oil pressure was down to 5 pounds. Haldeman discovered a broken oil line, which was impossible to repair in flight. They decided to ditch, and came down on the surface a quarter mile away from the *Barendrecht*, in a reasonably gentle landing. They had been aloft for 36 hours and had flown 2,623 miles from Roosevelt Field.

They'd failed, but it was a quiet, sunny day, and they were alive. The lifeboat pulled up, and Ruth said, "Take George first," since he did not have his safety suit on. Within minutes they were both aboard the *Barendrecht* and the crew had tied lines to the *American Girl*. Elder touched up her lipstick and turned to the captain. "Thank you very much," she said, and smiled.

But the tired little plane did not survive. As the ship tried to hoist her up, an ocean swell smashed her against the hull. Something exploded underwater, and flames broke through the surface. The Dutch tanker backed off, and they watched the burning plane slip beneath the waves.

Elder's reception at the city of Horta in the Azores was a success; nearly the entire population turned out to greet her. Docks and roofs were packed; she strolled down the gangplank and was greeted with cheers. Back at home, the reaction from older women was less friendly, but Elder ignored her critics this time. On November 11, Grover Whalen escorted the two pilots on their ticker tape parade up Broadway. They posed for a photo with the mayor. "Pulchritude is no bar to courage," said a beaming Beau James.

And as she predicted, the money rolled in. She'd already made $17,000 for news rights; now she signed a $100,000 contract for a vaudeville tour. The following March, she signed on with Paramount for a Flo Ziegfeld–produced picture entitled *Glorifying the American Girl*. Yet before that film was finally released, in 1929, she starred opposite heart-throb Richard Dix in the 1928 *Moran of the Marines*. The best offer Haldeman received during all this time was $10,000 for a lecture tour.

If anyone suffered, it was Elder's husband. When Ruth returned to New York, Lyle Womack tried to kiss her. "Don't be a damned fool," she snapped, and for the rest of the festivities treated him with scorn. After it was over, Womack flew back to his father's house in Panama to lick his wounds.

On September 6, 1928, Womack filed for divorce. He'd lost twelve pounds from stress, he claimed in court papers, and joined Richard Byrd's first Antarctic expedition aboard the *City of New York* as a fireman to forget the American Girl.

•

That left Frances Grayson to make the year's final try.

Life had never been easy for her. She'd had to work for everything, first as a journalist and then as a real estate agent, and often her fondest hopes fell through. She was not beautiful and young like Ruth Elder; she could not charm the press, and had little patience with stubborn men. Although financially secure, she was not rich and had no standing in New York society. She was an ardent feminist at a time when feminists were portrayed as frigid and frustrated or, worse, mannish and perverse. She wasn't old—only in her mid-thirties—but in newspaper stories, she sounded much older. Most photos showed a thin woman with a determined look on her face. Her quotes and journals often hinged on one theme: anything worth doing requires an act of will.

When Lindbergh flew across the ocean, she decided that a woman could do the same. She visited the factory of Igor Sikorsky, who showed her a seaplane he was building for a South American concern. She contacted a wealthy feminist—Aage Ancker, the daughter of a Pittsburgh steel manufacturer, who now lived with her husband in Copenhagen— and suggested a flight from New York to the Danish capital. Ancker backed her for the total cost of $50,000.

On October 14, the day after Elder's rescue, Grayson held a dinner for newsmen. Her plane symbolized the future of transatlantic flying, she claimed. Her pilot would be the well-known aviator Wilmer Stutz; her navigator, Brice Goldsborough, the compass expert with Pioneer Instruments who had calibrated the earth induction compasses of *Spirit* and *Columbia*. "I will prove that women can compete with men in his own undertakings," she declared.

But the weather refused to cooperate. Doc Kimball tried to talk her out of what he called a mad plan. He showed her the weather charts from years back: flying into the winter storms that historically lined her route was little short of suicide, he said. "Look at this," he pleaded, stabbing at the flowing isobars with his finger. "And this."

Grayson tried to maintain a smile. "They do look bad," she said. But that did not mean that *all* late-season flights were doomed.

On October 17, three days after the dinner with the press, *Dawn* made its first try. Stutz got the seaplane airborne, but it carried too much fuel in the tank and was nose-heavy. They were in the air only a few minutes before he returned.

On October 23 they tried again. Five hundred miles out, the sky grew dark and low. Engine trouble developed, and Stutz turned back once more. Grayson was furious; her fury grew worse when Stutz refused to make any other attempts so late in the year. She returned to Long Island to consult with Sikorsky. Everyone assumed her flight was off now that Stutz had bailed out, but instead, she enlisted the aid of Oscar Omdahl, a young Norwegian who had flown aboard the *Norge* with Amundsen. Bernt Balchen was his friend. When Balchen tried to talk him out of the flight, Omdahl countered that they could prevent ice from covering *Dawn*'s wings and struts by applying liberal layers of glycerin. There are so many other dangers, pleaded Balchen, but Oscar would not listen. He was convinced his big chance had come.

Grayson decided to head for Harbor Grace on Christmas Eve. This was the first leg of the trip; they would set down in Newfoundland and prepare the plane for the ocean crossing. In addition to Grayson, Omdahl, and Goldsborough, the *Dawn* carried engine expert Fred Koehler. He would inspect the engine after its initial flight, then stay behind.

As the date for takeoff approached, a dark inevitability gripped the *Dawn*. On the night of December 21, Gertrude Goldsborough noticed that her husband was acting strange. Brice had returned from a conference with Grayson, and for two hours he paced the floor. His hands were clammy. He did not answer when she asked what was wrong.

Brice returned home after a midnight conference the next day. They were taking off tomorrow, he said. By now Gertrude was terrified. She had to talk sense into her husband. "Do you think that damned woman is worth risking your life for?" she yelled.

"I do not consider that I am risking my life," Brice answered.

"I do."

But Brice was obviously scared. When they went to bed at 2:00 a.m., he clung all night to her. At 9:00 a.m. he left for Roosevelt Field. She did not see him again until four, when she went to the field to watch *Dawn* take off for Newfoundland. When she saw Brice, she could tell that something was wrong. He was so distracted that he nearly walked into the spinning propeller. He was about to board the plane, but came back, kissed her several times, then turned with terrible finality.

Before she took off, Grayson tucked a small automatic pistol in her pocket. The reporter who saw her do so asked if this was "a badge of authority for the commander of the expedition." She smiled, but did not reply. Instead, she mentioned the recent deaths of some sailors trapped in a submarine. "She spoke of the horror of a prolonged period of suffering, with no hope of relief before death intervened," the reporter later observed.

Dawn took off at 5:07 p.m. and rose after 2,500 feet with no apparent problem. At 7:10 p.m. employees of a French cable station at Orleans, on Cape Cod, thought they heard a plane pass overhead. It sounded as if it were heading out to sea.

Grayson's plane was never seen again.

As with the *White Bird*, there were rumors. At 9:45 p.m. a wireless station on Sable Island, southeast of Nova Scotia, thought they picked up the call letters and the message "Something wrong." On Christmas Day a wireless operator north of Harbor Grace thought he heard a message that could have been from a plane. It was garbled, and hard to interpret. "Where are we?" said the thin voice floating in space. "Can you locate us?"

No further message came through.

Somehow it made sense that these could be her parting words. On the night after the *Dawn*'s second failed attempt to cross the Atlantic, Frances Grayson returned to her cold hotel room in Old Orchard. She stared out the window, then began to scribble some private musings. She gave these to a *New York Times* correspondent to print "if something happens," she said.

"Waiting," she began. "Who am I?"

Sometimes I wonder.

Am I a little nobody? Or am I a great dynamic force—powerful—in that I have a God-given birthright and have all the power there is if only I will understand and use it?

Sometimes I am torn. . . .

It was a long series of thoughts, and it took some time to put them down. The Atlantic outside her window was troubled and gray—"gray fog, gray clouds, all is gray"—a description that matched her mood. The winds were against them, as was public opinion. "Aeronautical sages," the newspapers, and even her own pilot had called her mad.

"Are they right?" she wondered. "Can it be that I am wrong?"

She could not believe it, could not accept the fact that the "still, small voice" she had followed all these months might be misguided.

"I can't—I will not believe I am wrong."

True, there had been setbacks, but they had moved forward, "step by step, unfolding day by day." Wasn't that the pattern of life? How was that a failure? Winners were always called crazy. Lindbergh had been called insane.

"I am who or what I really am," she concluded, "a little nobody or a living, forceful power to carry out part of His great plan:

I will win.
I must not quit too soon.
Success is just ahead and the clouds between must disappear.

TWENTY-ONE

THE WAY
THE WIND SOCK BLOWS

By Christmas Day of 1927, the death toll of those trying to cross the North Atlantic had tripled: eighteen dead and five injured in eleven attempts that were either part of or inspired by the Orteig Prize. But there were others: two French fliers who died trying to cross the South Atlantic on the same day that Nungesser and Coli were lost; the ten in the Dole Race; Paul Redfern in his attempt to fly to Rio. "If this were in the name of progress, it might be worth it," lamented *The New York Times*. But the sad fact remained that during the flying seasons of 1926/1927, at least thirty-one aviators vanished or died in the grip of a strange obsession that no one understood but that excited the world. Though many declared such risks necessary and in the name of science, progress had veered in another direction: toward the development of big multi-engine planes that could ferry riders across a rapidly shrinking world. The doomed aviators of 1926 and 1927 weren't even sacrifices. They were the dying gasp of something more personal, a glimmer revealed to them, if only briefly, by Lindbergh and the others competing for the Orteig Prize.

Eighty-six years earlier, the Scottish barrister and journalist Charles Mackay wrote one of the first investigations of inexplicable mass behavior, those periodic bouts of public madness that leave their victims bruised, destitute, or dead. In his 1841 *Extraordinary Popular Delusions and the Madness of Crowds*, Mackay wrote:

> In reading the history of nations, we find that, like individuals, they have their whims and their peculiarities, their seasons of excitement and recklessness, when they care not what they do.

We find that while communities suddenly fix their minds upon one object, and go mad in its pursuit; that millions of people become simultaneously impressed with one delusion, and run after it, till their attention is caught by some new folly.

What were these follies? At first they seem dissimilar. Mackay detailed such financial madness as the South Sea Company bubble of 1711–20, the Mississippi Company bubble of 1719–20, and the Dutch "tulipomania" of the late seventeenth century, in which some varieties of tulip bulb became for a brief moment the most expensive object in the world. He listed movements that gripped societies in a cycle of violence: the Crusades and witch manias; the call of the "duello" for legions of young men. Every chapter asked the same question: How could good intentions go horribly wrong? Mackay looked at the individuals, not the greater societies, and in the process created one of the earliest and most enduring works of social psychology.

One thing that linked followers of the various manias was the uncompromising and irrational belief that the path they had taken would lead them to a better future. The Crusaders and hunters of witches believed, at least at first, that they could cleanse the world of evil; the investors in various bubbles felt they could free themselves and their families from a life of financial care. Followers of mystics, prophets, and seers all *knew* they could somehow touch a purer world. All were transported outside their frail bodies to become part of a larger, more glorious whole. Like Frances Grayson, they were a "living, forceful power." They were no longer little nobodies.

Two years after the Great Atlantic Derby, a new madness surfaced, this time with disastrous consequences for millions. In October 1929 a worldwide financial bubble, fueled by wild speculation, turned into panic, and the Dow Jones Industrial Average, which had reached the unheard-of height of 381 points, would plummet over the next three years to 300, then 250, 200, 150, 75, and finally 41. This bubble did not simply burst. It inverted, turning inside out, ruining fortunes and even modest savings throughout the world.

In 1932, at the absolute bottom of the stock market crash, financier Bernard Baruch wrote the foreword to a new edition of Mackay's tome. Baruch had always claimed that reading *Extraordinary Popular Delusions* put the fear of God into him and saved him millions, goading him to opt out of the wild speculation while there was still time. An un-named contemporary had told him how mystified he'd been by the be-havior of a flying cloud of midges, "hovering, apparently motionless, in a sunbeam." The entire cloud would shift to the right, then to the left, with no apparent cause; as this occurred, each midge maintained an exact distance from its thousands of fellows. What made them do that? wondered Baruch's friend. Great human movements might be slower in inception, but the effect was the same. The chance observer gets a glimpse of what is called, for lack of anything better, the "group mind." "I have always thought," said Baruch in reflecting upon the causes of the Great Depression, "that if...even in the presence of dizzily spiraling [stock] prices, we had all continuously repeated, *two and two still make four,* much of the evil might have been averted."

But the group mind adheres like glue.

In the flying season of 1926/27, the world held itself fast in a glorious dream of wings. The vision was as old as myth, but in that short space an extraordinary convergence of technology, communications, finance, and hype came together to make the dream seem flesh and to sweep all doubters away. The airplane would make the world a better place. It would release new freedoms for the oppressed and underprivileged. As flight transformed mankind, the old sins and pettiness would be left below. All that was needed was a savior, a hero, to lead us to that place. Lindbergh won the race and was revered. He is not revered today, at least not as blindly as he initially was, but he *is* remembered. But Lind-bergh did not take to the skies alone: a host of hopefuls, just as strong and weak and *human,* stepped up to the starting line, too.

They all paid for their fame. Somehow life in the Derby's aftermath did not measure up to the dream. Those who survived left something forever behind them in the trackless clouds.

•

If anything can be said to have prospered as a result of the race, it was commercial aviation. The decade following the Great Atlantic Derby saw the true beginning of the airline industry. In 1928 the Curtiss Aero-plane Company started an air taxi service to twenty-five cities with a $7.5 million capitalization. That same year, Clarence Chamberlin founded Chamberlin Airways, offering daily passenger service via flying boat between New York and Washington, D.C. Canada planned service between Quebec and Halifax; the Irish Free State, between Dublin and Paris. It was estimated that by 1929, forty planes would cart passengers to and from Chicago on a daily basis.

In 1928 air transport lines flew twice as many miles as they had in 1927; they carried three times the mail and four times more passengers, a figure that jumped from 12,599 to 52,934 paying customers in a single year. The number of licensed aviators exploded from about 1,500 in 1927 to more than 11,000 the following year. The number of cities with airports skyrocketed from a hundred to close to a thousand. Civilian, commercial, and government aircraft clocked nearly 66 million miles in 1928; A. J. Edwards, the sales manager for Ryan Airlines, said that in that year, he was able to sell about $400,000 worth of aircraft from "over my desk with but one trip into the field."

If 1928 was the year that commercial aviation finally took off, it was also the year when the men who made it possible began to feel or see the dark side of their fame. Floyd Bennett served as an early example of the consequences. He had never truly recovered from *America*'s crash, and continued to suffer weakness and bouts of pneumonia from his head injuries and pierced lung. Nevertheless, he and Balchen both planned to accompany Byrd on his first Antarctic expedition, starting out later that year. In April the two were testing the Ford trimotor airplane that Byrd expected to use when they got word that yet another transatlantic flight had gone down off the coast of Canada.

It was the *Bremen*, an all-metal Junkers manned by an Irish-German crew. And although it was the first European plane to survive the westward flight that had swallowed the *White Bird* and *St. Raphael*, it still could not make it to New York as planned. Instead, the *Bremen* flew straight into the face of a blizzard and was forced down on Greenly Island, off the coast of Labrador.

When news of the *Bremen*'s landing reached New York, the excitement over saving the fliers rivaled the effort to find Nungesser and Coli. Chamberlin planned to fly up, but Bennett and Balchen were already in the air. The New York *World* sponsored their flight, and sent Charles Murphy with them to cover the story. But Bennett and Balchen were suffering from the flu, Bennett more so than Balchen. When they flew to Detroit to pick up the airplane, Edsel Ford took one look and ordered them into the company hospital. Two days later, they checked out and took off for Labrador.

They never made it. On the trip out, Bennett sat mute, his face tinted yellow in the sunlight filtering through the oil-smudged windows. His hands dropped from the controls, and Balchen seized the wheel. They landed a hundred miles north of Quebec, in the little town of Sainte-Agnès. They put Bennett to bed in a farmhouse, and a doctor diagnosed him with pneumonia. Word came by wire that Lindbergh was flying in a serum to save him. Balchen dropped in to see his old friend before departing. Bennett lay in an old-fashioned four-poster bed, his face as white as the pillow. Balchen said he was going, but Bennett did not open his eyes. He ran his tongue over his lips. "Have a good trip," he said.

"I'll see you when I get back, Floyd."

"That depends on how the wind sock blows," he said, grinning weakly. Then his eyes sprang open. "One thing I want you to promise me, Bernt," he croaked. "No matter what happens, you fly to the South Pole with Byrd." When Balchen left, Bennett was moved to a hospital in Quebec. Lindbergh never made it with the serum: on April 28, 1928, Floyd Bennett died.

Byrd could not contain his grief, and was unable to complete his eulogy at the funeral. All the great rivals attended—Lindbergh, Chamberlin, Fonck. By this time, Byrd was well into the planning for his first of several trips to Antarctica. In time, he would take a stone from Bennett's grave and drop it over the South Pole.

They had planned the trip together, as far back as Spitzbergen. They would be the first to fly over the South Pole, and this time there would be no questioning their veracity. But as Bennett grew weaker throughout 1927 and 1928, he seemed to know it was only a dream. He would never see that southern land of ice; he would never resolve in his mind the growing doubts about whether they actually *had* flown over the North Pole.

Did Byrd ever harbor such doubts? There was one account that would claim that he did, but it is unconfirmed. In 1979 Finne Ronne, one of Byrd's Antarctic colleagues, wrote about an alleged confession that Byrd made in 1930 on a long walk with Dr. Isaiah Bowman, the president of the American Geographical Society. Different versions of this walk have surfaced, but according to Ronne, Byrd admitted to Bowman that he and Bennett had gotten no closer to the Pole than 150 miles. If the admission was true, Bowman never made it public. It would have ruined Byrd's career, and would also have sullied the memory of

Floyd Bennett. By the time that Ronne made his revelation in 1979, Bowman had been dead for twenty-nine years, making confirmation impossible.

Yet, for the rest of his life after the Derby, Byrd seemed a different man. At first he hid the change well. He maintained the pose of the officer and the gentleman, a guise important for both his public image and his conception of himself. But in private, his fame unleashed a darker strain in him. He danced at the edge of nativism and selective breeding; the man who'd refused to speak at the black church now corresponded with and was honored by the pro-eugenics "Aristogenic Association" of New York City. Byrd's musings about the "infinitesimal proportions of modern man" and his need consciously to evolve would be quoted in the association's "Statement of Purpose." "Races die for unsuccessful adaptation, untoward circumstances, and degeneration of stock," it claimed, code for the kind of selective breeding that would be extolled by Nazi Germany within the next decade. "The time will shortly come," wrote association chairman C. Ward Crampton to Byrd, "when man will sense his opportunity for racial management."

The "hero business" did not turn out as Byrd had dreamed. For the rest of the Jazz Age and into the 1950s, Byrd gave his life to the South Pole. He handled the expeditions as he had the transatlantic race, as full-scale scientific expeditions. The more he became engrossed in this second land of ice, the more he grew insulated. During the first Antarctic expedition of 1928–1930, he was frequently beset by doubt; for the first time, his drinking became noticeable. At one point it seemed that Balchen and some others might be lost in one of the expedition's two long-distance planes. "If they are lost, my work is done," he said, groaning, beside himself with anxiety, "and the public will never forget it either." He grew morose as the rescue party set out, staring at the floor and swinging his helmet between his knees. "Is there no end to it?" he pleaded. "I have had almost more than a man can bear."

During the second expedition of 1933–35, he decided to go it alone, as had Lindbergh. And while alone, he began to wonder how he had lost his way. It was 1934, seven years after the celebrated summer that had made them all gods. He crawled out of his solitary hut in Antarctica and stared into the night sky. The stars lent him a peace he had rarely known. He was at the world's end and near the axis of the earth, cut off from humanity in a land of darkness, ice, and cold.

This is what he had wanted for so long. After more than a decade in the limelight, Byrd craved solitude. For fourteen years he had planned or participated in six expeditions to some of the most remote places on earth. In between, he rushed from coast to coast on the lecture circuit, building his image or raising funds. From October 7, 1927, to March 29, 1928—during the lull between the Orteig race and his first Antarctic expedition—he gave seventy-seven lectures in colleges and theaters stretching from the Northeast to Texas and Oklahoma. And at so many of the venues, the audience asked about Lindbergh.

What was Lindy really like? Did he have a girlfriend? Byrd bit his tongue and steered their attention back to his own polar ambitions. It wore him down. He wanted a sanctuary, a "quiet place" where he could "reason undisturbed and take inventory."

Bolling Advance Base, named for his mother, proved to be that sanctuary. It was perched on the coast of the Ross Ice Shelf, 123 miles between the South Pole and Byrd's main exploratory base, "Little America." For six months during the perpetual dark of the 1934 polar winter, Byrd planned his solitude. It had not been his original intention. During his first Antarctic expedition in 1928, he had decided that the young science of polar meteorology could advance greatly if a winter weather post were established between the coast and the Transantarctic Mountains. Three men were needed, he said at the time: one man alone was too dangerous, while two trapped together in a hut no bigger than the spread of a man's arms would inevitably lead to friction.

Then he changed his mind. He brought a prefabricated hut from Little America and had the crew bury it under the ice, connected to two short tunnels that held fuel and food. He decided to stay there alone. His men said it was suicide; either that or a craving for publicity. But Byrd insisted that this was no "reckless whim."

On March 28, 1934, as he watched the squat polar tractors dwindle to specks, he had few misgivings. "Snow rolled on forever to meet the sky in a round of unbroken horizon," he wrote. He crawled down the ladder into his hut and began his monastic existence. He rose by the clock and cooked with a recipe book; he melted snow for daily baths and to wash his clothes. If the weather topside allowed it, he took walks in the endless night. Ice crystals, created by the bitter cold, twinkled in the platinum light. He imagined they were floating gems.

He felt that he had been transported to another world. In the deep polar silence, he witnessed the "imponderable procession and forces of the cosmos, harmonious and soundless." When he held his breath, "out of the silence I felt a gentle rhythm—the music of the spheres." Only in such silence could one understand the mainsprings of the universe, and Byrd saw himself as one of those lucky few. A Supreme Intelligence sought harmony in the cosmos, and that Intelligence sang to him alone.

Like Lindbergh, he'd become one of the chosen.

And like Lindbergh, he was nearly killed by the solitude. On May 31, 1934, little more than two months into his vigil, Byrd was making routine radio contact with Little America when he heard the gasoline engine skip a beat. He told his listeners to wait as he crawled to the adjoining tunnel to adjust the fuel mixture. The air was thick with exhaust, and he blacked out. Luckily he lost consciousness in a dip in the tunnel, beneath the fumes. When he came to, he staggered back to his radio to relay what he hoped was a calm and normal signal.

Thus began a nightmare of mental deterioration. Carbon monoxide poisoning was killing him. His forehead and eyes throbbed with pain. He discovered that the generator was not the main culprit. More deadly was a jury-rigged stovepipe that leaked carbon monoxide. His hut was a gas chamber. He couldn't escape the generator, his single source of heat. He couldn't escape the hut, his sole refuge from the cold. Two days after his blackout, on June 2, 1934, he wrote in his diary, "I am afraid it is the end." He scribbled notes telling his men where papers could be found, scrawled additional, red-pencilled instructions and taped them to the walls. He lost track of the days, but tried to hide his confusion during his regular radio messages. He feared that a rescue mission through the howling winter would kill someone. But as his radiograms grew more incoherent, his listeners knew he was in trouble.

Of his impending death he was certain, and so he began to examine his old certainties. He remembered the Orteig race: how he considered himself a forerunner of something greater. Everything he'd done had been for science, he often said. But what had they really done? Each aviator had been hailed as a modern Prometheus, bringing light and truth. But time was proving otherwise.

In this "sinister Ice Age at the bottom of the world," Byrd feared that their dreams would end differently. They'd seen themselves as messengers of hope, but what they'd called an instrument of peace was turning into one of war. Even now, in 1934, the rumors of war were heard. With Hitler in power, the Germans were building the most sophisticated air force ever imagined. In May 1933, bombing raids by Japanese fliers pushed the Chinese army south of the Great Wall. They'd helped shrink the world "with lightning-like rapidity," but instead of molding fraternity, they were promulgating an easier way to kill.

As progress leapt forward, "man's ability to get along with man has gone backwards," he thought. Their more orderly world seemed poised to lurch out of control.

His fears were real, but even Byrd could not imagine the suffering his and the others' advocacy during that "Summer of Eagles" would bring. World War II would be the aerial war to end all wars; it began and ended with death from above. The German bombing of Warsaw in 1939, and of Rotterdam, London, and Coventry in 1940, was denounced worldwide. Two years later, Britain unveiled its own new aerial weapon, incendiaries, which destroyed Hamburg in an unstoppable firestorm. The Japanese bombed Pearl Harbor with their air fleet, unleashing a cycle of violence from above. On March 9–10, 1945, 334 American aircraft attacked Tokyo with incendiaries, destroying 16 square miles of the city, leaving more than 1 million homeless, and causing up to 100,000 civilians to be "scorched and boiled and baked to death" in a firestorm so intense that buildings and people burst spontaneously into flame. A few months later, the world's first nuclear bombs were dropped on Hiroshima and Nagasaki. It has been estimated that the civilian death toll from the air raids and nuclear attacks on Tokyo, Hiroshima, and Nagasaki reached 400,000. The Orteig Prize had helped make it all possible.

Sometimes, when Byrd left his hut, the fears seemed to crush him from above. He thought of Floyd Bennett, of the transatlantic flight that nearly killed them, of the nightmares stalking Lindbergh after his victory and fame. They'd been so young and certain, so focused on their quest. The sky could not bind them then.

The air around the moon seemed to quake as he stared. Ice crystals saturated the night; a double halo pulsed in the silver refraction. Bright crosses formed in the outer ring. He'd felt like this in 1927, when he and the others rode a dark speck through the fog. Then, as now, he felt humbled and lonely. A man like him might establish facts, but mystery would always remain.

•

It was amazing how quickly and dramatically so many of them fell.

Lindbergh's descent was the most public and infamous, and has been chronicled ad infinitum. At first, however, it seemed the fairy tale would never end. He flew throughout the Americas, visited the great capitals of Europe, dined with royalty. On May 27, 1929, he married Anne Morrow, daughter of Dwight Morrow, ambassador to Mexico and partner in the Morgan bank. Now it was the "Lone Eagle and His Mate," and they flew all over the globe. A writer herself, Anne set down in her bestsellers the romance and exhilaration of living in the air. Their first child, Charles, was born in June 1930.

Soon after the Derby, there were murmurs of what would come. Fractures between Lindbergh and his followers began to form. People threw penknives and toy airplanes at his car during parades; they stole his laundry; they claimed to be a friend or relative to gain access to his hotel room. In response, he changed: he was rude to reporters and cameramen, and made demands to be left alone. The dislike was becoming mutual—if not from the public, then at least from the press—and eight months after the Paris flight, a New York editor wired a reporter covering Lindbergh's goodwill tour through Latin America: "NO MORE UNLESS HE CRASHES."

A dark and reckless side to Slim began to emerge, and because he was a god, the public looked aside. The first hint came in Washington in December 1927, when he took off for Mexico. The day was wet and muddy, and he deliberately swung the tail of his plane toward spectators, soaking them in the propeller's slipstream. In 1929 he jeopardized the lives of fourteen people at the Cleveland Air Races for the simple reason that he did not like to be kept waiting. As Lindbergh stunted with two navy fliers, a Detroit passenger plane came in on its regularly scheduled run. The ship was on time and clearly marked, but Lindbergh dove at her, roared under her wings and zoomed just ahead, catching the plane in the wake of his 400-horsepower engine. Only smart handling by the transport pilot prevented a catastrophe. There was talk of an investigation, but it never happened.

Perhaps the greatest, and most publicized, event in his life after the Derby was the kidnapping and murder of his infant son. On March 1, 1932, the boy was taken from the Lindberghs' new country home in

Hopewell, New Jersey; seventy-two days later, his body was found in a patch of woods in the same neighborhood. Within a few months, Congress passed the "Lindbergh law," which gave federal agents authority to chase kidnappers over state lines. In 1934, Bruno Hauptmann, a Bronx carpenter of German birth, was arrested, then convicted the next year. The investigation, arrest, and trial became a circus, and the Lindberghs secretly sailed for England on December 22, 1935, three months before Hauptmann walked to the electric chair.

Even before World War II, the change in Lindbergh was complete. His isolationist speeches for "America First" painted him in the public mind as a crude racist and a Nazi sympathizer. Even though he accepted a decoration from Hitler, he also informed the U.S. government about Germany's advanced aircraft capability. But the public could see him only in absolutes, never in shades of gray, and his swift fall from the sun was complete. The FBI investigated him as a subversive. The "Lindbergh Beacon" atop a Chicago skyscraper was renamed the "Palmolive Beacon"; "Lindbergh Peak" in Colorado's Rockies was changed to "Lone Eagle Peak." The fact that he would train, and fight, with American fighter pilots in the Pacific did not dispel the public's disenchantment with their former god.

In time, Lindbergh's family would feel that isolation, too. It was Anne Morrow Lindbergh who noted her husband's "tragedy & loneliness & frustration" in her unpublished diary. In kindergarten, one of Lindbergh's sons told a playmate that his father discovered America. "At about the same age, I dreamed that he was God," wrote his youngest child, Reeve. "If our father was God, it explained everything: why we called him 'Father,' when all our friends called their fathers 'Daddy'; why he had so little contact with the other families around us, and yet so many people spoke about him with a kind of reverence." It was not easy growing up in the shadow of The Hero. "In our family, it has always been hard to know what is right and what is wrong."

Charles Augustus Lindbergh died of lymphoma on August 26, 1974, on the Hawaiian island of Maui at the age of seventy-two. In the years before his death, there was a measure of public forgiveness for Lindbergh and a re-recognition of his greatest accomplishment, thanks in part to the comparison of his flight to the Apollo 11 moon landing. He probably empathized most with astronaut Michael Collins, who continued alone above the moon while Neil Armstrong and "Buzz" Aldrin walked upon its surface far below. He told Collins he valued the silence when one was alone.

He died peacefully, and only one local reporter showed up at the service, standing in the background.

But Lindbergh and Byrd were not alone in paying a heavy personal price for their fame. All during the 1930s, the casualty list of those who participated in the Derby expanded. In 1932 de Pinedo retired as Italy's exiled attaché to Buenos Aires, and on September 2, 1933, he took off from Long Island in a record-breaking attempt to fly from New York to Baghdad. His big Bellanca plane, the *Santa Lucia*, carried 1,025 gallons of fuel, 275 more than normal capacity. He feared sleep in what he said would be a 60-hour flight, so he rigged a device that would squirt cold water in his face and sound an alarm if he drifted off course by more than 5 degrees. "I'll do my best," he said, and started his engine at 7:01 a.m. The plane slewed off the runway, lost control in the grass, tore through a fence, and burst into flames. De Pinedo emerged from the cockpit badly burned, but then turned back, confused. The second explosion killed him.

For those who'd survived the race's first crash in 1926, the aftermath would be mixed. After months of on-again, off-again announcements, Fonck finally admitted that his Paris flight in the Sikorsky *Ville de Paris* was cancelled because of a lack of interest and funds. Lieutenant Lawrence Curtin, who'd planned to fly again as Fonck's copilot, would die in August 1936 when his navy plane crashed into the Panama Canal.

Though Igor Sikorsky's career stalled with the end of the race, he went on to build Pan American Airway's big ocean-conquering flying boats of the 1930s. In 1939 he designed and flew the Vought-Sikorsky VS-300, the first successful American helicopter. In 1942 he turned this into the Sikorsky R-4, the world's first mass-produced helicopter.

The star of that first doomed flight chose solitude. René Fonck never attempted another ocean flight. In 1936 he was made a lieutenant colonel in his nation's air reserves; three years later he retired as France's inspector of pursuit aircraft and disappeared. During the war, RAF Sergeant George Cole crashed near Malines, Belgium, and was hidden from the Germans in a monastery in which the brothers had taken a vow of perpetual silence. One monk drove the injured Cole to safety on a motorcycle, and during the nighttime ride broke his vow. It became apparent to Cole during the conversation that this little monk knew something about airplanes; it didn't take much prodding for him to reveal that he was Fonck. After the war, Fonck was accused of collaborating with the Germans, but the charges were quickly dropped when Cole revealed what Fonck had done for him. France's top ace lived quietly after that, and died in 1953 at age fifty-nine.

For those who'd cast their lot with *Columbia*, life after the race was filled with uncertainty, turmoil, and drama. Despite Giuseppe Bellanca's excellence as a designer, his aircraft company struggled for years, and in the 1950s it teetered on the edge of bankruptcy. In 1954 Albert and Sons, a midwestern plumbing supply company, came to his rescue for reasons that had nothing to do with aviation. Buying his company meant a tax write-off; in addition, the plumbing firm could now get on the New York Stock Exchange, where Bellanca was listed. The Sicilian retired with $2 million and started a new company with his son, designing experimental aircraft.

Clarence Chamberlin's fortunes continued to experience the same ups and downs as they always had. He started new businesses, just to see them fold. During World War II he trained mechanics for the air service, and after the war bought $2.5 million in surplus planes and parts for marine, farm, and industrial use. In time, he and Willda divorced; in 1936 he married Louise Ashby, the daughter of a state senator in Maine. That year, he and Louise planned to don electrically heated suits and oxygen masks and fly through the stratosphere to Europe in a sealed plane. This scheme never got off the ground. By 1947 he had retired to his farm in Connecticut, where he sold real estate and flew privately. A TV special in the 1950s showed him cradling a lamb in his arms while recalling the Orteig race. Each year, he wintered in Florida, where he gathered oysters. When friends came to visit, they reminisced about the "Golden Age of Flying," as it was coming to be called.

For Levine, everything he touched after the summer of 1927 turned to ashes. By 1934 he'd lost everything. In 1929 his fortune was wiped out in the stock market crash, and with it all his dreams of a transatlantic airline. By 1932 Grace had sued him for divorce and taken their daughters. In September 1934 he was found unconscious in a friend's kitchen in Boston. He'd turned on all five jets of the gas stove and closed the door. In his note he had written: "I just can't go on. You and your family have been awfully sweet to me and I deeply appreciate your kindness. Please forgive me. C.A.L."

A doctor from King's County Hospital was able to revive him, and by 1937 Levine seemed to find his feet again. He earned his second fortune in the development of experimental airplanes, but once again got into trouble with the law. That same year, he was convicted in federal court of conspiracy for trying to smuggle two thousand pounds of tungsten used in one of his projects across the Canadian border. He served eighteen months in prison. In 1942 he was again convicted of smuggling, but this time it was for humanitarian reasons. The charge was smuggling an illegal alien over the border: the alien was a German Jew who'd escaped from one of Hitler's concentration camps but had been denied an American visa. When Levine tried to sneak him across the Mexican border, he was caught, convicted, and sentenced to 150 days in jail.

In general, Levine's various indignities were treated as jokes and assigned to the back pages. The tone had never really changed since he first tried to win the Orteig Prize. After this last arrest, he seemed to disappear. Only the FBI was interested in his whereabouts, seeking restitution for an unpaid $5,000 fine levied as part of his tungsten conviction. Bureau records show they followed his scent through the grim world of New York's rooming houses and shady businesses. In 1956 the feds finally caught up with him, thanks to a tipster upset about an unpaid loan. But Levine was destitute, and the Bureau never collected a penny. They closed his case two years later.

Levine spent the rest of his days in poverty. In the 1960s an unidentified older woman gave him a home: she found him on the street and took pity on him when she remembered his name from the old headlines. He'd been *somebody*, he said. He'd made and lost two fortunes. He'd helped people worse off than he. But did those things matter if people called you a loser? Only the winners were remembered.

You're right, said the woman who fed and housed him. Life's not fair.

He died on December 6, 1991, forgotten and destitute—at ninety-four, the last Orteig rival.

Of all the competitors, those linked with *America* fared the worst as a group. Wanamaker died of a heart attack on March 9, 1928, a month after his sixty-fifth birthday. He survived just long enough to see one of his two *America*s make it to France, but died before he could invest in commercial airlines, which had been one of his original goals. Noville accidentally walked in front of a New York City taxicab on December 1, 1931, suffering a fractured skull and two broken legs. He mended in time to accompany Byrd on his ill-starred second Antarctic expedition, but his heavy drinking developed into alcoholism, and he would battle the disease for much of his remaining life.

Anthony Fokker continued to make planes, and for a while it seemed he would become the leading aircraft manufacturer in the United States and Europe. By 1929 his New Jersey factory was turning out a four-engine, thirty-two-passenger transport that at the time was the nation's largest. Eight airlines would be built with his planes, but differences with General Motors, which bought his company in the 1930s, caused him to resign as head of his American branch and withdraw the manufacturing and licensing use of his name.

His attempts at personal happiness seemed doomed as well. He'd divorced his first wife after coming to America. On February 9, 1929, his second wife, Viola, committed suicide by jumping from the bedroom window of their apartment on Riverside Drive. He was never the same, living by himself in his Alpine estate, sharing the house only with his old German gardener and dachsunds.

Fokker was said to be the first man to make a million dollars from aviation. By 1939 his planes had been used by twenty-five governments and more than fifty airlines throughout the world. But unlike the other rivals, Uncle Tony did not believe that aviation would bring peace on earth. In 1938 he returned from Europe with an apocalyptic vision. He saw war ahead, a future of fire and death, where "great air fleets of destruction" would dominate the skies. He predicted vast fleets of two hundred planes or more, each plane carrying three thousand pounds of high explosives. These fleets would fly high and fast, and "darken the sky over any city they pick." There would be no adequate defense against them, he said.

His prophecy came true, though he would not live to see its confirmation. When Raymond Orteig died after a long illness in June 1939, Fokker felt that a more gracious era had ended, to be replaced by one of brutality. That Christmas, he died of meningitis after three weeks of suffering. His ashes were sent to the Netherlands shortly before the German army invaded.

Bert Acosta's fate was as sad as Fokker's. His troubles had been building long before the Paris attempt, but in 1928 things began to fall apart. That year, the state of Connecticut suspended his pilot's license for zooming beneath a bridge in his hometown of Naugatuck; the next year, he was fined $500 for low flying and stunting. When he failed to pay the fine, the Department of Commerce revoked his license. But this failed to stop him, and in 1930 state police arrested him for flying without a license.

Flying was his life, his only means of livelihood, and without it, his life took a nosedive. His wife had him jailed in 1930 for nonsupport; he could not support anybody, not even himself, if he could not fly, he snapped at the judge. For that, he was sentenced to six months in jail. Levine bailed him out for $2,500, but jail failed to reform him, and in 1931 he was fined ten dollars for throwing empty liquor bottles at passersby. Levine came to his aid again and set him up in his own business, the Acosta Aircraft Corporation, but when Bert was charged in New York with selling fraudulent stock, the business failed.

What remained of his home life came to an end. When his wife discovered the old love letters from Reno divorcée Dorothy Walker, she sued Walker for alienation of affections, and filed for divorce. As would Levine, Acosta sought solace on Skid Row.

Despite all the turmoil in his personal life, Acosta could still fly rings around most other aviators. He would often sit in his car and watch the planes take off from Roosevelt Field. One day during this period, Joseph Terle, the builder of a homemade plane, had brought it in for a test but was unable to get it off the ground. Other pilots called the contraption hopeless, but Acosta took it up and nursed the ship through a series of banks, zooms, wingovers, and dives. Acosta stepped from the cockpit and announced, "I like it better than any airplane I ever flew." The grateful Terle named his ship the *Acosterle*.

In 1936 Acosta went off to fight in the Spanish Civil War. He headed the Yankee Squadron, which fought on the Loyalist side. The pilots flew ancient French and English commercial planes unarmed against German Heinkel He 51 fighters, each equipped with .30-caliber machine guns and flown by young Nazi aviators of the Condor Legion. Appropriately enough, Acosta and his fellows called themselves the "Suicide Squad."

One day, when returning from a raid, Acosta's patrol was jumped by a flight of Heinkels. One plane in Acosta's group went down, and suddenly he found himself in the middle of four powerfully equipped German fighters. His observer was armed with a rifle; Acosta, with an automatic pistol. The observer blasted away with his rifle while singing lewd Spanish songs. A Heinkel floated alongside for one last derisive look before delivering the coup de grace, and Acosta emptied a full clip into the pilot's face. His observer brought down another pilot with a well-aimed rifle shot. Both went down, and as the third Heinkel lined them up, the observer fired again. The German pilot rose, clutching his throat, and that plane went down. The other Germans fled.

Yet after a month of this, Acosta and the others came home. His enlistment had been tantamount to attempted suicide, given the equipment. And he was never paid.

During the 1940s, Acosta slid further into ruin. His daughters tried to save him, but he drifted from binge to lockup to fleabag rooming house in an alcoholic haze. He entered a sanatorium run by Franciscans, overlooking the Hudson River, but even the friars could not save him. In 1951 he collapsed in a New York City bar and was diagnosed with tuberculosis. When Byrd read of Bert's condition in the news, he set up a fund to save him. Acosta went from hospital to hospital, and in 1954 ended up at the Jewish Consumptive Relief Society in the foothills of the Rockies.

For months Acosta seemed to improve. He watched as the silver transcontinental planes rose into the azure sky above nearby Denver. He remembered his own flights, and the forty-two hours of hell in the *America*. What would it have been like to fly those big new planes? For a while he'd flown every plane that had been made in America, and there was no better life. "I had the opportunity," he told his daughter. "I blew it."

On September 1, 1954, he died at the age of fifty-nine.

By then, Byrd was entering his final, embittered years. Like Lindbergh, he'd floated on the inexhaustible fame of his flights, but his second Antarctic expedition, in which he nearly died alone, permanently changed him. As he tottered down the gangplank at Washington Navy Yard, a reporter asked about his next trip south. "I won't talk about going back now," he said. "I got enough of it for awhile."

Yet fame still called. From September 1935 to early 1937, *Time* reported, he "told 1,250,000 people in 250 cities about the South Pole." He wrote the book *Discovery* about the trip, and in 1938 the memoir *Alone*, about his near-death experience. He did go back, though more as an

administrator than as an explorer. And he fought off the rumors that
might have ruined his legacy.

Balchen, on the other hand, went on to have a distinguished career.
During World War II he commanded a staging base in Greenland for
U.S. bombers and fighters bound for England; he commanded a base in
Scotland that dropped tons of supplies to resistance fighters in Norway,
and flew out Allies interned in Sweden. He commanded the Tenth Rescue Squadron in Alaska, credited with 1,300 rescues. He was recommended for promotion to general seven times, and each time, he was
told, Byrd's powerful brother Harry—by then a senator and member of
the Senate Armed Services Committee—killed the promotion for "personal and special reasons."

By the early 1950s, Balchen decided to write his memoirs. *Come
North with Me* included his recollections of the race in Spitzbergen; his
cross-country tour with Bennett aboard the *Josephine Ford*; Bennett's
growing doubts about whether he and Byrd had actually made it to true
north; and the account of their flight aboard the *America*. He decided to
set the record straight, and the commander, by then in his sixties and a
kind of living monument, had gotten wind. In 1953 in a series of phone
calls and letters, Byrd threatened his old colleague. In an October 22,
1953, phone call, as Balchen prepared to fly to Norway to visit his sick
mother, Byrd told Balchen "to stop making statements about things that
I have never done and taking credit for things that I had not had anything to do with." On November 13 of that year, Byrd wrote, "Perhaps
you and your friends feel that I have become a weakling, with no ability
to defend myself?" Balchen chipped away at his book, and on March 11,
1957, he learned that Byrd had died at age sixty-eight.

Later in that year, he finished the manuscript and turned it over to
his New York publisher, E. P. Dutton, which ran an initial printing of
four thousand copies. By then Byrd's supporters—including Byrd's son
Richard Jr., Senator Harry Byrd, and the family lawyers—had a better
idea of the book's contents. The lawyers threatened Balchen with libel,
slander, and defamation of character; they talked of deporting him to
Norway, even though he was an American citizen. They began an inten-
sive lobbying campaign against the book and its author. Byrd's son enlisted the support of Fleet admiral William D. Leahy, U.S. representative
Carl Vinson, the National Geographic Society, the broadcaster Lowell
Thomas, the secretaries of the army and navy, Harry Guggenheim,

David Rockefeller, Admiral Arleigh Burke, Admiral Chester Nimitz, General George C. Marshall, General James Doolittle, the Henry Ford family, and General William Donovan. He left messages at the White House for President Dwight D. Eisenhower: "It would be very fine if the General could get a chance between now and then to call the publisher. I hate to bother the General with this problem, but I would appreciate very much anything he can do to help preserve the integrity of Adm Byrd." It is uncertain which of these noteworthies lent their aid, but Dutton buckled under pressure and released a heavily edited second edition with all the controversial sections excised or changed. Balchen was forced to pay for the rewrite, and said he did so because he thought it was the only way to keep his story alive. Near the end of his life, he donated his first draft, along with his other papers, to the Library of Congress. In 1971 the excised sections were published by writer Richard Montague.

It would appear that Byrd's fame had again prevailed. But like everyone else who achieved celebrity during the flying season of 1926/27, he endured huge costs that often came from unexpected quarters. Family fell prey to the costs just as readily as the fliers.

In October 1988 Byrd's son was found dead in an abandoned warehouse in Baltimore, his emaciated body clad in dirt-black clothes, one shoe on, the other cast to the side. The official cause of death was listed as malnutrition and dehydration, but in truth he had lived, as he died, in his father's shadow. He could never escape the weight. He was never "good enough," just as Byrd had been with his own father in Winchester. Celebrity keeps hostages, too, and Byrd's son became the collateral damage of dreams.

•

The aviator madness that rounded out the Jazz Age and continued through the Depression unleashed a desire for something that no one really understood. Lone fliers challenged old records and died, even as those records became more inconsequential. These people came out of nowhere—loners and dreamers, their heads in the clouds. In 1928, the year Amelia Earhart became the first woman to succeed in crossing the Atlantic, five aviators died in transatlantic attempts. Four died in 1929; in 1930, no fliers perished, but of the nine attempts, four crashed or were forced down. New Year's Day of 1931 began with two deaths, when a

Bellanca out of Hampton Roads, Virginia, vanished at sea. That year, eleven transatlantic flights carrying eleven people were planned. "Cold mathematics, based on a record of past performance, prove that 40% of these flights will fail," the magazine *Modern Mechanix* warned.

Yet the loners and dreamers persisted.

EPILOGUE: "IN THE CLOUDS"

In 1938 Douglas "Wrong Way" Corrigan became the first man to fly nonstop from New York to Dublin, doing so against all obstacles, including government officials. He did so, he claimed, by mistake, and the mistake brought him fame.

Ever since he'd helped build the *Spirit of St. Louis*, he'd wanted to be Lindbergh. Because he was Irish, he chose Dublin for his "first-flight." He was so inspired by his part in history that he wanted to make history himself. For the next decade, as the Orteig-inspired madness continued, Corrigan's flight to Dublin became his main reason to live.

But Corrigan traveled under a black cloud. He barnstormed the nation, borrowing gas or pieces of wood to mend his wing and landing gear. His Curtiss Robin monoplane was such a patchwork mess that every time he applied to fly across the Atlantic, government officials told him to reapply next year. Finally, they said his plane was so decrepit that he was lucky to fly it domestically. The plane itself was something of a character, a $900 "crate" that he dubbed *Sunshine*, likening it to "a ray of sunshine."

But after a decade of obsession and bad luck, Corrigan was growing tired. He'd been twenty and full of hope when he watched Lindbergh pirouette over the Ryan factory. That could be me up there, he often mused. Now he was thirty, and things weren't as easy any more. The Depression harried him. Flying was all he cared about, but the business had changed. Time was passing him by.

So, in 1937, he decided to go for broke. He took off for New York, but bad weather kept forcing him down. He landed in Podunk towns such as Arkadelphia, Arkansas, and Buckhannon, West Virginia, and gave people rides for gas money. By the time he made it to New York, it was too cold to fly, so he flew back to California nonstop to test whether *Sunshine* could last that long in the air. Though he made it, the plane was in such bad shape that she was grounded by authorities.

The next year was spent repairing *Sunshine*, and Corrigan obtained an "experimental" license to fly round trip from Los Angeles to New York. His real plan, however, was to continue east over the ocean. On July 7, 1938, he took off from Long Beach and ran straight into a massive New Mexican dust storm. He hit squalls with huge lightning bolts, but didn't have extra gas and plowed straight through. His tank sprang a leak. When he arrived in New York, 4 gallons of gas remained.

He stayed at Roosevelt Field for a week, preparing *Sunshine*. He found the leak in the fuel tank, but decided it wasn't that bad. More important to him was the fact that repairs would mean remounting the tank, and that would mean an extra week on the ground. Now and then reporters showed a little interest in the red-haired guy from California, but Corrigan did not tell them of his part in building the *Spirit of St. Louis*, nor give a hint of his plans. For the moment, he realized, the less he said, the better. At one point the aviatrix Ruth Nichols strolled up and eyed *Sunshine* with misgivings. She felt sorry for Corrigan, and concerned about his safety. Take my parachute, she said. "Thanks," said Corrigan, but there wasn't enough room for it in *Sunshine*. Besides, the plane was all he had to his name. If she went to pieces, he'd go with her.

He filed a flight plan from New York to Los Angeles, packed grease around the valve gear, and checked the valves. He filled the tanks and, at 4:00 a.m. on July 17, 1938, was ready to go. It was foggy in all directions, so foggy he'd have to fly by instruments. "Which way should I take off?" he asked the field manager.

"Any direction you want, except don't head toward the buildings on the west side of the field."

"I'll take off east," Corrigan said.

He rose after 3,000 feet, and was up 50 feet when he passed the edge of the field. At 500 feet, he noticed that his compass didn't seem to work, he later said. And so, instead of turning west toward Los Angeles, he mistakenly continued east into the fog.

He flew for two hours and occasionally saw breaks in the clouds. Usually, however, they formed a solid blanket beneath him. When he was ten hours out of New York, his feet started to get cold. He looked down and saw that the fuel tank leak had grown worse. Gas ran down his shoes, cooling his feet as it evaporated. He didn't worry much, because he figured that in a few hours the clouds would break and he could land, he later said. He was flying at 6,000 feet when the sky began to darken. He never adequately explained the fact that there would have been light in the west, the direction he thought he was headed. When asked to explain the mistake, he said that the light spread so diffusely through the clouds that it was hard to tell exactly where the sun was located. He pointed his flashlight at his feet and noticed that the gas was sloshing about an inch deep on the floor.

This was a problem, but Douglas Corrigan was always resourceful. He punched a hole in the floor with a screwdriver. The gas trickled out; the threat of explosion had passed, but now he was losing fuel. When he angled down to 3,500 feet, he saw water. Lots of water.

Now, this was strange, he said he realized. Where would this much water be found over America? He'd been flying for only twenty-one hours and shouldn't be over the Pacific yet. "I looked down at the compass, and now that there was more light I noticed that I had been following the wrong end of the compass on the whole flight," he told authorities. "As the opposite of west is east, I realized that I was over the Atlantic Ocean somewhere."

If he was telling the truth, as he always claimed, it had taken him quite a while to figure this out—yet he stayed remarkably calm. East? West? What's the difference to an aviator? At least he was still in the air. In a few minutes he saw a small fishing boat, and for some reason this reminded him of food. He gobbled down his provisions—some chocolate and a box of fig bars. A few more miles and he saw green hills unfold beneath him. It was like a dream—one he'd had so many times over the last ten years. In another few miles he passed over an airport with the name "BALDONNEL" marked in the grass field. "Having studied the map of Ireland two years before," he said, "I knew this was Ireland."

And so, in his mind, he'd won. He'd achieved his dream of being the first man to fly solo to Dublin, but he'd done so by breaking several federal and international laws. He apparently realized this for the first time, and the consequences frightened him. He could spend the next few years in jail. At the very least, he could be stripped of his pilot's license. Worst of all, he could lose *Sunshine*.

So he decided to fib. Corrigan would say he'd traveled twenty-six hours with nary a break in the clouds. He misread his compass so badly that he thought he was headed west until he saw the lights of Dublin. The story, not the flight, amazed everyone. To tell the world that you were so monumentally stupid as to fly over the Atlantic for twenty-six hours without knowing it took the past decade's aviation madness in an entirely new direction.

Yet Corrigan also represented something that struck a chord. The long slog of the Depression had worn down everyone. It drained rich and poor alike of money and means. The best one could hope for in times like these was some luck and a little native wit to help get through. Most of the gods were gone, and even Lindbergh was falling. In their place came the tricksters, and Corrigan was their king.

So he, too, was glorified. He got his "midsummer snowstorm of pa-per" as he took the Hero's Walk up Broadway. A band played the "Star-Spangled Banner" as he received the first of many compasses. A movie was made of him, and he wrote his autobiography. The cult of celebrity that had started with Lindbergh reached its bright-eyed apotheosis with Corrigan, who, after all, had helped to build Slim's world-famous plane.

But things had permanently changed. Eleven years earlier, the hero was a savior. But the new world had not come. People still looked to the sky when a plane passed over. But where there had once been an ec-stasy of hope, a knowing smile and a joke were the best one could hope for now.

So Corrigan stepped from his plane onto the green turf of his ances-tral land. An army officer walked out of the field office, and Corrigan asked if it was okay to stop here. The officer was unfailingly polite. "Yes, this is the correct field, all right," he said.

Corrigan sensed that something was wrong—the officer was taking this far too calmly, as if lost American fliers rolled up on his field every day. He asked, "Should I shut the motor off here or taxi up to the hangar?"

"It's all right to shut it off here. The lads'll pull the plane in the hangar."

"My name's Corrigan," Douglas said. When he'd left New York City yesterday morning, he thought he was headed for California.

Oh yes, they'd been expecting him, the army officer replied.

Corrigan was flabbergasted, and for a brief instant nearly lost his composure. "How come, how'd you find out?"

"Oh," the officer continued, "there was a small piece in the paper saying you might be flying this way." It was said with a straight face, though one could detect the hint of a smile. Without missing a beat, the officer asked, "So how did you end up here?"

"I got mixed up in the clouds," Corrigan replied. He looked the officer in the eyes and flashed the big, innocent smile that he'd use for the rest of his days. He'd tell the story often. People couldn't get enough of heroes. He, too, had been a hero—if only very briefly, and such a long time ago.

He cleared his throat and added, "I must have flown the wrong way."

TRANSATLANTIC TIME LINE

May 16–27, 1919, First Transatlantic Crossing: After eleven days and four stops, U.S. Navy lieutenant-commander Albert C. Read and a crew of five complete the first crossing of the Atlantic by air in the Navy Curtiss flying boat NC-4. They arrive in Lisbon on May 27 via the Azores. Two other flying boats had to give up.

May 18–19, 1919: Harry Hawker and Lieutenant-Commander Kenneth Mackenzie-Grieve attempt the first nonstop crossing, but after 1,400 miles of flight they ditch at sea beside a merchant vessel, which rescues them. They are 500 miles short of completion.

May 22, 1919: Raymond Orteig writes the president of Aero Club of America and offers a $25,000 prize to the first team of aviators to fly nonstop from New York to Paris, either way. This first offering has a time limit of five years.

June 14, 1919, First Nonstop Transatlantic Crossing: Captain John Alcock and Lieutenant Arthur Whitten Brown cross from St. John's in Newfoundland to Clifden in Ireland, in 16 hours, 27 minutes. Although they do not win the Orteig Prize, they do receive a £10,000 prize by London newspaper magnate Lord Northcliffe.

May 1924: Since no aviator has successfully flown nonstop from New York to Paris, Raymond Orteig renews his $25,000 prize offer for an indefinite time period.

1926: By this year, engines have been developed to such an extent that fliers believe it is possible to cross the Atlantic nonstop from New York to Paris. It is also the year Robert Goddard fires the first liquid-fuel rocket.

March 24, 1926: Top war ace René Fonck announces that he will come to the United States to compete for the Orteig Prize.

May 9, 1926: Navy fliers Richard E. Byrd and Floyd Bennett claim to be the first aviators to fly over the North Pole. Their claim will be disputed throughout the twentieth century.

September 21, 1926: Fonck takes off for Paris from Roosevelt Field in Long Island. His plane, a Sikorsky S-35, is severely overloaded and crashes at takeoff. Fonck and copilot Lawrence Curtin survive, but crew members Jacob Islamoff and Charles Clavier die.

Late October 1926: Department store magnate Rodman Wanamaker challenges Byrd to cross the Atlantic nonstop during a dinner he hosts in honor of the flight over the North Pole. Wanamaker offers to fund the effort for $100,000 in a plane named *America*.

Late 1926: François Coli and Paul Tarascon, early entrants for the Orteig Prize, crash during a test flight of their Potez 25 biplane. Tarascon is badly injured, and Coli will eventually team with fellow French war ace Charles Nungesser.

January 28, 1927: Noel Davis is the first American flier to officially apply for the Orteig Prize. His copilot is Stanton Hall Wooster. Both are navy men.

February 15, 1927: Francesco de Pinedo takes off from the southern tip of Italy on the first leg of his Four Continents flight.

February 28, 1927: Charles Lindbergh files his formal entry in the Orteig competition with the National Aeronautic Association. On March 1, a brief story appears on page 16 of *The New York Times*.

March 3, 1927: Byrd officially tells the press that he will attempt to cross the Atlantic and is being backed by Rodman Wanamaker. In the Vatican, Pope Pius XI gives his imprimatur to the use of airplanes in church work.

March 19–21, 1927: De Pinedo disappears over the Brazilian Amazon, then reappears in Manaus.

March 20, 1927: By now, five contestants have officially or unofficially declared their intention to compete for the Orteig Prize. A substantial feature story on the race appears in *The New York Times*.

April 6, 1927: De Pinedo lands at Roosevelt Dam, Arizona. His plane is accidentally destroyed when a teenage volunteer drops a lighted match into the oil-covered water surrounding the plane. The next day, Mussolini says he will send a new plane to New York Harbor.

April 10, 1927: Noel Davis unveils his plane, the *American Legion*, and takes it on its first trial spin. The powerful Keystone Pathfinder surpasses its maximum expected speed, Davis suddenly emerges as the front-runner, producing an urgency and interest in the race that had not been apparent previously.

April 12–14, 1927: Clarence Chamberlin and Bert Acosta set the world endurance record aloft in the Bellanca WB-2 monoplane *Columbia*. They stay in the air for 51 hours, 11 minutes, and 25 seconds, and cover 4,100 miles, considerably more than the 3,600 miles needed to cross from New York to Paris.

April 16, 1927: Noel Davis flies the *American Legion* from Langley Field in Virginia to Mitchel Field in Long Island. That same day, Richard Byrd's *America* crashes in its first test flight, severely injuring Floyd Bennett. Byrd, Tony Fokker, and George Noville suffer minor injuries.

April 20, 1927: Two new entrants are announced in the Orteig race: Lieutenant Winston W. Ehrgott of the New York National Guard and John H. Stelling. That same day, owner Charles Levine announces that airmail pilot Lloyd Bertaud will be the navigator of the Bellanca. On the morning of takeoff, Chamberlin and Acosta will draw straws to see who is pilot.

April 24, 1927: The Brooklyn Chamber of Commerce officially announces it will award $15,000 to the pilots of the *Columbia* if they win the New York–Paris competition. The plane is christened, and immediately after the ceremonies, two young girls—one, the daughter of Levine—jump into the cabin and ask for a ride. Chamberlin agrees, but immediately after takeoff the landing gear fails and he makes a daring landing, saving their lives. Nevertheless, the *Columbia*'s takeoff is delayed for repairs.

April 25, 1927: De Pinedo arrives in New York and is hailed as a hero. There is speculation that he might enter the lineup for the Orteig Prize.

April 26, 1927: Noel Davis and Stanton Wooster die during the final test of the *American Legion* in Virginia's Langley Field.

April 28, 1927: Bert Acosta withdraws from the *Columbia* team, leaving the field open to Chamberlin and Bertaud; soon afterward, he surfaces as a replacement pilot for Floyd Bennett aboard the *America*. On the same day, in San Diego, Lindbergh takes the *Spirit of St Louis* up on her maiden flight.

April 29, 1927: Two thousand antifascists riot on New York's Second Avenue while attempting to raid the Italian Legion Post where de Pinedo is speaking.

May 8, 1927: Charles Nungesser and François Coli take off from Le Bourget in Paris in the *White Bird*. The plane disappears sometime after reaching Newfoundland, and the two are never heard from again. They are officially listed as missing on May 10, and the search for wreckage continues late into the summer.

May 10–12, 1927: Lindbergh swoops from San Diego to New York in two legs, stopping at St. Louis. His first leg, from San Diego to St. Louis, sets a distance record for a nonstop flight by a single pilot. His arrival at New York completes a coast-to-coast flight of 21 hours and 20 minutes, breaking the 1923 record of two army fliers.

May 13, 1927: Chamberlin and Bertaud prepare to take off for Paris in the *Columbia* the next morning, but will be grounded by weather. That night, as they make their last-minute preparations, Levine hands them a contentiously worded contract that will cause major problems for the team in the week to come.

May 14–19, 1927: The three remaining planes—Lindbergh's *Spirit of St. Louis*, Byrd's *America*, and Chamberlin's *Columbia*—are all prepared to take off for Paris, but bad weather grounds them.

May 16, 1927: The battle over Levine's contract with the *Columbia*'s fliers becomes public and hits the papers. Levine threatens to fire Bertaud; in retaliation, Bertaud files an injunction in the Brooklyn courts, which results in the plane's being padlocked in her hangar until a judge hears the case on May 20.

May 17, 1927: Byrd adds the Norwegian test pilot Bernt Balchen to the crew of the *America*. The plane is ready to go, but Wanamaker insists that they not take off until "scientific" tests are completed and more certainty exists concerning the fate of Nungesser and Coli.

May 20–21, 1927: Lindbergh crosses the Atlantic in the *Spirit of St. Louis*, winning the Orteig Prize. His 3,610-mile flight takes 33 hours and 30 minutes.

May 22, 1927: De Pinedo leaves Newfoundland for the Azores islands, but has to be towed the last 200 miles. On June 16, he finally arrives in Ostia harbor, west of Rome.

June 4–6, 1927: Clarence Chamberlin and Charles Levine fly 3,930 miles nonstop in the *Columbia* from Roosevelt Field to Eisleben, Germany.

June 16, 1927: Raymond Orteig officially gives Lindbergh the $25,000 in prize money after the aviator returns to New York.

June 29–July 2, 1927: Richard Byrd, Bert Acosta, Bernt Balchen, and George Noville cross from New York to Paris, only to ditch off the coast of Normandy after overflying Paris in bad weather.

August 31, 1927: Leslie Hamilton and Fred Minchin, both of the Royal Air Force, and Princess Löwenstein-Wertheim, their financial backer, take off from England en route to Ottawa in Canada aboard a single-engine Fokker F-VIIa named the *St. Raphael*. She is seen over the Atlantic by a tanker, but vanishes in mists over Newfoundland and is never seen again.

September 6, 1927: Newspaper magnate William Randolph Hearst sponsors another Fokker F-VIIa, called *Old Glory*, crewed by Lloyd W. Bertaud and James DeWitt Hill. Philip Payne, editor of Hearst's New York *Daily Mirror*, goes along as a passenger. The plane takes off from Old Orchard Beach, Maine, and heads for Rome. The next day, a radio emergency message is received. Ships rush to the location, but they find only wreckage and no trace of the men.

September 6, 1927: On the same day of the *Old Glory*'s departure, the *Sir John Carling* takes off from Harbor Grace, Newfoundland. The plane is sponsored by the Carling Brewery of Canada and piloted by Captain Jerry Tully and Lieutenant James Medcalf. She, too, vanishes without a trace over the ocean.

October 11, 1927: Aspiring actress Ruth Elder and pilot George Haldeman take off from Roosevelt Field in Elder's bid to become the first woman to cross the ocean. They ditch their plane, the *American Girl*, about 300 miles short of the Azores when the engine develops an oil leak. They are rescued by a passing Dutch freighter. Elder's newfound fame helps her break into the movies.

December 23, 1927: Frances Wilson Grayson, the thirty-five-year-old niece of President Wilson, takes off in a Sikorsky S-36 amphibian named *Dawn* with three others aboard. They leave Roosevelt Field en route to Newfoundland, but the plane disappears within hours and is never found

April 25, 1928: Floyd Bennett dies.

May 20–21, 1932: Amelia Earhart makes the first solo crossing of the Atlantic by a woman.

May 20, 1939: Pan Am announces the inauguration of its first scheduled transatlantic passenger flight—a seventy-four-passenger, four-engine Boeing 314 seaplane. Although only freight is carried on this first flight, passenger service begins on June 28, 1939.

GLOSSARY

aerodrome: a regular flying field equipped with a runway, hangers, and other services for aviators.

aerodynamics· the branch of physics that deals with the properties of air (or any gas) in motion and the interactions between the air and a solid body (such as an airplane) moving through it.

aeronautics· the science of flight.

aileron: the movable parts of a wing that control or affect the roll of an aircraft by working opposite to one another—i.e., up-aileron on the right wing and down-aileron on the left wing.

airfoil: the shape of a flying surface seen in cross section. This term is most commonly used in reference to a wing.

air speed: the speed of an aircraft relative to the air.

altimeter: an instrument for measuring the altitude of an aircraft.

amphibian: an airplane designed to land and take off from either the ground or water. A seaplane or floatplane.

angle of attack· the acute angle at which an airfoil (a wing) meets a moving stream of air.

aspect ratio. the ratio of the span to the chord of an airfoil. A *high-aspect-ratio* wing has a wide span and narrow chord; vice versa for a *low-aspect-ratio* wing.

aviation: the art of operating a *heavier-than-air* craft.

bank: to tip an airplane laterally, along its longitudinal axis. Thus, to *right-bank* means to incline the plane with its right wing down.

barograph: an instrument for recording the barometric pressure of the atmosphere.

biplane: an airplane with two wings, one placed above the other.

ceiling: the height above the earth's surface of the lowest layer of obscuring clouds. This cloud cover is either described as *broken, overcast,* or *obscured* for it to be considered a ceiling; thus, a *thin* or *partial* cloud cover does not apply. Ceiling is also defined as either *absolute* or *service. Absolute ceiling* is the maximum height above sea level at which an airplane can maintain horizontal flight *Service ceiling* is the maximum height at which an airplane ceases to be able to rise at 100 feet per minute.

chandelle: an aircraft control maneuver in which the pilot combines a turn with a climb in a certain way. Practically speaking, it can be used to turn a plane within a minimal turn radius

chord: the measurable distance between the leading and trailing edge of a wing.

cockpit: the open spaces where the pilot and passengers ride. If enclosed, it is called a cabin.

control stick the vertical lever by means of which an airplane is controlled. *Pitch* is controlled by a fore-and-aft movement of the stick; *roll*, by a side-to-side movement. Also, *joystick*.

cowl, or cowling· the circular, removable housing, or *fairing*, placed around an aircraft engine, for streamlining and cooling.

dead reckoning: in the days of pioneer flight, before radios and beacons, this was essentially navigation by means of compass and watch over a set distance. The *dead* simply means "straight," as in the nautical *dead ahead*.

dead stick landing: descending flight with the engine and propeller stopped.

deviation: the error in a magnetic compass due to such inherent magnetic factors as the structure and equipment of an airplane.

dive: a steep descent in which the air speed is greater than the maximum speed in horizontal flight.

dope. the liquid applied to the cloth surfaces of an airplane that increased strength and produced tautness by shrinkage During the Jazz Age, a common dope was cellulose nitrate.

drag: the resisting force on an aircraft in its line of flight, but opposite its direction of motion.

drift: the angle between an aircraft's forward heading and its lateral track caused by wind.

Duraluminum: an aluminum alloy used by planes, as opposed to the traditional fabric and wood of the early days of flight. The original trade name was Dural, for a wrought aluminum-copper alloy created by the Bausch Machine Tool Company, but it fell into generic use for any aluminum alloy containing 3.0–4.5 percent copper, 0.4–1.0 percent magnesium, and 0.1–0.7 percent manganese. Alcoa's version was commonly called "Duraluminum."

elevator: the moving part of a horizontal airfoil that controls pitch. The fixed part of that airfoil is the *stabilizer*.

flare: a maneuver performed moments before landing in which the nose of an aircraft is pitched up to reduce the rate of speed at touchdown.

flying boat: a type of seaplane supported by a hull that rides on the surface of the water. Many of these were built with a large central hull, and lateral stability was provided by wing-tip floats.

fuselage: an aircraft's streamlined central structure, to which are attached the wings and tail. In general, the fuselage contains the engine, passengers, cargo, etc.

glide: a descent at a normal *angle of attack*, but without the engine power necessary to maintain level flight. Thus, engine thrust is replaced by the force of gravity along the line of flight.

ground effect. the increased lift produced by the interaction between a lift system and the ground when an aircraft is within a wingspan's distance above the ground. This affects low-winged aircraft more than mid- or high-winged aircraft because the wings are closer to the ground.

ground speed: the actual speed of an aircraft relative to the ground

Immelmann turn: a World War I dogfight maneuver in which a plane would climb and then, just short of a stall, the pilot would apply full rudder to turn the plane back down at an enemy aircraft, making possible a high-speed diving pass. Named after the first German ace, Max Immelmann.

landing gear. the undercarriage supporting the weight of the airplane upon landing. At the time, there were five common types. *boat-, float-, skid-, wheel-,* and *ski-type.*

leading edge: the foremost edge of a wing or propeller blade.

lift: the force exerted on the top of a moving wing as a low-pressure area, or vacuum, which causes it to rise. Wings do not float on a cushion of air, as is often assumed, but rather are pulled up by the vacuum.

load: the weight of and in the plane. There are four kinds of load: *Dead:* the weight of the empty airplane. *Full·* the sum of the dead load and the useful load, also called *gross weight. Pay.* That part of the useful load that generates revenue: (passengers and freight) *Useful.* The weight of the passengers, crew, oil, and fuel.

magneto: an accessory that produces and distributes a high-voltage spark for the ignition of a fuel charge in an internal combustion engine.

monoplane: a plane with one wing, although today this is often divided into two parts by the fuselage.

nacelle: a streamlined enclosure to protect the engine, landing gear, or crew.

nose-heavy: the condition of a plane in normal flight when the distribution of forces is such that if the controls were released, the nose would drop.

pitch. of the three axes in flight, the one that specifies the vertical, or up-and-down, motion.

pusher: a propeller mounted in the back of the engine, which pushes the aircraft through the air. Early aircraft were often of this design, as compared to today's more common *tractor* design, where the propeller is mounted in the front and pulls the plane behind it through the air.

ramjet. an aerodynamic duct in which fuel is burned to create a propulsive jet of high velocity. This needs to be accelerated to high speed before it becomes functional.

roll: a maneuver in which the plane revolves around its longitudinal axis while maintaining its horizontal direction.

rudder: the movable part of a vertical airfoil that controls *yaw.* The fixed part is the fin. The rudder is located in the tail.

rudder bar. the foot bar by which the cables controlling the rudder are operated.

sesquiplane: a biplane in which the lower wing is shorter than the upper, for lift.

side slip: a sideways movement of an aircraft, caused by a flow of air moving laterally to its flight path.

slipstream. the flow of air driven backward by a propeller or downward by a rotor.

stall· the condition in flight when for any reason a plane has lost the air speed necessary for support or control.

taxi· to run a plane over the ground, or a seaplane over the surface of the water, under its own power.

thrust: the driving force of the propeller in the forward line of its shaft, or the forward force produced by gases expelled to the rear by a jet or rocket engine. The opposite of *drag.*

turn indicator: an instrument indicating the forces acting on an aircraft in a banking turn, also called a *turn-and-bank indicator*.

true north: the northern direction of the axis of the Earth, as opposed to *magnetic north*.

yaw: to swing off course about the vertical axis because of wind gusts or a lack of directional stability. One of the three axes of flight, along with *pitch* and *roll*.

NOTES

PROLOGUE: WINGED MESSENGERS

3   Charles Augustus Lindbergh lined up the church in his gun sights: Charles A. Lindbergh, "Thoughts of a Combat Pilot," *The Saturday Evening Post*, October 2, 1954, 20, 22, 80; *Of Flight and Life* (New York: Charles Scribner's Sons, 1948), 49–50.

4   Between 1910 and 1950 two generations. Joseph J. Corn, *The Winged Gospel· America's Romance with Aviation* (Baltimore, Md.: Johns Hopkins University Press, 1983), 135–36, 37, 41, 39–40.

4   "the greatest factor for progress that has ever existed": Quoted in Leonard S. Reich, "Review: Farther and Faster: Aviation's Adventuring Years, 1909–1939," *Technology and Culture* 34, no. 2 (April 1993) 442.

4   "Of all the agencies that influenced men's minds": Quoted in Richard P. Hallion, *Taking Flight: Inventing the Aerial Age from Antiquity Through the First World War* (Oxford: Oxford University Press, 2003), 380.

5   the archetype of modern man: Richard D. Logan, "The Solitary Navigator as the Archetypical Modern Individual," *Journal of American Culture* 13, no. 4 (June 2004). 42; Carl Jung, *Modern Man in Search of a Soul* (New York. Harvest Books, 1933), 197.

5   "My cockpit is small": Charles Lindbergh, *The Spirit of St Louis* (New York: Scribner's, 1953), 227.

5   Of the 2,501 fatal accidents among private and student pilots: Paul A. Craig, *The Killing Zone: How and Why Pilots Die* (New York: McGraw-Hill, 2001), 13.

5   "[The pilot's] ego is writing checks": Ibid., 13, 7.

6   "It's not right until it looks right": Jerome C. Hunsaker, "A Half Century of Aeronautical Development," *Proceedings of the American Philosophical Society* 98, no. 2 (April 15, 1954): 123–24.

6   "Flying releases something almost uncontrollable": Leighton Collins, "The Dangers of the Air," in Wolfgang Langewiesche, *Stick and Rudder. An Exploration of the Art of Flying* (New York· McGraw-Hill, 1944, 1972), 329.

7   Just where did those early aeronauts think they were headed: Clive Hart, *The Dream of Flight: Aeronautics from Classical Times to the Renaissance* (London: Faber and Faber, 1972), 21; Peter Haining, *The Compleat Birdman: An Illustrated History of Man-Powered Flight* (New York: St. Martin's Press, 1976), 18.

7   "I am above them": Beryl Markham, *West with the Night* (New York. Farrar, Strauss and Giroux, 1983 [1942]), 284.

7   Antoine de Saint-Exupéry, the French Aéropostale pilot: Saint-Exupery is quoted in Janet B. Rollins, "Flight as Sea Voyage in Saint-Exupéry's 'Southern Mail' and 'Night Flight,'" *The Journal of American Culture* 7, no. 1–2 (Spring/Summer 1984): 75, 77.

9   "People who succeed are loved" Quoted in Scott A Sandage, *Born Losers A History of Failure in America* (Cambridge, Mass.: Harvard University Press, 2005), 277.

10 "Escape may be checked by water and land". Edith Hamilton, *Mythology· Timeless Tales of Gods and Heroes* (New York: New American Library, 1942), 139. Hamilton quotes from the account by the Greek poet Apollodorus.

ONE: STRANGE DAYS

13 Charles Lindbergh hooked his leg over the right side of the cockpit. A. Scott Berg, *Lindbergh* (New York· Berkeley Books, 1999), 35–38; Kenneth S. Davis, *The Hero. Lindbergh and the American Dream* (Garden City, N.Y.: Doubleday, 1959), 130–32; Assen Jordanoff, *Men and Wings* (Curtiss-Wright, 1942), 43–44, 45; "How It Feels to Drop from the Sky in a Parachute," *Literary Digest* 93, no. 8 (May 21, 1927): 72, 76; Lindbergh, *The Spirit of St Louis*, 5–7.

16 six years of Prohibition had taken their toll· "Orteig Is Dead, Donor of Prize Lindbergh Won," *New York Times*, June 8, 1939. Some of Broadway's great watering holes had been padlocked by Prohibition. the Hotel Knickerbocker, home of Manhattan's best free lunch, and the Manhattan Lounge, where the namesake cocktail was born.

16 In mid-August Rodolfo Alfonso Guglielmi di Valentina d'Antonguolla: George Walsh, *Gentleman Jimmy Walker: Mayor of the Jazz Age* (New York: Praeger, 1974), 79, 84–85, 85–86.

16 Maybe Mayor James J. Walker should have predicted: "Jimmy Walker," Wikipedia, en.wikipedia.org; Robert G. Folsom, *The Money Trail: How Elmer Irey and His T-Men Brought Down America's Criminal Elite*, uncorrected advance proof (Washington, D.C.: Potomac Books, 2010), 101.

17 New York determined its style: Walsh, *Gentleman Jimmy Walker*, 86–87.

17 Two days later, on August 27, the city gave a lavish ticker tape parade: Ibid., 87; *New York Times*, June 12, 1991, B1; *New York Times*, October 30, 1996, B1.

18 The audacious visitor was, in fact, one of the world's most famous fliers: "S-35," *Time*, August 23, 1926, www.time.com.

18 the "Unpuncturable": Laurence La Tourette Driggs, "Aces Among Aces," *National Geographic Magazine* 33, no. 6, (June 1918)· 569.

18 "I put my bullets into a target as if by hand": "René Fonck, Highest Scoring Allied Ace, 75 Kills," www.acepilots.com.

18 "One must be in constant training". Driggs, "Aces of Aces," 570; William E. Barrett, "Was Fonck a Faker?" *Cavalier*, February 1960, 27.

18 "Constantly I watch myself": Driggs, 570.

18 He watched himself that day· René Fonck, "My New York–Paris Flight," *Aero Digest*, June 1926, 320; "A Quiet Ace," *The New Yorker*, August 21, 1926, 10; Barrett, "Was Fonck a Faker?" 80.

18   He smiled easily at Walker: "S-35"; "A Quiet Ace," 10.

19   "I am surprised you didn't make a good mayor": "S-35."

19   he had lived alone in his room: "A Quiet Ace," 9–10; Barrett, "Was Fonck a Faker?" 80.

19   "the science of aeronautics has progressed": Fonck, "My New York–Paris Flight," 320.

20   There had been two previous transatlantic "hops": Percy Rowe, *The Great Atlantic Air Race* (Toronto: McClelland and Stewart, 1977), 63, 68; David Beaty, *The Water Jump. The Story of Transatlantic Flight* (New York: Harper and Row, 1976), 11, 29–31; Lt. Walter Hinton, "The First Transatlantic Flight," *Current History* (July 1927): 545–50; Richard K. Smith, *First Across! The U S. Navy's Transatlantic Flight of 1919* (Annapolis, Md.· Naval Institute Press, 1973).

20   According to Fonck, the idea to make such a flight: Fonck, "My New York–Paris Flight," 320; Barrett, "Was Fonck a Faker?" 80.

20   for two months sought additional French backing: "Fonck Plans New York–Paris Flight in May," *New York Times*, March 25, 1926, 1; March 31, 1926, 3; April 21, 1926, 7.

21   Fonck's announcement stunned the flying world: *New York Times*, April 4, 1926, 21; May 12, 1926, 4; May 14, 1926, 4.

21   Few paid them any mind: "Dinner to Capt. Fonck Is Given by Orteig," *New York Times*, May 5, 1926, 34; May 11, 1926, 11.

21   "Air transportation, bringing speed in communication": Fonck, "My New York–Paris Flight," 320.

21   All that summer, the plane took shape: "A Quiet Ace," 10.

22   Americans historically distrusted flight· Issac Kramnick, ed., *The Portable Enlightenment Reader* (New York: Penguin, 1995), xix; Alexis de Tocqueville, *Democracy in America*, ed. Richard D. Hoffner (New York: Penguin, 1956, 1984), 163; Jefferson to D. B. Lee, April 27, 1822, Container 52. "Jefferson, Thomas, General Correspondence," "Biographical Files, 1784–1962," Archives of the Institute of Aerospace Sciences in the American Institute of Aeronautics and Astronautics, Manuscript Division, Library of Congress, Washington, D.C. (hereafter AIAA Archives)

22   "may possibly give a new Turn to Human Affairs": Letter from Paris to Vienna, Franklin to Dr. Ingenhaus, January 16, 1784, Box OV45: "Franklin, Benjamin, Copies of Letters and Clippings," "Oversize, 1805–1955, n.d.," AIAA Archives.

23   "Pass on the Trans-Atlantic Air Line Railway". Container 174: "A pass on the Trans-Atlantic Air Line Railway, 1894," "Miscellaneous, 1804–1932," AIAA Archives.

23   the Harvard astronomer William Pickering: Hallion, *Taking Flight*, 400.

23   the victorious troops brought home the Spanish influenza: "1918 flu pandemic," Wikipedia, en.wikipedia.org.

23   That spring and early summer, as Fonck's shining gull took shape. *New York Times*, July 5, 1926, 1.

23   The North Atlantic is one of the harshest places on earth: "World InfoZone—Atlantic Facts," worldinfozone.com; David Beaty, *The Water Jump: The Story of Transatlantic Flight* (New York: Harper and Row, 1976), 8.

24   Fimbulwinter. Ragnarök, or the "Twilight of the Gods," is quoted in David B. Stephenson, Heinz Wanner, Stefan Brónnimann, and Jurg Luterbacher, "The

History of Scientific Research on the North Atlantic Oscillation," in James W. Hurrell, Yochanan Kushnir, Geir Ottersen, Martin Visbeck, eds., *The North Atlantic Oscillation: Climatic Significance and Environmental Impact* (Washington, D.C.: American Geophysical Union, 2003), 37.

24 The high winds in those clouds were known to push aircraft backward: Jan De Blieu, *Wind. How the Flow of Air Has Shaped Life, Myth, and the Land* (Boston: Houghton Mifflin, 1998), 145, Beaty, *The Water Jump*, 8.

24 Flying over the clouds was not an option either: Beaty, *The Water Jump*, 8.

25 Cunard liners such as the *Mauretania* made steady profits: Ibid.

25 the dream of flying the Atlantic had persisted. Smith, *First Across!* 4–6.

25 The first transatlantic flight to be reported as fact· Edward Jablonski, *Atlantic Fever* (New York: Macmillan, 1972), x.

26 St. Brendan of Clonfert sailed from Ardfert, in Ireland: The tale of Saint Brendan and his phantom island is taken from the following sources: "Brendan," en.wikipedia.org; "St. Brendan of Clonfert," www.irondequiot.catholic.org/index.php/St/BrendanofClonfert; Carl Selman, ed., *Navigatio Sancti Brendani Abbatus* (South Bend, Ind.. University of Notre Dame Press, 1959), "St. Brendan's Island," en.wikipedia.org.

26 short, bald, and risible: "Raymond Orteig, Hotel Man, Dies," *New York Times*, June 8, 1939; "No Tears," *The New Yorker*, April 2, 1949, 26–27; *Washington Daily News*, April 1, 1949, 34.

27 Like many immigrants, Raymond Orteig was stuck between two worlds. "Raymond Orteig, Hotel Man, Dies."

27 their owners belonged to the Tavern Club Scrapbook, "First Five Years of the Tavern Club, Jan. 15th, 1923–Jan. 15th, 1928," File, "Tavern Club Collection," BV Tavern Club, "Records of the Tavern Club, 1923–1964," New York Historical Society. The first time Orteig shows up as a member is in 1936 in the file "Dinner given by Raymond Orteig at the Hotel Lafayette. March 20, 1936."

27 the Aero Club of America hosted a banquet at the Lafayette: Leonard Mosley, *Lindbergh: A Biography* (New York: Doubleday, 1976), 73.

28 "As a stimulus for the courageous aviators": Orteig's note is quoted in many places. This appeared in Richard J. Beamish, *The Story of Lindbergh, the Lone Eagle* (Philadelphia: International Press, 1927), 165.

28 He could not foresee the consequences. Mosley, *Lindbergh*, 73–74; Alex Schroeder, *The Application and Administration of Inducement Prizes in Technology* (Golden, Colo.. Independence Institute, 2004), 3, "Orteig Is Dead, Donor of Prize Lindbergh Won," *New York Times*, June 8, 1939; "Orteig Dies at Age 69 after a Long Illness," *Newsweek* 13, no. 8 (June 19, 1939), "Inflation Calculator—U.S. Bureau of Labor Statistics," data.bls.gov/cgi-bin/cpicalc.pl. From the Raymond Orteig Historical Collection, National Air and Space Museum Archives, Washington, D.C. (hereafter Orteig Collection): René Fonck application; Paul Tarascon application; Letter from George W. Burleigh to C. F. Schory, May 28, 1925, Letter, Harry G. Young to C. F. Schory, September 25, 1925; Letter, George Burleigh to C. F. Schory, February 9, 1926; Letter, H. E. Hartney to C. F. Schory, April 13, 1926. Most sources state that Orteig renewed the prize in May 1924 for an unlimited amount of time, but *The Slipstream*, one of several American aviation magazines of the day, seemed to indicate that the prize was renewed on June 1, 1925, for another five years. The writer did not show much enthusiasm. "With all the

enthusiasm we can muster," it wrote, "we believe we can state, without fear of embarrassment that the prize will go begging as many more years, or at least during the period of extension of five years from June 1, 1925" ("The Orteig Prize," *The Slipstream* 6, no. 7 [July 1925]· 19).

28 The two nations whose hopes: Total casualties during World War I among all participants, military and civilian, totaled 37.5 million: 16.5 million dead and 21 million wounded. This means that nearly 2.1 percent of the world's population was injured or killed. From March 1918 to June 1920 the "Spanish flu" pandemic slew another 50 to 100 million. Although the war did not cause the flu, the worldwide demobilization of those infected spread it everywhere. Another 3 percent of the world's population died, making 1914–1920 the deadliest six years in human history. Statistics are drawn from "World Population 1918," wiki.answers.com; "World War I Casualties," Wikipedia, en.wikipedia.org.

29 America as the personification of The Machine: Georges Duhamel, *America the Menace· Scenes from the Life of the Future*, trans. Charles Miner Thompson (Boston: Houghton Mifflin, 1931), xiv, xiii; Frederick Lewis Allen, *The Big Change. America Transforms Itself, 1900–1950* (New York: Harper and Bros., 1952), 113, 115, 117.

30 Americans themselves seemed slow to notice: Lewis Mumford, *American Taste* (San Francisco: Westgate, 1929), 34; Waldo Frank, "The Perception of Power," in Loren Baritz, ed., *The Culture of the Twenties* (Indianapolis· Bobbs-Merrill, 1970), 373–74.

30 The airplane, like the tank and U-boat: Fred Erisman, *Boys' Books, Boys' Dreams, and the Mystique of Flight* (Fort Worth, Texas: Texas Christian University Press, 2006), 67.

30 With the war, we see a change in the public's perception: Erisman, *Boys' Books*, 51, 55, 64.

31 The French were ahead of their time. Hallion, *Taking Flight*, 386–87, 395.

32 More than in any other nation, aviation had become· Robert Wohl, *The Spectacle of Flight· Aviation and the Western Imagination, 1920–1950* (New Haven, Conn.: Yale University Press, 2005), 205.

32 a visitor to the United States in 1918: Hallion, *Taking Flight*, 388–91.

33 The military auctioned its surplus: Erisman, *Bad Boys'*, 85.

33 Some commercial interest did take shape: Ibid., 85–86.

33 military fliers, resented: Joseph R. Hamlen, *Flight Fever* (Garden City, N.Y.: Doubleday, 1971), 8; C. G. Grey and Leonard Bridgman, eds., *Jane's All the World's Aircraft, 1927* (London: Sampson Low, Marston, 1927), 62a.

34 "It is either fly or sink": "Dinner to Capt. Fonck Is Given by Orteig," 34.

TWO: THE SURE THING

35 Fonck charmed the sporting crowd: "Byrd Views Fonck Plane," *New York Times*, August 23, 1926; "Inflation Calculator—U.S. Bureau of Labor Statistics," data.bls.gov/cgr-bin/cpicalc.pl.

35 It was a huge silver beast, dwarfing the workers and spectators: "The Sikorsky Transatlantic Plane," *Aviation*, May 31, 1926, 834–35; "Specifications and Performance for the All-Metal Three-Motored Passenger or Freight Carrier S-35 'Special'—Model 1926," Sikorsky S-35, National Air and Space Museum Archives, Washington, D.C. (hereafter NASM Archives).

35 At 9:00 a.m. that clear Tuesday: "Fonck Takes Plane in Flight Over City," *New York Times*, August 24, 1926.

36 For Sikorsky, winning the prize meant everything: "In Philadelphia," *Time*, Monday, September 13, 1926, www.time.com.

37 What could he do?: Geoffrey T. Hellman, "The Winged S-11," *The New Yorker*, August 17, 1940, 26. There would eventually be four sons: George, Igor Jr., Nikolai, and Sergei. Sikorsky called them the "four rocketeers."

37 It was amazing to Sikorsky how quickly dreams could sour: Richard F. Dempewolff, "PM Salutes Igor Sikorsky," *Popular Mechanics* 112, no. 3 (Sept. 1959): 80.

37 Sikorsky feared the little things: "Igor Sikorsky," Wikipedia, en.wikipedia.org.

37 he was honored by the tsar. Dempewolff, "PM Salutes," 76; Dorothy Cochrane, Von Hardesty, and Russell Lee, *The Aviation Careers of Igor Sikorsky* (Seattle: University of Washington Press, 1989), 67.

38 There was no capital and little work for a man of his skills: Hellman, "Winged S-11," 20.

38 Vertical flight had been Sikorsky's first love: Igor Sikorsky, "Recollections of a Pioneer," transcript of an address to the Wings Club of New York City, November 16, 1964, 4, 6, CS-552500-01 Sikorsky, Igor Ivanovich (DR) (1991–20) Documents, NASM Archives; Dempewolff, "PM Salutes," 76; "Conquering Vertical Flight," unattributed manuscript that includes plans of Sikorsky's 1912 "B. N. Yuriev," CS-552500-01 Sikorsky, Igor Ivanovich (DR) (1991–20) Documents, NASM Archives.

38 In 1922 he showed these plans to W. A. Bary. Hellman, "Winged S-11," 20–22, Cochrane, Hardesty, and Lee, *Aviation Careers*, 70, 72, 76–80; Jablonski, *Atlantic Fever*, 35; Dempewolff, "PM Salutes," 77. Roscoe Turner would sell the S-29 to Howard Hughes in 1928 for use in his World War I movie epic *Hell's Angels* with Ben Lyon and Jean Harlow. The airplane was modified to resemble a huge German Gotha bomber, and was destroyed in a spectacular fiery crash. By then, it had flown 500,000 miles.

39 Sikorsky had every reason to think that the lean days were over· Hellman, "Winged S-11," 22.

40 Although this early S-35 was somewhat different: Letter, Harold E. Hartney to Maj. Ernest Jones, Assistant Secretary for Aeronautics, Department of Commerce, Oct. 6, 1926, Sikorsky S-35 (Fonck 1926 Transatlantic Attempt) Documents, AS-400249-01, NASM Archives.

40 Hartney could talk a good game. "Harold Evans Hartney," www.theaerodrome .com/aces/usa/hartney.php; Thomas G. Foxworth, "Bertrand B. Acosta, 1895– 1954," *Historical Aviation Album, All American Series*, vols. 6 and 7 (Temple City, Calif.: Historical Aviation Album, n.d.), 53.

40 Hartney formed the Argonauts, Inc.. Fonck, "My New York–Paris Flight," 320; "Col. Hartney Backs Berry in Fonck Row," *New York Times*, August 31, 1926, 1.

41 Berry saw the project as more than just a business proposition: "Col. Hartney Backs Berry," 1; Cochrane, Hardesty, and Lee, *Aviation Careers*, 82; "Aviation Pathfinders: Richard Byrd and Floyd Bennett," *A Century of Flight*, www.century -of-flight.freedom.com; "U.S. Air Force Fact Sheet· Berry, Homer Mulhall Papers," Air Force Historical Research Agency, www.afhra.af.mil.

41 Fonck had moved quickly from the very beginning: "Col. Hartney Backs Berry,"
    1; Letter, Hartney to Jones, October 6, 1926.

42 By March 1926 Hartney had arranged for the transport: "Col. Hartney Backs
    Berry," "Inflation Calculator—U S. Bureau of Labor Statistics," data.bls.gov/cgr
    -bin/cpicalc.pl.

42 Why was Fonck unable to keep his word: Robert L. Parrish, "René Fonck," tran-
    script for a series of short biographical sketches on World War I fliers, New Horizon
    Publishers, n.d., Fonck, René, Documents, CF-381000-01, NASM Archives.

42 he did have detractors, even during the war. "Fonck Plans New York–Paris Flight
    in May," 1; "René Fonck, Highest Scoring Allied Ace." cf: p. 45.

43 Such resentment seemed to continue: Barrett, "Was Fonck a Faker?" 80.

43 In June and July all seemed calm: "The Sikorsky Transatlantic Plane," 834–35;
    Hamlen, Flight Fever, 13; Norman F. Dacey, "A Biographical Sketch—Igor Ivan
    Sikorsky," Aeronautics, March 1930, 31–32.

43 Fonck did his part: Jablonski, Atlantic Fever, 78; letter, Hartney to Jones, Octo-
    ber 6, 1926; Jack Huttig, 1927: Summer of Eagles (Chicago: Nelson-Hall, 1980), 6.

44 Despite the calm, Hartney's patience wore thin: Letter, Hartney to Jones, Octo-
    ber 6, 1926.

44 it came too late to patch the divisions: Ibid.; Hamlen, Flight Fever, 13; Jablonski,
    Atlantic Fever, 78; "Col. Hartney Backs Berry," 1.

44 "The best thing for Capt. Berry to do is to keep quiet": "Col. Hartney Backs
    Berry," 1.

44 Soon others departed: Letter, Hartney to Jones, October 6, 1926; Jablonski, Atlan-
    tic Fever, 78.

45 "Fonck is irresponsible": Barrett, "Was Fonck a Faker?" 80.

45 Hartney's statement split the board down the middle: Letter, Hartney to Jones,
    October 6, 1926.

45 "Without the support of public opinion". "Transatlantic Flight Dissensions," New
    York Times, September 2, 1926.

45 "[T]he success of the flight is more important". Letter, Hartney to Jones, Octo-
    ber 6, 1926; Hamlen, Flight Fever, 15, "In Philadelphia," Time, Monday, Septem-
    ber 13, 1926, www.time.com.

45 During an August 30 test, the plane flew steadily. "Sikorsky Plane Tested," New
    York Times, August 30, 1926, Hamlen, Flight Fever, 15.

45 The next day, the plane was christened. "In Philadelphia," Hamlen, Flight Fe-
    ver, 15.

46 Around midnight on September 21, Igor Sikorsky: The account of the attempted
    takeoff and crash of S-35 comes from several sources: "Sikorsky Plane Crashes;
    Two Dead," Nassau Daily Review, September 21, 1926, 1; Hamlen, Flight Fever,
    16–20; Jablonski, Atlantic Fever, 79–84; Igor I. Sikorsky, The Story of the Winged-S:
    An Autobiography (New York: Dodd, Mead, 1958), 176–78; Barrett, "Was Fonck a
    Faker?" 80–82; Cochrane, Hardesty, and Lee, Aviation Careers, 86–92; Hell-
    man, "Winged S-11," 22; letter, Hartney to Jones, October 6, 1926; B. D. Foulois,
    Lt. Col., Commander of Mitchel Field, "Wreck of the Sikorsky S-35 Airplane,"
    report by Headquarters Mitchel Field and 9th Observation Group, Office of the
    Commanding Officer, Oct. 5, 1926, Sikorsky S-35 (Fonck 1926 Transatlantic
    Attempt) Documents, AS-400249-0, NASM Archives; Mosley, Lindbergh, 74–75;

"Cartwheel," *Time*, October 4, 1926, www.time.com; Paul Edward Garber, "Transatlantic Attempt Fails," *U.S. Air Services*, November 1926, 42–43; "Fonck Again Ready to Hop Off at Dawn," *New York Times*, September 21, 1926, 1; "Fonck Plane Burns; 2 Die at Start of Dawn Flight," *New York Times*, September 22, 1926, 1; "Experts Study Crash," *New York Times*, September 22, 1926, 4; "Airmen Cleared by Speedy Inquiry," *New York Times*, September 22, 1926, 1; "French Air Circles Grieved by Crash," *New York Times*, September 22, 1926, 4; Huttig, *1927*, 6–7.

53   The recriminations began immediately "Fonck Blames Aide Who Died in Crash," *New York Times*, September 23, 1926, 1.

53   Islamoff's was buried closer to where he died: "Cartwheel."

54   Sikorsky thought he himself was bankrupt: Sikorsky, *Story of the Winged-S*, 169–78; Hellman, "Winged S-11," 22.

THREE: "THIS HERO BUSINESS"

55   François Coli and Paul Tarascon. Paul Tarascon application, "Applications for the Raymond Orteig Prize," Orteig Collection; "Weekend Wings #18: The Struggle to Conquer the Atlantic," *Bayou Renaissance Man*, bayourenaissanceman.blogspot .com; "François Coli," Absolute Astronomy, www.absoluteastronomy.com; Robert de la Croix, *They Flew the Atlantic*, trans. Edward Fitzgerald (New York: Monarch, 1960 [1958]), 54, 61.

56   Four thousand miles to the west Mosley, *Lindbergh*, 76.

56   The moon reflected off a bend in the Illinois River: Lindbergh's decision to attempt the Orteig Prize comes from several sources· Lindbergh, *Spirit of St. Louis*, 11–15, 244; Berg, *Lindbergh*, 86–87, 92–93; Edmund T. Allen, "Flying Through Night and Fog," *Aviation* 27, no. 21 (November 21, 1927)· 1235.

58   On September 22, he wrote a letter of condolence. Letter, Sikorsky to Byrd, Oct. 2, 1926, Folder 4342, Box 115 "Transatlantic Flight," Byrd Polar Archives, Richard E. Byrd Collection, Ohio State University Libraries (hereafter "Byrd Collection").

58   "I'm looking for an aeroplane": Letter, Byrd to Sikorsky (misspelled "Zikosky"), Oct. 6, 1926, in Folder 4342, Box 115, "Transatlantic Flight," Byrd Collection.

58   Sikorsky did not waste time: Telegram, Sikorsky to Byrd, Oct. 11, 1926 Folder 4342, Box 115, "Transatlantic Flight," Byrd Collection; Letter, Sikorsky to Byrd, Oct. 23, 1926, Folder 4343, Box 115, "Transatlantic Flight," Byrd Collection.

59   "I am trying to buy a plane from you for a trans-atlantic flight": Letter, Byrd to Fokker, Oct. 11, 1926, Folder 4343, Box 115, "Transatlantic Flight," Byrd Collection.

59   a carefully crafted character or "personality"· Warren Susman, "Personality and the Making of Twentieth-Century Culture," www.h-net.org/~hst203/readings/ susman2, from Warren Susman, *Culture as History: The Transformation of American Society in the Twentieth Century* (New York: Pantheon, 1984), 271–85.

59   clad in the sheep-wool parka: "Outline of Film, Lt. Cdr. Byrd Flying in Northern Regions of the Arctic, 1925," n.d., File 4229, Box 13, "North Pole Flight," Byrd Collection.

59   In articles appearing in 1925 and 1926: Lisle A. Rose, *Explorer: The Life of Richard E. Byrd* (Columbia. University of Missouri Press, 2008), 109.

60   "Byrd is essentially a mystic": Charles J. V. Murphy, *Struggle: The Life and Exploits of Commander Richard E. Byrd* (New York. Frederick A. Stokes, 1928), 1.

60 "We must keep this up, Dick": Fitzhugh Green to Byrd, January 21, 1927, Folder 4343, Box 115, "Transatlantic Flight," Byrd Collection.

60 "He was very sensitive": Alden Hatch, *The Byrds of Virginia* (New York: Holt, Rinehart and Winston, 1969), 241–42.

60 "Wherever men live in contact". "Miscellaneous Thoughts," Numbers 193 and 95, an unpublished manuscript by Byrd dated May 22, 1950, Folder 3873, Box 92, Byrd Collection.

61 "I'll name this one". Pocahantas Wright Edmonds, *Virginians Out Front* (Richmond, Va.: Whitlet and Shepperson, 1972), 461; Rose, *Explorer*, 11–12.

62 "unshakeable conviction of self-worth": Ibid., 19.

62 Richard Byrd was raised in a violent family: Ibid., 12, 14; Murphy, *Struggle*, 25–26.

62 "I never expect to meet a man": Rose, *Explorer*, 12; Murphy, *Struggle*, 25.

63 "move and fly faster than the bird": Rose, *Explorer*, 16; Murphy, *Struggle*, 15.

63 "Danger was all that pleased him": Rose, *Explorer*, 15; Murphy, *Struggle*, 23.

63 On August 9, 1902, eleven weeks before his fourteenth birthday: Rose, *Explorer*, 16–17, 19; Murphy, *Struggle*, 30.

64 training in restlessness: Rose, *Explorer*, 16; Murphy, *Struggle*, 15.

64 Byrd was too restless to sit idle: Edmonds, *Virginians Out Front*, 467.

64 He desperately needed something: Rose, *Explorer*, 32.

65 Pensacola's influence: George F. Pearce, *The Navy in Pensacola: From Sailing Ships to Naval Aviation* (1825–1930) (Pensacola, Fla.: University of West Florida Books, 1980), 5, 122, 123, 127, 132.

66 the school's early seaplane trainers were man killers: Ibid., 131.

66 Lieutenant Byrd arrived in Pensacola: Ibid., 153, 155, 158, 161.

66 the planes had changed: "Admiral Byrd's Daughter Shares Her Memories of a Globe-Trotting Hero," *The Winchester Star*, November 19, 1993, A1; Pearce, *The Navy in Pensacola*, 157; Rose, *Explorer*, 35–36.

67 Clinicians in the budding field of aviation psychology: Harry G. Armstrong, M.D., "A Special Form of Functional Psychoneurosis Appearing in Airplane Pilots," *Journal of the American Medical Association* 106, no. 16 (April 18, 1936): 1348.

67 On July 30, 1921, he tried again: Byrd to Chief of Naval Operations, July 30, 1921, Folder 4343, Box 115, "Transatlantic Flight," Byrd Collection.

68 his chief opponent was Brigadier General William Mitchell: Rose, *Explorer*, 47; Edmonds, *Virginians Out Front*, 471.

68 When Mitchell pushed a bill before Congress: Edmonds, *Virginians Out Front*, 470; Ethan Mordden, *That Jazz! An Idiosyncratic Social History of the American Twenties* (New York: G. P. Putnam's Sons, 1978), 162–63.

69 His reach now extended· Memo, Byrd to Chief of Bureau of Navigation, March 26, 1925, Folder 4235, Box 113, "North Pole Flight," Byrd Collection.

FOUR: THE EXPLORER

70 the flight of the hot air balloon *Eagle*: David Roberts, *Great Exploration Hoaxes* (San Francisco: Sierra Club Books, 1982), 108; Richard Duncan, *Air Navigation and Meteorology* (Chicago: Goodheart-Willcox, 1929), 124.

71 Take Robert Peary, Byrd's personal hero: Barry Lopez, *Arctic Dreams: Imagination and Desire in a Northern Landscape* (New York: Bantam, 1987 [1986]), 345–46.

71 most suspicious of all was his mysterious burst of speed: Roberts, *Great Exploration Hoaxes*, 120–21.

72 Peary's face grew "long": Ibid., 124.

72 Crocker Land· "Aviation Pathfinders: Byrd and Bennett," www.century-of-flight .freeola.com, accessed March 17, 2010.

73 While Macmillan had substantial backing. Memo, Byrd to Chief of Bureau of Navigation, March 26, 1925, Letter, Byrd to Judge A. C. "Kit" Carson, March 31, 1925; and Letter, Byrd to Lt. Cmdr. Fitzhugh Green, April 10, 1925, Folder 4235, Box 113, "North Pole Flight," Byrd Collection.

73 A gloom fell over Byrd before the expedition began. Letter, David Rochford, American Legion of Massachusetts, to Byrd, June 16, 1925, File 4233, Box 113, "North Pole Flight," Byrd Collection; various household bills and letters, File 4235, Box 113, "North Pole Flight," Byrd Collection.

73 "Ederi": Typed pink note, "Ederi" to Byrd, n.d., 1925, File 4233, Box 113, "North Pole Flight," Byrd Collection.

74 it did not save the expedition. Edmonds, *Virginians Out Front*, 471–72; "Richard E. Byrd and the 1925 MacMillan Arctic Expedition," HistoryNet, www.history net.com; "Aviation Pathfinders Byrd and Bennett."

74 Warrant Officer Floyd Bennett: "Floyd Bennett," Wikipedia, en.wikipedia.org; Alice Booth, "Shall I Marry an Aviator?" *Good Housekeeping*, vol. 89, August 19, 1929, 80.

74 "[A]fter my first flight, I understood". Booth, "Shall I Marry," 80.

75 "Floyd, what shall I do?": Ibid., 81.

75 He wasn't much for words: Ibid., 179; Bernt Balchen, *Come North with Me* (New York: E. P. Dutton, 1958), 62.

75 They were flying over ice north of Greenland. Untitled manuscript about the MacMillan Expedition, n.d., Box 113, "North Pole Flight," File 4231, Byrd Collection.

76 Bennett was not home from Greenland a week. Booth, "Shall I Marry," 179.

76 Byrd made sure that he was in charge· Edmonds, *Virginians Out Front*, 472; Roberts, *Great Exploration Hoaxes*, 127; "Chantier, United States Shipping Board Emergency Fleet Corp., March 24, 1926," File 4256, Box 113, "North Pole Flight," Byrd Collection. Darrell V. Glines, *Bernt Balchen· Polar Aviator* (Washington, D.C.: Smithsonian Institute Press, 1999), 4.

76 Byrd thought he might use a dirigible. Raimund E. Goerler, ed., *To the Pole· The Diary and Notebook of Richard E. Byrd, 1925–1927* (Columbus: Ohio State University Press, 1998), 42–44; Byrd to J. Vincent Astor, January 13, 1926, File 4243, Box 113, "North Pole Flight," Byrd Polar Archives; "Statement Lt. Cdr. R. E. Byrd, Jan. 30, 1926," File 4256, Box 113, "North Pole Flight," Byrd Collection.

77 Spitzbergen, in Norway. Goerler, *To the Pole*, 45.

77 Yet Spitzbergen presented another challenge. Glines, *Bernt Balchen*, 4–5.

77 Lieutenant Bernt Balchen was quiet, athletic, blond, and wavy-haired: Ibid., 6–7, Goerler, *To the Pole*, 47.

78 Problems beset Byrd immediately. Glines, *Bernt Balchen*, 7–8; Goerler, *To the Pole*, 48–49.

78 Balchen saved Byrd's plane and his career: Byrd's flight and the controversy that followed come from these sources. Roberts, *Great Exploration Hoaxes*, 128–30; Cora Bennett, *Floyd Bennett* (New York William Farquhar Payson, 1932),

80–86; Glines, *Bernt Balchen*, 9–10; Goerler, *To the Pole*, 41–55; Raimund E. Goerler,"Richard E. Byrd and the North Pole Flight of 1926: Fact, Fiction as Fact, and Interpretation," an article submitted to the International Association of Aquatic and Marine Science Libraries and Information Centers, 24th Conference (Reykjavik, 1998), 363–76.

80 Two days later, on May 11, Amundsen's dirigible: Roberts, *Great Exploration Hoaxes*, 128.

80 Balchen suddenly found himself with plenty of spare time: Glines, *Bernt Balchen*, 10–11.

81 Yet amid the celebrations, Byrd glimpsed: Roberts, *Great Exploration Hoaxes*, 129; Byrd Polar Archives, "Polar Claim Questioned," May 9, 1996, *Los Angeles Times/Washington Post* News Service, Box 319, "Arctic Expedition, 1926," "Oversize Scrapbooks in Newspaper Account Series," Byrd Collection; no page or newspaper listed, though probably the *Los Angeles Times*. In 1996 the discovery of Byrd's flight diary in the Byrd Polar Archives revealed an erased, but still legible, sextant reading of the sun at 7:07:GCT of an apparent solar attitude of 19°25'30". Byrd's later typescript reports of his flight showed that his reading had been changed to 18°18'18", which put him at the Pole. On the basis of this and other data in the diary, astronomer-historian Dennis Rawlins, who had earlier debunked Peary's claims, concluded that Byrd had made it only 80 percent of the way to the Pole. Byrd erased the reading to falsify data and make it seem he had actually made it, Rawlins said. The public seems to accept Byrd's "duplicity," but not all experts agree. Lisle Rose, Byrd's most comprehensive biographer, believes that the disputed diary, the smoking gun in Rawlins's eyes, was actually a "scrap log," a kind of scratchpad kept by aviators in which they tried to figure out where they were in inexact and difficult conditions. Aviators and mariners had been keeping scrap logs since they first started trying to determine their location by the sun and the stars (Rose, *Explorer*, 133). Rose believes Byrd's claims, but Raimund E. Goerler, director of the Byrd Polar Research Center and the man who actually found the disputed diary, was not as sanguine as Rose. The issue of the Fokker's unexplained high speeds seems to bother him, as it did Balchen, several meteorologists, and possibly even Bennett himself (if one believes several later narratives by Balchen). In 1996 Goerler told a reporter in the just-mentioned newspaper account that he did not think Byrd had consciously lied when he said he made it to the Pole. However, added Goerler, Byrd "may well have realized after the expedition that he was short of the goal."

81 "the carping of foreigners made no difference". Quoted in Roberts, *Great Exploration Hoaxes*, 129.

82 "substantiate in every particular the claim of Commander Byrd": Gilbert Grosvenor, Frederick V. Coville, and Col. E. Lester Jones, "Report of the Special Committee Appointed by the Board of Trustees of the National Geographic Society to Examine the Records of Commander Byrd's Flight to the North Pole, May 9, 1926" (Washington, D.C.: National Geographic Society, June 28, 1926), File 4352, Box 113, "North Pole Flight," Byrd Collection.

82 "But do you think perhaps it would be better": Letter, Byrd to Dr. Isaiah Bowman, Nov. 24, 1926, File 4249, Box 113, "North Pole Flight," Byrd Collection.

82 "There is not the slightest doubt that you are wise": Letter, Bowman to Byrd, Nov. 29, 1926, File 4249, Box 113, "North Pole Flight," Byrd Collection.

83 "the first time in the history of journalism". "Notes and Comments," *The New Yorker*, May 27, 1926, 7.

83 The square-jawed, black-mustached Grover Whalen. Rose, *Explorer*, 144, 149; Alva Johnston, "The Gilded Copper," *The New Yorker*, January 12, 1929, 21.

83 It was the first of Byrd's three ticker tape parades. Rose, *Explorer*, 144–45; Johnston, "The Gilded Copper," 24.

83 "I believe aviation has pulled the teeth of the Arctic": Walsh, *Gentleman Jimmy Walker*, 78.

84 "Ukulele Dick": Ibid.

84 The next day, Whalen showed up again. Rose, *Explorer*, 150–51; *The New Wanamaker's· A Souvenir Guidebook of the Wanamaker Store in New York City* (1905?), Box 1: John Wanamaker (firm) John Wanamaker (firm) Collection, F128 T119100, New York Historical Society.

84 Balchen learned something else: Glines, *Bernt Balchen*, 28.

FIVE: "THE MOST SPECTACULAR RACE EVER HELD"

86 "He could make no announcement". "Byrd Hints at Flying Across the Atlantic," *New York Times*, October 29, 1926, 18.

87 George Palmer Putnam wrote a tribute: "Commander Byrd's Position," *New York Times*, Letters to the Editor, December 16, 1926, 26.

87 a new lecture called "The First North Pole Flight". "Screen Notes," *New York Times*, December 11, 1926, 14; "Lectures 1926–27". "Lt. Cdr. Byrd Flying in Northern Regions of the Arctic, 1926"; Letter, Byrd to H. W. August, editor of *The Times-Press*, Akron, Ohio, Feb. 18, 1927; Letter, Byrd to James P. Munroe, Twentieth-Century Club, March 23, 1927, Letter, Byrd to James Pond, March 18, 1927, File 490, Box 13, "North Pole Flight," Byrd Collection.

87 "My Grandmother Byrd, 87 years old". "Lectures". "Copy of Notes for Movie Lecture," File 491, Box 113, "North Pole Flight," Byrd Collection.

88 "the colored Methodist Episcopal Church in Ithaca, NY": Pond to Byrd, Oct. 9, 1926; Letter, Byrd to Pond, Oct. 10, 1926, File 491, Box 113, "North Pole Flight," Byrd Collection.

88 His notes included a segment entitled "Mess Attendants"· "Copy of Notes for Movie Lecture," File 491, Box 113, "North Pole Flight," Byrd Collection.

88 the Ku Klux Klan reached its political peak with 4.5 million members: Howard Zinn, *The Twentieth Century: A People's History* (New York: Harper and Row, 1980), 84.

88 there was a purpose to Byrd's seemingly gratuitous segment: Steven Loring Jones, "From 'Under Cork' to Overcoming: Black Images in Comics," www.ferris.edu/jimcrow/links/comics. Society columnist Cleveland Amory, who called Richard Byrd "perhaps the most pompous of all Twentieth Century Byrds," argued that Richard and his politician brother, Harry, were quite unsuccessful in hiding their prejudice, even from their brother Tom. Amory tells the story, in his *Who Killed Society?*, of a dinner at a friend's house, where Harry Byrd wished to compliment the cook. The black cook was summoned, and Harry asked his name "Byrd, sir," the cook replied. "'Byrd?' asked the Senator, surprised 'How do you spell it?' 'B-y-r-d,' spelled the cook." At this point, Tom Byrd broke in. "For a moment Tom said nothing, then, his eyes twinkling, he said, 'You are an excellent cook, Byrd,

and I want you to meet two very distinguished relations of yours—Senator Byrd and Admiral Byrd'" (Cleveland Amory, *Who Killed Society?* [New York. Harper and Bros., 1960], 286).

88   Byrd acknowledged the protests· Byrd, Richard, "Have Spectacular Flights Value?" uncorrected proof for the August 1926 issue of *World's Work* magazine, File 4238, Box 13, "North Pole Flight," Byrd Collection.

89   he personified the American faith in scientism. Thorstein Veblen's 1906 "The Place of Science in Modern Civilization" stated that in any large question which could affect mankind, "the final appeal is by common consent taken to the scientist," whose "answer is the only ultimately true one." He is quoted in Michael Adas, *Dominance by Design· Technological Imperatives and America's Civilizing Mission* (Cambridge, Mass Belknap, 2006), 203–207.

89   the *Josephine Ford* began a 7,000-mile cross-country tour: "Plan 7000-Mile Trip in Byrd Polar Plane," *New York Times,* October 1, 1926, 25.

89   Floyd Bennett piloted the three-engine Fokker. The tale of the *Josephine Ford's* cross-country tour comes from these sources: "Byrd Plane Ends Tour of Country," *The New York Times,* November 24, 1926, 3; "Floyd Bennett Pictures Aerial Lines of Future," *St. Louis Post-Dispatch,* November 14, 1926, n.p.; Balchen, *Come North with Me,* 62–67; Glines, *Bernt Balchen,* 31–33; Logbook October 7, 1926–November 23, 1926, File 3: "Logbooks, Josephine Ford (Airplane)," Box 4, Byrd Collection.

92   One company could do the job: Jablonski, *Atlantic Fever,* 87; Letter, Atlantic Aircraft Corporation to Byrd, Oct. 29, 1926, and Letter, Byrd to Wanamaker, Oct. 31, 1926, Folder 4343, Box 115, "Transatlantic Flight," Byrd Collection.

93   "Little Miss Ford rode to and from the North Pole": Jablonski, *Atlantic Fever,* 86–87.

93   "Uncle Tony" was uncouth. Anthony Fokker's biography can be found in several sources. Doree Smedley and Hollister Noble, "Flying Dutchman," *The New Yorker,* February 7, 1931, 20–21; Hamlen, *Flight Fever,* 36–40; Robert E. Martin, "Tony Fokker Captures America," *Popular Science Monthly* 119 (July 1931)· 38–39.

94   "total cost of the expedition": Letter, Byrd to Wanamaker, October 31, 1926, and Letter, Byrd to Wanamaker, December 28, 1926, Folder 4342, Box 115, "Transatlantic Flight," Byrd Collection.

95   "MR. W. FEARS COMMERCIALISM". Telegram, Grover Whalen to Byrd, Nov. 11, 1926, Folder 4342, Box 115, "Transatlantic Flight," Byrd Collection.

96   "Possibly the statements I made in my letters to you were too conservative": Letter, Byrd to Wanamaker, Nov. 16, 1926, Folder 4342, Box 115, "Transatlantic Flight," Byrd Collection.

96   "If we should buy the plane outright": Letter, Byrd to Whalen, Nov 16, 1926, Folder 4342, Box 115, "Transatlantic Flight," Byrd Collection.

96   Byrd knew who played adviser to the king· Telegrams: *Detroit News* to Byrd, January 13, 1927; Bennett to Byrd, January 14, 1927, Bennett to Byrd, Jan. 15, 1927; Bennett to Byrd, January 21, 1927, Folder 4342, Box 115, "Transatlantic Flight," Byrd Collection.

97   a $1 million life insurance policy: "15 Life Policies Each $4,000,000 or More," *New York Times,* February 21, 1927, 18; "Insurance Is Adapted to Our Complex Life," *New York Times,* March 20, 1927, Special Features, xx9.

97   "The Iron Lions of Bravery": Rodman Wanamaker, "The Iron Lions of Bravery: A

Message to the Citizens of New York City," (1923), and "Honor Rodman Wanamaker," *New York Times*, May 6, 1927, 23, Box 1, John Wanamaker (firm) Collection, F128T119100, New York Historical Society.

98   In an earlier day and place he would have been a merchant prince. "Rodman Wanamaker," Wikipedia, en.wikipedia.org; "A Salute to Rodman Wanamaker, 1863–1928," *Friends of the Wanamaker Organ at Macy's, Philadelphia*, wanamakerorgan .com; Joseph H. Appel, *The Business Biography of John Wanamaker, Founder and Builder* (New York: Macmillan, 1930), 160–76.

98   John Wanamaker, the "Founder": Appel, *Business Biography of John Wanamaker*, 126–29; John N. Ingham, "Wanamaker, John," *Biographical Dictionary of American Business Leaders, V–Z* (Westport, Conn.: Greenwood, 1983), 1543–47.

98   More than anything, Rodman resented the way that time had forgotten him. Interview, Ray Biswanger, executive director, Friends of the Wanamaker Organ, August 12, 2009; "New York Police Department Takes Pioneer Step Creating Aviation Section," *Aerial Age Weekly* 8 (Dec. 9, 1918). 654–55; Joshua Stoff, *Historic Aircraft and Spacecraft of the Cradle of Aviation Museum* (Toronto: General Publishing, Ltd., 2001), 8.

99   In February 1914 Wanamaker had proposed. Alan Wykes, *Air Atlantic: A History of Civil and Military Transatlantic Flying* (New York David White, 1968), 28; Appel, *Business Biography of John Wanamaker*, 162–64; Alden Hatch, *Glenn Curtiss: Pioneer of Aviation* (Guilford, Conn.. Globe Pequot, 1942), 235; "Untitled note on the *America*," *Scientific American*, June 27, 1914, 518, Wanamaker, Rodman Documents, CW-131000-01, NASM Archives.

99   "I have been planning a transatlantic flight since some time before 1914": "Wanamaker Hopes to Link Continents," *New York Times*, April 10, 1927, 25.

99   Lindbergh once again bailed out of his plane: Berg, *Lindbergh*, 89, 93; Davis, *The Hero*, 132–33; John Lardner, "The Lindbergh Legends," in Isabel Leighton, ed., *The Aspirin Age, 1919–1941* (New York: Simon and Schuster, 1949), 98.

101 the "New Woman". Allen, *Big Change*, 134–35.

101 "The word jazz in its progress". F. Scott Fitzgerald, "Echoes of the Jazz Age," *Scribner's Magazine* 90, no. 5 (November 1931): 459–65, quoted in Loren Baritz, ed., *The Culture of the Twenties* (Indianapolis: Bobbs-Merrill, 1970), 416, 419.

101 "the most expensive orgy in history": Ibid., 422.

101 The New Year would prove to be one of technical wonders: Kathleen Drowne and Patrick Huber, *The 1920s* (Westport, Conn.. Greenwood, 2004), xxiii–xxiv; David E. Kyvig, *Daily Life in the United States, 1920–1940: How Americans Lived Through the Roaring Twenties and the Great Depression* (Chicago: Ivan R. Dee, 2002), 83–84.

102 It would be a "year of wonders" especially for aviation: Drowne and Huber, *The 1920s*, 266; Charles Harvard Gibbs-Smith, *Aviation: An Historical Survey, from Its Origins to the End of World War II* (London: Her Majesty's Stationery Office, 1970), 182, 184, 192–93; Stephen L. McFarland, "Higher, Faster, and Farther: Fueling the Aeronautical Revolution, 1919–1945," in Roger D. Launius, ed., *Innovation and the Development of Flight* (College Station, Texas: Texas A&M University Press, 1999), 104–105.

102 Yet the most heralded improvement Gibbs-Smith, *Aviation*, 185, 193; Wright Aeronautical Corp., "Wright Air Cooled Aviation Engines, 'Whirlwind' Series"

(Patterson, N.J., 1926 or 1927), 2, Wright Whirlwind J-5 9-cyl Radial, Documents, BW-730580-01, NASM Archives; "Motor Feats Recorded," *New York Times*, December 20, 1926, 39.

103 the tiny Lawrance Aero-Engine Corporation of New York City: "History and Development of Wright Whirlwind," *The Slipstream* 8, no. 8 (August 1927) 10; Foster Ware, "Deus Ex Machina," *The New Yorker*, August 13, 1927, 18; Robert van der Linden, *The Boeing 247: The First Modern Airliner* (Seattle. University of Washington Press, 1991), 11–12.

103 this cornucopia of new inventions and their cheap production Drowne and Huber, *The 1920s*, 51–54, 59, 292–94; Merle Curti, *The Growth of American Thought* (New York: Harper and Bros., 1943), 697–704.

104 A new mantra: "The Roaring Twenties," www.sagehistory.net/twenties, "Euphoria Reigned in '27 Market," *Wall Street Journal* 227, no. 49, March 11, 1996, C1; Allen, *Big Change*, 140–42.

104 By 1927 the average man: "The Average Man," *Literary Digest* 93, no. 9 (May 28, 1927): 21–22.

104 "like a nervous beating of the feet". Fitzgerald, "Echoes of the Jazz Age," 421.

105 What could cause such darkness: John W. Ward, "The Meaning of Lindbergh's Flight," *American Quarterly* 10, no. 1 (1958) 6.

105 "That something is wrong with marriage today": Popenoe is quoted in Jill Lepore, "Fixed," *The New Yorker*, March 29, 2010, 95.

105 "What a civilization this is!": Reinhold Neibuhr, *Leaves from the Notebook of a Tamed Cynic* (New York: Richard R. South, 1930), 134, 143, 154–55.

105 *Buck v. Bell*: Lepore, "Fixed," 95; "Halt the Imbecile's Perilous Line," *The Literary Digest* 93, no. 8 (May 21, 1927): 11. The case concerned the forced tubal ligation of Connie Buck, a twenty-one-year-old inmate at the Virginia State Colony for the Feeble-Minded. As measured by intelligence tests of the time, Buck, her mother, and Buck's child born out of wedlock were all deemed "feeble-minded," a trait associated with "moral degeneracy." "Three generations of imbeciles are enough," wrote Justice Oliver Wendell Holmes Jr. for the 8-to-1 majority.

106 "something bright and alien flashed across the sky" Fitzgerald, "Echoes of the Jazz Age," 421.

106 "adjust and adorn": Plutarch's *Parallel Lives* is quoted in Tyler Cowen, *What Price Fame?* (Cambridge, Mass.: Harvard University Press, 2000), 46; Daniel J. Boorstin, *The Image, or What Happened to the American Dream* (New York. Atheneum, 1962), 57, 59, 61; "The Faustian Bargain," *The Economist* 344, no. 8033 (September 6, 1997).

106 information hunger: Boorstin, *The Image*, 38.

107 The rise of other media. Ibid.

107 Walter Winchell, the great gossip columnist: Neal Gabler, "Celebrity: The Greatest Show on Earth," *Newsweek*, Dec. 21, 2009, 65.

107 a stab at defining the American hero: Orrin E. Klapp, "The Creation of Popular Heroes," *American Journal of Sociology* 54, no. 2 (September 1948): 133; Boorstin, *The Image*, 51; Richard M. Huber, *The American Idea of Success* (New York: McGraw-Hill, 1971), 100, Joseph Campbell, *The Hero with a Thousand Faces* (Princeton, N.J. Princeton University Press, 1973 [1949]), 391.

108 "Year of the Big Shriek" Herbert Asbury, "The Year of the Big Shriek," in *Mirrors of the Year. A National Revue of the Outstanding Figures, Trends, and Events of*

1927–8, ed. Horace Winston Stokes (New York. Frederick A. Stokes, 1928), 196, 198, 202–203.

108   On Friday, January 30, 1925, the spelunker Floyd Collins: Mordden, *That Jazz!*, 196–99; Gary Alan Fine and Ryan D. White, "Creating Collective Attention in the Public Domain· Human Interest Narratives and the Rescue of Floyd Collins," *Social Forces* 81, no. 1 (September 2002): 62–63, 65–66, 68–70, 71, 73, 74.

110   "The hallmark of the American journalist": de Tocqueville, *Democracy in America*, 185.

110   "I was shadowed": Jablonski, *Atlantic Fever*, 87.

110   The story ran on March 1: "Mail Pilot Files Entry for Paris Flight, C. A. Lindbergh Will Fly a Ryan Monoplane," *New York Times*, March 1, 1927, 16.

111   On March 3, Byrd did as expected. "Flight to Paris Lures Noted Pilots of the Air," *New York Times*, March 20, 1927, Special Features, xx5; Richard Montague, *Oceans, Poles and Airmen. The First Flights over Wide Waters and Desolate Ice* (New York: Random House, 1971), 36.

111   Nungesser was easily the most glamorous. Interview, William Nungesser, September 19, 2009; source material from William Nungesser Private Collection.

112   what started out as René Fonck's one-man exhibition: "Davis to Join Byrd in Non-Stop Flight," *New York Times*, February 10, 1927, 2, "Crack Navy Pilots to Man Both Planes," *New York Times*, April 10, 1927, 1; "Flight to Paris Lures Noted Pilots of the Air," *New York Times*, March 20, 1927, Special Features, xx5; Montague, *Oceans, Poles and Airmen*, 63

SIX: THE FARM BOY

113   Douglas G. Corrigan walked onto the landing field. Douglas Corrigan, *That's My Story* (New York. E.P. Dutton, 1938), 87–89.

114   "Fame—Opportunity—Wealth": Anne Morrow Lindbergh, unpublished diary, January 25, 1953, quoted in Berg, *Lindbergh*, 5; Brendan Gill, *Lindbergh Alone* (New York: Harcourt Brace Jovanovich, 1977), Berg, *Lindbergh*, 6, 75, Dixon Wecter, *The Hero in America. A Chronicle of Hero Worship* (New York: Charles Scribners' Sons, 1941), quoted in Harold Lubin, ed., *Heroes and Anti-Heroes* (San Francisco: Chandler, 1968), 75.

115   "By the mechanics of hero worship"· Wecter, *Hero in America*, 75.

115   "Lindbergh was a commonplace person". Boorstin, *The Image*, 66–67.

115   "uncommonly sensible": Brian Horrigan, "'My Own Mind and Pen'· Charles Lindbergh, Autobiography, and Memory," *Minnesota History* 58, no. 1 (Spring 2002): 3.

115   He was a determinist· Berg, *Lindbergh*, 8.

116   "financial malfeasance, flight from justice". Ibid., 27.

116   "I don't like this flying business": Lardner, "Lindbergh Legends," 194–196.

116   when Charles was four, his father ran for Congress. Berg, *Lindbergh*, 41–42.

117   "That farm was one of the most important things in my life". Ibid., 33–34.

117   It was also the first place where he ever saw an airplane. Ibid., 34.

117   he developed his daredevil ways: Davis, *The Hero*, 26–27.

117   One was a horror of heights· Ibid., 26–27.

117   In 1915 C.A. helped found the Minnesota Farmer–Labor Party: Lardner, "Lindbergh Legends," 195; Walter W. Liggett, "The Lindbergh Who Was Almost Lynched," *Common Sense*, March 30, 1933, 10–11.

NOTES 435

118 a certain sternness was required: Davis, *The Hero*, 41; Lardner, "Lindbergh Legends," 195–96.
118 sometimes took C.A. up with him· Berg, *Lindbergh*, 71–72.
118 "I could see he was deeply moved": Lardner, "Lindbergh Legends," 196.
118 "stifled anger and sadness". Berg, *Lindbergh*, 77.
119 Lindbergh carried out one final promise Lardner, "Lindbergh Legends," 196.
119 "This sure is a great life". Berg, *Lindbergh*, 67; Randy Enshaw, "Barnstorming with Lindbergh," *Popular Science Monthly* 115, no. 4 (October 1929): 20.
120 The Jenny was a patchwork plane Paul O'Neil, *Barnstormers and Speed Kings* (Alexandria, Va.: Time-Life Books, 1981), part of the Time-Life series *The Epic of Flight*, 28–29.
120 A good barnstormer learned to read the signs: Ibid., 29; Robert J Hunter, M.D., "Cultivating the Balance Sense: A Prelude to Cloud Flying," a lecture given before the College of Physicians, Philadelphia, May 21, 1919, Folder 27, Box 88, Charles A. Lindbergh Collection, Missouri Historical Society, Columbia, Mo. (hereafter "C.A.L. Collection").
120 "It's a sociable place, under a wing": Lindbergh is quoted in Berg, *Lindbergh*, 67.
120 his infamous practical joking Enshaw, "Barnstorming with Lindbergh," 19–20.
121 Another oddity had to do with girls: Berg, *Lindbergh*, 192–93; Enshaw, "Barnstorming with Lindbergh," 20.
121 he was approached by talent scouts at Pathé: "Lost Star," *The New Yorker*, May 4, 1929, 17.
121 Lindbergh was apparently thinking of his future: Lardner, "Lindbergh Legends," 198; Berg, *Lindbergh*, 79
121 A mail pilot had to fly by night: Lardner, "Lindbergh Legends," 198; Allen, "Flying Through Fog and Night," 1234–35, "Lindbergh's Leap of Faith," *The Literary Digest*, 93, no. 10 (June 4, 1927). 7.
122 he made some lists: "Chas. Lindbergh, 2 handwritten pages of lists and 'propaganda,' ca. 1927," Folder 6, Box 11, C.A.L. Collection.
122 In some ways, his plan was vague: Joyce Milton, *Loss of Eden· A Biography of Charles and Anne Morrow Lindbergh* (New York: HarperCollins, 1993), 101.
122 He started with Earl Thompson: Lardner, "Lindbergh Legends," 199; Berg, *Lindbergh*, 93–95; Mosley, *Lindbergh*, 75–76.
123 One day that fall a Fokker representative. Lindbergh, *Spirit of St. Louis*, 28–29.
123 Lindbergh was floored: Ibid., 29.
123 What Lindbergh really wanted was a single-engine: Berg, *Lindbergh*, 54; Lindbergh, *Spirit of St. Louis*, 51–52.
123 Lindbergh visited Bellanca the next day: Lindbergh, *Spirit of St. Louis*, 53.
124 Like Sikorsky and Fokker, Bellanca was an immigrant: Leon Kelley, "Main Roads of Aviation," first draft ms., n.d., 2 File 3, Box 43, Giuseppe M. Bellanca Collection, National Air and Space Museum, Washington D.C. (hereafter Giuseppe M. Bellanca Collection).; William Weimar, "Wings Over America," *The New Yorker*, March 30, 1929, 22, 25, Giuseppe Lucrezio Monticelli, "Italian Emigration: Basic Characteristics and Trends with Special Reference to the Last Twenty Years," *International Migration Review* 1, no. 3 (Summer 1967): 11; "Biographical and Historical Notes" Giuseppe M. Bellanca Collection; "The Bellanca CF 5-Seater Cabin Airplane," *Aviation*, August 14, 1922, 183; Roscoe Deering, "Giuseppe Bellanca's Better Built Airplanes," unattributed magazine article, 51, File 2 Box 43,

Giuseppe M. Bellanca Collection; Letters Dorothy Brown to Bellanca, undated; Bellanca to Dorothy Brown, undated; Dorothy Brown to Bellanca, Feb. 8, 1921, File 3, "Personal Correspondence Between G. M. Bellanca and Dorothy Brown," Box 128, "Personal Correspondence," Giuseppe M. Bellanca Collection.

126 After Omaha, Bellanca designed wings: "Biographical and Historical Notes," Giuseppe M. Bellanca Collection.

126 The fates of the plane and of Bellanca were both in limbo. Lindbergh, *Spirit of St. Louis*, 53–54.

126 In December, Bellanca wired him that the WB-2: Berg, *Lindbergh*, 93–96, Milton, *Loss of Eden*, 103.

127 Knight looked at Lindbergh and felt sorry for him: Mosley, *Lindbergh*, 74.

127 Lindbergh hinted to his mother in Detroit: Berg, *Lindbergh*, 94–95.

127 "The experiences you are having seem very hard ones". Letter, Evangeline Lindbergh to Charles Lindbergh, Jan. 20, 1927, Folder 6A: "Personal Correspondence, Letters from Mother (1927 Jan. 17–May 18)," Box 11, "Correspondence, Transatlantic Flight," C.A.L. Collection.

127 "It will take a very trust-worthy plane". Letters: Evangeline to Charles, Jan. 31, 1927; Feb. 2, 1927; and Feb. 3, 1927, in Folder 6A, "Personal Correspondence, Letters from Mother (1927 Jan. 17–May 18)," Box 11, "Correspondence, Transatlantic Flight," C.A.L. Correspondence.

128 Giuseppe Bellanca wired with good news: Berg, *Lindbergh*, 96; Clarence D. Chamberlin, *Record Flights* (New York: Dorrance, 1928), 16.

128 No one would be more reviled. *Time*, October 31, 1927, www.time.com; Venlo Wolfsohn and Booton Herndon, "The Man Who Was Almost Lindbergh," *True*, May 1963, 57; Mordden, *That Jazz!*, 239; "Uncle Sam's Second Flying Hop Across the Pond," *The Literary Digest* (June 25, 1927). 41; "Levine Denies Rumor That He'll Forsake Judaism," *Brooklyn Daily Eagle*, November 25, 1927; *Time*, Oct. 24, 1927, www.time.com.

128 He did have supporters, but they were ignored: "Levine Nerviest Man He Ever Met," *Brooklyn Daily Eagle*, September 18, 1927; "Uncle Sam's Second Flying Hop Across the Pond," *The Literary Digest*, June 25, 1927, 41.

129 It was an anti-Semitic time: Henry Ford is quoted in Michael Alexander, *Jazz Age Jews* (Princeton, N.J.: Princeton University Press, 2001), 52, Eleanor Roosevelt is quoted on page 8.

129 Jews by the thousands were migrating. Harold W. Ribolaw, *Autobiographies of American Jews* (Philadelphia: Jewish Publication Society of America, 1973), 304–305.

130 tension between father and son: Hamlen, *Flight Fever*, 52–53; "Levine Keen on Thrills," *Brooklyn Daily Eagle*, June 5, 1927; "Levine Got Start as Aviation Worker," *New York Times*, June 5, 1927, 3; Levine, Charles A., Documents, CL-418000-01, NASM Archives; "Levine Got Started as Aviation Worker," 3.

131 The first time was on February 10: Berg, *Lindbergh*, 96; Lindbergh, *Spirit of St. Louis*, 72–73.

131 The second meeting occurs six days later: Lindbergh, *Spirit of St. Louis*, 75–76.

132 How much can we trust Lindbergh's version?: Berg, *Lindbergh*, 427; Neal Baldwin, *Henry Ford and the Jews· The Mass Production of Hate* (New York. Public Affairs, 2001), 288–89.

133 On January 20, 1927, she quotes a joke· Letter, Evangeline Lindbergh to Charles

Lindbergh, January 20, 1927, and letter, Evangeline Lindbergh to Charles Lindbergh, Jan. 31, 1927, Folder 69, "Personal Correspondence," Box 11, "Transatlantic Flight," C.A.L. Collection.

133 Lindbergh got down to business with the owner: Ev Cassagneres, *The Spirit of Ryan* (Blue Ridge Summit, Pa.: Tab, 1982), 43–44; Berg, *Lindbergh*, 98; Nick T. Spark, "Charles Lindbergh, Donald Hall, and the Plane That Made History," *American Aviation Historical Society Journal* 50, no. 2 (2005): 133.

134 Lindbergh liked Hall almost immediately: Spark, "Charles Lindbergh," 134.

134 They drove in Hall's Buick to the public library: Spark, "Charles Lindbergh," 134; Lindbergh, *Spirit of St. Louis*, 86–89; Berg, *Lindbergh*, 98–99.

135 A wave of relief seemed to wash over Lindbergh: Lindbergh, *Spirit of St. Louis*, 86; Berg, *Lindbergh*, 99.

135 She slept on the fact that her son had entered: Evangeline Lindbergh to Charles Lindbergh, March 4, 1927, Folder 6a, "Personal Correspondence, Letters from Mother (1927 Jan. 17–May 18)" Box 11, "Correspondence, Transatlantic Flight," C.A.L. Collection.

SEVEN: THE COWBOY

136 "A few years ago, we had 70 percent": "Noel Davis to Try New York–Paris Hop for Legion in June," *New York Times*, March 14, 1927, 1.

137 "an instinct for the key to a difficult situation": "Davis, Ocean Flier, Began as a Cowboy," *New York Times*, April 17, 1927, 1.

137 He was the most educated flier in the race: Ibid.; "Noel Davis," www.stjohns historiccemetery.com/pensacolas_heritages/naval_heritage.htm.

138 his chosen plane for the oceanic hop: "Davis, Ocean Flier," 1.

138 "On paper, at least": Ibid.

139 "The Mormons were never, in their church organization": Wallace Stegner, *Mormon Country* (Lincoln: University of Nebraska Press, 1970; first published 1942), 94.

139 Saints and Gentiles: Ibid., 282.

139 Davis seemed to hail from a family given to wanderlust: "Ogdenite was Boyhood Chum of Noel Davis," Ogden *Standard-Examiner*, April 26, 1927, 1; "Dead Fliers Ranked High in Air Service," *New York Times*, April 27, 1927, 13.

140 Davis was a Mormon, "though not a very good one": Phone interview with author, Noel Guy Davis Jr., July 8, 2010; Stegner, *Mormon Country*, 21–23.

140 He attended school when he could: Hamlen, *Flight Fever*, 22; "Davis, Ocean Flier," 1.

140 the Colt revolver, barbed wire: Wallace Stegner, *The American West as Living Space* (Ann Arbor: University of Michigan Press, 1987), 9.

140 Six applicants competed. "Six Applicants for Annapolis Cadetship," *Salt Lake Herald*, February 27, 1910, 17; "Davis, Ocean Flier," 1.

141 There were seven sections: "Davis, Ocean Flier," 1; "Going to Annapolis," *Deseret Evening News*, May 27, 1910, 12; "Eighty Graduates Receive Diplomas at L.D.S. High," *Salt Lake Telegram*, May 27, 1910, 2; "Noel Davis Surprised by Getting Life Job," *Salt Lake Herald*, May 27, 1910, 11.

141 Davis joked that he'd meant to go to Indianapolis: "Noel Davis"; "Davis, Ocean Flier," 1.

141 Instead, a measure of respect found him. "USS Illinois (BB-7)," Wikipedia, en.wikipedia.org; "Davis, Ocean Flier," 1; Kevin R Burns, *Noel Davis· The Father of the Naval Air Reserve* (American Institute of Aeronautics and Astronautics, 2008), a booklet prepared for the Forty-sixth Aerospace Sciences Meeting, January 2008, Reno, Nevada, 5, 11.

141 He called it luck: "Davis, Ocean Flier," 1.

142 Strauss took Davis to Great Britain: Noel Davis, "The Removal of the North Sea Mine Barrage," *National Geographic Magazine* 37, no. 2 (February 1920). 103–105.

142 One particularly perilous type of mine vexed him: "Davis, Ocean Flier," 1; "Utah Plane Victim Won Fame by his Mine Laying Exploits in World War," Ogden *Standard-Examiner*, April 26, 1927, 1, "Trophy Is Memorial to Early Aviator," *Navy Times*, April 25, 1977, 35; "Lt. Cdr. Noel Davis, USNR," "Davis, Noel (CDR) Documents". CD-075000-01, NASM Archives.

144 "You always had to take whatever he said with a grain of salt": Phone interview with author, Noel Davis Jr., July 8, 2010.

144 After earning his wings· Burns, Noel Davis; "Noel Davis", T. C. Lonquest, "Operation and Adjustment of the Davis-Radford Octant," Bureau of Aeronautics Technical Note, no. 178, February 6, 1928, 1–13; Lonquest, "Operation and Adjustment of the Mark II Model 2 Octant," Bureau of Aeronautics Technical Note, no. 207, November 22, 1929, 1–8.

144 He started haltingly, as had Lindbergh. Hamlen, *Flight Fever*, 23.

144 he met a like-minded ally: Burns, *Noel Davis*, 16; Suzanne K. Jones, phone interview with author, July 6, 2010; "Aircraft Propellor Blades—Request for application for United States Patent," July 29, 1923, CW-900500-01, Wooster, Stanton Hall—Documents, NASM Archives.

145 Wooster epitomized the kind of free spirit. Hamlen, *Flight Fever*, 23–24; "Dead Fliers Ranked High in Air Service," *New York Times*, April 27, 1927, 13. Suzanne K. Jones, phone interview with author, July 6, 2010; "Unfavorable Reports on Fitness, Ensign Stanton H. Wooster, U.S. Navy," December 15, 1920, CW-900500-01, Wooster, Stanton Hall—Documents. Suzanne Jones's mother, Helen Virginia Wooster Lewis Kemp, was Wooster's half sister. Wooster died when Helen Kemp was ten. Wooster's mother died sometime after he entered Yale; his father remarried after that and eventually moved to Tennessee.

145 Wooster appears to have quickly gained a reputation as a swashbuckler: Suzanne K. Jones, phone interview with author, quoting a family genealogy, July 6, 2010.

146 "in a general way something about what has been going on": "Dinner to Capt. Fonck is Given by Orteig," *New York Times*, May 5, 1926, 34; Letter, Byrd to Davis, January 1, 1927, Folder 4343, Box 115, "Transatlantic Flight," Byrd Collection.

146 Davis wrote his friend Lieutenant Bill Curtin Burns, *Noel Davis*, 22. Burns often quotes from the "Davis family archive," a collection of Noel Davis's journals and personal correspondence held by the Davis family.

146 He first attempted to buy a Fokker trimotor: Ibid., 21–22.

147 Major General Mason M. Patrick, chief of the Army Air Services. Hamlen, *Flight Fever*, 24.

147 Patrick promised secrecy. Ibid., 24–25.

147 Huff-Daland was a new company. Frank Kingston Smith and James P. Harrington, *Aviation and Pennsylvania* (Philadelphia, Pa : Franklin Institute Press, 1981), 115–16; Hamlen, *Flight Fever*, 24.

147 Davis got his plane, but he still needed backers: Burns, *Noel Davis*, 23–24; "Davis to Carry 20,000 Postcards," *New York Herald*, April 21, 1927, 3.

148 When Davis filed his Orteig Prize application. "Applications for the Raymond Orteig Prize," Orteig Collection, "Noel Davis to Try New York–Paris Hop," 1.

148 Davis's plane was big· Ibid., 1; *The Orteig Prize*, Collection of Suzanne K. Jones. This unlabelled film includes what seems to be an internal newsreel produced by Keystone Aircraft, possibly for promotion and sales. It shows the massive factory at Bristol and the plane taking shape inside.

148 The plane stretched: Smith and Harrington, *Aviation and Pennsylvania*, 116–17; "Davis Reveals New Features of Plane in Which He Will Attempt Non-Stop Flight to Paris," *New York Times*, March 24, 1927, 12; Hamlen, *Flight Fever*, 25–26; *The Orteig Prize*; "The Transatlantic Plane 'American Legion,'" *Aero Digest*, May 1927, 428.

149 "the *American Legion* may be the first": "Davis Plane in Test Flight," *New York Times*, April 10, 1927, 1.

149 It was a gray, cloudy day: Ibid.

150 "The plane handles beautifully": Ibid.

150 Davis pressed his advantage: "Crowds Cheer Take-Off," *New York Times*, April 11, 1927, 3; "Davis's Tests Stir Interest in Flight," *New York Times*, April 11, 1927, 3; "Fliers in Both Airplanes Will Report to the New York Times," *New York Times*, April 10, 1927, 1, Burns, *Noel Davis*, 25.

150 The *American Legion* flew the 160 miles: "Davis Is Delighted as His Ocean Plane Speeds 160 Miles," *New York Times*, April 11, 1927, 1; "Inspect Davis's Plane," *New York Times*, April 12, 29; Burns, *Noel Davis*, 25; "Noel Davis to Try New York–Paris Hop," 1.

151 the *American Legion* took off from Langley: "Davis's Big Plane Flies from Virginia," *New York Times*, April 17, 1927, 1; Noel Guy Davis Jr., phone interview with author, July 8, 2010. Davis was a flier like his father, and has collected all he could find about the crash and his father's life and career. Although he was only one year old during the events of 1927, his mother told him the story through the years.

EIGHT: THE PROFESSIONALS

153 A lively debate raged: Clarence D. Chamberlin, *Record Flights* (New York: Dorrance, 1928), 19; Robert R. Osborn, "Side Slips," *Aviation* 22, no. 17 (April 25, 1927): 858.

154 The steel *Columbia* rose with ease: Chamberlin, *Record Flights*, 19.

154 The world record the two hoped to beat Ibid.; "MacReady Is Elated," *New York Times*, April 15, 1927, 2; "French Admire Flight, But Want Record Back," *New York Times*, April 15, 1927, 1.

154 Macready sympathized with the pilots: "MacReady Is Elated," 2.

154 "a flier discovers whether he is running a ship": Randy Enslow, "How I Fly My Plane," *Popular Science Monthly*, December 1929, 46.

155 Dead stick landings called up every ounce: "Fliers Set New Record of 51 Hours in Air," *New York Times*, April 15, 1927, 1; Assen Jordanoff, "Meeting Emergencies in the Air," *Popular Science Monthly*, February 1930, 48.

155 the mental checklist· Hamlen, *Flight Fever*, 73; Chamberlin, *Record Flights*, 19; "Fliers Set New Record," 1; Jordanoff, "Meeting Emergencies," 48.

155 Cockpits were often tight, but the *Columbia*: Hamlen, "Flight Fever," 73; Chamberlin, *Record Flights*, 19–20.

156 The first day proved to be a dreary, bumpy ride: The account of the first day of the endurance flight comes from several sources: Hamlen, *Flight Fever*, 73–74; Chamberlin, *Record Flights*, 19–21; "Plane Up 42½ Hours Breaks U.S. Record and Keeps at Wind," *New York Times*, April 14, 1927, 1; "Fliers Set New Record of 51 Hours in Air," *New York Times*, April 15, 1927, 1; "Bellanca Monoplane Sets World Endurance Record," *Aviation*, April 25, 1927, 819–21.

158 Levine's search for an edge. Chamberlin, *Record Flights*, 16–18; "Fliers Set New Record of 51 Hours in Air," *New York Times*, April 15, 1927, 1; Hamlen, *Flight Fever*, 49, 58–59; Letter, Bellanca to Chamberlin, January 14, 1921, and Letter, E. A. Noblitt to Bellanca, April 2, 1921, Folder 5, "Correspondence 1921," Box 3, Giuseppe M. Bellanca Collection. Both letters show that by 1921, Bellanca and Chamberlin were a team: Bellanca designed his airplanes, and Chamberlin tested them. In 1921 this was more of an informal relationship, but it is also obvious that they had begun what would be a lifelong friendship.

158 he signed the thirty-year-old Leigh Wade· Chamberlin, *Record Flights*, 18; "Leigh Wade, Major General, United States Air Force," Arlington National Cemetery website, www.arlingtoncemetery.net/wleigh.htm.

158 On April 8, Wade "withdrew": Chamberlin, *Record Flights*, 18; "Wade Quits, Calls Paris Hop Untimely," *New York Times*, April 9, 1927, 21.

158 Thus began a theme· Chamberlin, *Record Flights*, 18–19; "Wade Quits," 21.

159 The *Columbia* was not that different in design from Bellanca's: Hamlen, *Flight Fever*, 50–51, "Bellanca Monoplane Sets World Endurance Record," *Aviation*, April 25, 1927, 819–21; "The Bellanca Monoplane—Holder of the World Endurance Record," *Aviation*, May 2, 1927, 908–10.

159 Chamberlin's career as a pilot: Chamberlin, *Record Flights*, 210; Iowa Aeronautics Commission, "Clarence D. Chamberlin, Denison, Iowa," Iowa Historical Society, 2. This is apparently a rough draft for a history of aviation in Iowa commissioned in the 1960s by the state aviation group.

160 His closest brush with death came in 1925: Chamberlin, *Record Flights*, 269–71.

160 "A man never got over a bad crack-up": Ibid., 271–72.

160 Chamberlin attributed such behavior to midwestern stubbornness: Ibid., 272, 183–85; "Denison, Iowa," Wikipedia, en.wikipedia.org. The population count was taken from the 1900 census.

161 Clarence's love of mechanics grew on him. "Clarence Chamberlin," unattributed source that appears to be a city history, Denison Public Library Archives, 126, 137, 138, 141, 163, 169; "Northwest Iowa Boy in Velvet Now, But Lived on Hamburger Not So Many Long Years Past," *Sioux City Index*, n.d.; Chamberlin, *Record Flights*, 187.

161 It was while driving Taber on a cross-country trip: Ibid., 188–89.

161 In 1917 he enlisted in the aviation section: "Clarence Chamberlin, 83, Pioneer in Ocean Flying," n.d. (no attribution but probably *New York Times*), Chamberlin, Clarence D., Documents, CC-196000-01, NASM Archives; Dick Totten, "Col. Clarence D. Chamberlin, Aviation Pioneer," n.d., unknown publication; Letter, Chamberlin to parents, June 12, 1918, "Clarence Chamberlin," Iowa Historical Society.

162 Flying changed him: Russell Owen, "The Dragon Hunters," *The New Yorker*, May 21, 1927, 34.

162 "Oh hell, war over". "Northwest Iowa Boy in Velvet Now."

162 But cleaning watches proved too tame: Chamberlin, *Record Flights*, 209.

162 "Colonel Hubert Fauntleroy Julian, M.D.": Morris Markey, "The Black Eagle—I," *The New Yorker*, July 11, 1931, 22–25; Hamlen, *Flight Fever*, 50. Chamberlin and Julian became close friends, close enough that in 1924, Julian asked Chamberlin to accompany him to Liberia in a fragile little seaplane named *Ethiopia I*. "Are you really going to try to get that thing off the water?" Chamberlin warily responded. Julian did, but not for long: Seconds after lifting off, the *Ethiopia I* crashed into the East River, and Julian spent the next week in the hospital.

163 Chamberlin also became the first-known pilot to take aerial photos: "Clarence Chamberlin, 83, Pioneer in Ocean Flying"; "Chamberlin Won Fame by Skill in Stunt Landing," *Brooklyn Daily Eagle*, June 6, 1927, 11.

163 He would prove this, often, while flying Levine· "Chamberlin Won Fame," 11.

163 The most famous instance occurred in 1926: Chamberlin, *Record Flights*, 273–74·

163 "I have flown often with Clarence": "Chamberlin Won Fame," 11.

164 By 1927 the dark and handsome Acosta: Foxworth, "Bertrand B. Acosta," 51–54; Norberto Cisneros, "Bert Acosta: Genius of Early Aviation," www.airmailpioneers .org/Pilots/Acosta.htm.

165 That June a group of navy brass gathered: "Bertrand Blanchard Acosta," Wikipedia, en.wikipedia.org; Foxworth, "Bertrand B. Acosta," 54.

166 He'd played the cuckold before: Foxworth, "Bertrand B. Acosta," 54.

166 In April 1922 a national flying meet. Ibid., 55.

166 His visitor was anything but an angel: Ibid., 53·

167 He'd badly misjudged her: Ibid., 55.

167 Acosta and Helen Pearsoll had apparently separated: Theirs would be a rocky marriage, with extended separations, though they would reconcile long enough to have two sons, Bertrand Jr. in 1922 and Allyn in 1924.

167 He began taking too many unnecessary chances: Ibid., 55; Lowell Thomas, *Thrills* (New York. Towner and Buranelli, 1933), 19–23.

167 "What time is it?": Ibid., 18–19; Foxworth, "Bertrand B. Acosta," 55.

169 both were battling sleep deprivation: The tale of the endurance flight comes from several sources: Chamberlin, *Record Flights*, 19–22; Foxworth, "Bertrand B. Acosta," 56; "Bertrand Blanchard Acosta"; Hamlen, *Flight Fever*, 75–76; "Plane Up 42½ Hours," *New York Times*, April 14, 1927, 1; "Pilot's Parents Confident," *New York Times*, April 15, 1927, 2; "French Admire Flight, But Want Record Back," 1; "Fifty-One Hours in the Air!" *Aero Digest*, May 1927, 371; "Bellanca Monoplane Sets World Endurance Record," 819–21; "Fliers Set New Record of 51 Hours in Air," 1.

169 In a 2000 study published in the *British Medical Journal*: Stanley Coren, *Sleep Thieves· An Eye-Opening Exploration into the Science and Mysteries of Sleep* (New York: Free Press, 1996), 48–59.

172 the French tempered their praise: "French Speed Plan to Make Hop First," *New York Times*, April 16, 1927, 3.

172 *Columbia's* backers had no questions about who would win: Hamlen, *Flight Fever*, 76.

172 "We intend to be the first across": "Air Race to Paris Promised by Backer of Bellanca Plane," *New York Times*, April 16, 1927, 1.

NINE: THE LORD OF DISTANCES

173 Perhaps the condors were a sign Francesco de Pinedo's introduction comes from several sources: "Map of de Pinedo's Flight," De Pinedo, Francesco (Cmdr): Documents, CD-132000-01, Manuscript Division, AIAA Archives; "Biographical Background, Francesco de Pinedo," www.italystl.com/pride, Max Gallo, *Mussolini's Italy· Twenty Years of the Fascist Era* (New York: Macmillan, Inc., 1964, 1973), 193; "De Pinedo's Milestone Flights," www.italystl.com/pride.

173 yet to be an airman in 1920s Italy meant belonging: Hamlen, *Flight Fever*, 22; Gallo, *Mussolini's Italy*, 168, 175–76; Paul David Pope, *The Deeds of My Fathers* (New York: Philip Turner, 2010), 107.

173 Mussolini had absorbed Italy's fledging Robert Wohl, *The Spectacle of Flight. Aviation and the Western Imagination, 1920–1950* (New Haven, Conn.. Yale University Press, 2005), 63; "Biographical Background," www.italystl.com/pride.

174 the idea of the flier as a natural leader. Wohl, "Spectacle of Flight," 60–61.

174 they gained wide credence. Ibid., 50–51, "Publisher's News Letter," *Aviation*, January 9, 1928, 109.

174 De Pinedo's twin-hulled seaplane: De Pinedo's encounter with the condors comes from several sources: "Andean Condor," Wikipedia, en.wikipedia.org; "De Pinedo's Milestone Flights," 4–5, "Francesco de Pinedo—When a Flock of Condors Imperiled de Pinedo," *Literary Digest*, n.d , n.p., AIAA Archives; Francesco de Pinedo, "By Seaplane to Six Continents," *National Geographic*, 54, no. 3 (September 1928). 253, 268–70. Just two years before de Pinedo's Four Continents Flight, the experienced British explorer Percy Fawcett had vanished in the vast Mato Grosso in his failed quest to discover the fabled City of Z.

176 Francesco de Pinedo (along with his journeys) was the most surreal: "Flight to Paris Lured Noted Pilots," xxx5.

176 In Italy, a cult formed around his name: "De Pinedo's Great Flight Makes Him Italian Idol," *New York Times*, April 6, 1927, 16.

176 his survival as an aviator: Jablonski, *Atlantic Fever*, 130–33; "Francesco de Pinedo," unattributed photocopy of magazine article, n.d., 35, AIAA Archives.

177 Il Duce and Balbo already harbored suspicions: "De Pinedo's Milestone Flights," 2; "Biographical Background," 1; Jablonski, *Atlantic Fever*, 130–33, "Francesco de Pinedo," unattributed photocopy of magazine article, n.d., 35, AIAA Archives. For example, before de Pinedo's first distance flight, Il Duce ordered him to keep Rome apprised of his progress; the aviator complied by wiring single-word telegrams announcing the place and time of his arrival. This annoyed the premier, since he had to rely on newspaper reports to learn more. The government wired stern instructions to the flier to relay a full account of his flight when he arrived in Tokyo. De Pinedo wired back. "FINISHED 2ND PART OF JOURNEY. ARRIVED LATE OWING TO GRAVE DIFFICULTIES IN ZUMBOANCA-TENSUI REGION DUE TO STORMS AND STRAIN ON MOTOR MACHINE AND CREW IN EXCELLENT CONDITION. AM OVERHAULING MACHINE. WILL WIRE WHEN READY TO RETURN." It was his longest communiqué.

177 the *Santa Maria* was an impressive ambassador: Jablonski, *Atlantic Fever*, 131; "De Pinedo's Milestone Flights," 3. De Pinedo packed top-flight navigational gear, a life raft, saltwater distiller, and fishing gear in the cabin, his plane also had room for 1,000 gallons of gas, but this meant that calculating the shortest route between points would always be essential.

177 its own logic: "Biographical Background," 2.

177 He had started, appropriately enough, as a sailor. Ibid., 1–2. Though considered a minor conflict today, the short Italo-Turkish War portended the future of military aviation. During the conflict, the Italians used powered aircraft for the first time in world history for military reconnaissance, and they used an airplane for the first time in at least one bombing run.

178 But de Pinedo was different. Ibid., 1.

178 The original idea for the Four Continents Flight: Zinn, The Twentieth Century, 77–78; David Cole, "Radical Aliens," London Review of Books, October 22, 2009, 26.

178 The battle for the South Atlantic: "De Pinedo's Milestone Flights," 2; de la Croix, They Flew the Atlantic, 40–46.

179 "Go ahead," urged the premier: "Francesco de Pinedo," AIAA Archives; Gallo, Mussolini's Italy, 126, 205.

179 the Savoia-Marchetti was christened the Santa Maria: "De Pinedo's Milestone Flights," 3; de Pinedo, "By Seaplane to Six Continents," 258.

179 They reached Bolama in Portuguese Guinea: "De Pinedo's Milestone Flights," 3; de Pinedo, "By Seaplane to Six Continents," 258–63.

179 De Pinedo entrusted the Santa Maria. "De Pinedo's Milestone Flights," 3; de Pinedo, "By Seaplane to Six Continents," 263.

180 they found themselves face-to-face: De Pinedo, "By Seaplane to Six Continents," 264; Joe Jackson, A Furnace Afloat. The Wreck of the Hornet and the 4300-mile Voyage of Its Survivors (New York: Free Press, 2003), 81–84. The waterspout's funnel was probably glowing, since subtropical spouts are known to lift tons of water filled with billions of phosphorescent microorganisms that blaze white or green when agitated.

180 the storm went on and on: "De Pinedo's Milestone Flights," 4, de Pinedo, "By Seaplane to Six Continents," 266–67.

180 Pope Pius XI was impressed: "Pope Considers Use of Planes in Church Work," New York Times, March 3, 1927, 6.

183 "across the stretches of Brazilian jungles". "Flies Over Snakes and Savages in Storm," New York Times, March 17, 1927, 2, "De Pinedo Disappears over Brazilian Wilds and Day and Night Pass Without News of Him," New York Times, March 19, 1927, 1.

183 Bugs tormented them: "De Pinedo's Milestone Flights," 5–6; de Pinedo, "By Seaplane to Six Continents," 270–72.

184 They swung west on the Guaporé River: "De Pinedo's Milestone Flights," 6; Michael Goulding, Ronaldo Barthem, and Efrem Ferreira, The Smithsonian Atlas of the Amazon (Washington, D.C.: Smithsonian Books, 2003), 147.

184 On March 20, the Santa Maria emerged: "De Pinedo's Milestone Flights," 6, Joe Jackson, The Thief at the End of the World: Rubber, Power, and the Seeds of Empire (New York: Viking, 2008), 249, 254–55, 277.

184 They started at dawn the next morning: "De Pinedo's Milestone Flights," 6; de Pinedo, "By Seaplane to Six Continents," 282–83.

185 They spent three days in Pará: Jackson, Thief at the End of the World, 122, 129; de Pinedo, "By Seaplane to Six Continents," 286.

185 They touched down on the city's banks: "De Pinedo Sweeps into New Orleans," New York Times, March 30, 1927, 12; "De Pinedo's Milestone Flights," 7.

185 Reporters and photographers swarmed. Ibid.

186 Some papers noted that even if de Pinedo: "A Great Italian Aviator," *New York Times*, March 31, 1927, 27.

186 But the French were just as likely. Hamlen, *Flight Fever*, 41–43, 57–58, 63–64; "French Speed Plans to Make Hop First," *New York Times*, April 16, 1927, 3.

187 Maybe de Pinedo, in his meandering way. The account of the explosion on the *Santa Maria*, and its aftermath, comes from several sources: "De Pinedo's Milestone Flights," 7–8; "Pinedo Plane Burns on Roosevelt Lake," *New York Times*, April 8, 1927, 1; "Charge Fascist Foe Fired Pinedo Plane," *New York Times*, April 8, 1927, 7; "Mussolini Reassures Fletcher," *New York Times*, April 8, 1927, 7; "An Accident, Says de Pinedo," *New York Times*, April 8, 1927, 7; "Pinedo's Adversity Will Add to Glory," *New York Times*, April 10, 1927, E9.

TEN: CRUEL DAYS

193 Charles Levine set the tone: "Air Race to Paris Promised by Backer of Bellanca Plane," *New York Times*, April 16, 1927, 1.

193 "It is hardly likely that the rules would be changed": Ibid.; Chamberlin, *Record Flights*, 28.

193 That was too slow for Levine: Ibid.

194 Levine did not consider him the "movie-type": Chamberlin, *Record Flights*, 15.

195 "I know quite a little about navigation". "Air Race to Paris Promised," 1.

195 "A man like Acosta would not need the undercarriage": Ibid.

195 Others were out there, waiting to compete. Letter, Winston Ehrgott to National Aeronautics Association, April 18, 1927, Orteig Collection, Montague, *Oceans, Poles and Airmen*, 42–43; "New Paris Flight Planned," *New York Times*, April 20, 1927, 11; Murphy, *Struggle*, 231.

196 "The *America* is in a much more advanced stage": Murphy, *Struggle*, 232.

196 "[K]eep the project absolutely confidential": Letter, Byrd to Bennett, January 15, 1927, Folder 4343, Box 115, "Transatlantic Flight," Byrd Collection.

196 "there is some danger of their attempting the Transatlantic flight" Letter, Byrd to Bennett, January 22, 1927 Folder 4343, Box 115, "Transatlantic Flight," Byrd Collection; G. H. Liljequist, "Did the 'Josephine Ford' Reach the North Pole?" *Interavia* 5 (1960): 589–91. This Fokker did not make the transpacific trip until June 1927, flying 25 hours and 43 minutes for an average speed of 81 knots. This airplane was equipped with even more powerful engines than the *Josephine Ford*. When Balchen read about her flight, he became even more suspicious that Byrd did not reach the North Pole as he said he had.

196 Balchen leapt at an offer: Letter, Western Canada Airways Ltd., to Bernt Balchen, March 12, 1927, Box OV1, "Scrapbooks, ca. 1920–ca. 1929," Record Group 401(97), Papers of Bernt Balchen, Manuscript Division, Library of Congress, Washington, D.C. (hereafter "Bernt Balchen Papers"); Alice McKay, "First Freight Flies North," *The Beaver*, September 1947, 18–21.

197 "I can't say much for Balchen": Letter, Byrd to Bennett, January 15, 1927, Folder 4343, Box 115, "Transatlantic Flight," Byrd Collection.

197 His distrust extended. Letter, Byrd to Wanamaker, March 18, 1927, Folder 4343, Box 115, "Transatlantic Flight," Byrd Collection; Murphy, *Struggle*, 230.

197 "Suppose he falls into the water?": Fitzhugh Green, "Dick Byrd—Gentleman,"

American Magazine, n.d., 77, File "Personages, Richard E. Byrd," Virginia Aeronautical Historical Society Archives.

198 The plane looked like the *Josephine Ford*: Richard Byrd, *Skyward: Man's Mastery of the Air as Shown by the Brilliant Flights of America's Leading Air Explorer, et al.* (New York: Penguin Putnam, 1928), 205–207; "Story of Byrd's Plans," *New York Times*, April 10, 1927, 1.

198 not so the myriad other details: Byrd, *Skyward*, 207–209; Rose, *Explorer*, 173–74; Letter, Byrd to Wanamaker, March 18, 1927, Folder 4343, Box 115, "Transatlantic Flight," Byrd Collection.

199 That was the crux of the matter: From Byrd Collection, Box 115, "Transatlantic Flight," Folder 4330: Letter, Byrd to Curtis Wilbur, secretary of the navy, December 24, 1926; Letter, Byrd to IRS, March 9, 1927; Letter, Byrd to Grover Whalen, March 10, 1927; Folder 4344: "Low Protein Diet," March 1927; "French Pledge Aid in Flight to Paris," *New York Times*, April 13, 1927, 2; "Byrd Now in Chicago," *New York Times*, April 13, 1927, 2; "Paris, April 14," *New York Times*, April 15, 1927, 3; "Aviation Progress Sketched by Byrd," *New York Times*, April 15, 1927, 3; "Byrd Rows in River in Rubber Lifeboat," *New York Times*, April 16, 1927, 3.

199 Hundreds of letters: Folders 4333 and 4334, Box 115, "Transatlantic Flight," Byrd Collection. These files contain hundreds of letters and telegrams from women and men asking to cross the ocean with Byrd. The number of posts from women seem, to the author, to outnumber those from men by about three or four to one, as described in the text.

199 "I have your telegram [or letter]": Letter, Byrd to Ruth Haviland, June 18, 1927, Folder 4333, Box 115, "Transatlantic Flight," Byrd Collection.

200 Fokker's mechanics trundled the *America*: Murphy, *Struggle*, 232.

200 Tony Fokker took the helm: The account of *America's* crash comes from several sources: "Byrd's Plane Crashes in Its First Trial," *New York Times*, April 17, 1927, 1; Murphy, *Struggle*, 232–35, Byrd, *Skyward*, 212–15; Bennett, *Floyd Bennett*, 116–18; George O. Noville, "Crash!" *Scientific American*, 138 (January 1928): 13–15; Robert E. Martin, "Tony Fokker Captures America," *Popular Science Monthly* 119 (July 1931): 38; Booth, "Shall I Marry an Aviator?" 80; Hamlen, *Flight Fever*, 67; Harry Bruno, *Wings Over America: The Inside Story of American Aviation* (New York: Robert M. McBride, 1942), 175.

201 Bennett lightened the load by about 200 pounds: "Bennett Cuts Load for Flight to Paris," *New York Times*, April 14, 1927, 3.

204 The *America* might be patched up: Jablonski, *Atlantic Fever*, 89.

205 Byrd fell into despondency: "Non-Stop Champions Deplore Byrd Crash," *New York Times*, April 17, 1927, 22, "Byrd Trip May be Cancelled," *New York Times*, April 18, 1927, 8; "Byrd Trip in Doubt, He Offers to Help Bellanca Flight," *New York Times*, April 18, 1927, 1; "Wanamaker Delays Byrd Flight Decision," *New York Times*, April 19, 1927, 29; Bennett's Recovery Slow," *New York Times*, April 20, 1927, 11; "Byrd's Future Undecided," *New York Times*, April 20, 1927, 11; "Bennett Frets in Hospital," *New York Times*, April 21, 1927, 29.

205 only Bennett remained, alone in his room: "Lt. Noville Leaves Hospital," *New York Times*, April 23, 1927, 19; "Visits Bennett in Hospital," *New York Times*, April 24, 1927, 21; Balchen, *Come North with Me*, 87–89.

206 Levine dropped a bomb· "Mail Flier Chosen for Bellanca Hop," *New York Times*, April 20, 1927, 11.

206 Levine tapped Lloyd Bertaud Hamlen, *Flight Fever*, 77–78; Chamberlin, *Record Flights*, 23; "Mail Flier Chosen," 11.

207 Clarence Chamberlin held no illusions. Chamberlin, *Record Flights*, 23; "Plus Fours," Wikipedia, en wikipedia.org.

207 the little Sicilian stood his ground: Chamberlin, *Record Flights*, 23–24.

207 the other rivals were moving forward: "Nungessser Plans to Start Sunday on Flight from Paris to New York," *New York Times*, April 21, 1927, 1; "Secret Hop Likely by Bellanca Plane," *New York Times*, April 22, 1927, 23; "Drouhin Bids Hard in Atlantic Hop," *New York Times*, April 24, 1927, 3.

208 The French threat caused Bellanca the greatest worry: "Bellanca Ready for Quick Start," *New York Times*, April 21, 1927, 29.

208 They planned their route and groomed their plane: Hamlen, *Flight Fever*, 78; "Bellanca Flight Mapped by Bertaud," *New York Times*, April 23, 1927, 19.

208 The Brooklyn Chamber of Commerce even did its part: "Brooklyn Is Backer of Bellanca Plane," *New York Times*, April 24, 1927, 3.

208 Sunday, April 24, was set as the plane's official christening: Chamberlin's deft rescue of the plane and the girls come from several sources: "A Famous Flyer's Impromptu Rescue Stunt," *The Literary Digest* 93, no. 8 (May 21, 1927): 62–66; Chamberlin, *Record Flights*, 29–33, "Chamberlin Saves Two Girls in Plane by Daring Landing," *New York Times*, April 25, 1927, 1; Hamlen, *Flight Fever*, 79–81, Wolfsohn and Herndon, "The Man Who Was Almost Lindbergh," *True*, May 1963, 60.

213 Chamberlin knew he had dodged a bullet. Owen, "Dragon Hunters," 32.

ELEVEN: A LITTLE PATCH OF GREEN

215 "A singular fatality seems to hang over"· "Chamberlin Saves Two Girls," 1.

215 By April 21, it was already assumed· "Ask Paris Greeting for Noel Davis," *New York Times*, April 22, 1927, 23.

215 Parisians began laying bets on the winner. "Paris Lays Bets on Ocean Flights," *New York Times*, April 23, 1927, 19.

216 "Coli understands the sea even better than the air". Ibid.

216 The field made a pleasant setting: "Langley Field," n.d., n.p., File "Personages, Davis & Wooster," Virginia Aeronautical Historical Society Archives.

216 "We are almost ready to get away": The tale of the *American Legion* comes from several sources: "Davis and Wooster Killed in Crash as Big Plane Falls on Virginia Swamp," *New York Times*, April 27, 1927, 1, Hamlen, *Flight Fever*, 69–71; Jablonski, *Atlantic Fever*, 90–91; "Yellow Giant," *Time*, May 9, 1927, www.time.com; "Stanton Wooster, Lieutenant, United States Navy," Arlington National Cemetery website, www.arlingtoncemetery.ney/swooster.htm; Burns, *Noel Davis*, 25–26; Leo C. Forrest Jr., interview with author, August 14, 2010, Poquoson, Va.

217 This would not be Mary's version· "Mrs. Davis Aids Flight," *New York Times*, April 13, 1927, 2; Noel Davis Jr., phone interview with author, July 8, 2010.

219 ground effect results from the physics of wingtip vortices· Linda D. Pendleton, "Ground Effect," AVWeb, www.avweb.com/news/airman; "Ground effect (aircraft)," Wikipedia, en.wikipedia.org; "Ground effect," www.pilotfriend.com. The

flight of the *American Legion* would be one of three flights the National Advisory Committee for Aeronautics would study to probe this mystery. It was a worrisome problem. Already the air services envisioned the use of bigger and bigger transports to move military equipment and troops all over the globe, but what good would that be if the planes could not get off the ground? "Let us suppose," wrote researchers Elliot Reid and Thomas Carroll in their July 1927 "A Warning Concerning the Take-Off with Heavy Load," that a heavily loaded "airplane has good flying speed and is at the point of leaving the ground: With the engine at full throttle the pilot finds that he gains altitude as rapidly as he would expect under the existing conditions. However, having reached a height approximately equal to the semi-span of the airplane, he notices that the rate of climb has decreased alarmingly. Slight changes of the attitude of the airplane are found to be of no avail. In the interim it is probable that he has passed the boundaries of the good landing surface of the airport and may then be confronted with the necessity of gaining still more altitude in order to avoid some obstacle. Finding this impossible, he can only choose between collision with the obstacle and the doubtful alternative of attempting a turn. In either case a serious accident is probable if not inevitable." Elliot G. Reid and Thomas Carroll, "Technical Note 258. A Warning Concerning the Take-Off with Heavy Load" (Washington, D.C. National Advisory Committee for Aeronautics, July 1927), 5.

221 "[F]or every young man whose eyes are fixed": Booth, "Shall I Marry an Aviator?" 80.
221 to speak to Davis's mother· "Davis Mother Takes News of Crash Bravely," *New York Times*, April 27, 1927, 2.

TWELVE: THE MAIDEN FLIGHT

222 The deaths of Davis and Wooster threw a pall. "Airmen Pay Tribute to Crash Victims," *New York Times*, April 27, 1927, 2.
222 Byrd's tribute was the most poignant: Ibid.
222 "they know that someday it will be done": "Ocean Flying Takes Heavy Toll," *New York Times*, May 1, 1927, xx4.
222 "Pioneers are always foolhardy": Ibid.
223 "[P]ilots are hoping that the jinx": Ibid.
224 Four people had died: "Transocean Flight Dogged by Bad Luck," *New York Times*, April 27, 1927, 2; "$150,000 in Prizes for Safer Aviation," *New York Times*, April 30, 1927, 2.
224 The fatal events affected spirits. "Davis's Crash Stirs Sympathy of Paris," *New York Times*, April 27, 1927, 2; "The Langley Field Disaster," *New York Times*, April 27, 1927, 24; "Nungesser and Coli Wary of Taking Off," *New York Times*, April 28, 1927, 25, "Plans Here Worry French," *New York Times*, April 28, 1927, 3.
224 That left the *Columbia*: "Bellanca Plane Tests Speed Today," *New York Times*, April 27, 1927, 3; "To Pick Second Pilot for Bellanca Tonight," *New York Times*, April 28, 1927, 25; "Bellanca Plane Ready in Six Days," *New York Times*, April 30, 1927, 21.
224 Chamberlin and Acosta sat alone at the Lambs Club· "Acosta Withdraws from Paris Flight," *New York Times*, April 29, 1927, 23; "The Lambs Club—New York City," www.nycago.org/Organs/NYC/html/LambsClub.html; National Air and Space Museum Archives. Letter, Bellanca to Levine, April 23, 1927, File 5, "Cor-

respondence 1927," Box 4, Giuseppe M. Bellanca Collection. The Lambs Club was a *Who's Who* of American entertainment, and its membership included such notables as Douglas Fairbanks, William S. Hart, and Will Rogers.

226 George Hughes of Elizabeth, New Jersey: "Drives Auto 107 Hours Without a Rest," *New York Times*, May 1, 1927, 5.

228 "a very large majority, even ninety-seven in a hundred". Sandage, *Born Losers*, 5–7.

228 Francesco de Pinedo was the next person: "De Pinedo Arrives in City Secretly," *New York Times*, April 25, 1927, 12.

229 The speech was a mistake, and more than a little naïve: "City Gives De Pinedo Rousing Welcome," *New York Times*, April 26, 1927, 3.

229 two thousand antifascists tried to break in. "Anti-Fascisti Riot Menaces De Pinedo," *New York Times*, April 29, 1927, 23.

230 He breathed a great sigh of relief. "De Pinedo's Milestone Flights."

232 the completed *Spirit of St. Louis*: Ev Cassagneres, *The Untold Story of the Spirit of St. Louis: From the Drawing Board to the Smithsonian* (New Brighton, Minn.: Flying Books International, 2002), 34–35. Jablonski, *Atlantic Fever*, 105.

233 The other distinctive feature: Beamish, *The Story of Lindbergh*, 182; Spark, "Charles Lindbergh," 138; Jablonski, *Atlantic Fever*, 106.

234 Ryan Airline's B-1 Brougham: Spark, "Charles Lindbergh," 135. Lindbergh's quotes are included in Spark.

234 About thirty-five people worked for Ryan. Cassagneres, *The Spirit of Ryan*, 49; Douglas Corrigan, *That's My Story* (New York: E.P. Dutton, 1938), 91–92.

235 in desperation he went out and bought charts: Cassagneres, *The Spirit of Ryan*, 59.

235 Lindbergh taught himself the fine points of navigation: Ibid., 58–59.

235 "People are all asking about you": Letter, Evangeline Lindbergh to Charles Lindbergh, March 18, 1927, Folder 6a, "Personal Correspondence, Letters from Mother (1927 Jan. 17–May 18)," Box 11, "Correspondence, Transatlantic Flight," C.A.L. Collection.

235 His flight had entered his mother's imagination: Letter, Evangeline Lindbergh to Charles Lindbergh, March 21, 1927; Letter, Evangeline Lindbergh to Charles Lindbergh, April 8, 1927, Folder 6a, "Personal Correspondence," Box 11, "Correspondence, Transatlantic Flight," C.A.L. Collection.

236 Lindbergh crawled into the cockpit: The account of *Spirit*'s maiden flight comes from these sources: Lindbergh, *Spirit of St. Louis*, 120–23; Cassagneres, *The Untold Story*, 43–45; Jablonski, *Atlantic Fever*, 106–109.

236 *Spirit* had already been gassed up when he crawled in: The fuel was Red Crown, supplied by Standard Oil's Richmond Refinery at San Francisco Bay. Five gallons of oil was poured in the oil tank; 50 gallons of gas in the big fuel tank for this first short flight. There would be no standard for aviation fuels until 1944, but by 1927 several chemicals were already being blended in to fight knock and give aviation fuel an average octane rating of 65 to 70.

THIRTEEN: THE WHITE BIRD

238 a famous soothsayer: "Rumors Stir Paris Over Start of Hop," *New York Times*, May 8, 1927, 25.

239 No object of adoration was ever uglier: "The Paris–New York Flight, Fate of Nungesser and Coli Still a Mystery," *Flight* 19, no. 19 (May 12, 1927): 297; "Levasseur PL.8. 'L'Oiseau Blanc,'" "Attaché's Report. Levasseur Seaplane to be Used by Nungesser re: Transatlantic Flight," NASM; "'Levasseur 8,' Transatlantic Plane," Aircraft Circular No. 5, National Advisory Committee for Aeronautics.

239 Everything about the *White Bird* had become a national obsession. "Nungesser May Take Off for New York Sunday," *New York Herald*, April 20, 1927, 1; "Nungesser Delays Flight to N.Y. Two Weeks," *New York Herald*, April 21, 1927, 1; Montague, *Oceans, Poles and Airmen*, 54.

239 The diverse crosswinds on their route could be deadly: Montague, *Oceans, Poles and Airmen*, 54; "Nungesser and Coli Wary of Taking Off," 25; "Nungesser Believed Ready to Take Off Immediately," *New York Herald*, April 25, 1927, 1, "Fliers Study Skies as Ready Planes Await Flights," *New York Herald*, May 2, 1927, 2; de la Croix, *They Flew the Atlantic*, 66–67; "Nungesser Plane Makes Speed Trial," *New York Times*, May 4, 1927, 3; "Hangar Fire Hurts Nungesser Plane," *New York Times*, May 5, 1927, 23; "Nungesser Is Ready: Waits on Weather," *New York Times*, May 7, 1927, 1; "Rumors Stir Paris Over Start of Hop," 25; "Ace's Mother Is Confident," *New York Times*, May 9, 1927, 2; "Atlantic Events," *Time*, May 23, 1927, n.p., www.time.com.

241 not so much of death as of failure. William Nungesser, interview with author, September 19, 2009; *L'Enigme de L'Oiseau Blanc*, 1997, Vincent Gielly, director.

242 the trajectory of his life: William Nungesser Private Collection; "Lt. Charles Nungesser," usfighter.tripod.com/nungesser.htm.

242 Charles seemed determined to distinguish himself. "Lt. Charles Nungesser," usfighter.tripod.com/nungesser.htm; Nungesser, Charles Eugene J. M. (Capt.), Documents, CN-105000-01, NASM; Henry Bates, "Charles Nungesser, Iron Ace of France," *Modern Man*, n.d., 22.

242 the uncle had disappeared: "Lt. Charles Nungesser," usfighter.tripod.com/nungesser.htm, Bates, "Charles Nungesser," 22–23.

243 A month after signing up. Nungesser's war record is compiled from several sources: William L. Nungesser, interview with author, September 19, 2009, "Lt. Charles Nungesser," usfighter.tripod.com/nungesser.htm; Bates, "Charles Nungesser," 21; William L. Nungesser, "Nungesser," *Over the Front* 6, no. 4 (Spring 1991): 17–24; Mark Surpin, *The Brave Men: Twelve Portraits of Courage* (New York: Platt and Munk, 1967), 229–55.

245 he drank two bottles of champagne and swam the Seine: Bates, "Charles Nungesser," 53; *L'Enigme de L'Oiseau Blanc*.

245 peace was not kind to him: William L. Nungesser, interview with author, September 19, 2009; Surpin, *The Brave Men*, 55–56; "Lt. Charles Nungesser," usfighter.tripod.com/nungesser.htm; Nungesser, "Nungesser," 24; "French Ace to Try for New Record in Egg-Shaped Plane," *Chicago Tribune*, Nov. 19, 1922; "Test New Flivver Plane," n.d., n.p., William L. Nungesser Private Collection.

246 love unexpectedly found him: William L. Nungesser, interview with author, September 19, 2009. William L. Nungesser Private Collection· "Picture of Consuelo Hatmaker in her flying suit standing beside Nungesser as he barnstorms in America", photo and caption, "Nungesser Amphibian N.U.A. Type"; "Miss Hatmaker Weds Captain Nungesser," n.d., n.p., but probably either *The New York Times* or the *New York Herald*. "Milestones," *Time*, May 28, 1923, www.time.com;

Chris Canter, "Re: Captain Charles Eugene Jule Marie Nungessser," genterum
.genealogy.com, posted March 20, 2002, "Nungesser," *Time*, May 28, 1923, www
.time.com.

247 He went to Hollywood: William L. Nungesser, interview with author, September 19, 2009; William L. Nungesser Private Collection. "Picture of Igor Sikorsky
in cockpit filming *Sky Raiders*"; "The Sky Raider," *Motion Picture News* 31, no. 14
(April 4, 1925): 1522, also full-page ad, 1382; "Charles Nungesser," Wikipedia,
en.wikipedia.org. Contrary to popular rumor, footage of Nungesser did not appear
in Howard Hughes's *Hell's Angels*, which was released in 1930, the same year as
Dawn Patrol. One rumor held that Nungesser was one of the stunt pilots killed in
the making of Hughes's film, but by then he had been missing for three years.

247 By 1926 the future seemed bright. William L. Nungesser, interview with author,
September 19, 2009; William L. Nungesser Private Collection: "Picture of Con-
suelo Hatmaker Standing Beside *White Bird*," copied from a photo at the Museé
Le Bourget; "American Wife Divorces Captain Nungesser," n.d., n.p.; Canter,
"Re: Captain Charles Eugene Jule Marie Nungessser"; *L'Enigme de L'Oiseau
Blanc*.

248 General Delcambre of the French meteorological service· Accounts of the *White
Bird*'s takeoff came from several sources: "Nungesser's 'White Bird' Fueling at
One a.m. for Dawn Atlantic Attempt," *New York Herald*, May 8, 1927, 1; Surpin,
The Brave Men, 257–59; Hamlen, *Flight Fever*, 88–90; de la Croix, 66–72; "Nun-
gesser Off on Paris–New York Hop at 5:17 a.m.," *New York Times*, May 8, 1927, 1;
"Storm in Nungesser's Path Over Atlantic," *New York Herald*, May 9, 1927, 1.

251 With four planes flanking her: Hamlen, *Flight Fever*, 90–91; "French Aviators
Somewhere Over Atlantic Ocean Nearing Goal of World's Record Dash," *New
York Herald*, May 9, 1927, 1; *L'Enigme de L'Oiseau Blanc*.

251 Nungesser's American rivals were taken. "Rivals Taken by Surprise," *New York
Times*, May 9, 1927, 1; Hamlen, *Flight Fever*, 91.

251 Levine was most admiring: "Storm in Nungesser's Path Over Atlantic," 1.

251 Raymond Orteig finally put to words: Ibid.

252 When the news made it to San Diego: Mosley, *Lindbergh*, 85.

252 Nungesser wired Captain René Bouygée: Hamlen, *Flight Fever*, 90–91; William L.
Nungesser, interview with author; Montague, *Oceans, Poles and Airmen*, 56.

253 One person was left out of the official lineup. William L. Nungesser Private Col-
lection: "Picture of Consuelo Hatmaker in photo montage at the Battery," *New
York Daily News*, n.d., n.p.; "Despair in Wake of Hope as Reports of Fliers' Safety
Are Denied," *Daily Mirror*, June 16, 1927, 17.

253 The crowds waited in miserable conditions. Hamlen, *Flight Fever*, 93–94; "Nungesser Missing Somewhere in Atlantic," *New York Herald*, May 10, 1927, 1.

253 James Kimball of the Weather Bureau: William Nungesser interview with author; *L'Enigme de L'Oiseau Blanc*; "Nungesser Missing Somewhere in Atlantic," 1;
"Should Be Nearing Land," *New York Times*, May 9, 1927, 1.

253 But conditions were worse than Kimball let on: "Storm Menaces Nungesser on
Flight in Mid-Atlantic," *Daily Mirror*, May 9, 1927, 2, Willis Day Gregg, "Metereol-
ogy of the North Atlantic and Transatlantic Flight," *Aviation* 23, no. 5 (Aug. 1,
1927). 263.

254 That day, 3,345 people called *The New York Times*: Hamlen, *Flight Fever*, 94;

"Nungesser Missing Somewhere in Atlantic," *New York Herald*, May 10, 1927, 9; Owen, "Dragon Hunters," *The New Yorker*, May 21, 1927, 32.

254 In Paris, *Le Presse* came out with an "extra" edition: "Rumors and False Reports Worry Anxious Parisians," *New York Herald*, May 10, 1927, 1; "U.S. Weather Bureau Denies Failure to Issue Bulletins," *New York Herald*, May 11, 1927, 1; "French Papers Defend Publication of Report," *New York Herald*, May 11, 1927, 1; William L. Nungesser, interview with author, Hamlen, "Flight Fever," 93–95; Montague, *Oceans, Poles and Airmen*, 57–59; "The Secret of the White Bird," *Aero-News Network*, www.aero-news.net. The collective note run by the French papers sounded simultaneously garbled and panic-stricken: "The undersigned evening papers, having come together in the same feeling of respect for their readers and for the reliability of the news which they owe to them, earnestly desire to affirm that yesterday afternoon they published only despatches successfully confirmed by the official manifestations of the Ministers of Commerce, of War, and of the Interior."

255 "Man is still thrilled and a little exalted": Owen, "Dragon Hunters," 32.

256 the two aviators apparently did conquer the Atlantic: William Nungesser interview with author; *L'Enigme de L'Oiseau Blanc*; Hamlen, *Flight Fever*, 96–97; Stephan Wilkinson, "The Search for L'Oiseau Blanc," *Air and Space Smithsonian* 1, no. 6 (February/March 1987): 87–95; "Sea Find Revives Mystery," *San Francisco Examiner*, January 25, 1961, 10; Letter, Richard E. Gillespie, executive director, TIGHAR, to Donald Lopez, deputy director of the National Air and Space Museum, August 15, 1986, Nungesser, Charles Eugene J.M. (Capt.), Documents, CN-105000-01, NASM, transcripts of sessions with psychic Ann Rylchenski, November 5, 1984 and November 6, 1986; "The White Bird," Wikipedia, en.wikipedia.org; Nungesser, "Nungesser," 24; Bill Wiggens, "Mystery of the White Bird," *Air Classics*, July 1999, retrieved from findarticles.com; "White Bird," *NUMA*, www.numa.net/expeditions/white_bird.htms; "Secret of the White Bird," Surpin, *The Brave Men*, 259–60; "New Evidence May Write Lindbergh Out of History as First to Fly Atlantic," *The Independent*, November 12, 2010, www.independent.co.uk. Clues, and possible pieces of the *White Bird*, have surfaced with the years. In the 1930s, rumors arose that parts of an aircraft engine had turned up in Maine. In 1961 a Maine lobsterman working his pots picked up a large piece of riveted aluminum, typical of the aircraft of the 1920s, off Jewell Island in the Casco Bay. It seemed to be part of an instrument panel, painted cream, with black edging.

There was renewed interest in the 1980s, largely because of the efforts of two rival investigative groups: author Clive Cussler's NUMA (the National Underwater and Marine Agency), and TIGHAR (The International Group for Historic Aircraft Recovery). NUMA checked the claims of Anson Berry, a woodsman from Machias, near the coast of Maine. On the afternoon of May 9, he said, he heard a sputtering plane pass overhead. The engine sounded erratic and it seemed to be in trouble. He looked up but could see not see anything through the fog. The plane drifted inland, and he heard what sounded like a crash about a mile away. Twenty-three years later another hunter would say that he came upon the remains of an old aircraft engine buried in the ground a mile from where Berry's camp had been. (Note: The two accounts of sightings in Machias, Maine, were rescued from obscurity by freelance writer Gunnar Hanson, best known for his role as Leatherface in Tobe Hooper's *The Texas Chainsaw Massacre*.)

Meanwhile, TIGHAR chased another rumor reports of a huge aircraft engine found by a hunter in Maine's Round Lake Hills district, also near Machias. Both investigations involved a lot of tromping around in the thick and boggy forest, and neither resulted in anything. In the mid-1980s, TIGHAR was given private money to continue the search for the *White Bird*, but the money came with strings: it was available only if they used the talents of a psychic at the American Society for Psychical Research in New York City. "Great," said Richard Gillespie, one of TIGHAR's founders, "there goes our credibility." Nevertheless, the psychic Ann Rylchenski made two tapings in the Society's Manhattan headquarters on November 5, 1984, and November 6, 1986. She claimed to be in the cockpit with two fliers about 100 miles off the coast of some northern woods. There was a small explosion under the right wing. They headed inland a few miles and crashed in a tall pine forest with a small mountain nearby. In 1984 she said that one flier suffered a broken back; the other's "chest was torn up." In 1986 she said the problem with the plane occurred very suddenly: "[I]t was at the very very last minute they realized how bad things were just before it went out of control."

257 "I am still waiting for my poor son": Letter from "La Maman du Capitaine Charles Nungesser" to Lindbergh, February 23, 1928, Folder 14, "Personal (CAL): Nungesser, Madame," Box 28, "Personal Correspondence 1927–1947, Personal (M-Wickersham)," C.A.L. Collection; "Mme. Nungesser Killed," *New York Times*, November 1, 1940, 5.

FOURTEEN: CURTISS FIELD

259 By Tuesday, May 10, the *White Bird* was officially listed as missing. "No Clue to Nungesser's Fate," *New York Herald*, May 11, 1927, 1, "'He'll Return,' Says Dauntless Mother of Flier," *New York Herald*, May 11, 1927, 8; William Nungesser interview with author; *L'Enigme de L'Oiseau Blanc*.

259 "Another loss": "Atlantic Events," *Time*, May 23, 1927, www.time.com; "No Word Received About Saint Romain," *New York Times*, May 8, 1927, n.p., www.nytimes.com; "News of St. Romain," *Evening Post*, May 7, 1927, 9. Nungesser and Coli were not France's only aviation losses that week. Three days before the *White Bird* took off, a Captain Saint-Romain and a Commander Mouneyres took off from Senegal in an attempt to fly nonstop to Brazil. Defying orders from the government, they'd removed the pontoons from their seaplane, making it impossible to land by sea. They sent two radio messages: one saying they were 200 miles from the mainland; the second, 120 miles. It was the last time they were ever heard from. Brazil dispatched two warships and some search planes, but they found nothing.

259 Byrd finally came out of seclusion: "Byrd to Try Paris Flight on Saturday in 'America,'" *New York Herald*, May 10, 1927, 1.

259 Some did not think this a good idea "Americans to Hop Off Saturday for Flight to Paris," *St. Louis Post-Dispatch*, May 11, 1927, 3.

260 As the wait stretched on: "Atlantic Events."

260 Lindbergh put *Spirit* through twenty-three test flights: Cassagneres, *Spirit of Ryan*, 64; Lindbergh, *Spirit of St. Louis*, 127–28; Hamlen, *Flight Fever*, 107–108.

260 Stories began to circulate: Berg, *Lindbergh*, 105; Lindbergh, *Spirit of St. Louis*, 132.

261 the first report of his maiden flight Davis, *The Hero*, 158–59; Lindbergh, *Spirit of St. Louis*, 123; "Lindbergh Plane Near Disaster," *New York Times*, April 30, 1927, 21; Lardner, "Lindbergh Legends," 199.

261 Lindbergh was clearly ready to go: Letter, Charles Lindbergh to Evangeline Lindbergh, May 7, 1927, Folder 6a, "Personal Correspondence, Letters from Mother (1927 Jan. 17–May 18)," Box 11, "Correspondence, Transatlantic Flight," C.A.L. Collection; Cassagneres, *Spirit of Ryan*, 54–55; Jablonski, *Atlantic Fever*, 108.

262 The first part of the trip passed easily: Lindbergh, *Spirit of St. Louis*, 136–42; Cassagneres, *Spirit of Ryan*, 56; Jablonski, *Atlantic Fever*, 109.

262 He taxied up to the black hangars. Lindbergh, *Spirit of St. Louis*, 143–46; Cassagneres, *Spirit of Ryan*, 67; Walter Sanford Ross, *The Last Hero: Charles A. Lindbergh* (New York: Harper and Row, 1967), 96–97; "1,550-Mile Flight Made by Lindbergh," *New York Times*, May 12, 1927, 2.

263 He catalogued his few possessions: Gary N. Smith, "The Charles Lindbergh Trunk: A Time Capsule of His St. Louis Years," *Gateway Heritage* 16, no. 1 (Summer 1995): 20–25.

263 He rose at five the next morning: Ibid., 20; Davis, *The Hero*, 170; Cassagneres, *Spirit of Ryan*, 56–57; Lindbergh, *Spirit of St. Louis*, 149.

264 From the air, the three airfields: Davis, *The Hero*, 170–71; Cassagneres, *Spirit of Ryan*, 67–68; Lindbergh, *Spirit of St. Louis*, 149–52; "Lindbergh Arrives After Record Hop," *New York Times*, May 13, 1927, 1.

265 Chamberlin gazed at the blond newcomer. "Flight Set for Saturday," *New York Times*, May 11, 1927, 1; "Hunt Hidden Flaws in Bellanca," *New York Times*, May 12, 1927, n.p., www.nytimes.com.

266 The first point of contention was the radio: "Should Atlantic Fliers Shun Radio to Save Weight?" *New York Times*, May 15, 1927, n.p., www.nytimes.com.

266 The wireless debate caused huge discord: Montague, *Oceans, Poles and Airmen*, 50–51.

267 normally brash journalists: Lindbergh, *Spirit of St. Louis*, 152.

267 It was actually a little frightening: Ibid.

267 It wasn't Richard Byrd who ferried *America*: Montague, *Oceans, Poles and Airmen*, 50–51; "May Start Tomorrow," *New York Times*, May 13, 1927, 1.

267 Balchen had not left Uncle Tony's factory: Balchen, *Come North with Me*, 90–91; Bennett, *Floyd Bennett*, 121.

268 Balchen had rarely seen Byrd: Balchen, *Come North with Me*, 91–92.

269 He seemed like a man reaching out for help: Letter, Byrd to Capt. Jerry H. Land, April 28, 1927, Folder 4354, Box 115, "Transatlantic Flight," Byrd Collection; "Byrd Denies Rumor," *New York Times*, May 10, 1927, n.p., "Byrd's Flight Anniversary," *New York Times*, May 10, 1927, n.p.

269 He wired Wanamaker: Telegram, Byrd to Wanamaker, May 11, 1927, Folder 4356, Box 115, "Transatlantic Flight," Byrd Collection.

269 Wanamaker was intrigued: Murphy, *Struggle*, 239–40.

269 So Byrd tried again: "The Trans-Atlantic Flight of the America," www.check-six .com.

270 like a man grown tired of addressing the same questions: "Byrd Flight to Await Fate of French Fliers," *New York Times*, May 12, 1927, n.p.

270 "haven't they got enough photographs?": Lindbergh, *Spirit of St. Louis*, 153–55.

FIFTEEN: THE WAITING GAME

271 "They're your buffers" Ross, *The Last Hero*, 99.

271 the Garden City provided a glimpse: "Garden City Hotel," Wikipedia, en.wikipedia .org; "The Garden City Hotel Our History," www.gardenccityhotel.com.

272 On the fringes stood some bankers: "Three Pilots Discuss Flight at Garden City," *The New York Times*, May 13, 1927, n.p., www.nytimes.com.

272 "When airmen talk, as they rarely do": Owen, "Dragon Hunters," 34.

273 "It was an unusual spectacle on a flying field": "Three Pilots Discuss Flight."

273 It was the opening note of a chorus: "Atlantic Events," "The Social Peek-a-Boo, A Reflection of Society Gossip That Makes the Rounds Every Week," *The Censor* (St. Louis), June 2, 1927, 11 Folder 39, Box 87, "Periodicals," C.A.L. Collection; Russell Owen, "Lindbergh's Epoch Making Flight from New York to Paris," *Current History* 26, no. 4 (July 1927): 506; Fitzgerald, "Echoes of the Jazz Age," 421.

274 the "mirror girl": Cassagneres, *Untold Story* 61–63.

274 All the other aviators were married: E-mail, Kevin Burns to Suzanne Jones, June 29, 2008, collection of Suzanne K. Jones. Although Wooster was getting a divorce from his first wife at the time of his death, he was engaged to marry a woman named Sally Finney soon after returning from Le Bourget.

275 several Jewish girls and boys stood looking: L. B. Linder, "What the Jew in the Street Thinks About the Jewish Flying Hero," *Der Tog* ("The Day," Brooklyn, N.Y.), June 9, 1927, quoted in Charles Albert Levine Bibliography, richard.arthur .norton.googlepages.com.

275 the spark that existed between Lindbergh and his fans. "Bad Weather Delays Flight Across Atlantic," *St. Louis Post-Dispatch*, May 14, 1927, 1.

275 "best we have to offer in clean-cut masculinity": "The Social Peek-a-Boo," 8, 10, 11; "America's Ideal Mother," *The Memphis Co-Operator* 5, no. 19 (May 7, 1928): 1–2.

276 "unvarnished Midwesterner": Mosley, *Lindbergh*, 94; Milton, *Loss of Eden*, 110; Mordden, *That Jazz!*, 245.

276 "'You can't wear it'": Bruno, *Wings Over America*, 182–83.

277 a case of "informational cascade": Ashley Mears, "What Makes Coco Rocha Hot?" *The Week*, August 13, 2010, 44–45, reprinted with permission from 3QuarksDaily .com.

277 They'd already put off their flight because of the weather: "May Start Tomorrow," *New York Times*, May 13, 1927, 1.

278 the excitement generated by *Columbia*'s imminent departure: "Bertaud's Career in the Air," *New York Times*, May 14, 1927, 2, "Chamberlin's Town Stirred," *New York Times*, May 14, 1927, 2; Letter, Concetina Bellanca to Giuseppe Bellanca, April 28, 1927, Folder 5, "Personal Correspondence," Box 142, Giuseppe M. Bellanca Collection.

278 The biggest noise came from Brooklyn. Linder, "What the Jew in the Street."

278 "Levine! With His Flying Machine": "Levine! With His Flying Machine," music by Sam Coslow, English words by Saul Bernie, Yiddish words by Joseph Tanzman, (New York: Spier and Coslow, 1927), Bella C. Landauer Collection of Aeronautical Sheet Music, NASM Archives.

279 "up to our necks in the inevitable last-minute preparations" Chamberlin, *Record Flights*, 37–38.

280 Every day, it was Dr. James Kimball who told the pilots. Foster Ware, "Forecaster

to the Fliers," *The New Yorker*, July 28, 1928, 20–22; James H. Kimball, "Telling Ocean Flyers When to Hop," *Popular Science Monthly* (July 1928): 16–17; Douglas W. Clephane, "Weather Bureau Aid in Ocean Flying," *Aviation* 23, no. 2, (July 11, 1927): 84–86; "Keeping Tabs on Ocean Weather to 'Tip Off' Ambitious Flyers," *The Literary Digest* 98, no. 3 (July 21, 1928). 52–53; Davis, *The Hero*, 172; "Weather Maps": May 11, 1927, 8 a.m.; May 12, 1927, 8 a.m., Byrd Collection; Murphy, *Struggle*, 242.

282 From Saturday, May 14, until the night of Thursday, May 19: The press coverage of the week leading up to Lindbergh's flight was quite extensive and often overlapping, yet the frustration of trying to craft a story out of essentially nothing led some magazines and newspapers to report what seemed like every rumor. Thus, the story of a little gray kitten that Lindbergh took a shine to in his hangar suddenly became the apocryphal story of the cat that flew with him to Paris. Another example· Tony Fokker's dislike of Byrd and frustration over *America*'s delays turned in one story into a fight in which Fokker decked the Explorer with a well-aimed jab to the jaw. Yet this is never mentioned anywhere else, so I have tried to stay away from such outriders. Finally, a lot of speculation was packaged as news. On the whole, however, the press coverage and later research were usually accurate and even microscopically focused, and the many sources include: "Rival Pilots Watchful," *New York Times*, May 14, 1927, 1; "Hope for Aviators Nears End in Paris," *New York Times*, May 15, 1927, 2; "Mrs. Lindbergh Bids Calm Good-Bye to Son," *New York Times*, May 15, 1927, n.p.; "Fliers Test Planes, Awaiting Good Day," *New York Times*, May 15, 1927, 1, "Wanamaker Offers Nungesser Award," *New York Times*, May 16, 1927, 1; "Paris Fliers Wait a Day or Two More for Skies to Clear," *New York Times*, May 17, 1927, 1, "Bertaud May Lose Post in Columbia," *New York Times*, May 18, 1927, 1, "Bertaud to Remain in Bellanca Crew," *New York Times*, May 19, 1927, 1; Berg, *Lindbergh*, 107–10; Milton, *Loss of Eden*, 110–13; Ross, *The Last Hero*, 100–105; Lindbergh, *Spirit of St Louis*, 148–72, Cassagneres, *Untold Story*, 60–67; "Roosevelt Field, New York," Wikipedia, en.wikipedia.org; "Oil Used on Trans-Atlantic Flight," *Aero Digest* 10, no. 6 (June 1927): 546; "Plywood on the Spirit of St. Louis," *Aero Digest* 10, no. 6 (June 1927): 546–48; "Fuel for the Transatlantic Hop," *Aero Digest* 10, no. 6 (June 1927): 548, "Goodrich Tires Put to Severe Test," *Aero Digest* 10, no. 6 (June 1927): 550; Arnold T. Blumberg, *The Big Big Little Book Book: An Overstreet Photo-Journal Guide* (Timonium, Md.. Gemstone, n.d.), 104; From C.A.L. Collection· "Papers, 1827–1969," A0904, Box 9, Folder 2, "Spirit of St. Louis Logbook (Holograph)"; "Spirit of St. Louis, Log of Flights at Curtiss Field"; Folder 6, "Pages Removed from the Spirit of St. Louis Flight Log"; Box 17, Folder 2, "Offers—1927, Animals, May 23–Aug. 10," Telegram, C. J. Haggard to Lindbergh, n.d. Chamberlin, *Record Flights*, 37–41; Wolfsohn and Herndon, "The Man Who Was Almost Lindbergh," 60, "American Flyers Again Delayed by Mid-Atlantic Fog," *St. Louis Post-Dispatch*, May 16, 1927, 1; Ratcliff, "Byrd's Bad Boy," 53; Byrd, *Skyward*, 216–17; "Bernt Balchen," *The New Yorker*, June 9, 1928, 10; Balchen, *Come North with Me*, 92–96, Montague, *Oceans, Poles and Airmen*, 68–71, 117; "Byrd Urges Flood Aid at Good-Will Meeting," *New York Times*, May 19, 1927, n.p ; George O. Noville, "Crash!" *Scientific American* 138 (January 1928): 15.

288 "That'll teach you to wear pajamas" Bruno, *Wings Over America*, 173; Davis, *The*

Hero, 180. Two versions of this story have been published, and they are direct opposites. Bruno and Blythe, who were closest to Lindbergh that week, said that Slim shouted, "That'll teach you to wear pajamas!" as recorded in the text. But most other accounts say the exact opposite—that Lindbergh cried, "That's what you get for sleeping without pajamas!" For his part, Lindbergh does not address the scene in his *Spirit of St. Louis.* Bruno's book would appear to be the story's primary source, but it is out of print and very hard to find. Thus, all subsequent tales seem to be the result of a misquote or typo in the later secondary sources. Yet there is another explanation, and I raise it only because so much cosmetic work was performed on Lindbergh's image over the years. The original line in Bruno's book could have had vague and disturbing homosexual overtones to readers of the time; after all, in this version, Lindbergh is punishing Blythe because he is *not* sleeping in the nude. That could have been a troubling ripple in the image of Lindbergh then developing as the apotheosis of the All-American Male. If this is true, the later change could have been less than accidental: After all, Byrd's early biographies were heavily edited to conform to his "hero" image. Thus, in these later versions, where Lindbergh douses Blythe for foregoing pajamas at bedtime, the message is far different: Lindbergh has become the ever-vigilant defender of male modesty, always ready to set things right with a healthy dose of ice water.

SIXTEEN: A BAD CASE OF NERVES

296 Bertaud's elation lasted at least eight hours: "Bertaud to Remain in Bellanca Crew," 1; Montague, *Oceans, Poles and Airmen,* 71.

297 "ambition of a man who 'discovers' a fighter": Chamberlin, *Record Flights,* 43.

297 "I have run into him here and there". Balchen, *Come North with Me,* 94.

297 Yet backing down and losing face: Stephen R. Murray, "FACE: Fear of Loss of Face and the Five Hazardous Attitudes Concept," *International Journal of Aviation Psychology* 9, no. 4 (1999): 405.

298 "To be ribbed by other mail flyers". Bruno, *Wings Over America,* 176.

298 He was extraordinarily sensitive to insult: Milton, *Loss of Eden,* 112–13; Bruno, *Wings Over America,* 176–77.

298 Blythe planned a tight schedule for that gloomy Thursday: Davis, *The Hero,* 180; Bruno, *Wings Over America,* 178–79; Mosley, *Lindbergh,* 96; *Rio Rita· A Musical Comedy,* produced by Flo Ziegfled, music and lyrics by Henry Tierney and Joseph McCarthy, book by Guy Bolton and Fred Thompson, Landauer Collection, New York Historical Society; Willis Day Gregg, "Meteorology of the North Atlantic and Transatlantic Flight," *Aviation,* 264.

299 But it's hard to keep secrets: Bruno, *Wings Over America,* 179; Ross, *The Last Hero,* 106.

299 "You got your weather, Slim". Bruno, *Wings Over America,* 179.

300 There were other matters to attend to· Cassagneres, *Spirit of Ryan,* 75; Berg, *Lindbergh,* 110–11; Ross, *The Last Hero,* 106–107.

300 Lindbergh was amazed to see no activity: Lindbergh, *Spirit of St. Louis,* 172–73.

300 All Slim could do now was go home. Ibid., 173–75; Cassagneres, *Spirit of Ryan,* 76–77; Ross, *The Last Hero,* 107–108.

301 Slim arrived at his hangar shortly before 3:00 a.m.. The account of *Spirit's* takeoff

is drawn from several sources: Berg, *Lindbergh*, 112–16; Lindbergh, *Spirit of St. Louis*, 177–78; Davis, *The Hero*, 186–91; Jessie E. Horsfall, "Lindbergh's Start for Paris," *Aero Digest* 10, no. 6 (June 1927)· 503–507; Cassagneres, *Spirit of Ryan*, 77–78; "Lindbergh Is Set to Fly at Daylight If Weather Conditions Remain Good," *New York Times*, May 20, 1927, 1; Robert Martin, "Tony Fokker Captures America," *Popular Science Monthly* 119 (July 1931): 132; Bruno, *Wings Over America*, 180–82; Ross, *The Last Hero*, 108–10; Balchen, *Come North with Me*, 97–98; Rose, *Explorer*, 157.

SEVENTEEN: THE CHOSEN

305 It is the twenty-second hour of his flight. Lindbergh, *Spirit of St. Louis*, 388–89.
305 "hypnagogic hallucination": Roger J. Broughton, "Behavioral Parasomnias," in Sudhansu Chokroverty, *Sleep Disorders Medicine: Basic Science, Technical Considerations, and Clinical Aspects* (Boston: Butterworth Heinemann, 1999), 638.
306 "extreme fatigue and subconscious ravings": Charles A. Lindbergh, *Autobiography of Values* (New York: Harvest, 1976), 12.
306 "The underwriters believe the risk is too great": Davis, *The Hero*, 192–93.
306 In Detroit, Slim's mother started. Ibid., 193.
307 All along the New England coast, people climbed up trees: Cassagneres, *Untold Story*, 71; Davis, *The Hero*, 193–94.
307 Judge Mitchell May of Brooklyn dismissed Bertaud's injunction: Wolfsohn, "The Man Who Was Almost Lindbergh," 90; Jablonski, *Atlantic Fever*, 138; Chamberlin, *Record Flights*, 43–44.
308 Lindbergh was winging over Nova Scotia: Berg, *Lindbergh*, 119; Cassagneres, *Untold Story*, 72–73.
308 "Tomorrow, Saturday, a holiday for me". Davis, *The Hero*, 194.
308 her son was flying over the open stretch of Atlantic: Lindbergh, *Spirit of St. Louis*, 235–36; Berg, *Lindbergh*, 119–20; Cassagneres, *Untold Story*, 75–76.
309 clear skies and good weather were just a memory: Clephane, "Weather Bureau Aid in Ocean Flying," 84.
309 Francesco de Pinedo and the *Santa Maria II*: "Francesco de Pinedo," unattributed photocopy of magazine article, n.d., 37, AIAA Archives; "De Pinedo's Milestone Flights," www.italystl.com/pride.
309 It would be his last contact with land until Ireland: Davis, *The Hero*, 195–96; Berg, *Lindbergh*, 121–22; Allan Keller, "Over the Atlantic Alone," *American History Illustrated* 9, no. 1 (April 1, 1974): 43.
310 Pioneer earth inductor compass· Charles Dixon, *The Conquest of the Atlantic by Air* (London. Sampson Low, Marston, 1931), 117–20; Bill Streever, "Five Minutes in the Arctic Ocean," *The Week*, August 14, 2009, 44.
311 dead reckoning: Dixon, *Conquest of the Atlantic by Air*, 114–15, 123.
311 Ice has been a deadly threat: Ibid., 326–27; Allen, "Flying Through Fog and Night," 1238; Duncan, *Air Navigation and Meteorology*, 127–31.
313 "The deepest sleep resembles death": I Samuel 26.12.
313 "They were dull-eyed, bodily worn": S. L. A. Marshall is quoted in Laverne C. Johnson and Paul Naitch, *The Operational Consequences of Sleep Deprivation and Sleep Deficit* (London: NATO Advisory Group for Aerospace Research and Development, 1974), 3.

314 "I saw them clearly": Lindbergh, *Autobiography of Values*, 12.
314 Lindbergh was not the first to spot such strange visitors. Jackson, *A Furnace Afloat: The Wreck of the Hornet and the 4300-mile Voyage of Its Survivors* (New York: Free Press, 2003), 74.
314 "phantom travelers". Tom Ogden, *The Complete Idiot's Guide to Ghosts and Hauntings* (Indianapolis, Ind.: Alpha, 1999), 243–56.
315 "border line of life and a greater realm beyond": Lindbergh, *Spirit of St. Louis*, 390.
315 Twelve-year-old George Reed: Don Engen, "A 70-year Question," *Air and Space Smithsonian* 12, no. 6 (Feb./Mar. '98): 4; Lindbergh, *Spirit of St. Louis*, 476–77.
315 "blue-jeaned peasants, white-aproned wives": Lindbergh, *Spirit of St. Louis*, 484–85.

EIGHTEEN: PASSENGERS

319 It was a bright Saturday afternoon Balchen, *Come North with Me*, 99; Montague, *Oceans, Poles and Airmen*, 77–78, Fitzhugh Green, "Dick Byrd— Gentleman," 77.
320 Levine ordered the plane towed to the field: Montague, *Oceans, Poles and Airmen*, 76–80; Chamberlin, *Record Flights*, 44–47; Jablonski, *Atlantic Fever*, 138–39; Kenneth Collings, *Just for the Hell of It* (New York: Dodd, Mead, 1938), 225–28.
322 he seemed like the only flier in the world. Allen, *Only Yesterday: An Informal History of the Nineteen-Twenties* (New York· Harper and Bros., 1931), 217–18; Boorstin, *The Image*, 67–68, Berg, *Lindbergh*, 136.
322 In the Roxy Theatre: *Charles A. Lindbergh, Hero of the Air*, Fox-Case Movietone, USA, 1927. On *Saved from the Flames. 54 Rare and Restored Films, 1896–1944*, Lobster Films/Blackhawk Collection, 2008.
322 The joy would spread worldwide: Berg, *Lindbergh*, 137.
323 "One had only to venture into any city street". Heywood Broun is quoted in "Lindbergh's Leap of Faith," *The Literary Digest* 93, no. 10 (June 4, 1927): 5–6.
323 Lindbergh was flooded with congratulatory telegrams: U.S. Department of State, *The Flight of Captain Charles A. Lindbergh from New York to Paris, May 20–21, 1927, as Compiled from the Official Records of the Department of State* (Washington, D.C.. U.S. Government Printing Office, 1927), a collection of congratulatory telegrams from heads of state; Allen, *Only Yesterday*, 218; Berg, *Lindbergh*, 162. From the C.A.L. Collection: Box 17, Folder 2, "Offers—1927, Animals, May 23–August 10". Telegram, C. T. Haggard to Lindbergh; Letter, Louis Melford Harkin of Melford Kennels to Lindbergh, June 9, 1927; Russell Becker to Lindbergh, May/June 1927. From Folder 3, "Offers—1927, Clothing, May 21–June 13": Telegram, Martin May, president Famous Barr Co., to Lindbergh. From Folder 4, "Offers—1927, Films/Lecture Tours, May 21–23": more letters and telegrams, including telegram, Carl Laemmle to Lindbergh, n.d.; Letter, Ed Milne to Lindbergh, May 23, 1927. From Folder 8, "Offers—1927, Involved in Business, May 24–June 30". Letter, Jordan Machine Tool Co. to Lindbergh, May 24, 1927; Telegram, Rush Jones Insurance Company to Lindbergh, May 26, 1927. From Folder 9, "Offers—1927, Personal Service, May 21–June 24"· miscellaneous offers, including Letter, Hans Bergmann, Masseuse, to Lindbergh, June 14, 1927. From

Folder 20, "Gifts—1927, May 21–24," miscellaneous offers of gifts. "Lindbergh to Refuse to Enter the Movies," *Toronto Star*, May 30, 1927, n.p.; Milton, *Loss of Eden*, 119.

324 Charles Nungesser had been right: Berg, *Lindbergh*, 165, 191; Boorstin, *The Image*, 67; Patrick L. Cox, "Charles Lindbergh and Mobil Oil," *Journalism History* 30, no. 2 (Summer 2004): 98; "Raymond Orteig, Hotel Man, Dies," *New York Times*, June 8, 1939, n.p.

325 "Lindbergh religion": Laura Robinson, "Lindbergh, the Messenger of Universal Brotherhood," *Reality: A Bahai Magazine* xiv, no. 1 (July 1927): 6; Alan Wykes, *Air Atlantic. A History of Civil and Military Transatlantic Flying* (New York: David White, 1968), 94–95; Owen, "Lindbergh's Epoch Making Flight," 506.

325 One feature that surprised everyone: Orrin E. Klapp, "Hero Worship in America," *American Sociological Review* 14, no. 1 (Feb. 1949): 60.

325 As the worship continued: Lamar Trotti, "Sending Lindbergh to the World Through the Motion Picture," *The Southern Club Woman* (Jacksonville, Fla.) 3, no. 4 (January 1928): 8, 19.

326 The French, at least at first, were the least taken: Wohl, *The Spectacle of Flight*, 11–12.

326 Lindbergh himself did a lot to defuse: Charles A. Lindbergh, *We* (Guilford, Conn.: Lyons, 2002 [G. P. Putnam's Sons, 1927], foreword by Myron T. Herrick), 10–11; Col. T. Bentley Mott, *Myron T. Herrick, Friend of France* (Garden City, N.Y.: Doubleday, Doran, 1929), 347–48; Wohl, *Spectacle of Flight*, 9.

326 Herrick housed and groomed Lindbergh: Raymond H. Fredette, "In Pursuit of Charles Lindbergh," *Air Power History* 46, no. 2 (Summer '99): 6, 7.

327 Lindbergh's landing in Le Bourget: Milton, *Loss of Eden*, 118; Wohl, *Spectacle of Flight*, 12–13; Fredette, "In Pursuit of Charles Lindbergh," 9.

327 But strange things began to happen: Mott, *Myron T. Herrick*, 341; Fredette, "In Pursuit of Charles Lindbergh," 10. A story long circulated that the "fake Lindbergh" was a *Herald American* reporter, but this seems mistaken, possibly because Lindbergh got it wrong in his book. The exchange between Harry Wheeler and Herrick is quoted from William L. Shirer, *20th Century Journey: A Memoir of a Life and the Times* (New York: Simon & Schuster, 1976), 323–44; Shirer wrote the monumental *The Rise and Fall of the Third Reich*. Although, as Fredette claims, the comic exchange was heard secondhand, Shirer was also known for carefully checking his sources.

328 Herrick finally met the *real* Lindbergh: Wohl, *Spectacle of Flight*, 20; Fredette, "In Pursuit of Charles Lindbergh," 19; Mott, *Myron T. Herrick*, 343.

328 Lindbergh rose at around 1:00 p.m.: Fredette, "In Pursuit of Charles Lindbergh," 16–17.

328 "I brought with me, gentlemen, the great sorrow": Ibid., 17, U.S. Department of State, *The Flight of Captain Charles A. Lindbergh from New York to Paris, May 20–21, 1927, as Compiled from the Official Records of the Department of State* (Washington, D.C.: U.S. Government Printing Office, 1927).

328 this was Lindbergh's last contribution: Fredette, "In Pursuit of Charles Lindbergh," 17.

328 His only other engagement: Ibid.; Beamish, *The Story of Lindbergh*, 50–51.

329 He would remain in Europe until June 4: Aeronautical Chamber of Commerce,

Aircraft Yearbook, 1928 (New York. Aeronautical Chamber of Commerce of America, 1927), 12–13.

330 "It would have been a wonderful thing": "Lindbergh's Leap of Faith," 8.

330 Lindbergh had won: Leonard Mlodinow, *The Drunkard's Walk· How Randomness Rules Our Lives* (New York: Vintage, 2008), 167, 204.

331 One day after *Spirit* landed in Paris: Michael Sassaman, "The Man Who Wasn't Lindbergh," *American Heritage of Invention and Technology* 22, no. 1 (Summer 2006)· 56; Jay Maeder, "Wings Levine and His Machine," www.nydailynews.com/archives.

331 General Marie Charles Duval, aviation expert for *Le Figaro·* Duval is quoted in Montague, *Oceans, Planes and Airmen*, 70.

332 "I'd rather come with you than stay at home and worry": "Clarence D. Chamberlin Recalls Historic Flight," *Yiddish Radio Project*, yiddishradioproject.org; Jablonski, *Atlantic Fever*, 141; "Mrs. Chamberlin Was to Have Been Flight Partner," *Brooklyn Daily Eagle*, June 5, 1927, 1, "Chamberlin's Wife Almost Made Hop," *New York Times*, June 5, 1927, 5.

332 Chamberlin announced he would take off at 4·00 a.m.: *Columbia's* takeoff and flight comes from several sources: Jablonski, *Atlantic Fever*, 139–46; Hamlen, *Flight Fever*, 135–53; "$5,000,000 Estate in Levine's Will," *New York Times*, June 5, 1927, n.p., www.nytimes.com; "Godspeed," *The New Yorker*, June 18, 1927, 11–12; Chamberlin, *Record Flights*, 51–97; "Chamberlin's Flight to Germany," *Aero Digest* (July 1927): 20–25; "Notes and Comments," *The New Yorker*, June 11, 1927, 9; Linder, "What the Jew in the Street"; Beamish, *The Story of Lindbergh*, 213–23; "The Chamberlin-Levine Flight from America to Germany," *Current History* (July 1927): 543–47; "Brooklyn Regards Flight as its Own; Rejoicing Is Wide," *Brooklyn Daily Eagle*, June 6, 1927, n.p.; "Uncle Sam's Second Flying Hop Across the Pond," 37–41; Horace Winston Stokes, *Mirrors of the Year: A National Revue of the Outstanding Figures, Trends and Events of 1927–1928* (New York: Frederick A. Stokes, 1928), 13; Chamberlin, "The Weather Conditions on My Flight to Germany," *Aero Digest* (November 1927). 513–14; Dixon, *Conquest of the Atlantic by Air*, 131; *Time*, June 9, 1927; "New York–Berlin (Nearly)," *Flight*, June 9, 1927, 376; Richard Montague, "How *Not* to· Fly the Atlantic," *American Heritage*, 22, no. 3 (1971) 42–47.

NINETEEN: FOUR MEN IN A FOG

344 In Germany, Levine's Judaism did not seem: "Congratulations by Coolidge for Iowan," *Sioux City Index*, n.d., n.p., State Historical Society of Iowa Library, "Chamberlin," file; Chamberlin, *Record Flights*, 114–19, "Berlin Greets Chamberlin and Levine," *Flight*, June 16, 1927, 401. *Der Tog* is quoted in *Time* magazine, June 20, 1927, www.time.com, and in "Charles Albert Levine Bibliography," richard.arthur.norton.googlepages.com.

345 The public seemed to have grown tired of him: Murphy, *Struggle*, 251; Byrd, *Skyward*, 218.

345 "Has not Lindbergh proved much that we set out to prove?": Letter, Byrd to Wanamaker, May 23, 1927, Folder 4344, Box 115, "Transatlantic Flight," Byrd Collection.

346   "If it is the desire of yourself and your crew to be relieved". Telegram, Wanamaker to Byrd, May 27, 1927, Folder 4344, Box 115, "Transatlantic Flight," Byrd Collection.

346   "The flights of Lindbergh and Chamberlin-Levine": Draft of letter or cable, Byrd to Wanamaker, n.d. (but after the *Columbia's* flight on June 6, 1927), Folder 4344, Box 115, "Transatlantic Flight," Byrd Collection.

346   The tests dragged on for days: Montague, *Oceans, Poles and Airmen,* 119.

346   the honors pile up on their rivals. *Aircraft Yearbook, 1927,* 13–14; "Colonel Lindbergh's Return," *Flight,* June 16, 1927, 401; Boorstin, *The Image,* 68; Horace Greeley Jr., "Lindbergh Month," *The New Yorker,* July 2, 1927, 28; Allen, *Only Yesterday,* 218.

347   Willda Chamberlin and Grace Levine took a liner: *Time* magazine, June 27, 1927, www.time.com; "Uncle Sam's Second Flying Hop Across the Pond," 37–38; Greeley, "Lindbergh Month," 30.

347   The wait to take off drove everyone: Murphy, *Struggle,* 251–52.

347   The wait may have been hardest on Acosta: "Pilot's Pilot," *Time,* June 10, 1935, n.p., www.time.com; Ratcliff, "Byrd's Bad Boy," 52; "Mrs. Acosta Asks Legal Bar to Her Rival's Love Making," *Evening Graphic,* November 23, 1928, n.p., Container 1: "Acosta, Bertram Blanchard, Newspaper clippings 1920s–1930s," "Biographical Files, 1784–1962," AIAA Archives.

348   Byrd used his idle time: Letter, North American Newspaper Alliance to Byrd, June 17, 1927, and Letter, *New York Times* to Byrd, June 21, 1927, Box 115, "Transatlantic Flight," Byrd Collection.

348   The delays drove Tony Fokker crazy. Montague, *Oceans, Poles and Airmen,* 119; Balchen, *Come North with Me,* 100.

349   Floyd Bennett showed up at the hangar: Balchen, *Come North with Me,* 101; Byrd, *Skyward,* 101.

350   The reports from seagoing ships on June 28–29: Ware, "Forecaster to the Fliers," 21; Kimball, "Telling Ocean Flyers When to Hop," 17.

350   *America* was the forerunner of transatlantic airlines. Montague, *Oceans, Poles and Airmen,* 120–21.

351   By 5:20 a.m. everyone was in the plane: Ibid., 122; Rose, *Explorer,* 158; Balchen, *Come North with Me,* 102–103.

351   From Long Island to Nova Scotia, the weather improved: This account of the cursed flight of the *America* comes from several sources. Richard E. Byrd, "Our Transatlantic Flight," *National Geographic* 52, no. 3 (September 1927). 346–68; Murphy, *Struggle,* 253–73, 281–82; James E. Mooney, *Air Travel* (New York: Scribner's Sons, 1930), 238–39; Goerler, ed. *To the Pole,* 111–14; Rose, *Explorer,* 158–61; Byrd, "My Flight Across the Atlantic," in James Edward West, *The Lone Scout of the Sky. The Story of Charles A. Lindbergh* (Philadelphia: Boy Scouts of America, by John C. Winston, 1928), 202–15; Montague, *Oceans, Poles and Airmen,* 122–26; Balchen, *Come North with Me,* 102–12; Byrd, *Skyward,* 227–39; "Anxious Crowd at Le Bourget Awaits Arrival of Fliers," *New York Herald,* July 1, 1927, 11; "National Affairs: Four Men in a Fog," *Time,* July 11, 1927, n.p., www.time .com; Norman D. Vaughan with Cecil B. Murphey, *With Byrd at the Bottom of the World: The South Pole Expedition of 1928–1930* (Harrisburg, Pa.. Stackpole, 1990), 88–90. Charles J. V. Murphy's 1939 account in *Life* states, "Whether it was Byrd himself or Bernt Balchen who knocked Acosta from the controls and whether the

weapon used was a flashlight or a wrench, no one but the four men on the *America* can say; and they have seldom discussed the episode. In his official log of the flight, Byrd, who has a deep respect and liking for Acosta, never mentioned it. As a Virginian, Byrd esteems loyalty above all other qualities and many of the men who have served him know that they can count on his help in any emergency 'on the beach.'" It must be remembered that the Murphy and Mooney accounts are essentially from Byrd's point of view, a lens that almost always embellishes his own role and that of his friends, while diminishing that of any perceived "enemies."

356   the team wasn't that far off their original flight plan: Murphy, *Struggle*, 282–83; Montague, *Oceans, Poles and Airmen*, 131; Balchen, *Come North with Me*, 115–16; Byrd, *Skyward*, 242–43.

357   "[T]here is nothing more glorious" Noville, "Crash!" 13.

357   For five hours that night, the four flew over France. The crash of the *America* comes from several sources. Balchen, *Come North with Me*, 117–21, "National Affairs Four Men in a Fog," *Time*, July 11, 1927; "Plane's Windows Torn Out to Help Escape After Fall," *New York Herald*, July 4, 1927, 1; Noville, "Crash!" 14–15; Byrd, *Skyward*, 246–50, Murphy, *Struggle*, 284–89.

TWENTY: "THE CLOUDS BETWEEN MUST DISAPPEAR"

361   Myrtle Brown of Omaha decided to fly. "Island Girl to Fly Atlantic," *The Staten Islander*, December 16, 1927, 1.

361   Few "lady flyers" existed at the time Helena Huntington Smith, "New Woman," *The New Yorker*, May 10, 1930, 28, Judith Thurman, "Missing Woman," *The New Yorker*, September 14, 2009, 103–108

362   the Orteig Prize had unleashed a new sense of possibility Allen, *Only Yesterday*, 221–23; Boorstin, *The Image*, 68; Berg, *Lindbergh*, 167–68; Cassagneres, *Untold Story*, 123–24; "American Idol," *Columbia· The Magazine of Northwest History* 21, no. 3 (Fall 2007). 33; "Lindbergh as a Columbus," *Literary Digest* 93, no. 12 (June 18, 1927): 20.

362   When the *Columbia* took off, Myrtle could see the worry: "Chamberlin's Flight to Germany," *Aero Digest* (July 1927): 24–25; "Chamberlin-Levine Appear Near Break," *New York American*, June 23, 1927, n.p.; Clarence Chamberlin, "Air Mail Across the Atlantic," *The Rotarian* 46, no 1 (January 1935). 7.

363   The aftermath of the *Columbia's* flight certainly did not hurt Bellanca "Biographical and Historical Notes," The Giuseppe M. Bellanca Collection, www.nasm.si.edu.

363   they planned to sue Levine for $500,000: "Levine, Facing $300,000 Suit by U.S. Plans Counteraction," *New York Herald*, July 2, 1927, n.p., Container 10, "Byrd, Richard E., Biographical Files, 1784–1962," AIAA Archives.

363   Yet Levine's European dalliance: Lester D. Gardner, "The Schneider Trophy Race Through American Eyes," *Aviation* 23, no. 18 (October 31, 1927). 1052; "Levine on Visit to Pope Breaks Vatican Dress Rule; Wears Old Familiar Suit," *Brooklyn Daily Eagle*, October 3, 1927, 3, "Levine's Flight Cost Him $125,000," *Brooklyn Daily Eagle*, October 20, 1927, n.p.

365   Once again, he was the conquering hero: Balchen, *Come North with Me*, 121–23; Rose, *Explorer*, 163–65; "Bernt Balchen," 10; Letter, Albert Buhler to Byrd, July 7, 1927, Folder 4345, Box 115, "Transatlantic Flight," Byrd Collection; various letters

and cables of congratulations to Byrd, Folder 4360, Box 116, Byrd Collection. Buhler's letter to Byrd read, "Dear Sir, you are the luckiest man in France, I am the unhappiest." Buhler's wife was sick, and he was unemployed, he'd left Strasbourg looking for work, but he had failed and his family starved. "Hunger is nothing against the bitter feeling that wife and children are in a helpless situation," he said. Byrd's response, if any, is not preserved.

366 "Physically he suggests a delicate instrument": "'Dick' Byrd as a Mercury of Modern Flying Science," *The Literary Digest*, July 23, 1927, 34.

366 "Take my hand and lift me": Murphy, *Struggle*, 20–21.

367 the army aviator Lester J. Maitland and Albert Hegenberger: "Byrd Far Out to Sea, Fighting Wind and Fog; Army Pilots Make Hawaii Leap in 25 Hours," *New York Herald Tribune*, June 30, 1927, 1; "The New Craze—Flying the Atlantic," *Flight*, June 23, 1927, 420.

367 Their explanations, when they tried to make them: "Island Girl to Fly Atlantic," 1; "Wilmington Aviatrix Falls in $100 Worth of Spinach," *The Evening Journal* (Wilmington, Del.), March 15, 1930, 1; Untitled article, *New York Telegram*, January 4, 1928, n.p., Box 164, "News Clippings," Giuseppe M. Bellanca Collection.

369 James D. Dole, president of the Hawaiian Pineapple Company: Hamlen, *Flight Fever*, 213.

369 Fifteen planes entered. Ibid., 213–15, Byrd, "That 'Big Parade' in the Air," in Stokes, *Mirrors of the Year*, 16–17; Montague, *Oceans, Poles and Airmen*, 166–67.

369 Ten people died in the race: "Counting the Cost of Stunt Flying," *Literary Digest* 94, no. 10 (September 3, 1927): 10.

370 They wanted more races and they wanted more Lindbergh. "Over the Foaming Billows (To the Land of Parlez Vous)," Lyrics by J. Calder Bramwell, Music by Carl Dillon, Bandmaster of the Third U.S. Infantry (St. Paul, Minn.: J. Calder Bramwell, 1927), Folder 54, Box 106, "Sheet Music," "Papers, 1827–1969," A0904 C.A.L. Archives; Anna Fitzin, "Ave Lindbergh," a mounted and matted poem dated June 13, 1927, Outsize Folder 31, "Poems," Box 106, "Sheet Music," C.A.L. Collection; *Norfolk Virginian-Pilot* quoted in "Counting the Cost of Stunt Flying," *The Literary Digest* (September 3, 1927), 10.

371 Paul Redfern, a young man of barely 108 pounds. Montague, *Oceans, Poles and Airmen*, 167; Murphy, *Struggle*, 296.

371 the first woman to brave the Atlantic: Montague, *Oceans, Poles and Airmen*, 175–77; "Sad Secrets of the Port of the Port of Missing Planes," *The Literary Digest* 94, no. 13 (September 24, 1927): 60; "Atlantic Airmen Who Failed," in *The Book of Famous Flyers*, James Mollison, ed. (London: Collins' Clear-Type Press, 1934), 87–88; "Princess at Sea," *New York Herald-Tribune*, September 1, 1927, 1; Hamlen, *Flight Fever*, 245–50.

372 the *Sir John Carling*: Jablonski, *Atlantic Fever*, 181–82; "Sir John Carling Wings Way over Atlantic Without Radio," *New York Herald-Tribune*, September 8, 1927, 1.

372 Lloyd Bertaud again tried to cross the ocean: Hamlen, *Flight Fever*, 264–70; Montague, *Oceans, Poles and Airmen*, 182–83; "Lloyd W. Bertaud, Early Christofferson Aviator-Instructor" File: "Personages, Lloyd Bertaud"; Virginia Aeronautical Historical Society Archives; Cecil Roseberry, *The Challenging Skies: The Colorful Story of Aviation's Most Exciting Years, 1919–1939* (Garden City, N.Y.: Doubleday, 1966), 105; "Old Glory Sought Vainly in Rain and Fog," *New York*

Herald-Tribune, September 8, 1927, 1; "Wireless S.O.S. Is Dispatched by Old Glory," *Christian Science Monitor*, September 7, 1927, 1; "Hearst Urged Flyers Abandon Flight to Rome," *New York Times*, September 8, 1927, 1.

375 Ruth Elder: The tale of Ruth Elder comes from several sources· Hamlen, *Flight Fever*, 296–314, Montague, *Oceans, Poles and Airmen*, 191–204; "The American Girl, Ruth Elder's Transatlantic Flight," *Aero Digest* 11, no. 5 (November 1927): 515; "Elder, Ruth, Newspaper Clippings": "Miss Elder's Zeal Defeats Hop Delays," *New York Telegram*, n.d., n.p.; "Womack, on Polar Expedition, Is Divorced from Ruth Elder," *Washington Evening Star*, December 12, 1928, n.p.; "Going to Reno," *Washington Star*, September 29, 1939, n.p.—all from Container 26, "Biographical Files, 1784–1962," Kathleen Brooks-Pazmany, "United States Women in Aviation, 1919–1929," *Smithsonian Studies in Air and Space*, no. 5.

380 That left Frances Grayson to make the year's final try: Montague, *Oceans, Poles and Airmen*, 205–18; Pazmany, "United States Women," 23; "Atlantic Airmen Who Failed," 91; Kimball, "Telling Ocean Fliers When to Hop," 17; Dixon, *Conquest of the Atlantic by Air*, 146–50; "Mrs. Grayson Took Automatic Pistol on Dawn's Flight," *Newark Sunday Call*, December 25, 1927, n.p., and "Dawn's Navigator Foresaw Death," *The World*, May 22, 1929, n.p., Grayson, Frances Wilson, Documents, CG-605000-01, NASM Archives.

TWENTY-ONE: THE WAY THE WIND SOCK BLOWS

384 "In reading the history of nations": Charles Mackay, *Extraordinary Popular Delusions and the Madness of Crowds* (New York: Harmony, 1980 [London, 1841, rev. ed. 1852]), xix.

385 financier Bernard Baruch wrote the foreword: Ibid., xiii–xiv.

386 it was commercial aviation: "Anywhere, Everywhere," *Time*, September 17, 1928, www.time.com; *Aircraft Yearbook*, 1929, 1–6, 371–72; Edgar C. Wheeler, "Breaking into Aviation," *Popular Science Monthly*, July 1928, 44.

387 Floyd Bennett served as an early example: Montague, *Oceans, Poles and Airmen*, 219–21; Murphy, *Struggle*, 327–28; "The 'Bremen's' Epic Flight," *Literary Digest* 97, no. 4 (April 28, 1928): 5–7; "Rescuing 'The Three Musketeers of the Air,'" *Literary Digest* 97, no. 6 (May 12, 1928): 32–47; "Bennett Expires; Lindbergh's Flight with Serum Futile," *New York Times*, April 25, 1928, 1.

388 Did Byrd ever harbor such doubts?· Rose, *Explorer*, 126.

389 Byrd seemed a different man: Balchen, *Come North with Me*, 177; Letter, Byrd to C. Ward Crampton, Aristogenic Association, New York City, Oct. 17, 1927; Letter, Crampton to Byrd, Oct. 26, 1927; Pamphlet, "The Aristogenic Association, New York City," both from Folder 481, "Lectures," Box 13, Byrd Collection.

389 "If they are lost, my work is done": Balchen, *Come North with Me*, 177; Rose, *Explorer*, 245–46.

389 The stars lent him a peace: Richard E. Byrd, *Alone* (New York. Kodansha International, 1995 [1938]), afterword by David G. Campbell, 56–57; also, Richard Byrd, "Adventures in the Realms of Imagination and Thought," a manuscript that may have been published by the Grolier Society in 1950, Folder 3868, Box 91: "Published Writings," Byrd Collection.

390 he gave seventy-seven lectures: "Commander Byrd's Lecture Engagements, 1927–28," Folder 480, "Lecture invitations and schedules," Byrd Collection.

390 "quiet place": Byrd, *Alone*, 4.

390 It had not been his original intention: Lisle A. Rose, "Exploring a Secret Land: The Literary and Technological Legacies of Richard E. Byrd," *Virginia Magazine of History and Biography* 110, no. 2 (2002). 8, accessed at EBSCOhost.

390 or a craving for publicity· Finn Ronne, *Antarctica, My Destiny· A Personal History by the Last of the Great Polar Explorers* (New York· Hastings House, 1979), 44. Ronne had little love and only a grudging respect for Byrd, but Norman Vaughan remained loyal throughout. Nevertheless, Vaughan was heartbroken by his leader's solitary choice and stayed home when Byrd took him aside before the departure. Vaughan and Murphey, *With Byrd at the Bottom of the World*, 173–75.

390 no "reckless whim": Byrd, *Alone*, 36.

390 "Snow rolled on forever to meet the sky": Byrd, *Alone*, 36.

390 He crawled down the ladder into his hut: Byrd, "Adventures in the Realms of Imagination and Thought," 1.

391 imponderable procession and forces of the cosmos: Ibid., 2.

391 A Supreme Intelligence sought harmony in the cosmos: Byrd, *Alone*, 85; Edmonds, *Virginians Out Front*, 497.

391 he was nearly killed by the solitude: Byrd, *Alone*, 163–65.

391 on June 2, 1934. Thomas Charles Poulter, "The Long, Lonely Vigil of Richard E. Byrd," unpublished manuscript, Folder 3872, Box 92, Byrd Collection. Poulter was the second-in-command and senior scientist at Little America during the Byrd Antarctic Expedition II from 1933 to 1935, in which Byrd almost died.

391 "sinister Ice Age at the bottom of the world": Byrd, "Adventures in the Realms of Imagination and Thought," 3–4.

392 World War II would be the aerial war to end all wars: John W. Dower, *War Without Mercy· Race and Power in the Pacific War* (New York: Pantheon, 1986), 39–41.

393 Lindbergh's descent was the most public: Boorstin, *The Image*, 69, 73; Lardner, "Lindbergh Legends," 201, 204–206; Morris Markey, "Young Man of Affairs—I," *The New Yorker*, September 20, 1930, 28; Markey, "Young Man of Affairs—II," *The New Yorker*, September 27, 1930, 31; Leo Braudy, *The Frenzy of Renown: Fame and Its History* (New York: Oxford University Press, 1986), 23; Berg, *Lindbergh*, 362; Jan Jacobi and Sharon Smith, "Charles Lindbergh: A Journey of the Spirit," *Gateway Heritage* 22, no. 4 (2002)· 15.

394 "I dreamed that he was God": Reeve Lindbergh, *Under a Wing: A Memoir* (New York: Simon and Schuster, 1998), 11, 13.

395 In 1932 de Pinedo retired: "Francesco de Pinedo," unattributed story, 34–43 AIAA Archives; "Ashes Reveal Princess' Love for De Pinedo," *New York Daily News*, September 6, 1933, 1.

395 Lieutenant Lawrence Curtin· "William Curtin, Navy Pilot, Dies in Plane Crash," *Army Tribune*, August 15, 1936, n.p., Curtin, Lawrence W.: Documents, CC833500–01, NASM Archives.

395 The star of that first doomed flight chose solitude: "Flier Finds Fonck, Ace of 1918, Is Silent Monk," *New York Times*, n.d., n.p., and "René Fonck Dead; World War I Ace," *New York Times*, June 19, 1953, n.p., Container 29: "Fonck, René, Newspaper clippings," "Biographical Files, 1784–1962," AIAA Archives.

396 Despite Giuseppe Bellanca's excellence as a designer: Montague, *Oceans, Planes and Airmen*, 268; Collection: "Biographical and Historical Notes," Giuseppe M. Bellanca Collection.

396   Clarence Chamberlin's fortunes: Montague, *Oceans, Planes and Airmen*, 268–69;
       "Clarence Duncan Chamberlin," Wikipedia, en.wikipedia.org; "Chamberlin
       Named as City's Air Engineer," *New York Times*, June 5, 1928, n.p.; "Made to Fit
       in Ordinary Garage," *New York Times*, October 29, 1929, n.p.; "New Airline Is
       Formed," *New York Times*, December 3, 1932, n.p.; "By Stratosphere to Europe,"
       New York Times, January 27, 1937, n.p.; "Chamberlin Back in Air," *New York Times*,
       June 24, 1946, n.p.—all from Container 12: "Chamberlin, Clarence," "Biographi-
       cal Files, 1784–1962," AIAA Archives.
396   By 1934 he'd lost everything. "Charles A. Levine, Aviation Pioneer," *Washington
       Jewish Week*, January 2, 1992, 18, "Charles Levine," Yiddish Radio Project, www
       .yiddishradioproject.com; Montague, *Oceans, Poles and Airmen*, 269–72,
       "Charles A. Levine, 94, Is Dead," *New York Times*, December 18, 1991, www
       .nytimes.com; Charles A. Levine, Case File No. 93–7651 and 105–108975, Federal
       Bureau of Investigation, Washington, D.C.
397   those linked with *America* fared the worst as a group: Ingham, "Wanamaker,
       John," *Biographical Dictionary of American Business Leaders, V–Z*, 1543, 1547; "Lt.
       Noville Improving," *Washington Post*, December 8, 1931, n.p., Container 98, "Nou-
       ville [sic], George O., Miscellany," "Biographical Files, 1784–1962," AIAA Ar-
       chives; Rose, *Explorer*, 385.
398   Anthony Fokker continued to make planes· "Young Wife of Fokker, Air King,
       Leaps 15 Stories to Her Death," *New York Daily News*, February 9, 1929, n.p.;
       "Fokker Sees Wars Decided in Air," *New York Times*, March 19, 1938, n.p.; " Tony
       Fokker's Yacht $250,000 Fire Ruin," *New York Daily News*, October 9, 1939, n.p.;
       "Fokker, Airplane Pioneer, Dies," *New York Journal-American*, December 23,
       1939, n.p.; "Anthony H. G. Fokker, 49, Dies; Plane Designer and Builder," *New
       York Herald-Tribune*, December 24, 1939, n.p.; "Anthony H. G. Fokker Dies," *New
       York Sun*, December 24, 1939, n.p., "Fokker Dies in New York," *Time*, January 1,
       1940, n.p.; "Orteig Is Dead, Donor of Prize Lindbergh Won," *New York Times*,
       June 8, 1939, n.p.—all from Container 29. "Fokker Anthony, Newspaper clippings
       1939–1940," "Biographical Files," 1784–1962," AIAA Archives.
398   His troubles had been building: Montague, *Oceans, Poles and Airmen*, 273; Fox-
       worth, "Bertrand B. Acosta, 1895–1954," 109–12; "Acosta Stunts Hour in Plane
       Built by Novice," *New York Herald Tribune*, n.d., n.p., Container 1· "Acosta, Ber-
       tram Blanchard, Newspaper clippings 1920s–1930s," "Biographical Files, 1784–
       1962," AIAA Archives; "Pilot's Pilot," *Time*, June 10, 1935, n.p., Acosta, Bertrand
       B.: Documents, CA-04300–01, NASM Archives.
400   By then, Byrd was entering his final, embittered years: Rose, *Explorer*, 384, 385;
       David Roberts, "Heroes and Hoaxes. Commander Byrd's Polar Flight of Fancy,"
       Outside, October 1981, 68; "Body of Adm. Byrd's Son, 68, Found in Empty Ware-
       house," *New York Times*, October 9, 1988, www.nytimes.com; Montague, *Oceans,
       Poles and Airmen*, 273–74; Memo, Lt Richard Byrd Jr. to General E. R. Quesada,
       May 2, 1958, "Subject: Additional Information, by Way of Background, regard-
       ing 'Come North with Me' by Bernt Balchen"; Message, Lt. Byrd to President
       Dwight Eisenhower, on White House stationery, May 7, 1958, 11.25 a.m.; "Plan
       B—Destroying the Lie," a list of allies drafted by Lt. Byrd; "Those who have been
       after this matter"—all from Folder 263, "Bernt Balchen," Box 7, Byrd Collection;
       a second list of allies drafted by Lt. Byrd, Letter, Byrd to Balchen, October 12,

1931, and letter, Byrd to Balchen, November 13, 1953, File 1095, "Correspondence," Byrd Collection.

403 "Cold mathematics, based on a record of past performance": Lew Holt, "How Many Will Die Flying the Atlantic This Season?" *Modern Mechanix*, August 1931, blog .modernmechanix.com; Jablonski, *Atlantic Fever*, 295–301.

EPILOGUE: "IN THE CLOUDS"

405 In 1938 Douglas "Wrong Way" Corrigan became the first man: Corrigan, *That's My Story*, 186–99; Jablonski, *Atlantic Fever*, 285–86.

BIBLIOGRAPHY

PRINT SOURCES

"About Colonel Lindbergh." *The New Yorker*, December 17, 1927, 18.

Adas, Michael. *Dominance by Design: Technological Imperatives and America's Civilizing Mission* (Cambridge, Mass.: The Belknap, 2006).

———. *Machines as the Measure of Men· Science, Technology, and Ideologies of Western Dominance*, (Ithaca, N.Y.: Cornell University Press, 1990).

Aeronautical Chamber of Commerce. *Aircraft Yearbook, 1927* (New York: Aeronautical Chamber of Commerce of America, 1927).

———. *Aircraft Yearbook, 1928* (New York: Aeronautical Chamber of Commerce of America, 1928).

———. *Aircraft Yearbook, 1929* (New York: Aeronautical Chamber of Commerce of America, 1929).

"Air-Minded." *The New Yorker*, May 4, 1929, 16.

Alexander, Michael. *Jazz Age Jews* (Princeton, N. J.: Princeton University Press, 2001).

Allen, Edmund T. "Flying Through Fog and Night," *Aviation*, 23, no. 21 (Nov. 21, 1927): 1234–39.

Allen, Frederick Lewis. *The Big Change: America Transforms Itself, 1900–1950* (New York: Harper and Bros., 1952).

———. *Only Yesterday: An Informal History of the Nineteen-Twenties* (New York: Harper and Bros., 1931).

"America and Germany Reunited by Air." *Literary Digest* 93, no. 12 (June 18, 1927): 5–7.

"America's Ideal Mother." *The Memphis Co-Operator* 5, no. 19 (May 7, 1928): 1–2.

"The American Girl, Ruth Elder's Transatlantic Flight." *Aero Digest* 11, no. 5 (November 1927): 515–16.

"American Idol." *Columbia: The Magazine of Northwest History*, Fall 2007, 21(3), 33.

"American Legion," *Aero Digest* 10, no. 5 (May 1927): 428.

Amory, Cleveland. *Who Killed Society?* (New York: Harper and Bros., 1960).

Appel, Joseph H. *The Business Biography of John Wanamaker, Founder and Builder* (New York: Macmillan, 1930).

Armstrong, Harry G., M.D. "A Special Form of Functional Psychoneurosis Appearing in Airplane Pilots." *Journal of the American Medical Association* 106, no. 16 (April 18, 1936): 1347–54.

Asbury, Herbert. "The Year of the Big Shriek." In Horace Winston Stokes, ed. *Mirrors of the Year. A National Revue of the Outstanding Figures, Trends, and Events of 1927–8* (New York. Frederick A. Stokes Co., 1928), 196ff

"Atlantic Airmen Who Failed." In *The Book of Famous Flyers.* Ed. James Mollison (London: Collins' Clear-Type Press, 1934), 86–115.

Atlas, James. "The Art of Failing." *The New Yorker*, May 25, 1998, 67–73.

"The Average Man." *Literary Digest* 93, no. 9 (May 28, 1927): 21–22.

Balchen, Bernt. *Come North with Me* (New York: E. P. Dutton, 1958).

Baldwin, Neal. *Henry Ford and the Jews· The Mass Production of Hate* (New York· Public Affairs, 2001).

Baritz, Loren, ed. *The Culture of the Twenties* (Indianapolis. Bobbs-Merrill, 1970).

Barrett, William E. "Was Fonck a Faker?" *Cavalier* (February 1960). 72.

Beamish, Richard J. *The Story of Lindbergh, the Lone Eagle* (Philadelphia The International Press, 1927).

Beard, Charles. "Introduction," *Whither Mankind* (New York· Longmans, Green, 1928), 1–24. In Baritz, Loren, ed. *The Culture of the Twenties* (Indianapolis. Bobbs-Merrill, 1970), 388–99.

Beaty, David. *The Water Jump· The Story of Transatlantic Flight* (New York: Harper and Row, 1976).

Beck, Richard, and Ryan K. Jessup. "The Multidimensional Nature of Quest Motivation." *Journal of Psychology and Theology* 32, no. 4 (2004): 283–94.

"The Bellanca CF 5-Seater Cabin Airplane." *Aviation* (Aug. 14, 1922) 183.

"The Bellanca Monoplane—Holder of the World Endurance Record." *Aviation* (May 2, 1927): 908–10.

"Bellanca Monoplane Sets World Endurance Record." *Aviation* (April 25, 1927): 819–21

Bennett, Cora L. *Floyd Bennett* (New York: William Farquhar Payson, 1932).

Berg, A. Scott. *Lindbergh* (New York· Berkeley Books, 1999).

"Berlin Greets Chamberlin and Levine." *Flight*, June 16, 1927, 401.

Bernard, André. "Flight." *American Scholar* 68, no. 3 (Summer '99): 12.

"Bernt Balchen." *The New Yorker*, June 9, 1928, 10–11.

Berry, Frederic W. "The Fear of Failure." *The Cosmopolitan* 35 (June 1903): 233.

"Beyond Keewee and Modock." *The New Yorker*, January 7, 1928, 11–12.

Blair, William R. "Meteorology for Aviation." *Proceedings of the American Philosophical Society* 67, no. 3 (1928): 287–96

Blumberg, Arnold T. *The Big Big Little Book Book. An Overstreet Photo-Journal Guide* (Timonium, Md.: Gemstone, 2004).

Bond, Douglas D., M.D. *The Love and Fear of Flying* (New York: International Universities Press, 1952). Preface by General James H. Doolittle.

Boorstin, Daniel J. *The Exploring Spirit. America and the World, Then and Now* (New York· Random House, 1975).

———. *The Image, or What Happened to the American Dream* (New York. Atheneum, 1962).

Booth, Alice. "Shall I Marry an Aviator?" *Good Housekeeping* 89, August 19, 1929, 80ff.

Borden, Morton, ed. *Voices of the American Past: Readings in American History.* (Lexington, Mass.: D. C. Heath, 1972)

Braudy, Leo. *The Frenzy of Renown: Fame and Its History* (New York: Oxford University Press, 1986).

"The 'Bremen's' Epic Flight." *Literary Digest* 97, no. 4 (April 28, 1928). 5–7.

Brooks-Pazmany, Kathleen. "United States Women in Aviation, 1919–1929." *Smithsonian Studies in Air and Space* 5.

Broughton, Roger J. "Behavioral Parasomnias." In Sudhansu Chokroverty. *Sleep Disorders Medicine· Basic Science, Technical Considerations, and Clinical Aspects* (Boston: Butterworth Heinemann, 1999), 635–60.

Bruno, Harry. *Wings Over America. The Inside Story of American Aviation* (New York: Robert M. McBride, 1942).

Burns, Kevin R. *Noel Davis: The Father of the Naval Air Reserve* (American Institute of Aeronautics and Astronautics, 2008). A booklet prepared for the Forty-sixth Aerospace Sciences Meeting, January 2008, Reno, Nevada.

Busch, Niven, Jr. "New Post Road." *The New Yorker*, May 25, 1929, 30–36.

"Byrd and Maitland Planes Alike in Design." *Aviation* 23, no. 2 (July 11, 1927): 74–76.

Byrd, Richard E. *Alone* (New York Kodansha International, 1995 [1938]). Afterword by David G. Campbell.

———. "First Flight to the North Pole." *National Geographic* 50, no. 3 (September 1926).

———. *Little America* (New York: G. P. Putnam's Sons, 1930).

———. "My Flight Across the Atlantic." In James Edward West, *The Lone Scout of the Sky· The Story of Charles A. Lindbergh* (Philadelphia. John C. Winston for Boy Scouts of America, 1928), 202–15.

———. "Our Transatlantic Flight." *National Geographic* 52, no. 3 (September 1927): 346–68.

———. *Skyward: Man's Mastery of the Air as Shown by the Brilliant Flights of America's Leading Air Explorer et al.* (New York: Penguin Putnam, 1928).

———. "That 'Big Parade' in the Air." In Horace Winston Stokes. *Mirrors of the Year: A National Revue of the Outstanding Figures, Trends and Events of 1927–1928* (New York: Frederick A. Stokes, 1928), 1–33.

Campbell, Joseph. *The Hero with a Thousand Faces* (Princeton, N.J.. Princeton University Press, 1973 [1949]).

Cassagneres, Ev. *The Spirit of Ryan* (Blue Ridge Summitt, Pa.: Tab Books, 1982).

———. *The Untold Story of the Spirit of St. Louis· From the Drawing Board to the Smithsonian* (New Brighton, Minn.. Flying Books International, 2002).

Chamberlin, Clarence D. "Air Mail Across the Atlantic," *The Rotarian* 46, no. 1 (January 1935): 6–7.

———. *Give 'em Hell!* (New York: Beechwood, 1942).

———. *Record Flights* (New York: Dorrance, 1928).

———. "The Weather Conditions on My Flight to Germany." *Aero Digest* (November 1927): 513–14.

"The Chamberlin-Levine Flight from America to Germany." *Current History* (July 1927): 543–47.

"Chamberlin's Flight to Germany." *Aero Digest* (July 1927): 20–25.

"Chance Writes the Lindbergh Saga." *Literary Digest* 93, no. 12 (June 18, 1927): 28–29.

"Charlie Lindbergh Gets a Job." *Literary Digest* 97, no. 10 (June 9, 1928): 34–41.

Chidester, T. R. *Mood, Sleep, and Fatigue Effects in Flight Operations.* Unpublished doctoral dissertation, University of Texas, Austin.

Chokroverty, Sudhansu. *Sleep Disorders Medicine: Basic Science, Technical Considerations, and Clinical Aspects* (Boston: Butterworth Heinemann, 1999).

Clephane, Douglas W. "Weather Bureau Aid in Ocean Flying." Aviation 23, no. 2 (July 11, 1927). 84.

Cochrane, Dorothy, Von Hardesty and Russell Lee. The Aviation Careers of Igor Sikorsky (Seattle: University of Washington Press, 1989).

Cole, David. "Radical Aliens." London Review of Books, October 22, 2009, 26–27.

Collings, Kenneth. Just for the Hell of It (New York: Dodd, Mead, 1938).

Collins, Leighton. "The Dangers of the Air." In Wolfgang Langewiesche. Stick and Rudder: An Exploration of the Art of Flying (New York: McGraw-Hill, 1944, 1972), 323–50.

Collinson, Clifford, and Capt. F. McDermott. Through Atlantic Clouds: The History of Atlantic Flight (London: Hutchinson, 1934).

"Colonel Lindbergh's Return." Flight, June 16, 1927, 401.

"Conquest of Antarctica Is Resumed." Literary Digest (October 14, 1933): 14.

Corn, Joseph J. The Winged Gospel· America's Romance with Aviation (Baltimore, Md.: Johns Hopkins University Press, 1983).

Corrigan, Douglas. That's My Story (New York: E. P. Dutton, 1938).

Cotter, Charles H. The Atlantic Ocean (Glasgow: Brown, Son and Ferguson, 1974).

"Counting the Cost of Stunt Flying." Literary Digest 94, no. 10 (September 3, 1927): 10–11.

Cowen, Tyler. What Price Fame? (Cambridge, Mass.: Harvard University Press, 2000).

Cox, Patrick L. "Charles Lindbergh and Mobil Oil." Journalism History 30, no. 2 (Summer 2004)· 98–106.

Craig, Paul A. The Killing Zone. How and Why Pilots Die (New York: McGraw-Hill, 2001).

Cram, Ralph. "The Romance of Flying, Facts and Figures." Aero Digest 10, no. 6 (June 1927). 572.

Cramer, Deborah. Great Waters: An Atlantic Passage (New York: W. W. Norton, 2001).

Curti, Merle. The Growth of American Thought (New York· Harper and Bros., 1943).

Dacey, Norman F. "A Biographical Sketch—Igor Ivan Sikorsky." Aeronautics, March 1930, 31–32.

Dalton, Stephen. The Miracle of Flight (New York: McGraw-Hill, 1977).

Davis, Kenneth S. The Hero: Lindbergh and the American Dream (Garden City, N.Y.: Doubleday, 1959).

Davis, Lennard J. Obsession: A History (Chicago: University of Chicago Press, 2008).

Davis, Noel. "The Removal of the North Sea Mine Barrage." National Geographic Magazine 37, no. 2 (February 1920): 103–105.

De Bleu, Jan. Wind: How the Flow of Air Has Shaped Life, Myth, and the Land (Boston: Houghton Mifflin, 1998).

De la Croix, Robert. They Flew the Atlantic (New York: Monarch, 1960 [1958]). Trans. Edward Fitzgerald.

Dempewolff, Richard F. "PM Salutes Igor Sikorsky." Popular Mechanics 112, no. 3 (Sept. 1959). 73.

Denenberg, Barry. An American Hero: The True Story of Charles A. Lindbergh (New York: Scholastic, 1996).

De Pinedo, Francesco. "By Seaplane to Six Continents," National Geographic 54, no. 3 (September 1928). 247–302.

De Tocqueville, Alexis. *Democracy in America*. Ed. Richard D. Hoffner (New York: Penguin, 1956, 1984).

"'Dick' Byrd as a Mercury of Modern Flying Science." *The Literary Digest* (July 23, 1927): 34.

Dixon, Charles. *The Conquest of the Atlantic by Air* (London: Sampson Low, Marston, 1931).

Dorfman, John R. "Euphoria Reigned in '27 Market." *Wall Street Journal* 227, no. 49, March 11, 1996, C1.

Dower, John W. *War Without Mercy: Race and Power in the Pacific War* (New York: Pantheon, 1986).

Driggs, Laurence La Tourette. "Aces Among Aces." *National Geographic Magazine* 33, no. 6 (June 1918).

Drowne, Kathleen, and Patrick Huber. *The 1920s* (Westport, Conn.: Greenwood, 2004).

Duhamel, Georges. *America the Menace· Scenes from the Life of the Future* (Boston: Houghton Mifflin, 1931). Trans. Charles Miner Thompson.

Duncan, Richard. *Air Navigation and Meteorology* (Chicago: Goodheart-Willcox, 1929).

Earhart, Amelia. *20 Hrs. 40 Min.* (New York: Arno, 1980 [1928]).

"An Early Atlantic Flight That Came to Grief," *Literary Digest* 98, no. 12 (September 22, 1928): 64–69.

Edmonds, Pocahantas Wright. *Virginians Out Front* (Richmond, Va.: Whitlet and Shepperson, 1972).

"An Eight-Point Roman Holiday." *The New Yorker*, July 23, 1927, 28.

Empson, Jacob. *Sleep and Dreaming* (New York. Harvester Wheatsheaf, 1993).

Engen, Don. "A 70-year Question." *Air and Space Smithsonian* 12, no. 6 (Feb./Mar. '98): 4.

Enslow, Randy. "Barnstorming with Lindbergh." *Popular Science Monthly* 115, no. 4 (October 1929): 19–21.

———. "How I Fly My Plane." *Popular Science Monthly* (December 1929): 46–48.

"Epitaph for the 1920s: by James T. Adams, 1931." From James T. Adams, *The Epic of America* (Boston: Atlantic-Little, Brown, 1931). In *Morton Borden, Voices of the American Past: Readings in American History* (Lexington, Mass.: D. C. Heath, 1972), 397–400.

Erisman, Fred. *Boys' Books, Boys' Dreams, and the Mystique of Flight* (Fort Worth: Texas Christian University Press, 2006).

Evans, Nancy. "Good-by, Bohemia," *Scribner's Magazine* 89, no. 6 (June 1931): 643–46. In Baritz, Loren, ed. *The Culture of the Twenties* (Indianapolis: Bobbs-Merrill, 1970), 409–13.

"A Famous Flyer's Impromptu Rescue Stunt." *Literary Digest* 93, no. 8 (May 21, 1927) 62–66.

"The Faustian Bargain." *The Economist* 344, no. 8033 (September 6, 1997).

Ferris, Kerry O. "Through a Glass, Darkly: The Dynamics of Fan-Celebrity Encounters." *Symbolic Interaction* 24, no. 1 (2001), 25–47.

Fiedler, Leslie A. *Love and Death in the American Novel* (New York: Criterion, 1960).

"Fifty-One Hours in the Air!" *Aero Digest* (May 1927): 371.

"Fifty-One Hours in the Air." *Literary Digest* 93, no. 5 (April 30, 1927): 13.

"The Final Speeches of Sacco and Vanzetti to the Court, April 9, 1927." From Marion D. Frankfurter and Gardner Jackson, eds. *The Letters of Sacco and Van-*

zetti (New York). In *Morton Borden, Voices of the American Past: Readings in American History* (Lexington, Mass.: D. C. Heath, 1972), 361–77.

Fine, Gary Alan, and Ryan D. White. "Creating Collective Attention in the Public Domain: Human Interest Narratives and the Rescue of Floyd Collins." *Social Forces* 81, no. 1 (September 2002): 57–85.

Fitzgerald, F. Scott. "Echoes of the Jazz Age." *Scribner's Magazine* 90, no. 5 (November 1931): 459–65. In Baritz, Loren, ed. *The Culture of the Twenties* (Indianapolis: Bobbs-Merrill, 1970), 413–24.

Flanner, Janet. "Paris Letter." *The New Yorker*, June 11, 1927, 53–55.

Fleischer, Suri, and Arleen Keylin, eds. *Flight: as Reported by the New York Times* (New York: Arno, 1977).

"Flying Home?" *The New Yorker*, October 15, 1927, 18.

"Flying Over," *The New Yorker*, November 24, 1928, 18–19.

Flynn, John T. "The Dwindling Dynasties." *The North American Review* 230, no. 6 (December 1930): 645–50.

Folsom, Robert G. *The Money Trail: How Elmer Irey and His T-Men Brought Down America's Criminal Elite*. Uncorrected advance proof (Washington, D.C.: Potomac, 2010).

Fonck, René. *Ace of Aces* (New York: Ace, 1967).

———. "My New York–Paris Flight." *Aero-Digest* (June 1926): 320.

Foxworth, Thomas G. "Bertrand B. Acosta, 1895–1954," *Historical Aviation Album, All American Series*, vols. 6 and 7 (Temple City, Calif.: Historical Aviation Album, n.d.), 51–112.

Frank, Waldo. *The Re-Discovery of America* (New York: Charles Scribner's Sons, 1929), 90–105. In Baritz, Loren, ed. *The Culture of the Twenties* (Indianapolis: Bobbs-Merrill, 1970), 371–82.

Fredette, Raymond H. "In Pursuit of Charles Lindbergh." *Air Power History* 46, no. 2 (Summer '99). 4–19.

"Fuel for the Transatlantic Hop." *Aero Digest* 10, no. 6 (June 1927): 548.

Gabler, Neal. "Celebrity: The Greatest Show on Earth." *Newsweek*, Dec. 21, 2009, 62–67.

Gallo, Max. *Mussolini's Italy: Twenty Years of the Fascist Era* (New York: Macmillan, 1964, 1973).

Garber, Paul Edward. "Transatlantic Attempt Fails." *U.S. Air Services*, November 1926, 42–43.

Gardner, Lester D. "The Schneider Trophy Race Through American Eyes." *Aviation* 23, no. 18 (Oct. 31, 1927): 1050–53.

Gibbs-Smith, Charles Harvard. *Aviation: An Historical Survey, from Its Origins to the End of World War II* (London: Her Majesty's Stationery Office, 1970).

Giles, David. *Illusions of Immortality: A Psychology of Fame and Celebrity* (New York: St. Martin's, 2000).

Gill, Brendan. *Lindbergh Alone* (New York: Harcourt Brace Jovanovich, 1977).

Glines, Darrell V. *Bernt Balchen: Polar Aviator* (Washington, D.C.: Smithsonian Institute Press, 1999).

"Godspeed." *The New Yorker*, June 18, 1927, 11–12.

Goerler, Raimund E. "Richard E. Byrd and the North Pole Flight of 1926. Fact, Fiction as Fact, and Interpretation." An article submitted to the 24th Conference of the International Association of Aquatic and Marine Science Libraries and Information Centers (Reykjavik, 1998), 363–76.

Goerler, Raimund E., ed. *To the Pole: The Diary and Notebook of Richard E. Byrd, 1925–1927* (Columbus: Ohio State University Press, 1998).

"Goodrich Tires Put to Severe Test." *Aero Digest* 10, no. 6 (June 1927): 550.

Goulding, Michael, Ronaldo Barthem, and Efrem Ferreira. *The Smithsonian Atlas of the Amazon* (Washington, D.C.: Smithsonian Books, 2003).

Greeley Horace, Jr. "Lindbergh Month." *The New Yorker*, July 2, 1927, 28–30.

Gregg, Willis Day. "Meteorology of the North Atlantic and Transatlantic Flight." *Aviation* 23, no. 5 (Aug. 1, 1927): 242.

Grey, C. G., and Leonard Bridgman, eds. *Jane's All the World's Aircraft, 1927* (London: Sampson Low, Marston, 1927).

———. *Jane's All the World's Aircraft, 1928.*

Haining, Peter. *The Compleat Birdman: An Illustrated History of Man-Powered Flight* (New York: St. Martin's, 1976).

Hallion, Richard P. *Taking Flight: Inventing the Aerial Age from Antiquity Through the First World War* (Oxford: Oxford University Press, 2003).

"Halt the Imbecile's Perilous Line." *Literary Digest* 93, no. 8 (May 21, 1927): 11.

Hamlen, Joseph R. *Flight Fever* (Garden City, N.Y.: Doubleday, 1971).

Hart, Clive. *The Dream of Flight: Aeronautics from Classical Times to the Renaissance* (London: Faber and Faber, 1972).

Hatch, Alden. *The Byrds of Virginia* (New York: Holt, Rinehart and Winston, 1969).

———. *Glenn Curtiss: Pioneer of Aviation* (Guilford, Conn.: Globe Pequot, 1942)

"Hectic Seconds in the Cockpit." *Literary Digest* 97, no. 6 (May 12, 1928): 66–69.

Hegener, Henri. *Fokker—The Man and the Aircraft* (Fallbrook, Calif.: Aero, 1961).

Heibling, Mark. "The Meaning of Lindbergh's Flight in France." *Research Studies: A Quarterly Publication of Washington State University* 50, no. 2 (June 1982): 90–98.

Hellman, Geoffrey T. "The Winged S-11." *The New Yorker*, August 17, 1940, 21.

Hertzberg, Arthur. *The Jews in America: Four Centuries of an Uneasy Encounter: A History* (New York: Columbia University Press, 1997).

Hinton, Lt. Walter. "The First Transatlantic Flight." *Current History* (July 1927): 545–50.

"His Private Life." *The New Yorker*, January 14, 1928, 10.

"History and Development of Wright Whirlwind." *The Slipstream* 8, no. 8, (August 1927): 10.

"Hopping Off." *The New Yorker*, November 17, 1928, 20.

Horrigan, Brian. "'My Own Mind and Pen': Charles Lindbergh, Autobiography, and Memory." *Minnesota History* 58, no. 1 (Spring 2002). 2–15.

Horsfall, Jessie E. "Lindbergh's Start for Paris." *Aero Digest* 10, no. 6 (June 1927). 503.

"How Commander Byrd Forecasts the Coming Age of the Air." *Literary Digest* 97, no. 1 (April 7, 1928). 5–6.

Howe, Irving. *World of Our Fathers: The Journey of the East European Jews to America and the Life They Found and Made* (New York: Simon and Schuster, 1976).

Howe, Irving, and Kenneth Libo. *How We Lived: A Documentary History of Immigrant Jews in America, 1880–1930* (New York: Richard Marek, 1979).

"How It Feels to Drop from the Sky in a Parachute." *Literary Digest* 93, no. 8 (May 21, 1927): 70–78.

Huber, Richard M. *The American Idea of Success* (New York: McGraw-Hill, 1971).

Hunsaker, Jerome C. "A Half Century of Aeronautical Development." *Proceedings of the American Philosophical Society* 98, no. 2 (April 15, 1954): 121–30.

Huttig, Jack. *1927: Summer of Eagles* (Chicago: Nelson-Hall, 1980).

Ingham, John N. "Wanamaker, John," *Biographical Dictionary of American Business Leaders*, V-Z (Westport, Conn.: Greenwood, 1983), 1543–47.

Jablonski, Edward. *Atlantic Fever* (New York: Macmillan, 1972).

Jackson, Joe. *A Furnace Afloat. The Wreck of the Hornet and the 4300-mile Voyage of Its Survivors* (New York· The Free Press, 2003).

———. *The Thief at the End of the World: Rubber, Power, and the Seeds of Empire* (New York: Viking, 2008).

Jacobi, Jan, and Sharon Smith. "Charles Lindbergh: A Journey of the Spirit." *Gateway Heritage* 22, no. 4 (2002) 6–15.

Johnson, Laverne C., and Paul Naitch. *The Operational Consequences of Sleep Deprivation and Sleep Deficit* (London: NATO Advisory Group for Aerospace Research and Development, 1974).

Johnston, Alva. "The Gilded Copper." *The New Yorker*, January 12, 1929, 21–24.

Jordanoff, Assen. "Meeting Emergencies in the Air," *Popular Science Monthly*, February 1930, 47–48.

———. *Men and Wings* (Curtiss-Wright, 1942).

Jung, Carl. *Modern Man in Search of a Soul* (New York: Harvest, 1933).

Kaplan, Sidney. "Social Engineers as Saviors. The Effects of WWI on Some American Liberals." *Journal of the History of Ideas* 17, no. 4 (1956): 347–69.

Karp, Abraham J. *A History of Jews in America* (Northvale, N.J.: Jason Aronson, 1997).

"Keeping Tabs on Ocean Weather to 'Tip Off' Ambitious Flyers." *Literary Digest* 98, no. 3 (July 21, 1928): 52–54.

Keller, Allan. "Over the Atlantic Alone." *American History Illustrated* 9, no. 1 (April 1, 1974): 38–45.

Kern, Tony. *Darker Shades of Blue· The Rogue Pilot* (New York: McGraw-Hill, 1999).

Kimball, James H. "Telling Ocean Flyers When to Hop." *Popular Science Monthly*, July 1928, 16–17.

Kinert, Reed. *Racing Planes and Air Races· A Complete History*—vol. 1, *1909–1923*; vol. 2, *1924–1931* (Fallbrook, Calif.. Aero, 1967).

Kinkade, T. H. "Doc." "Tuning Up Transatlantic Motors." *Scientific American* 139 (February 1928). 105–107.

Klapp, Orrin E. "The Creation of Popular Heroes." *American Journal of Sociology* 54, no. 2 (September 1948): 133–41.

———. "Hero Worship in America." *American Sociological Review* 14, no. 1 (Feb. 1949)· 53–62.

Knoles, George Harmon. *The Jazz Age Revisited: British Criticism of American Civilization During the 1920s* (Stanford, Calif.: Stanford University Press, 1955).

Kramnick, Isaac, ed. *The Portable Enlightenment Reader* (New York: Penguin, 1995).

Krutch, Joseph Wood. "The Modern Temper." *The Atlantic Monthly* 139 (February 1927). 167–75. In Baritz, Loren, ed. *The Culture of the Twenties* (Indianapolis: Bobbs-Merrill, 1970), 355–71.

Kyvig, David E. *Daily Life in the United States, 1920–1940: How Americans Lived Through the Roaring Twenties and the Great Depression* (Chicago. Ivan R. Dee, 2002).

Lardner, John. "The Lindbergh Legends." In Isabel Leighton, ed. *The Aspirin Age, 1919–1941* (New York: Simon and Schuster, 1949), 190–213.

Lepore, Jill. "Fixed." *The New Yorker*, March 29, 2010, 93.

Lester, Lewis F., and Deborah H. Bombaci. "The Relationship Between Personality and Irrational Judgment in Civil Pilots." *Human Factors* 26, no. 5 (1984): 565–72.

Liggett, Walter W. "The Lindbergh Who Was Almost Lynched," *Common Sense* (March 30, 1933): 9–11.

Liljequist, G. H. "Did the 'Josephine Ford' Reach the North Pole?" *Interavia* 5, (1960)· 589–91.

"Lindbergh as a Columbus." *Literary Digest* 93, no. 12 (June 18, 1927). 20.

Lindbergh, Charles A. *Autobiography of Values* (New York. Harvest, 1976).

———. *Of Flight and Life* (New York. Charles Scribner's Sons, 1948).

———. *The Spirit of St. Louis* (New York: Scribner, 1953).

———. "Thoughts of a Combat Pilot." *The Saturday Evening Post*, October 2, 1954, 20–22.

———. *We* (Guilford, Conn.. Lyons, 2002 [G. P. Putnam's Sons, 1927]).

Lindbergh, Reeve. "Charles Lindbergh." *Time* 153, no. 23 (June 14, 1999): 75.

———. *Under a Wing: A Memoir* (New York: Simon and Schuster, 1998).

"Lindbergh's Flight." *Aero Digest* 10, no. 6 (June 1927): 542.

"Lindbergh's Leap of Faith." *The Literary Digest* 93, no. 10 (June 4, 1927): 5–8.

Logan, Richard D. "The Solitary Navigator as the Archetypical Modern Individual." *Journal of American Culture* 13, no. 4 (June 2004): 41–45.

Lonquest, T. C. "Operation and Adjustment of the Davis-Radford Octant." *Bureau of Aeronautics Technical Note* 178 (February 6, 1928). 1–13.

———. "Operation and Adjustment of the Mark II Model 2 Octant." *Bureau of Aeronautics Technical Note* 207 (November 22, 1929). 1–8.

Lopez, Barry. *Arctic Dreams: Imagination and Desire in a Northern Landscape* (New York, Bantam, 1987 [1986]).

"Lost Star." *The New Yorker*, May 4, 1929, 17.

Luckett, Perry D. "Technology and Modern Leadership: Charles Lindbergh, A Case Study." *Air University Review* 34, no. 6 (1983): 64–72.

McFarland, Stephen L. "Higher, Faster, and Farther: Fueling the Aeronautical Revolution, 1919–1945." In Roger D. Launius, ed. *Innovation and the Development of Flight* (College Station: Texas A&M University Press, 1999), 100–31.

Mackay, Charles. *Extraordinary Popular Delusions and the Madness of Crowds* (New York: Harmony Books, 1980 [London, 1841; rev. ed. 1852]).

McMains, Howard F. "The Guest of the Nation: Politics and Charles Lindbergh's Return to the United States in 1927." *New York History* 66, no. 3 (July 1985), 262–79.

March, H. Colley. "The Mythology of Wise Birds." *The Journal of the Anthropological Institute of Great Britain and Ireland* 27 (1898): 209–32.

Markey, Morris. "The Black Eagle—I." *The New Yorker*, July 11, 1931, 22–25.

———. "The Black Eagle—II." *The New Yorker*, July 18, 1931, 20–23.

———. "The Shouts Having Died." *The New Yorker*, December 3, 1927, 40–44.

———. "World Cruise: New Style." *The New Yorker*, March 21, 1931, 50–54.

————. "Young Man of Affairs—I." *The New Yorker*, September 20, 1930, 26–29.

————. "Young Man of Affairs—II." *The New Yorker*, September 27, 1930, 30–33.

Markham, Beryl. *West with the Night* (New York: Farrar, Straus and Giroux, 1983 [1942]).

Martin, Paul. *Counting Sheep. The Science and Pleasure of Sleep and Dreams* (New York: Thomas Dunne, 2004).

Martin, Robert E. "Tony Fokker Captures America." *Popular Science Monthly* 119 (July 1931)· 38.

Mears, Ashley. "What Makes Coco Rocha Hot?" *The Week*, August 13, 2010, 44–45. Reprinted by permission from 3QuarksDaily.com.

Miller, William. "American Historians and the Business Elite." *Journal of Economic History* 9 (1949). 184–208.

"A Million-Dollar Attack on the South Pole." *Literary Digest* 98, no. 11 (September 15, 1928): 34–52.

Milton, Joyce. *Loss of Eden· A Biography of Charles and Anne Morrow Lindbergh* (New York: HarperCollins, 1993).

Mitchell, William, "What Trans-Atlantic Flights Augur for the Future." *Aero Digest* 11, no. 5 (Nov. 1927): 517.

————. *Winged Defense: The Development and Possibilites of Modern Air Power* (New York: G. P. Putnam's Sons, 1925).

Mlodinow, Leonard. *The Drunkard's Walk. How Randomness Rules Our Lives* (New York: Vintage, 2008).

Montague, Richard "How *Not* to Fly the Atlantic." *American Heritage* 22, no. 3 (1971): 42–47.

————. *Oceans, Poles and Airmen. The First Flights Over Wide Waters and Desolate Ice* (New York: Random House, 1971).

Monticelli, Giuseppe Lucrezio. "Italian Emigration: Basic Characteristics and Trends with Special Reference to the Last Twenty Years." *International Migration Review* 1, no. 3 (Summer 1967)· 10–24.

Mooney, James E. *Air Travel* (New York: Scribner's Sons, 1930).

Mordden, Ethan. *That Jazz! An Idiosyncratic Social History of the American Twenties* (New York· G. P. Putnam's Sons, 1978).

Mosley, Leonard. *Lindbergh. A Biography* (New York. Doubleday, 1976).

Mott, Col. T. Bentley. *Myron T. Herrick, Friend of France* (Garden City, N.Y.. Doubleday, Doran, 1929).

Muha, Laura. "Charles A. Lindbergh," *Biography* 2, no. 12 (Dec. '98): 96.

Mumford, Lewis. *American Taste* (San Francisco. Westgate, 1929), 16–34. In Baritz, Loren, ed. *The Culture of the Twenties* (Indianapolis: Bobbs-Merrill, 1970), 399–405.

Murphy, Charles J. V. *Struggle: The Life of Commander Byrd* (New York· Stokes, 1928).

Murray, Stephen R. "FACE: Fear of Loss of Face and the Five Hazardous Attitudes Concept." *International Journal of Aviation Psychology* 9, no. 4 (1999): 403–11.

Neibuhr, Reinhold. *Leaves from the Notebook of a Tamed Cynic* (New York. Richard R. South, 1930).

Neville, Lee. "A 20th-Century Hero." *US News and World Report* 122, no. 19 (May 19, 1997): 12.

"The New Craze—Flying the Atlantic." *Flight* (June 23, 1927): 420.

"The New Duration Record, Some Particulars of the Equipment Used." *Flight* 19, no. 18 (May 5, 1927): 271.

"New York–Berlin (Nearly)." *Flight*, June 9, 1927, 376.

"New York Police Department Takes Pioneer Step Creating Aviation Section." *Aerial Age Weekly* 8 (Dec. 9, 1918). 654–55.

North, R. A., and G. R. Griffin. *Aviator Selection 1919–1977* (Pensacola, Fla.: Naval Aerospace Medical Research Lab, NAMRL SR 77, Naval Air Station).

"No Tears." *The New Yorker*, April 2, 1949, 26–27.

"Notes and Comments." *The New Yorker*, May 22, 1926, 7–8; May 28, 1927, 9; June 11, 1927, 9–10; and June 18, 1927, 9.

Novello, J. R., and I. Z. Youssef. "Psycho-social Studies in General Aviation I: Personality Profile of Male Pilots." *Aerospace Medicine* 45, no. 2 (1974a): 185–88.

———. "Psycho-social Studies in General Aviation II: Personality Profile of Female Pilots." *Aerospace Medicine* 45, no. 6 (1974b): 630–33.

Noville, George O. "Crash!" *Scientific American* 138 (January 1928): 13–15.

Nungesser, William L. "Nungesser." *Over the Front* 6, no. 4 (Spring 1991). 17–25.

"Ocean Flights Declared Well Worth the Cost." *Literary Digest* 95, no. 10 (December 3, 1927): 23–24.

Ogden, Tom. *The Complete Idiot's Guide to Ghosts and Hauntings* (Indianapolis, Ind.: Alpha, 1999).

"Oil Used on Trans-Atlantic Flight." *Aero Digest* 10, no. 6 (June 1927). 546.

O'Neil, Paul. *Barnstormers and Speed Kings* (Alexandria, Va.: Time-Life Books, 1981). Part of the Time-Life series *The Epic of Flight*.

"Orteig Dies at Age 69 After a Long Illness." *Newsweek* 13, no. 8 (June 19, 1939).

"The Orteig Prize." *The Slipstream* 6, no. 7 (July 1925): 19.

Osborn, Robert R. "Side Slips." *Aviation* 22, no. 17 (April 25, 1927). 858.

Oswald, Ian. *Sleeping and Waking. Physiology and Psychology* (Amsterdam: Elsevier, 1962).

"The Outcry for a Curb on 'Death Flights.'" *Literary Digest* 94, no. 13 (September 24, 1927). 5–7.

Owen, Russell. "The Dragon Hunters." *The New Yorker*, May 21, 1927, 32–38.

———. "Lindbergh's Epoch Making Flight from New York to Paris." *Current History* 26, no. 4 (July 1927): 506–12.

"The Paris–New York Flight, Fate of Nungesser and Coli Still a Mystery." *Flight* 19, no. 19 (May 12, 1927): 297.

Parrish, Michael E. *Anxious Decades: America in Prosperity and Depression, 1920–1941* (New York· W. W. Norton, 1992).

Pearce, George F. *The Navy in Pensacola: From Sailing Ships to Naval Aviation (1825–1930)* (Pensacola, Fla.. University of West Florida Books, 1980).

Pessen, Edward. "The Egalitarian Myth and American Social Reality: Wealth, Mobility, and Equality in the 'Era of the Common Man,'" *American Historical Review* 76 (Oct. 1971): 989–1034.

Phillips, Kevin. *Wealth and Democracy· A Political History of the American Rich* (New York: Broadway, 2002).

Pitkin, Walter B. *The Secret of Achievement* (New York. Grosset and Dunlap, 1936). Originally published as *The Psychology of Achievement*, 1930

"Plywood on the Spirit of St. Louis." *Aero Digest* 10, no. 6 (June 1927). 546–48.

Pope, Paul David. *The Deeds of My Fathers* (New York. Philip Turner, 2010).

"Popular Literature on Aviation." *Aero Field* 2, no. 6 (Oct. 1927). 123–26.

Portnoy, Joseph. "The Polar Flap: Byrd's Flight Confirmed." *Journal of the Institute of Navigation* 20, no. 3 (1973): 208–18.

"Publisher's News Letter." *Aviation* (January 9, 1928): 109.

"A Quiet Ace." *The New Yorker*, August 21, 1926, 9–10.

Ratcliff, J. D. "Byrd's Bad Boy." *Esquire*, July 1936, 52.

Rawlins, Dennis. "Byrd's Heroic 1926 Flight and Its Faked Last Leg." *DIO. The International Journal of Scientific History* 10 (January 2000). 2–106.

Reich, Leonard S. "Review. Farther and Faster: Aviation's Adventuring Years, 1909–1939." *Technology and Culture* 34, no. 2 (April 1993): 441–42.

Reid, Elliot G., and Thomas Carroll. *Technical Note 258. A Warning Concerning the Take-Off with Heavy Load* (Washington, D.C.. National Advisory Committee for Aeronautics, July 1927).

"Reinhold Niebuhr on American Society, 1927." From Reinhold Niebuhr, *Leaves from the Notebook of a Tamed Cynic* (New York: Richard R. Smith, 1930). In Morton Borden, *Voices of the American Past. Readings in American History* (Lexington, Mass.: D. C. Heath, 1972), 273–75.

"Rescuing 'The Three Musketeers of the Air.'" *Literary Digest* 97, no. 6 (May 12, 1928): 32–47.

Ribolaw, Harold W. *Autobiographies of American Jews* (Philadelphia. Jewish Publication Society of America, 1973).

Roberts, David. *Great Exploration Hoaxes* (San Francisco· Sierra Club Books, 1982).

———. "Heroes and Hoaxes: Commander Byrd's Polar Flight of Fancy." *Outside*, October 1981, 62–70.

Robertson, James Oliver. *American Myth, American Reality* (New York: Hill and Wang, 1980).

Robinson, Laura. "Lindbergh, the Messenger of Universal Brotherhood." *Reality: A Bahai Magazine* 14, no. 1 (July 1927): 6–7.

Rodahl, Kåre. *North: The Nature and Drama of the Polar World* (New York: Harper and Bros., 1953).

Rollins, Janet B. "Flight as Sea Voyage in Saint-Exupery's 'Southern Mail' and 'Night Flight.'" *The Journal of American Culture* 7, nos. 1–2 (Spring/Summer 1984)· 75–78.

Rollins, Peter. "Will Rogers on Aviation: A Means of Fostering Frontier Values in an Age of Machines and Bunk?" *Journal of American Culture* 7 (Spring/Summer 1984)· 85–92.

Ronne, Finn. *Antarctica, My Destiny A Personal History by the Last of the Great Polar Explorers* (New York: Hastings House, 1979).

Rose, Lisle A. *Explorer. The Life of Richard E. Byrd* (Columbia, Mo.: University of Missouri Press, 2008).

Rose, Susan. *The Medieval Sea* (New York Hambledon Continuum, 2007).

Roseberry, Cecil R. *The Challenging Skies. The Colorful Story of Aviation's Most Exciting Years, 1919–1939* (Garden City, N.Y.. Doubleday, 1966).

Rosenblatt, Roger. "The Deep and Quiet Continents of Ice." *U.S. News and World Report* 105, no. 16 (October 24, 1988)· 20.

Ross, Walter Sanford. *The Last Hero: Charles A. Lindbergh* (New York. Harper and Row, 1967).

Rovit, Earl. "A Touch of Greatness." *Sewanee Review* 108, no. 3 (Summer 2000): 399.

Rowe, Percy. *The Great Atlantic Air Race* (Toronto: McClelland and Stewart, 1977).

Rutan, Bert. "Confidence in Nonsense." *Aviation Week and Space Technology* 158, no. 12 (March 24, 2003): 50.

"Sad Secrets of the Port of Missing Planes." *Literary Digest* 94, no. 13 (September 24, 1927): 56–68.

Samuel, Larry. *Rich. The Rise and Fall of American Wealth Culture* (New York: American Management Association, 2009).

Sandage, Scott A. *Born Losers: A History of Failure in America* (Cambridge, Mass.: Harvard University Press, 2005).

Sassaman, Michael. "The Man Who Wasn't Lindbergh." *American Heritage of Invention and Technology* 22, no. 1 (Summer 2006). 56.

Scammell, Henry. "Across the Atlantic." *Air & Space Smithsonian* 11, no. 1 (1996): 32–40.

Schlaifer, Robert, and S. D. Heron. *Development of Aircraft Engines; Development of Aviation Fuels: Two Studies of Relations between Government and Business* (Boston: Maxwell Reprint, 1950).

Schroeder, Alex. *The Application and Administration of Inducement Prizes in Technology* (Golden, Colo.: Independence Institute, 2004).

Selman, Carl, ed. *Navigatio Sancti Brendani Abbatus* (South Bend, Ind.: University of Notre Dame Press, 1959).

Shaffer, Laurance F. "Fear and Courage in Aerial Combat." *Journal of Consulting Psychology* 9, no. 1 (Jan.–Feb. 1947): 137–43.

"Should Trans-Oceanic Flights Be Regulated?" *The Slipstream* 8, no. 10 (October 1927): 7–9.

Sikorsky, Igor I. *The Story of the Winged-S· An Autobiography* (New York: Dodd, Mead, 1958).

"The Sikorsky Transatlantic Plane." *Aviation* (May 31, 1926). 834–35.

"The Sky Raider." *Motion Picture News* 31, no. 14 (April 4, 1925): 1522; also full-page ad, 1382.

Sloan, S. J., and C. L. Cooper. *Pilots Under Stress* (London· Routledge and Kegan Paul, 1986).

Smedley, Doree, and Hollister Noble. "Flying Dutchman." *The New Yorker*, February 7, 1931, 20–24.

Smith, Frank Kingston, and James P. Harrington. *Aviation and Pennsylvania* (Philadelphia: Franklin Institute Press, 1981).

Smith, Gary N. "The Charles Lindbergh Trunk: A Time Capsule of His St. Louis Years," *Gateway Heritage* 16, no. 1 (1995): 20–25.

Smith, Helena Huntington. "New Woman," *The New Yorker*, May 10, 1930, 28–31.

Smith, Michael L. "Air-Conditioned Daydreams: The Airplane in American Culture." *American Quarterly* 36, no. 5 (Winter 1984): 713–18.

Smith, Richard K. *First Across! The U.S. Navy's Transatlantic Flight of 1919* (Annapolis, Md.: Naval Institute Press, 1973).

Spark, Nick T. "Charles Lindbergh, Donald Hall, and the Plane That Made History." *American Aviation Historical Society Journal* 50, no. 2 (2005): 132–46.

Stegner, Wallace. *Mormon Country* (Lincoln: University of Nebraska Press, 1970). First published 1942.

Stephenson, David B., Heinz Wanner, Stefan Bronnimann, and Jürg Luterbacher.

"The History of Scientific Research on the North Atlantic Oscillation." In James W. Hurrell, Yochanan Kushnir, Geir Ottersen, Martin Visbeck, eds. *The North Atlantic Oscillation: Climatic Significance and Environmental Impact* (Washington, D.C.. American Geophysical Union, 2003), 37–50.

Stoff, Joshua. *The Aerospace Heritage of Long Island* (Interlochen, N.Y.: Heart of the Lakes, 1989).

———. *Historic Aircraft and Spacecraft of the Cradle of Aviation Museum* (Toronto: General Publishing, 2001).

———. *Long Island Airports* (Charleston, S.C.. Arcadia, 2004).

Stokes, Horace Winston. *Mirrors of the Year: A National Revue of the Outstanding Figures, Trends and Events of 1927–1928* (New York: Frederick A. Stokes, 1928).

Streever, Bill. "Five Minutes in the Arctic Ocean." *The Week*, August 14, 2009, 44–45. Excerpted from Streever, *Cold: Adventures in the World's Frozen Places* (New York: Little, Brown, 2009).

Surpin, Mark. *The Brave Men: Twelve Portraits of Courage* (New York: Platt and Munk, 1967).

Thomas, Lowell. *Thrills* (New York: Towner and Buranelli, 1933).

Thurman, Judith. "Missing Woman." *The New Yorker*, September 14, 2009, 103–108.

"A Transatlantic Flight," *Nature* 121, no. 3061 (June 30, 1928): 1033.

"The Transatlantic Plane 'American Legion.'" *Aero Digest* (May 1927): 428.

Trotti, Lamar. "Sending Lindbergh to the World Through the Motion Picture." *The Southern Club Woma*n (Jacksonville, Fla.) 3, no. 4 (January 1928): 8.

Tversky, Amos, and Daniel Kahneman. "The Framing of Decisions and the Psychology of Choice," *Science* 211, no. 30 (January 1981): 453–58.

"Uncle Sam's Second Flying Hop Across the Pond." *The Literary Digest* (June 25, 1927): 37–41.

U.S. Department of State. *The Flight of Captain Charles A. Lindbergh from New York to Paris, May 20–21, 1927, as Compiled from the Official Records of the Department of State* (Washington, D.C.: U.S. Government Printing Office, 1927). "Presented by the Secretary of State Frank B. Kellogg, June 11, 1927, to CAPTAIN LINDBERGH, In commemoration of his epochal achievement."

Van der Linden, Robert. *The Boeing 247: The First Modern Airliner* (Seattle: University of Washington Press, 1991).

Vaughan, Norman D., and Cecil B. Murphey. *With Byrd at the Bottom of the World The South Pole Expedition of 1928–1930* (Harrisburg, Pa.: Stackpole, 1990).

Veblen, Thorstein. "The Place of Science in Modern Civilization." *American Journal of Sociology* 11, no. 5 (1906): 585–99.

Walsh, George. *Gentleman Jimmy Walker. Mayor of the Jazz Age* (New York: Praeger, 1974).

"Wanted: New Poles for Byrd to Conquer." *Literary Digest* 106, no. 11 (July 5, 1930): 38–41.

Ward, John W. "The Meaning of Lindbergh's Flight." *American Quarterly* 10, no. 1 (1958): 3–16.

Ware, Foster. "Deus Ex Machina." *The New Yorker*, August 13, 1927, 16–19.

———. "Forecaster to the Fliers." *The New Yorker*, July 28, 1928, 20–22.

Wecter, Dixon. *The Hero in America: A Chronicle of Hero Worship* (New York: Charles Scribners' Sons, 1941). Quoted in Harold Lubin, ed. *Heroes and Anti-Heroes* (San Francisco: Chandler, 1968), 74–87.

Weimar, William. "Wings Over America." *The New Yorker*, March 30, 1929, 22–25.

West, James Edward. *The Lone Scout of the Sky· The Story of Charles A. Lindbergh* (Philadelphia: Boy Scouts of America, John C. Winston, 1928).

Westcott, Malcolm R. *Toward a Contemporary Psychology of Intuition: A Historical, Theoretical, and Empirical Inquiry* (New York: Holt, Rinehart and Winston, 1968).

"What Byrd Found." *Literary Digest* 106, no. 2 (July 12, 1930): 24.

"What Germany Thinks of the 'Bremen' Flight." *Literary Digest* 97, no. 6 (May 12, 1928): 14–15.

"What Nungesser's Mother Thinks of Ocean Flights." *Literary Digest* 97, no. 6 (May 12, 1928): 69–71.

Wheeler, Edgar C. "Breaking into Aviation." *Popular Science Monthly*, July 1928, 43–44.

White, Lynn, Jr. "Medieval Uses of Air." *Scientific American* 223, no. 2 (August 1970): 92–100.

White, T. H. *The Book of Beasts: Being a Translation from a Latin Bestiary of the Twelfth Century* (New York: Dow, 1984 [1954]).

"Why They Failed." *Success*, November 1898, 24.

Wiggens, Bill. "Mystery of the White Bird." *Air Classics*, July 1999. Available at findarticles.com.

Wilkinson, Stephan, "The Search for L'Oiseau Blanc," *Air & Space Smithsonian* 1, no. 6 (Feb./March 1987): 86–95.

Wohl, Robert. *The Spectacle of Flight· Aviation and the Western Imagination, 1920–1950* (New Haven, Conn.: Yale University Press, 2005).

Wolfsohn, Venlo, and Booton Herndon. "The Man Who Was Almost Lindbergh." *True*, May 1963, 57–60.

"Wright J5-C Engine." *Aero Digest* 10, no 6 (June 1927).

Wykes, Alan. *Air Atlantic: A History of Civil and Military Transatlantic Flying* (New York: David White, 1968).

Zinn, Howard. *The Twentieth Century· A People's History* (New York: Harper and Row, 1980).

NEWSPAPERS (ARTICLES IN CHRONOLOGICAL ORDER)

CHICAGO TRIBUNE

"French Ace to Try for New Record in Egg-Shaped Plane," November 19, 1922.

THE CHRISTIAN SCIENCE MONITOR

"Wireless S.O.S. Is Dispatched by Old Glory," September 7, 1927, 1.

DAILY MIRROR (NEW YORK)

"Storm Menaces Nungesser on Flight in Mid-Atlantic," May 9, 1927, 2.

"Despair in Wake of Hope as Reports of Fliers' Safety Are Denied," June 16, 1927, 17.

DAILY NEWS (NEW YORK)

"Ashes Reveal Princess' Love for De Pinedo," September 6, 1933, 1.

DESERET EVENING NEWS

"Going to Annapolis," May 27, 1910, 12.

THE EVENING JOURNAL (WILMINGTON, DEL.)
"Wilmington Aviatrix Falls in $100 Worth of Spinach," March 15, 1930, 1.

EVENING POST (WELLINGTON, N.Z.)
"News of St. Romain," May 7, 1927, 9.

NASSAU DAILY REVIEW
"Sikorsky Plane Crashes, Two Dead," September 21, 1926, 1.

NAVY TIMES
"Trophy Is Memorial to Early Aviator," April 25, 1977, 35.

NEW YORK AMERICAN
"Chamberlin-Levine Appear Near Break," June 23, 1927, n.p.

THE NEW YORK HERALD
"Nungesser May Take Off for New York Sunday," April 20, 1927, 1.
"Davis to Carry 20,000 Postcards," April 21, 1927, 3.
"Nungesser Delays Flight to N.Y. Two Weeks," April 21, 1927, 1.
"Nungesser Believed Ready to Take Off Immediately," April 25, 1927, 1.
"Fliers Study Skies as Ready Planes Await Flights," May 2, 1927, 2.
"Nungesser's 'White Bird' Fueling at One a.m. for Dawn Atlantic Attempt," May 8, 1927, 1.
"French Aviators Somewhere Over Atlantic Ocean Nearing Goal of World's Record Dash," May 9, 1927, 1.
"Storm in Nungesser's Path Over Atlantic," May 9, 1927, 1.
"Byrd to Try Paris Flight on Saturday in 'America,'" May 10, 1927, 1.
"Nungesser Missing Somewhere in Atlantic," May 10, 1927, 1.
"Rumors and False Reports Worry Anxious Parisians," May 10, 1927, 1.
"French Papers Defend Publication of Report," May 11, 1927, 1.
"'He'll Return,' Says Dauntless Mother of Flier," May 11, 1927, 8.
"No Clue to Nungesser's Fate," May 11, 1927, 1.
"U.S. Weather Bureau Denies Failure to Issue Bulletins," May 11, 1927, 1.
"Byrd Far Out to Sea, Fighting Wind and Fog; Army Pilots Make Hawaii Leap in 25 Hours," June 30, 1927, 1.
"Anxious Crowd at Le Bourget Awaits Arrival of Fliers," July 1, 1927, 11.
"Plane's Windows Torn Out to Help Escape After Fall," July 4, 1927, 1.
"Princess at Sea," September 1, 1927, 1.
"Old Glory Sought Vainly in Rain and Fog," September 8, 1927, 1.
"Sir John Carling Wings Way Over Atlantic Without Radio," September 8, 1927, 1.

NEW YORK TIMES
These are by no means the only articles in the *Times* devoted to coverage of the Orteig Prize. There were many, many more. This list, alone, however, shows how much space the newspaper devoted to the race, a remarkable output for the nearly year and a half that the events described occurred. Since bylines were rare at that time, it is impossible to tell from this which specific reporters were assigned to the fliers

in the race. But it would make an interesting study—how the style and prejudices of the individual writer shaped the public perceptions of the rivals in something that was so often related in near-mythic terms.

"French Ace Says America Leads All Other Nations in Aviation," January 24, 1926, E1.

"Fonck Plans New York–Paris Flight in May," March 25, 1926, 1.

"Dinner to Capt. Fonck Is Given by Orteig," May 5, 1926, 34.

May 11, 1926, 11.

May 12, 1926, 4.

May 14, 1926, 4.

"Byrd Views Fonck Plane," August 23, 1926.

"Fonck Takes Plane in Flight Over City," August 24, 1926.

"Sikorsky Plane Tested," August 30, 1926.

"Col. Hartney Backs Berry in Fonck Row," August 31, 1926, 1.

"Transatlantic Flight Dissensions," September 2, 1926.

"Fonck Again Ready to Hop Off at Dawn," September 21, 1926, 1.

"Airmen Cleared by Speedy Inquiry," September 22, 1926, 1.

"Experts Study Crash," September 22, 1926, 4.

"Fonck Plane Burns; 2 Die at Start of Dawn Flight," September 22, 1926, 1.

"French Air Circles Grieved by Crash," September 22, 1926, 4.

"Fonck Blames Aide Who Died in Crash," September 23, 1926, 1.

"Plan 7000-Mile Trip in Byrd Polar Plane," October 1, 1926, 25.

"Byrd Hints at Flying Across the Atlantic," October 29, 1926, 18.

"Byrd Plane Ends Tour of Country," November 24, 1926, 3.

"Screen Notes," December 11, 1926, 14.

"Commander Byrd's Position," Letters to the Editor, December 16, 1926, 26.

"Motor Feats Recorded," December 20, 1926, 39.

"Davis to Join Byrd in Non-Stop Flight," February 10, 1927, 2.

"15 Life Policies Each $4,000,000 or More," February 21, 1927, 18.

"Mail Pilot Files Entry for Paris Flight, C. A. Lindbergh Will Fly a Ryan Monoplane," March 1, 1927, 16.

"Pope Considers Use of Planes in Church Work," March 3, 1927, 6.

"Noel Davis to Try New York–Paris Hop for Legion in June," March 14, 1927, 1.

"Flies Over Snakes and Savages in Storm," March 17, 1927, 2.

"De Pinedo Disappears Over Brazilian Wilds and Day and Night Pass Without News of Him," March 19, 1927, 1.

"Flight to Paris Lures Noted Pilots of the Air," March 20, 1927, Special Features, xx5.

"Insurance Is Adapted to Our Complex Life," March 20, 1927, Special Features, xx9.

"Davis Reveals New Features of Plane in Which He Will Attempt Non-Stop Flight to Paris," March 24, 1927, 12.

"De Pinedo Sweeps into New Orleans," March 30, 1927, 12.

"A Great Italian Aviator," March 31, 1927, 27.

"De Pinedo's Great Flight Makes Him Italian Idol," April 6, 1927, 16.

"An Accident, Says de Pinedo," April 8, 1927, 7.

"Charge Fascist Foe Fired Pinedo Plane," April 8, 1927, 7.

"Mussolini Reassures Fletcher," April 8, 1927, 7.

"Pinedo Plane Burns on Roosevelt Lake," April 8, 1927, 1.

"Wade Quits, Calls Paris Hop Untimely," April 9, 1927, 21.
"Crack Navy Pilots to Man Both Planes," April 10, 1927, 1.
"Davis Plane in Test Flight," April 10, 1927, 1.
"Fliers in Both Airplanes Will Report to the New York Times," April 10, 1927, 1.
"Pinedo's Adversity Will Add to Glory," April 10, 1927, E9.
"Story of Byrd's Plans," April 10, 1927, 1.
"Wanamaker Hopes to Link Continents," April 10, 1927, 25.
"Crowds Cheer Take-Off," April 11, 1927, 3.
"Davis Is Delighted as His Ocean Plane Speeds 160 Miles," April 11, 1927, 1.
"Davis's Tests Stir Interest in Flight," April 11, 1927, 3.
"Inspect Davis's Plane," April 12, 1927, 29.
"Byrd Now in Chicago," April 13, 1927, 2.
"French Pledge Aid in Flight to Paris," April 13, 1927, 2.
"Mrs. Davis Aids Flight," April 13, 1927, 2.
"Bennett Cuts Load for Flight to Paris," April 14, 1927, 3.
"Plane Up 42½ Hours Breaks U.S. Record and Keeps at Grind," April 14, 1927, 1.
"Aviation Progress Sketched by Byrd," April 15, 1927, 3.
"Fliers Set New Record of 51 Hours in Air," April 15, 1927, 1.
"French Admire Flight, But Want Record Back," April 15, 1927, 1.
"MacReady Is Elated," April 15, 1927, 2.
"Paris, April 14," April 15, 1927, 3.
"Pilot's Parents Confident," April 15, 1927, 2.
"Air Race to Paris Promised by Backer of Bellanca Plane," April 16, 1927, 1.
"Byrd Rows in River in Rubber Lifeboat," April 16, 1927, 3.
"French Speed Plan to Make Hop First," April 16, 1927, 3.
"Byrd's Plane Crashes in its First Trial," April 17, 1927, 1.
"Davis, Ocean Flier, Began as a Cowboy," April 17, 1927, 1.
"Davis's Big Plane Flies from Virginia," April 17, 1927, 1.
"Non-Stop Champions Deplore Byrd Crash," April 17, 1927, 22.
"Byrd Trip in Doubt, He Offers to Help Bellanca Flight," April 18, 1927, 1.
"Byrd Trip May be Cancelled," April 18, 1927, 8.
"Wanamaker Delays Byrd Flight Decision," April 19, 1927, 29.
"Bennett's Recovery Slow," April 20, 1927, 11.
"Byrd's Future Undecided," April 20, 1927, 11.
"Mail Flier Chosen for Bellanca Hop," April 20, 1927, 11.
"New Paris Flight Planned," April 20, 1927, 11.
"Bellanca Ready for Quick Start," April 21, 1927, 29.
"Bennett Frets in Hospital," April 21, 1927, 29.
"Nungessser Plans to Start Sunday on Flight from Paris to New York," April 21, 1927, 1.
"Ask Paris Greeting for Noel Davis," April 22, 1927, 23.
"Secret Hop Likely by Bellanca Plane," April 22, 1927, 23.
"Bellanca Flight Mapped by Bertaud," April 23, 1927, 19.
"Lt. Noville Leaves Hospital," April 23, 1927, 19.
"Paris Lays Bets on Ocean Flights," April 23, 1927, 19.
"Brooklyn Is Backer of Bellanca Plane," April 24, 1927, 3.
"Drouhin Bids Hard in Atlantic Hop," April 24, 1927, 3.
"Visits Bennett in Hospital," April 24, 1927, 21.

"Chamberlin Saves Two Girls in Plane by Daring Landing," April 25, 1927, 1.

"De Pinedo Arrives in City Secretly," April 25, 1927, 12.

"City Gives De Pinedo Rousing Welcome," April 26, 1927, 3.

"Airmen Pay Tribute to Crash Victims," April 27, 1927, 2.

"Bellanca Plane Tests Speed Today," April 27, 1927, 3.

"Davis and Wooster Killed in Crash as Big Plane Falls on Virginia Swamp," April 27, 1927, 1.

"Davis Mother Takes News of Crash Bravely," April 27, 1927, 2.

"Davis's Crash Stirs Sympathy of Paris," April 27, 1927, 2.

"Dead Fliers Ranked High in Air Service," April 27, 1927, 13.

"The Langley Field Disaster," April 27, 1927, 24.

"Transocean Flight Dogged by Bad Luck," April 27, 1927, 2.

"Nungesser and Coli Wary of Taking Off," April 28, 1927, 25.

"Plans Here Worry French," April 28, 1927, 3.

"To Pick Second Pilot for Bellanca Tonight," April 28, 1927, 25.

"Acosta Withdraws from Paris Flight," April 29, 1927, 23.

"Anti-Fascisti Riot Menaces De Pinedo," April 29, 1927, 23.

"Bellanca Plane Ready in Six Days," April 30, 1927, 21.

"Lindbergh Plane Near Disaster," April 30, 1927, 21.

"$150,000 in Prizes for Safer Aviation," April 30, 1927, 2.

"Drives Auto 107 Hours Without a Rest," May 1, 1927, 5.

"Ocean Flying Takes Heavy Toll," May 1, 1927, xx4.

"Nungesser Plane Makes Speed Trial," May 4, 1927, 3.

"Hangar Fire Hurts Nungesser Plane," May 5, 1927, 23.

"Honor Rodman Wanamaker," May 6, 1927, 23.

"Nungesser Is Ready: Waits on Weather," May 7, 1927, 1.

"Nungesser Off on Paris–New York Hop at 5.17 a.m.," May 8, 1927, 1.

"Rumors Stir Paris Over Start of Hop," May 8, 1927, 25.

"No Word Received About Saint Romain," May 8, 1927, n.p.

"Ace's Mother Is Confident," May 9, 1927, 2.

"Rivals Taken by Surprise," May 9, 1927, 1.

"Should Be Nearing Land," May 9, 1927, 1.

"Byrd Denies Rumor," May 10, 1927, n.p.

"Flight Set for Saturday," May 11, 1927, 1.

"Byrd Flight to Await Fate of French Fliers," May 12, 1927, n.p.

"Hunt Hidden Flaws in Bellanca," May 12, 1927, n.p.

"1,550-Mile Flight Made by Lindbergh," May 12, 1927, 2.

"Lindbergh Arrives After Record Hop," May 13, 1927, 1.

"May Start Tomorrrow," May 13, 1927, 1.

"Three Pilots Discuss Flight at Garden City," May 13, 1927, n.p.

"Bertaud's Career in the Air," May 14, 1927, 2.

"Chamberlin's Town Stirred," May 14, 1927, 2.

"Rival Pilots Watchful," May 14, 1927, 1.

"Fliers Test Planes, Awaiting Good Day," May 15, 1927, 1.

"Hope for Aviators Nears End in Paris," May 15, 1927, 2.

"Mrs. Lindbergh Bids Calm Good-By to Son," May 15, 1927, n.p.

"Should Atlantic Fliers Shun Radio to Save Weight?" May 15, 1927, n.p.

"Wanamaker Offers Nungesser Award," May 16, 1927, 1.
"Paris Fliers Wait a Day or Two More for Skies to Clear," May 17, 1927, 1.
"Bertaud May Lose Post in Columbia," May 18, 1927, 1.
"Bertaud to Remain in Bellanca Crew," May 19, 1927, 1.
"Byrd Urges Flood Aid at Good-Will Meeting," May 19, 1927, n.p.
"Lindbergh Is Set to Fly at Daylight If Weather Conditions Remain Good," May 20, 1927, 1.
"Chamberlin's Wife Almost Made Hop," June 5, 1927, 5.
"$5,000,000 Estate in Levine's Will," June 5, 1927, n.p.
"Levine Got Start as Aviation Worker," June 5, 1927, 3.
"Hearst Urged Flyers Abandon Flight to Rome," September 8, 1927, 1.
"Bennett Expires; Lindbergh's Flight with Serum Futile," April 25, 1928, 1.
"Orteig Is Dead, Donor of Prize Lindbergh Won," June 8, 1939.
"Raymond Orteig, Hotel Man, Dies," June 8, 1939, n.p.
"Mme. Nungesser Killed," November 1, 1940, 5.
"Charles A. Levine, 94, Is Dead," December 18, 1991.

THE OGDEN STANDARD-EXAMINER
"Ogdenite Was Boyhood Chum of Noel Davis," April 26, 1927, 1.
"Utah Plane Victim Won Fame by His Mine Laying Exploits in World War," April 26, 1927, 1.

ST. LOUIS POST-DISPATCH
"Floyd Bennett Pictures Aerial Lines of Future," November 14, 1926, n.p.
"Americans to Hop Off Saturday for Flight to Paris," May 11, 1927, 3.
"Bad Weather Delays Flight Across Atlantic," May 14, 1927, 1.
"American Flyers Again Delayed by Mid-Atlantic Fog," May 16, 1927, 1.

SALT LAKE HERALD
"Six Applicants for Annapolis Cadetship," February 27, 1910, 17.
"Noel Davis Surprised by Getting Life Job," May 27, 1910, 11.

SALT LAKE TELEGRAM
"Eighty Graduates Receive Diplomas at L.D.S. High," May 27, 1910, 2.

SAN FRANCISCO EXAMINER
"Sea Find Revives Mystery," January 25, 1961, 10.

THE STATEN ISLANDER
"Island Girl to Fly Atlantic," December 16, 1927, 1.

TORONTO STAR
"Lindbergh to Refuse to Enter the Movies," May 30, 1927, n.p.

WALL STREET JOURNAL
"Euphoria Reigned in '27 Market" 227, no. 49 (March 11, 1996)· C1.

WASHINGTON DAILY NEWS
April 1, 1949, 34.

WASHINGTON JEWISH WEEK
"Charles A. Levine, Aviation Pioneer," January 2, 1992, 18.

WINCHESTER STAR
"Admiral Byrd's Daughter Shares Her Memories of a Globe-Trotting Hero," November 19, 1993, A1.

ARCHIVAL SOURCES
BROOKLYN PUBLIC LIBRARY, THE BROOKLYN COLLECTION, CLIPPING FILES OF
THE BROOKLYN DAILY EAGLE, 1927–1928
   "Levine Keen on Thrills," June 5, 1927.
   "Mrs. Chamberlin Was to Have Been Flight Partner," June 5, 1927, 1.
   "Brooklyn Regards Flight as Its Own; Rejoicing Is Wide," June 6, 1927, n.p.
   "Chamberlin Won Fame by Skill in Stunt Landing," June 6, 1927, 11.
   "Levine Nerviest Man He Ever Met," September 18, 1927.
   "Levine on Visit to Pope Breaks Vatican Dress Rule; Wears Old Familiar Suit,"
      October 3, 1927, 3.
   "Levine's Flight Cost Him $125,000," October 20, 1927, n.p.
   "Levine Denies Rumor That He'll Forsake Judaism," November 25, 1927.

BYRD POLAR ARCHIVES, OHIO STATE UNIVERSITY LIBRARIES, RICHARD E. BYRD
COLLECTION
   Box 4
      File 3: "Logbooks, Josephine Ford (Airplane)"
         Logbook October 7, 1926–November 23, 1926.
   Box 7
      Folder 263, "Bernt Balchen"
         Memo, Lieutenant Richard Byrd Jr. to General E. R. Quesada, May 2,
            1958. "Subject: Additional Information, by Way of Background, regarding 'Come North with Me' by Bernt Balchen."
         Message, Lieutenant Byrd to President Dwight Eisenhower, on White
            House stationery, May 7, 1958, 11:25 a.m.
         "Plan B—Destroying the Lie," a list of allies drafted by Lieutenant
            Byrd.
         "Those who have been after this matter," a second list of allies drafted by
            Lieutenant Byrd.
   Box 13
      Folder 480, "Lecture invitations and schedules"
         "Commander Byrd's Lecture Engagements, 1927–28"
         Letter, Louis J Alber to Richard E. Byrd, August 22, 1928.
      File 481, "Lectures"
         Letter, Byrd to C. Ward Crampton, The Aristogenic Association, New
            York City, October 17, 1927

Letter, Crampton to Byrd, October 26, 1927.
Pamphlet, "The Aristogenic Association, New York City."
File 490, "Lectures 1926–27"
. "Lt. Cdr. Byrd Flying in Northern Regions of the Arctic, 1926"
Letter, Byrd to H. W. August, editor of *The Times-Press,* Akron, Ohio, February 18, 1927.
Letter, Byrd to James Pond, March 18, 1927.
Letter, Byrd to James P. Munroe, The Twentieth-Century Club, March 23, 1927.
File 491, "Lectures"
"Copy of Notes for Movie Lecture"
Letter, James Pond to Byrd, Oct. 9, 1926.
Letter, Byrd to Pond, October 10, 1926.
File 1095, "Correspondence"
Letter, Byrd to Balchen, October 12, 1931
Letter, Byrd to Balchen, November 13, 1953.
Box 91
Folder 3868
Richard Byrd, "Adventures in the Realms of Imagination and Thought," a manuscript that may have been published by The Grolier Society in 1950.
Box 92
Folder 3872
Thomas Charles Poulter, "The Long, Lonely Vigil of Richard E. Byrd," unpublished manuscript.
Folder 3873
Richard E. Byrd, "Miscellaneous Thoughts," Number 95, p. 193, an unpublished manuscript by Byrd dated May 22, 1950.
Box 113, "North Pole Flight"
File 4229
"Outline of Film, Lt. Cdr. Byrd Flying in Northern Regions of the Arctic, 1925," n.d.
File 4231
Untitled manuscript about the MacMillan Expedition, n.d.
File 4233
Letter, David Rochford, American Legion of Massachusetts, to Byrd, June 16, 1925.
Typed pink note, "Ederi" to Byrd, n.d., 1925.
File 4235
Memo, Byrd to Chief of Bureau of Navigation, March 26, 1925.
Letter, Byrd to Judge A C. "Kit" Carson, March 31, 1925.
Letter, Byrd to Lt. Cmdr. Fitzhugh Green, April 10, 1925.
Various household bills and letters, 1925.
File 4238
Byrd, Richard. "Have Spectacular Flights Value?" Uncorrected proof for the August 1926 issue of *World's Work* magazine.
File 4243
Letter, Byrd to J. Vincent Astor, January 13, 1926.

File 4249
>   Letter, Byrd to Dr. Isaiah Bowman, November 24, 1926.
>   Letter, Bowman to Byrd, November 29, 1926.
File 4252
>   Gilbert Grosvenor, Frederick V. Coville, and Col. E. Lester Jones. "Report of the Special Committee Appointed by the Board of Trustees of the National Geographic Society to Examine the Records of Commander Byrd's Flight to the North Pole, May 9, 1926" (Washington, D.C.: National Geographic Society, June 28, 1926).
File 4256
>   "Statement Lt. Cdr. R.E. Byrd, January 30, 1926."
>   "Chantier, United States Shipping Board Emergency Fleet Corp., March 24, 1926"
Box 115, "Transatlantic Flight"
Folder 4330
>   Letter, Byrd to Curtis Wilbur, Secretary of the Navy, December 24, 1926.
>   Letter, Byrd to IRS, March 9, 1927.
>   Letter, Byrd to Grover Whalen, March 10, 1927.
Folder 4333 and 4334
>   These are filled with requests from admirers to accompany Byrd on his transatlantic flight. The majority of the letters and telegrams were written by women.
Folder 4333
>   Letter, Byrd to Ruth Haviland, June 18, 1927.
Folder 4342
>   Letter, Sikorsky to Byrd, October 2, 1926.
>   Letter, Byrd to Sikorsky (misspelled "Zikosky"), October 6, 1926.
>   Telegram, Sikorsky to Byrd, October 11, 1926.
>   Letter, Byrd to Wanamaker, October 31, 1926.
>   Telegram, Grover Whalen to Byrd, November 11, 1926.
>   Letter, Byrd to Wanamaker, November 16, 1926.
>   Letter, Byrd to Whalen, November 16, 1926.
>   Letter, Byrd to Wanamaker, December 28, 1926.
>   Telegram, *Detroit News* to Byrd, January 13, 1927.
>   Telegram, Bennett to Byrd, January 14, 1927.
>   Telegram, Bennett to Byrd, January 15, 1927.
>   Telegram, Bennett to Byrd, January 21, 1927.
Folder 4343
>   Letter, Byrd to Chief of Naval Operations, July 30, 1921.
>   Letter, Byrd to Fokker, October 11, 1926.
>   Letter, Sikorsky to Byrd, October 23, 1926.
>   Letter, Atlantic Aircraft Corporation to Byrd, October 29, 1926.
>   Letter, Byrd to Rodman Wanamaker, October 31, 1926.
>   Letter, Byrd to Davis, January 1, 1927.
>   Letter, Byrd to Bennett, January 15, 1927.
>   Letter, Fitzhugh Green to Byrd, January 21, 1927.
>   Letter, Byrd to Bennett, January 22, 1927.
>   Letter, Byrd to Wanamaker, March 18, 1927.

Folder 4344: "Low Protein Diet," March 1927.
    Letter, Byrd to Wanamaker, May 23, 1927.
    Telegram, Wanamaker to Byrd, May 27, 1927.
    Draft of letter or cable, Byrd to Wanamaker, n.d., but after the *Columbia's* flight on June 6, 1927.
    Letter, North American Newspaper Alliance to Byrd, June 17, 1927.
    Letter, *New York Times* to Byrd, June 21, 1927.
Folder 4345
    Letter, Albert Buhler to Byrd, July 7, 1927.
Folder 4354
    Letter, Byrd to Capt. Jerry H. Land, April 28, 1927.
Folder 4356
    Telegram, Byrd to Wanamaker, May 11, 1927.
Box 116
    Folder 4360
    Various letters and cables of congratulations to Byrd.
Box 319, "Arctic Expedition 1926"
    "Polar Claim Questioned," May 9, 1996, *Los Angeles Times/Washington Post* News Service. No page or newspaper listed, though probably the *Los Angeles Times*.
    "Weather Maps": May 11, 1927, 8 a.m., May 12, 1927, 8 a.m.

DENISON PUBLIC LIBRARY ARCHIVES, DENISON, IOWA, "CLARENCE CHAMBERLIN"
    "Northwest Iowa Boy in Velvet Now, But Lived on Hamburger Not So Many Long Years Past," *Sioux City Index*, n.d.
    Unattributed photocopy that appears to be a city history, 126, 137, 138, 141, 163, 169.

FEDERAL BUREAU OF INVESTIGATION, *CHARLES A. LEVINE*, CASE FILE NO. 93-7651 AND 105-108975

IOWA HISTORICAL SOCIETY, "CLARENCE CHAMBERLIN"
    "Congratulations by Coolidge for Iowan," *Sioux City Index*, n.d., n.p.
    Iowa Aeronautics Commission, "Clarence D. Chamberlin, Denison, Iowa."
    Letter, Chamberlin to parents, June 12, 1918.

SUZANNE K. JONES PRIVATE COLLECTION
    E-mail, Kevin Burns to Suzanne Jones, June 29, 2008.

LIBRARY OF CONGRESS, MANUSCRIPT DIVISION, ARCHIVES OF THE INSTITUTE OF AEROSPACE SCIENCES IN THE AMERICAN INSTITUTE OF AERONAUTICS AND ASTRONAUTICS, "AIRCRAFT COMPANY FILES"
    Container 155: "Huff, Daland and Co., Miscellany"

LIBRARY OF CONGRESS, MANUSCRIPT DIVISION, ARCHIVES OF THE INSTITUTE OF AEROSPACE SCIENCES IN THE AMERICAN INSTITUTE OF AERONAUTICS AND ASTRONAUTICS, "BIOGRAPHICAL FILES, 1784–1962"
    Container 1: "Acosta, Bertram [*sic*] Blanchard, Newspaper clippings 1920s–1930s"

"Mrs. Acosta Asks Legal Bar to Her Rival's Love Making," *Evening Graphic,* November 23, 1928, n.p.

"Acosta Stunts Hour in Plane Built by Novice," *New York Herald Tribune,* n.d., n.p.

Container 7: "Bellanca, Giuseppe"

Container 10: "Byrd, Richard E."

"Levine, Facing $300,000 Suit by U.S. Plans Counteraction," *New York Herald,* July 2, 1927, n.p.

Container 12: "Chamberlin, Clarence"

"Chamberlin Named as City's Air Engineer," *New York Times,* June 5, 1928, n.p.

"Made to Fit in Ordinary Garage," *New York Times,* October 29, 1929, n.p.

"New Airline Is Formed," *New York Times,* December 3, 1932, n.p.

"By Stratosphere to Europe," *New York Times,* January 27, 1937, n.p.

"Chamberlin Back in Air," *New York Times,* June 24, 1946, n.p.

Container 17: "Davis, Noel, Newspaper Clippings"

Container 26: "Elder, Ruth, Newspaper Clippings"

"Miss Elder's Zeal Defeats Hop Delays," *New York Telegram,* n.d., n.p.

"Womack, on Polar Expedition, Is Divorced from Ruth Elder," *Washington Evening Star,* December 12, 1928, n.p.

"Going to Reno," *Washington Star,* September 29, 1939, n.p.

Container 29: "Fokker, Anthony, Newspaper clippings 1939–1940"

"Young Wife of Fokker, Air King, Leaps 15 Stories to Her Death," *New York Daily News,* February 9, 1929, n.p.

"Fokker Sees Wars Decided in Air," *New York Times,* March 19, 1938, n.p.

"Tony Fokker's Yacht $250,000 Fire Ruin," *New York Daily News,* October 9, 1939, n.p.

"Fokker, Airplane Pioneer, Dies," *New York Journal-American,* December 23, 1939, n.p.

"Anthony H.G. Fokker, 49, Dies; Plane Designer and Builder," *New York Herald-Tribune,* December 24, 1939, n.p.

"Anthony H. G. Fokker Dies," *New York Sun,* December 24, 1939, n.p.

"Fokker Dies in New York," *Time,* January 1, 1940, n.p.

Container 29. "Fonck, René, Newspaper clippings"

"Flier Finds Fonck, Ace of 1918, Is Silent Monk," *New York Times,* n.d., n.p.

"René Fonck Dead; World War I Ace," *New York Times,* June 19, 1953, n.p.

Container 52: "Jefferson, Thomas, General Correspondence"

Letter, Jefferson to D. B. Lee, April 27, 1822.

Container 53: "Johnson, Samuel, Miscellany"

Container 64: "Lindbergh, Charles A., Clippings 1928"

Container 98: "Nouville [sic], George O., Miscellany"

"Lt. Noville Improving," *Washington Post,* December 8, 1931, n.p.

Container 98: "Nungesser, Charles O., Miscellany"

Container 98: "Ortig [sic], Raymond, Newspaper Clippings"

Container 101: "De Pinedo, Francisco, Miscellany"

Container 113: "Sikorsky, Igor Ivan, Newspaper Clippings"

LIBRARY OF CONGRESS, MANUSCRIPT DIVISION, ARCHIVES OF THE INSTITUTE OF
AEROSPACE SCIENCES IN THE AMERICAN INSTITUTE OF AERONAUTICS AND
ASTRONAUTICS, "FRANCESCO DE PINEDO"
"Francesco de Pinedo," unattributed photocopy of magazine article, n.d., 34–43.
"Map of de Pinedo's Flight."
"When a Flock of Condors Imperiled de Pinedo," *Literary Digest*, n.d., n.p.

LIBRARY OF CONGRESS, MANUSCRIPT DIVISION, ARCHIVES OF THE INSTITUTE OF
AEROSPACE SCIENCES IN THE AMERICAN INSTITUTE OF AERONAUTICS AND
ASTRONAUTICS, "MISCELLANEOUS, 1804–1932"
Container 174: "A Pass on the Trans-Atlantic Air Line Railway, 1894"

LIBRARY OF CONGRESS, MANUSCRIPT DIVISION, ARCHIVES OF THE INSTITUTE OF
AEROSPACE SCIENCES IN THE AMERICAN INSTITUTE OF AERONAUTICS AND
ASTRONAUTICS, "OVERSIZE, 1805–1955, N.D."
Box OV45 "Franklin, Benjamin, Copies of Letters and Clippings"
Letter from Paris to Vienna, Franklin to Dr. Ingenhaus, January 16, 1784.

LIBRARY OF CONGRESS, MANUSCRIPT DIVISION, ARCHIVES OF THE INSTITUTE OF
AEROSPACE SCIENCES IN THE AMERICAN INSTITUTE OF AERONAUTICS AND
ASTRONAUTICS. "SCRAPBOOKS, 1784–1962". "CHAMBERLIN, CLARENCE, MAY 13,
1927 TO JANUARY 23, 1933"

LIBRARY OF CONGRESS, MANUSCRIPT DIVISION, PAPERS OF BERNT BALCHEN,
RECORD GROUP 401(97)
Box OV1. "Scrapbooks, ca. 1920–ca. 1929"
Letter, Western Canada Airways Ltd., to Bernt Balchen, March 12, 1927.
McKay, Alice. "First Freight Flies North," *The Beaver*, September 1947, 18–21.

MISSOURI HISTORICAL SOCIETY, CHARLES A. LINDBERGH COLLECTION
Box 11. "Correspondence, Transatlantic Flight"
Folder 6, "Chas. Lindbergh, 2 handwritten pages of lists and 'propaganda,'
ca. 1927"
Folder 6a, "Personal Correspondence, Letters from Mother (1927 January
17–May 18)"
Letter, Evangeline Lindbergh to Charles Lindbergh, January 20, 1927.
Letter, Evangeline Lindbergh to Charles Lindbergh, January 31, 1927.
Letter, Evangeline Lindbergh to Charles Lindbergh, February 2, 1927.
Letter, Evangeline Lindbergh to Charles Lindbergh, February 3, 1927.
Letter, Evangeline Lindbergh to Charles Lindbergh, March 3, 1927.
Letter, Evangeline Lindbergh to Charles Lindbergh, March 4, 1927.
Letter, Evangeline Lindbergh to Charles Lindbergh, March 18, 1927
Letter, Evangeline Lindbergh to Charles Lindbergh, March 21, 1927.
Letter, Evangeline Lindbergh to Charles Lindbergh, April 8, 1927.
Letter, Charles Lindbergh to Evangleine Lindbergh, May 7, 1927.
Box 17
Folder 2, "Offers—1927, Animals, May 23–August 10"

Telegram, C. T. Haggard to Lindbergh.

Letter, Louis Melford Harkin of Melford Kennels to Lindbergh, June 9, 1927.

Russell Becker to Lindbergh, May/June 1927.

Folder 3, "Offers—1927, Clothing, May 21–June 13"

Telegram, Martin May, president Famous Barr Co., to Lindbergh.

Folder 4, "Offers—1927, Films/Lecture Tours, May 21–23"

More letters and telegrams, including telegram, Carl Lammle to Lindbergh, n.d.

Letter, Ed Milne to Lindbergh, May 23, 1927.

Folder 8, "Offers—1927, Involved in Business, May 24–June 30"

Letter, Jordan Machine Tool Co. to Lindbergh, May 24, 1927.

Telegram, Rush Jones Insurance Company to Lindbergh, May 26, 1927.

Folder 9, "Offers—1927, Personal Service, May 21–June 24"

Miscellaneous offers, including letter, Hans Bergmann, Masseuse, to Lindbergh, June 14, 1927.

Folder 20, "Gifts—1927, May 21–24"

Miscellaneous offers of gifts.

Box 28, "Personal Correspondence 1927–1947, Personal (M-Wickersham)"

Folder 14, "Personal (CAL): Nungesser, Madame"

Letter from "La Maman au Capitaine Charles Nungesser" to Lindbergh, February 23, 1928.

Box 87, "Periodicals"

Folder 39

"The Social Peek-a-Boo, A Reflection of Society Gossip That Makes the Rounds Every Week," *The Censor* (St. Louis), June 2, 1927, 8–11.

Box 88

Folder 27

Robert J. Hunter, M.D., "Cultivating the Balance Sense. A Prelude to Cloud Flying," a lecture given before the College of Physicians, Philadelphia, May 21, 1919.

MISSOURI HISTORICAL SOCIETY, LINDBERGH, CHARLES AUGUSTUS: "PAPERS, 1827–1969," A0904

Box 9

Folder 2

"Spirit of St. Louis Logbook (Holograph)"

"Spirit of St. Louis, Log of Flights at Curtiss Field"

Folder 6, "Pages Removed from the Spirit of St. Louis Flight Log"

Box 17

Folder 2, "Offers—1927, Animals, May 23–Aug. 10"

Telegram, C. J. Haggard to Lindbergh, n.d.

Box 106, "Sheet Music"

Folder 54

"Over the Foaming Billows (To the Land of Parlez Vous)," lyrics by J. Calder Bramwell, music by Carl Dillon, bandmaster of the Third U.S. Infantry (St. Paul, Minn.: J. Calder Bramwell, 1927).

Outsize Folder 31, "Poems"
Anna Fitzin, "Ave Lindbergh," a mounted and matted poem dated June 13, 1927.

NATIONAL AIR AND SPACE MUSEUM, ARCHIVES, ACOSTA, BERTRAND B.·
DOCUMENTS, CA-004300-01
Foxworth, Thomas G. "Bertrand B. Acosta, 1895–1954." *Historical Aviation Album, All American Series.* Vol. 6 and 7 (Temple City, Calif.: Historical Aviation Album, n.d.), 51–112.
Letter, S. Rolfe Gregory, Fairchild Aircraft Corp., Hagerstown, Md., to Russ Brinkley, OX5 Club of America, Sept 25, 1958.
Letter, Pete Goff to Bert Acosta, Oct. 4, 1961. This was returned unanswered with the note attached: "Dear Phil: Can you shed any light on this? Is Acosta dead or alive? The original of the above letter was returned 'not known.' Pete"
"Pilot's Pilot," *Time,* June 10, 1935, n.p.
"Plane Now in Air for 50-Hour Flight," unattributed newspaper.

NATIONAL AIR AND SPACE MUSEUM ARCHIVES, CHAMBERLIN, CLARENCE D.:
DOCUMENTS, CC-196000-01
"Clarence Chamberlin, 83, Pioneer in Ocean Flying," no date or attribution, but probably *New York Times.*
Totten, Dick, "Col. Clarence D. Chamberlin, Aviation Pioneer," no date or attribution.

NATIONAL AIR AND SPACE MUSEUM ARCHIVES, CURTIN, LAWRENCE W.:
DOCUMENTS, CC833500-01
"William Curtin, Navy Pilot, Dies in Plane Crash," *Army Tribune,* August 15, 1936, n.p.

NATIONAL AIR AND SPACE MUSEUM ARCHIVES, DAVIS, NOEL (CDR). DOCUMENTS,
CD-075000-01
"Lt. Cdr. Noel Davis, USNR," no date or attribution.

NATIONAL AIR AND SPACE MUSEUM ARCHIVES, DE PINEDO, FRANCESCO (CMDR).
DOCUMENTS, CD-132000-01

NATIONAL AIR AND SPACE MUSEUM ARCHIVES, FONCK, RENÉ, DOCUMENTS,
CF-381000-01
"Fonck (66 Boches)" Hoo/1. This appears to be one in a set of collectible cards about World War I aces.
Parrish, Robert L. "René Fonck," transcript for a series of short biographical sketches on World War I fliers, New Horizon Publishers, n.d.

NATIONAL AIR AND SPACE MUSEUM ARCHIVES, GIUSEPPE M. BELLANCA
COLLECTION: "BIOGRAPHICAL AND HISTORICAL NOTES"
Box 3
Folder 5, "Correspondence 1921"

Letter, Bellanca to Chamberlin, January 14, 1921.
Letter, E. A. Noblitt to Bellanca, April 2, 1921.
Box 4
    File 5, "Correspondence 1927"
    Letter, Bellanca to Levine, April 23, 1927.
Box 43
    File 2
    Roscoe Deering, "Giuseppe Bellanca's Better Built Airplanes," unattrib-
        uted magazine article, 46.
    File 3
    Leon Kelley, Main Roads of Aviation, first draft ms., n.d.
Box 128, "Personal Correspondence"
    File 3, "Personal Correspondence Between G. M. Bellanca and Dorothy
    Brown (Bellanca)"
    Letter, Bellanca to Dorothy Brown, undated
    Letter, Dorothy Brown to Bellanca, February 8, 1921.
    Letter, Dorothy Brown to Bellanca, undated.
Box 142, "Personal Correspondence"
    Folder 5· Letter, Concetina Bellanca to Giuseppe Bellanca, April 28, 1927.
Box 164, "News Clippings"
    Untitled article, New York Telegram, January 4, 1928, n.p.

NATIONAL AIR AND SPACE MUSEUM ARCHIVES, GRAYSON, FRANCES WILSON,
DOCUMENTS, CG-605000-01
    "Mrs. Grayson Took Automatic Pistol on Dawn's Flight," Newark Sunday Call,
        December 25, 1927, n.p.
    "Dawn's Navigator Foresaw Death," The World, May 22, 1929, n.p.

NATIONAL AIR AND SPACE MUSEUM ARCHIVES, BELLA C. LANDAUER COLLECTION
OF AERONAUTICAL SHEET MUSIC
    "Levine! With His Flying Machine," music by Sam Coslow, English words by Saul
        Bernie, Jewish words by Joseph Tanzman (New York· Spier and Coslow, Inc.,
        1927).

NATIONAL AIR AND SPACE MUSEUM ARCHIVES, "LAVASSEUR [sic] PL.8, 'L'OISEAU
BLANC'"
    "Attaché's Report: Levasseur Seaplane to be Used by Nungesser re: Transatlantic
        Flight."
    "National Advisory Committee for Aeronautics, Aircraft Circular No. 5. 'Levas-
        seur 8,' Transatlantic Plane."

NATIONAL AIR AND SPACE MUSEUM ARCHIVES, LEVINE, CHARLES A.,
DOCUMENTS, CL-418000-01
    "Levine Got Started as Aviation Worker," unattributed newspaper clipping, pos-
        sibly New York Times, n.d.

NATIONAL AIR AND SPACE MUSEUM ARCHIVES, NUNGESSER, CHARLES EUGENE J. M.
(CAPT.), DOCUMENTS, CN-105000-01
Bates, Henry. "Charles Nungesser, Iron Ace of France," *Modern Man*, n.d.,
22–54.
Letter, Richard E. Gillespie, executive director, TIGHAR, to Donald Lopez, dep-
uty director of the National Air and Space Museum, August 15, 1986.
Transcripts of sessions with psychic Ann Rylchenski, November 5, 1984, and No-
vember 6, 1986.

NATIONAL AIR AND SPACE MUSEUM ARCHIVES, RAYMOND ORTEIG HISTORICAL
COLLECTION
Applications for the Raymond Orteig Prize.
Letter, George W. Burleigh to C. F. Schory, May 28, 1925.
Letter, Harry G. Young to C. F. Schory, September 25, 1925.
Letter, George Burleigh to C. F. Schory, February 9, 1926.
Letter, H. E. Hartney to C. F. Schory, April 13, 1926.
Letter, Winston Ehrgott to National Aeronautics Association, April 18, 1927.

NATIONAL AIR AND SPACE MUSEUM ARCHIVES, SIKORSKY, IGOR IVANOVICH (DR)
(1991–20) DOCUMENTS, CS-552500-01
"Conquering Vertical Flight," unattributed manuscript, including plans of
Sikorsky's 1912 "B. N. Yuriev."
Sikorsky, Igor. "Recollections of a Pioneer." Transcript of an address to the Wings
Club of New York City, November 16, 1964, 4, 6.

NATIONAL AIR AND SPACE MUSEUM, ARCHIVES, SIKORSKY S-35 (FONCK
1926 TRANSATLANTIC ATTEMPT) DOCUMENTS, AS-400249-01
Foulois, B. D., Lt. Col., Commander of Mitchel Field. "Wreck of the Sikorsky
S-35 Airplane." Report by Headquarters Mitchel Field and Ninth Observation
Group, Office of the Commanding Officer, Oct. 5, 1926.
Letter, Harold E. Hartney to Maj. Ernest Jones, Assistant Secretary for Aeronau-
tics, Department of Commerce, Oct. 6, 1926.
"Specifications and Performance for the All-Metal Three-Motored Passenger or
Freight Carrier S-35 'Special'—Model 1926."

NATIONAL AIR AND SPACE MUSEUM, ARCHIVES, WANAMAKER, RODMAN
DOCUMENTS, CW-131000-01
"Untitled note on the *America*," *Scientific American*, June 27, 1914, 518.

NATIONAL AIR AND SPACE MUSEUM, ARCHIVES, WOOSTER, STANTON HALL,
DOCUMENTS, CW-900500-01
"Unfavorable Reports on Fitness, Ensign Stanton H. Wooster, U.S. Navy," De-
cember 15, 1920.
"Aircraft Propellor Blades–Request for application for United States Patent," July
29, 1923.

NATIONAL AIR AND SPACE MUSEUM, ARCHIVES, WRIGHT WHIRLWIND J-5 9-CYL
RADIAL, DOCUMENTS, BW-730580-01
Wright Aeronautical Corp., "Wright Air Cooled Aviation Engines, 'Whirlwind'
Series" (Patterson, N.J., 1926 or 1927).

NEW YORK HISTORICAL SOCIETY, JOHN WANAMAKER (FIRM) COLLECTION,
F128 T119100
Box 1
Wanamaker, John (firm). *The New Wanamaker's: A Souvenir Guidebook of the
Wanamaker Store in New York City* (1905?).
Wanamaker, Rodman. "The Iron Lions of Bravery: A Message to the Citizens
of New York City" (1923).
Wanamaker, Rodman. *A Record of the Christening of the Great Monoplane
"America"* (1927).

NEW YORK HISTORICAL SOCIETY, LANDAUER COLLECTION
Ziegfeld, Florenz. *Rio Rita: A Musical Comedy.*" Produced by Florenz Ziegfeld.
Music and lyrics by Henry Tierney and Joseph McCarthy. Book by Guy Bolton
and Fred Thompson. At the Ziegfeld Theatre, Sixth Avenue and Fifty-fourth
Street, 1927

NEW YORK HISTORICAL SOCIETY, FILE: "NEW YORK (CITY)—PARADES"
Gustaitis, Joseph. "A Thanksgiving Tradition." *American History*, Dec. 1995,
32–37.
New York Times, June 16, 1963, A1; Aug. 31, 1986, n.p.; June 12, 1991, B1; October 30, 1996, B1; February 8, 2008, B6; March 30, 2009, n.p.

NEW YORK HISTORICAL SOCIETY, RECORDS OF THE TAVERN CLUB, 1923–1964,
BV TAVERN CLUB
File, "Tavern Club Collection"
Scrapbook, "First Five Years of the Tavern Club, Jan. 15, 1923–Jan. 15, 1928."
The first time Orteig shows up as a member is in 1936 in the file "Dinner
given by Raymond Orteig at the Hotel Lafayette. March 20, 1936."

WILLIAM L. NUNGESSER PRIVATE COLLECTION
"American Wife Divorces Captain Nungesser," n.d., n.p.
"Miss Hatmaker Weds Captain Nungesser," n.d., n.p., but probably either *The
New York Times* or *The New York Herald*.
"Nungesser Amphibian N.U.A. Type," photo and caption.
"Picture of Consuelo Hatmaker in her flying suit standing beside Nungesser as he
barnstorms in America"
"Picture of Consuelo Hatmaker in photo montage at the Battery," *New York Daily
News*, n.d., n.p.
"Picture of Consuelo Hatmaker Standing Beside *White Bird*," copied from a photo
at Museé Le Bourget.
"Picture of Igor Sikorsky in cockpit filming *Sky Raiders*."
"Test New Flivver Plane," n.d., n.p.

VIRGINIA AERONAUTICAL HISTORICAL SOCIETY ARCHIVES
    File: "Personages, Davis & Wooster"
    "Langley Field," n.d., n.p.

VIRGINIA AERONAUTICAL HISTORICAL SOCIETY ARCHIVES
    File: "Personages, Lloyd Bertaud"
    "Lloyd W. Bertaud, Early Christofferson Aviator-Instructor"

VIRGINIA AERONAUTICAL HISTORICAL SOCIETY ARCHIVES
    File: "Personages, Richard E. Byrd"
    Green, Fitzhugh. "Dick Byrd—Gentleman." *American Magazine*, n.d.,
    77–81.

WORLD WIDE WEB

"Andean Condor," Wikipedia, en.wikipedia.org.
"Anywhere, Everywhere." *Time*, September 17, 1928, www.time.com.
"Atlantic Events." *Time*, May 23, 1927, n.p., www.time.com.
"Aviation Pathfinders· Richard Byrd and Floyd Bennett." *A Century of Flight*, www
    .century-of-flight.freedom.com.
"Bertrand Blanchard Acosta." Wikipedia, en.wikipedia.org.
"Biographical and Historical Notes," The Giuseppe M. Bellanca Collection, www
    .nasm.si.edu.
"Biographical Background, Francesco de Pinedo," www.italystl.com/pride/page9.htm.
"Brendan." Wikipedia, en.wikipedia.org.
Canter, Chris. "Re: Captain Charles Eugene Jule Marie Nungessser," genterum
    .genealogy.com. Posted March 20, 2002.
"Cartwheel." *Time*, October 4, 1926, www.time.com.
"Charles Augustus Lindbergh, 1902–74, American aviator." *Columbia Encyclopedia*,
    search.ebscohost.com/login.aspx?direct=true&db=a9h&AN=IXBLindbergC
    son&site=ehost-live">Charles Augustus Lindbergh, 1902 _74, American aviator.
"Charles Levine." *Yiddish Radio Project*, www.yiddishradioproject.com.
"Charles Nungesser," Wikipedia, en.wikipedia.org.
Cisneros, Norberto. "Bert Acosta: Genius of Early Aviation," www.airmailpioneers
    .org/Pilots/Acosta.htm.
"Clarence D. Chamberlin Recalls Historic Flight." *Yiddish Radio Project*, yiddishradio
    project.org.
"Clarence Duncan Chamberlin." Wikipedia, en.wikipedia.org.
"Crocker Land." "Aviation Pathfinders: Byrd and Bennett." www.century-of-flight
    .freeola.com.
"Denison, Iowa." Wikipedia, en.wikipedia.org.
"De Pinedo's Milestone Flights." www.italystl.com/pride/page11.htm.
"Floyd Bennett." Wikipedia, en.wikipedia.org.
"François Coli." *Absolute Astronomy*. www.absoluteastronomy.com.
"Garden City Hotel." Wikipedia, en.wikipedia.org.
"The Garden City Hotel: Our History." www.gardencityhotel.com.
"Ground effect (aircraft)." Wikipedia, en.wikipedia.org.

"Ground effect." www.pilotfriend.com.

"Harold Evans Hartney." www.theaerodrome.com/aces/usa/hartney.php.

Holt, Lew. "How Many Will Die Flying the Atlantic This Season?" *Modern Mechanix*, August 1931, blog.modernmechanix.com.

"Igor Sikorsky." Wikipedia, en.wikipedia.org.

"Inflation Calculator—U.S. Bureau of Labor Statistics," data.bls.gov/cgr-bin/cpicalc.pl/.

"In Philadelphia." *Time*, Monday, September 13, 1926, www.time.com.

"Jimmy Walker." Wikipedia, en.wikipedia.org.

Jones, Steven Loring. "From 'Under Cork' to Overcoming: Black Images in Comics," www.ferris.edu/jimcrow/links/comics.

"The Lambs Club—New York City," www.nycago.org/Organs/NYC/html/LambsClub.html.

"Leigh Wade, Major General, United States Air Force." Arlington National Cemetery Website, www.arlingtoncemetery.net/wleigh.htm.

Linder, L. B. "What the Jew in the Street Thinks About the Jewish Flying Hero." *Der Tog* ("The Day," Brooklyn, N.Y.), June 9, 1927. Quoted in Charles Albert Levine Bibliography, richard.arthur.norton.googlepages.com.

"Lt. Charles Nungesser," usfighter.tripod.com/nungesser.htm.

Maeder, Jay. "Wings Levine and His Machine," www.nydailynews.com/archives.

"Milestones." *Time*, May 28, 1923, www.time.com.

"National Affairs: Four Men in a Fog." *Time*, July 11, 1927, n.p., www.time.com.

"New Evidence May Write Lindbergh out of History as First to Fly Atlantic." *The Independent*, November 12, 2010, www.independent.co.uk.

"1918 flu pandemic." Wikipedia, en.wikipedia.org.

"Noel Davis." www.stjohnshistoriccemetery.com/pensacolas_heritages/naval_heritage.htm.

"Nungesser." *Time*, May 28, 1923, www.time.com.

Pendleton, Linda D. "Ground Effect," AVWeb, World's Premier Independent Aviation News Resource, www.avweb.com/news/airman.

"Pilot's Pilot." *Time*, June 10, 1935, n.p., www.time.com.

"Plus Fours." Wikipedia, en.wikipedia.org.

"René Fonck, Highest Scoring Allied Ace, 75 Kills," www.acepilots.com.

"Richard E. Byrd and the 1925 MacMillan Arctic Expedition." HistoryNet, www.historynet.com.

"The Roaring Twenties," www.sagehistory.net/twenties.

"Rodman Wanamaker." Wikipedia, en.wikipedia.org.

"Roosevelt Field, New York." Wikipedia, en.wikipedia.org.

Rose, Lisle A. "Exploring a Secret Land: The Literary and Technological Legacies of Richard E. Byrd." *Virginia Magazine of History and Biography* 110, 2 (2002): 8. Accessed on EBSCOhost on August 4, 2009.

"S-35." *Time*, August 23, 1926, www.time.com.

"St. Brendan of Clonfert," www.irondequiot.catholic.org/index.php/St/Brendanof Clonfert.

"St. Brendan's Island." Wikipedia, en.wikipedia.org.

"A Salute to Rodman Wanamaker, 1863–1928." Friends of the Wanamaker Organ at Macy's, Philadelphia, wanamakerorgan.com.

"The Secret of the White Bird." *Aero-News Network*, www.aero-news.net.
"Stanton Wooster, Lieutenant, United States Navy." Arlington National Cemetery website, www.arlingtoncemetery.ney/swooster.htm.
Susman, Warren. "Personality and the Making of Twentieth-Century Culture," www.h-net.org/~hst203/readings/susman2. From Warren Susman, *Culture as History: The Transformation of American Society in the Twentieth Century* (New York: Pantheon Books, 1984), 271–85.
Time. Oct. 24, 1927; October 31, 1927, www.time.com.
"Transport: Transatlantic Tradition." *Time*, September 28, 1936, n.p., www.time.com.
"The Trans-Atlantic Flight of the America," www.check-six.com.
"U.S. Air Force Fact Sheet. Berry, Homer Mulhall Papers." Air Force Historical Research Agency, www.afhra.af.mil.
"USS Illinois (BB-7)." Wikipedia, en.wikipedia.org.
"Weekend Wings #18: The Struggle to Conquer the Atlantic." *Bayou Renaissance Man*, bayourenaissanceman.blogspot.com.
"White Bird," NUMA, www.numa.net/expeditions/white_bird.htms.
"The White Bird," Wikipedia, en.wikipedia.org.
"World InfoZone—Atlantic Facts," worldinfozone.com.
"World Population 1918," wiki.answers.com.
"World War I Casualties," Wikipedia, en.wikipedia.org.
"Yellow Giant." *Time*, May 9, 1927, www.time.com.

INTERVIEWS

Belote, Harvey "Windy." Flight and interviews. Cape Charles, Virginia, October 2009.
Biswanger, Ray, executive director, Friends of the Wanamaker Organ. Series of e-mails, beginning August 12, 2009.
Davis, Noel Guy, Jr. Phone interview. Plymouth, Minnesota, July 8, 2010.
Forrest, Leo G., Jr. Interview. Poquoson, Va., August 14, 2010.
Jones, Suzanne K. Phone interview. Danville, Va., July 6, 2010.
Nungesser, William L. Interview. Riverhead, N.Y., September 19, 2009.

FILMS AND DVDS

Captain Charles A. Lindbergh of America. Kinograms, 1927. National Air and Space Film Archives, VE 00295.
Charles A. Lindbergh, Hero of the Air. Fox-Case Movietone, USA, 1927. On *Saved from the Flames. 54 Rare and Restored Films, 1896–1944.* Lobster Films/Blackhawk Collection, 2008.
L'Enigme de L'Oiseau Blanc. 1997, Vincent Gielly, director.
The Orteig Prize. Collection of Suzanne K. Jones. Although mostly composed of newsreel footage, this also contains what seems to be company footage of the *American Legion*'s construction in the Keystone Aircraft Corporation's factory in Bristol, Pennsylvania.
We Saw It Happen. Igor Sikorsky and Clarence Chamberlin. United Technologies, 1952 (silent, 35 mm). National Air and Space Museum Film Archives, FC 04131 and 04197.

We Saw It Happen: Igor Sikorsky, Clarence Chamberlin, and Clarence Chamberlin &
Carl Spaatz (wild tracks). United Technologies, 1952 and 1953 (sound, 35 mm).
FC 04130, FC 04155, FC 04196, and FC 04240. This and the silent film clips
in the previous citation are outtakes for the TV documentary *We Saw It Hap-*
pen. However, the sound track is out of sync and requires the aid of a film
archivist to view.

.

ACKNOWLEDGMENTS

What would a writer do without the kindness of experts and strangers? You call them out of the blue, invade their lives, then pick their brains. This was the sixth nonfiction narrative in which I pestered pleasant, unsuspecting people with all manner of questions. Such continuing patience confirms one's faith in humanity.

Though reams have been written about Charles Lindbergh and Richard Byrd, digging out details on the other participants in the race proved a little more difficult. However, as an old newspaper editor once told me, there are experts on everything—the challenge is just to track them down. In this case, descendants of the fliers were more than willing to talk about their ancestors. Suzanne K. Jones of Danville, Virginia, was a storehouse of information on Stanton Wooster; her mother had been Wooster's half sister, and she filled in gaps that would have been impossible to fill otherwise. She put me in touch with Noel Davis's son, Noel Guy Davis Jr. of Plymouth, Minnesota, who was barely a year old when his father died. Yet Davis's mother kept the flier's memory alive for him. In time, Noel Jr. would become an aviator like his father, join the military, and become an honorary member of the Quiet Birdmen, a private club for aviators, founded in 1921 by World War I pilots, which included in its ranks such luminaries as Lindbergh and Eddie Rickenbacker.

And then there is William L. Nungesser of Riverhead, New York, the American cousin of the famous French ace. Billy Nungesser probably knows more about his famous relative than anyone else in the world; his house is filled, top to bottom, with Nungesser files and photos, and he was more than generous in sharing them with me. A lot of new information appears in this book about Charles Nungesser that apparently had not surfaced previously in the United States. Much of that came from Billy. If he did not know something, he pointed me in the right direction.

Not every expert had a family connection. Dr. Susan Wansink, Professor of German and French at Virginia Wesleyan College, has helped me before. This time she translated the sad letter of Leontine Nungesser, thus adding a tragic dimension to the story. Ray Biswanger, executive director of the Friends of the Wanamaker Organ, helped me put enigmatic department store magnate Rodman Wanamaker into perspective. Leo G. Forrest Jr., a local historian in Poquoson, Virginia, helped me map out the fatal progress of the *American Legion*'s last flight.

One real treat was my introduction to veteran crop duster Harvey "Windy" Belote of Virginia's Eastern Shore. To residents of that rural peninsula, Windy is something of a legend. More than one person told me of watching as he inserted his big yellow biplane, a Grumman Ag-Cat with a roaring radial engine, into what seemed an impossibly tight space, then taking her out again. He'd been spraying fields for more than thirty years and was contemplating retirement when I showed up on his runway. Nevertheless, he explained the most basic concepts of flying and took me up in his little two-seater Piper Cub to get a feel for the wind and the air. It always helps to have a "feel" for your subject; I don't think that would have been possible if not for Windy's knowledge and generosity.

I've found over the years that archivists and librarians are possibly a writer's best friends. This time was no exception. At the Missouri Historical Society Library and Archives in St. Louis, Bascom curator Sharon Smith was a great help, especially during our conversations about the popular response to Lindbergh; while associate archivists Molly Kodner and Jaime Bourassa kept me supplied with a constant flow of Lindbergh esoterica. At the Byrd Polar Archives of the Ohio State University in Columbus, Ohio, archivist Laura Kissel helped me tackle the complexities of the famous explorer. In addition, Dr. Dave Bromwich, a research meteorologist at the Byrd Polar Research Institute, was kind enough to explain the mechanics of the turbulent weather over the Grand Banks of Newfoundland. At the archives of the Smithsonian Institute's National Air and Space Museum—both on the National Mall and at the Gerber Facility out of town—I was aided by what seemed an endless flow of experts. In particular, I'd like to thank acquisitions archivist Patricia Williams, film archivist Mark Taylor, chief photo archivist Melissa Keiser, and staff and volunteer archivists Brian Nicklas, Phil Edwards and Pedro Turina. Further thanks go out to Jennifer Melton, archivist for the Virginia Aeronautical Historical Society in Richmond; Hank Zalatel, librarian of the Iowa Department of Transportation Library at Iowa State University's Institute for Transportation; Chela Weber, chief archivist of the Brooklyn Historical Society; Jean Coffee, archivist at the Brooklyn Public Library's Brooklyn Collection; J. Gail Nicola, chief of the Ike Skelton Library at the Joint Forces Staff College in Norfolk, Virginia; and the reference staffs of the Utah States Archives in Salt Lake City, Utah; the Winchester Public Library in Winchester, Virginia; and the Denison Public Library in Denison, Iowa.

As always, I'd like to thank my literary agent, Noah Lukeman, who keeps me on the straight and narrow while seeing to the bread and butter. And I'd like to thank my editors at Farrar, Straus and Giroux, Jonathan Galassi and Jesse Coleman, who believed in this airy tale of tragedy while exhibiting a patience and understanding that went far beyond the call of duty when things got a little rough and slow.

INDEX

Butler, Katie, 303
Byrd, Beatrice Evelyn, 199
Byrd, Eleanor Bolling Flood, 61, 62, 63
Byrd, Evelyn, 199
Byrd, Harry, 61, 62, 68, 83, 320, 401
Byrd, Marie Ames, 64, 66
Byrd, Richard, 35, 41, 59–69, 86–91,
   114–15, 128, 163, 365–67, 370,
   400–401; Antarctic expedition of, 74,
   77, 85, 86, 205, 236, 345, 350, 355,
   379, 387–92, 398, 400–401; Balchen's
   memoirs and, 401–402; Bennett's
   injury and, 203–205, 268–69; birth
   of, 61; blacks as viewed by, 88, 389;
   crippled aviators visited by, 366–67;
   Davis and, 141, 144, 146; Davis's
   death and, 222, 268–69; death of,
   401, drinking of, 389; "Ederi" note
   and, 73–74; Fokker and, 93, 94,
   204–205; hangar of, 283, 301, 319–20;
   image of, 59–60, 389; injuries and
   health problems of, 64; on lecture
   circuit, 87–88, 95; letters from
   women to, 166, 199–200; Lindbergh's
   takeoff and, 302–303, 304, 321;
   Mitchell and, 68–69; Nungesser's
   flight and, 251, 252, 269–70;
   North Pole flight of, 9–10, 14–15, 17,
   41, 44, 58–61, 63, 69, 71–85, 87, 89,
   92, 93, 344, 346, 355, 388–89; Peary
   and, 71; at Pensacola, 64–65, 66;
   Sikorsky and, 58–59, 92; transpacific
   flight offers and, 369; tributes to,
   365–66; violent family life of, 62
Byrd, Richard, transatlantic flight of,
   344–60; Byrd's flight diary, 352;
   Byrd's injury on practice flight, 202,
   204, 205; estimated costs of, 94; the
   flight, 348–60; landing and
   reception, 365–67; Lindbergh's
   flight compared with, 366;
   Lindbergh's victory and, 319–20,
   345–46; Orteig Prize competition, 5,
   9–10, 37, 58–59, 78, 85, 86–87,
   91–96, 110–12, 126, 136, 146, 148, 149,
   172, 179, 182, 194–200, 208, 215, 225,

231, 259, 267–70, 281–85, 288, 293,
   297, 300, 319–20, 330; planning for,
   195–99; test flights for, 200–205,
   282; Wanamaker's sponsorship of,
   85, 86, 92, 94–97, 99, 110, 111, 194,
   196–99, 206, 223, 282–83, 285, 296,
   344, 345–46; see also America (Byrd's
   airplane)
Byrd, Richard, Jr., 401, 402
Byrd, Richard Evelyn, 61, 62–63, 73
Byrd, Tom, 61, 62, 320, 350

C

Cabral, Sacadura, 178–79
Cactus Kitten, 166
Campbell, Joseph, 107, 114
Camp Kearney, 260
Canada, 23–24
Cannon, Henry W., 71
Carisi, John, 158, 168, 170, 171–72, 266,
   308, 320, 333–36, 363; on Columbia
   christening flight, 208–12
Carling Brewery, 372
Carmania, 374–75
Carpentier, Georges, 250
Castle, Virginia, 199
celebrity culture, 106, 107, 272
Celestina, Angelina, 17
Chamberlin, Clarence Duncan, 47,
   159–63, 207, 236, 361, 362, 364, 396;
   aviation career of, 159–64; Balchen
   and, 292–93; Bellanca and, 160; on
   Columbia christening flight, 209–13,
   215, 223, 225, 231; on endurance-
   testing flight, 153–59, 168–72, 235;
   on Grand Tour of Europe, 362; land-
   on-a-dime ability of, 163; Levine's
   contract and legal battles with,
   279–80, 289–95, 296–97, 307, 321;
   Lindbergh's takeoff and, 302, 304;
   Lindbergh's victory and, 320–22;
   mail service and, 362–63; as news
   photographer, 163; Nungesser's flight